Studia epigraphica et historica in honorem Ioannis Pisonis

Herausgegeben von
Lucrețiu Mihailescu-Bîrliba, Radu Ardevan,
Rada Varga, Florian Matei-Popescu
und Ovidiu Țentea

2024
Harrassowitz Verlag · Wiesbaden

Bis Band 60: Philippika. Marburger altertumskundliche Abhandlungen.

This book was supported by a grant of the Romanian Ministry of Research, Innovation and Digitization, CNCS-UEFISCDU, project number PN-III-P 1-1-TE-2021-0165, within PNCDI III.

Bibliografische Information der Deutschen Nationalbibliothek
Die Deutsche Nationalbibliothek verzeichnet diese Publikation in der Deutschen Nationalbibliografie; detaillierte bibliografische Daten sind im Internet über https://dnb.de/ abrufbar.

Bibliographic information published by the Deutsche Nationalbibliothek
The Deutsche Nationalbibliothek lists this publication in the Deutsche Nationalbibliografie; detailed bibliographic data are available on the internet at https://dnb.de/.

Informationen zum Verlagsprogramm finden Sie unter
https://www.harrassowitz-verlag.de/

Gedruckt auf alterungsbeständigem Papier.
Druck und Verarbeitung: Hubert & Co., Göttingen
Printed in Germany

ISSN 1613-5628 eISSN 2701-8091
ISBN 978-3-447-12209-2 eISBN 978-3-447-39547-2

Le Professeur Ioan Piso

Table des matières

Tabula Gratulatoria

Raffaele D'Amato, Ferrara
Dan Aparaschivei, Iași
Adrian Ardeț, Caransebeș
Carmen-Lucia Ardeț, Caransebeș
Radu Ardevan, Cluj-Napoca
Mátyás Bajusz, Sf. Gheorghe
Giulia Baratta, Macerata
Marius Barbu, Deva
Vitalie Bârcă, Cluj-Napoca
Eugenia Beu-Dachin, Cluj-Napoca
Yann LeBohec, Paris
Dilyana Boteva, Sofia
George Bounegru, Alba Iulia
Laurent Bricault, Toulouse
Livia Buzoianu, Constanța
Juan Ramón Carbó García, Murcia
Antonio Caballos Rufino, Sevilla
Chiara Cenati, Wien
Andrei Cîmpeanu, București
Sorin Cociș, Cluj-Napoca
Victor Cojocaru, Iași
Mireille Corbier, Paris
Cătălin Cristescu, Deva
Roxana Gabriela Curcă, Iași
Dan Deac, Cluj-Napoca
Piotr Dyczek, Warszawa
Michał Duch, Poznań
Werner Eck, Köln
José D'Encarnação, Lisboa
Carmen Fenechiu, Cluj-Napoca
Gelu Florea, Cluj-Napoca
Florin Fodorean, Cluj-Napoca
Péter Forisek, Debrecen
Regula Frei-Solba, Lausanne
Cristian Găzdac, Cluj-Napoca
Darius Groza, Alba Iulia
Manfred Hainzmann, Graz
Ana Honcu, Iași
Marietta Horster, Mainz
Jeremy M. Hutton, Madison
Zofia Kaczmarek, Poznań
Ted Kaizer, Durham
Anne Kolb, Zürich
Péter Kovács, Piliscsaba
Krysztof Królczyk, Poznań
Peter Kruschwitz, Wien
Anamarija Kurilić, Zadar
Vlad Lăzărescu, Cluj-Napoca
Marc Mayer i Olivé, Barcelona
Yolande Marion, Bordeaux
Attilio Mastino, Sassari
Răzvan Mateescu, Cluj-Napoca
Florian Matei-Popescu, București
Lucrețiu Mihailescu-Bîrliba, Iași
Virgil Mihailescu-Bîrliba, Iași
Stephen Mitchell †, Exeter
Fritz Mitthof, Wien
Leszek Mrozewicz, Poznań
Zsolt Molnár, Cluj-Napoca
Denisa Murzea, Wien
Silvia Mustață, Cluj-Napoca
Eduard Nemeth, Cluj-Napoca
György Németh, Budapest
Coriolan Horațiu Opreanu, Cluj-Napoca
Ioan C. Opriș, București
Silvia Orlandi, Roma
Radu Ota, Alba Iulia
Andreas Pangerl, Köln
Annamária – I. Pázsint, Cluj-Napoca
Liviu Mihai Petculescu, București

Constantin C. Petolescu, București
David Petruț, Cluj-Napoca
Alexandru Rațiu, București
Michel Reddé, Paris
Cecilia Ricci, Campobasso
Isabel Rodà de Llanza, Barcelona / Tarragona
Alexander Rubel, Iași
Joaquin Ruiz de Arbulo, Tarragona
Dan Ruscu, Cluj-Napoca
Ligia Ruscu, Cluj-Napoca
Viorica Rusu-Bolindeț, Cluj-Napoca
Marjeta Šašel-Kos, Ljubljana
Michael Sommer, Oldenburg
Michael A. Speidel, Istanbul / Zürich
Liliana Suciu-Mateescu, Cluj-Napoca
Ádám Szabó, Budapest
Csaba Szabó, Szeged
Ernő Szabó, Pécs
Hans Taeuber, Wien
Francis Tassaux, Bordeaux
Tiberiu Tecar, Cluj-Napoca
Agnieszka Tomas, Warsaw
Călin Timoc, Timișoara
Ivo Topalilov, Sofia
Ovidiu Țentea, București
Rada Varga, Cluj-Napoca
Zsolt Visy, Pécs
Javier Velaza, Barcelona
Ekkehard Weber, Wien
Heinrich Zabehlicky, Wien
Susanne Zabehlicky-Scheffenegger, Wien
Claudio Zaccaria, Trieste
Petronel Zahariuc, Iași
Livio Zerbini, Ferrara
Boaz Zissu, Ramat Gan

L'Anniversaire d'un grand Professeur

Huit dizaines d'années de vie et six dizaines d'années d'activité représentent toujours un moment de bilan. Dans le cas du Professeur Ioan Piso, ce bilan est extrêmement impressionnant et riche – non seulement en achèvements professionnels, mais aussi en significations axiologiques, valides pour tous qui servent notre domaine, ainsi que pour tous qui respectent leur statut intellectuel.

Nous ne rappelons que brièvement les repères biographiques déjà connus du Professeur. Le jeune Ioan Piso appartenait dès le début à un monde d'une formation intellectuelle distinguée et d'un haut profil moral[1]. Son enfance dans la Vallée du Jiu (qui à l'époque était essentiellement différente d'aujourd'hui, un univers dominé par le sérieux, par la compétence professionnelle et par un solide esprit éthique), le lycée à Petroşani et l'atmosphère à la maison lui ont fourni une très bonne éducation, complétée dans l'ambiance de l'*Alma Mater Napocensis*, sous la coordination de vrais maîtres (comme C. Daicoviciu, M. Macrea, N. Lascu, K. Horedt, A. Bodor et d'autres). Il a choisi d'emblée l'étude de l'histoire ancienne, en s'approchant d'elle par l'intermédiaire des langues anciennes et des sciences humaines, dont la culture juridique ne manquait non plus. Et justement ces fondements lui ont permis plus tard les approches archéologiques proprement-dits des réalités antiques.

Ayant la chance de rester juste après la fin de ses études dans l'enseignement supérieur, il a pleinement confirmé les espoirs légitimes du milieu académique, par une exceptionnelle carrière didactique et scientifique. Ioan Piso a parcouru tous les degrés universitaires jusqu'à la plus haute position, celle de professeur et de directeur de thèses doctorales. Encore plus, il a occupé plusieurs ans la fonction importante de directeur du Musée Nationale de l'Histoire de Transylvanie de Cluj-Napoca. Aujourd'hui il dirige le Centre d'Études Romaines de l'Université de Cluj, fondé par ses propres efforts et doué d'une bibliothèque de spécialité constituée par les donations appartenant aux illustres savants, qui ont personnellement connu et apprécié Ioan Piso.

Nous évoquons en premier lieu sa performance didactique. Ses cours ont resté dans la mémoire des étudiants et ont mené à la formation de leurs compétences. Il a dirigé de nombreuses thèses doctorales, certaines devenues aujourd'hui des travaux cités dans notre domaine. Plusieurs générations d'archéologues et d'enseignants se sont formées sous l'influence incitative du Professeur. On n'oublie pas, bien sûr, les invitations en tant que "visiting professor" aux prestigieuses universités européennes (Vienne, Cologne, Bordeaux, Paris, Graz, León).

---

1 Voir Orbis Antiqus. Studia in honorem Ioannis Pisonis, Cluj-Napoca 2004, 7–14.

Le travail du Professeur a été toujours accompagné par la recherche exceptionnelle du monde ancien (particulièrement de la Dacie romaine). À côté des études érudites sur les inscriptions, des fouilles déroulées d'une manière rigoureuse à Ulpia Traiana Sarmizegetusa et des investigations vraiment novatrices dans notre domaine, ses contributions sur la vie sociale et culturelle du monde gréco-romain, de Dacie et des autres provinces, utilisant toutes les catégories de sources, se sont imposées comme des modèles pour tout le monde scientifique. Mais Ioan Piso reste d'abord un épigraphiste d'un très haut niveau. Il faut juste rappeler qu'il a été élu et réélu comme représentant de la Roumanie dans le comité scientifique de l'Association Internationale d'Épigraphie Grecque et Latine (2007–2017)[1].

Pour le derniers vingt ans[2] on peut constater une évolution ascendante de ces efforts: encore neuf livres et plus de 100 études et articles de spécialité, publiés chez des maisons éditrices prestigieuses d'Europe, ainsi que plusieurs programmes et projets de recherche – en Roumanie ou à l'étranger, dont quelques-uns continuent encore. Depuis sa retraite (2012), qui a fait cesser son activité didactique, Ioan Piso est devenu encore plus actif en recherche: il est une présence habituelle aux congrès et symposions internationaux, où son opinion reste encore appréciée et respectée. Le Professeur a bénéficié également de nombreuses bourses de recherche aux institutions renommées[3].

Sur plan professionnnel, on peut affirmer que Ioan Piso jouit de la plus large appréciation internationale. Aux distinctions antérieures[4] et en tant que membre des institutions académiques prestigieuses[5] on peut ajouter la réception dans l'Académie Royale de Barcelone (2007), la médaille "Oszkár Hahn" de l'Université de Budapest (2010) et la décoration " Service fidèle"en rang de commandeur (2016).

Mais le profile du Professeur reste incomplet sans sa dimension civique, d'engagement courageux pour la défense du patrimoine culturel de son pays. Dans de moments de confusion des valeurs et du chaos institutionnel, Ioan Piso s'est fait remarqué par ses interventuions dans l'espace public, en confrontant des préjugements et des clichés déjà fort présents dans la société roumaine. À partir de 2002 il est président de la Fondation Culturelle "Roșia Montană". Il a défendu le patrimoine de Roșia Montană comme membre des commissions nationales d'archéologie ou des monuments historiques. Dans toute situation il a défendu l'éthique professionnelle et les valeurs de l'humanité.

On ne peut pas finir ce petit profil du Professeur sans parler de son côté humain. Nous, les éditeurs de ce volume, sommes ses élèves, même si certains d'entre nous n'ont pas suivi les cours de l'Université de Cluj. Il faut parler d'abord de sa grande générosité. Non seulement nous avons bénéficié de son aide dans les moments le plus importants de nos

1 Il avait occupé cette position de 1982 à 2002 aussi, mais avant 1990 le régime dictatorial lui avait interdit les voyages à l'extérieur. Ioan Piso a été membre de ce comité de 2012 à 2017.

2 C'est-à-dire à partir de 2004; voir la bibliographie annexée.

3 Il est devenu boursier "Humboldt" en 1983, mais il a effectivement bénéficié de ce statut à partir de 1991.

4 Décoration « Service fidèle » au grade d'officier (2000); le prix «Vasile Pârvan» de l'Académie roumaine (2003).

5 L'Institut Archéologique Allemand (1993); La Société Belge d'Études Celtes (1993); La Société Nationale des Antiquaires de France (1997); L'Institut Archéologique Autrichien (1998).

carrières, mais aussi des générations de jeunes chercheurs, devenus ultérieurement des spécialistes importants dans les domaines d'archéologie et de l'épigraphie, ont eu son appui généreux. Il serait nécessaire, peut-être, encore un volume pour énumérer tous ceux qui ont effectivement eu le support du Professeur et de raconter les histoires de ces expressions de la munificence spirituelle de Ioan Piso. C'était vraiment une pure munificence, car il ne demandait rien en échange. Son exigence était renommée, mais c'était dans le meilleur sens du mot et nous avons beaucoup appris de cette exigence. Derrière son visage parfois sévère, mais jamais avec une expression d'acharnement, et derrière sa voix profonde, nous avons découvert un humour flamboyant et une chaleur qui nous avait, en paraphrasant Brassens, chauffé le corps et l'esprit. Et à tout cela s'ajoutaient un amour profond pour sa famille et pour sa patrie.

Les mots sont insuffisants pour exprimer nos sentiments de reconnaissance et pour faire parler la reconnaissance des autres. Au Professeur Ioan Piso, nous lui souhaitons tout simplement beaucouop de santé et de force de nous faire apprendre encore de nouvelles choses et de partager des moments inoubliables avec sa familles et tous ceux qui lui sont chers!

Ad multos annos felices faustosque !

24.08.2023

Radu Ardevan
Lucrețiu Mihailescu-Bîrliba
Rada Varga
Florian Matei-Popescu
Ovidiu Țentea

Œuvres Publiées du Professeur Ioan Piso

Livres

Inscriptiones Daciae Romanae III/2 (Sarmizegetusa), Ed. Academiei, Bucureşti 1980 (avec I. I. Russu, V. Wollmann).
Fasti provinciae Daciae I. Die senatorischen Amtsträger, Habelt Verlag, Bonn 1993.
Inscriptions d'Apulum (Inscriptions de la Dacie Romaine III/5), Mémoires de l'Académie des Inscriptions et Belles-Lettres, I-II, Ed. Frères Boccard, Paris 2001.
Das Heiligtum des Jupiter Optimus Maximus auf dem Pfaffenberg / Carnuntum, 1. Die Inschriften, Akademie Verlag, Wien 2003.
An der Nordgrenze des Römischen Reiches. Ausgewählte Studien (1972–2003), Habes 41, Steiner Verlag, Stuttgart 2005.
Le forum vetus de Sarmizegetusa, Ed. Academiei, Bucureşti 2006.
Der Marmor im römischen Dakien, Ed. Mega, Cluj-Napoca 2012 (avec H. Müller, B. Schwaighofer, M. Benea).
Fasti provinciae Daciae II. Die ritterlichen Amtsträger, Habelt Verlag, Bonn 2013.
Inscriptiones Daciae Romanae, Appendix I. Inscriptiones laterum musei Zilahensis, Ed. Mega, Cluj-Napoca 2016 (avec D. Deac).
Inscriptiones Daciae Romanae, Appendix II. Inscriptiones laterum musei Napocensis, Ed. Mega, Cluj-Napoca 2016 (avec F. Marcu).
Lexikon epigraphicum Daciae, Ed. Mega, Cluj-Napoca 2016 (avec R. Ardevan, C. Fenechiu, E. Beu-Dachin, St. Lalu).
Inscriptiones Daciae Romanae, Appendix III. Inscriptiones laterum museorum Banatus Temesiensis, Ed. Mega, Cluj-Napoca 2019 (avec A. Ardeţ, C. Timoc).
Istoria elenistică şi istoria Romei, Cluj-Napoca 2000 (university textbook).
Unter dem Siegel Roms. Ausgewählte Schriften (2004– 2020), Akademie Verlag, Wien, 2023.

Articles et études

Publius Furius Saturninus, AMN 9, 1972, 463–471.
Două piese romane de la Botorca (Tîrnăveni), AMN 9, 1972, 473–476 (avec V. Pepelea).
Descoperiri monetare antice în Transilvania, Apulum 10, 1972, 719–720 (avec E. Chirilă).
Certains aspects de l'organisation de la Dacie romaine, RevRoumHist 12/6, 1973, 999–1015.
Un complex de construcţii în terase din aşezarea dacică de la Feţele Albe, AMN 10, 1973, 65–96 (avec H. Daicoviciu, I. Glodariu).
Votorum nuncupatio de Sarmizegetusa, RevRoumHist 13/5–6, 1974, 723–733.

Războiul lui Philippus cu carpii, in: In memoriam Constantini Daicoviciu, Cluj 1974, 301–309.
Sur la vie municipale de Sarmizegetusa, StCl 16, 1974, 235–244.
O inscripţie funerară de la Beriu, Apulum 12, 1974, 580–582.
Principalele rezultate ale săpăturilor din 1973–1974 la Ulpia Traiana Sarmizegetusa şi semnificaţia lor, Sargetia 11–12, 1974–1975, 225–231 (avec H. Daicoviciu, D. Alicu, E. Nemeş, C. Pop, A. Rusu).
Epigraphica (I), Sargetia 11–12, 1974–1975, 57–79.
Epigraphica (II), Apulum 13, 1975, 677–682.
Sarmizegetusa şi războaiele marcomanice, AMN 12, 1975, 159–163 = Sarmizegetusa et les guerres marcomannes, RevRoumHist 16/1, 1977, 155–159 (avec H. Daicoviciu).
Epigraphica (III), AMN 12, 1975, 165–178.
P. Furius Saturninus, légat de Dacia Superior, in: Actes de la XIIème Conférence internationale d'Etudes Classiques «Eirene» (Cluj-Napoca 2–7 octobre 1972), Bucureşti – Amsterdam 1975, 679–685.
Zur Laufbahn des Calpurnius Iulianus, RömÖsterr 3, 1975, 175–182.
La carrière équestre de P. Aelius Hammonius, Dacia 20, 1976, 251–257.
Epigraphica (IV), Apulum 14, 1976, 441–453.
Carrières sénatoriales (I), RevRoumHist 15/3, 1976, 465–481.
Inscripţii din Sarmizegetusa, AMN 13, 1976, 89–97 (avec H. Daicoviciu).
Epigraphica (V), AIIA 19, 1976, 259–265.
Publius Aelius Antipater, in: Epigraphica. Travaux dédiés au VIIe Congrès d'épigraphie grecque et latine (Constantza, 9–15 septembre 1977), Bucureşti 1977, 75–78 (avec H. Daicoviciu).
La carrière de Ti. Claudius Claudianus, in: Epigraphica. Travaux dédiés au VIIe Congrès d'épigraphie grecque et latine (Constantza, 9–15 septembre 1977), Bucureşti 1977, 167–176.
Epigraphica (VII). Inscripţii din Sarmizegetusa, Apulum 15, 1977, 643–657.
Un relief din Sarmizegetusa cu reprezentarea lui Silvanus şi a nouă Silvane, AMN 14, 1977, 155–158 (avec A. Rusu).
Epigraphica (VIII). Inscripţii din Sarmizegetusa aflate la Ostrovul Mare, Apulum 16, 1978, 189–197.
Epigraphica (IX). Inscipţii votive recent descoperite la Sarmizegetusa, AIIA 21, 1978, 279–287.
Die Laufbahn eines Ritters aus Pamphylien, Chiron 8, 1978, 515–527.
Epigraphica (X), AMN 15, 1978, 179–187.
Epigraphica (VI), StCl 18, 1979, 137–144.
La carrière de Aurelius Tuesianus, in: Actes du VIIe Congrès International d'Épigraphie Grecque et Latine (Constantza 1977), Bucureşti, 1979, p. 441–442.
Principalele rezultate ale săpăturilor din 1975–1977 la Ulpia Traiana Sarmizegetusa, Sargetia 14, 1979, 139–154 (avec H. Daicoviciu, D. Alicu, C. Pop).
Carrières sénatoriales (II), AMN 16, 1979, 69–86.

Şantierul Ulpia Traiana Sarmizegetusa (campania 1978), MatCercArh 13, 1979, 231–233 (avec H. Daicoviciu, D. Alicu, C. Pop, A. Rusu).
Epigraphica (XI), Potaissa 2, 1980, 123–131.
Epigraphica (XII), AMN 17, 1980, 81–89.
Beiträge zu den Fasten Dakiens im 3. Jahrhundert, ZPE 40, 1980, 273–282.
Săpăturile de la Ulpia Traiana Sarmizegetusa, MatCercArh 14, 1980, 276–282 (avec H. Daicoviciu, D. Alicu, C. Pop, A. Rusu).
Die spätrömische Inschrift von Gornea, ZPE 42, 1981, 263–272.
Epigraphica (XIII). Inscriptions de Apulum, AMN 18, 1981, 443–449.
Un chevalier romain patron de la colonia Drobeta, Apulum 19, 1981, 125–126.
Carrières sénatoriales (III), AMN 19, 1982, 39–57.
La place de la Dacie dans les carrières sénatoriales, in: Epigrafia e ordine senatorio (Tituli 4), Roma 1982, 369–395.
Notes épigraphiques, in: Epigrafia e ordine senatorio (Tituli 4), Roma 1982, 489–493.
Maximinus Thrax und die Provinz Dazien, ZPE 49, 1982, 225–238.
Epigraphica (XIV). Inscripţii din Apulum, AMN 20, 1983, 103–111.
Castrul roman de la Căşei, MatCercArh 15, 1983, 297–298 (avec D. Isac, Al. Diaconescu, C. Opreanu).
Săpăturile din 1980 de la Ulpia Traiana Sarmizegetusa, MatCercArh 15, 1983, 246–277 (avec H. Daicoviciu, D. Alicu, C. Pop, A. Soroceanu, C. Ilieş).
Inschriften von Prokuratoren aus Sarmizegetusa (I), ZPE 50, 1983, 233–251.
Das Militärdiplom von Drobeta, ZPE 56, 1984, 263–295 (avec D. Benea).
Diploma militară de la Drobeta, AMN 21, 1984, 111–124 (avec D. Benea).
Ein Apolloheiligtum in der Nähe von Tibiscum, ZPE 58, 1985, 211–218 (avec P. Rogozea).
Zur Entstehung der Provinz Dacia Porolissensis, in: Römische Geschichte, Altertumskunde und Epigraphik. Festschrift für Artur Betz zur Vollendung seines 80. Lebensjahres, Wien 1985, 471–481.
Epigraphica (XV). Inscripţii din Apulum, AMN 22–23, 1985–1986, 489–501.
Forurile din Ulpia Traiana Sarmizegetusa, AMN 22–23, 1985–1986, 161–183 (avec Al. Diaconescu).
Săpăturile arheologice de la Ulpia Traiana Sarmizegetusa (1985), in: Documente recent descoperite şi informaţii arheologice. Material documentar în sprijinul cadrelor didactice şi catedrelor de ştiinţe sociale, Bucureşti 1986, 23–31.
Săpăturile arheologice din 1981 la Ulpia Traiana Sarmizegetusa, MatCercArh 16, 1986, 121–134 (avec H. Daicoviciu, D. Alicu, C. Pop, S. Cociş).
Prosopographia coloniae Dacicae Sarmizegetusae (I), AMN 24–25, 1987–1988, 163–170.
Nymphaeum-ul de la Germisara, RMI 59, 1, 1990, 9–17 (avec A. Rusu).
Les deux forums de la colonia Ulpia Traiana Augusta Dacica Sarmizegetusa, REA 92/3–4, 1990, 273–296 (avec R. Etienne, Al. Diaconescu).
Les propylées du forum civil de Sarmizegetusa (Roumanie), CRAI janvier-mars 1990, 91–113 (avec R. Etienne, Al. Diaconescu).
Die Inschriften vom Pfaffenberg und der Bereich der Canabae legionis, Tyche 6, 1991, 131–160.

Municipium Vindobonense, Tyche 6, 1991, 171–177.
Apulum, in: La politique édilitaire dans les provinces de l'empire romain, Cluj-Napoca 1993, 67–82 (avec Al. Diaconescu).
Zum Kultus der Dea Caelestis, ZPE 99, 1993, 223–236.
Monumente romane descoperite la Alba Iulia, Apulum 27–30, 1990–1993, 227–239 (avec M. Blăjan).
Die soziale und ethnische Zusammensetzung der Bevölkerung în Sarmizegetusa und in Apulum, in: Prosopographie und Sozialgeschichte. Studien zur Methodik und Erkenntnismöglichkeit der kaiserlichen Prosopographie (Kolloquium Köln 24.–26. November 1991), Köln – Wien – Weimar 1993, 315–337.
La tablette de Baudecet (Gembloux, Belgique): éléments d'étude comparative, Latomus 52/4, 1993, 826–841.
Ein Militärdiplom aus der Provinz Dacia Porolissensis, ZPE 100, 1994, 577–591 (avec W. Eck, D. Isac).
Ein unechter beneficiarius in Apulum, ZPE 103, 1994, 207–208.
Le forum en bois de Sarmizegetusa (Roumanie), CRAI janvier-mars 1994, 147–164 (avec R. Etienne, Al. Diaconescu).
Săpăturile arheologice din 1984 de la Ulpia Traiana Sarmizegetusa, AMN 31/I, 1994, 433–460 (avec H. Daicoviciu, D. Alicu, S. Cociş, C. Ilieş, C. Meylan, A. Paki).
Ein neuer Statthalter von Noricum Mediterraneum, ZPE 107, 1995, 299–304.
L'aristocratie municipale en Dacie et la grande propriété foncière, in: Du Latifundium au Latifondo (Actes de la Table ronde internationale du CNRS organisée à l'Université Michel de Montaigne Bordeaux III les 17–19 décembre 1992), Paris 1995, 437–444.
Epigraphische Beiträge zum Pfaffenberger Heiligtum, in: Römische Inschriften – Neufunde, Neulesungen und Neuinterpretationen. Festschrift für Hans Lieb (= Arbeiten zur römischen Epigraphik und Altertumskunde 2), Basel – Berlin 1994, 341–346.
Zur Tätigkeit des L. Aelius Caesar in Pannonien, CJ 1993/1994 (1995), 197–202.
Eine Parallele zwischen den Praetoria der Statthalter in Carnuntum und in Apulum, CJ 1993/1994 (1995), 203–209.
Le territoire de la Colonia Sarmizegetusa, EN 5, 1995, 63–82. 75.
Eine Votivinschrift aus Caransebeş, EN 5, 1995, 83–86.
Zum Munizipalleben von Apulum und Sarmizegetusa, SpecNova 11, 1995, 155–164.
Eine Votivinschrift vom Pfaffenberg (Carnuntum) für das Wohl des Tetrarchen Maximianus, CJ 1995, 95–99.
Marbles in the Roman Province of Dacia, in: Actes de la IVème Conférence internationale Asmosia, Bordeaux 1995, 131–140 (avec H.W. Müller, B. Schwaighofer, M. Benea, Al. Diaconescu).
Les estampilles tégulaires de Sarmizegetusa, EN 6, 1996, 153–199.
Un graffite sur une brique de Teregova, EN 6, 1996, 201–203.
Provenance of marble objects from the Roman province of Dacia, JÖAI 66, 1997, 430–454 (avec H.W. Müller, B. Schwaighofer, M. Benea, Al. Diaconescu).
Zwei fragmentarische Laufbahnen aus dem Forum Vetus von Sarmizegetusa, ZPE 120, 1998, 272–276.

Inschriften von Prokuratoren aus Sarmizegetusa (II), ZPE 120, 1998, 253–271.
Quatre monuments épigraphiques d'Apulum découverts dans le lit de Mureş, AMN 35/I, 1998, 109–118 (avec V. Moga, M. Drîmbărean).
Epigraphica (XVI). Inscriptions de Sarmizegetusa, Sargetia 17/I, 1998, 261–266.
Un bureau du publicum portorium Illyrici à Apulum, AMN 35/I, 1998, 105–108 (avec V. Moga).
Die Legio XV Apollinaris in den markomannischen Kriegen, AMN 35/I, 1998, 97–104.
Un Archelaus à Apulum, Apulum 35, 1998, 147–150 (avec Cl. Băluţă).
Different voices in: Traiano ai confini dell'Impero, Milano 1998, 125–128 (Provincia Dacia), 134–136 (Colonia Dacica Sarmizegetusa), 138–142 (Apulum), 271–274 nr. 206–209, 276 nr. 212, 280 nr. 221, 281 nr. 223/1–4, 286 nr. 233. 8 (others).
Ein Bruchstück eines Militärdiploms aus Apulum, ZPE 126, 1999, 243–248.
Ein Celeianer als Decurio von Sarmizegetusa, în Steine und Wege. Festschrift für Dieter Knibbe zum 65. Geburtstag, Wien 1999, 379–382.
Epigraphica Tibiscensia, AMN 36/I, 1999, 91–107 (avec D. Benea).
Fulgur conditum, AMN 36/I, 1999, 109–110 (avec M. Drîmbărean).
L'ala Flavia en Dacie, AMN 36/I, 1999, 81–89.
Les chevaliers romains dans l'armée impériale et les implications de l'imperium, in: L'ordre équestre. Histoire d'une aristocratie (IIe siècle av. J.-C. – IIIe siècle ap. J.-C.), Collection de l'Ecole Française de Rome 257, Rome 1999, 321–350.
Testo epigrafico, supporto architettonico e contesto archeologico nei fori di Sarmizegetusa, in: Atti del XI Congresso Internazionale di Epigrafia Greca e Latina, Roma 18–24 settembre 1997, Roma 1999, 125–137 (avec Al. Diaconescu).
Les légions dans la province de Dacie, in: Actes du Congrès sur les légions romaines (Lyon 1998), Lyon 2000, 203–224.
I pomarenses di Sarmizegetusa, in: Miscellanea Epigrafica in onore di Lidio Gasperini, Macerata 2000, 743–750.
Colonia Ulpia Traiana Augusta Dacica Sarmizegetusa, in: Kulturparks. Erbe und Entertainment (ed. Eugen Scherer, Ilona Slawinski), St. Pölten 2000, 67–75.
Ti. Claudius Constans, procurateur de Dacie Inférieure et de Maurétanie Césarienne, AMN 37/I, 2000, 231–242.
Des fistulae plumbeae à Sarmizegetusa, AMN 37/I, 2000, 223–229 (avec G. Băeştean).
Epigraphica (XVI), Sargetia 27/I, 1997–1998 (2001), 261–266.
Les inscriptions du sanctuaire de Pfaffenberg, BSNAF 1997 (2001), 51–53.
Colonia Ulpia Traiana Augusta Dacica Sarmizegetusa. Brève présentation et état de recherche, TransRev 10, 2, 2001, 16–37.
De nouveau sur les Lucii Antonii de Sarmizegetusa, in: Studii de istorie antică. Omagiu profesorului Ion Glodariu, Cluj-Napoca 2001, 363–370.
Trei inscripţii din Apulum, Apulum 38, 2001, 189–192 (avec Cl. Băluţă).
Studia Porolissensia (I). Le temple dolichénien, AMN 38/I, 2001, 221–237.
Greek marbles in the Roman Province of Dacia, in: Archaeometry Issues in Greek Prehistory and Antiquity, Athens 2001, 199–211 (avec H. W. Müller, B. Schwaighofer, M. Benea, Al. Diaconescu).

Il Pfaffenberg di Carnuntum e le sue iscrizioni, in: Roma sul Danubio. Da Aquileia a Carnuntum lungo la via dell'ambra (ed. M. Buora, W. Jobst), Roma 2002, 87–91.

L'urbanisation des provinces danubiennes, in: La naissance de la ville dans l'Antiquité, Paris 2003, 285–298.

Die römische Provinz Dacia, in: Reallexikon der germanischen Altertumskunde (éd. R. Müller), Berlin – New York 2003, 483–489.

Sarmizegetusa, in: Reallexikon der germanischen Altertumskunde (éd. R. Müller), Berlin – New York 2004, 513–518.

Gli Illiri ad Alburnus Maior, in: Dall'Adriatico al Danubio. L'Illirico nell'età greca e romana (Atti del convegno internazionale Cividale del Friuli, 25–27 settembre 2003, ed. G. Urso), Pisa 2004, 271–307.

Le dieu Yarhibôl, in: Studia Historica et Archaeologica in honorem Magistrae Doina Benea, Timişoara 2004, 299–303.

Les fouilles du forum vetus de Sarmizegetusa. Rapport général, AMN 39–40/I, 2002–2003 (2004), 59–154 (avec R. Étienne, A. Diaconescu)

Epigraphica (XVII), AMN 39–40/I, 2002–2003 (2004), 201–219.

Der Tribun C. Valerius Valerianus in Germisara, AMN 39–40/I, 2002–2003 (2004), 197–200 (avec A. Pescaru, E. Pescaru).

Inschriften für Kaiser Hadrian in Sarmizegetusa, in: Epigraphica II. Mensa rotunda epigraphiae Dacicae Pannonicaeque (ed. G. Németh, I. Piso), Debrecen 2004, 81–88.

Der Prätorianerpräfekt Q. Marcius Turbo und seine Söhne, ZPE 150, 2004, 265–280.

The Roman Empire at the Origin of Romania's and the Nederlands' Present Territory, in: 2000 Years of Inter-European East-West Relations. Case Study: Romania –The Nederlands, Bucureşti 2004, 417–421.

Zu den Fasten Dakiens unter Trajan, in: Ad fontes! Festschrift für Gerhard Dobesch zum fünfundsechzigsten Geburtstag am 15. September 2004, Wien 2004, 515–518.

Die Cohors III Campestris in Porolissum, in: „Eine ganz normale Inschrift" ... und Ähnliches zum Geburtstag von Ekkehard Weber, Wien 2005, 325–331.

La Mésie Supérieure et les débuts de Sarmizegetusa, in: Römische Städte und Festungen an der Donau. Akten der regionalen Konferenz (Beograd 16–19 Oktober 2003), Beograd 2005, 119124.

Apulum, Dacie, Dalmatie, Drobeta, Germisara, Histria, Napoca, Porolissum, Potaissa, Sarmizegetusa Regia, Sarmizegetusa Ulpia Traiana, Tropaeum Traiani, in: Dictionnaire de l'Antiquité (ed. J. Leclant), Paris 2005, 168–169, 623, 624, 626–627, 726, 979, 1082–1083, 1500–1501, 1774, 1781, 1962–1963, 2230.

Die Augustalen in Sarmizegetusa, in: Epigraphica III. Politai et cives (ed. G. Németh, P. Forisék), Debrecen 2006, 101–116.

Nouvelle discussion sur la carrière de Calpurnius Iulianus, in: Miscellanea numismatica Antiquitatis. In honorem septagenarii magistri Virgilii Mihăilescu-Bîrliba oblata, Honoraria 4, Iaşi 2007, 231–237.

La legio I Adiutrix à Sarmizegetusa Regia?, in: Dacia felix. Studia Michaeli Bărbulescu oblata, Cluj-Napoca 2007, 279–283.

Un nouveau conductor salinarum en Dacie, AMN 41–42/I, 2004–2005 (2007), 179–182.

Studia Porolissenssia (II), AMN 41–42/I, 2004–2005 (2007) 183–188.
Aus der Geschichte der Archäologie und Epigraphik, in: Imperium an der Peripherie. Österreichische Spuren in Siebenbürgen (ed. H. Balomiri, I. Etzersdorfer), Wien – Sibiu 2007, 150–161.
Le cursus honorum de São Miguel d'Odrinhas, SEBarc VI, 2008, 155–168.
Il processo di urbanizzazione della Dacia Romana, in: L'eredità di Traiano (Atti del Convegno internazionale di Studi, Bucarest 6–7 giugno 2007, ed. A. Castaldini), Bucarest 2008, 28–44.
Les débuts de la province de Dacie, in: Die römischen Provinzen. Begriff und Gründung (Colloquium Cluj-Napoca, 28. September – 1. Oktober 2006), Cluj-Napoca 2008, 297–331.
L'inscription monumentale de l'entrée dans le forum vetus de Sarmizegetusa, AMN 43–44/I, 2006–2007 (2008), 151–161.
Note sur le territorium Arcobadarense, AMN 43–44/I, 2006–2007 (2008), 163–166.
La cohors I Augusta Ituraeorum en Dacie, AMN 43–44/I, 2006–2007 (2008), 167–175 (avec F. Marcu).
L'aigle de la legio XIII Gemina, AMN 43–44/I, 2006–2007 (2008), 177–182 (avec V. Moga, M. Drîmbarean).
Sarmizegetusa, Forum novum 2007, CCA 2007, 2008, 265–269 (avec C. Roman, F. Marcu, O. Țentea, G. Cupcea).
Sarmizegetusa, Forum novum, Capitoliu, templul lui Yarhibol, CCA 2008, 2009, 189–191 (avec F. Marcu, O. Țentea, M. Barbu, G. Cupcea, R. Varga).
Inscriptiones submersae, in: Epigrafi romane di Transilvania raccolte da Giuseppe Ariosti e postillate da Scipione Maffei. Biblioteca Capitolare di Verona. Manoscritto ccxlvii. Studi e ricerche (a cura di G. P. Marchi e J. Pál), Verona 2010, 169–178.
La liste d'un college de Sarmizegetusa, in: Identități culturale și regionale în context european. Studii de arheologie și antropologie istorică / Local and regional cultural identities in European context. Archaeology and historical antropology. In memoriam Alexandri V. Matei, Cluj-Napoca 2010, 439–442.
Note sur cinq bornes milliares de Dacie, in: Scripta classica. Radu Ardevan sexagenario dedicata, Cluj-Napoca 2011, 321–330.
Il Capitolium, l'Epulum Iovis e il Dies Iovis nella Dacia Romana, in: Roma e le province del Danubio. Atti del I Convegno Internazionale Ferrara – Cento, 15–17 Ottobre 2009 (a cura di L. Zerbini), Soveria Manelli 2010, 269–278.
Das Forum von Brigetio, ACD 46, 2010, 71–77.
Un nouveau temple palmyrénien à Sarmizegetusa, Dacia 55, 2011, 111–121 (avec O. Țentea).
Le Capitole de Sarmizegetusa, Dacia 56, 2012, 129–134 (avec F. Marcu, O. Țentea, G. Cupcea, R. Varga).
Die Laufbahn des T. Flavius T. fil. Palatina Priscus Gallonius Fronto Q. Marcius Turbo und seine Aufgaben im dakischen und im mauretanischen Raum, StudiaUBB Historia, 57/1, 2012, 90–100.
The archaeological patrimony of Roșia Montană, in: Roșia Montană in Universal History (Hrsg. Pompei Cocean), Cluj-Napoca 2012, 25–30.

Zum Judenkrieg des Q. Marcius Turbo, ZPE 187, 2013, 255–262.

Die Inschrift aus Albertirsa, in: Studia epigraphica in memoriam Géza Alföldy, Bonn 2013, 275–284.

Studia Porolissensia (III), AMP 35, 2013, 159–176.

Une inscription funéraire des environs de Napoca, Tibiscum 3, 2013, 33–35 (avec T. Tecar).

Studia Porolissensia (IV), RB 27, 2013, 39–51.

A funerary stele from Miercurea Sibiului, BrukenthalAM IX/1, 2014, 67–71 (avec Gh. Natea, V. Palaghie).

Sur le statut municipal de Potaissa, in: Archäologische Beiträge. Gedenkschrift zum hundertsten Geburtstag von Kurt Horedt, Cluj-Napoca 2014, 69–75.

Die Trajansfora: politische Botschaft, in: Trajan und seine Städte. Colloquium Cluj-Napoca (29. September – 2. Oktober 2013), Cluj-Napoca 2014, 255–273.

Die palmyrenischen Truppen in Dakien. Monumente und Öffentlichkeit, in: Öffentlichkeit – Monument – Text. XIV Congressus Internationalis Epigraphiae Graecae et Latinae 27.–31. Augusti MMXII, Berlin – Boston 2014, 479–480 (avec O. Țentea).

Le siège du gouverneur de Mésie Inférieure, in: Interconnectivity in the Mediterranean and Pontic World during the Hellenistic and Roman Periods III. Pontica et Mediterranea, Cluj-Napoca 2014, 489–504.

Ein centurio regionarius aus der legio X Fretensis in Dakien, Tyche 29, 2014, 115–123 (avec G. Cupcea).

Zur Reform des Gallienus anläßlich neuer Inschriften aus Potaissa, Tyche 29, 2014, 125–146.

L'aigle en argent de Micia, SAA 20, 2014, 219–229.

Les listes de centurions de Potaissa et la participation des légions daciques à la guerre parthique de Caracalla, in: Ad fines Imperii Romani. Studia Thaddaeo Sarnowski septuagenario ab amicis, collegis discipulisque dedicata, Varsaviae 2015, 81–91.

Studia Porolissensia V, RB 28, 2014, 124–130.

Epigraphica Potaissensia, in: Culti e religiosità nelle province danubiane (Atti del II Convegno Internazionale Ferrara 20–22 Novembre 2013, éd. L. Zerbini), Bologna 2015, 423–438.

Bemerkungen zu Dexippos Vindobonensis (I), Göttinger Forum für Altertumswissenschaft, Göttingen, 18, 2015, 199–215.

Studia Porolissensia VI, AMP 37, 2015, 193–213.

Epigraphica Porolissensia (I), AMP 37, 2015, 215–229 (avec D. Deac, R. Zagreanu).

Germisarensia, Tibiscum 5, 2015, 223–234.

Une famille de pérégrins à Potaissa, in: Archaeologia Transylvanica. Studia in honorem Stephani Bajusz, Cluj-Napoca – Târgu Mureș Budapest 2015, 165–167.

Ein Gebet für die Nymphen aus Germisara, AMN 52/I, 2015, 47–68.

Nochmals zur spätrömischen Inschrift von Gornea, in: From Polites to Magos. Studia György Németh sexagenario dedicata, Budapest – Debrecen 2016, 255262.

Ein sextarium aus Potaissa, in: „Voce concordi". Scritti per Claudio Zaccaria (= Antichità Altoadriatiche 85). Festschrift Claudio Zaccaria, Trieste 2016, 555–559.

Das Heiligtum der Zollstation von Porolissum, ZPE 200, 2016, 544–548 (avec C. H. Opreanu, D. Deac).

Die rätselhafte cohors I Augusta aus der Dacia Porolissensis, in: Mensa rotunda epigraphica Napocensis, Cluj-Napoca 2016, 35–46.

War die Eroberung Dakiens eine Notwendigkeit?, in: Columna Traiani. Traianssäule – Siegesmonument und Kriegsbericht in Bildern (= Tyche Sonderband 9), Wien 2017, 333–342.

Zur Inschrift des primus pilus G. Baienius Ianuarius aus Novae, Studia Europaea Gnesnensia, Gniezno, 16, 2017, 57–69.

L'inscription de Villadecanes et le dies Iovis en Espagne Tarraconnaise, CCGG 28, 2017, 135–150.

Colonia Dacica Sarmizegetusa, short introduction; The forum of Trajan (forum vetus); The forum of Antoninus Pius (forum novum) and the Capitol, in: The exhibition Sarmizegetusa – the beginning of the Roman Dacia (ed. O. Țentea, Al. Rațiu), București 2017, 14–37.

Das verhängnisvolle Jahr 262 und die amissio Daciae, in: Proceedings of the first International Roman and Late Antique Thrace Conference. "Cities, Territories and Identities" (Plovdiv, 3rd–7th October 2016), Sofia 2018, 427–440.

Kleinasiatische Götter und Kolonisten in Dakien, Gephyra 15, 2018, 37–70.

Un avium inspex et le statut d'Asturica Augusta, Anuari de Filologia. Antiqua et Mediaevalia, Barcelona, 8, 2018, 747–755.

Eine neue kaiserliche Statuenbasis von Buciumi und Caracallas Reise nach Dakien, in: Limes XXIII. Proceedings of the 23rd International Congress of Roman Frontier Studies Ingolstadt 2015. Akten des 23. Internationalen Limeskongresses in Ingolstadt 2015. Beiträge zum Welterbe. Limes Sonderband, Mainz 2018, 756–762 (avec D. Deac).

Ulpia Traiana Sarmizegetusa – Edificiul de cult al zeilor palmyreni, CCA 2017, 2018, 112117 (avec O. Țentea, F. Matei-Popescu).

Une dédicace à Ratiaria pour le salut du gouverneur P. Mummius Sisenna Rutilianus, in: La Dacie et l'Empire Romain. Mélanges d'épigraphie et d'archéologie offerts à Constantin C. Petolescu, București 2018, 97–104.

Eine Weihung aus Porolissum für das Wohl des Severischen Kaiserhauses, ZPE 209, 2019, 295–296 (avec C. H. Opreanu).

Die Göttin Hekate in Sarmizegetusa, in: L. Mihailescu-Bîrliba (Hrsg.), Limes, Economy and Society in the Lower Danubian Provinces (= Colloquia Antiqua 25), Leuven – Paris – Bristol 2019, 139–157 (avec Cs. Szabó).

Traianus Decius und die Provinz Dakien, in: Panegyrikoi logoi. Festschrift für Johannes Nollé zum 65. Geburtstag, Bonn 2019, 53–61.

Les beneficiarii consularis de Samum, in: Roman Army and Local Society in the Limes Provinces of the Roman Empire (= Pharos 42), Rahden 2019, 109–129.

Epigraphica Porolissensia (II), AMP 41, 2019, 253–261 (avec D. Deac).

Les estampilles militaires de Războieni-Cetate, AMP 41, 2019, 263–289 (avec R. Varga).

Une statio de beneficiarii consularis à Teregova, AB 27 (In memoriam Alexandri Szentmiklosy), 2019, 197–199.

Bemerkungen zu Dexippos Vindobonensis (II), in: Empire in Crisis: Gothic Invasion and Roman Historiography (= Tyche Supplementband 12), Wien 2020, 337–355.
Si defit aurum: l'initiation dans un Serapeum de Sarmizegetusa, Bibliotheca Isiaca 4, Bordeaux 2020, 127–137.
L'inscription de construction de l'Iseum de Savaria, Bibliotheca Isiaca 4, Bordeaux 2020, 139–142.
La legio III Gallica à Potaissa, in: Studia honoraria archaeologica. Zbornik radova u prigodi 65. rođendana prof. dr. sc. Mirjane Sanader, Zagreb 2020, 325–331.
L'affranchi impérial Philomusus et le temple palmyrénien de Sarmizegetusa, in: Varia epigraphica et archaeologica. Volume dédié à la mémoire de Maria Bărbulescu (= Pontica 52, Suppl. 6), Constanța 2020, 245–254 (avec O. Țentea, F. Matei-Popescu).
Die Ziegelstempel als Quelle für die Geschichte der Provinz Dakien, in: Ad ripam fluminis Danuvi. Papers of the 3rd International Conference on the Roman Danubian Provinces (= Tyche Supplementband 11), Wien 2020, 279–295 + Pl. 41.
Les cultes isiaques à Sarmizegetusa, in: Africa, Egypt and the Danubian Provinces of the Roman Empire. Population, Military and Religious Interactions (2nd–3rd centuries AD), B.A.R. Int. Ser. 3058, Oxford 2021, 45–63 (avec L. Bricault, D. Deac).
Isis myrionima à Micăsasa, in: Pro merito laborum. Miscellanea epigrafica per Gianfranco Paci, Tivoli 2021, 515–521.
Deux inscriptions rupestres d'Arulis sur l'Euphrate et la supposée participation de la Legio IIII Flavia Felix à l'expédition parthique de Trajan, in: Antiquitas Aeterna. Classical Studies Dedicated to Leszek Mrozewicz on His 70th Birthday, Wiesbaden 2021, 339–344.
Liber frugifer im Auxiliarkastell von Romita?, in: K. Matijević (Hg.), Miscellanea historica et archaeologica. Festschrift zu Ehren von Rainer Wiegels anlässlich seines 80. Geburtstages, Computus Druck Satz Verlag, Gutenberg 2021, 175–181, 282.
N(umerus) P(almyrenorum) O(---), RömÖsterr 44, 2021, 199–205.
Colonia Dacica Sarmizegetusa, die erste römische Stadt nördlich der Donau, in: K. Matijević, R. Wiegels (Hg.), Kultureller Transfer und religiöse Landschaften. Zur Begegnung zwischen Imperium und Barbaricum in der römischen Kaiserzeit (= AAWG 52), Berlin – Boston 2022, 213–254.
Studia Porolissensia VII, in: Defending the polis defending the empire. The ancient Greek and Roman military strategy and inscriptions (éd. I. Piso, P. Forisék), Budapest 2022, 145–158.
Harietto und Dagalaifus in Emona. Ein Beitrag zur Geschichte des spätrömischen Heeres, in: Emperor, Army, and Society. Studies in Roman Imperial History for Anthony R. Birley, Bonn 2022, 327–336 (avec Anja Ragolić).
Der Palmyrener P. Aelius Theimes, duumviralis der colonia Dacica Sarmizegetusa, ZPE 223, 2022, 277–284 (avec O. Țentea).
Dakerkriege Trajans, in: L. Burckhardt, M. Al. Speidel (Hrsg.), Militärgeschichte der griechisch-römischen Antike. Lexikon (Der Neue Pauly Suppl. 12), Stuttgart 2022, 487–489.

La Dacie poétique (I), in: Romans and Natives in the Danubian Provinces (1st–6th C. AD) (eds. L. Mihailescu-Bîrliba, I. Piso), Wiesbaden 2023, 309–324.

Beitrag zur palmyrenischen Onomastik in Dakien, in: Religion und Epigraphik. Kleinasien, der griechische Osten und die Mittelmeerwelt. Festschrift zum 65. Geburtstag von Walter Ameling (Asia Minor Studien Band 102), Bonn 2023, 401–406 + Taf. 15.

Les numeri Palmyrenorum, in: Alfred von Domszewski. Latin Epigraphy in the Roman Empire (eds. S. Nemeti, C. Timoc). Acts of the Colloquium held in Timișoara in December 14th–17th 2022, Cluj-Napoca 2024, 171–184 (avec Ovidiu Țentea).

Volumes édités

Acta Musei Napocensis 35–44, 1998–2007.

Epigraphica II. Mensa rotunda epigraphiae Dacicae Pannonicaeque, Debrecen 2004 (avec Gy. Németh) .

Die römischen Provinzen. Begriff und Gründung (Colloquium Cluj-Napoca, 28. September – 1. Oktober 2006), Cluj-Napoca 2008.

Scripta classica. Radu Ardevan sexagenario dedicata, Cluj-Napoca 2011 (avec V. Rusu-Bolindeț, R. Varga, S. Mustață, E. Beu-Dachin, L. Ruscu).

Trajan und seine Städte. Colloquium Cluj-Napoca, (29. September – 2. Oktober 2013), Cluj-Napoca 2014 (avec Rada Varga).

Defending the polis defending the empire. The ancient Greek and Roman military strategy and inscriptions, Budapest 2022 (avec P. Forisek).

Romans and Natives in the Danubian Provinces (1st–6th C. AD), Wiesbaden, Harrasowitz Verlag, 2023 (avec L. Mihailescu-Bîrliba).

Abréviations

Tout le reste des abréviations dans ce volume est selon l'Année Philologique, l'Annér Épigraphique et le Supplementum Epigraphicum Graecum.

AAWG = Abhandlungen der Akademie der Wissenschaften zu Göttingen. Neue Folge, Göttingen.
AB = Analele Banatului, Timișoara.
ACD = Acta Classica Universitatis Scientiarum Debreceniensis, Debrecen.
AIIA = Anuarul Institutului de Istorie și Arheologie, Cluj-Napoca.
AMN = Acta Musei Napocensis, Cluj-Napoca.
AMP = Acta Musei Porolissensis, Zalău.
Apulum = Apulum. Acta Musei Apulensis, Alba Iulia.
BrukenthalAM = Brukenthal. Acta Musei, Sibiu.
CCA = Cronica cercetărilor arheologice din România, București.
CCGG = Cahiers du Centre Gustave Glotz, Paris.

Chiron = Chiron. Mitteilungen der Kommission für Alte Geschichte und Epigraphik des Deutschen Archäologischen Institus, München.
CJ = Carnuntum Jahrbuch. Zeitschrift für Archäologie und Kulturgeschichte des Donauraumes, Wien.
CRAI = Comptes rendus de l'Académie des Inscriptions et Belles-Lettres, Paris.
Dacia = Dacia. Revue d'archéologie et d'histoire ancienne, București.
EN = Ephemeris Napocensis, Cluj-Napoca.
Gephyra = Gephyra. Research Centre for Mediterranean Languages and Cultures of Akdeniz University, Antalya.
JÖAI = Jahreshefte des Österreichischen Archäologischen Instituts, Wien.
Latomus =Latomus. Revue d'études latines, Bruxelles.
MatCercArh = Materiale și cercetări arheologice, București.
Pontica = Pontica, Constanța.
Potaissa = Potaissa. Studii și comunicări, Turda.
RB = Revista Bistriței. Complexul muzeal județean Bistrița-Năsăud, Bistrița.
REA = Revue d'Études Anciennes, Paris – Bordeaux.
RevRoumHist = Revue roumaine d'histoire, București.
RMI = Revista monumentelor istorice, București.
RömÖsterr = Römisches Österreich, Graz.
SAA = Studia Antiqua et Archaeologica, Iași.
Sargetia = Sargetia. Acta Musei Devensis, Deva.
SEBarc = Sylloge Epigraphica Barcinonensis, Barcelona.
SpecNova = Specimina nova dissertationum ex Instituto Historico Universitatis Quinqueecclesiensis de Iano Pannonio nominatae, Pécs.
StCl = Studii Clasice, București.
StudiaUBB Historia = Studia Universitatis "Babeș-Bolyai", series Historia, Cluj-Napoca.
Tibiscum =Tibiscum – Serie Nouă. Istorie – Arheologie – Etnografie, Caransebeș.
Tituli = Tituli. Pubblicazioni di epigrafia e antichità greche e romane dell'Università di Roma Sapienza, Roma.
TransRev = Transylvanian Review / Center for Transylvanian Studies, Cluj-Napoca.
Tyche = Tyche. Beiträge zur Alten Geschichte, Papyrologie und Epigraphik, Wien.
ZPE = Zeitschrift für Papyrologie und Epigraphik, Bonn.

Epigraphica

Contribution to the Prosopography of Kalchedon*

Annamária I. Pázsint

Kalchedon was a Megarian foundation,[1] and according to Eusebius,[2] it was founded as a *polis* in 685 BC, while Herodotus[3] specifies that it was founded 17 years before the foundation of Byzantion. Due to it having been founded before Byzantion, Kalchedon was designated as *caecorum oppidum*,[4] the location of Byzantion being much more advantageous. In its turn, Kalchedon[5] founded a colony, that of Astakos, while along with Megara it founded Mesambria; additionally, it might have been also involved in the foundation of Byzantion.[6]

Given its geographical location, as well as its regional importance, a focus on the prosopography of Kalchedon seems to be an auspicious endeavour. For the Black Sea area, there are several reference prosopographical works. A. Avram[7] has dealt extensively with the topic, the *Prosopographia Ponti Euxini Externa*,[8] which focuses on the *Pontikoi* attested in other cities, is mandatory for anyone interested in the mobility of the *Pontikoi*. For Kalchedon in particular, the works of M. Dana[9] and A. Robu[10] are of reference. Additionally, in the last years, the author has also tried to bring a contribution to this field by discussing the prosopography of multiple Greek *poleis* from the Black Sea.[11]

* Acknowledgements: This work was supported by a grant of the Babeş-Bolyai University – UBB Starting Research Grant project number SRG-UBB 32912/22.06.2023.

1 See, especially Robu 2014a, 222–242.

2 Euseb. *Chron.* 93b.

3 Hdt. 4.144.1.

4 Plin. *HN* 5.149.

5 On the history of Kalchedon see, Avram 2004; Merle 1916; Robu 2014a. Merle 1916; Robu 2014a.

6 Avram 2004, 981.

7 To mention some: Avram 2011; Avram 2012; Avram 2013.

8 Avram 2013. See also, Avram 2011; Avram 2012.

9 Dana 2011.

10 Robu 2007/2009; Robu 2012; Robu 2012/2018; Robu 2013a; Robu 2013 b; Robu 2014a; Robu 2014b.

11 Pázsint 2022a; Pázsint 2022b; Pázsint 2023; Pázsint 2024.

Overview of the population

As it results from the prosopographical catalogue below, the available epigraphic sources record 194 persons (attested as Καλχηδόνιοι/Καλαηδόνιοι/Χαλχηδόνιοι), who seem to have been attested at Kalchedon and its territory,[12] from around the 4th century BC and up to the 3rd century AD. From a chronological point of view, the inscriptions are almost evenly distributed between the Hellenistic and the Roman period, the dating of inscriptions being in many instances rather general.

From a gender perspective, the epigraphic representativeness is not surprising. The epigraphically attested male population represents most of the population (158, or 81%), followed at a great distance by the female population (37, or 19%). Among the attested women, not many stand out, which is not surprising, and when they do, it is because of the religious offices that they held, their economic power, or their appurtenance to a certain family. There is only one priestess, respectively Ἀριστονίκα daughter of Μοσχ[---] (3rd century BC),[13] who is mentioned on a contract concerning the acquisition of the priestly office for Μήτηρ (Ὀρέα?).[14] Ἀριστονίκα bought it for 300 drachmas, and a tenth of [30?] drachmas (?), payment made at once. According to the contract, the priestess was allowed to resell the priestly office, stipulation which is missing from the two other regulations attested at Kalchedon.[15] Nevertheless, besides the priestess, an inscription from the Roman period mentions also a προφῆτις of Apollo Chresterios, respectively Ἄπφη, who was the master of Ὀρβανίλλα.[16]

Women are mostly visible at their death, but here epithets (γλυκυτάτη[17]) are rarely used to describe them. Two of the women were, nevertheless, mourned in moving funerary epigrams.[18] From 340/339 BC we have the well-known funerary epigram[19] dedicated to Βοίδιον, the wife of the Athenian στρατηγός Χάρης.[20] She was from Athens and accompanied her husband overseas, in the Athenian aid brought to Byzantion, which was besieged by king Philip II of Macedon. As it results, she died during the expedition, being laid to rest on the Asiatic shore of the Bosphorus.

Later, from the 2nd century BC comes another funerary epigram of a woman, respectively Στρατονίκα daughter of Ἀπολλώνιος and of an *ignota*.[21] Her parents set up her fu-

---

12 For its territory see Robu 2014b, 190–193.
13 IK Kalchedon 11.
14 For this regulation see, LSAM 4.
15 Sokolowski 1955, 17.
16 IK Kalchedon 61. See below for other prophets.
17 IK Kalchedon 69. Term used also for children: IK Kalchedon 69; IK Kalchedon 71.
18 In total, there are five funerary epigrams attested at Kalchedon, the other three being dedicated to men (IK Kalchedon 31 = SEG 28, 1662; IK Kalchedon 34), one of them being an ephebe (IK Kalchedon 32 = SEG 38, 1274).
19 *The Anthologia Palatina* VII 169 reports on the epigram dedicated by Χάρης to his wife.
20 IK Kalchedon 35.
21 IK Kalchedon 33 = SEG 28, 1661.

nerary monument, the text of the inscription being an epigram in which her death is lamented, stipulating that she was just about to get married.

From the Roman period, the funerary inscriptions mentioning two women and their family members, record also their *agnomina*, following the formula ἡ καὶ [---]. It is the case of Στρατήγια ἡ καὶ Ἔλπις, wife of Ἑρμιανός son of Ἑρμόδωρος, mother of Ὀνήσιμος, Πώσφορος, and Ἑρμιανός;[22] and Αὐρηλία Ὀνησικράτεια ἡ καὶ Δυσκόλιον, daughter of Αὐρήλιος Ἀγάπητος and Αὐρηλία Εὐτυχιανή, sister of Αὐρήλιος Ἱμέριος.[23] The other funerary inscriptions mentioning women are more laconic, recording only the personal name and the patronymic,[24] sometimes along with the person whom set up the monument to their memory (mostly their parents, husbands, and in a case the son[25]), or to whom they set up the monument to.

Despite having only these two occurrences, among the women who were part of elite families we probably have also Γύκεια wife of Ἀρίστων son of Ἀρίστων. According to the editors of the inscription, given the iconography of the sarcophagus, Ἀρίστων was very likely a ἱερεύς, ἀγωνοθέτης, ἀγορανόμος, γυμνασίαρχος and στρατηγός.[26] The personal name and patronymic[27] is also one of prestige, which could have been chosen exactly given the position of the family in the local society.

In what concerns age, at Kalchedon, only 16 persons have their age mentioned (out of whom six are women) on their funerary monument, ranging from the age of one to 60. In one case, the age is not given in a concise manner, but reference is made of a young age. As such, Στρατονίκα daughter of Ἀπολλώνιος died when she was about to get married, which indicates that she was young.[28] The funerary epigram[29] of the ephebe Ἑκαταῖος son of Ἑκαταῖος,[30] stipulates that he died οὔπω ἐφειβήην θηκάμενος χλαμύδα, but adds also his age at death (XVIII). Most of the inscriptions recording age stipulate, besides it, only the personal name and the patronymic. Age rounding is encountered here as well, as part of an epigraphic habit specific for the ancient world regarding the knowledge of exact dates of birth. Unfortunately, no reason for their death is given.

Occupations are rarely attested in the inscriptions from Kalchedon. Besides the above-mentioned ἰατρός ([---]νος son of Θευγένης), and ship builder (Πεισίστρατος son of Ἡλιόδωρος) from Cos, there is only one Χαλχηδόνιος attested at Istros as *negotiator* (see

22 IK Kalchedon 63.
23 IK Kalchedon 69.
24 IK Kalchedon 39; IK Kalchedon 47.
25 IK Kalchedon 62.
26 IK Kalchedon 65. See also Dana 2011, 43.
27 At Callatis, from the relatively same timeframe, there are a father and son part of the elite, with the same personal name and patronymic: ISM III 40 = IG X,3,3,1 34a; ISM III 41 = IG X,3,3,1 34b; ISM III 42= IG X,3,3,1 33bc; ISM III 43 = IG X,3,3,1 35; ISM III 44 = IG X,3,3,1 32; ISM III 45 = SEG 27, 384 = IG X,3,3,1 36.
28 IK Kalchedon 33 = SEG 28, 1661.
29 IK Kalchedon 32 = SEG 38, 1274.
30 See Dana 2011, 46.

below). Given the location of the *polis*, and the fact that it had two harbours,[31] other *negotiatores* certainly carried out their activity there, as well as shippers. Nevertheless, from the territory of Kalchedon, respectively from Chrysopolis, there is evidence of a group of ναῦται (practicing fishing with nets),[32] that was active in the 1st–2nd century AD. It seems that the members were mostly slaves (9), with one citizen being mentioned along them, Κοΐντος Λόλλιος Κάτος, who was very likely related to the Lolii attested at Byzantion during the same period.[33] Moreover, he might have held the citizenship of both Byzantion and Kalchedon.[34]

Overview of the society

In terms of juridical status, we can identify slaves, freedmen, citizens and Roman citizens. There are ten identifiable slaves;[35] one is Ὀρβανίλλα, who was the θρεπτή of Ἄπφη and daughter of Τυραννίς.[36] The funerary monument dedicated to her stipulates her age at death (XXVII). The other nine, are the above-mentioned ναῦται, who are attested only through their personal name, and also through the term φιλοδέσποτες.[37] One of them, Λόλλιος, is recorded as ἰσαγέμων, respectively as a deputy in the hierarchy, bearing the same *nomen* as the citizen who was likely their master.

The citizen body is divided into ἑκατοστύες (Ἀ[---], Ἀσωποδώρηα, Ἀτθίς, Δίασπις Δρο[---], Ἡρακλήα, Ἱππωνήα, Καλλιχορεατήα, Ὀλιδνήα, Παρτε[---], Πολιατήα/Πολητήα, Ποττωι, Σειρο, Τρίασπις).[38] Only a small percentage of the population is composed of Roman citizens (23, or 11,85%), out of which seven are Aurelii, four are Iulii and three are Flavii. Noteworthy to mention is the fact that out of them, only six are women. Unfortunately, as each person is attested through only one inscription, we cannot identify cases of social mobility.

Not negligible is the percentage of foreigners. More precisely, there are 34 persons at Kalchedon who display an origin marker. Most of them originate from Cos (28 – due to the finding of a list),[39] while the others from Olbia,[40] Byzantion,[41] Seleucia.[42] Nevertheless,

---

31 Avram 2004, 980. For the Byzantine period, see also, Belke 2021.

32 Demirkök 2010, 163–167.

33 See, Robu 2012/2018, 160–161.

34 See, Robu 2012/2018, 161.

35 There are also iconographic representations of slaves, but these were not necessarily a demographic reality: IK Kalchedon 31; IK Kalchedon 32; IK Kalchedon 49; IK Kalchedon 57.

36 IK Kalchedon 61 = CIG 3796.

37 Robu 2012/2018, 159; Robu 2014a, 342–347.

38 IK Kalchedon 6; IK Kalchedon 7. See, Robu 2014a.

39 IK Kalchedon 15.

40 IK Kalchedon 16.

41 IK Kalchedon 2.

42 IK Kalchedon 1.

they are attested in decrees. Among the foreigners there is also a *proxenos*, who was likely an Ὀλβιανὸς τῶν πρὸς Ὕπανιν.[43]

On the other way around, approximately 15 Χαλχηδόνιοι are attested in other cities from the Pontic area (Olbia,[44] Panticapaeum,[45] possibly at Istros,[46] Odessus[47]), or beyond it (Iasos,[48] Delos,[49] Lindus,[50] Carthaea,[51] island of Samothrace,[52] Seleucia,[53] Alexandria,[54] Theba,[55] unknown location[56]), as a sign of permanent or temporary mobility, for reasons which can sometimes only be presumed. Some of them are attested as *proxenoi*: it is the case of the Χαλχηδόνιοι attested at Olbia (an *ignotus* son of [---]ικος from the 3rd century BC), at Panticapaeum (an *ignotus* from 344–310 BC) and at Carthaea (an *ignotus* from the 4th century BC). The *proxenos* from Carthaea is attested in an honorary inscription[57] dedicated to a long list of other *proxenoi*, but instead of a Χαλχηδόνιος, it might actually be a Χαλκ[ιδεύς], as the names and ethnics are grouped on the list according to the geographical area, in this case Euboea.

The Χαλχηδόνιος attested at Istros, an *ignotus* son of [Διοσκου]ρίδης was honoured in around 200 BC, for his role as *negotiator*, as he brought to the city a grain transport, and sold it for a reasonable price. According to D. M. Pippidi,[58] it seems that the city was faced with one of the food crises, therefore it is this context that led to the *negotiator*'s honouring. Further away, at Lindus, a Χαλχαδόνιος is mentioned on a list of foreigners, who are mentioned with one exception ([---]του Τύριος) only with their personal names and the origin markers.

In what concerns the local magistrates,[59] there are only a few attestations. These officials are mostly common for other Megarian foundations as well.[60] First of all there is the βασιλεύς,[61] the eponymous magistrate here, and in the Megarian colonies. Several βασιλεῖς are attested at Kalchedon, between the Hellenistic period and the 1st century AD.

43 IK Kalchedon 4.
44 SEG 53, 785 = PPE 2271.
45 IosPE II 2 = CIRB 2 = PPE 2272.
46 ISM I 20 = PPE 2269. In the PPE, Alexandru Avram corrects the origin from Καρχηδόνιος to Χαλχηδόνιος.
47 IGB I²172. See also, Ruscu 2004.
48 IK Iasos 163.
49 IG XI.4, 618.
50 ILindos 275 = PPE 2289.
51 IG XII 5, 542 = PPE 2293.
52 IG XII 8, 152 = PPE 2301; IG XII 8, 152 = PPE 2302; ISamothrace 22 = PPE 2303.
53 RIG 535 = IK Kalchedon 1.75–78 = PPE 2314.
54 SB XVI 2858.6 = PPE 2319.
55 Syringes 1375 = PPE 2320.
56 PPE 2343.
57 On this list of *proxenoi* see, Mack 2011.
58 See the commentary of ISM I 20.
59 On the civic organisation of Kalchedon see, Robu 2007/2009; Robu 2014a, 366–406.
60 Avram 2004, 980.
61 Robu 2014a, 367–375.

The earliest attestation is that of Προμαθίων son of Θεόδοτος,[62] who is mentioned along with other local magistrates, such as the ἱερομνάμων, the προφήτας, three νομοφύλακες, the αἰσιμνῶντες, the ἀγεμόνα βουλᾶς, and the γραμματεὺς βουλᾶς καὶ δάμου. The inscription is honorary, representing the crowning of their ἀγεμών. From a similar timeframe is the attestation of another βασιλεύς, Ἀντίφιλος son of Θεόγειτος,[63] who is mentioned on a dedication to Hestia made by three ἀνκριτῆρες (officials of Megarian origin). From the 3rd-2nd century BC we have another mention of a βασιλεύς, Ὀλυμπιόδωρος,[64] whose office dates the inscription concerning the acquisition of a priestly office for Hermes (see above). The last attestation is that of Αὖλος Ὀκτάιος (attested between 27 BC and AD 14), who was not once, but four times βασιλεύς, and additionally an unreadable number of times προφήτας, an unreadable number of times ἱερομνάμων, twice priest of Caesar Augustus, six times ἀγωνοθέτης of the Pythian games, priest, twice ἀγωνοθέτης of the *Aktia* and of competitions of *paides*.[65] The offices which he held are considerable, even if we compare the evidence to other Pontic cities, where the evidence is more abundant. Αὖλος Ὀκτάιος was, without any doubt, an important local figure.

Then, there is the ἱερομνάμων,[66] an official who was in charge of religious matters, and who accompanied the βασιλεύς[67] (official not attested at Megara). The official was in charge of proposing the decrees, action which in the 2nd century BC seems to have been fulfilled by the στρατηγοί.[68] Besides the above-mentioned example, there is another one (an *ignotus*) who was also προφήτας (of Apollo Chresterios),[69] being attested through his funerary monument, sometimes in the Hellenistic period, but as the inscription is extremely fragmentary, we cannot tell more on the person who held the office.

Besides the eponymous magistrates, we have groups of magistrates, such as the αἰσυμνᾶται,[70] who were elected members of the Council for one month. Several are mentioned in the Hellenistic period through the collective dedications that they make, along with other officials.[71] One of the αἰσυμνᾶται, Διονύσιος son of Διονύσιος, Πολητήας, seems to have also been ἀγεμὼν βουλᾶς.[72]

Στρατηγοί[73] are also specific for the Megarian colonies, at Kalchedon these are only mentioned in a proxeny decree.[74] Nevertheless, the earliest evidence concerns a στρατηγός,

62 IK Kalchedon 7.

63 IK Kalchedon 8.

64 IK Kalchedon 10 = LSAM 3.

65 IK Kalchedon 19. See, Dana 2011, 127–128.

66 Robu 2014a, 375–382.

67 Avram 2004, 980.

68 Robu 2013a, 151.

69 IK Kalchedon 42

70 Robu 2014a, 382=387.

71 IK Kalchedon 6; IK Kalchedon 7. One of the αἰσυμνᾶται, Τυνδάριχος son of Καλλίας, has a personal name that is of Doric origin, which comes from the name of Tyndaridai (Dioskouroi). This is the sole attestation of the name at Kalchedon. For it see, Robu 2013b, 291–292.

72 IK Kalchedon 7.

73 Robu 2014a, 391–401.

74 IK Kalchedon 1.

but not of local origin; it is *Χάρης*, an Athenian *στρατηγός*, who is mentioned on the funerary monument of his wife (*Βοίδιον*[75]).

The *νομοφύλακες*[76] were officials who watched over the laws, and their observance. At Kalchedon there are more than three *νομοφύλακες* from the Hellenistic period. Three of them are attested on the same inscription,[77] along with other officials, while an unreadable number of *νομοφύλακες* are attested on a fragmentary inscription.[78]

Besides these offices, sometime in the Roman period, there is also an attestation of an *οἰκονόμος Χαλχηδονίων* (respectively the treasurer of the city),[79] office[80] which was held by *Διονύσιος*, husband of *Εὐτυχία* and father of *Θεόδοτος* (who lived for four years), as it results from the funerary inscription set up by them for themselves.

Additionally, two inscriptions[81] mention the office of *ἀγωνοθέτης*, in connection to the honouring of *proxenoi*, more precisely for their role in announcing the crowning of the *proxenoi* in the theatre (*Εὔδαμος* son of *Νίκων*, *Σελευκεύς*[82] and E[---] son of *ignotus*, *Βυζάντιος*).[83]

The office of *γραμματεύς* is briefly mentioned by the above-mentioned inscription,[84] recording several local officials. More precisely, *Μέμνων* son of *Μενεκράτης* was *γραμματεὺς βουλᾶς καὶ δάμου* sometime in the Hellenistic period. Reference to the *βουλά* and the *δᾶμος* is made through several inscriptions, beginning with the 3rd century BC.[85]

Besides these officials, we also mention the attestation of several priests. From the 3rd-2nd century BC, an inscription[86] records the existing regulation for the acquisition of a priestly office. A certain *Μενέμαχος* son of [---]*λος* pays 7500 drachmas, most likely for the priesthood of Heracles. Payments are made also to other priests, as follows: to the priest of an unreadable deity, to the priest of Hermes, to the priest of Ammon, to the priest of Heracles, to the priest of the Samothrace Gods, to the priest of Zeus Boulaios. Another inscription recording the regulation[87] concerning the acquisition of a priesthood (Asclepios),[88] comes from the 1st century BC – 1st century AD. *Μᾶτρις* son of *Μήνιος* is the one mentioned as having bought the priesthood of Asclepios for around 5038 drachmas and four obols (payment made in two instalments). According to the regulation, the pur-

75 IK Kalchedon 35.
76 Robu 2014a, 404–405.
77 IK Kalchedon 7.
78 IK Kalchedon 11 = LSAM 4.
79 IK Kalchedon 101.
80 On this office see, Landvogt 1908.
81 IK Kalchedon 1; IK Kalchedon 2.
82 The representative of Antiochos IV Epiphanes; see, Dana 2011, 73, 119.
83 See, Dana 2011, 71.
84 IK Kalchedon 7.
85 IK Kalchedon 1; IK Kalchedon 2; IK Kalchedon 5; IK Kalchedon 7; IK Kalchedon 10; IK Kalchedon 11; IK Kalchedon 12.
86 IK Kalchedon 10 = LSAM 3.
87 For this regulation see, LSAM 5.
88 IK Kalchedon 12.

chaser of the priesthood was to be exempt from military service[89] and all liturgies, except if he wishes to undertake them. He was also to wear a wreath at festivals, and to take part in public feasts. In addition, he was also able to farm the land around the sanctuary and had the right to access magistracies and public offices. The priesthood might have been bought only for the person's son.

In terms of **networks**,[90] as most of the inscriptions are funerary,[91] the predominant relations are those between family members. Nevertheless, one θίασος has been attested (worshipping the Twelve Gods[92]), to which we might add another possible association (φράτερες – possibly a religious association[93]). The θιασῶται are attested in the 3rd century BC, the inscription mentioning them records the regulations of the association and the rights of the priest. It seems that they had a common building described here as *κοινὸν Νικομάχειον*, but also a *βωμὸς τῶν θεῶν τῶν δυώδεκα*, which implies the making of sacrifices. Considering the choice of the name for the building, it is likely that Νικόμαχος was the founder of the association. Networks based on a common occupation might be suggested in the case of the *ναῦται* (who shared also a common juridical status), and it can be presumed also in the case of Dubitatius Attianus, the heir of Severius Acceptus.[94] As Severius Acceptus was a *miles legionis VIII Augustae*, who served for six years and lived for XXVI, Dubitatius Attianus was very likely also active in the same legion.

In terms of **family networks**, the predominant relations are, as expected, those between husbands and wives, or parents and children.[95] As opposed to the evidence from other *poleis*, at Kalchedon the inscriptions mention at the most three children,[96] with the predominance of two.[97] As we encounter in the inscriptions from other Pontic cities, here as well, a case of adoption is specified. More precisely, on the funerary inscription of Ἀπολλᾶς (who was likely *ἱερεύς*, *στρατηγός* and *γυμνασίαρχος*[98]), we find the mentioning of the fact that he was the son of Κρατῖνος and the adopted son of a certain Περιγένης.[99]

89 Such an exemption is attested also in an inscription from 4th/3rd century BC Sinope concerning the priesthood of Poseidon Heliconios (IK Sinope 8 = LSAM 1).

90 For the political networks see especially, Robu 2012; Robu 2014b. For the cultural networks see especially, Dana 2011.

91 Two of the inscriptions have as their closing line, prescriptions against the violation of the tomb (IK Kalchedon 67 and IK Kalchedon 69). One of them (IK Kalchedon 69), also specifies the amount to be paid to the *Fiscus* (10.00 *denarii*) and to the city (5.000 *denarii*) in case of violation.

92 IK Kalchedon 13 = LSAM 2 = AGRW 13204 = Poland B 418 = CAP Inv. no. 539.

93 Öğüt-Polat/Şahin 1985 = CAP Inv. no. 717.

94 IK Kalchedon 41.

95 IK Kalchedon 57; IK Kalchedon 63; IK Kalchedon 64; IK Kalchedon 67 (sarcophagus); IK Kalchedon 68 (sarcophagus); IK Kalchedon 69 (sarcophagus).

96 IK Kalchedon 63.

97 IK Kalchedon 66; IK Kalchedon 68; IK Kalchedon 69.

98 Dana 2011, 44, 156.

99 IK Kalchedon 45.

While in the Pontic area, the specification of adoption[100] is not so frequently attested,[101] this is more common for Asia Minor and Greece. Less frequently are the monuments set up for,[102] or by brothers. One such example is a 2nd century AD sarcophagus, with an inscription set up by Ἀρίζηλος son of Χρυσέρως to himself, to his brother Χρυσέρως, and to his sister-in-law Μόσχιον.[103]

The personal **military networks** are rarely encountered both in the Hellenistic and in the Roman period, as at Kalchedon the presence of the military personnel is rarely attested epigraphically. The earliest inscription, from 82 BC, attests several members of a quadrireme,[104] who were from Cos, and who were under the commandment of Aulus Terentius Varron (πρεσβευτής). Besides their personal name and patronymic, their rank is specified (ναύαρχος, τριήραρχος, κυβερνάτας, πρωρεύς, κελευστάς, πεντηκόνταρχος, ἰατρός, ἐπιβάται). Given the context, the ἰατρός ([---]νος son of Θευγένης[105]) was probably a military physician. Mentioned along with them is also the builder of the ship (Πεισίστρατος son of Ἡλιόδωρος). The attestation of the inscription at Kalchedon is to be explained through the presence of the ship for the defence of the Bosphorus, as a consequence of the expedition of Sylla against Mithradates VI Eupator, but very likely also against pirates.[106] Later, there are only brief mentions of members of the Roman army. One is the above-mentioned Severius Acceptus, *miles* of the *legio VIII Augusta*, who lived for only XXVI years, and whose heir (Dubitatius Attianus) could have been himself part of the unit. Besides them, we have C. Iulius Valens, *centurio classis praetoria Ravennas*, who lived for XL years and served for XXII years.[107] His funerary monument was set up by C. Iulius Flavianus, his *amicus*, who was probably active in the same *classis*. Next, a *miles* of the *cohors II Lucensium* (Aurelius Saturninus) has his funerary monument[108] set up by a certain Menefron, who might have been his slave.

The **religious networks** can be partially reconstructed.[109] For example, in the 3rd century BC, an embassy from Histria is sent to Kalchedon[110] in order to consult the oracle of Apollo, probably concerning the introduction of the cult of Sarapis.[111] Or, still in the 3rd century BC, when Kalchedon asks at Delphi the recognition of its sanctuary as ἄσυλος καὶ

100 On the adoptive and polyonymous nomenclature in the Roman Empire see, Salomies 1992; Salomies 2014.
101 Attested at Odessus (IGB I² 50; IGB I² 175); Dionysopolis (IGB I² 14(2)); possibly at Istros (ISM I 123 = SEG 24, 1134).
102 IK Kalchedon 41.
103 IK Kalchedon 66.
104 IK Kalchedon 15.
105 See also, Samama 2003, 415–416, no. 312.
106 Dana 2011, 195.
107 IK Kalchedon 54.
108 IK Kalchedon 56.
109 For an ampler discussion se, Robu 2013a, 143–157; Robu 2014b.
110 ISM I 5 = SEG 24, 1091 = SEG 58, 682 = SEG 51, 936(1).
111 Ruscu 2002, 212; Robu 2013, 144.

φύκτιμος,[112] which was recognised by Phokaia and Tenedos as well.[113] On the other way around, Kalchedon recognizes the sanctuary of Asclepios of Cos as ἄσυλος (242 BC).[114]

Certainly, the epigraphic sources provide only glimpses on the population, archaeological studies on the size of the territory, along with anthropological studies, and the literary sources provide additional information on the population. Consequently, the epigraphic sources are silent on significant historical moments, on representative members of the elite, or various persons known from the literary sources, such as the philosophers Θρασύμαχος (5th century BC),[115] and Ξενοκράτης son of Ἀγαθήνωρ (4th century BC);[116] the physicians Ἡρόφιλος (4th/3rd century BC)[117] and Φαλέας (4th century BC);[118] the sculptor Βόηθος son of Ἀθαναίων (2nd century BC)[119] etc.

Conclusions

Overall, the evidence is rather evenly distributed between the Hellenistic and Roman period. As expected, the male population is the best represented, even though the inscriptions are rather laconic, and offer very few prosopographical information on them, beyond the familial appurtenance. In terms of society, we notice the lack of permeability into the elite of Roman citizens. The officials are those specific for the Megarian colonies, and once with the coming of the Romans, we see no significant change. The networks reflected in the inscriptions are those to be expected, respectively between family members, rarely do we encounter network that surpass the family nucleus, and this is recorded in the case of officials, or of persons whose occupation is known. The Καλχηδόνιοι who record their existence do so especially as a last remembrance, for themselves or for their loved ones; but some express also their piety, or more rarely their local importance. Visible are also those actors, whose actions lead to the help of the city or its citizens. Overall, the epigraphic evidence offers a snippet view on the population who lived at Kalchedon, and the networks that they developed between the 4th century BC and the 3rd century AD.

112 FDelphes III 4 372; Dana 2011, 96–97; Robu 2013a, 144.
113 Robu 2013a, 146.
114 Robu 2013a, 151.
115 Dana 2011, 282–283.
116 Dana 2011, 284–287.
117 Dana 2011, 195, 305–306.
118 Dana 2011, 284.
119 Dana 2011, 210.

Prosopographical catalogue

A

1. Αὐρήλιος Ἀγάπητος husband of Αὐρηλία Εὐτυχιανῇ; father of Αὐρηλία Ὀνησικράτεια and Αὐρήλιος Ἱμέριος; funerary inscription; after AD 212; Kalchedon; IK Kalchedon 69; http://romansıbyı.com/rpeople/23339.
2. Ἀγήσανδρος son of Ἐργοτέλης; he was from Cos; he was πεντηκόνταρχος in the *classis* [---]; dedication; 82 BC; Kalchedon; IK Kalchedon 15; http://romansıbyı.com/rpeople/23245.
3. Ἀθηνοκλῆς son of Μηνόδωρος; he was νομοφύλαξ; dedication; Hellenistic period; Kalchedon; IK Kalchedon 7; http://romansıbyı.com/rpeople/23216.
4. Ἀθαναίων son of Ἀπολλοφάνης; he was προφήτας (of Apollo Chresterios); dedication; Hellenistic period; Kalchedon; IK Kalchedon 7; http://romansıbyı.com/rpeople/23212.
5. Ἀθαναίων son of Ἀσκλαπιόδωρος; dedication; Hellenistic period; Kalchedon; IK Kalchedon 7; http://romansıbyı.com/rpeople/23224.
6. Ἄκκα; wife of Φιλισκίων; she lived for XL years; funerary inscription; unknown dating; Kalchedon (Panteichion); IK Kalchedon 119; http://romansıbyı.com/rpeople/23362.
7. Severius Acceptus; he lived for XXVI years; he was *miles* in the *legio VIII Augusta*; unspecified relationship with Dubitatius Attianus; funerary inscription; Roman period; Kalchedon; IK Kalchedon 55; http://romansıbyı.com/rpeople/23302.
8. Ἀνδρότιμος son of Μενεκλῆς; he was from Cos; he was ἐπιβάτης in the *classis* [---]; dedication; 82 BC; Kalchedon; IK Kalchedon 15; http://romansıbyı.com/rpeople/23266.
9. [Ἄ]ντανδρος son of Μενεκράτης; dedication; Hellenistic period; Kalchedon; IK Kalchedon 6; http://romansıbyı.com/rpeople/23211.
10. Ἀντίγονος son of Ἀντίγονος; he was from Cos; he was ἐπιβάτης in the *classis* [---]; dedication; 82 BC; Kalchedon; IK Kalchedon 15; http://romansıbyı.com/rpeople/23262.
11. Ἀ̣ντίοχος son of Εὐφάνης; he was from Cos; he was ἐπιβάτης in the *classis* [---]; dedication; 82 BC; Kalchedon; IK Kalchedon 15; http://romansıbyı.com/rpeople/23252.
12. Ἀντίφιλος son of Θεόγειτος; he was βασιλεύς; dedication; Hellenistic period?; Kalchedon; IK Kalchedon 8; http://romansıbyı.com/rpeople/23228.
13. Ἀντώνιος son of Αὐρήλιος Δημόφιλος son of Μουκιανός and Ἄφη daughter of Νουμᾶς; brother of Νομωνιανή; funerary inscription; Roman period; Kalchedon; IK Kalchedon 68; http://romansıbyı.com/rpeople/23337.
14. Ἀπολλᾶς son of Διονύσιος; funerary inscription; Hellenistic period; Kalchedon; IK Kalchedon 41; http://romansıbyı.com/rpeople/23288.

15. Ἀπολλᾶς son of Κρατῖνος (*nat.*); he was the adopted son of Περιγένης (*ad.*); funerary inscription; Hellenistic period; Kalchedon; IK Kalchedon 45; http://romansıby1.com/rpeople/23289.
16. Ἀπολλώνιος son of Θεόμναστος; dedication; Hellenistic period; Kalchedon; IK Kalchedon 6; http://romansıby1.com/rpeople/23209.
17. Ἄπφη; *patrona* of Ὀρβανίλλα; she was πρφῆτις (of Apollo Chresterios); funerary inscription; Roman period; Kalchedon; IK Kalchedon 61; http://romansıby1.com/rpeople/23314.
18. Ἀρέσκουσα; wife of Ἀσίννις Ἰνγένους; mother of Θεόδωρος; funerary inscription; Roman period; Kalchedon; IK Kalchedon 57; http://romansıby1.com/rpeople/23307.
19. Ἀρίζηλος son of Χρυσέρως; brother of Χρυσέρως; brother-in-law of Μόσχιον; funerary inscription; 2nd centuruy AD; Kalchedon; IK Kalchedon 66; http://romansıby1.com/rpeople/23328.
20. Ἀριστονίκα daughter of Μοσχ[---]; she was a ἱέρεια; regulation; 3rd century BC; Kalchedon; IK Kalchedon 11; http://romansıby1.com/rpeople/23235.
21. Ἀριστοκράτης son of Ἀριστοκράτης; he was from Cos; he was κελευστάς in the *classis* [---]; dedication; 82 BC; Kalchedon; IK Kalchedon 15; http://romansıby1.com/rpeople/23244.
22. Ἀριστομένης; funerary inscription; unknown dating; Kalchedon; IK Kalchedon 34; http://romansıby1.com/rpeople/23276.
23. Ἀρίστων son of Διονύσιος; dedication; Hellenistic period; Kalchedon; IK Kalchedon 6; http://romansıby1.com/rpeople/23206.
24. Ἀρίστων son of Ἀρίστων; husband of Γύκεια; according to the editors, given the iconography, Ἀρίστων was probably ἱερεύς, ἀγωνοθέτης, ἀγορανόμος, γυμνασίαρχος and στρατηγός; sarcophagus; 1st century BC; Kalchedon; IK Kalchedon 65; http://romansıby1.com/rpeople/23326.
25. Ἀρτεμᾶς; he was part of the ναῦται; dedication; 1st–2nd century AD; Chrysopolis; Demirkök 2010, 163–167.
26. Dubitatius Attianus; he was the heir of Severius Acceptus; funerary inscription; Roman period; Kalchedon; IK Kalchedon 55; http://romansıby1.com/rpeople/23303.
27. Ἄφη daughter of Νουμᾶς; wife of Αὐρήλιος Δημόφιλος son of Μουκιανός; mother of Ἀντώνιος and Νομωνιανή; funerary inscription; Roman period; Kalchedon; IK Kalchedon 68; http://romansıby1.com/rpeople/23336.
28. Ἀφφοῦς; husband of Ἰουλία Λύδη; father of Καπετωλεῖνος; funerary inscription; Roman period; Kalchedon; IK Kalchedon 62.

B

29. Βαθύλος son of Παρθένιος; funerary inscription; Hellenistic period; Kalchedon; IK Kalchedon 46; http://romansıby1.com/rpeople/23290.

30. Βοίδιον; she was the wife of the Athenian strategos Χάρης; funerary inscription; 340/339 BC; Kalchedon; IK Kalchedon 35; http://romansıbyı.com/rpeople/23277.
31. Βουκόλις; husband of Εὐσεβία; father of Παμφίλη; funerary inscription; Roman period; Kalchedon; IK Kalchedon 125; http://romansıbyı.com/rpeople/23371.
32. Βυρίχος son of Αἰσχηΐδας; dedication; Hellenistic period; Kalchedon; IK Kalchedon 7; http://romansıbyı.com/rpeople/23220.

Γ

33. Γύκεια; wife of Ἀρίστων son of Ἀρίστων; sarcophagus; 1st century BC; Kalchedon; IK Kalchedon 65; http://romansıbyı.com/rpeople/23327.

Δ

34. Δαμᾶς son of Μηνόδοτος; dedication; Hellenistic period; Kalchedon; IK Kalchedon 7; http://romansıbyı.com/rpeople/23226.
35. [Δ]αμάτριος son of Ἀπολλόδωρος; dedication; Hellenistic period; Kalchedon; IK Kalchedon 6; http://romansıbyı.com/rpeople/23210.
36. Δαμοκράτης son of Ἀθαναίων; dedication; Hellenistic period; Kalchedon; IK Kalchedon 6; http://romansıbyı.com/rpeople/23204.
37. Δαμόκριτος son of Ἐκφαντίδας; he was from Cos; he was ἐπιβάτης in the *classis* [---]; dedication; 82 BC; Kalchedon; IK Kalchedon 15; http://romansıbyı.com/rpeople/23247.
38. Αὐρήλιος Δημόφιλος son of Μουκιανός; husband of Ἄφη; father of Ἀντώνιος and Νομωνιανή; funerary inscription; Roman period; Kalchedon; IK Kalchedon 68; http://romansıbyı.com/rpeople/23335.
39. Διονύσιος son of Πυθᾶς; dedication; Hellenistic period; Kalchedon; IK Kalchedon 6; http://romansıbyı.com/rpeople/23208.
40. Διονύσιος son of Διονύσιος; he was ἀγεμὼν βουλᾶς; dedication; Hellenistic period; Kalchedon; IK Kalchedon 7; http://romansıbyı.com/rpeople/23218.
41. Διονύσιος son of Διονύσιος; funerary inscription; unknown dating; Kalchedon; IK Kalchedon 53; http://romansıbyı.com/rpeople/23299.
42. Διονύσιος son of Ἀμυνάδας; dedication; Hellenistic period?; Kalchedon; IK Kalchedon 8; http://romansıbyı.com/rpeople/23229.
43. Διονύσιος; husband of Εὐτυχία; father of Θεόδοτος; he was οἰκονόμος Χαλχηδονίων; funerary inscription; Roman period; Kalchedon; IK Kalchedon 101; http://romansıbyı.com/rpeople/23354.

44. Διονύσιος son of Εὐφρόνιος; funerary inscription; 1st century BC; Kalchedon; IK Kalchedon 102; http://romans1by1.com/rpeople/23357.
45. Διονύσιος son of Ἀπολλώνιος; unspecified relationship with Λευκίς; funerary inscription; Roman period; Kalchedon; IK Kalchedon 1031; http://romans1by1.com/rpeople/23375.
46. Διονύσιος; he was part of the ναῦται; dedication; 1st–2nd century AD; Chrysopolis; Demirkök 2010, 163–167.
47. Διότιμος son of Διονύσιος; dedication; Hellenistic period?; Kalchedon; IK Kalchedon 8; http://romans1by1.com/rpeople/23231.

E

48. Ἑκαταῖος son of Ἑκαταῖος; he was an ephebos; he won 11 competitions; he died at XVIII years; funerary inscription; 2nd-3rd century AD; Kalchedon; IK Kalchedon 32 = SEG 38, 1274; http://romans1by1.com/rpeople/23274.
49. Ἐλειθύης; unspecified relationship with Νικογένεια; funerary inscription; Archaic period; Kalchedon; IK Kalchedon 30 = SEG 27, 816; http://romans1by1.com/rpeople/23271.
50. Ἑλίκιον; wife of Θεοκλείδας; unspecified relationship with Κέρδων; funerary inscription; Hellenistic period; Kalchedon; IK Kalchedon 49; http://romans1by1.com/rpeople/23293.
51. Ἐπικράτης son of Ἐπικράτης; he was from Cos; he was ἐπιβάτης in the *classis* [---]; dedication; 82 BC; Kalchedon; IK Kalchedon 15; http://romans1by1.com/rpeople/23250.
52. Μέμμιος Ἔραστος; unspecified relationship with Μέμμια Καλλίστη; he lived for LX years; funerary inscription; 3rd century AD; Kalchedon; IK Kalchedon 70; http://romans1by1.com/rpeople/23344.
53. Ἕρμαιος son of Ἕρμαιος; he was ἱερομνάμων; dedication; Hellenistic period; Kalchedon; IK Kalchedon 7; http://romans1by1.com/rpeople/23213.
54. Ἑρμιανός son of Ἑρμόδωρος; husband of Στρατήγια; father of Ὀνήσιμος, Πώσφορος, and Ἑρμιανός; funerary inscription; Roman period; Kalchedon; IK Kalchedon 63; http://romans1by1.com/rpeople/23318.
55. Ἑρμιανός son of Ἑρμιανός son of Ἑρμόδωρος and Στρατήγια ἡ καὶ Ἔλπις; brother of Ὀνήσιμος, Πώσφορος, and Ἑρμιανός; funerary inscription; Roman period; Kalchedon; IK Kalchedon 63; http://romans1by1.com/rpeople/23322.
56. Ἔρως; he was part of the ναῦται; dedication; 1st–2nd century AD; Chrysopolis; Demirkök 2010, 163–167.
57. Ἔρως; he was part of the ναῦται; dedication; 1st–2nd century AD; Chrysopolis; Demirkök 2010, 163–167.
58. Εὔạινος son of Νικοκλῆς; he was from Cos; he was ἐπιβάτης in the *classis* [---]; dedication; 82 BC; Kalchedon; IK Kalchedon 15; http://romans1by1.com/rpeople/23264.

59. Εὔδαμος son of Νίκων; Σελευκεύς; decree; 174 BC; Kalchedon; IK Kalchedon 1; http://romansiby1.com/rpeople/23197.
60. Εὔδαμος son of *ignotus*; he was from Cos; he was ναύαρχος *classis* [---]; dedication; 82 BC; Kalchedon; IK Kalchedon 15; http://romansiby1.com/rpeople/23239.
61. Εὐσεβία; wife of Βουκόλις; mother of Παμφίλη; funerary inscription; Roman period; Kalchedon; IK Kalchedon 125; http://romansiby1.com/rpeople/23372.
62. Ἀβιάνιος Εὐτύχης; husband of Λαμ[---]; funerary inscription; Roman period; Kalchedon; IK Kalchedon 124; http://romansiby1.com/rpeople/23369.
63. Φλαούιος Εὐτύχης; father of Φλαούιος [---] and Φλαούιος [---]; he was προτήκτωρ; funerary inscription; 3rd century AD; Kalchedon; IK Kalchedon 71; http://romansiby1.com/rpeople/23345.
64. Εὐτυχία; wife of Διονύσιος; mother of Θεόδοτος; funerary inscription; Roman period; Kalchedon; IK Kalchedon 101; http://romansiby1.com/rpeople/23355.
65. Αὐρηλία Εὐτυχιανή; wife of Αὐρήλιος Ἀγάπητος; mother of Αὐρηλία Ὀνησικράτεια and Αὐρήλιος Ἱμέριος; funerary inscription; after AD 212; Kalchedon; IK Kalchedon 69; http://romansiby1.com/rpeople/23340.
66. Εὐτυχίς; wife of Μόσχος son of Ζώτιχος; mother of Σωσίβιος and Θησεύς; funerary inscription; 2nd century AD; Kalchedon; IK Kalchedon 67; http://romansiby1.com/rpeople/23332.
67. Εὔφαμος son of Ἀντίλοχος; dedication; Hellenistic period; Kalchedon; IK Kalchedon 6; http://romansiby1.com/rpeople/23201.
68. Εὐφημία; wife of Φιλισκίων; she lived for an unreadable number of years; funerary inscription; unknown dating; Kalchedon (Panteichion); IK Kalchedon 119; http://romansiby1.com/rpeople/23363.
69. Εὔφημος son of Ἐπιθύμητος; father of Μίκκη; funerary inscription; Roman period; Kalchedon (Chalkitis Isl.); IK Kalchedon 122; http://romansiby1.com/rpeople/23364.

Z

70. Ζωΐλος son of Φιλίσσκος; funerary inscription; Hellenistic period; Kalchedon; IK Kalchedon 51; http://romansiby1.com/rpeople/23297.
71. Ζωπυρίων son of Μεσσάνιος; dedication; Hellenistic period; Kalchedon; IK Kalchedon 6; http://romansiby1.com/rpeople/23205.
72. Ζώσιμος; he was part of the ναῦται; dedication; 1st–2nd century AD; Chrysopolis; Demirkök 2010, 163–167.
73. Ζωτᾶς son of Ἐπικράτης; dedication; Hellenistic period; Kalchedon; IK Kalchedon 6; http://romansiby1.com/rpeople/23203.

74. Ζωτίχος son of Ἀθαναίων; he was νομοφύλαξ; dedication; Hellenistic period; Kalchedon; IK Kalchedon 7; http://romans1by1.com/rpeople/23217.
75. Ζωτίχος son of Σιλιανός; he lived for I year; funerary inscription; Hellenistic period; Kalchedon; IK Kalchedon 50; http://romans1by1.com/rpeople/23296.

Ἡ

76. Ἡραγόρας son of Πραξίφαντος; he was from Cos; he was ἐπιβάτης in the *classis* [---]; dedication; 82 BC; Kalchedon; IK Kalchedon 15; http://romans1by1.com/rpeople/23255.
77. Ἡράκων; he was part of the ναῦται; dedication; 1st–2nd century AD; Chrysopolis; Demirkök 2010, 163–167.
78. Ἡρίλαος son of Ἀνδροκλῆς; brother of Ὀλυμπιάδας; funerary inscription; Hellenistic period; Kalchedon; IK Kalchedon 41; http://romans1by1.com/rpeople/23285.

Θ

79. Θεάφιλος son of Διονύσιος; dedication; Hellenistic period; Kalchedon; IK Kalchedon 7; http://romans1by1.com/rpeople/23225.
80. Θεόδοτος son of Διονύσιος and Εὐτυχία; he lived for IV years; funerary inscription; Roman period; Kalchedon; IK Kalchedon 101; http://romans1by1.com/rpeople/23356.
81. Θεόδωρος son of Ἀσίννις Ἰνγένους and Ἀρέσκουσα; funerary inscription; Roman period; Kalchedon; IK Kalchedon 57; http://romans1by1.com/rpeople/23308.
82. Θεοκλείδας son of Θεοκλείδας; husband of Ἑλίκιον; unspecified relationship with Κέρδων; funerary inscription; Hellenistic period; Kalchedon; IK Kalchedon 49; http://romans1by1.com/rpeople/23294.
83. Θεόπομπος son of Διονύσιος; funerary inscription; Hellenistic period?; Kalchedon; IK Kalchedon 36; http://romans1by1.com/rpeople/23278.
84. Θησεύς son of Μόσχος son of Ζώτιχος and Εὐτυχίς; brother of Σωσίβιος; funerary inscription; 2nd century AD; Kalchedon; IK Kalchedon 67; http://romans1by1.com/rpeople/23334.
85. Θρασύδαμος son of Θρασύμαχος; he was from Cos; he was ἐπιβάτης in the *classis* [---]; dedication; 82 BC; Kalchedon; IK Kalchedon 15; http://romans1by1.com/rpeople/23248.

I

86. Αὐρήλιος Ἱμέριος son of Αὐρήλιος Ἀγάπητος and Αὐρηλία Εὐτυχιανή; brother of Αὐρηλία Ὀνησικράτεια; funerary inscription; after AD 212; Kalchedon; IK Kalchedon 69; http://romans1by1.com/rpeople/23342.

87. Ἀσίννις Ἰνγένους; husband of Ἀρέσκουσα; father of Θεόδωρος; funerary inscription; Roman period; Kalchedon; IK Kalchedon 57; http://romansıbyı.com/rpeople/23306.
88. Ἵππων son of Διονύσιος; he was νομοφύλαξ; dedication; Hellenistic period; Kalchedon; IK Kalchedon 7; http://romansıbyı.com/rpeople/23215.

K

89. Καλλικράτης son of Ἀριστόπαππος; he was from Cos; he was ἐπιβάτης in the *classis* [---]; dedication; 82 BC; Kalchedon; IK Kalchedon 15; http://romansıbyı.com/rpeople/23259.
90. Καλλικράτης son of Χαρίστιος; he was from Cos; he was ἐπιβάτης in the *classis* [---]; dedication; 82 BC; Kalchedon; IK Kalchedon 15; http://romansıbyı.com/rpeople/23263.
91. Μέμμια Καλλίστη; unspecified relationship with Μέμμιος Ἔραστος; she lived for XXXII years; funerary inscription; 3rd century AD; Kalchedon; IK Kalchedon 70; http://romansıbyı.com/rpeople/23343.
92. Κάνωβος son of Θρασυδάμας; he was from Olbia; decree; 4th century BC; Kalchedon; IK Kalchedon 16; http://romansıbyı.com/rpeople/23267.
93. Καπετωλεῖνος son of Ἀφφοῦς and Ἰουλία Λύδη; funerary inscription; Roman period; Kalchedon; IK Kalchedon 62; http://romansıbyı.com/rpeople/23316.
94. Καρτιμένης son of Ἀριστώνουμος; he was κυβερνάτας in the *classis* [---]; dedication; 82 BC; Kalchedon; IK Kalchedon 15; http://romansıbyı.com/rpeople/23242.
95. Δημέας Καστηνός; boundary inscription; 2nd-3rd century AD; Kalchedon; SEG 37, 1036; http://romansıbyı.com/rpeople/23377.
96. Κοΐντος Λόλλιος Κάτος; dedication; 1st–2nd century AD; Chrysopolis; Demirkök 2010, 163–167.
97. Κέρδων son of Βίων; unspecified relationship with Θεοκλείδας son of Θεοκλείδας; unspecified relationship with Ἑλίκιον; funerary inscription; Hellenistic period; Kalchedon; IK Kalchedon 49; http://romansıbyı.com/rpeople/23295.
98. Κλεόνικος son of Εὔκαρπος; he was from Cos; he was τριήραρχος in the *classis* [---]; dedication; 82 BC; Kalchedon; IK Kalchedon 15; http://romansıbyı.com/rpeople/23240.
99. Κλωδία; mother of Τιμόθεος; funerary inscription; Roman period; Kalchedon; IK Kalchedon 58; http://romansıbyı.com/rpeople/23311.
100. Κρατῖνος son of Ζωΐλος; dedication; Hellenistic period; Kalchedon; IK Kalchedon 6; http://romansıbyı.com/rpeople/23207.
101. Αὐρηλία Κρατίστη; wife of *ignotus*; funerary inscription; AD 212; Kalchedon; IK Kalchedon 73; http://romansıbyı.com/rpeople/23351.

102. Κριτόλας son of Ἄγγελος; unspecified relationship with Σαμιάδας son of Πύρρος; funerary inscription; Hellenistic period; Kalchedon; IK Kalchedon 40; http://romans1by1.com/rpeople/23282.

Λ

103. Λευκίς son of Λευκίς; unspecified relationship with Διονύσιος son of Ἀπολλώνιος; funerary inscription; Roman period; Kalchedon; IK Kalchedon 1031; http://romans1by1.com/rpeople/23376.
104. Λόλλιος; ἰσαγέμων; he was part of the ναῦται; dedication; 1st–2nd century AD; Chrysopolis; Demirkök 2010, 163–167.
105. Λούκιος?; husband of *ignota*; father of *ignotus*; funerary inscription; Roman period; Kalchedon; IK Kalchedon 64; http://romans1by1.com/rpeople/23323.
106. Ἰουλία Λύδη; wife of Ἀφφοῦς; mother of Καπετωλεῖνος; funerary inscription; Roman period; Kalchedon; IK Kalchedon 62; http://romans1by1.com/rpeople/23317.

M

107. Μάξιμος son of Μουκιανός; dedication; AD 206; Kalchedon; IK Kalchedon 103; http://romans1by1.com/rpeople/23358.
108. Ματρίκων son of Μήνιος; dedication; Hellenistic period; Kalchedon; IK Kalchedon 7; http://romans1by1.com/rpeople/23221.
109. Ματρίκων son of Προμαθίων; he lived for LIV? years; funerary inscription; Roman period; Kalchedon; IK Kalchedon 58; http://romans1by1.com/rpeople/23309.
110. Μᾶτρις son of Μήνιος; he was ἱερεύς; decree; 1st century BC – 1st century AD; Kalchedon; IK Kalchedon 12; http://romans1by1.com/rpeople/23236.
111. Ματροδώρα daughter of Πρόξενος; funerary inscription; Hellenistic period; Kalchedon; IK Kalchedon 39; http://romans1by1.com/rpeople/23281.
112. Πώλλα Ἀτέλλια Μελιτίνη; funerary inscription; Roman period; Kalchedon; IK Kalchedon 60; http://romans1by1.com/rpeople/23312.
113. Μέμνων son of Μενεκράτης; he was γραμματεὺς βουλᾶς καὶ δάμου; dedication; Hellenistic period; Kalchedon; IK Kalchedon 7; http://romans1by1.com/rpeople/23227.
114. Μενέμαχος son of [---]λος; decree; 3rd-2nd century BC; Kalchedon; IK Kalchedon 10 = LSAM 3; http://romans1by1.com/rpeople/23234.
115. Μενέμαχος son of Δίφιλος; funerary inscription; Hellenistic period; Kalchedon; IK Kalchedon 43; http://romans1by1.com/rpeople/23287.
116. Μήνιος son of Σκέψων; father of Μήνιος; he lived for XXV years; funerary inscription; 3rd century BC; Kalchedon; IK Kalchedon 31 = SEG 28, 1662; http://romans1by1.com/rpeople/23273.

117. Μήνιος son of Μήνιος; he lived for XXV years; funerary inscription; 3rd century BC; Kalchedon; IK Kalchedon 31 = SEG 28, 1662; http://romans1by1.com/rpeople/23272.
118. Μήνιος son of Φανίων; funerary inscription; Hellenistic period?; Kalchedon; IK Kalchedon 37; http://romans1by1.com/rpeople/23279.
119. Μήνιος son of Δαμάτριος; funerary inscription; Hellenistic period; Kalchedon; IK Kalchedon 52; http://romans1by1.com/rpeople/23298.
120. Menefron; he was *miles* in the *cohors II Lucensium*; unspecified relation with Aurelius Saturninus; funerary inscription; Roman period; Kalchedon; IK Kalchedon 56; http://romans1by1.com/rpeople/23305.
121. Μίκκη daughter of Εὔφημος son of Ἐπιθύμητος; she lived for XX years; funerary inscription; Roman period; Kalchedon (Chalkitis Isl.); IK Kalchedon 122;
122. Μόσχιον; wife of Χρυσέρως son of Χρυσέρως; sister-in-law of Ἀρίζηλος; funerary inscription; 2nd century AD; Kalchedon; IK Kalchedon 66; http://romans1by1.com/rpeople/23330.
123. Μόσχος son of Ζώτιχος; husband of Εὐτυχίς; father of Σωσίβιος and Θησεύς; funerary inscription; 2nd century AD; Kalchedon; IK Kalchedon 67; http://romans1by1.com/rpeople/23331.

N

124. Νικαγόρας son of Νικαγόρας; he was from Cos; he was ἐπιβάτης in the *classis* [---]; dedication; 82 BC; Kalchedon; IK Kalchedon 15; http://romans1by1.com/rpeople/23253.
125. Νικαγόρας son of Διογένης; he was from Cos; he was ἐπιβάτης in the *classis* [---]; dedication; 82 BC; Kalchedon; IK Kalchedon 15; http://romans1by1.com/rpeople/23260.
126. Νίκανδρος son of *ignota*; brother of Νικομᾶς; funerary inscription; Roman period; Kalchedon; IK Kalchedon 123; http://romans1by1.com/rpeople/23367.
127. Νικίας son of Μενίσκος; dedication; Hellenistic period; Kalchedon; IK Kalchedon 7; http://romans1by1.com/rpeople/23219.
128. Νικογένεια; unspecified relationship with Ἐλειθύης; funerary inscription; Archaic period; Kalchedon; IK Kalchedon 30 = SEG 27, 816; http://romans1by1.com/rpeople/23270.
129. Νικοκλῆς son of Κλεινίας; he was from Cos; he was ἐπιβάτης in the *classis* [---]; dedication; 82 BC; Kalchedon; IK Kalchedon 15; http://romans1by1.com/rpeople/23249.
130. Νικομᾶς son of *ignota*; brother of Νίκανδρος; funerary inscription; Roman period; Kalchedon; IK Kalchedon 123; http://romans1by1.com/rpeople/23366.
131. Νικόμαχος son of Νικόμαχος; he was from Cos; he was ἐπιβάτης in the *classis* [---]; dedication; 82 BC; Kalchedon; IK Kalchedon 15; http://romans1by1.com/rpeople/23261.

132. Νικόμαχος; he was probably the founder or the leader of an association (θίασος) who had a common building (κοινὸν Νικομάχειον); regulation; 3rd century BC; Kalchedon; IK Kalchedon 13;
http://romans1by1.com/rpeople/4231.
133. Νικώ daughter of Μήνιος; funerary inscription; Hellenistic period; Kalchedon; IK Kalchedon 47;
http://romans1by1.com/rpeople/23291.
134. Νομωνιανή daughter of Αὐρήλιος Δημόφιλος son of Μουκιανός and Ἄφη daughter of Νουμᾶς; sister of Ἀντώνιος; funerary inscription; Roman period; Kalchedon; IK Kalchedon 68;
http://romans1by1.com/rpeople/23338.
135. Νόσσων son of Τιμοκλῆς; he was from Cos; he was ἐπιβάτης in the *classis* [---]; dedication; 82 BC; Kalchedon; IK Kalchedon 15;
http://romans1by1.com/rpeople/23257.

Ξ

136. Ξενιάδας son of Ἑρμόκριτος; funerary inscription; 3rd/2nd century BC; Kalchedon; SEG 35, 1299;
http://romans1by1.com/rpeople/23374.
137. Ξενόδοκος son of Τιμοκράτης; he was from Cos; he was ἐπιβάτης in the *classis* [---]; dedication; 82 BC; Kalchedon; IK Kalchedon 15;
http://romans1by1.com/rpeople/23254.
138. Ξενόδοκος son of Ἐχεκρατίδης; he was from Cos; he was ἐπιβάτης in the *classis* [---]; dedication; 82 BC; Kalchedon; IK Kalchedon 15;
http://romans1by1.com/rpeople/23256.
139. Ξενότιμος son of [---]της; he was from Cos; he was ἐπιβάτης in the *classis* [---]; dedication; 82 BC; Kalchedon; IK Kalchedon 15;
http://romans1by1.com/rpeople/23258.

O

140. Αὖλος Ὀκτάιος; he was four times βασιλεύς; an unreadable number of times προφήτας (of Apollo Chresterios); an unreadable number of times ἱερομνάμων; twice priest of Caesar Augustus; six times ἀγωνοθέτης of the Pythian games; ἱερεύς; honorary inscription; 27 BC – AD 14; Kalchedon; IK Kalchedon 19;
http://romans1by1.com/rpeople/23269.
141. Ὀλυμπιάδας son of Ἀνδροκλῆς; brother of Ἡρίλαος; funerary inscription; Hellenistic period; Kalchedon; IK Kalchedon 41;
http://romans1by1.com/rpeople/23284.
142. Ὀλυμπιόδωρος; he was βασιλεύς; decree; 3rd-2nd century BC; Kalchedon; IK Kalchedon 10 = LSAM 3;
http://romans1by1.com/rpeople/23233.
143. Αὐρηλία Ὀνησικράτεια ἡ καὶ Δυσκόλιον; daughter of Αὐρήλιος Ἀγάπητος and Αὐρηλία Εὐτυχιανή; sister of Αὐρήλιος Ἱμέριος; funerary inscription; after AD 212; Kalchedon; IK Kalchedon 69;
http://romans1by1.com/rpeople/23341.
144. Ὀνήσιμος son of Ἑρμιανός son of Ἑρμόδωρος and Στρατήγια ἡ καὶ Ἔλπις; brother of Ὀνήσιμος, Πώσφορος, and Ἑρμιανός; funerary inscription; Roman period;

Kalchedon; IK Kalchedon 63;
http://romansıbyı.com/rpeople/23320.

145. Ὀρβανίλλα daughter of Τυραννίς; she was a θρεπτή; she lived for XXVII years; she was the θρεπτή of Ἄπφη; funerary inscription; Roman period; Kalchedon; IK Kalchedon 61;
http://romansıbyı.com/rpeople/23313.
146. Caius Iulius Valens; amicus of Caius Iulius Flavianus; he lived for XXII years; he was a *centurio* in the *Classis Ravennas*; funerary inscription; Roman period; Kalchedon; IK Kalchedon 54;
http://romansıbyı.com/rpeople/23300.
147. Αὖλος Τερέντιος Οὐάρρων son of Οὐάρρων; he was *legatus* in the *classis* [---]; dedication; 82 BC; Kalchedon; IK Kalchedon 15;
http://romansıbyı.com/rpeople/23238.

Π

148. Παμφίλη; son of Βουκόλις and Εὐσεβία; funerary inscription; Roman period; Kalchedon; IK Kalchedon 125;
http://romansıbyı.com/rpeople/23373.
149. Παπίας son of Διόγνητος; dedication; Hellenistic period; Kalchedon; IK Kalchedon 7;
http://romansıbyı.com/rpeople/23223.
150. Πεισίστρατος son of Ἡλιόδωρος; he was from Cos; he built the ship; dedication; 82 BC; Kalchedon; IK Kalchedon 15;
http://romansıbyı.com/rpeople/23241.
151. Πηροβρης son of Ἀνδρέας; he was a ἱερεύς; boundary inscription; 2nd-3rd century AD; Kalchedon; SEG 37, 1036;
http://romansıbyı.com/rpeople/23378.
152. Πομπώνιος son of *ignotus*; honorary inscription; unknown dating; Kalchedon; IK Kalchedon 17;
http://romansıbyı.com/rpeople/23268.
153. Πραξίας son of Θεύδαμος; he was from Cos; he was ἐπιβάτης in the *classis* [---]; dedication; 82 BC; Kalchedon; IK Kalchedon 15;
http://romansıbyı.com/rpeople/23265.
154. Πρῖμος; he was part of the ναῦται; dedication; 1st–2nd century AD; Chrysopolis; Demirkök 2010, 163–167.
155. Προμαθίων son of Θεόδοτος; he was βασιλεύς; dedication; Hellenistic period; Kalchedon; IK Kalchedon 7;
http://romansıbyı.com/rpeople/23212.
156. Προμαθίων son of Προμαθίων; dedication; Hellenistic period; Kalchedon; IK Kalchedon 7;
http://romansıbyı.com/rpeople/23222.
157. Πρόξενος son of Παρμένων; funerary inscription; Hellenistic period; Kalchedon; IK Kalchedon 38;
http://romansıbyı.com/rpeople/23280.
158. Πώσφορος son of Ἑρμιανός son of Ἑρμόδωρος and Στρατήγια ἡ καὶ Ἔλπις; brother of Ὀνήσιμος, and Ὀνήσιμος Ἑρμιανός; funerary inscription; Roman period;

Kalchedon; IK Kalchedon 63;
http://romansiby1.com/rpeople/23321.

Σ

159. Σαμιάδας son of Πύρρος; unspecified relationship with Κριτόλας son of Ἄγγελος; funerary inscription; Hellenistic period; Kalchedon; IK Kalchedon 40; http://romansiby1.com/rpeople/23283.
160. Aurelius Saturninus; he was *miles* in the *cohors II Lucensium*; unspecified relation with Menefron; funerary inscription; Roman period; Kalchedon; IK Kalchedon 56; http://romansiby1.com/rpeople/23304.
161. Σεῖος son of Χρῆστος; husband of Χρύσα; funerary inscription; 2nd century BC; Kalchedon; IK Kalchedon 72;
http://romansiby1.com/rpeople/23348.
162. Στρατήγια ἡ καὶ Ἔλπις; wife of Ἑρμιανός son of Ἑρμόδωρος; mother of Ὀνήσιμος, Πώσφορος, and Ἑρμιανός; funerary inscription; Roman period; Kalchedon; IK Kalchedon 63;
http://romansiby1.com/rpeople/23319.
163. Στρατονίκα daughter of Ἀπολλώνιος; funerary inscription; 2nd century BC; Kalchedon; IK Kalchedon 33 = SEG 28, 1661;
http://romansiby1.com/rpeople/23275.
164. Σωσίβιος son of Μόσχος son of Ζώτιχος and Εὐτυχίς; brother of Θησεύς; funerary inscription; 2nd century AD; Kalchedon; IK Kalchedon 67;
http://romansiby1.com/rpeople/23333.
165. Σωσιγένης son of Σωσιγένης; dedication; Hellenistic period?; Kalchedon; IK Kalchedon 8;
http://romansiby1.com/rpeople/23230.

Τ

166. Τερτία daughter of Ἀν[---]; unreadable relationship with [---]ηνια? [---]; funerary inscription; Roman period; Kalchedon; IK Kalchedon 74;
http://romansiby1.com/rpeople/23353.
167. Τιμόθεος son of Τιμόθεος; he was from Cos; he was ἐπιβάτης in the *classis* [---]; dedication; 82 BC; Kalchedon; IK Kalchedon 15;
http://romansiby1.com/rpeople/23251.
168. Τιμόθεος son of Κλωδία; funerary inscription; Roman period; Kalchedon; IK Kalchedon 58;
http://romansiby1.com/rpeople/23310.
169. Τίμων son of Γλαῦκος; he was from Cos; he was πρωρεύς in the *classis* [---]; dedication; 82 BC; Kalchedon; IK Kalchedon 15;
http://romansiby1.com/rpeople/23243.
170. Τυνδάριχος son of Καλλίας; dedication; Hellenistic period; Kalchedon; IK Kalchedon 6;
http://romansiby1.com/rpeople/23202.
171. Τυραννίς; mother of Ὀρβανίλλα; funerary inscription; Roman period; Kalchedon; IK Kalchedon 61;
http://romansiby1.com/rpeople/23315.

Φ

172. Φιλισκίων; husband of Ἄκκα and Εὐφημία; he lived or L years; funerary inscription; unknown dating; Kalchedon (Panteichion); IK Kalchedon 119; http://romansıbyı.com/rpeople/23361.
173. Φίλων son of Ἀντίπατρος; dedication; 1 BC; Kalchedon; IK Kalchedon 14; http://romansıbyı.com/rpeople/23237.
174. Φίλων son of Ποσειδώνιος; funerary inscription; Hellenistic period; Kalchedon; IK Kalchedon 48; http://romansıbyı.com/rpeople/23292.
175. Caius Iulius Flavianus; amicus of Caius Iulius Valens; he lived for XXII years; he was a *centurio* in the *Classis Ravennas*; funerary inscription; Roman period; Kalchedon; IK Kalchedon 54; http://romansıbyı.com/rpeople/23301.

Χ

176. Χρύσα; wife of Σεῖος son of Χρῆστος; she lived for XXXI years; funerary inscription; 2nd century BC; Kalchedon; IK Kalchedon 72; http://romansıbyı.com/rpeople/23349.
177. Χρυσέρως son of Χρυσέρως; brother of Ἀρίζηλος; husband of Μόσχιον; funerary inscription; 2nd centuruy AD; Kalchedon; IK Kalchedon 66; http://romansıbyı.com/rpeople/23329.

Ignoti

178. *Ignota*; wife of Λούκιος?; mother of *ignotus*; funerary inscription; Roman period; Kalchedon; IK Kalchedon 64; http://romansıbyı.com/rpeople/23325.
179. *Ignota*; mother of Νικομᾶς and Νίκανδρος; funerary inscription; Roman period; Kalchedon; IK Kalchedon 123; http://romansıbyı.com/rpeople/23368.
180. *Ignotus* son of Νικόμαχος; he was part of an association who had a common building (κοινὸν Νικομάχειον); regulation; 3rd century BC; Kalchedon; IK Kalchedon 13; http://romansıbyı.com/rpeople/4231.
181. *Ignotus* son of *ignotus*; he was part of an association who had a common building (κοινὸν Νικομάχειον); regulation; 3rd century BC; Kalchedon; IK Kalchedon 13; http://romansıbyı.com/rpeople/4232.
182. *Ignotus*; decree; Hellenistic period; Kalchedon; IK Kalchedon 3; http://romansıbyı.com/rpeople/23199.
183. *Ignotus*; Ὀλβιανὸς τῶν πρὸς Ὕπανιν; decree; Hellenistic period; Kalchedon; IK Kalchedon 4; http://romansıbyı.com/rpeople/23200.
184. *Ignotus*; he was a ἱερομνάμων and προφήτας; funerary inscription; Hellenistic period; Kalchedon; IK Kalchedon 42; http://romansıbyı.com/rpeople/23286.
185. *Ignotus* son of Λούκιος? and *ignota*; funerary inscription; Roman period; Kalchedon; IK Kalchedon 64; http://romansıbyı.com/rpeople/23324.

186. *Ignotus*; husband of Αὐρηλία Κρατίστη; funerary inscription; AD 212; Kalchedon; IK Kalchedon 73;
http://romansıbyı.com/rpeople/23350.
187. *Ignotus*; dedication; unknown dating; Kalchedon; IK Kalchedon 104;
http://romansıbyı.com/rpeople/23359.

Fragmentary

188. Διογ[---] son of *ignotus*; he lived for an unreadable number of years; funerary inscription; unknown dating; Kalchedon; IK Kalchedon 113;
http://romansıbyı.com/rpeople/23360.
189. E[---] son of *ignotus*; Βυζάντιος; decree; 2nd century BC; Kalchedon; IK Kalchedon 2;
http://romansıbyı.com/rpeople/23198.
190. Λαμ[---]; wife of Ἀβιάνιος Εὐτύχης; funerary inscription; Roman period; Kalchedon; IK Kalchedon 124;
http://romansıbyı.com/rpeople/23370.
191. Γάϊος Ἰούλιος Μο[---]; construction; unknwon dating; Kalchedon; IK Kalchedon 9;
http://romansıbyı.com/rpeople/23232.
192. Φλαούιος [---] son of Φλαούιος Εὐτύχης; brother of Φλαούιος [---]; funerary inscription; 3rd century AD; Kalchedon; IK Kalchedon 71;
http://romansıbyı.com/rpeople/23346.
193. Φλαούιος [---] son of Φλαούιος Εὐτύχης; brother of Φλαούιος [---]; funerary inscription; 3rd century AD; Kalchedon; IK Kalchedon 71;
http://romansıbyı.com/rpeople/23347.
194. [---]ηνια? [---]; unreadable relationship with Τερτία; funerary inscription; Roman period; Kalchedon; IK Kalchedon 74; http://romansıbyı.com/rpeople/23352.
195. [--]ης; he was part of the ναῦται; dedication; 1st–2nd century AD; Chrysopolis; Demirkök 2010, 163–167.
196. [---]νος son of Θευγένης; he was from Cos; he was ἰατρός in the *classis* [---]; dedication; 82 BC; Kalchedon; IK Kalchedon 15;
http://romansıbyı.com/rpeople/23246.

Bibliography

Avram, A. 2004. The Propontic Coast of Asia Minor, in M.H. Hansen, Th. H. Nielsen (eds.), An Inventory of Archaic and Classical *Poleis*, Oxford, 979–981.

Avram, A. 2011. Pour une prosopographie externe des ressortissants du Pont-Euxin, Ancient civilizations from Scythia to Siberia 17, 1–23.

Avram, A. 2012. Contribution à la prosopographie externe des cités grecques et des peuples indigènes du nord et de l'est du Pont-Euxin, in A. Hermary, G.R. Tsetskhladze, J.-P.M. Morel (eds.), From the pillars of Hercules to the footsteps of the Argonauts, Leuven, 279–313.

Avram, A. 2013. Prosopographia Ponti Euxini Externa, Leuven.

Belke, K. 2021. Gates to Asia Minor: The Harbours of Chalcedon, Chrysopolis, Hiereia and Eutroiu Limen Opposite Constantinople, in F. Daim, E. Kislinger (eds.), The Byzantine Harbours of Constantinople, Mainz, 223–233.

Dana, M. 2011. Culture et mobilité dans le Pont-Euxin, Bordeaux.
Dana, M. 2013. Ἔχω δὲ πατρίδας νῦν δύω (CIRB 134): relații și rețele în orașele grecești din sudul mării Negre și vecinii lor pontici, in F. Panait-Bîrzescu, I. Bîrzescu, F. Matei-Popescu, A. Robu (eds.), Poleis în Marea Neagră. Relații interpontice și producții locale, București, 45–86.
Demirkök, F. 2010. Four Inscriptions Discovered in the Marmaray Excavations, in U. Kocabaş (ed.), Istanbul Archaeological Museums. Proceedings of the 1st Symposium on Marmaray-Metro Salvage Excavations, 5th–6th May 2008, Istanbul, 163–167.
Landvogt, P. 1908. Epigraphische Untersuchungen über die Oikonomos: ein Beitrag zum hellenistischen Beamtenwesen.
Mack, W. 2011. The proxeny-lists of Karthaia, Revue des Études Anciennes 113/2, 319–344.
Merle, H. 1916. Die Geschichte der Städte Byzantion und Kalchedon: von ihre Gründung bis zum Eingreifen der Römer in die Verhältnisse des Ostens, Kiel.
Öğüt-Polat, S., Şahin, S. 1985. Katalog der bithynischen Inschriften im archäologischen Museum von Istanbul, Epigraphica Anatolica 5, 97–121.
Pázsint, A.-I. 2022a. Contribution to the Prosopographia Ponti Euxini Externa. Kallatianoi et Odessitai, Journal of Ancient History and Archaeology 9/3, 5–16.
Pázsint, A.-I. 2022b. Prosopographia Ponti Euxini. Dionysopolis, Acta Musei Napocensis 59/I, 9–51.
Pázsint, A.-I. 2023. Contributions à la prosopographie de Tomis. Les femmes, in L. Mihailescu-Bîrliba, I. Piso (eds.), Romans and Natives in the Danubian provinces. Papers of the 5th International Conference on Roman Danubian Provinces, Wiesbaden, 429–454.
Pázsint, A.-I. 2024. Population at Callatis and Odessus. The Roman Soldiers, *Electrum* 31, *in print.*
Poland, F. 1909. Geschichte des griechischen Vereinswese, Leipzig.
Robu, A. 2007/2009. Traditions et innovations institutionnelles : l'organisation civique de Byzance et de Chalcédoine, Il Mar Nero VII, 149–166.
Robu, A. 2012. Les établissements mégariens de la Propontide et du Pont-Euxin : réseaux, solidarités et liens institutionnels, Pallas. Revue d'études antiques 89, 181–195.
Robu, A. 2012/2018. Cultes et groupes de pêcheurs en Propontide : note sur une dédicace de Chalcédoine, Il Mar Nero IX, 159–165.
Robu, A. 2013a. Sanctuare și relații între cetăți în lumea elenistică: Exemplul cetăților Chalcedon și Byzantion, in F. Panait-Bîrzescu, I. Bîrzescu, F. Matei-Popescu, A. Robu (eds.), Poleis în Marea Neagră. Relații interpontice și producții locale, București, 143–157.
Robu, A. 2013b. Traditions et rapprochements onomastiques dans les cités grecques de la mer Noire : quelques exemples tirés du « monde mégarien », in A. Avram, I. Bîrzescu (eds.), Mélanges d'archéologie et d'histoire ancienne a la mémoire de Petre Alexandrescu, Roma, 281–293.
Robu, A. 2014a. Mégare et les établissements mégariens de Sicile, de la Propontide et du Pont-Euxin : histoire et institutions, Bern/New York.

Robu, A. 2014b. Byzance et Chalcédoine à l'époque hellénistique : entre alliances et rivalités, in V. Cojocaru, A. Coşkun, M. Dana (eds.), Interconnectivity in the Mediterranean and Pontic world during the Hellenistic and Roman periods. Cluj-Napoca, 187–206.

Ruscu, L. 2002. Relaţiile externe ale oraşelor greceşti de pe litoralul românesc al Mării Negre, Cluj-Napoca.

Ruscu, L. 2004. Personal External Relations of the Western Pontic Cities in pre-Roman Period, in S. Panova (ed.), *Cerno More mezhdu istoka i zapada. Reka Dunav most mezhdu narodi i kultury. IX Pontijski cetenija*, Varna, 16–17 maj 2003, Varna, 144–160.

Salomies, O. 1992. Adoptive and polyonymous nomenclature in the Roman Empire, Helsinki.

Salomies, O. 2014. Adoptive and polyonymous nomenclature in the Roman Empire, in M.L. Caldelli, G.L. Gregori (eds.), Epigrafia e ordine senatorio, 30 anni dopo (Atti della XIXe Rencontre sur l'épigraphie du monde romain : Roma 21–23 marzo 2013), Roma, 511–536.

Samama, É. 2003. Les Médecins dans le monde grec. Sources épigraphiques sur la naissance d'un corpus médical, Geneva.

Sokolowski, F. 1955. Lois sacrées de l'Asie Mineure, Paris.

La reflexión amarga de un *homo novus* en el momento culminante de su carrera: Cicerón y la aristocracia romana

Marc Mayer i Olivé

Cicerón en el *Pro Murena* pronuncia unas ácidas palabras criticando en la figura de Servio Sulpicio la arrogante preponderancia del patriciado en virtud de su noble cuna. La ocasión es la defensa de Lucio Licinio Murena, cónsul designado por las elecciones para el consulado del 62 a. C.[1], que son impugnadas por uno de los candidatos derrotados, el jurista patricio Servio Sulpicio Rufo[2], fundamentándose en la *lex Tullia de ambitu* atribuyendo la elección de Murena a la corrupción. En apoyo de la pretensión de Silano se situó en un principio ni más ni menos que el prestigioso y austero Marco Porcio Catón[3], flanqueado por un casi desconocido Gneo Postumio y un jovencísimo Servio Sulpicio del que no tenemos otras noticias que las que nos ofrece el propio discurso de Cicerón[4].

No es este el caso de tratar sobre la legitimidad o no de este proceso, sino de volver la vista a la actuación de Cicerón ante uno de los acusadores[5], quizás el menos importante, sobre el que vuelca su parecer sobre la aristocracia romana y puesto que se atreve a poner en duda la elección de Murena, plebeyo, lanuvino y primer cónsul de su estirpe. La situación es especialmente arriesgada ya que se produce en un momento en que han tenido éxito algunos procesos de este género, especialmente en el 66 a. C. que había comportado la deposición de los cónsules designados. Pensemos también en que en el fondo de la escena planea la figura del gran derrotado en dos elecciones sucesivas al consulado: el patricio

1 MRR II 169, 172–173 y 580–581, MRR III, 123–124.

2 MRR II, 624.

3 MRR II, 606.

4 Cabe sospechar sin embargo que pesara en la actitud que refleja el discurso la derrota en estas mismas elecciones del jurisconsulto Servio Sulpicio Rufo en quien el joven pudo haber depositado algunas esperanzas.

5 Un libro reciente traza ágilmente a grandes rasgos el cuadro de estos momentos complicados de la vida de Cicerón que ya ha triunfado, después de la condena de Verres, como abogado, Roman 2020, 76–101. Un resumen biográfico útil en May 2002, 1–21. Para una bibliografía más completa cf. Mayer Olivé 2019, 7–20. Es siempre útil volver la vista a las páginas de un clásico en el análisis de la actuación de Cicerón, cf. Ciaceri 1939², 281–283, para este proceso.

Lucio Sergio Catilina[6]. No resulta necesario recordar aquí el desenlace de aquellos dificilísimos sucesos.

Los términos con los cuales refuta Cicerón la autoridad para emprender la acusación de Servio Sulpicio, al que llama, "cum grano salis" *adulescens ingeniosus et bonus de equitum centuriis*[7], son los que siguen: *Tua vero nobilitas, Ser. Sulpici, tametsi summa est, tamen hominibus litteratis et historicis est notior, populo vero et suffragatoribus obscurior. Pater enim fuit equestri loco, avus nulla inlustri laude celebratus. Itaque non ex sermone hominum recenti sed ex annalium vetustate eruenda est nobilitatis tuae y; descarga algo la crudeza y el peso de sus duras palabras al continuar: Quare ego te semper in nostrum numero adgregare soleo, quod virtute industriaque perfecisti ut, cum equitis Romani esse filius, summa tamen amplitudine dignus putarere*[8].

Una crítica demoledora al personaje, pero también a quienes sin más razón que la antigüedad y nobleza de sus antepasados pretenden enfrentarse a una nueva situación y dar juicios basados únicamente en su alcurnia, aunque esta fuera indudablemente reconocida y respetada por el pueblo[9]. Recordemos en este punto que entre los años 94 y 64 a.C. todos los cónsules habían sido de origen noble, sin presencia de plebeyos, y el hecho de que de todas maneras, como se ha sobradamente demostrado, era difícil llegar al consulado sin haber tenido antecesores directos que hubieran ejercido la pretura, como era el caso de Murena[10].

Cicerón se permite en esta ocasión además mencionar con un cierto punto de desdén a los historiadores eruditos y a los anales, unas crónicas claramente aristocráticas al servicio de una clase social que se ve reflejada en ellas y que en cierta medida toma los hechos y actitudes descritas como ejemplo de conducta que se deben extender a toda la clase dirigente. A esta creencia inveterada opone Cicerón la realidad política del momento, fruto de una larga época convulsa en la que la relativa estabilidad en el consulado de una única clase social ha hecho que esta olvide aparentemente las circunstancias concomitantes.

Resulta evidente que en este momento, y el discurso resulta claro, el sistema se halla definitivamente en crisis, sin que por ello podamos pensar que el Arpinate, hombre de su tiempo, aunque su invectiva pueda ser considerada, como así debe de ser, de ámbito general y ampliada a mayor escala, tenga en su mente otra cosa más allá de preconizar una apertura y ampliación de esta oligarquía, que permita la ascensión de una nueva clase política conservadora ya emergente y no tan condicionada por su origen familiar[11].

La defensa de Murena permite que el cónsul, desde su nuevo prestigio como tal[12], intente preconizar con su defensa la superación política de algunos de los diversos tópicos implí-

6 MRR II, 147, 155 y 617; MRR III, 192.

7 Cic. *Mur.* 26, 54, citamos según la edición de la Collection des Universités de France de Boulanger 1946, 64.

8 Cic. *Mur.* 7, 16, según la edición mencionada en la nota anterior p. 39

9 Gruen 1974, 505.

10 Gruen 1974, 508–523, esp. 522 para el acceso al consulado entre el 78 y el 49 a.C., el cálculo estadístico muestra como el 88,5% de los 61 cónsules elegidos proceden de familias consulares.

11 Dos trabajos relativamente recientes se ocupan de la ideología del político en aquel momento: Pina Polo, 2005, 247–266; Roman 2020, 229–260, con una buena selección de pasajes significativos.

12 Cf. para el carácter marcadamente político de esta defensa Cape 2002, 113–158, esp. 118–119.

citos al acceso a los cargos de gobierno, entre ellos el linaje, abriendo el camino a un nuevo concepto que se consolidará más tarde en su pensamiento político en el que frente a los denominados *optimates* juegan sin duda un papel referencial los *boni* y la *concordia ordinum*[13].

Evidentemente en el proceso de Murena prevaleció el criterio de la defensa[14], que Cicerón ejerció conjuntamente a Quinto Hortensio Hortal y Marco Licinio Craso, lo cual no deja de ser muy significativo[15].

Se ha señalado repetidamente el carácter eminentemente político del proceso de Murena, pero quizás no se ha insistido suficientemente en la afirmación de Cicerón respecto al linaje del joven Servio Sulpicio, una invectiva judicial que, no obstante, va mucho más allá de la persona, a la que pretende respetar y se vuelca sobre la situación política anterior contra cuyas dificultades había luchado victoriosamente el orador como *homo novus*.

No nos cabe duda de que, como harán después los satíricos en un momento en que la nobleza tradicional empieza a ser anecdótica[16], nos hallamos ante la explicitación de un sentimiento de rechazo, que seguramente fue compartido por una parte substancial de la sociedad, el cual indica la proximidad del final de una república aristocrática, que ha pesar de los problemas de todo tipo que la habían desafiado, había sobrevivido hasta aquel momento con un apoyo social muy notable.

Como última observación no dejemos de recordar como al final mismo del régimen republicano a las puertas del principado todavía Gayo Julio César indicaba con orgullo su origen patricio[17] y como la abreviatura que indica el origen patricio en la fórmula onomástica perdura en la epigrafía y en la nomenclatura de época imperial[18], momento en el cual la *adlectio inter patricios* será un honor codiciado, cuya concesión alargará su prestigio hasta el final del imperio romano e incluso más allá[19].

Bibliografía

Badel, C. 2007. Épigraphie et mobilité sociale: l'adlectio inter patricios, en M. Mayer i Olivé, G. Baratta, A. Guzmán Almagro (eds.), Acta XII Congressus internationalis epigraphiae Graecae et Latinae. Provinciae imperii Romani inscriptionibus descriptae, vol. I, Barcelona, 93–98.

13 Cf. Schofield 2021, 193–203, para el papel atribuido a los *boni*. Una buena antología de pasajes relativos a la visión política de la sociedad por parte de Cicerón en Lacey, Wilson 1978, que aunque no se ocupa del Pro Murena es útil para ver las referencias al proceso electoral fundamentalmente sobre todo en el Pro Plancio, 253–273.

14 Cf. para la técnica de Cicerón de defensa en el caso de Murena, Corbeill 2002, 197–217, esp. 201-204.

15 Cf. *MRR* II, 573, para el primero y 580, para el segundo.

16 Para un examen de esta tendencia y sus antecedentes, véase Mayer i Olivé 2021, 97–105.

17 Cf. Batstone 2018, 43–57, para la conciencia de la autoconstrucción de un personaje. Véase para este aspecto Mayer 2011, 189–232, esp. 194–211. Para el orgullo familiar cf. Meier 1982, 70–75.

18 Cf. Pistor 1965; Badel 2007, 93–98; Buongiorno 2020, 67–78.

19 Picotti 1928, 3–80.

Batstone, W. 2018. Caesar Constructing Caesar, en L. Grillo, C. B. Krebs (eds.), The Cambridge Companion to the Writings of Julius Caesar, Cambridge, 43–57.
Boulanger, A. (ed.) 1946.Cicéron, Discours tome XI, Pour L. Murena – Pour P. Sylla (Collection des Universités de France), Paris.
Buongiorno, P. 2020. La tabula Lugdunensis e i fondamenti ideologici e giuridici dell'adlectio inter patricios di Claudio, en O. Licandro, C. Giuffrida, M. Cassia (eds.), Senatori, cavalieri e curiali fra privilegi ereditari e mobilità verticale (Fra Oriente e Occidente, 8), Roma, 67–78.
Cape Jr., R. W. 2002. Cicero's consular Speeches, en J. M. May (ed.), Brill's Companion to Cicero. Oratory and Rhetoric, Leiden, Boston, Köln, 113–158.
Ciaceri, E. 1939[2]. Cicerone ed i suoi tempi, vol. I Dalla nascita al consolato (a. 106–63 a. C.), Milano, Genova, Roma, Napoli (reimpr. Roma 1964).
Corbeill, A. 2002. Ciceronian invective, en J. M. May (ed.), Brills Companion to Cicero. Oratory and Rhetoric, Leiden, Boston, Köln, 197–217.
Gruen, E. S. 1974. The Last Generation of the Roman Republic, Berkeley, Los Angeles, London (reimpr. 1995).
Lacey, W. K., Wilson, B. W. J. G. 1978. Res publica: Roman Politics and Society according to Cicero, Bristol.
May, Cicero J. M. 2002. His Life and Career, en J. M. May (ed.), Brill's Companion to Cicero. Oratory and Rhetoric, Leiden, Boston, Köln, 1–21.
Mayer, M. 2011. Caesar and the Corpus Caesarianum, en G. Marasco (ed.), Political Autobiographies and Memoirs in Antiquity. A Brill Companion, Leiden, Boston 189–232.
Mayer Olivé, M. 2019. Cicerón en el jardín, Rivista di Archeologia XLIII, 7–20.
Mayer i Olivé, M. 2021. Aut pastor fuit aut illud quod dicere nolo. La superbia de las gentes aristocráticas en Juvenal, en M. A. Coronel Ramos, R. Hernández Pérez (eds.), Priscorum interpres. Homenaje al profesor Jaime Siles (Studia Philologica Valentina, Anejo 2), Valencia, 97–105.
Meier, C. 1982. Caesar, Berlin.
MRR II: Broughton, T. R. S., The Magistrates of the Roman Republic, vol II, 99 B. C.–31 B. C. (Philological Monographs. American Philological Association, XV, vol. II) Cleveland, Ohio 1952 (reimpr. 1968).
MRR III: Broughton, T. R. S., The Magistrates of the Roman Republic, vol III Supplement, (Philological Monographs. American Philological Association, XV, vol. III), Atlanta, Georgia 1986.
Picotti, G. B. 1928. Il "patricius" nell'ultima età imperiale e nei primi regni barbarici d'Italia, Archivio Storico Italiano 86 (ser. 7, vol.9) n. 1 (325), 3–80.
Pina Polo, F. 2005, Marco Tulio Cicerón (Biografías), Barcelona.
Pistor, H.-H. 1965. Prinzeps und Patriziat in der Zeit von Augustus bis Commodus, Freiburg i. Breisgau (tesis doctoral).
Roman, Y. 2020, Cicéron, Paris.
Schofield, M. 2021. Cicero. Political Philosophy (Founders of Modern Political and Social Thought), Oxford.

Flora, (k)eine unbekannte Gottheit

Marietta Horster

Ioan Piso, meinem seit gemeinsamen
Kölner Tagen geschätzten Kollegen

Eine italische Göttin in Rom

M. Terentius Varro (116–27 v. Chr.) bietet in seinem Kompendium über die von der lateinischen Sprache geprägte römische Kultur, *De lingua Latina*, eine Erläuterung zur räumlichen Gliederung der Stadt Rom (Var. ling. 5, 41–58). Er erklärt dabei beispielsweise, wieso der eine Berg *Capitolinus*, der andere *Saturnius* heißt (5, 41–42) und kommt dann zu den Charakteristika der auf die vier Teile (Suburbana, Esquilina, Collina, Palatina) der Stadt verteilten Orte (*loca*), die auf den früheren Standorten der 27 Heiligtümern der Argeier (*Argeorum sacraria*) beruhen. Das ist der Auftakt, um sich Götter- und Ortsnamen weiter zu widmen und dabei *en passant* auch auf deren Heiligtümer und Kulte einzugehen. Dazu gehören auch die Gottheiten, die die Römer von den Sabinern übernommen hätten; zumindest deren Benennung sei, so Varro, auf die sabinische Sprache (*Sabinum linguam olent*) zurückzuführen, auch wenn Saturn und Diana, die in diese Gruppe gehören, durchaus auch Wurzeln in einer zweiten Sprache, derjenigen der Latiner, haben dürften (Varr. ling. 5, 74). Danach soll König Tatius, seinem Gelübde entsprechend, die folgenden Altäre (*arae*) in Rom geweiht haben: für Ops, Flora, Vediovis, Saturnus, Sol, Luna, Volcanus und Summanus, ebenso auch für Larunda, Terminus, Quirinus, Vortumnus, die Laren, Diana und Lucina.[1]

Die Gottheit, der dieser Beitrag gewidmet ist, wird dann noch ein zweites Mal im Werk des Varro genannt, ähnlich marginal erscheinend wie beim ersten Mal. Aber immerhin erfährt der Leser so, wo offenbar ein Heiligtum für Flora gelegen war: gleich neben oder am sogenannten *Clivus Proximus*, der wiederum den sich erhebenden Weg zur Anhöhe des *Capitolium Vetus* bezeichne. An diesem „Alten Kapitol“ soll der früheste Tempel der

1 Varr. ling. 5, 74 (ed. De Melo): *Et arae Sabinum linguam olent, quae Tati regis voto sunt Romae dedicatae: nam, ut annales dicunt, vovit Opi, Flor<a>e, Vediovi Saturnoque, Soli, Lunae, Volcano et Summano, itemque Larundae, Termino, Quirino, Vortumno, Laribus, Dianae Lucinaeque; e quis nonnulla nomina in utraque lingua habent radices, ut arbores quae in confinio natae in utroque agro serpunt: potest enim Saturnus hic de alia causa esse dictus atque in Sabinis, et sic Diana, de quibus supra dictum est.*

Trias Iupiter, Iuno und Minerva gelegen haben, deutlich älter als der, der auf dem zur Zeit Varros *Capitolium* genannten Hügel lag.[2] Unmittelbar zuvor im selben Abschnitt (5, 158) widmet sich Varro auch dem *Clivus Publicus. Clivus Publicus* und *Clivus Proximus* liegen demnach nebeneinander und der Kultort für Flora am Hang (*susus*) des *Clivus Proximus* auf dem Weg in Richtung altem Kapitol.

Nicht nur über dieses frühe Heiligtum und seine Lage,[3] dessen Funktion und die Art der Verehrung für Flora wird seit langem diskutiert,[4] sondern auch über das, was zumindest theoretisch neben literarischen Zeugnissen auch Spuren in der materiellen Überlieferung hinterlassen haben dürfte, aber nicht archäologisch bzw. kaum numismatisch und epigraphisch erkennbar ist: Die individuelle Verehrung für die Göttin Flora selbst und den kollektiven, ihr geweihten, von Augustus renovierten Tempel in Rom, von dessen Existenz auch noch im 4. Jh. n. Chr. die Rede ist.

Ein Priestertum in Rom

Nach den augusteischen *Fasti Praenestini* geht es bei den Ritualen für Flora um die Fruchtbarkeit der blühenden Natur.[5] In Rom soll es laut Ennius dafür einen „Flamen Floralis" gegeben haben, der zusammen mit anderen Priestern für einzelne Gottheiten

2 Varr. ling 5, 158 (ed. De Melo): *Clivos Publ<i>cius ab aedilibus plebei Publici<i>s qui eum publice aedificarunt. Simili de causa Pullius et Cosconius, quod ab his viocuris dicuntur aedificati. Clivus proximus a Flora susus versus Capitolium Vetus, quod ibi sacellum Iovis Iunonis Minervae, et id antiquius quam aedis quae in Capitolio facta.*

3 Im LTUR gibt es zwei Beiträge – Flora, aedes und Flora, templum (in Colle) –, die nicht aufeinander abgestimmt zu sein scheinen. Beide gehen von dem nahe dem „alten" Kapitol gelegenen Heiligtum aus (Papi 1995; Coarelli 1995). Sie ergänzen sich aber vorzüglich in den Hinweisen auf die Überlieferung, unabhängig davon, ob die jeweilige Zuschreibung sich nun auf ein oder zwei Heiligtümer bezogen hat Weitere Zeugnisse sind u.a.: Vitr. 7, 9, 4 (Büros, die sich zwischen den Heiligtümern der Flora und des Quirinus befinden); Tac. ann. 2, 49 (Tempel der Flora ist in der Republik von L. und M. Publicii gestiftet worden); Vell. Pat. 1, 14, 8 (die *Ludi florales* wurden anlässlich der Einweihung des Tempels der Flora im Jahr 240 v. Chr. initiiert); vgl. unten zu den *Fasti Praenestini*: das Heiligtum der Flora, Göttin über/für alles Blühende (*quae rebus florescendis praeest*) ist geweiht worden wegen der Unfruchtbarkeit der Pflanzen (*propter sterilitatem fru[g]um*). Die Formulierung dürfte auf den unmittelbaren Anlass nach schlechten Ernten in den 240er Jahren zurückgehen. Die Fruchtbarkeit der gesamten Natur, für die Ceres zuständig ist, wird hier durch den besonderen Fokus auf die blühenden Bäume und Sträucher, die Früchte tragen sollen, ergänzt. Zur Verbindung der Göttinnen, zum Kult im Sabinerland und zum Ritus für Flora in der Republik u.v.a. mehr vgl. Cels Saint-Hilare 1977, vgl. auch Fabbri 2019, 31–37.

4 Von Wissowa 1909a bis Fabbri 2019.

5 I. It. XIII 2, 17 für den 28. April: *F IIII n(efas) p(iaculum) ludi Florae feriae ex s(enatus) c(onsulto) quod eo di[e fanu]m et [ara] / Vestae in domu Imp(eratoris) Caesaris Augu[sti po]ntif(icis) max(imi) / dedicatast Quirinio et Valgio co(n)s(ulibus) eodem / die aedis Florae quae rebus florescendis praeest / dedicata est propter sterilitatem fru[g]um.*

erstmals von Numa Pompilius, einem der sagenhaften Könige, eingesetzt worden war.[6] Es wurde vermutet, dass sich ein Hinweis auf diese besondere Priesterschaft im Jahr 53 v. Chr. findet, als auf einer Münze des Münzmeisters C. Servilius C. f. der Hinweis auf FLORAL PRIMVS (RRC 423/1) zu lesen ist.[7] Die sehr viel ausführlichere Legende MEMMIVS AED CERIALIA PREIMVS FECIT, die wohl im Jahr 56 v. Chr. geprägt worden sein dürfte und die erstmalige Feier der Ceralia durch den Aedilen Memmius hervorhebt (RRC 427/1), ist einer der Gründe, wieso der von Servilius geprägte Denar mit einer deutlich kürzeren Legende verständlich war: Kein Flamen Floralis, sondern ein ebenfalls erstmals in bestimmter Art und Weise ausgerichtetes Floralia-Fest dürfte gemeint sein – sofern die spätere Datierung (53 v. Chr.) nach dem Memmius-Denar stimmt. Das ursprünglich eintägige Fest, das wohl in nicht regelmäßiger Form nach dem Ende des 1. Punischen Krieges eingerichtet und ab dem Jahr 173 v. Chr. dann jährlich gefeiert wurde,[8] könnte sich nun in Richtung der später auch von Ovid beschriebenen Form der mehrtägigen Aufführungen im Theater in Verbindung mit einem abschließenden Zirkus-Event (von *venationes* von Ziegen und Hasen ist bei Ovid, *Fast.* 5, 371–374 die Rede) vom 28. Mai bis 2. April entwickelt haben.

Unabhängig von der Datierung ist aber auf keinen Fall die vermeintliche Existenz einer über Münzähnlichkeiten der Servilii konstruierten Familientradition für ein Flora-Priesteramt nachvollziehbar.[9] Im Gegenteil scheint es vielmehr der Augurat zu sein, über den sich die Familie im 2. und 1. Jh. v. Chr. präsentiert. Mit seinem Denar (RRC 264/1),

---

6 Ennius, ann. fr. 116–118 (ed. Skutsch) überliefert bei Varr. ling. 7, 45 (ed. De Melo): *Eundem [= Ennius] Pompilium ait fecisse flamines, qui cum omnes sunt a singulis deis cognominati, in quibusdam apparent etyma, ut cur sit Martialis et Quirinalis; sunt in quibus flaminum cognominibus latent origines, ut in his qui sunt versibus plerique: Volturnalem, Palatualem, Fur<r>inalem, Floralemque Falacrem<que> et Pomonalem fecit. Hic idem, quae o<b>scura sunt; eorum origo Volturnus, diva Palatua, Furrina, Flora, Falacer pater, Pomo[rum]na[m].*

7 Mit Kommentar zur Münze und ihrer Relevanz für ein mögliches Flaminat des Servilier-Vorfahren M. Servilius Pulex Geminus, Rüpke 2005, vol. 2, 1284 Nr. 3069. Zu den Verwandtschaftsverhältnissen der Servilii vgl. Zmeskal 2009, 252–254. In den Priesterlisten bei Rüpke 2005, vol. 1, 589 werden zwei Priester als Flamines Floralis aufgeführt: der u.a. als Augur und Konsul bezeugte M. Servilius Pulex Geminus (s. oben im Text) und der aus Apulien stammende M. Numisius M.f. M.n. Quintianus, dessen kaiserzeitliches Flaminat auch ein städtisches in Teanum Apulum sein könnte, CIL IX 705, im Katalog bei Rüpke 2005, vol. 2, 1177 Nr. 2551, der ihn in das 2. Jh. datiert und der Stadt Rom zuordnet.

8 Mit Hinweisen zu Quellen und Literatur Fabbri 2019, 28–29. Etwas anders die Argumente von Ryan 2008, der versucht, die Tradition der Servilii und die Abbildung des Lituus auf einigen von deren Münzen mit den *Floralia* bzw. den *Ludi Florales* durch die Verantwortung der Auguren für die rituelle Korrektheit solcher Veranstaltungen zu erklären.

9 So aber Crawford 1974 und Rüpke 2005 (s. Anm. 7). Crawford 1974 datiert RRC 423/1 in das Jahr 57 v. Chr., dagegen Hersh, Walker 1984 mit einer Datierung ins Jahr 53 v. Chr., der sich Hollstein 1993, 256–260 anschließt (übernommen auch in https://www.ikmk.uni-tuebingen.de/object?id=ID1264). Die „Digital Prosopography of the Roman Republic" hat den Münzmeister nicht in ihre Datenbank aufgenommen. Zu den verschiedenen identifizierten Genealogien der Münzprägenden von RRC 370 und 423 von Th. Mommsen über F. Münzer bis zu den Autoren nach M. Crawford und seinem RRC siehe Hollstein, ibid.

Abb. 1: RRC 423/1 © Institut für Klassische Archäologie der Eberhard Karls Univ. Tübingen, Inv. nr. III 317/12, Foto St. Krmnicek

der auf der Vorderseite neben der Legende ROMA den Kopf des Apolls und einen Lituus darstellt, dürfte sich C. Servilius M.f.M.n. Vatia, Münzmeister 127 v.Chr.,[10] und ähnlich auch C. Servilius in der Zeit 82/80 v.Chr. (RRC 370/1) auf seinem Denar, mit ROMA, Lituus und Apoll-Kopf, wohl kaum auf das eigene Karriere-Potential beziehen, sondern vielmehr anknüpfen an seinen Vorfahren M. Servilius C.f.P.n. Pulex Geminus, cos. 202, der nach 211 als Augur kooptiert worden war.[11] Und der schon genannte etwa 150 Jahre später prägende Münzmeister C. Servilius aus derselben Familie prägt „seinen" Denar ebenfalls mit Lituus, allerdings findet sich auf dem Avers nicht mehr die Legende ROMA, sondern FLORAL PRIMUS (s. Abb. 1) und ein idealisierter Kopf der durch den Blütenkranz charakterisierten Flora.

Wahrscheinlich ist zumindest ein stadtrömischer Priester für Flora bekannt, M. Numisius Quintianus.[12] Wenig überraschend ist er aus der Kaiserzeit überliefert, nachdem Augustus die in Rom vorhandenen Kulte und deren Kultstätten zu neuem Leben erweckt und offenbar deren Pflege öfter Rittern anvertraut hatte. Auch von den übrigen „flamines", die Ennius in seinem annalistischen Gedicht nennt, die Volturnus, Palatua, Furrina, Flora, Falacer und Pomona geweiht gewesen sein sollen, finden sich kaum Spuren und, wenn doch, dann in der Kaiserzeit wie bei Flora.[13] Numisius' Priestertum der *Laurentes Lavinates* dürfte mit dem Ritter-Status verbunden gewesen sein. Neben dem Stadtpatronat von Teanum Apulum, wohl seiner Heimatstadt, werden für den Ehegatten der von dieser Stadt geehrten Pomponia Drusilla lediglich jene beiden Priestertümer genannt. Das ist wohl ein ausreichender Grund, ihn mangels weiterer munizipaler Bezüge im Text nicht als einen Priester für Flora in Teanum Apulum, sondern als stadtrömischen *flamen Floralis* zu identifizieren.[14]

---

10 Datierung von Crawford 1974, RRC 264/1 für den Münzmeister C. Servilius in das Jahr 127 v.Chr. und ebd. auch der Identifizierungsvorschlag mit C. Servilius Vata.

11 C. Servilius M.f.M.n. Vatia war circa 102 v.Chr. selber Augur, so Rüpke 2005, 1284–1285 Nr. 3071.

12 CIL IX 705, eine Statuenbasis aus (lokalem?) Stein: *Pomponiae / C(ai) f(iliae) Drusillae / M(arcus) Numisius / M(arci) f(ilius) M(arci) n(epos) Cor(nelia) / Quintianus / Laurens Lavinas / flamen floralis / patronus munic(ipii) / co(n)iugi rarissimae / l(ocus) d(atus) d(ecreto) d(ecurionum).*

13 Keine Nachweise finden sich für einen Priester des Volturnus, der Furrina und des Falacer. In Rüpke 2005, vol. 1, 589 sind immerhin zwei *pontifices* für Palatua (Anonymus 94 aus der Kaiserzeit, CIL XI 5031; der Ritter L. Egnatuleius P.f. Sabinus, 2. Jh. n.Chr, CIL VIII 10500 in Thysdrus) und einer für Pomona (der Ritter C. Iulius Silvanus Melanio, Ende 2./Anfang 3. Jh., CIL III 12732 in Gradina) angegeben.

14 Scheid, Granino Cecere 1999, 81; Pasqualini 2008, 225 mit Anm. 22. Scheid, Granino Cecere 1999, 103 argumentieren zudem, dass die meisten der nicht-ritterlichen Priester *Laurentes Lavinates* in den Zeitraum zwischen dem Ende des 2. Jhs. und dem Anfang des 3. Jhs. datieren (ibid., 155–158 mit 10 solcher Personen). Die Studie von Granino Cecere 2008 unterstreicht dagegen den hohen Anteil

Ovids Flora und das Fest *Floralia*

Ovid hat mit seinen Fasten den augusteischen Aufschwung der Kulte und Rituale begleitet. Die so offensichtlichen Interessen an den kultischen Traditionen Roms hat er durch aufwändige Recherchen literarisch-poetisch geformt und dabei zum Teil auch die von Varro wenige Jahrzehnte zuvor gesetzten Akzente durchaus verändert. Der Göttin bekrönt von 1000 Blüten, *mille venit variis florum dea nexa coronis* (Ov. Fast. 4, 945), der Herrin der Blumen, *arbitrium tu, dea, floris habes* (5, 212), Flora und ihrer Abkunft von Mars, vor allem aber ihrer Wirkmacht für die Fruchtbarkeit und das Blühen der Pflanzen widmet er sich in Fast. 5, 183–274. Er bietet dann eine Beschreibung des Festes *Floralia* als zunächst durchaus seriös plebeisch, was dann später als jährlich etabliert wird (5, 275–330, jährlich 5, 295–296: *annua crediderim spectacula facta; negavit*);[15] es sticht durch seinen ausgelassenem Charakter hervor, ist mit Banketten und Alkohol verbunden (5, 331–348, zur Trunkenheit *ebrius* und Unterstützung von Bacchus 5, 337–340) und da besonders die „leichten Damen" erwähnt werden (5, 349–376), dürften auch diese kräftig mitgefeiert haben. Bei letzteren ist der Kontext das nächtliche Feiern, von denen Fackeln zeugen (361–368).[16] Spuren dieses Festes finden sich zwar in zahlreichen literarischen Zeugnissen,[17] aber in den verschiedenen Darstellungsmedien, von Vasen über Reliefs bis zu Gemälden, sind die Göttin und ihr Fest nicht präsent, eine Ausnahme bilden ihre seltenen Porträts auf Münzen.[18] Zwar ist Flora mit dem überaus gewichtigen Thema der Frucht und Fruchtbarkeit verbunden, dennoch wird sie bei Ovid und bei vielen anderen Autoren nicht zuletzt durch die Ausgestaltung des Festes seit der späten Republik und in der Kaiserzeit als eine eher „leichte" Göttin charakterisiert. Dies entspricht nicht dem von Fabbri 2019 zuletzt unterstrichenen, sehr viel agrarisch-gewichtigeren Bild einer Göttin, die über das Werden und Gedeihen der Pflanzen wacht. Bei einem christlichen Augustinus bleibt von Flora kaum noch etwas übrig an Zuständigkeit: bis auf den guten Blütenstand und damit das kleine Zeitfenster der Blütezeit, für das sie verantwortlich ist, wird sie von ihm

---

der lediglich auf munizipaler Ebene aktiven Priester dieser Art in der Regio X, auch schon in der Mitte des 2. Jhs.

15 Im Jahr 173 v. Chr., dem Konsulat von L. Postumius Albinus und M. Popilius Laenas, Ov. Fast. 5, 329. Zur Datierung und zum Charakter des Festes in republikanischer Zeit mit seiner Nähe mehr zu den Bacchanalien als zu den *Cerialia*, die aber etwa zeitgleich jährlich gefeiert worden sein dürften, vgl. Cels Saint-Hilaire 1977, 260–272. Sie stellt den Kontext zur Agrarkrise und zu den Problemen der stadtrömischen Plebs her, ibid. 261–265.

16 Hierzu und zum Folgenden vgl. Foulon 2010 und Fabbri 2019, 39–71 (zur Göttin v.a. bei Ovid) und 115–185 (zu den *Floralia* in Rom).

17 Zusammenstellung der vielfältigen literarischen Quellen zum Fest bis in die Spätantike bei Wissowa 1909b; Hošek 1988, 137–138.

18 Vgl. Hošek 1988, 138–139. Er führt neben den Abbildungen des blumenbekränzten Kopfes der Flora auf den republikanischen Denaren RRC 447; 423/1; 521; 512/1–2 nur eine der trajanischen Restitutionsmünzen BMC Emp III Taf. 22, 19 auf. Hinzu kommt lediglich eine Statuenbasis, CIL VI 30867 (s. hierzu unten), die nahelegt, dass auf ihr eine Statue der Flora gestanden haben könnte, von der aber nichts erhalten ist. Fabbri 2019, 201–217 diskutiert noch einige Kleinbronzen, die in der Forschung als Flora angesprochen (interpretiert?) worden sind.

in eine lange Liste von mehr oder weniger unbekannten Gottheiten eingereiht, die in einer von Augustinus auf diese Weise lächerlich gemachten, nicht-christlichen Sicht für das Gedeihen der Natur zuständig waren.[19]

Flora in Inschriften

Zeugnisse aus Rom und Italien für eine durch Gruppen oder Individuen verehrte Gottheit Flora sind ausgesprochen selten, wenn man vom gemeinschaftlich organisierten Fest der *Floralia* einmal absieht.[20] Auch die Gebete und Opfer für Flora durch die Arvalbrüder und andere Priestergruppen geben keinen Hinweis auf eine individuelle Verehrung der Flora. Zudem bettet sich Flora bei den priesterlichen Vorgaben in eine lange Liste von anderen Göttern, die vergleichbare oder auch größere Gaben erhielten, ein.[21]

Abgesehen von einer ungewöhnlichen Inschrift aus dem 16. Jh., die allerdings auf einem antiken Stein eingeschrieben wurde und deswegen wahrscheinlich als ‚falsus' in das *Corpus Inscriptionum Latinarum* überhaupt aufgenommen wurde,[22] gibt es eine Gruppe von Bronzetäfelchen, die einem Weihobjekt angehängt oder anders beigegeben waren. Dabei handelt es sich wahrscheinlich um einige genuine wie auch um nachgemachte (antik oder spätere) flache Bronzen, insgesamt mindestens um sechs. Sie sind jeweils in Form einer Tabula Ansata gearbeitet und haben mit ihrer Größe von 6–7 cm × 19–20 cm möglicherweise drei unterschiedliche Provenienzen aus dem südlichen Italien und vielleicht Mittelitalien. Nicht nur die äußere Erscheinung ist identisch, sondern auch der Text: *Florae / Tib(erius) Plautius Drosus / mag(ister) II / v(otum) s(olvit) l(ibens) m(erito).*[23] Sofern

19 Aug. Civ. Dei 4, 8: *praefecerunt ergo Proserpinam frumentis germinantibus, geniculis nodisque culmorum deum Nodutum, inuolumentis folliculorum deam Volutinam; cum folliculi patescunt, ut spica exeat, deam Patelanam, cum segetes nouis aristis aequantur, quia ueteres aequare hostire dixerunt, deam Hostilinam; florentibus frumentis deam Floram, lactescentibus deum Lacturnum, maturescentibus deam Matutam; cum runcantur, id est a terra auferuntur, deam Runcinam.* Zu dieser Verkleinerungs- und Verzettelungsstrategie durch Augustinus vgl. Cameron 2010, 621–622.

20 Die *ludi Florales* wurden zumindest zeitweilig auch im numidischen Cirta gefeiert, CIL VIII 6958 (2. Jh.), mit weiteren Hinweisen zu den *Floralia* und *ludi Florales* außerhalb der Stadt Rom, vgl. Fabbri 2019, 195. Die aus Pompeii gemalten Inschriften des 1. Jhs., die Flora bezeichnen, könnten sich ebenfalls auf das Fest beziehen, e. g. CIL IV 7073 und 7988e cf. p. 1531.

21 Der Göttin werden wie vielen anderen Gottheiten auch *oves II* durch die Arvalbrüder geweiht, vgl. etwa CIL VI 2099 = 32386 aus dem Jahr 183 und VI 2104 = 32388 aus dem Jahr 218.

22 CIL V *415 *Genio / Iucunditatis / Musis / Floraeque / sacrum*, mit Erläuterungen und Fotografie ediert in Modonesi 1995, Nr. 91.

23 *Florae / Tib(erius) Plautius Drosus / mag(ister) II / v(otum) s(olvit) l(ibens) m(erito),* cf. Cooley 2018. Eines der Täfelchen befindet sich im Museum von Neapel (inv. 2570), A. Parma, in: Camodeca, Solin et al. 2000, Nr. 575. Es dürfte mit CIL XIV 3486 aus unbekannter Herkunft identisch sein. Ein weiteres Exemplar befand sich im Ashmolean Museum von Oxford, ist aber dort nicht mehr vorhanden. Es ist unklar, ob es dasjenige ist, das aus der Villa des Horaz in Licentia stammt. Das jetzt im Thermenmuseum in Rom aufbewahrte Exemplar (inv. 65029) ist dasjenige, das ursprünglich aus der Sammlung der Königin Christina von Schweden, die sich nach ihrer Abdankung 1654 bis zu ihrem Tod 1689 in Rom aufhielt, schließlich in das Museum Kirchneriana kam, um nun in

mehr als eine der Täfelchen eine echte Weihbeischrift des Tib. Plautius Drosus war, der entfernt mit der senatorischen Familie der Tib. Plautii aus Trebula Sufenas verbunden gewesen sein könnte, so zumindest der Vorschlag von A. Parma (s. Anm. 21), war jener ein echter Flora-Anhänger. Vor allem aber war er als *magister II* zum zweiten Mal Vorsitzender einer Vereinigung, vielleicht von Händlern oder Handwerkern. Da wohl mehrere der Täfelchen authentisch zu sein scheinen, könnten deren Verbreitung im südlichen und mittleren Italien mit seinen beruflichen Aktivitäten verbunden gewesen sein. Die einzige ‚Berufsgruppe', von der wir hören, dass sie in besonderem Maße mit den *Floralia*, nicht aber zwangsläufig mit Flora assoziiert war, waren die *meretrices* (Ov. *Fast.* 5, 349). Da es wohl kaum eine Berufsvereinigung der Bordellbesitzer gab und wir auch von keiner der Blumen- oder auch Früchtehändler hören, stehen wir bei Kontext und persönlicher Motivation von Drosus' Flora-Verehrung ohne jeden Anhaltspunkt da, obwohl die Wahrscheinlichkeit der Verbindung zu seiner Tätigkeit für den Verein, dem er angehörte, naheliegt.

Es bleiben nun neben der vermeintlichen Flora-Weihung aus Mainz (s. unten) überhaupt nur zwei erhaltene antike Inschriften auf Stein, die eine solche Verehrung der Göttin bezeugen. Ein vermeintlich drittes Exemplar ist eine Editionsdublette (ILJug 1204 aus Veliki Bruon, zur Gemeinde Pula gehörig, identisch mit AE 1983, 425 aus Brijuni). Der Weihaltar ist in Zweitverwendung im byzantinischen Castrum am Strand des kroatischen Brijuni (früher *regio X, Venetia et Histria*) gefunden worden: *Flor(a)e Aug(ustae) M(arcus) Aure(lius) / Iustus / [[- - -]]? / v(otum) s(olvit) l(ibens) [m(erito)?] f(ecit).*[24] Die Verbindung einer Gottheit mit einem *Augustus* oder einer *Augusta* als eine Art Epiklese verändert deren Charakter nicht. Da es für eine solche Kombination regionale Trends und Zeiträume gab, in denen dieser Zusatz besonders beliebt wurde oder gar als Standard bei Weihung galt, scheint auch „Flora Augusta" darauf zu deuten, dass hierdurch weniger die göttliche Fürsorge oder Verbindung einer Gottheit mit dem jeweiligen Kaiser und seiner Familie bzw. Herrschaft zum Ausdruck gebracht werden sollte, als vielmehr die zeitgemäße und loyale Haltung des Weihenden demonstriert wurde. M. Aurelius Iustus nutzte daher nicht nur die römische Ausdrucksform des Votum, sondern er wählte hierfür noch die am Ende des 2., wenn nicht gar im 3. Jh. in seiner Umgebung übliche und angemessene Form – wenn auch für eine keineswegs übliche Gottheit, Flora.

Zudem weihte ein Mann in Rom auf einer Basis für Flora, Fortuna und Panthea stehend ein unbekanntes Objekt. Es wurde vermutet, dass es sich dabei um eine Statue der Flora gehandelt haben könnte:[25] *A(ulus) Herennuleius Soteric<u>us</u> <u>voto</u> <u>su</u>[c]/cepto basim posuit*

---

die Sammlung der Diokletiansthermen aufgenommen zu werden. Dies erschließt sich aus den von M.G. Granino Cecere, in: Friggeri, R. et al. 2012, I 10 (hier als identisch mit EphEp IX p. 467 bezeichnet). Parma verweist zudem auf zwei Fälschungen gleicher Machart, die sich im Museum von Verona und in der Bibliotheca Vaticana befinden sollen.

24 AE 1983, 425 aus der Publikation von Mlakar 1979, dort mit Foto fig. 5. In ILJug 1204 wird der Text auf möglicher Rasur so wie in der Erstpublikation entsprechend in Z. 5–6 wie folgt wiedergegeben: *v. l. s. v. / l [-4-] f.*

25 CIL VI 30867 cfr. p. 3758 und p. 4142 = EDR161306. Das Stück ist nicht in den Katalog von Friggeri, R. et al. 2012 aufgenommen worden, obwohl von A. Ferraro 2017 in EDR das Thermenmuseum in Rom als letzter bekannter Aufbewahrungsort angegeben wird. Die Interpretation als eine nur

deae Florae Fortunae Panthea[e]. Schließlich schließt die magere Ausbeute der drei Weihungen mit einer Steininschrift im umbrischen Mevania. Dort wird im 2. Jh. der Flora ein Altar von einem gewissen C. Caesius Hermes geweiht:[26] *Florae / sacr(um) / C(aius) Caesius / Hermes.*[27]

Am Ende sind es lediglich diese zwei kurz vorgestellten Altäre und die eine Basis aus Stein für eine Weihung, die – alle in Italien – als Ausdruck individueller Verehrung der Flora errichtet wurden, ob nun zur Erfüllung eines Votums oder aus anderen Gründen.

Flora in Mainz?

- - - ? / [Fl]or(a)e(?) sacr/[u]m G(aius) Sextius / [F]elix in suo / [- - - ?] / [v(otum) s(olvit)] l(ibens) [l(aetus)?] m(erito).[28]

Der Stein aus Mainz ist somit in jedem Fall eine Rarität. Erhalten ist in der ersten Zeile lediglich ein gut lesbares ORESACR. Es gibt keinen Spielraum, die gut lesbaren Buchstaben der ersten Zeile anders zu deuten als Teil von zwei Wörtern]ORE SACR[.[29] Auch der Fundort und -kontext aus dem Jahr 1880 gibt keinerlei Hinweise, handelt es sich doch um eine Zweitverwendung als Treppenstufe.

Das Monument selbst ist klein (ca. 38 cm hoch), aus lokalem Stein, mit sorgfältiger Schrift gearbeitet. Der obere Teil ist zu einem unbekannten späteren Zeitpunkt abgearbeitet worden und könnte eine weitere Textzeile oder auch dekorative Elemente getragen haben, wie die unten am Rand sichtbare Leiste. Der Rest eines runden Ornaments scheint vor dem L in der letzten Zeile sichtbar zu sein und könnte mittig zwischen zwei bis drei (?) Buchstaben rechts und links davon gestanden (?) haben, die die Erfüllung eines Gelübdes (*votum libens* oder *laetus merito*) anzeigten. Allerdings kann der erhaltene Rest eines Halbrunds auch das Ergebnis eines späteren Eingriffs darstellen.

Mit oder ohne Reliefs, die meisten der zeitlich genauer eingrenzbaren Weihaltäre und der weiteren steinernen Weihobjekte aus Mainz und Umgebung datieren aus dem 2. und 3. Jh. Auch wenn die Paläographie in diesem privaten Kontext wenig aussagekräf-

---

für Flora als Schicksals- und Allgöttin geweihte Basis mit Statue ist dagegen wegen des Charakters der Göttin und des ihr zugewiesenen Funktionsbereiches nicht naheliegend. Nur in diesem Fall wäre davon auszugehen, dass einzig Flora sich auf der Basis als Statue befunden habe. Naheliegender ist, ein einziges Objekt zu erwarten, das als angemessen für alle drei Göttinnen empfunden wurde.

26 Größe 97cm hoch, 44 cm breit.

27 Sein Vater oder ein möglicher naher männlicher Verwandter hatte im nahegelegenen Tuficum zuvor eine Weihung für Silvanus gestiftet, AE 2008, 502 = EDR111687: *Sacr(um) Silvano / C(aius) Caesius Hermes sen(ior) / v(otum) s(olvit).* Mit 91,2cm Höhe und einer Breite von 57cm vergleichbar dimensioniert wie der Altar für Flora, datiert die Inschrift allerdings in das spätere 1. Jh.; im 2. Jh. kam eine zweite Inschrift hinzu.

28 CIL XIII 6673, gefunden als Treppenstufe der Futtermagazine in der früheren Bilhildisstr.

29 Sinnvolle, aber auch grober Datierung und Charakter des Textes nicht angemessene Textergänzungen würden als letzten lesbaren Buchstaben ein T und nicht ein R erfordern (wie etwa ein für aus spätantik-kaiserlichen Kontext stammendes *victores ac triumphatores*, das ebenso wenig angemessen wäre wie die aus römischen Rechtstexten bekannte Formulierung *venditores actum*).

tig ist, scheint der aus Kalkstein gearbeitete kleine Weihealtar mit Inschrift für Bellona vergleichbar zu sein, der in die 1. Hälfte des 2. Jhs. datiert wird. Die Bellona-Weihung hat keine Worttrenner in den drei Zeilen Text, sondern fügt solche *puncta* erst in der vierten Zeile mit V S L M ein,[30] während deutliche Worttrenner ein häufiges Merkmal der Mainzer Weihinschriften im Verlauf des 2./3. Jhs. sind.

Zwischen den erhaltenen Resten der ersten drei und der mit nur noch zwei Buchstaben sichtbaren letzten Zeile scheint eine weitere gestanden zu haben, die, so die Vermutung des CIL-Editors K. Zangemeister, vom Steinmetz selber korrigierend wieder entfernt worden sei. Allerdings ist vielmehr das Inschriftenfeld der Zeilen 1–3 mit dem darunterliegenden Platz insgesamt vertieft im Verhältnis zur letzten Zeile, so dass hier wohl nicht mit einer Rasur einer weiteren Zeile zu rechnen ist. Da die Buchstabenform der Zeilen 1–3 zu derjenigen der letzten passt, ist auch nicht davon auszugehen, dass der leicht vertiefte obere Textteil aus einer zweiten Nutzung des Steins stammt, die letzte Zeile dagegen zu einer ursprünglichen Inschrift gehört. Der Text ist also abgesehen von dem fehlenden vorderen Teil, der vielleicht anders als wie oben in der Edition von CIL XIII wiedergegeben eher länger gewesen sein dürfte, gleichzeitig entstanden und hatte dementsprechend auch nur – abgesehen von einem möglichen abgearbeiteten Anfang des Textes – vier Zeilen. Für eine Symmetrie könnte eine erste Zeile vor der noch erhaltenen gestanden haben, die dann ähnlich wie die letzte, nicht im leicht vertieften Hauptfeld des Textes, sondern auf der etwas erhabenen stehengebliebenen Oberfläche eingemeißelt worden war.

------?
[---]ORESACR
[---]MGSEXTIVS
[---]ELIXINSVO
[---]L [.?] M

Ein möglicher (ursprünglich mittiger?) Ornamentrest am Rand des Bruchs der letzten Zeile könnte darauf deuten, dass die rechte Hälfte von etwa gleicher Breite wie die linke fehlt. Ein zu erwartendes V oder V S oder auch V S L davor müsste, zumindest in den letzten beiden Fällen, wenn ähnlich sorgfältig ordiniert wie der Rest des Texte, entsprechenden Raum gehabt haben. Dann allerdings kann die bisherige Ergänzung nicht überzeugen, was sowohl den Anfang mit der Nennung einer Gottheit mit kurzem Namen (wie Flora) als auch die Menge der beteiligten Personen beträfe – es müssten dann eher zwei Personen als nur eine sein.

Die Namensteile in den erhaltenen Resten von Zeilen 2 und 3 sind gut erkennbar, Sextius ebenso wie [F]elix. Mehr als eine Person zu vermuten, die für die Inschrift und Weihung verantwortlich war, widerspricht aber dem in Zeile 3 erhaltenen *in suo*, das unabhängig von der Gesamtlänge des Textes, wie in vielen anderen Fällen in den beiden Germanien auf die Errichtung eines Weihobjektes auf privatem, eigenen Grund eines einzelnen

30 CIL XIII 6666, vgl. die Beschreibung, Datierung und Abbildung bei Frenz 1992, 67–68 Nr. 14 mit Taf. 15, 1.2.3.

Abb. 2: © CIL XIII-Projekt Flensburg

Stifters hinweist.[31] Scheint also die Ordinatio des noch erhaltenen Inschriftenteiles auf einen längeren Text zu weisen als auf einen, dem nur drei bis vier Buchstaben fehlen, so passt diese Vermutung nicht so recht zum noch erhaltenen Textrest.

Für Flora spricht zudem, dass immerhin eine Weihung FLOR(A)E mit einer ebensolchen Auslassung des A in Brijuni (s. oben) überliefert ist; eine Weihung an eine andere Göttin, wie etwa an die ähnlich falsch geschriebene Diana als [NEM**O]RE SACR**VM in Nordafrika,[32] statt wie zu erwarten an *Dianae Nemorensi sacrum*, kann daher noch weniger überzeugen als die eines *sacrum Flor(a)e*.

Die Mainzer „Flora"-Weihung kann und muss daher in Ermangelung überzeugenderer Vorschläge weiterhin als eine solche untersucht werden, auch wenn sie nicht als ein „Beweis" für die Erweiterung des seltenen Flora-Kultes aus Italien nach Germania Superior gelten sollte. Angesichts der Präsenz von Legionssoldaten in Mainz mit (ober-)italischer Herkunft im 1. Jh. ist jedoch ein solcher Transfer von Göttervorlieben in dieser und der Zeit danach nicht auszuschließen. Das letzte Wort zu Flora in Mainz ist daher sicher noch nicht gesprochen.

31 Spickermann 2008, 316 mit Anm. 54 weist neben 16 Iupitersäulen mit „in suo" noch auf 19 weitere Weihobjekte bzw. Altäre mit Inschriften aus den beiden Germanien hin, davon 5 alleine aus Mainz inklusive der „Flora"-Weihung. Denkbar ist allerdings auch, dass ein „in suo" sich dann nur auf den letzten Namen bzw. den Besitzer bezieht, so dass dann eine weitere Personennennung nicht grundsätzlich ausgeschlossen ist.

32 Marcillet-Jaubert 1968 schlägt in I. Altava 228 aus Hadjar Roum in Mauretania Caesariensis das Folgende vor: *[Dianae(?) s]anctae / [Nemo]re(?) sacrum / [vota d]eddi(t) C(aius) Teren/[tius ...]teus ex p[.]*. Zwar ist ähnlich wie in Mainz auch an diesem Ort ein Gestaltungsspielraum der lateinischen Sprache für eine römische Gottheit möglich, aber nicht naheliegend. Wenn wie auch hier ohne Parallele, dann kann das ebenso wenig überzeugen – auch wenn die Autorin des Beitrags keine bessere Lösung zu bieten hat. Nahe läge es, das *[- - - S]ANCTAE / [- - -]RE SACRVM* zu einer gänzlich anderen, möglicherweise christlich inspirierten, spätantiken Inschrift zu ergänzen, aber dafür müsste eine genauere Untersuchung des Objektes, der Inschrift und ihrer Datierung erfolgen.

Literaturverzeichnis

Cameron, A. 2010. The Last Pagans of Rome, Oxford.

Camodeca, Solin, H. et al. 2000. Catalogo delle iscrizioni latine del Museo Nazionale di Napoli, ILMN. 1: Roma e Latium, Neapel.

Cels Saint-Hilaire, J. 1977. Le fonctionnement des Floralia sous la République, Dialogues d'histoire ancienne 3, 253–286.

Coarelli, F. 1995. Flora, templum, in E.M. Steinby, Lexicon Topographicum Urbis Romae. Vol. II D–G, Rom, 254.

Cooley, A. 2018. The curious case of Flora, in A. Guzmán and J. Martínez (eds.), Animo Decipiendi? Rethinking Fakes and Authorship in Classical, Late Antique and Early Christian Works, Groningen, 285–90.

Crawford, M. 1974. Roman Republican Coinage, Cambridge.

De Melo, W.D.C. 2019. Varro : De lingua Latina. Introduction, Text, and Translation, Oxford.

Fabbri, L. 2019. Mater Florum: Flora e il suo culto a Roma. Florenz.

Foulon, A. 2010. Flora et le Floralia chez Ovide, in D. Briquel, C. Février, Ch. Guittard (eds.), Varietates fortunae. Religion et mythologie à Rome : hommage à Jacqueline Champeaux, Paris, 45–54.

Frenz, H.G. 1992. Denkmäler römischen Götterkultes aus Mainz und Umgebung (Corpus Signorum Imperii Romani, Deutschland II 4, Germania Superior), Mainz.

Friggeri, R. et al. 2012. Terme di Diocleziano. La collezione epigrafica. Milano.

Granino Cecere, M.G. 2008. I Laurentes Lavinates nella X regio, in P. Basso, A, Buonopane, A. Cavarzere, S. Pesavento Mattioli (eds.), Est enim ille flos Italiae: vita economica e sociale nella Cisalpina romana. Atti delle Giornate di Studi in onore di Ezio Buchi (Verona 30 novembre – 1 dicembre 2006), Verona, 169–190.

Hersh, Ch., Walker, A. 1984. The Mesagne Hoard, ANSMN 29, 103–134.

Hollstein, W. 1993. Die stadtrömische Münzprägung der Jahre 78–50 v. Chr. zwischen politischer Aktualität und Familienthematik: Kommentar und Bibliographie, München.

Hošek, R. 1988, Flora, in Lexicon Iconographicum Mythologiae Classicae (LIMC) IV 1, Zürich / München, 137–139.

Marcillet-Jaubert, J. 1968. Les Inscriptions d'Altava, Aix-en-Provence.

Mlakar, S. 1979, Neki prilozi poznavanju antičke topografije Istre, Histria Archaeologica 10/2, 9–42.

Modonesi, D. 1995, Museo Maffeiano: iscrizioni e rilievi sacri latini, Rom.

Papi, E. 1995. Flora, aedes, in E.M. Steinby, Lexicon Topographicum Urbis Romae. Vol. II D–G, Rom, 253–254.

Pasqualini, A. 2008. Mappa liturgica dei flamini minori di Roma, in M. Caldelli, G. Gregori, S. Orlandi (eds.), Epigrafia 2006 : Atti della XIVe Rencontre sur l'épigraphie in onore di Silvio Panciera, con altri contributi di colleghi, allievi e collaboratori, Rom, 437–452.

Rüpke, J. 2005. Fasti Sacerdotum. Die Mitglieder der Priesterschaften und das sakrale Funktionspersonal römischer, griechischer, orientalischer und jüdisch-christlicher Kulte in der Stadt Rom von 300 v. Chr. bis 499 n. Chr., Stuttgart.

Ryan, F. X. 2008. Der Denar des C. Serveilius C. F. mit Florakopf und Krummstab, Numismatica e Antichità Classiche 37, 193–199.

Scheid, J., Granino Cecere, M. G. 1999. Les sacerdoces publics équestres, in L'ordre équestre. Histoire d'une aristocratie (IIe siècle av. J.-C. – IIIe siècle ap. J.-C.). Actes du colloque internationale de Bruxelles – Leuven, Rom, 79–189.

Spickermann, W. 2008. Kultplätze auf privatem Grund in den beiden Germanien, in A. Sartori (ed.), Dedicanti e Cultores nelle Religioni Celtiche (Quaderni di Acme 104), Milano, 305–328.

Wissowa, G. 1909a. Flora, RE VI 1, 2747–2749.

Wissowa, G. 1909b. Floralia, RE VI 1, 2749–2752.

Zmeskal, K. 2009. Adfinitas: die Verwandtschaften der senatorischen Führungsschicht der römischen Republik von 218–31 v. Chr., Passau.

Osiris *ex Aegypto* à l'époque impériale : l'apport de l'épigraphie

Laurent Bricault

Fondateur de Viterbe, et par suite de la civilisation étrusque, Osiris aurait profité de son séjour dans la péninsule pour enseigner aux Italiens (*sic*) à labourer, semer et faire du vin[1]. C'est du moins ce que laisse entendre une colonne couverte de soi-disant hiéroglyphes égyptiens[2] découverte vers 1490 dans la cathédrale San Lorenzo de Viterbe, et bientôt expliquée par son inventeur, le Dominicain Annius de Viterbe, dans ses *Antiquités* publiées en 1498[3]. Une belle inscription latine rappelant ces hauts faits fut d'ailleurs gravée sous le bas-relief en 1587 à l'initiative du sénat et du peuple de Viterbe (Fig. 1). Tout ceci n'est évidemment que fable inventée par le faussaire dominicain pour affermir ses thèses et autres développements sur les origines de l'Italie et l'antiquité plus que vénérable de certaines familles aristocratiques qu'il servait[4]. On retrouve des traces de ces élucubrations généalogiques dans les peintures fameuses mettant en scène Isis, Osiris et même Apis – qui donna son nom à la chaîne des Apennins, comme chacun le sait ! – que Pinturicchio réalisa pour une salle de l'*appartimento* d'Alexandre VI Borgia au Vatican, sur un synopsis du même Annius[5]. Si la renommée de ces falsifications s'estompa bien vite[6] et avec elle le souvenir de la geste osirienne, qu'en fut-il réellement de la présence d'Osiris en Italie et dans les provinces romaines à l'époque impériale ?

En Égypte, Osiris[7] est le souverain du royaume des morts, auquel s'assimile le roi défunt, puis, à partir du Moyen Empire, les particuliers qui en sont dignes. Le mythe tel que l'a rapporté Plutarque dans le *De Iside et Osiride* précise comment Osiris, tué par son frère Seth et découpé en morceaux dispersés dans le Nil, fut retrouvé par ses sœurs Isis

1 Annius de Viterbe 1491 ; cf. Curran 2018, 55–74.
2 Sur les néo-hiéroglyphes, voir Winand 2022a, 2022b et 2023.
3 Annius de Viterbe 1498 ; cf. Baffioni, Mattiangieli 1981, 296–303 ; Curran 1998/1999, 172–176 ; Curran 2018, 61–70 ; Collins 2000 ; Rolet 2008, 223–229. Pour une traduction en français de la lecture du texte « égyptien » par Annius de Viterbe, voir Rolet 2008, 226 ; Fournet 2022, 28. Les différents éléments sculptés qui composent cette fantaisie historique datent du XIIe-XIIIe (la lunette) et du XVe siècle (les portraits).
4 Crahay 1983 ; Ligota 1987 ; Popper 2011.
5 Cieri-Via, Blamoutier 1991 ; Curran 1998/1999, 166–171 ; Curran 2018, 30–54.
6 Stephens 2013 ; Rothstein 2018 ; Paoli 2023.
7 Sur le dieu, Gwyn Griffiths 1980 ; Malaise 2005, 139–141 ; Smith 2017.

Fig. 1: Bas-relief de Viterbe commémorant la geste d'Osiris (ph. L. Bricault)

et Nephthys, puis reconstitué et embaumé par Anubis. Isis, par le battement de ses ailes, revivifia le corps de son frère-époux défunt et en conçut un fils, Horus, qui finit par venger son père en triomphant de Seth. Maître de l'au-delà, dieu qui préside à l'immortalité, Osiris se trouve également associé à l'eau, à l'inondation du Nil, et par suite au renouveau de la végétation et à la fertilité, sa destinée se renouvelant chaque année dans le cycle de la nature. Il meurt lorsque le Nil se retrouve à l'étiage, et renaît avec l'inondation, prêt à féconder Isis, la terre d'Égypte.

Aux premiers temps de l'époque hellénistique, la diffusion initiale du culte d'Isis et de son nouveau parèdre Sarapis, conçu comme une forme hellénisante d'Osiris[8], bientôt accompagnés du fidèle dieu-chacal Anubis et du dieu-enfant Harpocrate[9] semble laisser Osiris sur le quai d'Alexandrie[10]. L'intégration de l'Égypte dans l'Empire romain, après la disparition de Cléopâtre VII, ne lui est guère plus propice. Le Nil ne paraît pas se déverser soudainement dans le Tibre, pourrait-on écrire en paraphrasant Juvénal[11]. Il est toutefois possible de repérer sa présence au sein du cercle isiaque, dans quelques contextes particuliers révélés par l'épigraphie.

Osiris et l'Arétalogie d'Isis

L'historiographie, au cours du XXe siècle, a pris l'habitude d'appeler *Arétalogie d'Isis*, souvent avec un "A" majuscule, un texte rédigé en grec, connu par cinq exemplaires quasi identiques retrouvés en Méditerranée orientale et repris, partiellement, par Diodore de Sicile dans sa *Bibliothèque historique* au milieu du Ier s. av. J.-C. Ce texte, dont une version semble-t-il complète fut retrouvée en 1925 dans les ruines d'un temple d'Isis à Kymè, en Éolide, sur la côte égéenne de l'actuelle Turquie, apparaît comme une mise en forme active et en partie novatrice d'une tradition littéraire égyptienne, l'autobiographie laudative, ici concentrée autour de la figure de la déesse Isis[12]. La cristallisation d'éléments variés que l'on y lit correspond certainement à une stratégie d'écriture conditionnée par des enjeux et des objectifs précis : accompagner et renforcer les premiers pas d'Isis et de son culte *ex Aegypto*, dans le contexte de la compétition que se livrent en Méditerranée orientale, aux IIIe-IIe s. av. J.-C., les diadoques et épigones successeurs d'Alexandre. Les cinq exemplaires de ce texte d'une cinquantaine de lignes, pour la plupart fragmentaires, que l'on a jusqu'ici retrouvés sont à dater entre le Ier et le IIIe s. apr. J.-C.[13]. Toutefois, l'*Urtext* qui leur a donné naissance est bien antérieur, puisque l'on connaît aussi et déjà, à la fin du IIe et au Ier s. av. J.-C., à Maronée en Thrace et sur l'île d'Andros, des adaptations versifiées et davantage encore hellénisées de cette arétalogie. Dans ce texte probablement rédigé au IIIe s. av. J.-C., peut-être à Memphis, Sarapis n'apparaît pas, contrairement à Osiris, qui y est cité deux fois en tant que frère et époux d'Isis. C'est encore pour des impératifs généalogiques qu'Osiris est mentionné dans deux hymnes écrits en grec, celui de Kios, en Bithynie, au Ier

8 C'est probablement en ce sens qu'il faut comprendre la formule onomastique Sérapis Osiris sur une dédicace datée des années 20 du premier siècle apr. J.-C. récemment mise au jour sur l'île de Pag, en Dalmatie. Voir Grisonic *et al.* 2022 ; Grisonic *et al.* 2024 (à paraître).

9 Bricault 2004.

10 Sur Osiris hors d'Égypte durant la période hellénistique, voir Touloumtzidou & Christodoulou (à paraître).

11 Juvénal, *Saturae* III, 62 : « In Tiberim defluxit Orontes ».

12 Bricault 2022.

13 RICIS 302/0204 (Kymè) et 113/0545, 113/1201, 202/1101, 306/0201 pour les quatre autres copies.

Fig. 2: Hymne de de Kios à Osiris (d'après L. Bricault, *RICIS*, Paris 2005, n° 308/0302)

s. apr. J.-C.[14], dont le principal protagoniste est Anubis (Fig. 2), et celui bien plus tardif de Chalcis, en Eubée qui, au IVe s. apr. J.-C., s'adresse en premier à Karpocrate[15].

Osiris et la fête des *Isia*

Les Ménologes rustiques du Ier s. apr. J.-C.[16], le calendrier peint sous Sainte-Marie-Majeure possiblement à la fin du IIe s.[17], le calendrier dit du « Chronographe de 354 »[18] indiquent qu'à l'automne, sept jours durant, du 28 octobre au 3 novembre[19], se déroulait, du moins à Rome, la fête des *Isia*. Commencées le 28 octobre dans la douleur de la perte d'Osiris, les *Isia* s'achevaient le 3 novembre par les *Hilaria* (appelés aussi *Heuresis* dans les Ménologes) célébrant la renaissance du dieu. Cette dernière date, qui correspond à la fête égyptienne osirienne du 19 Hathyr, fut fixée officiellement dans le calendrier romain, soit

14 RICIS 308/0302.

15 RICIS 104/0206.

16 Ils sont connus par deux inscriptions : CIL I², p. 280–281 ; VI, 2305–2306 ; Degrassi 1963, 284–298 ; RICIS 501/0129.

17 Magi 1972 ; Stern 1973 ; Mielsch 1976 ; Mols & Moormann 2010, avec discussion approfondie de la bibliographie antérieure.

18 Stern 1953 ; Divjak & Wischmeyer 2014.

19 Jean le Lydien, *De mens.* IV, 48.

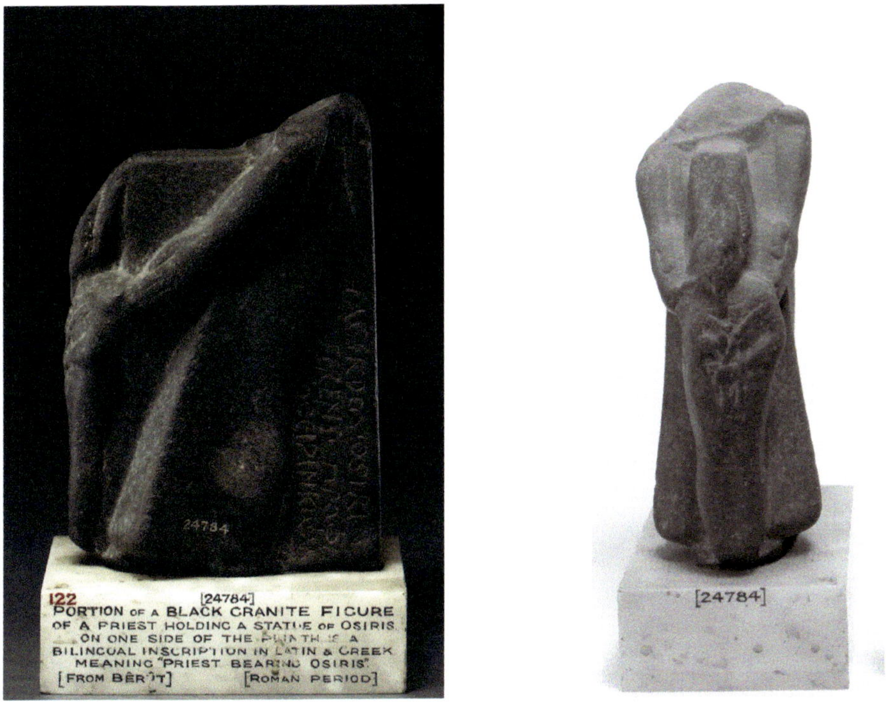

Fig. 3a–b: Statue théophore de Tyr (BM EA24784 © Trustees of the British Museum)

entre 25 et 28 apr. J.-C., soit plus vraisemblablement lors du principat de Caligula entre 37 et 39 apr. J.-C.

Le contenu précis de ces fêtes, en dehors des grandes lignes – quête d'Isis assistée du chasseur Anubis pour retrouver son époux assassiné puis renaissance de ce dernier –, nous échappe quelque peu, sauf à vouloir transposer à Rome des rites proprement égyptiens. Cela n'est d'ailleurs pas totalement inconcevable, si l'on considère par exemple une scène figurée sur une peinture de l'Iséum de Pompéi évoquant Isis cherchant son époux sur une barque bien plus égyptienne qu'italienne. Il est fort probable que les informations livrées par Plutarque en divers passages de son traité se rapportent à des manifestations égyptiennes, comme lorsque les participants à la fête, à l'unisson, s'exclament qu'Osiris est retrouvé[20], avant de façonner puis de parer une figurine en forme de croissant. La majeure partie des cérémonies devait avoir lieu dans l'enceinte des sanctuaires, voire dans les théâtres proches, sans être toutefois ouvertement publiques. Seule la partie terminale, avec la proclamation de la redécouverte d'Osiris (*inventio Osiridis*)[21], devait donner lieu à des festivités extra-muros. C'est essentiellement au travers de ce final que de nombreux

20 Plutarque, *De Iside et Osiride* 39 ; cf. i.a. Brenk 2001.
21 Bricault 2013, 386–394.

auteurs latins, chrétiens ou non, livrent leur opinion sur les *Isia*, principalement dans une optique polémique[22].

La présence d'Osiris dans les processions isiaques d'époque impériale est confirmée par un document singulier qui proviendrait de Tyr (Fig. 3a–b)[23]. Il s'agit d'une statue fragmentaire – la tête et la partie inférieure manquent – en basalte, de facture égyptienne, d'un prêtre (*ḥm-ntr*) agenouillé et portant une statue d'Osiris. L'inscription hiéroglyphique du pilier dorsal mentionnant la « prêtrise des 4 phylè » est antérieure au décret de Canope de 238 av. J.-C. qui en instaure une cinquième. Quatre siècles plus tard, probablement après 198 apr. J.-C., date à laquelle Septime Sévère fonde la *Colonia Septimia Severa Tyrus*, un texte bilingue latin/grec est gravé sur l'un des côtés du pilier dorsal. Celui-ci désigne sobrement le personnage statufié comme un « prêtre porteur d'Osiris » (*sacerdos Osirim ferens*), un « prophète portant l'image d'Osiris en procession » (προφή[της] Ὄσειριν κωμ[ά]ζ(ω)[ν]). Cette statue d'un prêtre théophore a pu prendre place dans le temple tyrien dont l'existence est suggérée par une dédicace du IIIe s. av. J.-C. adressée à Sarapis et aux dieux qui partagent le même naos[24].

L'importation, sans doute à l'époque romaine, de statues osiriphores égyptiennes destinées à certains sanctuaires isiaques, attestée par plusieurs autres documents[25], participe d'un mouvement qui paraît vouloir (re)donner à Osiris une place plus importante dans le cercle divin entourant Isis, quitte à réinterpréter le sens premier de ce type de représentations. Comme Michel Malaise l'a justement noté[26], la figure divine n'est pas réellement portée, mais touchée, en un geste de protection qui appelle assurément une réciprocité. Cette signification première, en contexte isiaque hors d'Égypte, semble laisser place à la perception de l'image comme celle d'un prêtre chargé de porter Osiris lors des processions, à l'instar des Anubophores porteurs (du masque cynocéphale) d'Anubis[27]. Une inscription romaine[28] datable du Ier ou du IIe s. apr. J.-C. indique que la corporation des *pausarii* et des *argentarii* a fait édifier une *mansio* pour Isis et Osiris. Les *pausarii* étant les adeptes chargés de marquer les pauses durant les processions isiaques[29], la *mansio* en question pourrait bien être à identifier à un reposoir pour les images cultuelles transportées lors de la *pompè*. Isis, tout comme Osiris, devaient figurer parmi les dieux ainsi présentés à la vue de la population réunie le long du parcours sacré, au moins lors des *Isia*[30].

---

22 Ainsi Sénèque, *De superstitione* ap. Augustin, *Civ. Dei* VI, 10, 2, ou encore Minucius Felix, *Octavius* XXII, 1.

23 RICIS 402/0802. Voir également Parlasca 2002, 1–3, pl. I.

24 RICIS 402/0801.

25 Malaise 2004 ; Pétigny 2008.

26 Malaise 2004, 75–79.

27 Bricault 2001/2.

28 RICIS 501/0136.

29 Bricault 2012, 94–96.

30 Mentionnons ici l'offrande, par deux hiéraphores de Pergame, d'un grand nombre de représentations divines appartenant à la sphère isiaque, peintes ou sculptées, dont une d'Osiris, qui ont pu être portées en procession lors de cérémonies publiques (RICIS 301/1202 ; Ier s. apr. J.-C. ?).

Osiris et Isis de Taposiris

La déploration par Isis de la perte d'Osiris, commémorée au premier jour des *Isia*, s'est également traduite visuellement comme l'atteste une série de représentations d'Isis *dolens*[31]. Le principal témoignage de la popularité de cet aspect du mythe osirien provient de *Faesulae* (Fiesole), en Étrurie. En 1883, lors de travaux agricoles, les ruines de ce qui a pu être un *sacellum* livrent une statue d'Isis dolente, inscrite sur sa base, ainsi que la base également inscrite d'une statue d'Osiris dont ne subsistent que les pieds, disposés selon une posture égyptienne caractéristique (Fig. 4)[32]. Toutes deux sont offertes par Caius Gargennius Maximus, fils de Spurius, de la tribu Scaptia, au nom de son frère Marcus Gargennius Macrinus, deux vétérans qui ont fort probablement servi en Égypte au cours du IIe s. apr. J.-C. La statue de la déesse est dédiée à la *domina Isis Taposiris*[33], celle du dieu au *dominus Osiris*[34]. L'attribut onomastique *Taposiris* (en grec Ταποσειρίας / ἐν Ταποσίρι) est attesté par plusieurs inscriptions et papyrus. La plus ancienne se lit sur une dédicace mise au jour dans l'enceinte du grand sanctuaire de Taposiris Magna. Datée du règne de Ptolémée IV et Arsinoé III (220–204 av. J.-C.), elle est adressée à Sarapis, Isis de Taposiris et Apollon Maréotis, c'est-à-dire la triade Osiris-Isis-Horus « habillée » à la grecque[35]. Hors d'Égypte, cette épiclèse toponymique apparaît à Délos en 110/9 av. J.-C., à Chéronée et à Athènes au IIIe s. apr. J.-C.[36], sans toutefois qu'Osiris soit nommé dans ces trois inscriptions. Le mythe osirien, ou du moins cerains mythèmes, étaient suffisamment connus pour que l'on consacre au dieu sa statue, éventuellement placée dans une chapelle abritant également sa sœur-épouse éplorée[37].

Le dossier épigraphique du sanctuaire isiaque de Thessalonique, riche de plus de 75 inscriptions, révèle qu'il en allait de même dans le grand port de Macédoine. Au IIe s.

31 Bricault 1992a ; Parlasca 2003 ; Bricault 2006, 75–83.

32 Il n'existe aucune description, même sommaire, de la structure mise au jour lors de la plantation d'une vigne. La découverte est mentionnée par G.F. Gamurrini (1883), puis reprise la même année dans diverses publications qui s'attachent essentiellement aux deux inscriptions. Sur cette courte historiographie, voir Wild 1984, 1777. La datation des inscriptions est proposée par Gamurrini d'après la paléographie.

33 RICIS 511/0102.

34 RICIS 511/0101.

35 Martinez *et al.* 2020, 1010–1012 n° 3. Du même site proviennent deux autres inscriptions fragmentaires d'époque romaine mentionnant Isis de Taposiris : Boussac 2010, 70 ; Martinez *et al.* 2020, 1013 n° 5 ; à Oxyrhynchos furent découverts deux papyrus la nommant : *P. Oxy.* XII 1434 (107/8 apr. J.-C.) ; *PSI* IX 1036 (192 apr. J.-C.) ; enfin, pour une plaque achetée à Louxor, mais dont la provenance pourrait être toute autre, voir Brashear 1975 (217–204 av. J.-C.).

36 RICIS 202/0313 (Délos), 105/0895 (Chéronée) et 101/0216 (Athènes).

37 À l'exception de la dédicace de Vibia Calidia à Isis et Osiris gravée en lettres pointées sur une petite plaque de bronze mise au jour à Veleia, en Gaule Cisalpine (RICIS 512/0801 ; IIe s. apr. J.-C.), le couple divin n'apparaît toutefois jamais associé dans le même texte propitiatoire ou gratulatoire. À Scarbantia, en Pannonie, les fouilles de ce qui a pu être un lieu de culte isiaque à forte tonalité égyptienne ont livré quant à elles une dédicace du IIe s. apr. J.-C. à Osiris Auguste émanant d'un *sacerdos Isidis* (AE 2006, 1041 ; RICIS Suppl. II, 613/0602 ; Mráv & Gabrieli 2011, 219–222, n° 4 et fig. 10).

Fig. 4: Base d'une statue d'Osiris de Fiesole (d'après L. Bricault, *RICIS*, Paris 2005, n° 511/0101)

apr. J.-C., une dame Pétrônia Okellina consacre un autel au dieu Osiris, tandis qu'une dédicace fragmentaire adressée au dieu, peut-être de même époque, fait mention d'un *dromos*, une allée qui pouvait conduire à l'espace (ou l'un des espaces) cultuel(s) où l'on vénérait le dieu[38]. Dans cet important sanctuaire où l'on adorait principalement Isis, Sarapis, Anubis et Harpocrate, Osiris était présent dès l'époque hellénistique[39]. Vers 120 av. J.-C., un certain Phylakidès y fait élever pour le divin Osiris un enclos bâti à l'intérieur duquel est déposé un coffre ouvragé qui rappelle la dérive du dieu enfermé dans un sarcophage de bois par son frère Seth[40], une iconographie que l'on retrouve en image sur un mur du « sacrarium » de l'Iséum de Pompéi[41]. En 39/8 av. J.-C., c'est un Osirieon et sa colonnade que font édifier deux représentants de l'importante *gens* des Salarii, un bâtiment destiné à conserver le διδυμαφόριον, sans doute un récipient renfermant les parties génitales du dieu[42]. Ces éléments mobiliers et immobiliers sont certainement à mettre en rapport avec la fête de l'*inventio Osiridis*. À Thessalonique, un culte spécifique était donc rendu à Osiris sous son aspect de dieu ressucité et revivificateur. Deux années plus tard, en 37/6 av. J.-C., les deux mêmes dédicants, un père et son fils, font cette fois le don d'un *hydreion* destiné à recevoir l'eau du Nil divinisé[43]. Quelques décennies plus tôt, un autre *hydreion* avait été consacré à Délos. Ce bâtiment, identifié par Hélène Siard à la structure monumentale excavée à l'extrémité du *dromos* du Sarapieion C[44], renvoie clairement à la nature hydriaque du frère-époux d'Isis et constitue, en quelque sorte, une forme helléni-

38 RICIS 113/0553 (l'autel) et 113/0554 (le *dromos*).
39 Touloumtzidou & Christodoulou (à paraître).
40 RICIS 113/0506.
41 Voir Veymiers 2021, 140–141 et fig. 6.4.
42 RICIS 113/0520.
43 RICIS 113/0521.
44 Siard 2007. Dans une étude récente qui ignore malheureusement toute la littérature francophone et germanophone sur le sujet, G. Aristodemou (2019) identifierait l'*hydreion* à une fontaine.

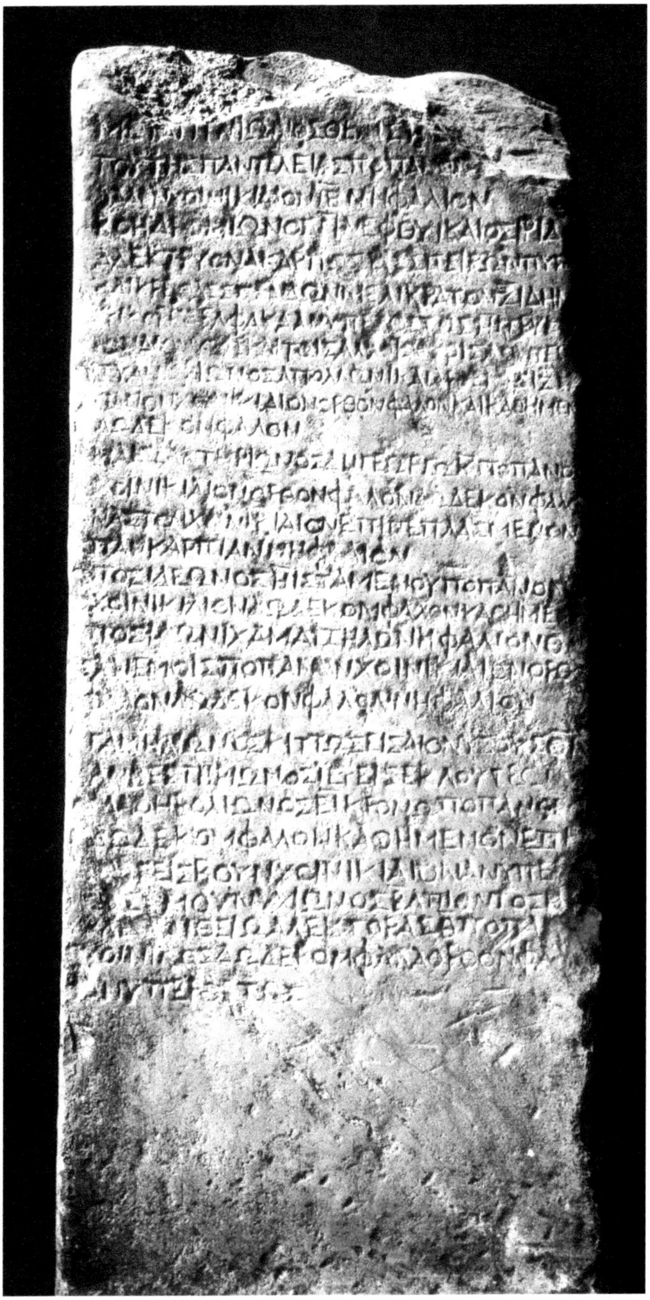

Fig. 5: Calendrier d'une association athénienne
(d'après L. Bricault, *RICIS*, Paris 2005, n° 101/0225)

Fig. 6: Dédicace au roi Osiris de Troade (© T. Özhan)

sée d'Osiris qui se matérialise par la suite, au moins à partir du principat d'Auguste, sous la forme de l'hydrie sacrée que l'on rencontre notamment à Rome[45].

Osiris et Nephthys

Isis n'est toutefois pas la seule de la fratrie nommée avec Osiris dans l'épigraphie d'époque impériale. L'autre sœur d'Osiris, Nephthys, apparaît en effet aux côtés de son frère dans deux documents singuliers. Le premier est un calendrier sacrificiel gravé sur une grande stèle de marbre brisée à la partie supérieure (Fig. 5)[46]. Datable du IIe s. apr. J.-C., il énumère les sacrifices et offrandes à faire tout au long de l'année par ce qui semble être une association d'agriculteurs[47]. Quand la plupart des divinités honorées reçoivent, mois après mois, des offrandes de gâteaux et des libations sans vin, le 13 du mois de Boedromion, Osiris et Nephthys se voient sacrifier un coq, offrir du blé et de l'orge et verser une libation de *melikraton*, une mixture à base de miel. Plusieurs des puissances divines honorées par cette association sont liées d'une manière ou d'une autre aux divinités éleusiniennes, comme un certain nombre de dates rituelles le sont avec le calendrier officiel d'Athènes. Ainsi, la date du sacrifice pour Osiris et Nephthys coïncide avec le début de la fête des Mystères et peut alors apparaître comme un sacrifice préliminaire aux festivités.

45 Malaise 1985.
46 RICIS 101/0225.
47 Voir le riche commentaire de Chr. de Lisle (2020), 20–35 n° 2.

Fig. 7: *Defixio* de Rome(?) (BM 1878,1019.2r ; © Trustees of the British Museum)

Le choix d'honorer ensemble Osiris et Nephthys doit s'expliquer par le fait qu'ils sont parfois considérés comme les parents adultérins d'Anubis[48] – Osiris étant officiellement l'époux d'Isis et Nephthys l'épouse de Seth –, en Égypte comme dans le monde grec[49] ; Anubis, le dieu de la momification, celui qui permet aux défunts de vivre à nouveau[50], dont la présence en tête du cortège lors des *Isia* est fondamentale. Le lien avec les Mystères d'Éleusis apparaît alors clairement. Le second provient d'Asie Mineure. Lors de travaux agricoles, un fragment de base inscrite a été mis au jour dans une localité de Troade du Nord[51]. Seule la partie droite de l'inscription, gravée sur trois lignes, est conservée (Fig. 6). L'auteur anonyme consacre à Osiris le roi (et peut-être à Isis) l'image d'Aphrodite Ourania et de Nephthys, voire d'une troisième divinité. Le texte est malheureusement trop lacunaire pour pouvoir en dire davantage.

Seth, le quatrième enfant de Geb et Nout, n'est pas oublié puisqu'il apparaît lui aussi dans un texte dont le protagoniste principal est Osiris. Dans une *defixio* inscrite sur une lamelle de plomb, peut-être de provenance romaine (Fig. 7)[52], le *defigens* ordonne au nom d'Osiris de punir un certain Nikomédès, accusé d'avoir brûlé le lit de papyrus d'Osiris et d'avoir mangé du poisson sacré, deux métaphores qui l'assimilent à Seth. Osiris le grand, ignoblement capturé par l'impie Typhon (*i.* e. Seth) est invoqué dans le texte comme celui

48 Plut., *De Iside*, 14 et 38. Voir Gwyn Griffiths 1970, 316–319, 447 ; Quaegebeur 1977, 122.

49 Voir aussi l'hymne à Anubis de Kios (RICIS 308/0302), qui fait d'Osiris le père d'Anubis.

50 Anubis, dans l'inscription de Pag citée *supra* (p. 45 n. 8), y est d'ailleurs invoqué comme *inventor et custos sacrorum*.

51 Özhan 2018.

52 Mais voir les doutes émis par Jordan 2004. La *defixio* ayant appartenu à la collection de Francis Douce au début du XIXe s., sa provenance romaine ne peut être assurée.

« s'est emparé du commandement et du sceptre royal des dieux souterrains »[53]. Cette malédiction s'inspire directement d'un recueil de formules magiques égyptiennes que l'on connaît notamment par un papyrus de provenance fayoumique[54]. Sous une forme ou une autre (nominale ou visuelle), Osiris apparaît de fait sur de nombreuses autres *defixiones* mises au jour sur le territoire de l'Empire. Il y est invoqué comme une puissance souterraine, capable de punir et de faire souffrir les vivants.

Osiris et l'eau fraîche

Mais s'il peut punir et faire mourir, Osiris est aussi, en Égypte et hors d'Égypte, capable d'intervenir en faveur des morts. En effet, parmi les prérogatives du dieu figure l'offrande d'eau fraîche au défunt. La formule « Qu'Osiris te donne l'eau fraîche », qui semble voir le jour au Ier s. apr. J.-C., se lit sur divers supports (pierres, lamelles de métal) à Césarée Maritime, Rome, Carthage ou encore Alexandrie[55]. Cette offrande trouve sa source dans une croyance égyptienne ancestrale qui voulait que les morts, dans l'au-delà, puissent souffrir de la faim et de la soif. Grâce à cette libation d'eau, puisée dans le Nil ou les substituts du fleuve et assimilée au dieu lui-même, le défunt accédait à l'immortalité[56]. Elle traduit combien l'aspect funéraire d'Osiris demeure fondamental dans l'espace gréco-romain, n'hésitant pas à se combiner avec la référence aux dieux Mânes, comme dans l'épitaphe de Iulia Politikè, à Rome (Fig. 8)[57]. Partie intégrante des libations effectuées sur la tombe, tout comme des cérémonies et des banquets commémorant la mémoire du disparu, l'eau offerte au mort au nom d'Osiris apparaît à la fois comme symbole de régénération et de renaissance. Garante de l'immortalité promise au défunt devenu ainsi un Osiris, l'offrande de l'eau doit probablement être mise en rapport avec les figurations d'Osiris-Hydreios, qui représente symboliquement l'eau du Nil, et le vase à bec qui la contenait lors des cérémonies et que décrit Apulée (*Métamorphoses* XI, 11)[58].

Le caractère (ré)affirmé, hors d'Égypte, d'Osiris en tant que puissance funéraire lui (p)réservait un rôle essentiel, quoique limité, auprès des populations de l'Empire mais aussi de celles soumises aux pouvoirs politiques qui le supplantèrent en Occident au cours

53 IG XIV, 1047 ; RICIS 501/0202 ; voir Bevilacqua 1992/3 et surtout Jordan 2004.

54 PGM LVIII, 8–14. Voir Gordon & Gasparini 2014, 48–49 ; Gasparini 2016.

55 RICIS 403/0401 (Césarée), 501/0164, 0178, 0196, 0198, 0199 (Rome) et 703/0111 (Carthage) ; *SB* I (1915) 335, 1415, 3449 et 3467, *I.Métriques* n° 47 et Łukaszewicz 1989 (Alexandrie). La même idée se retrouve, semble-t-il, dans l'hymne hélas très fragmentaire de Gomphoi, en Thessalie, datable du Ier–IIe s. apr. J.-C. (RICIS 112/0201, ll. 9–10) ; sur ce texte, voir désormais Lanna 2024 (à paraître).

56 Delia 1992.

57 RICIS 501/0198. La formule D.M. se lit aussi, par exemple, sur l'épitaphe de la chrétienne Licinia Amias, datée du début du IIIe s. apr. J.-C. et qui provient de la nécropole du Vatican (ICUR II, 4246).

58 Voir supra p. 50 pour Osiris-Hydreios et les *hydreia*.

Fig. 8: Inscription funéraire de Iulia Politikè (d'après L. Bricault, *RICIS*, Paris 2005, n° 501/0198)

du Ve siècle, comme l'attestent les nombreuses statuettes de bronze retrouvées en milieu funéraire, encore aux VIe et VIIe siècles[59].

Conclusion

Les sources épigraphiques d'époque impériale mentionnant Osiris hors d'Égypte brossent le portrait d'une puissance divine qui conserve un caractère très égyptien, ce que ne contredit d'ailleurs pas la documentation iconographique[60]. Les textes évoquent en général la généalogie du dieu, ou certains éléments du mythe osirien qui, ritualisés, étaient célébrés dans des bâtiments particuliers comme à Thessalonique ou lors des processions de l'*inventio Osiridis*. Ce sont clairement ses aspects de maître de l'au-delà et de dieu de la renaissance, agraire notamment, que retient le monde gréco-romain en l'intégrant parfois à la famille isiaque. Dans ce cercle divin, Osiris se distingue la plupart du temps de Sarapis et intervient dans des contextes où le parèdre alexandrin d'Isis n'apparaît pas. Cette forme de complémentarité fonctionnelle illustre toute la complexité des rapports entre les deux divinités[61] et, finalement, la place relativement secondaire occupée par Osiris dans le succès des cultes isiaques à l'époque impériale.

Bibliographie

Annius de Viterbe, Viterbiae Historiae Epitoma, MS Vat. lat. 6263, 346r–371v, 1491.

Annius de Viterbe, Commentaria fratris Ioannis Annii Viterbensis ordinis predicatorum Theologiae professoris super opera diversorum auctorum de Antiquitatibus loquentium, Roma, Eucharius Silber, 1498.

Aristodemou, G. 2019. Invisible Monuments of a City. The so-called Hydreion of the Sarapeion of Thessaloniki, in N. Ακαμάτης *et al.* (eds.), Τῷ διδασκάλῳ. Τιμητικός τόμος για τον Καθηγητή Ιωάννη Ακαμάτη, Thessaloniki, 69–78.

Baffioni, G., Mattiangieli, P. 1981. Annio da Viterbo : documenti e ricerche, 1, Roma.

Bevilacqua, G. 1992–1993. Il «papiro di Osiride» in una *defixio* di Roma, Scienze dell'Antichità 6/7, 143–151.

Boussac, M.-F. 2010. À propos des divinités de Taposiris Magna à l'époque hellénistique, in P. Carlier, C. Lerouge-Cohen (eds.), Paysage et religion en Grèce antique. Mélanges offerts à Madeleine Jost, Paris, 69–74.

59 Cf. Leclant 1974 ; Bricault 1992b ; Clerc & Leclant 1994. L'étude de ces représentations hors d'Égypte reste à faire.

60 Pour de rares manifestations de ce que j'appellerais une deségyptianisation visuelle d'Osiris, voir Clerc & Leclant 1994.

61 Sur ces rapports complexes, voir déjà Cacace 2017 et la thèse de ce jeune savant intitulée « Étude comparée des couples divins Osiris-Isis et Isis-Sarapis dans la documentation égyptienne d'époque gréco-romaine ».

Brenk, F. E. 2001. In the Image, Reflection and Reason of Osiris: Plutarch and the Egyptian Cults, in A. Pérez Jiménez, F. Casadesús Bordoy (eds.), Estudios sobre Plutarco. Misticismo y religiones mistéricas en la obra de Plutarco, Madrid, 83–98.
Bricault, L. 1992a. Isis dolente, BIFAO 92, 37–49.
Bricault, L. 1992b. Deux nouveaux Osiris dans le nord de la Gaule, Revue du Nord-Archéologie LXXIV n° 296, 179–183.
Bricault, L. 2001/2. Les Anubophores, Bulletin de la Société égyptologique de Genève 24, 29–42.
Bricault, L. 2004. La diffusion isiaque : une esquisse, in P. C. Bol *et al.* (eds.), Fremdheit – Eigenheit. Ägypten, Griechenland und Rom. Austausch und Verständnis, Stuttgart, 548–556.
Bricault, L. 2006. Du nom des images d'Isis polymorphe, in C. Bonnet et al. (eds.), Religions orientales – culti misterici. Neue Perspektiven – nouvelles perspectives – prospettive nuove, Stuttgart, 75–95.
Bricault, L. 2012. Associations isiaques d'Occident, in A. Mastrocinque, C. Giuffrè Scibona (eds.), Demeter, Isis, Vesta, and Cybele. Studies in Greek and Roman Religion in Honour of Giulia Sfameni Gasparro, Stuttgart, 91–104.
Bricault, L. 2022. L'Arétalogie d'Isis : biographie d'un texte canonique, in D. Agut-Labordère, M.J. Versluys (eds.), Canonisation as Innovation. Anchoring Cultural Formation in the First Millennium BCE, Leiden-Boston, 243–262.
Cacace, N. 2017. King Osiris and Lord Sarapis, Archiv für Religionsgeschichte 18–19, 285–306.
Christodoulou, P. 2021. The Isiac Sanctuary in Thessaloniki from its beginnings to the age of Augustus: a brief overview, in Ancient Macedonia VIII: Macedonia from the death of Philip II to Augustus' rise to power, Thessaloniki, 451–472.
Cieri-Via, C., Blamoutier, N. 1991. "Characteres et figuras in opere magico". Pinturicchio et la décoration de la "camera segreta" de l'appartement Borgia, Revue de l'Art 94, 11–26.
Clerc, G., Leclant, J. 1994. art. *Osiris*, LIMC VII, Zürich-München, 107–116 et pl. 79–82.
Collins, A. 2000. Renaissance Epigraphy and Its Legitimating Potential: Annius of Viterbo, Etruscan Inscriptions, and the Origins of Civilization, in A. Cooley (ed.), The afterlife of inscriptions: reusing, rediscovering, reinventing & revitalizing ancient inscriptions, Bulletin of the Institute of Classical Studies. Supplement 75. London, 57–76.
Crahay, R. 1983. Réflexions sur le faux historique : le cas d'Annius de Viterbe, Bulletin de la Classe des lettres et des sciences morales et politiques 69, 241–267.
Curran, B. 1988/1999. "De sacrarum litterarum Aegyptiorum interpretatione." Reticence and hubris in Hieroglyphic studies of the Renaissance: Piero Valeriano and Annius of Viterbo, Memoirs of the American Academy in Rome 43/44, 139–182.
Degrassi, A. 1963. Inscriptiones Italiae 13 : Fasti et elogia. Fasc. 2: Fasti anni Numani et Iuliani, accedunt ferialia, menologia rustica, parapegmata, Roma.
Delia, D. 1992. The Refreshing Water of Osiris, Journal of the American Research Center in Egypt 29, 181–190.
de Lisle, C. 2020. Attic Inscriptions in UK Collections 11. Ashmolean Museum, Oxford.

Divjak, J., Wischmeyer, W. (eds.) 2014. Das Kalenderhandbuch von 354 – Der Chronograph des Filocalus, 2 vols., Wien.
Fournet, J.-L. 2022. L'Égypte pharaonique de la fin de l'Antiquité à Champollion : une civilisation muette, in J.-L. Fournet *et al.* (dir.), Champollion 1822. Et l'Égypte ancienne retrouva la parole, Catalogue de l'exposition au Collège de France du 17 septembre au 25 octobre 2022, Paris, 16–47.
Gamurrini, G. F. 1883. Fiesole, NSA, 75–76.
Gasparini, V. 2016. "I will not be thirsty. My lips will not be dry": Individual Strategies of Re-constructing the Afterlife in the Isiac Cults, in K. Waldner, R. Gordon, W. Spickermann (eds.), Burial Rituals, Ideas of Afterlife, and the Individual in the Hellenistic World and the Roman Empire, Stuttgart, 125–150.
Gordon, R. L., Gasparini, V. 2014. Looking for Isis "the Magician" (ḥkȝy.t) in the Graeco-Roman World, in L. Bricault, R. Veymiers (eds.), Bibliotheca Isiaca III, Bordeaux, 39–53.
Grisonic, M., Cesarik, N., Vilogorac Brčić, I., Štrmelj, D. 2022. Calpurnia L. Pisonis filia, Cn. Pisonis neptis and the votive altar dedicated to Isis, Serapis, Osiris and Anubis in Caska Cove, on the island of Pag, VAMZ 3e s., LV, 231–255.
Grisonic, M., Cesarik, N., Vilogorac Brčić, I., Štrmelj, D., Bricault L. 2024. Calpurnia L. Pisonis filia, Cn. Pisonis neptis, Isis et suis, in L. Bricault, R. Veymiers (eds.), Bibliotheca Isiaca V (à paraître).
Gwyn Griffiths, J. 1970. Plutarch's De Iside et Osiride, Swansea.
Gwyn Griffiths, J. 1980. The Origins of Osiris and his Cult, Leiden.
Jordan, D. R. 2004. Magia nilotica sulle rive del Tevere, Mediterraneo antico 7.2, 693–710.
Lanna, S. 2024. *L'Inno a Iside* di Gomphoi (*RICIS* 112/0201). Testo, traduzione e commento, in L. Bricault, R. Veymiers (eds.), Bibliotheca Isiaca V (à paraître).
Leclant, J. 1974. Osiris en Gaule, in Studia Aegyptiaca I, Budapest, 263–285.
Ligota, C. R. 1987. Annius of Viterbo and Historical Method, Journal of the Walburg and Courtauld Institutes 50, 44-56.
Łukaszewicz, A. 1989. An Osiris "Cool Water" Inscription von Alexandria, ZPE 77, 195–196.
Magi, F. 1972. Il Calendario dipinto sotto S. Maria Maggiore, MemPontAcc XI.1, 1–103.
Malaise, M. 1985. Ciste et hydrie, symboles isiaques de la puissance et de la présence d'Osiris, in J. Ries (ed.), Le symbolisme dans le culte des grandes religions. Actes du colloque de Louvain-la-Neuve, 4–5 octobre 1983, Louvain-la-Neuve, 125–155.
Malaise, M. 2004. Statues égyptiennes naophores et cultes isiaques, Bulletin de la Société égyptologique de Genève 26, 65–80.
Malaise, M. 2005. Pour une terminologie et une analyse des cultes isiaques, Bruxelles.
Martinez, K., Pfeiffer, S., von Recklinghausen, D. 2020. New Evidence for the Worship of Isis and Osiris from Taposiris Magna, in J. Kamrin et al. (eds.), Guardian of Ancient Egypt. Studies in Honor of Zahi Hawass, Prague, vol. II, 1001–1022.
Mielsch, H. 1976. Review of F. Magi, Il Calendario dipinto sotto S. Maria Maggiore, Gnomon 48, 499–504.
Mols, S T. A. M., Moormann, E. 2010. L'edificio romano sotto S. Maria Maggiore a Roma e le sue pitture: proposta per una nuova lettura, MDAIR 116, 469–506.

Mráv, Z., Gabrieli, G. 2011. A Scarbantiai Iseum és feliratos emlékei, Arrabona 49.1, 201–238.
Özhan, T. 2018. A Dedication to Βασιλεὺς Ὄσιρις from the Inner Troad, Gephyra 15, 95–99.
Paoli, L. 2023. Re-Forging a Forgery: The French Editions of Annius of Viterbo's Antiquitates, in P. Lavender, M. Amundsen Bergström (eds.), Faking It! The Performance of Forgery in Late Medieval and Early Modern Culture, Leiden, 75–118.
Parlasca, K. 2002. Ägyptische Skulpturen als Griechische Votive in Heligtümern des Ostmittelmeerraums und des Nahen Ostens, in B. Bol, D. Kreikenbom (eds.), Sepulkral und Votivdenkmälern östlicher Mittelmeergebiete (7. Jh. v. Chr. – 1. Jh. n. Chr.) Kulturbegegnungen im Spannungsfeld von Akzeptanz und Resistenz, Mainz.
Parlasca, K. 2003. Trauernde Isis, Euthenia oder „Aegyptus capta". Zu einer „alexandrinischen" Bronzegruppe in Privatbesitz, Antike Welt fasc. 2, 161–164.
Pétigny, A. 2008. Une statue égyptienne de la XXIXe dynastie à Tyr, BAAL 12, 1–13.
Popper, N. 2011. An Ocean of Lies: The Problem of Historical Evidence in the Sixteenth Century, Huntington Library Quarterly 74.3, 375–400.
Quaegebeur, J. 1977. Anubis, fils d'Osiris, le vacher, in Studia Aegyptiaca III, Budapest, 119–130.
Rolet, S. 2008. La « Tabula Bembi » et le bas-relief « osirien » d'Annius de Viterbe : deux figures contradictoires de la mystérieuse Égypte, in D. Martin, P. Servet, A. Touron (coord.), L'énigmatique à la Renaissance : formes, significations, esthétiques, Paris, 215–231.
Siard, H. 2007. L'hydreion du Sarapieion C de Délos : la divinisation de l'eau dans un sanctuaire isiaque, in L. Bricault, M. J. Versluys, P. G. P. Meyboom (eds.), Nile into Tiber. Egypt in the Roman World, Leiden, Boston, 417–447.
Smith, M. 2017. Following Osiris: Perspectives on the Osirian Afterlife from Four Millennia, Oxford.
Stern, H. 1953. Le Calendrier de 354. Étude de son texte et de ses illustrations, Paris.
Stern, H. 1973. Le calendrier de Sainte-Marie-Majeure, REL 51, 41–48.
Touloumtzidou, A., Christodoulou, P. 2024. Tracing Osiris in the Hellenistic Mediterranean, in L. Bricault, R. Veymiers (eds.), Bibliotheca Isiaca V (à paraître), Bordeaux.
Veymiers, R. 2021. Les mystères isiaques et leurs expressions figurées. Des exégèses modernes aux allusions antiques, in N. Belayche, F. Massa (eds.), Mystery Cults in Visual Representation in Graeco-Roman Antiquity, Leiden, 123–168.
Wild, R. A. 1984. The Known Isis – Sarapis Sanctuaries of the Roman Period, ANRW II 17.4, 1739–1851.
Winand, J. 2022a. La réception de l'Antiquité classique, in J. Winand, G. Chantrain (dir.). Les hiéroglyphes avant Champollion. Depuis l'Antiquité classique jusqu'à l'Expédition d'Égypte, Liège, 37–58.
Winand, J. 2022b. Hiéroglyphes et néo-hiéroglyphes à la Renaissance, in J. Winand, G. Chantrain (dir.), Les hiéroglyphes avant Champollion. Depuis l'Antiquité classique jusqu'à l'Expédition d'Égypte, Liège, 83–142.
Winand, J. 2023. Hieroglyphs in the Renaissance: Rebirth or New Life? (Part 1), Hieroglyphs 1, 45–107.

Iscrizioni senatorie di Roma: novità, ritrovamenti, riletture

Silvia Orlandi

Pubblicando, nel 2000, l'aggiornamento al fascicolo di CIL, VI dedicato ai *Magistratus populi Romani*, Géza Alföldy ha reso un enorme servizio alla comunità scientifica, offrendo l'edizione, la riedizione o l'aggiornamento bibliografico di moltissimi testi epigrafici fondamentali per la nostra conoscenza della prosopografia e della storia sociale e istituzionale del mondo romano.

Ma come ben sa chi l'epigrafia la pratica "di prima mano", ogni edizione, anche la più ricca e completa, è destinata fatalmente ad essere superata, nel giro di qualche anno, dal susseguirsi di studi e scoperte, come hanno ben dimostrato David Nonnis e Maurizio Giovagnoli nel loro contributo all'aggiornamento proprio del fascicolo di CIL, VI relativo alle iscrizioni senatorie[1].

Qualche volta, però, le novità – piccole o grandi che siano – emergono non da nuovi cantieri o nuove pubblicazioni, ma dall'attività, più oscura ma non meno utile, di progressiva digitalizzazione del nostro patrimonio epigrafico, soprattutto se questa è condotta non su semplice base bibliografica, ma in stretta relazione con la verifica degli originali e il controllo dei documenti d'archivio.

È quanto stiamo facendo, ormai da 20 anni, con l'inserimento delle iscrizioni latine e greche dell'Italia antica nella banca dati EDR (Epigraphic Database Roma: www.edr-edr.it), attività da cui sono nate ormai diverse pubblicazioni scientifiche edite in varie sedi e che mi vede coinvolta non solo in qualità di responsabile scientifica del progetto, insieme ai colleghi Giuseppe Camodeca e Giovanni Cecconi, ma spesso anche in prima persona, come schedatore. Tale attività ha conosciuto un periodo particolarmente felice nel triennio 2013–2016, quando un finanziamento della Commissione Europea ha permesso la creazione del progetto EAGLE: Europeana network of Ancient Greek and Latin Epigraphy (www.eagle-network.eu), del cui consorzio faceva parte anche l'università Babeş-Bolyai di Cluj-Napoca, sotto la responsabilità del nostro Ioan Piso.

Memore di quell'entusiasmante triennio, in cui ci è sembrato di poter realizzare il sogno di avere in un unico archivio gran parte delle banche dati epigrafiche d'Europa, vorrei dedicare al collega qualche novità sulle iscrizioni senatorie di Roma, nata proprio

1 Giovagnoli, Nonnis 2014.

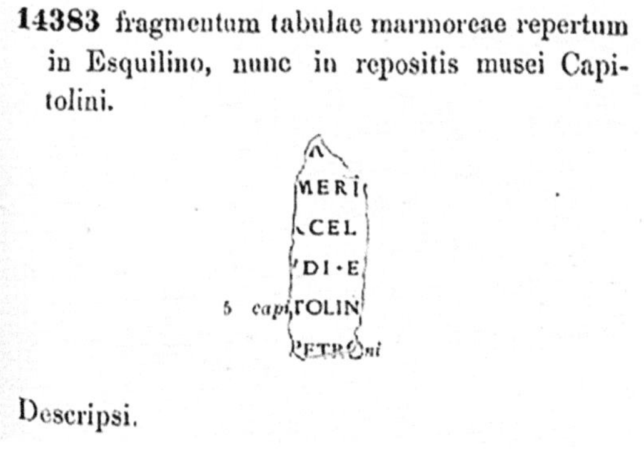
14383 fragmentum tabulae marmoreae repertum in Esquilino, nunc in repositis musei Capitolini.

Descripsi.

Fig. 1: CIL, VI 14383

Fig. 2: Foto Archivio di Epigrafia Latina Silvio Panciera, neg. 7236. © Roma, Sovrintendenza Capitolina ai Beni Culturali

dal lavoro per l'implementazione dell'Epigraphic Database Roma e del server del portale EAGLE, che dal 2016 continua a funzionare e ad ospitare sempre nuovi records. In particolare, le novità che qui si presentano nascono dalla parallela attività di digitalizzazione della documentazione fotografica relativa alla parte della collezione epigrafica dell'Antiquarium Comunale del Celio attualmente in deposito presso il Museo della Civiltà Romana, che da alcuni anni l'Archivio di Epigrafia Latina Silvio Panciera sta svolgendo in collaborazione con la Sovrintendenza Capitolina ai Beni Culturali.

Marcella ritrovata

Nella cassa 250, un tempo immagazzinata nel Palazzo delle Esposizioni di via Nazionale, e ora in deposito presso il Museo della Civiltà Romana, si conserva, con l'inv. 3223, un frammento di lastra marmorea mutila su tutti i lati (38 × 21 × 3,5). Il pezzo è stato identificato con l'iscrizione pubblicata sotto il numero CIL, VI 14383, tra i *tituli sepulcrales reliqui*, dove non vengono sostanzialmente avanzate proposte di lettura e integrazione, fatto salvo il riconoscimento della presenza del *cognomen Capitolinus* e del gentilizio *Petronius* (figg. 1–2).

Si tratta, in realtà, dell'indebita reduplicazione del frammento a dell'iscrizione sepolcrale relativa alla figlia di un console, pubblicato insieme al frammento b, ad esso contiguo, sotto il numero CIL, VI 31697, quando entrambi i pezzi erano conservati nel Palazzo dei Conservatori dei Musei Capitolini, "in scalis" (fig. 3).

Lo smantellamento dei frammenti un tempo murati lungo le pareti dello scalone deve aver portato alla dispersione del materiale, se già nell'*addendum* pubblicato a p. 3805 del supplemento a CIL, VI edito nel 1933, Martin Bang dava per irreperibile il frammento destro, mentre il sinistro era nel frattempo "migrato" nell'Antiquarium Comunale del Celio, dove fu visto nel 1913 "horti muro applicitum". Né più fortunato è stato Géza Alföldy,

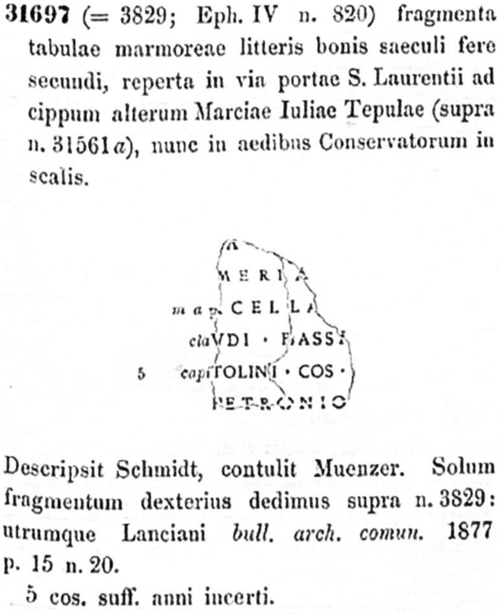
31697 (= 3829; Eph. IV n. 820) fragmenta tabulae marmoreae litteris bonis saeculi fere secundi, reperta in via portae S. Laurentii ad cippum alterum Marciae Iuliae Tepulae (supra n. 31561*a*), nunc in aedibus Conservatorum in scalis.

Descripsit Schmidt, contulit Muenzer. Solum fragmentum dexterius dedimus supra n. 3829: utrumque Lanciani *bull. arch. comun.* 1877 p. 15 n. 20.
5 cos. suff. anni incerti.

Fig. 3: CIL, VI 31697

che ha ripubblicato il testo in CIL, VI 41154 dandone per la prima volta una trascrizione interpretativa, e proponendone alcune integrazioni sulla base della foto del frammento superstite, allora conservato presso il Palazzo delle Esposizioni[2], e dell'apografo del testo più integro, edito in precedenza. Con il ritrovamento o, meglio, il riconoscimento del frammento che si credeva perduto, la lettura di Alföldy trova ora conferma e può essere riproposta integralmente, senza più parti sottolineate:

- - - - - -
[Cl]a[udiae Bassae?]
[Nu]meriạ[e - - -]
[Ma]rcella[e - - -]

[Cla]udi Bassị [- - -]
[Capi]tolini co(n)s(ulis) f̣[iliae]
[et -] Petrọnịọ [- - -]
- - - - - -

2 Ora anch'esso in deposito presso il Museo della Civiltà Romana, cassa 166.

Fig. 4: Ricomposizione dei frammenti dell'iscrizione di Marcella

Siamo, dunque, di fronte alla dedica posta a una dama di alto rango, nella cui onomastica si riconoscono il gentilizio Numeria e il *cognomen* Marcella, che si definisce – come era consuetudine per le donne dell'ordine senatorio – figlia del console *Claudius Bassus Capitolinus*, e a un altro personaggio di cui si individua nell'ultima riga conservata, il gentilizio Petronio. Il console è senz'altro da mettere in relazione, anche se verosimilmente non da identificare, con il senatore originario dell'Asia Minore *Claudius Capitolinus*, vissuto all'inizio del III secolo[3], cioè in un'epoca più tarda di quella che le caratteristiche paleografiche della nostra iscrizione, ascrivibile alla seconda metà del II secolo, suggeriscono[4].

Quel che la ricomposizione, sia pure virtuale, dei due frammenti (fig. 4)[5] permette di apprezzare maggiormente, tuttavia, è la rilevanza monumentale dell'iscrizione che doveva costituire la lastra di arredo parietale esterno di un sepolcro di notevoli dimensioni, adeguato alla posizione sociale ed economica dei defunti in essa menzionati. Degna di nota anche la localizzazione di questa tomba, ipotizzabile sulla base del luogo di ritrova-

3 Su cui vd. Halfmann 1982, 637.

4 Vd. in proposito le osservazioni di Alföldy in CIL, VI p. 4962 ad 41154, con discussione della bibliografia precedente.

5 La rielaborazione grafica è merito di Angela Mincuzzi, che colgo l'occasione per ringraziare.

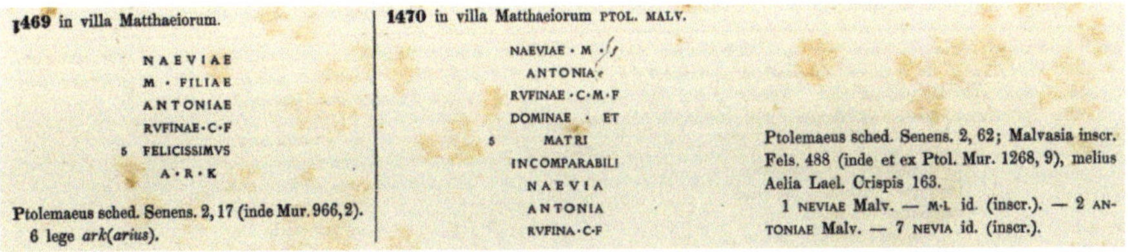

1469 in villa Matthaeiorum.

NAEVIAE
M · FILIAE
ANTONIAE
RVFINAE · C · F
FELICISSIMVS
A · R · K

Ptolemaeus sched. Senens. 2, 17 (inde Mur. 966, 2).
6 lege *ark(arius)*.

1470 in villa Matthaeiorum PTOL. MALV.

NAEVIAE · M ·
ANTONIA
RVFINAE · C · M · F
DOMINAE · ET
MATRI
INCOMPARABILI
NAEVIA
ANTONIA
RVFINA · C · F

Ptolemaeus sched. Senens. 2, 62; Malvasia inscr. Fels. 488 (inde et ex Ptol. Mur. 1268, 9), melius Aelia Lael. Crispis 163.
1 NEVIAE Malv. — M·L id. (inscr.). — 2 ANTONIAE Malv. — 7 NEVIA id. (inscr.).

Fig. 5a–b: CIL, VI 1469–1470

mento dei frammenti[6], nell'allora via di Porta San Lorenzo corrispondente all'attuale via Marsala, all'altezza di largo Montemartini. Ci troviamo immediatamente all'esterno delle Mura Serviane, in una zona non lontana dal percorso antico della via Nomentana, dove si hanno notizie dell'esistenza di altre tombe monumentali dedicate a membri dell'ordine senatorio, come quella di Tacito[7] e – con tutte le cautele del caso – quella dei Licini e dei Calpurni[8]. Un'ulteriore conferma di come anche il paesaggio funerario della "città dei morti" prevedesse gerarchie di rilevanza e visibilità che rispecchiavano quelle valide e operanti nella città dei vivi.

Rufina ritrovata

Il senese Francesco Tolomei, visitando Roma nel 1666, documentò la presenza, nella villa Mattei sul Celio, di due iscrizioni dedicate alla stessa donna, la *clarissima femina Naevia Antonia Rufina*: la prima[9] postale quando era ancora in vita dal suo tesoriere (*arkarius*), lo schiavo *Felicissimus*; la seconda[10] dopo la sua morte (dal momento che è ricordata come *clarissimae memoriae femina*) dalla figlia omonima. Di entrambe le iscrizioni si persero le tracce fino alla fine del XIX secolo, se Wilhelm Henzen le pubblicò nel primo fascicolo del *Corpus* sulla base della sola tradizione manoscritta (fig. 5 a–b).

Già nel Supplemento pubblicato nel 1902, tuttavia, Christian Hülsen documentava la presenza della parte inferiore dell'iscrizione CIL, VI 1469 nella Galleria Lapidaria dei Musei Vaticani[11], mentre è di qualche anno più tardi, nel 1905, la ri-scoperta, in via S. Agata dei Goti, di un altro piccolo frammento della stessa epigrafe, confluita nella collezione epigrafica dell'Antiquarium Comunale del Celio[12].

6 Da mettere in relazione con quello del cippo dell'*Aqua Marcia* pubblicato in CIL, VI 31561a = EDR123651.
7 Da cui proviene la monumentale iscrizione sepolcrale CIL, VI 1574 = 41106 = EDR093379.
8 Con il gruppo di are sepolcrali CIL, VI 31721–31728, sulle cui problematiche vicende vd. la sintesi in CIL, VI p. 4778.
9 CIL, VI 1469 = EDR032708.
10 CIL, VI 1470 = EDR110970.
11 Vd. la scheda accessibile al link https://catalogo.museivaticani.va/index.php/Detail/objects/MV.8976.0.0.
12 La cui foto è pubblicata in SupplIt Imagines – Roma, 2, 3136.

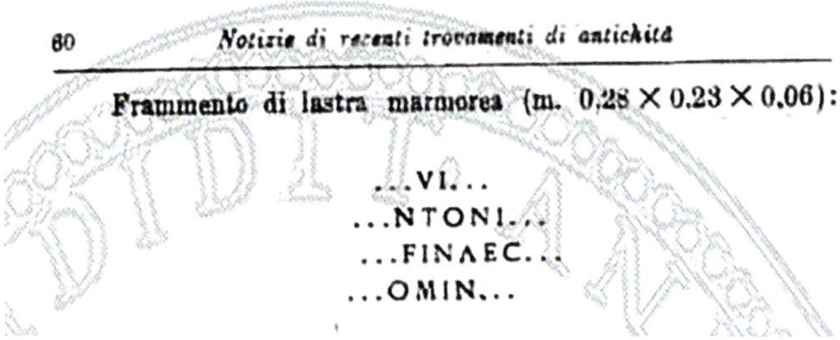

60 *Notizie di recenti trovamenti di antichità*

Frammento di lastra marmorea (m. 0,28 × 0,23 × 0,06):

...VI...
...NTONI...
...FINAEC...
...OMIN...

Fig. 6: Frammento della dedica a Rufina nell'edizione del Bullettino Comunale 1915

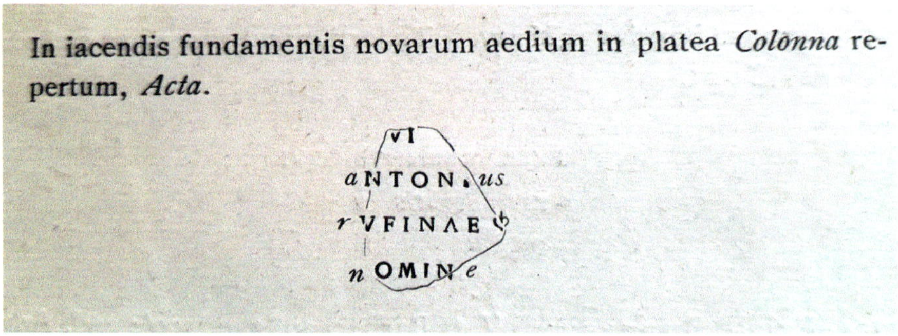

In iacendis fundamentis novarum aedium in platea *Colonna* repertum, *Acta*.

VI
*a*NTON·*us*
*r*VFINAE
*n*OMIN*e*

Fig. 7: Frammento della dedica a Rufina nell'edizione delle ICUR, 3758

Possiamo ora dire che vicende simili accomunano questa iscrizione all'altra dedica posta alla stessa Rufina. Anche questa, infatti, dopo essere stata documentata nella collezione Mattei, dovette andare in frantumi, e i pezzi che originariamente la componevano si dispersero, rimanendo a lungo irreperibili, finché, nel 1915, un frammento pertinente alla parte centrale della lastra non fu rinvenuto, tra materiali di scarico, a piazza Colonna, nell'area dove sorgeva palazzo Piombino e dove in seguito sarebbe stata costruita la Galleria Colonna, oggi Galleria Alberto Sordi. Il frammento fu pubblicato da Luigi Cantarelli nel Bullettino della Commissione Archeologica Comunale di quell'anno, ma non riconosciuto come pertinente all'iscrizione già nota, tanto che la trascrizione che l'autore ne dà non contiene alcun tentativo di integrazione o interpretazione del testo (fig. 6).

Il ritrovamento è registrato anche nei Giornali di scavo del maggio di quell'anno (faldone 7, pagina 3265)[13], e da documentazione d'archivio dipende anche la pubblicazione dello stesso pezzo nel primo volume della nuova serie delle *Inscriptiones Christianae Urbis Romae*, curato nel 1922 da Angelo Silvagni. Qui, sotto il numero 3758, tra le iscrizioni

13 Disponibili in formato e-book sul sito dell'Archivio di Documentazione Archeologica al link http://ada.beniculturali.it/en/258/excavation-diaries/7#7.

Fig. 8: Foto Archivio di Epigrafia Latina Silvio Panciera, neg. 6782.
© Roma, Sovrintendenza Capitolina ai Beni Culturali

incertae originis, troviamo di nuovo il nostro frammento, anche in questo caso non riconosciuto come già edito, né nel CIL, né nel Bullettino Comunale (fig. 7).

Benché nessuno degli editori ne segnali la collocazione, il frammento in questione si trova tra i materiali di competenza della Sovrintendenza Capitolina ai Beni Culturali, e più precisamente nella cassa 225 in deposito presso il Museo della Civiltà Romana (fig. 8).

Il recupero di questa porzione della lastra – forse originariamente inserita nella fronte di una base – consente ora di proporre una trascrizione aggiornata del testo, che continua, in ogni caso, a basarsi in gran parte sull'accurato apografo del Tolomei:

Naeviae M(arci) [f(iliae)]
Antonia[e]
Rufinae, c(larissimae) m(emoriae) f(eminae),
dominae et
matri
incomparabili
Naevia
Antonia
Rufina, c(larissima) f(emina).

Ma, soprattutto, la storia collezionistica di questi frammenti conferma quanto, a volte, sia utile ricostruire tali vicende per risalire alla probabile provenienza archeologica dei monumenti iscritti. Lo stesso *Felicissimus* che pose a *Rufina* la dedica pubblicata in CIL, VI 1469, infatti, compare come dedicante anche dell'iscrizione in onore di un *T. Aelius Naevianus*[14], proveniente dalla vigna Santarelli sull'Esquilino[15]. Nella stessa vigna, nel 1663, fu scoperta anche una dedica a *T. Aelius Naevius Antonius Severus*[16], in cui è probabilmente da riconoscere un figlio della nostra Rufina, postagli, quando era ancora giovane[17], dal suo *nutritor*, il liberto Pao[18]. È possibile, dunque, che, prima di giungere a far parte della collezione Mattei, anche le iscrizioni in onore di *Naevia Antonia Rufina* si trovassero nell'area del Cispio da cui provengono le altre iscrizioni relative a membri della stessa *gens*, dove doveva sorgere la *domus* di famiglia. In seguito, divenuto adulto, il senatore *Naevius Antonius Severus* si sarebbe trasferito in una *domus* indipendente sul Quirinale, da localizzare nella zona – corrispondente all'attuale Villino Hüffer in via Nazionale 191 – da cui proviene un'altra iscrizione in suo onore[19], postagli intorno alla metà del III secolo da due militari che avevano verosimilmente prestato servizio nella provincia da lui governata[20]. Un puzzle complesso e interessante, cui il ritrovamento del nostro frammento contribuisce con l'aggiunta di una nuova tessera.

Una nuova iscrizione per *Rufus*

Sempre nel Museo della Civiltà Romana, nella cassa 252, si trova un altro documento di piccole dimensioni, ma di grande interesse. Si tratta di due frammenti contigui di una lastra di marmo bigio, di cui si conserva parte del margine superiore e di quello destro, rinvenuti in piazza del Colosseo (fig. 9)[21].

Vi si leggono poche lettere, sicuramente pertinenti alla parte superiore di un testo, che si possono trascrivere come segue:

[- - -]o L(uci) f(ilio) Ru+[- - -]
[- - -]+A+[- - -]
\- - - - - -

14 Su cui vd. PIR², A, 225.
15 CIL, VI 9147 = EDR168608.
16 Su cui vd. PIR², N, 5.
17 Nel testo dell'iscrizione figura ancora come *quaestor*.
18 CIL, VI 1332 = EDR109213.
19 IGUR, I 58 = EDR170698.
20 Vd. in proposito le osservazioni di Panciera 2003, 359–360 = Panciera 2006, 1195–1196.
21 Anche in questo caso la ricomposizione virtuale dei due frammenti è opera di Angela Mincuzzi.

Fig. 9: Ricomposizione dei frammenti. Foto Archivio di Epigrafia Latina Silvio Panciera, negg. 7528 e 7545. © Roma, Sovrintendenza Capitolina ai Beni Culturali

r. 1: sul margine destro della lastra si conserva il tratto verticale di una lettera che doveva essere incisa quasi interamente sulla lastra marmorea adiacente a questa, consentendo così di ricostruire un testo di notevoli dimensioni, che si sviluppava su più lastre giustapposte.
r. 2: oltre alla traccia di una A, si conservano solo le parti superiori di due tratti verticali.

Troppo poco, apparentemente, per proporre qualsiasi integrazione, se non del *cognomen* – verosimilmente *Ruf[o]* – del personaggio. Tuttavia, le caratteristiche paleografiche dell'iscrizione (lettere in capitale molto elegante, con apicature a spatola e sapiente uso del chiaroscuro, osservabile soprattutto nell'ingrossarsi e assottigliarsi del tratto curvo della O, interpunzioni regolari a forma di "spina di rosa", spaziatura tra le lettere) la avvicinano molto al frammento superstite dell'iscrizione bilingue posta in onore del senatore [---]*us Rufus*, proconsole della provincia di Ponto e Bitinia in un anno incerto dell'inizio dell'età agustea, da un cospicuo gruppo di città orientali che lo avevano scelto come patrono (fig. 10).

L'iscrizione del proconsole *Rufus* è stata pubblicata in CIL, VI 1508 e nelle IGUR 71 sulla base della sola tradizione manoscritta del XVI secolo, quando le lastre che componevano l'iscrizione furono viste reimpiegate in varie parti della chiesa di S. Lorenzo in Lucina.

È merito di Luigi Moretti aver pubblicato, negli anni 70 del secolo scorso, un frammento di questo monumento, rinvenuto nei lavori di restauro della chiesa del Camposan-

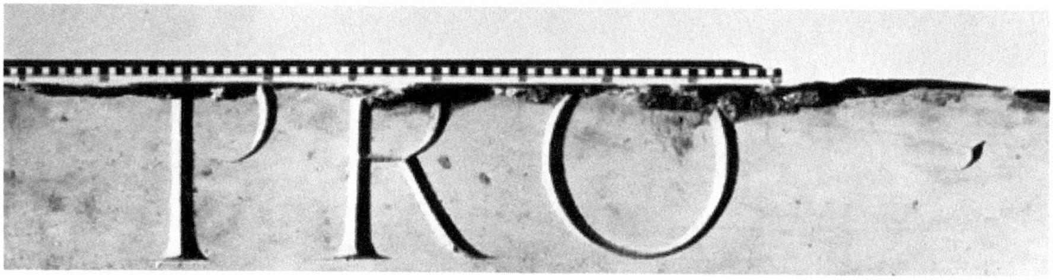

Fig. 10: Dettaglio della prima riga superstite di CIL, VI 1508

to Teutonico nella Città del Vaticano, e lì tuttora conservato[22]. Alla luce di questa importante scoperta, che ha consentito, tra l'altro, di rivalutare il discusso apografo ligoriano dell'iscrizione, tutto il testo è stato poi ripubblicato da Werner Eck[23], che ne ha proposto una ricostruzione grafica, sostanzialmente ripresa nel supplemento del CIL del 2000, sotto il numero 41054 (fig. 11)[24].

Si tratta, come si vede, di un imponente monumento onorario, di cui le lastre marmoree dovevano costituire il rivestimento, che raggiungeva una lunghezza di circa 8, se non addirittura 9 metri e che dobbiamo immaginare completato da una o più statue raffiguranti l'onorato e i membri della sua famiglia o forse le personificazioni delle città dedicanti[25].

Purtroppo il frammento del Museo della Civiltà Romana non è, come si sarebbe tentati di pensare, un'altra parte già nota del monumento, anche se la lettura *[- - -]o L(uci) f(ilio) Ruf[o - - -]* si adatterebbe perfettamente al frammento a, noto da tradizione manoscritta. La diversa dimensione dei caratteri (8 cm. nel nostro caso, ben 25 per il frammento del Camposanto Teutonico), infatti, impedisce di pensare a due parti della stessa sequenza di lastre. Ma l'affinità paleografica, la disposizione del testo sulla superficie scrittoria, priva di cornice, la forma particolare delle interpunzioni e la sua pure parziale coincidenza testuale suggeriscono la possibilità che si tratti di un altro monumento (o di un'altra parte dello stesso monumento) con la medesima struttura e per il medesimo personaggio, che va ad aggiungersi al già noto frammento pubblicato dallo stesso Alföldy in CIL, VI 41055[26], in cui si legge *[- - - o L(uci) f(ilio)] Ruf[o procos(n)s(uli)] / [- - -]ini pat[rono].* Il fatto che quest'ultima lastra sia stata rinvenuta reimpiegata in una struttura dell'età di Claudio conferma sia la datazione alla primissima età imperiale proposta per il nostro personaggio, sia l'ipotesi che il suo monumento onorario, troppo ingombrante per non essere sgradito all'imperatore, sia stato distrutto in concomitanza con la costruzione della meridiana di Augusto in Campo Marzio, e i suoi pezzi dispersi in vari punti della città.

22 Moretti 1980.
23 Eck 1984.
24 Vd. anche EDR093337.
25 Per quest'ipotesi vd. in part. Eck 1984, 207–208.
26 Vd. foto e ulteriore bibliografia in EDR093338.

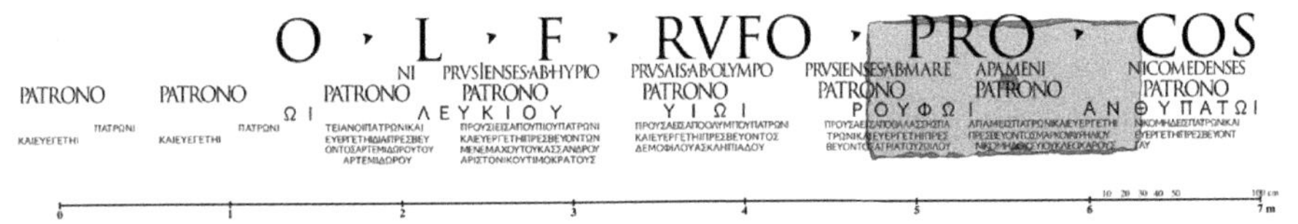

Fig. 11: Ricostruzione grafica dell'iscrizione in CIL, VI 41054

I nuovi frammenti, se l'interpretazione che qui si propone fosse corretta, andrebbero a corroborare ulteriormente tali ipotesi, ampliando, nel loro piccolo, la nostra base documentaria per la conoscenza dell'aristocrazia di età augustea.

Bibliografia abbreviata

Eck, W. 1984. CIL VI 1508 (Moretti, IGUR 71) und die Gestaltung senatorischer Ehrenmonumente, Chiron 14, 201–217.

Giovagnoli, M., Nonnis, D. 2014. CIL, VI: un aggiornamento al supplemento senatorio di Géza Alföldy. Testi editi e inediti, in M. L. Caldelli, G. L. Gregori (eds.), Epigrafia e ordine senatorio, 30 anni dopo, Roma, 217–232.

Halfmann, H. 1982. Die Senatoren aus den kleinasiatischen Provinzen des Römischen Reiches vom 1. Bis 3. Jahrhundert (Asia, Pontus-Bithynia, Lycia-Pamphilia, Galatia, Cappadocia, Cilicia), in Epigrafia e ordine senatorio, II (Tituli 5), Roma, 603–650.

Moretti, L. 1980. A proposito di Pirro Ligorio e di IGUR 71, in M. J. Fontana , M. T. Piraino, F. P. Rizzo (eds.), Φιλίας χάριν. Miscellanea di studi classici in onore di E. Manni, Roma, V, 1583–1592.

Panciera, S. 2003. Domus a Roma: altri contributi alla loro inventariazione, in Serta antiqua et mediaevalia, VI. Usi e abusi epigrafici, 355–374 = Panciera 2006, 1193–1206.

Panciera, S. 2006. Epigrafi, epigrafia, epigrafisti. Scritti vari editi e inediti (1956–2005), con note complementari e indici, Roma.

Tellus e non *Terra*
Considerazioni su alcune iscrizioni latine di età imperiale*

Cecilia Ricci

Breve premessa

Abbiamo tutti in mente la rappresentazione più nota e diffusa della *Tellus*: una giovane donna, seduta o semidistesa, che tiene in mano una cornucopia, simbolo di abbondanza e prosperità, che nutre (o è circondata da) due o più bambini. Tale rappresentazione la avvicina a Cerere, alla quale la dea era associata, sin dai tempi più antichi: le due divinità femminili venivano celebrate in occasioni di feste connesse con la ricchezza del suolo e in particolare nel corso dei *Fordicidia*, all'inizio della primavera[1].

A oggi, lo studio più completo sulle caratteristiche di *Tellus/Terra Mater*, sulla diffusione del culto e sulle trasformazioni intercorse nella lunga durata della storia di Roma è quello condotto da Tamás Gesztelyi nel 1981[2]. In apertura del contributo, lo studioso proponeva una breve rassegna bibliografica, mettendo in evidenza questioni fondamentali, quali il carattere agricolo e/o ctonio della dea, la sua origine (greca/italica/romana), la sua natura di *mater*. Gesztelyi forniva dunque un quadro d'insieme del culto di *Tellus*, sulla base delle fonti a disposizione (letterarie, iconografiche, numismatiche, epigrafiche), non trascurando di considerare l'immagine della dea restituita dalla speculazione filosofica

---

* Cecilia Ricci (Università del Molise – IT). Il ricordo del prof. Piso è legato per me al 1981, il mio primo anno di università, alla giovinezza e alla gioia della ricerca. I suoi interventi pacati, la sua sapienza non ostentata, il suo impegno civile sono stati, da allora, una compagnia silenziosa ma costante nei miei studi. Per questo lo ringrazio e gli rivolgo i miei auguri più cari.

1 Le celebrazioni per la *Tellus* sono registrate nei fasti anziati, ostiensi e prenestini (Degrassi 1963; Dumézil 2001, 325–330; Carandini 2003², 559–576). Il 13 dicembre, in occasione del *dies Natalis* del tempio, Cerere e *Tellus* venivano celebrate con un *lectisternium* (Arn. *Nat.* 7.32.8). Si vedano Prescendi 2015 (in particolare sulla connessione con Ceres e sui *Fordicidia*) e Marcattili 2020.1, entrambi con ampia bibliografia precedente. Sull'opportuna distinzione tra Tellus e Terra mater, si vedano Jennings-Rose, Scheid 2016: "Secondo Ovidio (Fast. 1. 671 ss.), *Tellus* era patrona del luogo di coltivazione, *Ceres* delle origini della coltivazione; e mentre *Terra* descrive l'elemento 'terra', *Tellus* è il nome della sua divinità protettrice (Serv. *Aen.* 1. 171; 12. 778)...".

2 Lo stesso Gesztelyi aveva già pubblicato (e pubblicherà successivamente) altri contributi sempre dedicati a *Terra Mater*: Gesztelyi 1971, 1972, 1977, 1981–82.

della tarda repubblica – sottolineando in particolare l'apporto di Lucrezio e Varrone – e, grazie in particolare alle iscrizioni, dalla politica religiosa degli imperatori e dalle manifestazioni della religiosità privata a Roma e nelle province.

Lo studioso ungherese metteva in giusta evidenza lo snodo fondamentale segnato dal principato augusteo: è ben noto infatti che in questo periodo, quando la dea diventa la personificazione della terra che assicura all'Italia la prosperità dell'età dell'oro, le fonti su *Tellus* sono particolarmente numerose[3]. Un'altra fase di buona fortuna del culto, testimoniata soprattutto dalle monete, è compresa tra la metà del II secolo e l'epoca severiana.

Per quanto riguarda le testimonianze epigrafiche, Gesztelyi passava in rassegna quelle dell'Occidente romano, dando rilievo ai documenti africani e, per ragioni diverse, a quelli restituiti dalle province danubiane e balcaniche; al carattere di culto astrale e/o misterico talvolta assunto dalla dea; alla sua forte valenza simbolica, riferibile al ciclo di morti e rinascite, attestato diffusamente nei monumenti funerari, a partire dal II secolo. Nel complesso, Gesztelyi metteva in giusta evidenza i diversi significati attribuiti a Terra, il suo legame ora con il modo agricolo, ora con una specifica area regionale; e la sua relativa popolarità nel contesto della religione privata (anche al di fuori della formula augurale *sit tibi terra levis*).

Ritengo sia utile tornare a sottolineare il numero esiguo delle testimonianze epigrafiche (in tutto poco meno di un centinaio) che si riferiscono a *Terra mater* o *Tellus*, da sola o insieme ad altre divinità, con o senza ulteriori epiteti. Alcune di esse ricordano l'esistenza di *aedes* e/o di sacerdoti della dea, anche se un solo tempio (in Africa Proconsolare) è tuttora conservato[4]. Inoltre, nel saggio di Gesztelyi, la documentazione della città di Roma e quella dell'Italia romana, riceveva un'attenzione parziale[5], come è d'altronde pienamente giustificabile, in considerazione del carattere sistematico della sua trattazione[6].

Nelle iscrizioni dell'Italia romana, la dea è ricordata quasi esclusivamente come *Terra* (*mater*). Solo in tre di esse si parla di *Tellus*: in questa sede, ci si concentra su queste testimonianze, per meglio analizzarle e per cercare eventualmente di individuare le ragioni di tale peculiarità.

---

3 Ghisellini 1994. Accanto alle citazioni poetiche di Virgilio, Ovidio e Orazio, in quest'epoca, per la prima volta, abbiamo la più celebre rappresentazione iconografica della dea nel celeberrimo rilievo sull'*ara Pacis* (Gesztelyi 1981, 440 s. con bibliografia). Sulla rappresentazione 'classica' della *Tellus* (*ara Pacis*, corazza dell'Augusto di Prima Porta, gemma augustea), prima di Gesztelyi, già Strong 1937.

4 Le province africane hanno restituito il maggior numero di testimonianze del culto di *Tellus/Terra mater*, come dea del grano (e, più in generale, dei frutti della terra), che, nelle parole di Duncan Fishwick, "personifica la germinazione, la nascita, la morte e la resurrezione" (Fishwick 1996, 32, con fonti e ricca bibliografia). L'alto numero e l'eloquenza delle testimonianze africane erano già stati sottolineati da Gesztelyi 1981, 431, 446–450. Per culto di *Tellus/Terra Mater* nel Nordafrica, oltre a Gesztelyi 1972, si veda il recente intervento sistematico di Bel Faïda 2008.

5 Gesztelyi 1981, 450–51.

6 È partendo da tali considerazioni che, di recente, ho condotto una rassegna sistematica delle (poche) testimonianze epigrafiche del culto di *Tellus/Terra mater* nell'Italia augustea, in considerazione delle loro peculiarità e del fatto che, in prospettiva comparativa, esse gettano luce su alcuni aspetti degli atti votivi. Lo scopo era quello di cogliere, per quanto possibile e in relazione ai diversi contesti, alcune specificità dei caratteri divini di *Terra Mater* e delle manifestazioni religiose che la riguardano: Ricci c.s.

La dedica urbana

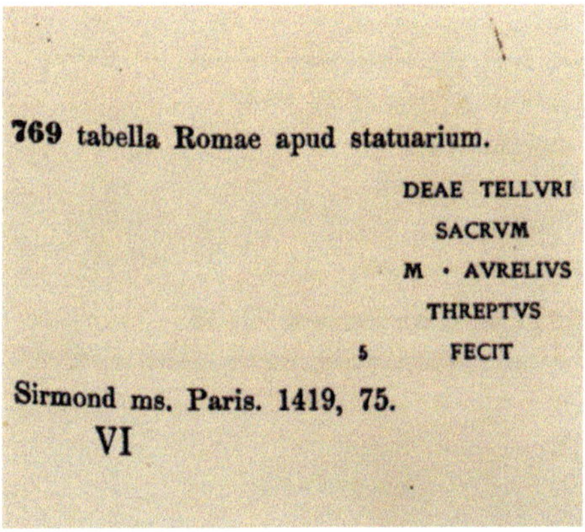
769 tabella Romae apud statuarium.

DEAE TELLVRI
SACRVM
M · AVRELIVS
THREPTVS
5 FECIT

Sirmond ms. Paris. 1419, 75.
VI

Fig. 1: *CIL*, VI 769, cfr. pp. 838, 3757, 30827 = *CIL*, VI 30827 = *ILS* 3956 (iscrizione perduta: immagine tratta dal Corpus)

Prima di presentare l'unica dedica romana di questo piccolo corpus, va ricordato che le iscrizioni di *Tellus/Terra* (*Mater*) a Roma sono in tutto una decina[7]. La maggior parte di esse – se si esclude naturalmente il cospicuo numero di epitaffi in cui la Terra è in vario modo invocata perché accolga e protegga il defunto, anche attraverso espressioni formulari – è di carattere votivo, come quella analizzata in questa sede. Purtroppo la quasi totalità delle dediche è di provenienza ignota ed è impossibile ricondurle, con una qualche verisimiglianza, al più noto *aedes Telluris*, che nel 268 a.C. venne dedicato a Roma nella zona delle *Carinae*[8]. Dopo alcuni interventi di ripristino e abbellimento nella tarda repubblica, una ricostruzione e forse una nuova configurazione del tempio e del quartiere della *Tellus* si ebbe certamente con i Severi: oltre al frammento della *Forma Urbis*, varie fonti ci parlano in tal senso, testimoniando una fase in cui il culto della Terra (Madre), non solo a Roma, conobbe un nuovo impulso.

A Roma *Tellus* è venerata attraverso tabella votiva, forse relativa a un donario, di provenienza e conservazione ignota[9] (fig. 1).

Deae Telluri
sacrum.
M(arcus) Aurelius
Threptus
fecit.

7 *CIL*, VI 29609 = 34191= *CLE* 974; EDR144568; *CIL*, VI 35887, cfr. p. 3920 = *CLE* 1532 = *ILS* 8168; *CIL*, VI 770, cfr. pp. 3006, 3757 = 30828 = *CIL*, I^2 995 = *ILS* 3950; Solin 1975, 6 nr. 1; *CIL*, VI 84, cfr. p. 3755 = *ILS* 3950; EDR121362; *CIL*, VI 16398 cfr. p. 3914 = *ILS* 08008 = SupplIt Imagines – Roma 05, 4892; EDR 162083; *CIL*, VI 31171 = *ILS* 4832 = Speidel 1994, pp. 59–60, nr. 25; EDR029237; *CIL*, VI 772 cfr. p. 3757 = *ILS* 1522; EDR149374; *CIL*, VI 3731, cfr. pp. 3007, 3728 = 31052 = *ILS* 3951; EDR121650; *CIL*, VI 771, cfr. pp. 3006, 3757; EDR148411; oltre a *CIL*, VI 769, presentata e commentata più avanti.

8 È ancora discussa l'ubicazione esatta delle *Carinae* (Serv. *Aen*. 8.361) e, di conseguenza, quella del tempio di *Tellus*. Si vedano, con diverse posizioni: Ziolkowski 1992, 155–162; Palombi 1997, 140–168; Coarelli 2000, 2010 e 2019, 3; *CIL*, VI 113; EDR14898059–376; Amoroso 2007; Färber 2012, tutti con fonti e ampia bibliografia.

9 *CIL*, VI 769, cfr. pp. 838, 3757, 30827 = *CIL*, VI 30827 = *ILS* 3956.

Nell'*additamentum* al Corpus (30827) si ricorda come, nella *Descrittione della città di Rieti* di Pompeo Angelotti (1635), la lapide risulti conservata a Rieti, a casa Vecchiarelli; lo stesso Angelotti inoltre trascrive gli elementi onomastici del dedicante e il verbo di dedica su un'unica riga.

Marcus Aurelius Threptus è un liberto imperiale o un suo discendente; il suo cognome a Roma conosce ampia diffusione. Conosciamo due suoi omonimi: il primo, con ogni probabilità vissuto un secolo più tardi, commemora a Ostia (la moglie?) *Faustina*[10]; il secondo è un liberto procuratore di Frigia. Questo secondo personaggio compare in una lunga iscrizione di *Eulandra* (attuale Sülmenli-Akar Çay, in Turchia), che ricorda la disputa in tre tempi intercorsa tra due villaggi (*Anossa* e *Antimacheia*), confinanti con una grande proprietà imperiale che si estendeva tra *Synnada* e *Docimium*. *Aurelius Threptus* è uno dei tre procuratori attivi in epoca severiana, chiamati a intervenire nella contesa tra i due centri a proposito delle *angareia* che ciascun villaggio doveva fornire per il *cursus publicus*[11].

L'iscrizione di *Eulandra* è stata più volte riconsiderata, di recente anche da Marco Vitale[12], che si sofferma sul profilo amministrativo della Frigia in epoca imperiale, suggerendo l'ipotesi che si trattasse di una vera e propria sotto-provincia dell'Asia, affidata a procuratori di rango libertino, che rispondevano soltanto al governatore senatorio e godevano di una sostanziale autonomia di azione.

I compiti affidati a questi procuratori liberti sono di notevole interesse e possono costituire, a mio avviso, un trait d'union con la nostra iscrizione: essi erano incaricati di risolvere dispute legali anche relative a confini (come nel caso dell'iscrizione di *Eulandra*), di occuparsi delle requisizioni e di garantire l'esportazione di prodotti locali, in particolare il celebre 'marmo frigio' ricavato dalle cave di *Docimium*.

Ora, noi sappiamo dalla documentazione provinciale (in particolare dalla Dalmazia e delle province danubiane) che buona parte delle dediche alla Terra sono realizzate da funzionari imperiali e personale subalterno (in qualche caso anche da magistrati locali), incaricati di amministrare miniere/cave/saline[13].

---

10 *CIL*, XIV 668; EDR145910 (con datazione compresa tra il III e la metà del IV secolo): *D(is) M(anibus). / M(arcus) Aur(elius) Thre/ptus Faustinae / fecit / b(ene) m(erenti)*.

11 Frend 1956.

12 Levick 2002, 63–65 nr. 57; Hirt 2010; Vitale 2015 (che cita *Aurelius Threptus* alle pp. 37 nr. 11 e 39).

13 Anche nelle province di area danubiana (in Dalmazia, nelle Pannonie, in Dacia e nella *Moesia superior*), *Terra Mater* ricorre con relativa frequenza, esclusivamente in dediche votive e quasi sempre ha connotazioni ben riconoscibili, essendo diffusa nei distretti minerari: si distingue la serie di sei altari offerti alla dea per la salvezza dell'imperatore regnante e della famiglia imperiale (da Settimio Severo a Filippo l'Arabo), rinvenuta presso l'odierno villaggio di Ljubija (Bosnia), al centro del distretto delle miniere di ferro dalla valle della Sana. Il fatto che le dediche venissero fatte sempre nello stesso giorno, il 21 aprile, ha fatto pensare a una cerimonia annuale (forse legata al *dies Natalis Romae*). Si vedano al riguardo, oltre a Gesztelyi 1971, 1977 e 1981: Sanader 1996; Dusanic 1999; Piso 2004, 296; Mráv, Ottományi 2005; Nemeti e Nemeti 2010, 119–123; e, da ultimo, Vitelli Casella 2017. Su *Terra Mater* e le miniere di sale, si rimanda agli studi di Lucrețiu Mihalescu-Bîrliba, in particolare Mihailescu-Bîrliba 2018. In un numero più contenuto di testimonianze, prevalentemente concentrate in Pannonia, *Terra* (da sola o invocata con *Iuppiter Optimus Maximus* o con l'intera triade capitolina) è la *Genetrix*, la terra d'origine, identificata con il territorio di provenienza (Gesztelyi 1981, 448–449).

L'omonimia del procuratore di Frigia e del dedicante alla *Tellus* di Roma naturalmente non dà certezza sull'identificazione del personaggio, cui tuttavia il legame tra l'attività estrattiva del marmo nella regione dove il procuratore era operativo e la dedica con la divinità 'patrona' di tale attività darebbe sostanza. A questa considerazione è da aggiungere l'onomastica del dedicante romano: prenome e gentilizio rimandano in ogni caso a un orizzonte cronologico di fine II e inizi del III secolo (cui certamente appartiene il *Threptus* frigio)[14].

Le due dediche dall'Italia romana

Nel resto della Penisola (e in territorio istriano) le iscrizioni di *Terra Mater* sono solo sette, molto disperse e così distribuite: una dall'*ager Beneventanus* e una da *Volsinii*, qui di seguito considerate; una da *Altinum*[15], una da Aquileia[16], due da *Pula* e dal territorio[17]; una da Ostia[18]. La loro natura è esclusivamente sacra. Solo l'iscrizione ostiense ricorda esplicitamente l'offerta nel 142 d. C. di un *signum* della dea per la sede dei dendrofori.

La prima (e più antica) delle iscrizioni italiche è stata rinvenuta nell'*ager Beneventanus*[19]. Si tratta di una lastra di provenienza ignota, un tempo utilizzata come stipite di finestra nella casa del barone Latini a Santa Maria a Toro, nella provincia, appunto, di Benevento e ora forse perduta. La lapide fu vista da Dressel che fornì la scheda a Mommsen per il *CIL*; la riporto completa di apparato per la discussione sulle integrazioni suggerite (fig. 2).

L. Septim[ius . f(ilius)],
L. Coc(c)eiu[s . f(ilius)],
IIIvir(i) [i(ure) d(icundo)],
[l]ucar T[elluri (?)],
d(e) s(enatus) s(ententia), [dederunt?].

---

14 Priva di fondamento, a mio avviso, l'idea di Gesztelyi 1981, 450, il quale propone una datazione di epoca claudia.

15 *AE* 1953, 97b, località Canevere (*Altinum*): *Terrae matri.*

16 Brusin 1991–1993, vol. I 359 = *ILS* 3952; EDR093896, Aquileia. Cfr. Alföldy 1984, 93, nr. 67: *Terrae Matri. / C(aius) Baebius C(ai) f(ilius) Pal(atina) / Antiochianus, / eq(uo) p(ublico), decur(io) / Aquil(eiensis) et / C(aius) Baebius Antiochus, / IIIIII vir Aquileiae, / ius IIII liberorum / consecutus, ex voto.*

17 Inscriptiones Italiae X.1, 653 (da cui è tratto il disegno ricostruttivo); EDR139394, , *Pula*: *Terrae Matri, e[x] / imperatu, Sex. Tettiu[s ..]*; Inscr. Ital. X.1, 23 (da cui è tratto il disegno ricostruttivo); EDR072567, isola di S. Caterina, presso Pula: *Terra[e] Matri / Flavi[a M]oschis / [v(otum) s(olvit)]*.

18 *CIL*, XIV 67 = *CIMRM* 286 = *CCCA* III, 413; EDR144050, Ostia (ora conservata ai Musei Vaticani): *Sex(tus) Annius Merops, / honoratus, dendrophoris / Ostiensium signum Terrae Matris / d(ono) d(edit). Dedicat(um) XIII K(alendas) Mai(as) L(ucio) Cuspio Rufino, / L(ucio) Statio Quadrato co(n)s(ulibus).*

19 *CIL*, IX 2117 = *CIL*, I² 1730 (p. 1030) = *ILLRP* 556, S. Maria del Toro.

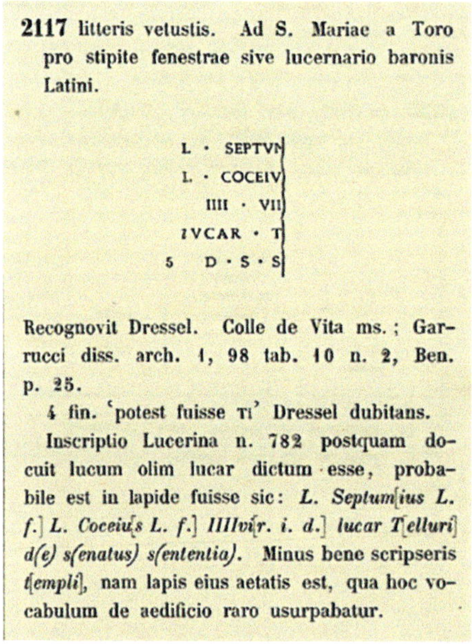

2117 litteris vetustis. Ad S. Mariae a Toro pro stipite fenestrae sive lucernario baronis Latini.

L · SEPTVN
L · COCEIV
IIII · VII
*l*VCAR · T
D · S · S

Recognovit Dressel. Colle de Vita ms.; Garrucci diss. arch. 1, 98 tab. 10 n. 2, Ben. p. 25.

4 fin. 'potest fuisse TI' Dressel dubitans.

Inscriptio Lucerina n. 782 postquam docuit lucum olim lucar dictum esse, probabile est in lapide fuisse sic: *L. Septum[ius L. f.] L. Coceiu[s L. f.] IIIIvi[r. i. d.] lucar T[elluri] d(e) s(enatus) s(ententia).* Minus bene scripseris *t[empli]*, nam lapis eius aetatis est, qua hoc vocabulum de aedificio raro usurpabatur.

Fig. 2: *CIL*, IX 2117 = *CIL*, I 1730 (p. 1030) = *ILLRP* 556, S. Maria del Toro (iscrizione perduta: immagine tratta dal Corpus)

Il carattere lacunoso dell'iscrizione non consente di determinare con certezza se la divinità nominata sia *Tellus*. Anche se, va detto, l'ipotesi, avanzata da Mommsen in apparato, pare cogliere nel vero, per ragioni diverse: oltre che per lo spazio a disposizione per integrazioni nelle righe precedenti e nella successiva, per il presumibile luogo di origine della lastra, dove la presenza di *Tellus* ben si spiega, per l'epoca di appartenenza dell'iscrizione. L'offerta di un bosco sacro (a *Tellus*?) è fatta, in ottemperanza a una delibera del senato locale, dai quattuorviri *Lucius Septimius* e *Lucius Cocceius*, ricordati prima del nome della divinità: i loro gentilizi ricorrono entrambi a *Beneventum*, anche se in epoca ampiamente successiva[20]. Resta difficile, per l'irreperibilità dell'iscrizione, definire a quale monumento la lastra appartenesse.

Nel lemma del Corpus si parla di *litterae vetustae* che, considerate insieme all'uso del termine *lucar* in luogo di *lucus* – raro ed epigraficamente non attestato oltre il I secolo d.C. – e alla probabile assenza di cognome dei due magistrati, orienta per un inquadramento cronologico entro i primi decenni del I sec. d.C.

La terza e ultima dedica del nostro piccolo corpus è riportata su una lastra di rivestimento rinvenuta nella basilica flavia a *Volsinii* (nell'augustea *regio VII*)[21] (fig. 3).

A(ulus) L(ucius) Seii A(uli) f(ilii), curatores aquae,
ex aere conlato
Fonti Telluri sacr(um).

Due *curatores aquae*, membri della medesima *gens* e fratelli, *Aulus Seius* e *Lucius Seius* (anche loro, come i quattuorviri beneventani, senza cognome), con fondi appositamente raccolti, dedicano un monumento a *Fons* e *Tellus*, due divinità telluriche. Raymond Bloch osservava che tale associazione aveva un precedente in area osca, presso il santuario di

20 *CIL*, IX 1538 = *ILS* 4185, 228 d.C. (*Septimius*); *CIL*, IX 1887; EDR103692 (II sec. d.C.); *NSA* 2008/2009, p. 352 s. nr. 16; EDR129418, III sec. d.C. (*Cocceius*).

21 Corbier 1983 = *AE* 1983, 395 e Bloch 1987 = *AE* 1987, 362; EDR079087.

Mefitis a Rossano di Vaglio; un elemento che lo induceva a far risalire a epoca pre-romana il legame tra le due personificazioni. La sua ipotesi tuttavia si fondava su un'errata lettura del documento RV-52 del corpus epigrafico del santuario di *Mefitis* a Rossano di Vaglio; una recente e più verosimile lettura del testo ha portato a escludere tale abbinamento e dunque il collegamento con la dedica di *Volsinii*[22].

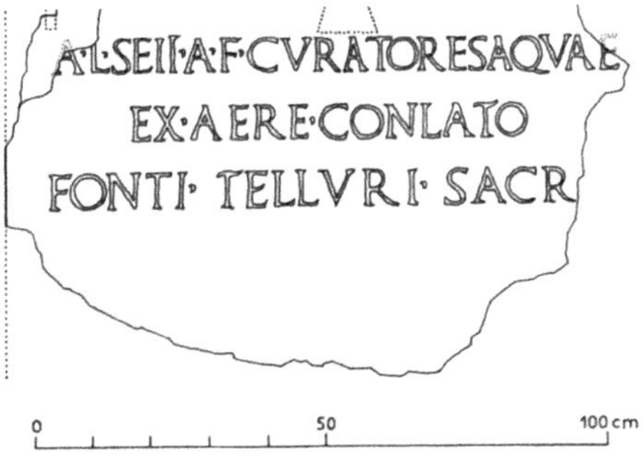

Fig. 3: Corbier 1983 = *AE* 1983, 395; EDR07907 con altra bibliografia (disegno ricostruttivo tratto dall'articolo di M. Corbier, p. 722, fig. 3)

La datazione della lastra volsiniese è resa possibile dall'indicazione della *cura aquae* che non può essere precedente la comparsa a Roma nell'II a.C. del *curator aquarum*, come giustamente osservato da Mireille Corbier (la quale mette anche in rilievo la conferma, grazie al nostro testo, dell'origine volsiniese della *gens Seia*). Siamo dunque tra fine I a.C. e primi decenni del I d.C.

Sono ben consapevole che il numero assai ridotto di iscrizioni che compongono il dossier epigrafico su *Tellus* non consenta osservazioni di carattere generale; alcune puntualizzazioni paiono tuttavia opportune.

In nessuno dei tre casi considerati il nome della *Tellus* è accompagnato da un epiteto; laddove non di rado, nelle iscrizioni in lingua latina, *Terra mater* è ricordata come *sancta*, *genetrix* o *conservatrix*, protettrice del riposo dei defunti e garanzia del ciclo vitale.

La provenienza delle iscrizioni è varia: la dedica di Roma, della quale non conosciamo dettagli, si può tuttavia senz'altro riferire alla città e non al territorio; così come la dedica di *Volsinii*, rinvenuta nella basilica flavia. La dedica dei quattuorviri di S. Maria a Toro, se il luogo di collocazione originaria non era troppo distante da quello di conservazione, era originariamente situata nel territorio di *Beneventum*, dove evidentemente si trovava il *lucus* e forse un sacello consacrati alla dea.

Se le due dediche italiche provengono da aree tra loro assai lontane e non disponiamo di elementi per avanzare ipotesi attendibili sui monumenti a cui appartenevano (are? basi di statue? Si vd. più avanti), comune è tuttavia l'orizzonte cronologico, compreso tra l'epoca triumvirale e l'inizio dell'età imperiale.

Pare particolarmente preziosa l'indicazione dei dedicanti in tutte e tre le offerte considerate: va detto infatti che, in buona parte delle dediche imperiali a *Terra Mater*, essi non sono esplicitati, lasciando immaginare l'espressione devozionale collettiva di una comunità o di un'associazione; o la volontà del dedicante privato di rimanere anonimo (un orientamento, d'altronde, tutt'altro che raro nell'epigrafia sacra). Nelle iscrizioni di *Volsinii* e di S. Maria a Toro si tratta di magistrati, evidentemente incaricati e in rappresentanza della

22 L'iscrizione RV-52 è compresa nella raccolta di Lejeune 1980, 445 s. (con immagini). La nuova lettura si deve a Del Tutto Palma 1989–1990, part. 179–184 (con bibliografia precedente), ed è accolta da Crawford et alii 2011, vol 3, 1397 s.: *Potentia* 21.

comunità di appartenenza. A Roma viceversa l'offerente è un privato, che agisce a titolo personale, e non ricorda dati biografici né un'eventuale carica rivestita.

Resta da rivolgersi il quesito al quale è (in parte) più complesso rispondere: perché *Tellus* e non *Terra mater*?

A *Volsinii* la divinità è abbinata a *Fons* e sono la natura del territorio e in particolare le sue particolarità geologiche (una faglia profonda e la sorgente) della collina di Civita a chiarire il motivo dell'offerta, posta in luogo pubblico. Non sappiamo se i *curatores aquae* abbiano offerto un *signum* della dea; forse più semplicemente hanno monumentalizzato il luogo da dove l'acqua scaturiva, scegliendo di rivolgersi non solo a *Fons* ma anche alla *Tellus*, che ne rende possibile la fuoriuscita.

A *Beneventum*, fatta salva la natura lacunosa dell'iscrizione e l'incertezza che permane sulle integrazioni – e in particolare quella relativa al nome della dea -, viene da pensare a un culto rurale, forse risalente. L'iscrizione poteva essere apposta a una base o direttamente su un edificio.

Del protagonista del documento urbano si è detto: è tutt'altro che certo che *M(arcus) Aurelius Threptus* possa identificarsi con il procuratore severiano, così come, ancora una volta, è impossibile definire il luogo dove la dedica è stata posta e il monumento relativo (un'ara?). L'accostamento con il *Threptus* di *Eulandra*, in considerazione del suo ruolo, contribuirebbe a individuare il carattere che della dea si voleva sottolineare (in Grecia e in Oriente, ancora nel III secolo, più *Tellus* che Terra e molto vicina a Demetra)[23], connesso alla stabilità della terra e al sottosuolo.

Come opportunamente sottolinea Gesztely, le poche testimonianze (epigrafiche, numismatiche, archeologiche) di cui disponiamo non consentono di chiarire cosa la Terra rappresentasse nei tempi più antichi; e se i caratteri originari di una potente dea (di origine italica?) fossero stati progressivamente accantonati per conferirle, grazie all'interpretazione filosofica della tarda repubblica e all'azione della politica augustea, una nuova fisionomia[24].

Per quel che le tre epigrafi di *Tellus* di Roma e dell'Italia romana ci permettono di rilevare, non sembra un caso che esse si concentrino in due momenti chiave: l'epoca triumvirale, quando tale nuova fisionomia si stava definendo e *Terra Mater* era andata affiancandosi alla *Tellus*, ancora prevalente[25]; e, a distanza di un paio di secoli, l'età severiana, quando il culto della *Tellus*, in particolare a Roma (dove il grande tempio a lei dedicato e l'area in cui sorgeva ottennero una nuova sistemazione) e nelle province africane, ebbe un nuovo impulso e conobbe una ripresa degna di attenzione.

23 Weinstock 1933 e 1934; Opelt 1962; Gesztelyi 1981.

24 Gesztelyi 1981, 455; Id.1981–1982.

25 *Terra mater*, "Madre Terra", è attestata solo a partire dal II sec. a. C.: Jennings-Rose, Scheid 2016.

Bibliografia

Alföldy, G. 1984. Römische Statuen in Venetia et Histria. Epigraphische Quellen, Heidelberg.

Amoroso, A. 2007. Il tempio di Tellus e il quartiere della praefectura urbana, Workshop-ArchClass 4, 53–84.

Bel Faïda, A. 2008. Le culte de la fertilité en Afrique romaine: Tellus – Terra Mater; témoignages épigraphiques, in P. Ruggeri, J. González, C. Vismara, R. Zucca (eds.), Le ricchezze dell'Africa: risorse, produzioni, scambi (Atti del XVII convegno di studio 'L'Africa romana', Sevilla, 14–17 dicembre 2006), Roma, 183–193.

Bloch, R. 1987. Fons et Tellus et la Civitas, MEFRAnt 99.2, 563–571.

Brusin, G. B. 1991–1993. Inscriptiones Aquileiae, 3 voll., Udine.

Carandini, A. 2003[2]. La nascita di Roma. Dèi, lari, eroi e uomini all'alba di una civiltà, Torino, 559–576.

Coarelli, F. 2000. Tellus, aedes, LTUR 5, 24 sq.

Coarelli, F. 2010. La basilica di Massenzio e la Praefectura Urbis, in G. Bonamente, R. Lizzi (eds.), Istituzioni, carismi ed esercizio del potere (IV–VI secolo d. C.), Bari, 133–146.

Coarelli F. 2019. Statio. I luoghi dell'amministrazione nell'antica Roma, Roma.

Corbier, M. 1983. La famille de Séjan à Volsinii: la dédicace des Seii, curatores aquae, MEFRAnt 95.2, 719–756.

Crawford, M. H. et alii 2011. Imagines Italicae. A Corpus of Italic Inscriptions (Bulletin of the Institute of Classical Studies, Supplement 110), 3 voll., London.

Degrassi, A. 1963. Fasti anni Numani et Iuliani. InscrItal, 13.2, Roma.

Del Tutto Palma, L. 1989–1990. Due 'voces nihili': lucani *udo e *numulo, StudEtr 57, 179–186.

Dumézil, G. 2001. La religione romana arcaica, Milano (ediz. ital. del testo francese del 1974).

Dušanić, S. 1999. The miners'cults in Illyricum, Pallas 50, 129–139.

Färber, R. 2012. Die Amtssitze der Stadtpräfekten im spätantiken Rom und Konstantinopel, in F. Arnold, A. Busch, R. Haensch, U. Wulf-Rheidt (eds.), Orte der Herrschaft. Charakteristika von antiken Machtzentren, Leidorf, 49–71.

Fishwick, D. 1996. On the origins of Africa Proconsularis III: the era of the Cereres again, Antiquités africaines 32, 13–36.

Frend, W. H. C. 1956. A third-Century Inscription relating to angareia in Phrygia, JRS 46, 46–56.

Gesztelyi, T. 1971. The Cult of Terra Mater in the Danubian Basin lands, ACD 7, 85–90.

Gesztelyi, T. 1972. The Cult of Tellus-Terra Mater in North-Africa, ACD 8, 75–84.

Gesztelyi, T. 1977. Eine singuläre Terra Mater Darstellung aus Sopianae, ACD 13, 45–49.

Gesztelyi, T. 1981. Terra mater in der Zeit des Prinzipats, ANRW II 17.1, 429–456.

Gesztelyi, T. 1981–1982. Terra Mater in der Religionspolitik des Augustus, ACD 17, 141–147.

Gesztelyi, T. 1996. Zur Religiosität der spaträmischen heidnischen Aristokratie (Datierungsversuch der Precatio Terrae Matris), SpecNova 11.1, 49–58.

Ghisellini, E. 1994. Tellus, LIMC VII.1, 879–889.
Hirt, A.M. 2010, Imperial Mines and Quarries in the Roman World: Organizational Aspects 27 BC-AD 235, Oxford.
Jennings Rose, H., Scheid, J. 2016. Tellus, in Oxford Classical Dictionary online [https://doi.org/10.1093/acrefore/9780199381135.013.6270; ultima consultazione 20.09.2023).
Lejeune, M. 1980. Inscriptions de Rossano di Vaglio 1974–1979, Atti della Accademia Nazionale dei Lincei. Classe di Scienze Morali, Storiche e Filologiche. Rendiconti, Roma, ser. VIII, 35, 445–466.
Levick, B. 2002. The Government of the Roman Empire. A Sourcebook, London.
Marcattili, F. 2020. Il cibo e la dea: il magmentarium di Tellus e il lectisternium di Cerere, RA 69, 103–115.
Mihailescu-Bîrliba, L. 2018. The importance of salt exploitation in Roman Dacia. The case of Ocna Mures, JAHA 5.4, 32–36.
Mráv, Z., Ottományi, K. 2005. A pagus Herculius és vicusainak Terra Mater oltára Budaörsről, *SpecNova* 19, 2005, 71–118.
Nemeti, I., Nemeti, S. 2010. The Barbarians within. Illyrian colonists in Roman Dacia, Studia historica 28, 109–133.
Opelt, I. 1962. Tellus/Terra mater, RAC 5, 433.
Palombi, D. 1997. Tra Palatino ed Esquilino: Velia, Carinae, Fagutal. Storia urbana di tre quartieri di Roma antica, Roma.
Piso, I. 2004. Gli Illiri ad Alburnus Maior, in G. Urso (ed.), Dall'Adriatico al Danubio. L'Illirico nell'età greca e romana (Atti del convegno internazionale Cividale del Friuli, 25–27 settembre 2003), Pisa, 271–308.
Prescendi, F. 2015. Tellus, i semi e la vacca pregna, in M. Bettini, G. Pucci (eds.), Terrantica. Volti, miti e immagini della terra nel mondo antico (Mostra, Roma, Colosseo 23 aprile – 11 ottobre 2015), Milano, 180–187.
Ricci, C. cs. Tellus/Terra mater nell'epigrafia di Roma e dell'Italia romana, Studi e Materiali di Storia delle Religioni (2024, in stampa).
Sanader, M. 1996, Novi aspekti kulta božice Terra Mater, Opvscvla archaeologica 20, 1, 119–130.
Solin, H. 1975. Epigraphische Untersuchungen in Rom und Umgebung, Helsinki.
Speidel, M.-P. 1994. Die Denkmäler der Kaiserreiter. Equites singulares Augusti, Köln.
Strong, E. 1937. Terra Mater or Italia, JRS 27, 114–126.
Vitale, M. 2015. Imperial Phrygia. A Procuratorial Province governed by liberti Augusti, Philia 1, 33–45.
Vitelli Casella, M. 2017. Un esempio di comunicazione politica nell'Antichità: le iscrizioni pro salute nella provincia romana di Dalmazia, in M. Corbier, G. Sauron (eds.), Langages et communication: écrits, images, sons, Paris, 35–47.
Weinstock, St. 1933. Tellus, Glotta 22, 153–162.
Weinstock, St. 1934. Tellus, RE V.A.1, 791–806.
Ziolkowski, A. 1992. The temples of mid-Republican Rome and their historical and topographical context, Roma.

Cn. Piso Cn. F. IIIVIR
Una problematica tessera in avorio da Aquileia e la presenza dei Calpurnii Pisones in Istria e Liburnia

Claudio Zaccaria

La felice occasione di rendere omaggio a Ioan Piso mi ha suggerito di riprendere in esame un singolare piccolo oggetto conservato nel caveau del Museo Archeologico Nazionale di Aquileia[1], che mi ripromettevo da tempo di ripubblicare, tentando una rilettura, un inquadramento e un commento[2].

Si tratta di una *tessera* in avorio a doppio tronco di cono (∅ cm 1,75; spess. cm 65), che presenta al centro di entrambe le facce un foro da compasso e sfregi di varie dimensioni sul dritto e particolarmente sul rovescio, interessato anche da una vistosa scheggiatura. Le superfici sono levigate e recano due iscrizioni a caratteri incisi (alt. lett.: D/ 0,3 cm; R/ 0,9 cm).

D/ (fig. 1a): CN. PISO. CN. f. IIIVIR, tracciata ad andamento circolare lungo il bordo con lettura dal centro; lettere leggermente apicate con solco profondo e modulo regolare, tranne VIR che presenta tratti più leggeri e irregolari con le tre lettere compresse nello spazio ridotto, indizio di un'esecuzione non calibrata; interpunzioni regolarmente disposte.

R/ (fig. 1b): nelle edizioni precedenti si è proposto di leggere un nesso VR ad andamento retrogrado, interpretato dubitativamente come *V(rbs) R(oma)*; diversamente dalla grande V tracciata al centro del campo epigrafico con solco profondo e pronunciate apicature, la presunta R risulta incisa con tratto incerto, e potrebbe essere uno sfregio come altri, meno profondi, visibili sulla superficie.

---

1 Come si ricava dal numero di inventario (R.C. 1497), l'oggetto, rinvenuto ad Aquileia in data e circostanze non note era già presente nella Raccolta Comunale che ha preceduto l'Imperial Regio Museo dello Stato inaugurato nel 1882, ma è stato reso noto solo nel catalogo della mostra "Instrumenta inscripta Latina: sezione aquileiese" tenutasi ad Aquileia dal 22 marzo al 12 maggio 1992 (Blason Scarel 1992) e ripresentato nel catalogo della mostra "Made in Roma and Aquileia", tenutasi ad Aquileia dal 12 febbraio al 31 maggio 2017 (Fedele 2017).

2 Ringrazio la Direttrice del Museo, dott.ssa Marta Novello, per la concessione a pubblicare qui le immagini e la dott.ssa Annarita Lepre, funzionario archivista, per avermi fornito sollecitamente le ottime foto.

Fig. 1a: Tessera d'avorio (MAN Aquileia, inv. R. C. 1497, foto di Gianluca Baronchelli)

A quanto posso vedere, l'oggetto non trova confronti puntuali e non si inserisce nelle serie tipologiche delle *tesserae* finora studiate, che comunque sono per lo più di incerta interpretazione[3].

Come per altri oggetti simili rinvenuti ad Aquileia[4], non è nemmeno da escludere la possibilità che si tratti dell'opera di un falsario, anche se in questo caso non se ne coglie lo scopo e non vi sono elementi per individuarne l'aggancio nella tradizione aquileiese ed eventualmente l'autore.

Mentre la scritta sul rovescio rimane problematica[5], anche se è probabile che si tratti di un'indicazione numerale, la legenda sul dritto va evidentemente sciolta con *Cn(aeus) Piso Cn(aei) f(ilius) (trium)vir* e il personaggio, che presenta l'omissione del gentilizio tipica dei *Calpurnii Pisones* sia nelle fonti letterarie sia nelle testimonianze epigrafiche e numismatiche, può essere identificato con il *Cn. (Calpurnius) Piso* che fu console nel 7 a. C., governatore dell'*Hispania citerior*, dell'*Africa proconsularis* e della *Syria*[6], ed è soprattutto

3 Ancora valida la casistica esposta in Rostovtzew 1905 e in RE V A.l, 1934, 851–854, s.v. Tessera (K. Regling). Vedi anche Gülbay, Kireç 2008, 6–19 e 48–54; Küter 2019, 84, figg. 18–20 e 92.

4 Ad es. la tessera plumbea con l'effigie di Aquileia e la legenda CHRYSOPOLIS AQVILEIA (Maionica 1899; falsa per Kubitschek 1909, 38–39 [= trad. it. 101–102] e Buora 2008).

5 Eck, Caballos, Fernandez 1996, nota 71.

6 RE III, 1 (1897), cc. 1380–1382, s.v. Calpurnius 70 e Suppl. I (1903), c. 271 (A. Groag); PIR² (1936), 58–61: C 287 Cn. Calpurnius Piso, consul a. 747 = 7 a. C. (E. Groag). Su di lui vedi Eck, Caballos, Fernandez 1996, 71–77.

Fig. 1b: Tessera d'avorio (MAN Aquileia, inv. R. C. 1497, foto di Gianluca Baronchelli)

famoso per essere stato sospettato dell'uccisione di Germanico ed essersi suicidato durante il processo, che si concluse comunque con una condanna. Le vicende, su cui abbiamo le testimonianze delle fonti letterarie[7] e delle copie in bronzo del *Senatus consultum de Gnaeo Pisone patre* rinvenute quasi tutte nella penisola iberica[8], sono troppo note per essere qui ripetute[9]. Egli ricoperse all'inizio della carriera senatoria, la carica di *triumvir aere argento auro flando feriundo*, facendo coniare, da solo o con i colleghi *L. Naevius Surdinus* e *C. Plotius Rufus,* diverse emissioni per Augusto, che oggi si tende a datare nel 15 a. C.[10]. Si è pertanto ritenuto che si riferisse a questa carica la menzione del triumvirato presente nella legenda del dritto[11]. Ma è stato osservato che la semplice dicitura III VIR (priva della consueta specificazione A. A.A. F.F che è sempre presente nelle legende monetali) potreb-

7 Tac., Ann. 2, 55–58 e 69–82; 3, 7–18. Vedi anche Suet., Tib. 52; Calig. 2; Vitell. 2; Plin., n. h. 11, 187; Dio 57,18, 9–10.

8 Edizioni con commento: Eck, Caballos, Fernandez 1996; Caballos, Eck, Fernandez 1996; Cooley 2023. Riassume la storia dei ritrovamenti e della pubblicazione dei nove frammenti noti Manni 2016, 52–54, note 37–38.

9 Un'utile sintesi in Manni 2016, 40–52.

10 RIC I² Augustus 380–382, 390–396; vedi anche Online Coins of the Roman Empire (OCRE: http://numismatics.org/ocre/results?q=authority_facet%3A%22Augustus%22+AND+issuer_facet%3A%22Cn.+PISO+Cn.F%22&lang=en). Tradizionalmente erano datate nel 23 o 22 a. C.: per i problemi di datazione vedi Burnett 1977, 48–52.

11 Blason Scarel 1992; Fedele 2017.

be anche riferirsi ad altri collegi di tre membri istituiti in varie occasioni, ad esempio "per i provvedimenti nelle città fuori Roma che venivano avviati dal Senato o forse anche da Augusto" e, a Roma stessa, nelle operazioni della *lectio senatus* o nella *recognitio equitum*, "ad esempio come strumento con cui i singoli cavalieri venivano assegnati (o sorteggiati) a uno dei triumviri per la *recognitio*" [12].

Allo stato della questione non è comunque possibile proporre una soluzione certa per la carica di *Cn. Piso* menzionata nella legenda ed è anche problematico stabilire quale fosse la funzione della *tessera*.

In via del tutto ipotetica è stato proposto di interpretare la *tessera* come "contrassegno ufficiale utilizzabile in ambito monetale/bancario"[13], ma non è chiaro quale potesse essere una sua utilizzazione in quel contesto ed è difficilmente spiegabile perché sarebbe giunta ad Aquileia[14].

Un eventuale impiego nelle procedure della *recognitio equitum* potrebbe spiegare teoricamente la presenza ad Aquileia: infatti, come è stato osservato, "una tessera di questo tipo poteva essere facilmente portata a casa da un cavaliere di Aquileia" [15]. La mancanza di confronti concreti impedisce però di considerare questa eventualità come risolutiva.

Rimanendo nel campo delle ipotesi, e ammettendo che al rovescio sia incisa un'indicazione numerale, si potrebbe pensare di praticare un'altra via per prospettare un'interpretazione dell'oggetto.

La tessera, infatti, potrebbe essere stata un contrassegno di riconoscimento per l'ingresso a luoghi di spettacolo o di svago e benessere oppure una di quelle *tesserae* che venivano distribuite al popolo dall'autorità centrale o locale o da eminenti personaggi (e in età imperiale soprattutto dall'imperatore) in occasione di particolari ricorrenze pubbliche e che poi potevano venir esibite da chi le aveva ricevute per riscuotere il corrispettivo del donativo in denaro o servizi[16].

Entrambe queste soluzioni presuppongono, però, di ammettere che in qualche circostanza *Cn. Piso* fosse stato presente ad Aquileia, dove, però, la documentazione epigrafica offre solo testimonianze di *Calpurnii* che non possono essere messi in relazione con il nostro personaggio.

Uno spiraglio, comunque, si apre considerando le prime fasi della carriera di *Cn. Piso*.

È stato, infatti, suggerito che il giovane Pisone, più o meno coetaneo di Tiberio, potrebbe aver prestato servizio con lui come tribuno militare nelle guerre spagnole di Augusto (26–25 a.C.) e in seguito potrebbe aver partecipato alle campagne dalmato-illiriche[17], forse anche come uno dei *legati* di Tiberio tra il 16 e il 15 a.C.[18]. In quelle occasioni e

12 Eck, Caballos, Fernandez 1996, 73, con la bibliografia precedente.
13 Blason Scarel 1992; Fedele 2017.
14 Eck, Caballos, Fernandez 1996, 73.
15 Eck, Caballos, Fernandez 1996, 73 nota 74.
16 Per alcuni esempi vedi Kuhn 2014 (a proposito di Gülbay, Kireç 2008, nn. 225, 230, 233, 235); Geelmuyden Bulgurlu, Hazinedar Coşkun 2023.
17 Syme 1986, 369; Eck, Caballos, Fernandez 1996, 76.
18 Hofmann-Löbl 1996, 237.

negli anni successivi, considerati i suoi stretti legami col Princeps [19], egli avrebbe potuto frequentare Aquileia dove Augusto e Tiberio soggiornarono a più riprese[20]. Una possibile partecipazione alle operazioni militari in Dalmazia potrebbe essere una ragionevole motivazione anche per il dono a lui fatto da Augusto di un *saltus in Hillirico*[21], di cui si apprende l'esistenza nel *S.c. de Cn. Pisone patre*, con la precisazione che ne fu richiesta – ufficialmente per por fine agli abusi suoi e dei suoi servi e liberti che avevano provocato proteste da parte delle comunità confinanti – la restituzione da parte di Tiberio, che così lo sottrasse al *patrimonium* confiscato a *Cn. Piso*, che invece poi fu diviso per iniziativa del Senato tra i due figli maschi[22], con un legato a titolo di dote e di *peculium* per la figlia[23].

La presenza dei *Pisones* in Liburnia è testimoniata anche dai possedimenti sull'isola di Pag (l'antica *Cissa*) di *Calpurnia, L(uci) Pisonis aug(uris) / f(ilia), Cn(aei) Pisonis neptis*[24], che appare come committente di ben tre offerte votive rinvenute in località Caska (Novalja)[25]. La proprietà l'aveva evidentemente ereditata dal padre, *L. Cornelius Piso augur*[26], console nel 1 a.C. e fratello del nostro *Cn. Piso* (entrambi figli di *L. Calpurnius Piso Frugi*, console nel 23 a.C.[27]: a lui si dovrebbe riferire anche la *fistula aquaria*, rinvenuta presso Caska nelle rovine dell'acquedotto, che recava un marchio, visto nel XVI secolo e tramandato con lettura errata[28], che deve essere necessariamente corretto in *Calpurni Pisonis*[29]. Nell'area di Caska sono state rinvenute anfore e tegole con impressi i nomi di senatori romani[30], tra cui

19 Eck, Caballos, Fernandez 1996, 76.

20 Halfmann 1986, 90 e 162; Buchi 2003, 177–178; Rossi 2003, 169–170.

21 Eck, Caballos, Fernandez 1996, 76 e 205. Vedi anche Andermahr 1998, 201, nota 9.

22 *Cn.* (*L.* dopo la condanna del padre) *Calpurnius Piso*: PIR^2 (1936), C 293; vedi Eck, Caballos, Fernandez 1996, 77–80; *M. Calpurnius Piso*: PIR^2 (1936), C 296; vedi Eck, Caballos, Fernandez 1996, 80–83.

23 *S.c. de Cn. Pisone patre* A 93–94: *filio eius Pisoni maiori*; A 100 = B 78: *M(arco) etiam Pisoni*, A 113 = B 86: *M(arco) filio*; 104–105: *Calpurniae Cn. Pisonis filiae*. Sulla trasmissione del patrimonio e sull'identità di questa *Calpurnia* vedi Eck, Caballos, Fernandez 1996, 83–86; Lamberti 2006; Platschek 2009.

24 RE Suppl. XIV (1974), 85, s.v. Calpurnius 127a (W. Eck); per i testi vedi EDCS-15100101, EDCS-67500106, EDCS-83800075, EDCS-10000337 con i rimandi alle edizioni precedenti. Vedi anche Andermahr 1998, 201, nota 9.

25 Sulle scoperte delle dediche e le diverse letture vedi Sticotti 1940; Šonje 1958; Šašel 1962–63; Šašel 1964, 363–367; Kurilić 1994, 206–210, nn. 17–19; Zović, Kurilić 2015, 426–427, nn. 44–46; Grisonić et al. 2022; sulle proprietà dei Pisones già Wilkes 1969, 199–200, 331; Vitelli Casella 2022, 281–284.

26 RE III 1 (1897), 1383, s.v. Calpurnius 74 e Suppl. I (1903), 271 (A. Groag); PIR^2 (1936) C 290 L. Calpurnivs Piso augur, consul a. 753 = 1 a.C. (E. Groag)

27 RE III 1 (1897), 1391–1392, s.v. Calpurnius 95 (A. Groag); PIR^2 (1936), C 286 Cn. Calpurnivs Piso, consul a. 731 = 23 a.C. (E. Groag).

28 Ljubić 1877, 261: "È nell'isola una valle detta Cesca, nella quale fù già una città chiamata da Plinio Issa, non ignorabilis civitas, le cui vestigie si vedono hoggidì parte sotto aqua et parte in terra, con mura et musaichi bellissimi. V'è ancora un aquadotto longo più di otto miglia, per lo quale era condutta l'aqua d'una villa detta Colane fin alla detta città d'Issa, nel qual aquidotto fù trovato pochi dì sono un canone di piombo, sopra il quale erano scritte queste parole: Calphornius Pisanus, dal che si comprende, che l'isola fusse colonia di Romani com'era Zara città a quella vicina".

29 Grisonić et al. 2022, 248.

30 Grisonić 2017; Konestra, Kurilić, Lipovac Vrkljan 2021, 150–152, figg. 5–7.

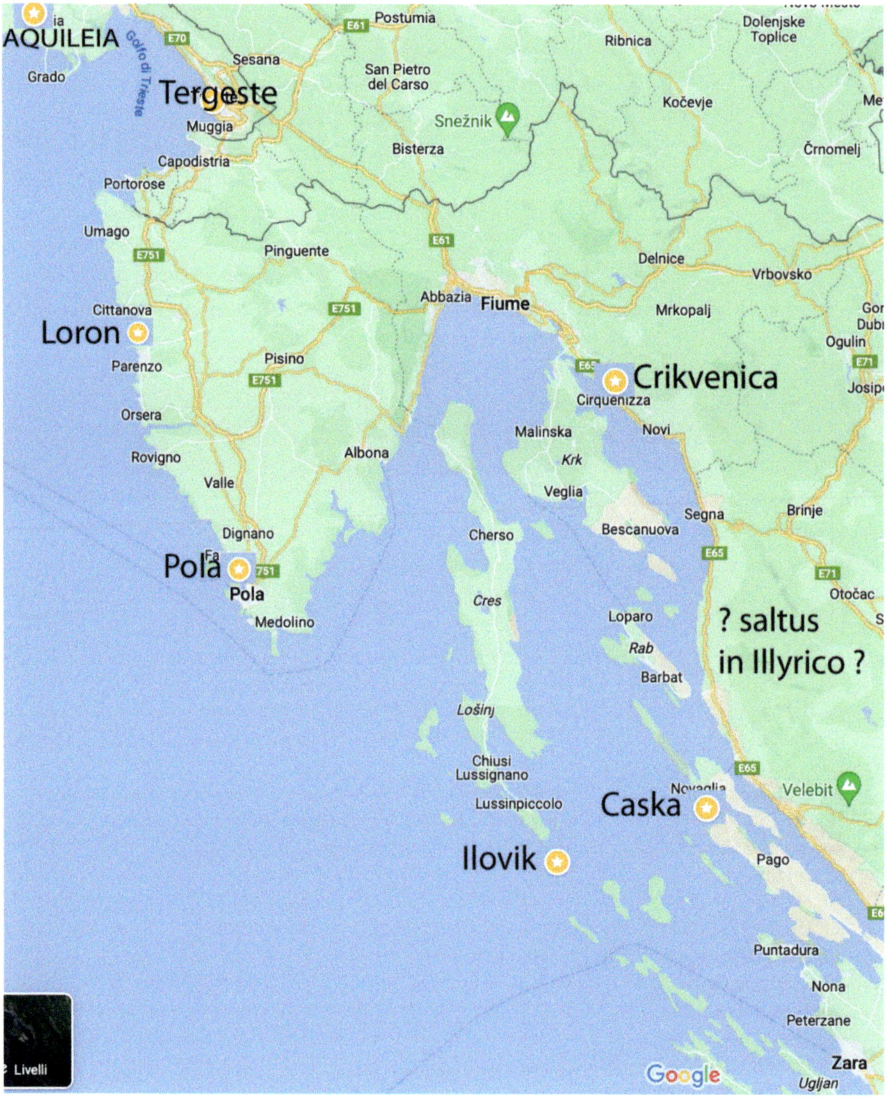

Fig. 2: Carta dell'alto Adriatico, rielaborata da Google maps

si segnalano particolarmente un'anfora e una tegola con il bollo SEX. APPVLEIO COS (console nel 29 a.C. con Ottaviano e governatore dell'Illirico nell'8 a.C.), un'anfora con il bollo M. IVNIO SILANO (console nel 25 a.C. con Augusto), una tegola con il bollo LIBON[---] (forse il console del 34 a.C. con M. Antonio, cognato di Ottaviano e di stanza nell'Illirico nel 49 a.C.), e soprattutto una tegola con il marchio [--- C]AESAR III COS, con tutta probabilità da sciogliere come *[Imp(erator) C]aesar III co(n)s(ul)* e da riferire a una produzione proveniente da una proprietà del futuro Augusto, che fu console nell'anno 31 a. C.[31]. Si può supporre che anche questi possedimenti, almeno per una parte, venissero in seguito in possesso di *L. Piso augur, liberalitate divi Augusti*[32], come compensazione dei servizi resi nelle campagne militari e del supporto all'ascesa del Princeps.

I due fratelli *Pisones* bene si inseriscono nella rete dei personaggi legati ad Augusto che figurano come beneficiari di terre in Liburnia e Istria[33]. Va anche ricordato che *L. Piso augur* aveva preso in moglie una *Statilia*[34], figlia del famoso generale *Ti. Statilius Taurus*[35], che aveva preso parte alle campagne contro i *Delmatae* (34–33 a. C.) e alla battaglia di Azio (31 a. C.), ed era padre del *Sisenna Statilius Taurus*[36], di cui si conosce la proprietà fondiaria in Istria, nel territorio a sud del fiume *Ningus* (Quieto / Mirna), dove sono state indagate in località Loron fornaci per anfore, laterizi e terra sigillata[37].

Per completare il quadro, vanno ricordati gli altri due rami dei *Calpurnii* che si erano stabiliti già alla fine del periodo repubblicano in Istria[38]. *L. Calpurnius Piso Caesoninus*, suocero di Cesare, figura, infatti, insieme a *C. Cassius Longinus* come cofondatore della colonia di Pola[39], mentre nel nord della penisola è attestato già negli ultimi decenni del I sec. a. C. un terzo ramo di questa *gens*, i *Pisones Frugi*[40], che possono essere messi in relazione con i *Licinii Crassi* dell'Istria citati da Tacito[41].

I rapporti reciproci tra la Liburnia e Aquileia sono ormai ben documentati dalle recenti evidenze epigrafiche e archeologiche che testimoniano proprietà aquileiesi nell'area liburnica e scambi di prodotti[42]. Ad esempio, sembra probabile che appartenesse ai *Mutillii* aquileiesi[43], membri dell'aristocrazia municipale che in seguito ascenderà all'*ordo*

---

31 Kurilić 2016.

32 Plin., nat. hist., 18, 37, a proposito dell'origine delle ricchezze di *L. Tarius Rufus*, tra cui c'erano anche proprietà in Dalmazia e/o in Liburnia; vedi Tassaux 1985, 149–153; Andermahr 1998, 445–446.

33 Tassaux 1984; Tassaux 1985; Tassaux 2003; Tassaux 2005; Starac 1999, 53–54, 58–59, 72–73, 77–79, 85–87; Starac 2000, 41–42.

34 Herrmann 1960, 130–134, n. 30, App. 46, fig. 1 = IG XII,6_1, 364 (Samos) = SEG 45, 1169; cf. 46, 1172 = Mc Cabe, Samos 390 = PHI-PH254549.

35 RE III A-2 (1929), 2199–2203, s.v. Statilius 34 (A. Stein); PIR^2 (2006) S 853 (K. Wachtel).

36 RE III A-2 (1929), 2197–2199, s.v. Statilius 33 (A. Stein); PIR^2 (2006) S 851 (K. Wachtel).

37 Tassaux, Matijašić, Kovačić (eds.) 2001; Maggi, Marion, 2002; Maggi, Marion 2011. Per le attestazioni epigrafiche di schiavi e liberti degli *Statilii Tauri* a *Parentium*, Montona, *Piquentum* e *Aquileia* vedi Andermahr 1998, 437.

38 Andermahr 1998, 199–201; Tassaux 2003, 98; Tassaux 2005, 141.

39 CIL, V 54 = Inscr.It. X, 1, 81 = ILLRP 639 = EDR135433: *L(ucius) Cassius C(ai) f(ilius) Longin(us) L(ucius) Calpurnius L(uci) f(ilius) Piso / IIvir(i) quinq(uennales)*; vedi anche CIL I^2, 2512 = Inscr.It. X, 1, 65 = ILLRP 423 = EDR072430: *L(ucius) Calpụ[rnius L(uci) f(ilius)] / Piso Cae̥[soninus] / co(n)ṣ(ul)*; Inscr.It. X, 1, 708 = ILLRP 424 = EDR073747: *[--- L(ucius) Cal]purn[ius L(uci) f(ilius)] / [Cae]son[inus co(n)s(ul)? ---]*. Vedi anche Andermahr 1998, 200.

40 Se ne conosce un liberto nel territorio di Capodistria: *C(aius) Calpurnius / C(ai) Frugi l(ibertus) Alexsa(nder?)*(CIL, V 495 = Inscr.It. X, 3, 15 = EDR007641).

41 Tac., Hist., 2, 72, 2: vedi Syme 1960 [= Syme 1979, 496–509]; Tassaux 1985, 154; Tassaux 2005, 141. Discusso in Andermahr 1998, 201, nota 8 e 320–321, nota 7.

42 Konestra, Kurilić, Lipovac Vrkljan 2021, 152.

43 Chiabà 2003, passim.

senatorius[44], il *saltus* dove operavano le fornaci per anfore e laterizi rinvenute a Crikvenica, sulla costa liburnica di fronte a Veglia (Krk)[45], i cui prodotti sono stati rinvenuti ad Aquileia[46]. Inoltre, un magistrato aquileiese risulta aver avuto proprietà a Ilovik, l'isola più meridionale dell'arcipelago di Lussino, passaggio obbligato sulla rotta marittima da Iader e Cissa a Pola e Aquileia[47]. Sembra logico pensare che Aquileia costituisse un centro di attrazione anche per i senatori che erano divenuti proprietari terrieri e produttori in Istria e Liburnia, specialmente all'inizio del Principato, quando la città nordadriatica era il principale porto di scambio della regione[48].

Anche alla luce di queste evidenze, una presenza ad Aquileia di *Cn. Piso Cn. f. IIvir*, proprietario di un *saltus* in Illirico, anche se non dimostrabile con certezza, rientra nella categoria del possibile. Posto naturalmente che l'oggetto che ha generato questo contributo sia autentico e che i ragionamenti qui sviluppati non risultino mera speculazione.

Sarà stato comunque un ottimo pretesto per portare all'attenzione degli specialisti un oggetto problematico e soprattutto per porgere un piccolo amichevole omaggio a uno studioso che entra di diritto nella serie degli illustri *Pisones*.

Bibliografia

Andermahr, A.M. 1998. Totus in Praediis: Senatorischer Grundbesitz in Italien in der frühen und hohen Kaiserzeit, Bonn.

Blason Scarel, S. 1992. Tessera, in Instrumenta inscripta Latina: sezione aquileiese, Catalogo della Mostra (Aquileia, 22 marzo-12 maggio 1992), Mariano del Friuli, 37–38, nr. 50.

Buchi, E. 2003. Aquileia da Tiberio ad Antonino pio (14–161 d.C.), Antichità Altoadriatiche 54, 177–219.

Buora, M. 2008. Aquileia chrysopolis. Geschichte einer Legende, Anodos. Studies on ancient World, 8, In Honour of Werner Jobst [2010], 109–114.

Burnett, A.M. 1977. The Authority to Coin in the Late Republic and Early Empire, The Numismatic Chronicle 17, 37–63.

Caballos, A., Eck, W., Fernandez, F. 1996. El senadoconsulto de Gneo Pisón padre, Sevilla.

Chiabà, M. 2003. Spunti per uno studio sull' origo delle gentes di Aquileia Repubblicana, Antichità Altoadriatiche 54, 79–118.

Cooley, A.E. 2023. The senatus consultum de Cneo Pisone patre. Text, Translation, and Commentary, Cambridge.

Eck, W., Caballos, A., Fernandez, F. 1996. Das senatus consultum de Cneo Pisone patre, München.

44 Andermahr 1998, 349–350.

45 Lipovac Vrkljan 2009; Pietruszka, Wypijewski 2016: *de salt(u) // Sex(ti) M(u)tilli Max(imi).*

46 Maggi 2018.

47 Kurilić, Serventi 2015.

48 Da ultimo Mainardis 2021, con la bibliografia precedente.

Fedele, I. 2017. Tessera, in Made in Roma and Aquileia: marchi di produzione e di possesso nella società antica, Catalogo della Mostra di Roma (Mercati di Traiano – Museo dei Fori imperiali, 13 maggio – 20 novembre 2016), a cura di L. Ungaro, M. Milella, S. Pastor; Catalogo della Mostra di Aquileia (Palazzo Meizlik, 12 febbraio – 31 maggio 2017), a cura di A. Giovannini, Roma, 224, A10.3.

Geelmuyden Bulgurlu, V., Hazinedar Coşkun, T. 2023. A Group of Lead Tokens in the Ephesos Museum Collection, in M. E. Gkikaki (ed.), Tokens in Classical Athens and Beyond, Liverpool, 275–338.

Gülbay, O., Kireç, H. 2008. Efes KurşunTesseraelari / Ephesian Lead Tesserae, Selçuk Belediyesi.

Grisonić, M. 2017. Amphorae from Caska in the Augusto-Tiberian Period: Imports and Local Productions?, in G. Lipovac Vrkljan, I. Radić Rossi, A. Konestra (eds.), Adri-Amphorae. Amphorae as a Resource for the Reconstruction of Economic Development in the Adriatic Region in Antiquity: Local Production, Proceedings of the Workshop, Zagreb, 21st April 2016, Zagreb 2017, 68–79.

Grisonić, M. et al. 2022. Calpurnia L. Pisonis filia, Cn. Pisonis neptis i zavjetna ara, posvećena Izidi, Serapisu, Ozirisu i Anubisu iz uvale Caska na otoku Pagu / Calpurnia L. Pisonis filia, Cn. Pisonis neptis and the Votive Altar Dedicated to Isis, Serapis, Osiris and Anubis in Caska Cove, on the Island of Pag, Vjesnik Arheološkog Muzeja u Zagrebu 55, 1–2, 231–255.

Halfmann, H. 1986. Itinera principum. Geschichte und Typologie der Kaiserreisen im römischen Reich, Stuttgart.

Herrmann, P. 1960: Die Inschriften romischer Zeit aus dem Heraion von Samos, Athenische Mitteilungen 75, 68–193.

Hofmann-Löbl, I. 1996. Die Calpurnii. Politisches Wirken und familiäre Kontinuität, Frankfurt am Main.

Konestra, A., Kurilić, A., Lipovac Vrkljan, G. 2021. Tiles and Amphorae in the Roman Province of Dalmatia: Evidence of Stamps, in D. Rigato, M. Mongardi, M. Vitelli Casella (eds.), Adriatlas 4. Produzioni artigianali in area adriatica: manufatti, ateliers e attori (III sec. a. C. – V sec. d. C.), Atti della Tavola Rotonda di Bologna, 23–25 maggio 2019, Pessac, 145–166.

Kubitschek, W. 1909. CHRYSOPOLIS, Numismatische Zeitschrift 42, 1909, 38–46 [trad. it. CHRYSOPOLIS. Piombo da Aquileia, Bullettino di archeologia e storia dalmata 32, 101–113].

Küter, A. 2019. Roman tesserae with Numerals: Some Thoughts on Iconography and Purpose, in A. Crisà, M. Gkikaki, C. Rowan (eds.), Tokens: Culture, Connections, Communities, Royal Numismatic Society, Special Publication No. 57, London, 79–93.

Kuhn, C. T. 2014. Prosopographical Notes on Four Lead Tesserae from Roman Ephesos. Zeitschrift für Papyrologie und Epigraphik 190, 137–140. https://www.jstor.org/stable/23850689

Kurilić, A. 1994. Latinski natpisi antičkog, kasnoantičkog i ranosrednjovjekovnog razdoblja na otoku Pagu i zadarsko-šibenskom otočju, Radovi Zavoda za povijesne znanosti HAZU u Zadru 36, 191–246.

Kurilić, A. 2016. Roman Tile Stamped [C]AESAR III COS, in Studi in onore di Claudio Zaccaria, Antichità Altoadriatiche 85, 377–386.

Kurilić, A., Serventi, Z. 2015. Natpis Gaja Kornelija s Ilovika i Cornelii u Liburniji / Caius Cornelius's Inscription from Ilovik and Cornelii in Liburnia, Opuscula archaeologica 37–38, 219–247.

Lamberti, F. 2006. Questioni aperte sul SC. de Cn. Pisone patre, in M. Silvestrini, T. Spagnuolo Vigorita, G. Volpe (eds.), Studi in onore di Francesco Grelle, Bari, 201–226.

Lipovac Vrkljan, G. 2009. L'officina ceramica di Crikvenica, in: S. Pesavento Mattioli, M.-B. Carre (eds.), Olio e pesce in epoca romana. Produzione e commercio nelle regioni dell'alto Adriatico, Atti del Convegno, Padova, 16 febbraio 2007, Antenor Quaderni 15, Roma, 309–314.

Ljubić, Š. 1877. Commissiones et relationes Venetae: Tomus II: Annorum 1525–1553, Monumenta spectantia historiam Slavorum meridionalium 8, Jugoslavenska Akademija Znanosti i Umjetnosti, Zagrabiae.

Maggi, P. 2018. Crikvenica amphorae from Canale Anfora: First Evidence of Liburnian Wine at Aquileia, in G. Lipovac Vrkljan, A. Konestra (eds.), Pottery Production, Landscape and Economy of Roman Dalmatia. Interdisciplinary approaches, Oxford, 57–61.

Maggi, P., Marion, Y. 2002. Sénateurs et activités économiques: l'enseignement des timbres de Loron (Croatie), in Acta XII Congressus Internationalis Epigraphiae Graecae et Latinae: Provinciae Imperii Romani inscriptionibus descriptae (Barcelona, 3–8 Septembris 2002), Barcelona, 857–862.

Maggi, P., Marion, Y. 2011. Le produzioni di anfore e di terra sigillata a Loron e la loro diffusione, in G. Lipovac Vrkljan, I. Radić Rossi, B. Šiljeg (eds.) , Rimske keramičarske i staklarske radionice: proizvodnja i trgovina na jadranskom prostoru. Zbornik I. međunarodnog arheološkog kolokvija, Crikvenica, 176–187.

Mainardis, F. 2021. Aquileia (Regio X) nelle reti commerciali mediterranee: persone e merci dalla documentazione epigrafica, in L. Chioffi, M. Kajava, S. Örmä (eds.), Il Mediterraneo e la storia III. Documentando città portuali – Documenting Port Cities, Atti del convegno internazionale, Capri 9–11 maggio 2019, Acta Instituti Romani Finlandiae 48, Roma, 153–175.

Maionica, E. 1899. Chrysopolis Aquileja, Jahreshefte des Österreichischen Archäologischen Institutes 2, Beibl., 105–106.

Manni, A. 2016. Il senatus consultum de Cnaeo Pisone patre come fonte di cognizione del diritto di Roma antica, in G. D. Merola, A. Franciosi (eds.), Manentibus titulis. Studi di epigrafia e papirologia giuridica, Napoli, 39–72.

Martínez Caballero, S. 2017. El asesinato del praetor L. Calpurnius Piso por un termestino (Tac. Ann.4.45): ¿persecución de la libertas y la alta nobleza romana en época de Tiberio César?, Gerión 35/1, 203–228.

Pietruszka, W., Wypijewski, I. 2016. Sextus Mutillius Maximus: In Search of the Owner of a Liburnian saltus, ZPE, 198, 283–286.

Platschek, J. 2009. Römisches Recht in Bronze – Der Senatsbeschluss de Cn. Pisone patre als Quelle des römischen Familien- und Erbrechts, forum historiae iuris (Feb. 6, 2009), https://forhistiur.net2009-02-platschek.

Rossi, R. F. 2003. Aquileia in età cesariana ed augustea, Antichità Altoadriatiche 54, 155–176.
Rostovtzew, M. 1905. Interprétation des tessères en os avec figures, chiffres et légendes, Revue Archéologique 5, 110–124.
Starac, A. 1999. Rimsko vladanje u Histriji i Liburniji: društveno i pravno uređenje prema literarnoj, natpisnoj i arheološkoj građi. I: Histrija, Pula.
Starac, A. 2000. Rimsko vladanje u Histriji i Liburniji: društveno i pravno uređenje prema literarnoj, natpisnoj i arheološkoj građi. II: Liburnija, Pula.
Sticotti, P. 1940. Pago, in Serta Hoffilleriana. Commentationes gratulatorias Victori Hoffiller sexagenario obtulerunt collegae amici discipuli a. d. XI Kal. Mar. 1937, Zagreb, 179–180.
Syme, R., 1960. Piso Frugi and Crassus Frugi, JRS, 50 13–20 [= Id., Roman Papers, 2, Oxford 1979, 496–509].
Syme, R. 1986. The Augustan Aristocracy, Oxford.
Šašel, J. 1962–63. Calpurnia L. Pisonis auguris filia, Živa antika /Antiquité vivante 12, 387–390.
Šašel, J. 1964. Probleme und Möglichkeit onomastischer Forschung, in Akten des IV Internationalen Kongresses der griechischen und lateinischen Epigraphik, Wien, 363–367.
Šonje, A. 1958. Nalaz rimskog natpisa na Caski kod Novalje na otoku Pagu / Die Auffindung einer römischen Inschrift in Caska der Novalja auf der Insel Pag, Živa antika 8, 311–322.
Tassaux, F. 1984. L'implantation territoriale des grandes familles d'Istrie sous le Haut-Empire romain, in Problemi storici ed archeologici dell'Italia nordorientale e delle regioni limitrofe dalla preistoria al medioevo (Atti dei Civici Musei di Storia ed Arte di Trieste, Quaderno, 13/2), Trieste, 193–229.
Tassaux, F. 1985. Sur quelques rapports entre l'Istrie et la Liburnie dans l'antiquité, Antichità Altoadriatiche 26, 129–158.
Tassaux, F. 2003. Élites locales, élites centrales. Approche économique et sociale des grands propriétaires au nord de l'Italie romaine (Brescia et Istrie), Histoire & Sociétés Rurales 19, 1, 91–120.
Tassaux, F. 2005. Patrimoines sénatoriaux de la Decima Regio, Cahiers Glotz 16, 139–164.
Tassaux, F., Matijašić, R., Kovačić, V. (eds.) 2001. Loron (Croatie), un grand centre de production d'amphores à huile istrienne (Ier–IVe s. ap. J.-C.), Ausonius Mémoires 6, Bordeaux.
Vitelli Casella, M. 2022. La Liburnia settentrionale nell'antichità: geografia, istituzioni e società, Bologna.
Wilkes, J. J. 1969. Dalmatia, London.
Zović, V., Kurilić, A. 2015. The Structure of Votive Inscriptions from Roman Liburnia, Arheološki Vestnik 66, 399–453.

Die *nomina legionum* auf einer Säule vom Forum Romanum Zu CIL VI 3492

Michael A. Speidel

Auf dem Forum Romanum, bei der Basilica Aemilia, wurden um die Mitte des 16. Jahrhunderts bei Grabungen die Bruchstücke zweier Säulen aus Marmor gefunden, auf denen zwei identische Inschriften eingemeisselt waren (Abb. 1): Auf beiden Säulen stand je eine Liste aller 33 Legionen des Imperium Romanum, die seit der Regierungszeit des Septimius Severus existierten.[1] Während eine der beiden Säulen offenbar schon früh verloren ging, ist die andere erhalten geblieben und befindet sich heute in den Vatikanischen Museen in Rom. Sie ist rund 60 cm hoch und hat einen Durchmesser von knapp 40 cm. Der Text besteht aus einer Überschrift (*nomina legionum*) und aus den Ziffern und Namen von in drei Kolumnen geordneten 33 Legionen. Die Buchstabenhöhe der Legionsnamen beträgt knapp 3 cm, die der Überschrift rund 3,7 cm. Man liest:

Nomina leg(ionum)

II Aug(usta)	*II Adiut(rix)*	*IIII Scyth(ica)*
VI Victr(ix)	*IIII Flav(ia)*	*XVI Flav(ia)*
XX Victr(ix)	*VII Claud(ia)*	*VI Ferrat(a)*
VIII Aug(usta)	*I Italic(a)*	*X Frete(nsis)*
XXII Prim(igenia)	*V Maced(onica)*	*III Cyren(aica)*
I Min(ervia)	*XI Claud(ia)*	*II Traian(a)*
XXX Ulp(ia)	*XIII Gem(ina)*	*III Aug(usta)*
I Adiut(rix)	*XII Fulm(inata)*	*VII Gem(ina)*
X Gem(ina)	*XV Apol(linaris)*	*II Italic(a)*
XIIII Gem(ina)	*III Gall(ica)*	*III Italic(a)*
I Parth(ica)	*II Parth(ica)*	*III Parth(ica)*

1 CIL VI 3492 a (erhalten) und b (verloren) = VI 32901a und b = ILS 2288 = AE 1994, 37 = AE 1995, 44. Zur Inschrift siehe auch den ausführlichen Kommentar und die umfassende Bibliographie bei Cosme 1994 (dort 176 zum Fundort). Ferner: Petolescu 1996, 61–62, Nr. 24. Mosser 2003, 283, Nr. 241. Reuter 2012, Nr. 149. Garofalo 2019, 328–330, Nr. 12.

Abb. 1: CIL VI 3492 a. = EDCS-19000504

Abb. 2: Abklatsch CIL EC0004940 (Foto PEC0004940)

Wie schon E. Borman und G. Henzen, die Herausgeber der Inschrift im *Corpus Inscriptionum Latinarum,* erkannten, enthält die Liste verschiedene chronologische Schichten, deren jüngste in die Zeit nach der Gründung der drei parthischen Legionen unter Septimius Severus gehört und die damit, nach allgemeiner Ansicht, die Inschrift als Ganzes in die Zeit dieses Kaisers datiert.[2] Folgende Abschnitte lassen sich erkennen:[3]

Die ersten 28 Legionen sind im Uhrzeigersinn in der geografischen Reihenfolge ihrer Stationierungsprovinzen aufgeführt, wobei die als *superior* benannten Provinzen immer ihren als *inferior* bezeichneten Gegenstücken voranstehen:

II Augusta, VI Victrix, XX Victrix	*Britannia*
VIII Augusta, XXII Primigenia	*Germania superior*
I Minervia, XXX Ulpia	*Germania inferior*
I Adiutrix, X Gemina, XIIII Gemina	*Pannonia superior*
II Adiutrix	*Pannonia inferior*
IIII Flavia, VII Claudia	*Moesia superior*
I Italica, V Macedonica, XI Claudia	*Moesia inferior*
XIII Gemina	*Dacia*

2 Cosme 1994, 173. Siehe ebd. 172: „La datation de l'inscription ne pose guère de problèmes". Garofalo 2019, 330: „databile intorno al 200 d. C."

3 Dazu ausführlich Cosme 1994, bes. 172–175.

XII Fulminata, XV Apollinaris	*Cappadocia*
III Gallica, IIII Scythica, XVI Flavia	*Syria*
VI Ferrata, X Fretensis	*Syria Palaestina*
III Cyrenaica	*Arabia*
II Traiana	*Aegyptus*
III Augusta	*Africa / Numidia*
VII Gemina	*Hispania citerior.*

Die Namen der Provinzen sind in der Liste nicht angegeben, doch werden die Legionen innerhalb des jeweiligen Provinzkommandos immer in aufsteigender Reihenfolge ihrer Nummern aufgeführt. Offensichtlich wurde dieser Hauptteil der Liste somit nach einheitlichen Grundsätzen erstellt. Die Aufzählung scheint zudem für den Zeitpunkt ihrer Entstehung den Bestand der Legionen genau wiederzugeben. So fehlt etwa die vermutlich zwischen 132 und 136 während des Bar Kochba-Aufstandes vernichtete *legio XXII Deiotariana* ebenso wie die *legio IX Hispana*, die im Jahr 161 in der Nähe von Elegia in Armenien aufgerieben wurde.[4] Die Liste kann somit erst nach dem Untergang der 9. Legion entstanden sein.[5]

Bisher vielleicht nicht genügend beachtet wurde, dass die geographische Ordnung der Legionen in diesem Hauptteil aus der Zeit vor 168/70 stammt, als Mark Aurel die *legio V Macedonica* von Troesmis in *Moesia inferior*, wo die Legion gemäss unserer Liste noch ihr Standlager hatte, nach Potaissa in *Dacia* verlegte.[6] Dazu passt nicht nur die Nennung der nach etwa 165/166 neu aufgestellten Legionen *II* und *III Italica* sondern auch deren Stellung ausserhalb der geographischen Ordnung am Ende der Liste. Denn in den ersten Jahren ihrer Existenz scheinen diesen beiden Legionen ihre späteren festen Garnisonsplätze in Noricum und Raetia noch nicht zugewiesen worden zu sein.[7] Es entsprach der römischen administrativen Praxis solche neuen Einheiten am Ende bestehender Listen anzufügen, wie vor allem Beispiele aus der *Notitia Dignitatum* zeigen.[8] Es ist jedenfalls überaus wahrscheinlich, dass die Namen der beiden *Italica*-Legionen der Liste hinzugefügt wurden, bevor diese auf die Säule geschrieben wurde, zumal es auch nur durch deren Nennung möglich war, die *nomina legionum* in genau drei Spalten zu je zehn Zeilen anzuordnen. Möglicherweise stand der Zweck der Inschrift sogar mit der Aufstellung der beiden neuen Legionen in einem Zusammenhang.

Wie dem auch sei, aus den beschriebenen Beobachtungen wird ersichtlich, dass die Liste der römischen Legionen vom Forum Romanum, als sie in der zweiten Hälfte der 160er Jahre in Stein gemeisselt wurde, der damaligen Realität entsprach. Dass solche Legionslisten von den zuständigen Büros in Rom tatsächlich regelmässig auf den neuesten

4 Zum Untergang der 9. Legion siehe: Dio 71,2,1. Eck 1972, 459–462. Birley 2005, 229.

5 Bemerkenswerterweise wurde der Name der im Jahr 219 von Kaiser Elagabal aufgelösten *legio III Gallica* (Dio 80,7,1–3) nicht gelöscht.

6 Piso 1993, 88–89, 98–99.

7 Birley 1987, 249. Dietz 2000, 133.

8 Dazu demnächst ausführlich Speidel, im Druck.

Stand gebracht wurden, legen auch die literarisch von Josephus, Tacitus, und Cassius Dio überlieferten Beispiele nahe.[9] Im Falle der epigraphisch überlieferten Legionsliste vom Forum Romanum wird jedoch nicht angenommen, dass sie in severischer Zeit von einer solchen aktuellen Liste der Reichsverwaltung abgeschrieben wurde, sondern dass sie die Kopie einer auf vergänglichem Material in drei Kolumnen notierten Liste aus der Zeit zwischen ca. 165/66 und 168/70 war, der die Namen der drei um 195 von Septimius Severus aufgestellten Partherlegionen in der letzten Zeile hinzugefügt waren.[10] Denn die Paläographie und der Anordnung der Inschrift auf der Säule schienen nahezulegen, dass der Text in einem Zug eingemeisselt wurde, einschliesslich der letzten (11.) Zeile mit den drei parthischen Legionen.[11]

Diese Lösung ist allerdings kaum wahrscheinlich. Denn einerseits fällt es schwer zu glauben, dass unter Septimius Severus die Abschrift einer veralteten Legionsliste verwendet worden sein soll, wenn doch in Rom aktuelle Listen der Legionen vorhanden und erhältlich waren.[12] Gegen diese Deutung spricht auch der Umstand, dass die beiden *Italica*-Legionen bei dieser Gelegenheit, rund dreissig Jahre nach ihrer Aufstellung, nicht in die geographische Reihenfolge der Liste integriert worden sind. Dasselbe gilt schliesslich auch für die fehlende Umgestaltung der drei Spalten von je zehn zu je elf Zeilen, so dass die parthischen Legionen am Ende der Liste hätten stehen können, wie es zuvor mit den *Italica*-Legionen geschehen war und wie es für nachgetragene Einheiten bei Truppenlisten offenbar üblich war.

Wenn es schwer fällt zu glauben, dass der Aufwand gescheut wurde, eine aktuelle Liste aller Legionen zu besorgen oder zu erstellen, so zeigt eine weitere Beobachtung, dass die bisher angenommene Entstehungsgeschichte der Liste tatsächlich kaum das Richtige trifft. Denn ein genauer Blick auf die Textverteilung zeigt, dass die Namen der drei parthischen Legionen in einer durchgehenden Zeile unter die drei bestehenden zehnzeiligen Spalten eigemeisselt wurden, ohne die Namen der *legiones Parthicae* am linken Rand der Spalten auszurichten (Bild 1 und 2). Die parallelen Spalten umfassen somit nur 10 Zeilen, die letzte Zeile mit den Partherlegionen gehört nicht zur ursprünglichen Textverteilung. Daraus folgt mit grosser Wahrscheinlichkeit, dass die Namen dieser Legionen erst nach der Vollendung der ursprünglich nur dreissig *nomina legionum* umfassenden Inschrift aus der Zeit zwischen ca. 165/66 und 168/70 nachgetragen wurden. Das geschah vermutlich kurze Zeit nach der Gründung der drei *legiones Parthicae* um 195.

Die Liste der Legionen des Römischen Reichs vom Forum Romanum ist unter den erhaltenen lateinischen Inschriften einzigartig. Der genaue architektonische Kontext der

9 Jos., BJ 2,16,4 (366–387). Tac., *Ann.* 4,5. Dio 55,23–24. Dazu demnächst ausführlich Speidel, im Druck.

10 Cosme 1994, 173 and 184. Zum Zeitpunkt der Gründung der *legiones Parthicae*: Speidel 2009, 187–189.

11 CIL VI 3492: „uno tempore, eadem manu." Siehe etwa auch H. Dessau in ILS 2288. A. Passerini, *Dizionario Epigrafico* IV 2, s.v. *legio*, 557. Auch die elektronischen Datenbanken Clauss / Slaby (EDCS-19000504. 17.9.2023) und Epigraphic Database Roma (EDR174557. 17.9.2023) präsentieren die Inschrift, wie alle Editionen, als Text aus einem Guss.

12 Speidel, im Druck.

beiden Säulen ist leider nicht erhalten, womit auch der Zweck der Listen in ihrem grösseren baulichen und textlichen Zusammenhang nicht unmittelbar ersichtlich ist.[13] Man hat deshalb versucht, aus dem Fundort der beiden Säulen bei der Basilica Aemilia Hinweise zu ihrer Bedeutung zu gewinnen. So wurde etwa vermutet, dass die Basilica Aemilia von Augustus, zusammen mit einem Bildprogramm zur Verherrlichung seiner «Unterwerfung» der Parther im Jahre 20 v. Chr. auch zwei Säulen mit den Namen aller damals existierenden Legionen erhalten habe. Diese beiden Inschriften seien dann unter Septimius Severus, vielleicht anlässlich von dessen Triumph über die Parther im Jahre 203, ersetzt worden, wobei die geographische Verteilung der Legionen in diesem neuen Text bewusst so gewählt worden sei, dass ein Bezug zu Mark Aurel, ja sogar zu dessen Triumph über die Parther entstand, den er gemeinsamen mit Lucius Verus im Jahre 166 feierte.[14]

Bevor die Inschriften mit den Listen des Augustus jedoch ersetzt worden seien, hätten sie Kaiser Traian zur Errichtung einer weiteren in Stein gemeisselten Liste von Legionen im Zentrum Roms angeregt.[15] Traians Legionenliste, von der sich nur wenige Bruchstücke erhalten haben, war zusammen mit Sockeln, auf denen die Namen weiterer Einheiten eingemeisselt waren, an der Basilica Ulpia auf dem Traiansforum zu sehen.[16] Diese Inschrift war allerdings nicht in drei Spalten sondern in einer einzigen, viele Meter langen Zeile geschrieben gewesen und gehörte mit ihren 15 cm hohen Buchstaben in einen monumentalen architektonischen Kontext.[17] Denn trotz der Unsicherheiten, die vor allem dem bruchstückhaften Zustand dieser Inschrift geschuldet ist, ist sicherlich zurecht vermutet worden, dass es sich hier nicht um eine vollständige Liste aller Legionen Roms handelte, sondern nur um die Namen jener Einheiten, die vollständig oder als Abteilung unter Traian an den beiden Kriegen zur Eroberung Dakiens teilgenommen hatten.[18] Für das Verständnis dieser Inschrift(en) ist es schliesslich von grosser Bedeutung, dass sie nicht als schlichte Liste konzipiert war, sondern dass sich die Namen der Legionen offenbar auf vergoldete Kopien der Feldzeichen der genannten Einheiten bezogen, die auf den Blöcken mit den eingemeisselten Namen aufgestellt waren.[19]

Das traianische Beispiel der monumentalen Verherrlichung eines römischen Sieges und der daran beteiligten Truppen kann somit kaum zum besseren Verständnis der ungleich kleineren Legionslisten vom Forum Romanum beitragen. Die Vollständigkeit der Listen auf den Säulen schliesst zudem aus, dass sie sich auf einen bestimmten Sieg bezogen. Ihre bescheidene Grösse kann schliesslich kaum mit dem monumentalen An-

---

13 Siehe dazu die Ausführungen und Überlegungen bei Cosme 1994, 174–186.

14 Cosme 1994, 183–184. Nach Chioffi 1996, 50–53 sollen die Säulen zu einem „avancorpo“ oder „padiglione“ am östlichen Ende der Porticus der Basilica Aemilia gehört haben, wo sie mit anderen bedeutenden Inschriften aus der Zeit des Augustus zu sehen gewesen seien. Dazu passt allein schon die Datierung der Legionslisten nicht.

15 Ebd. 184.

16 CIL VI 3493 = 32902 = AE 2019, 113–115. Dazu zuletzt Pastor 2019.

17 Pastor 2019, 98 vermutet eine Länge von 65 Metern. Siehe die Rekonstruktion ebd. 103.

18 Pastor 2019. Siehe dazu etwa auch Strobel 1984, 100–101, Anm. 11. Bérard 1988, 161–162.

19 Gell. 13,25,1–2: *In fastigiis fori Traiani simulacra sunt sita circumundique inaurata equorum atque signorum militarium, subscriptumque est:* (2) *"ex manubiis"*.

spruch der Basilica Ulpia und dem Traiansforum verglichen werden. Es ist auch nicht zu erkennen, wie die beiden kleinen Säulen in der Architektur der Basilica Aemilia integriert gewesen wären und wie die nur knapp 45 cm hohen Inschriften mit ihren 3 cm hohen Buchstaben dort eine Wirkung hätten entfalten können, die jenen in der Basilica Ulpia irgendwie vergleichbar gewesen wären.

Der kleine Säulendurchmesser und die geringen Masse der Inschrift lassen jedenfalls kaum einen Zweifel daran, dass diese nicht zu einem monumentalen kaiserlichen oder staatlichen Bauwerk gehörten, sondern zu einem bescheideneren, privaten Bau. Natürlich können erst weitere Hinweise verlässliche Aussagen zum inhaltlichen und architektonischen Zusammenhang der Säulen und ihrer Legionslisten ermöglichen. Dennoch lassen sich auch beim jetzigen Stand der Kenntnisse einige, wenn auch vielleicht teils spekulative Überlegungen anstellen. Denn möchte man nach den Massen des erhaltenen Säulenbruchstücks urteilen, kommt als zugehöriges Bauwerk wohl vor allem eine *aedicula* in Frage. Die beiden Legionslisten dürften dann inhaltlich mit dem kultischen Zweck des anzunehmenden Schreins verbunden gewesen sein. Da die Listen der *nomina legionum* aber im Nominativ und ohne syntaktischen Zusammenhang auf den Säulen stehen, waren sie dem Monument wohl am ehesten als erklärende oder ergänzende Beischriften hinzugefügt worden. Denn es ist zweifellos auszuschliessen, dass das Monument, zu dem die beiden Säulen gehörten, keinen weiteren Bezug zu den Legionen Roms aufwies.

Treffen diese beiden Annahmen das Richtige, so führen sie zu folgender Lösung. Die Liste der *nomina legionum* bezog sich vermutlich auf in der *aedicula* sichtbaren, aber unbeschriebenen Symbole der Legionen. Dabei kann es sich dann aber, ähnlich wie bei der Basilica Ulpia, nur um Darstellungen der Feldzeichen (*signa legionum*) gehandelt haben, denn diese waren nicht nur die wichtigsten Symbole ihrer Legionen, sondern ihnen galt auch die kultische Verehrung der Legionsangehörigen. Tatsächlich ist ein Kult für die *signa legionum* in Rom durch zwei Altäre aus Marmor mit identischen Inschriften aus der Regierungszeit des Septimius Severus bezeugt.[20] Der Stifter dieser Altäre war ein Iulius Proculus, *centurio frumentarius a (castris) peregrinis*.[21] Die *frumentarii* und die meisten übrigen Soldaten und Offiziere, die im Lager der *castra peregrina* auf dem mons Caelius untergebracht waren, waren von ihren Legionen überall im Reich abgeordnet und dienten in Rom weit weg von ihren Stammlagern, wo die Feldzeichen ihrer Einheiten kultisch verehrt wurden.[22] Aus diesem Grund wurde in den *castra peregrina* offenbar ein Kult für die Gesamtheit aller Legionsfahnen eingeführt.[23] Es ist deshalb wahrscheinlich,

20 AE 1994, 248 und 249 (gefunden beim Mithraeum der *castra peregrina* (S. Stefano Rotondo), wo sie wohl in zweiter Verwendung standen [so Panciera 2006, 1462]): *Signis legionum / Severi et Antonini / [[[et Getae]]] / Augg(ustorum) nn(ostrorum) / Iulius Proculus |(centurio) fr(umentarius) / a peregr(inis).*

21 Dazu Panciera 2006.

22 Siehe nur AE 1993, 1571: *Aquilae / et signis / leg(ionis) II Part(hicae) / [Se]ver(ianae).* CIL III 6224= ILS 2295: *Dis militaribus, / Genio, Virtuti, A/quilae sanc(tae) signis/que leg(ionis) I Ital(icae) Seve/rianae.* RIB 1263 = ILS 2557: *Genio et Signis / coh(ortis) I F(idae) Vardul(lorum) / c(ivium) R(omanorum) eq(uitatae) m(illiariae).* AE 2003, 1406: *Signis coh(ortis) I / Alp(inorum) p(editatae) Antonin(i)/an(a)e All(ius?) Exsupe/ratus praef(ectus) d(onum) d(edit).* Etc.

23 Dazu ausführlich Panciera 2006, 1455–56.

dass die angenommene Aedicula mit den Namen aller Legionen auf ihren Säulen ebenfalls den *signa legionum* gewidmet war und vermutlich auch von einem oder mehreren Legionsangehörigen der *castra peregrina* gestiftet wurde,[24] zumal Soldaten und Offiziere ähnliche Schreine in Rom offenbar öfters gestiftet haben.[25] Ob freilich die Aedicula mit den Legionslisten auf dem Forum Romanum errichtet wurde oder ob die beiden Säulenbruchstücke dorthin verschleppt worden sind, um in einem Kalkofen verbrannt zu werden, muss offen bleiben.[26]

Literaturverzeichnis

Bérard, F. 1988. Le role militaire des cohortes urbaines, MEFRA 100, 159–182.
Birley, A.R. 1987. Marcus Aurelius. A Biography. Revised Edition. Yale.
Birley, A.R. 2005. The Roman Government of Britain. Oxford.
Chioffi, L. 1996. Gli elogia augustei del foro Romano: Aspetti epigrafici e topografici. Roma.
Cosme, P. 1994. Les légions romaines sur le Forum : recherches sur la Colonnette Maf-féienne, MEFRA 106, 167–196.
Dietz K. 2000. Legio III Italica, in Y. Le Bohec (ed.), Les légions de Rome sous le Haut-Empire, Paris, 133–143.
Eck, W. 1972. Zum Ende der legio IX Hispana, Chiron 2, 459–462.
Garofalo, P. 2019. Un manoscritto inedito con inscrizioni latine e greche, ovvero ricerche intorno all'Anonymus Vallicellianus (S.Borr.Q.VI.188), Epigraphica 81, 299–332.
Mosser, M. 2003. Die Steindenkmäler der legio XV Apollinaris. Wien.
Panciera, S. 2006. Signis legionum – Insegne, immagini imperiali e centuriones frumentarii a peregrinis, in Epigrafi, epigrafia, epigrafisti. Scritti vari editi e inediti (1956–2005) con note complementari e indici, Roma, 1453–1464.

24 Zu gemeinsamen Stiftungen siehe etwa CIL VI 1110 (p. 3778, 4324): *[Corneliae Saloninae] / [Sanctissimae Augustae coniugi] (...) [centuriones] deputati et supernume/[rarii et f]rumentari(i) cum / [---] et Iusto tribb(unis) et Aurelio / [- principe pe]regrinorum et Aurelio / [- subprincipe] peregrinorum (...).*

25 Siehe z.B. CIL VI 207 = 30715: *Genio centuriae C(ai) Tu[- aram] / et aediculam omni im[pensa cum colum]nis et cancello aereo cum [-] / A(ulus) Pontius L(uci) f(ilius) Scap(tia) Pris[cus -] (...) d(onum) [d(edit)].* CIL 212 = ILS 2100: *Gen(io) |(centuriae) // Signum Genium centuriae cum aedicula et marmoribus ex/ornata et aram sua pecunia fecer(unt) |(centurio) C(aius) Veturius C(ai) f(ilius) Pol(lia) Rufinus L(epido) R(egio?) / item evocati et milites quorum nomina et medicus coh(ortis) in ara et aedicul(a) / scripta sunt (...).* Siehe ferner etwa auch CIL VI 177. VI 213 = ILS 2099. VI 214 = 30716. VI 215 = 30717. VI 218 = ILS 2107. VI 219 = ILS 2162. VI 221 = ILS 2160. VI 229. VI 30931.

26 Auf dem Forum: vgl. CIL VI 32415 = ILS 4932: *Flaviae L(uci) f(iliae) Publiciae / religiosae / sanctitatis v(irgini) V(estali) max(imae) / cuius egregiam morum / disciplinam et / in sacris peritissimam / operationem merito / res publica in dies / feliciter sentit / Ulpius Verus et Aurel(ius) / Titus |(centuriones) deputati / ob eximiam eius erga se / benivolentiam / g(ratis?) p(osuerunt).* Verschleppt: vgl. bes. CIL VI 37260, das Bruchstück eines marmornen Grabsteins eines *frumentarius*, das ebenfalls bei der Basilica Aemilia gefunden wurde. Siehe ferner CIL VI 32722 und 37242.

Pastor, S. 2019. L'esercito di marmo. Analisi e nuove interpretazioni delle attestazioni epigrafiche dal Foro di Traiano. Bull. Comm. Arch. Rom. 120, 95–108.

Petolescu, C.C. 1996. Inscriptiones Daciae Romanae. Inscriptiones extra fines Daciae repertae, Bd. I. Bucarest.

Piso, I. 1993. Fasti Provinciae Daciae I. Die senatorischen Amtsträger. Bonn.

Reuter, M. 2012. Legio XXX Ulpia Victrix. Ihre Geschichte, ihre Soldaten, ihre Denkmäler. Darmstadt.

Speidel, M.A. 2009. Heer und Herrschaft im Römischen Reich der Hohen Kaiserzeit. Stuttgart.

Speidel, M.A. im Druck. Unit lists and Roman bureaucratic traditions in the Notitia Dignitatum (pars Orientis), in M. Jelusić, A. Kaiser, S. Roggo (eds.), Ruling an Empire in a Changing World – Studies on Origin, Impact, and Reception of the Notitia Dignitatum.

Macenio

Ligia Ruscu

Es wird im Allgemeinen angenommen, dass von den uns bekannten Veteranen der römischen Armee etwa 20–25% an ihren Heimatsort zurückkehrten; ca. 75–80% zogen es vor, sich in oder nahe dem Ort niederzulassen, wo sie zuletzt gedient hatten; nur sehr wenige wählten eine dritte Möglichkeit[1]. Ein Beispiel herausragender geographischer Mobilität eines Militärs findet sich in einer Inschrift aus Novae[2]. Eine Grabstele wurde von Marcus Valerius Macenio seinem Vater Marcus (?) Aurelius Macenio errichtet. Dieser gibt seine Herkunft mit *domo [.]app.* an, was zu *domo [C]app(adocia)* ergänzt wurde[3], hatte in der *legio I Minervia*[4] gedient, die in Bonn stand, und sich in Novae unweit des Lagers der *legio I Italica* niedergelassen. Damit hätten wir hier einen Mann, der sich zu Rekrutierungszwecken beinahe so weit von seinem Heimatort entfernte, wie es nur irgend möglich war, und es dann vorzog, für seinen Ruhestand einen Ort auszuwählen, der weder sein Heimat- noch sein Dienstort war und der sich auf halbem Wege zwischen beiden befindet.

Gesondert betrachtet, lässt sich jeder dieser Punkte erklären. Dass der Veteran seine Herkunft mit einer Provinz und nicht mit einer Stadt oder einem sonstigen Ort angab, ist zwar weniger gewöhnlich, es konnte jedoch gezeigt werden, dass solche Angaben nicht abwegig sind[5]. Dass Soldaten aus Kleinasien desöfteren in Einheiten dienten, die außerhalb Kleinasiens und manchmal weit davon entfernt standen, ist wohlbekannt[6]. Dass es keine Zeugnisse zu Legionssoldaten mit der Herkunft in Kappadokien gibt[7] und keine zu Auxiliareinheiten, die in Kappadokien rekrutiert wurden[8], ist zwar überraschend, kann aber eine Folge des Forschungsstandes sein. Dass sich gelegentlich ein Veteran an einem Ort niederließ, der keine Verbindung zu seiner Heimat oder seinem (letzten) Standort

1 Forni 1953, 41–42; Forni 1974, 359; Raepsaet-Charlier 1978; Roxan 1981; Roxan 1989; Derks, Roymans 2006; Wesch-Klein 2007, 446.

2 ILBulg 309 = IDRE 2, 325 = IGLNovae 76 = PLINovae S. 173 = AE 1987, 861.

3 Siehe dazu Gerov, *ad* ILBulg 309, und den Kommentar zu IGLNovae 76.

4 Nicht der *legio XIII Gemina*, wie anfangs angenommen; siehe dazu Gerov, *ad* ILBulg 309, und den Kommentar zu IGLNovae 76. Zur *legio I Minervia* siehe Ritterling 1925, 1420–1434; Le Bohec 2000; Eck 2000.

5 Dazu besonders Mrozewicz 1985; vgl. Speidel 1986.

6 Dazu Eck 2009; Eck 2014; Speidel 2007.

7 Speidel 1980, bes. 741–743.

8 Siehe dazu Speidel 2014.

aufzuweisen scheint, ist auch nicht unerhört[9]. Zusammengenommen aber haben so viele Ungewöhnlichkeiten in Verbindung mit ein und derselben Person kumulative Wirkung und erfordern nähere Betrachtung.

Es sind im römischen Armeemilieu allerdings Fälle ähnlich spektakulärer Mobilität bezeugt. Ein solches Beispiel ist C. Iulius Gratus, ein Veteran der Prätorianergarde, der seine Herkunft mit Berytus angab und in Philippopolis begraben wurde[10]. Das Grabmal wurde ihm von seinem Erben (und Verwandten?) C. Iulius Gratus, Veteran der *legio IIII Scythica*, errichtet, was die Inschrift zwischen der Gründung der Provinz Thracia durch Claudius (45/6 n. Chr.) und die Versetzung dieser Legion in den Osten durch Corbulo[11] (56/7 n. Chr.) datiert. In solchen Fällen hat man es jedoch mit Vernetzungen von Veteranen zu tun, die diesen den Umzug im Reiche wesentlich erleichterten: Berytus war römische Kolonie und als solche guter Rekrutierungsgrund für neue Soldaten. Die Legionen, aus deren Veteranen vor nicht so langer Zeit (kurz nach Actium) die neue Kolonie gegründet wurde, waren die *V Macedonica* und die *III Gallica*[12]; erstere hatte, wie auch die *IIII Scythica*, vorhin auf dem Balkan gestanden: zunächst in Macedonia, danach in Moesien[13]. Die Familien der beiden Iulii Grati, die ihr Bürgerrecht wahrscheinlich von Augustus erhalten hatten, waren vermutlich mit dieser Gegend eng verbunden und die Beziehungen bestanden noch eine Generation später weiter, weshalb die beiden im Ruhestand Philippopolis wählten. Macenio steht aber außerhalb eines solchen Netzwerkes.

Die Inschrift wurde im IGLN in die erste Hälfte des 3. Jh. datiert, wohl hauptsächlich wegen des Nomens Aurelius des Verstorbenen. Der Text bietet keinen sonstigen Datierungsanhaltspunkt. Das Nomen ist jedoch nicht abgekürzt, wie man es bei einer Datierung später als die *constitutio Antoniniana* wohl erwarten könnte. Der Sohn trägt ein vom Vater unterschiedliches Nomen. Dies lässt sich dadurch erklären, dass der Sohn zu einem Zeitpunkt geboren wurde, als der Vater noch im aktiven Militärdienst stand und somit das *conubium* nicht besaß; der Sohn trägt wahrscheinlich den Namen seiner Mutter. Da aber Septimius Severus auch den aktiven Militärs das *conubium* verlieh[14], erhält man damit eine vorseverische Datierung zumindest für die Geburt des jungen Valerius.

Höchst ungewöhnlich ist das Cognomen Macenio, das beide Männer tragen. (Dies ist die Nominativform: Die Herausgeber des IGLN nahmen im Falle des Sohnes einen Fehler des Steinmetzen an und sprachen sich für die Form Macenius aus. Dafür gibt es nicht ausreichende Gründe. Dass der Name des Verstorbenen im Nominativ stehen kann, ist ausreichend bezeugt; die Inschrift ist zwar nicht elegant eingemeisselt, aber deutlich, und enthält keine sonstigen Fehler.) Dass eine solche Diskussion überhaupt nötig ist, geschieht

9 Siehe zu einigen solchen Beispielen Ruscu 2017.

10 AE 2001, 1750. Es ist fast gewiss, dass eine Gürtelplatte (ohne bekannten Fundort) eines C. Iulius Gratus aus der 5. prätorischen Kohorte, diesem Mann gehörte: Eck, Pangerl 2015, 120.

11 Ritterling 1925, Sp. 1559–1560.

12 Sartre 1991, 123, 337–338; Hall 2004, 46–47.

13 Ritterling 1925, Sp. 1159–1160, 1573–1574; Campbell 1999, 16–17.

14 Herodian III 8, 5; zur Verheiratung der römischen Soldaten am umfassendsten Phang 2001; dagegen jedoch Eck 2011.

deshalb, weil der Name in dieser Form sonst nirgends bezeugt ist[15]. Im OPEL[16] ist dies der einzige Eintrag dieses Namens. Etruskische, keltische oder orientalische Herkunft wurden dafür vorgeschlagen[17], letztere wahrscheinlich allein wegen der vermuteten kappadokischen Herkunft das Aurelius Macenio; allerdings ist bei Zgusta[18] ein solcher oder ähnlicher Name nicht zu finden.

Die keltische Herkunft des Namens ist bei weitem die wahrscheinlichere. Bei Holder[19] findet sich die Variante *Macena*. Die nächststehenden Analogien für den Namen, in der Form Macenus oder Macenius, kommen ausschließlich aus Gallien und Hispanien[20]. Falileyev[21] diskutiert den Namen, verweist noch auf *Maceius* und *Macer* und akzeptiert seine keltische Struktur, spricht sich aber schließlich doch gegen eine keltische Deutung aus, im wesentlichen wegen der vermutlichen orientalischen Herkunft des Veteranen.

Davon ausgehend ist es angemessener, statt einer kappadokischen Provenienz des Macenio eine Herkunft in den westlichen Provinzen mit keltischem Hintergrund zu akzeptieren. Es lassen sich dort durchaus andere Herkunftsangaben finden, die die Buchstabenfolge [.]APP enthalten. Am passendsten ist Vappincum (oder Vapincum), Hauptort der Avantici im Stammesverband der Vocontii in Gallia Narbonensis (heute Gap, Dép. Hautes-Alpes), *vicus*, danach römische *civitas*[22]. Fälle von Veteranen aus der Narbonensis, die sich in den balkanischen Provinzen niederließen, sind nicht ungewöhnlich: Da ist M. Licinius M. f. Voltinia tribu Optatus[23], der aus Lucus (am wahrscheinlichsten Lucus Augusti Vocontiorum in der Narbonensis) stammte. Er wurde in die *legio I Italica* rekrutiert, wahrscheinlich während die Legion noch in Lugdunum stand, und ließ sich nach der Entlassung aus dem Militärdienst, wahrscheinlich durch Domitian, in Scupi nieder[24]. Ebenfalls aus Lucus Vocontiorum stammen L. Valerius L. f. Galeria Galenus[25], Veteran der *legio IIII Macedonica* (rekrutiert während die Legion noch in Mogontiacum stand) und C. Iulius C. f. Voltinia Velox[26], Veteran der *legio V Alaudae*, die sich beide ebenfalls in Scupi niederließen[27].

Solche Fälle zeigen, dass die Bewegungen römischer Militäreinheiten im späten 1. und frühen 2. Jh. n. Chr., besonders während der Dakerkriege Trajans, den westkeltischen und den Balkanraum näher zueinander brachten, als es geographisch naheliegend erschiene.

15 Vgl. Minkova 2000, 198–199.
16 OPEL III 42.
17 Minkova 1999.
18 Zgusta 1964, *passim*; Zgusta 1984, *passim*.
19 Holder II 377.
20 Keramische Stempel: *Macen(i)* CIL II 6349,27 Hispania citerior, Elche; *of(ficina) Maceni* Provost 1988, 102 Lugudunensis, Tours.
21 Falileyev 2013, s. v. Macenio.
22 Talbert 2000, 17 G4 FRA. Siehe dazu Goessler 1955; Walde 2012.
23 CIL III 8198 = IMS VI 37.
24 Siehe zu ihm Matei-Popescu 2010, 80.
25 IMS VI 39 = AE 1984, 760.
26 IMS VI 41.
27 Siehe zu ihnen Ferjančić 2002, 282, Nr. 320–321; Matei-Popescu 2010, 80.

Eine Verbindung zwischen der *legio I Minervia* und Novae ist schon seit langem bekannt. Die Legion nahm an den Dakerkriegen Trajans teil und das Vorhandensein einer Vexillation im Lager von Novae wird durch mehrere Funde von Ziegelstempeln bezeugt[28].

Damit lässt die keltische Herkunft des Namens des Macenio auch eine keltische Herkunft des Mannes wahrscheinlicher erscheinen, und diese ihrerseits erlaubt die Umgehung der Absonderlichkeiten, die eine kappadokische Herkunft mit sich bringt. Es kann folgender Sachverlauf wiederhergestellt werden: Aurelius Macenio mag noch in der Regierungszeit Neros geboren sein, trat wohl kurz nach 80 der *legio I Minervia* bei, kam unter Trajan mit einer Vexillation daraus an die untere Donau, erhielt hier seine *honesta missio* und beschloss, sich in Novae, seinem (vermutlich) letzten Standort, niederzulassen.

Damit erhält man einen Fall nicht mehr gar so ungewöhnlicher Mobilität. Eine westliche keltische Herkunft für Macenio hat den Vorteil, so manches an seinen Wanderungen auf viel einfachere Weise zu erklären. Er bräuchte dann nicht mehr am östlichsten Ende des Reiches für eine Legion an dessen westlichem Ende rekrutiert zu werden, sondern könnte (vergleichsweise) mühelos in eine der Legionen am Rhein eingetreten und mit ihr in den Balkanraum gelangt sein.

Literaturverzeichnis

Campbell, J. B. 1999. s. v. *legio*, DNP VII, Stuttgart 1999, 7–22.

Derks, T., Roymans, N. 2006. Returning Auxiliary Veterans: Some Methodological Considerations, Journal of Roman Archaeology 19, 121–135.

Eck, W. 2000. Die *legio I Minervia*. Militärische und zivile Aspekte ihrer Geschichte im 3. Jh., in Y. Le Bohec (Hrsg.), Les légions de Rome sous le Haut-Empire. Actes du Congrès de Lyon (17–19 septembre 1998) I, Lyon, 87–94.

Eck, W. 2009. Rekrutierung für das römische Heer in den Provinzen Kleinasiens. Das Zeugnis der Militärdiplome, in O. Tekin (Hrsg.), Ancient History, Numismatics and Epigraphy in the Mediterranean World. Studies in Memory of Clemens E. Bosch and Sabahat Atlan and in Honour of Nezahat Baydur, Istanbul, 137–142.

Eck, W. 2011. Septimius Severus und die Soldaten. Das Problem der Soldatenehe und ein neues Auxiliardiplom, in B. Onken, D. Rohde (Hrsg.), *In omni historia curiosus*. Studien zur Geschichte von der Antike bis zur Neuzeit. Festschrift für Helmuth Schneider zum 65. Geburtstag, Wiesbaden, 63–77.

Eck, W. 2014. Das römische Heer und die kleinasiatischen Provinzen während der Hohen Kaiserzeit, in J. Fischer (Hrsg.), Der Beitrag Kleinasiens zur Kultur- und Geistesgeschichte der griechisch-römischen Antike. Akten des internationalen Kolloquiums, Wien 3.–5. November 2010 (TAM Ergänzungsband 27), Wien, 87–97.

28 Siehe dazu Ritterling 1925, 1426–27; Gostar 1965; Sarnowski 1987; AE 1987, 865; Strobel 1988; Matei-Popescu 210, 260.

Eck, W., Pangerl, A. 2015. Inschriften auf metallenen militärischen Gebrauchsgegenständen, in P. Henrich, Ch. Miks, J. Obmann, M. Wieland (Hrsg.), *Non solum ... sed etiam*. Festschrift für Thomas Fischer zum 65. Geburtstag, Rahden/Westf., 113–126.

Falileyev, A. 2013. The Celtic Balkans, Aberystwyth.

Ferjančić, S. 2002. Naseljavanje legijskih veterana u balkanskim provincijama: I–III vek n. e., Beograd.

Forni, G. 1953. Il reclutamento delle legioni da Augusto a Diocleziano, Milano.

Forni, G. 1974. Estrazione etnica e sociale dei soldati delle legioni nei primi trei secoli dell' Impero, ANRW II 1, 339–391.

Goessler, P. 1955. s. v. *Vapincum*, RE VIII 1, 354–359.

Gostar, N. 1965. *Legio I Minervia* în estul Daciei, AUI 11, 1–8.

Hall, L. J. 2004. Roman Berytus. Beirut in Late Antiquity, London.

Holder, A., 1904. Alt-celtischer Sprachschatz, Leipzig 1904.

Le Bohec, Y. 2000. *Legio I Minervia* (Ier- IIe siècles), in Y. Le Bohec (Hrsg.), Les légions de Rome sous le Haut-Empire. Actes du Congrès de Lyon (17–19 septembre 1998) I, Lyon, 83–86.

Matei-Popescu, F. 2010. The Roman Army in Moesia Inferior, Bucharest.

Minkova, M. 2000. The Personal Names of the Latin Inscriptions in Bulgaria, Frankfurt/Main.

Phang, S. E. 2001. The Marriage of Roman Soldiers (13 B. C.–A. D. 235). Law and Family in the Imperial Army, Leiden.

Provost, M. 1988. Carte archéologique de la Gaule 37: L'Indre-et-Loire, Paris.

Raepsaet-Charlier, M.-T. 1978. Le lieu d'installation des vétérans auxiliaires romains d'après les diplômes militaires, L'Antiquité Classique 47.2, 557–565.

Ritterling, E. 1925. s. v. *legio*, RE XII, Sp. 1186–1829.

Roxan, M. M. 1981. The Distribution of Roman Military Diplomas, Epigraphische Studien 12, 265–286.

Roxan, M. M. 1989. Findspots of Military Diplomas of the Roman Auxiliary Army, University College London Institute of Archaeology Bulletin 26, 127–181.

Ruscu, L. 2017. Über Sex. Vibius Gallus aus Amastris, Istraživanja (Novi Sad) 28, 58–68.

Sarnowski, T. 1989. Zur Truppengeschichte der Dakerkriege Traians. Die Bonner Legio I Minervia und das Legionslager Novae, Germania 65, 107–122.

Sartre, M. 1991. L'Orient romain, Paris.

Speidel, M. A. 2007. Rekruten für ferne Provinzen. Der Papyrus ChLA X 422 und die kaiserliche Rekrutierungszentrale, ZPE 163, 281–295.

Speidel, M. A. 2014. Connecting Cappadocia. The Contribution of the Roman Imperial Army, in V. Cojocaru, A. Çoşkun, M. Dana (Hrsg.), Interconnectivity in the Mediterranean and Pontic World During the Hellenistic and Roman Periods, Cluj-Napoca, 625–640.

Speidel, M. P. 1980. Legionaries from Asia Minor, ANRW II 7, 730–746.

Speidel, M. P. 1986. The Soldiers' Homes, in W. Eck, H. Wolff (Hrsg.), Heer und Integrationspolitik. Die römischen Militärdiplome als historische Quelle, Köln, 467–481.

Strobel, K. 1988. Anmerkungen zur Truppengeschichte des Donauraumes in der hohen Kaiserzeit I: Die neuen Ziegelstempel der Legio I Minervia aus dem Lager der Legio I Italica in Novae in Moesia Inferior, Klio 70, 501–511.
Talbert, R.J.A. 2000. Barrington Atlas of the Greek and Roman World, Princeton.
Walde, C. 2012. s.v. *Vapincum*, DNP XII 1, Stuttgart, Sp. 1124.
Wesch-Klein, G. 2007. Recruits and Veterans, in P. Erdkamp (Hrsg.), A Companion to the Roman Army, Oxford, 435–450.
Zgusta, L. 1964. Kleinasiatische Personennamen, Prag.
Zgusta, L. 1984. Kleinasiatische Ortsnamen, Heidelberg.

La mobilité des militaires recrutés du milieu rural de Mésie inférieure: les unités et leur aire d'action

Lucrețiu Mihailescu-Bîrliba

1 Introduction

Les militaires recrutés du milieu rural de la Mésie Inférieure sont de plus en plus attestés dans les sources épigraphiques (surtout dans les diplômes militaires) dans les dernières décennies. Ils peuvent être identifiés selon la mention explicite de leur origine rurale, selon le lieu de découverte lorsqu'ils rentrent chez eux et (avec un degré plus élevé d'incertitude) selon leurs ethnonymes (*Thracus*, *Bessus*, *Dacus*). Si dans le cas de *Dacus*, la probabilité que le personnage soit originaire de Mésie Inférieure est plus élevée, dans les cas de *Thracus* et de *Bessus* il est possible que les personnes dont ces ethnonymes sont attachés proviennent de Thrace et de Mésie Inférieure. Dans la plupart écrasante des cas le lieu de découverte des diplômes militaires n'est pas mentionné, puisqu'ils proviennent du marché des antiquités, mais il y a toujours un degré de probabilité que beaucoup de ces diplômes proviennent toujours du milieu rural de la province. J'analyserai un aspect de la mobilité de ces soldats, y compris les situations « probables », en suivant les unités où ils ont servi et leur aire d'action.

2 L'évidence des sources

Les **Annexes 1–6** de la fin de l'article référencent les unités où ont agi les soldats originaires du milieu rural de la Mésie Inférieure ou encore pour certains d'entre eux, dans lesquelles ils ont achevé leur service. On observe que dans les légions sauf pour une exception, les sources attestent de recrutements à la fin du IIe siècle ou au IIIe siècle (**Annexe 1**). Les recrutements locaux dans les *legiones* ont commencé assez tôt en Mésie Inférieure. Dans le cas de la *legio V Macedonica*, on peut parler de ce phénomène vers la fin du Ier siècle[1]. Pourtant, ces recrutements deviennent plus fréquents à partir du règne d'Hadrien[2] et particulièrement dans la période qui est également enregistrée pour notre échantillon-

1 Mihailescu-Bîrliba 2016, 75.
2 Mihailescu-Bîrliba 2016, 72–74.

nage. Quant à l'exception, le recrutement dans l'armée romaine date de 44–46[3] mais il est certain que le militaire a servi d'abord dans l'une des flottes prétoriennes puis dans la *legio II Adiutrix*. Zurazis Decebali f., un Dace provenant certainement du sud du Danube, est libéré en 70, avant le terme, de la légion ci-dessus mentionnée à cause de ses blessures, à côté d'autres soldats *qui bello inutiles facti*. Le même jour, le 7 mars 70 et un jour avant ont reçu la *honesta missio* deux autres soldats dans la même situation, dont les diplômes ont été trouvés en Mésie Supérieure : un Dace anonyme[4] et un Thrace, Dules Datui f.[5]. Un troisième soldat, Nerva Laidi f. de Dalmatie, a reçu la *honesta missio* le 6 mars 70[6]. Il s'agit de la fin de la guerre civile de 68–69. La légion était constituée des marins de la flotte de Ravenne qui, selon Tacite, avaient demandé de servir dans une légion : leur élite était envoyée dans l'armée de Vespasien tandis que la flotte était complétée par des marins originaires de Dalmatie[7]. Après la fin de la guerre, Vespasien a récompensé les marins et les nouveaux soldats des légions en leur accordant le droit de cité[8]. En ce qui concerne la *legio II Adiutrix*, elle est fondée le 7 mars 70 lorsque les soldats transférés des flottes reçoivent la citoyenneté[9].

Du côté des flottes romaines, on constate que les recrutements ont compris à partir de Claude un grand nombre de soldats provenant du milieu rural de l'espace balkano-danubien. L'**Annexe 6** en présente une situation statistique. La plupart des recrues, 44 au nombre, ont été envoyées dans la flotte de Misène et 14 seulement dans la *classis Ravennas*. Quatre inscriptions sont trop fragmentaires pour apprendre de quelle flotte il s'agit dans le texte. Pour autant, le premier diplôme militaire provenant de la Mésie Inférieure est celui qui atteste la libération de Sparticus Diuzeni f. le 11 décembre 52[10]. Nous avons auparavant argumenté des circonstances des recrutements. Il n'est pas lieu ici de les reprendre. La flotte accueille de nouvelles recrues les années suivantes comme il en résulte d'une *constitutio* de 54 où les témoins sont des Thraces encore actifs, probablement dans la flotte de Misène[11]. Les individus originaires – certainement ou probablement – du milieu rural de la Mésie Inférieure ont été enrôlés en 44–46 dans les flottes de Misène et de Ravenne (voir l'**Annexe 6**). De la deuxième moitié du Ier siècle et du IIe siècle datent la plupart des textes (**Annexe 6**). Les soldats ont servi, mises à part quelques exceptions, dans la flotte de Misène. Ils sont attestés en grande majorité avec l'ethnonyme *Thracus* ou *Bessus* ; il est par conséquent difficile d'affirmer s'ils sont de façon certaine originaires de Mésie Inférieure. De plus, comme D. Dana l'a correctement remarqué, le terme *Bessus* est utilisé pour dé-

3 Sharankov 2006, 37–46.
4 RMD V, 323.
5 CIL XVI 10.
6 CIL XVI 11.
7 Tacite, Hist. 3, 50.
8 CIL XVI 13 ; RMD IV, 203; Chiriac, Mihailescu-Bîrliba, Matei 2004, 265–269 etc.
9 Ritterling 1925, 1439–1440.
10 CIL XVI 1.
11 ISM IV, 1.

signer une personne provenant des régions habitées par les Thraces[12]. Enfin, la dernière période est illustrée par l'époque des Sévères et surtout par le règne de Septime, seul ou conjointement avec ses fils. De cette période sont issus les diplômes qui spécifient l'origine rurale des marins tout en indiquant aussi le village – *uicus Bres[---]*[13], *uicus Dizerpera*[14], *uicus Zinesdina Maior*[15], *uicus [---]tsitsi*[16]. Dans l'écrasante majorité des cas, les *uici* font partie du milieu rural de Nicopolis ad Istrum.

En ce qui concerne la mobilité des militaires recrutés dans la flotte, les sources sont assez précises. Ils proviennent de Mésie Inférieure ou au moins, d'un territoire habité par les Thraces ou les Daces et ont effectué leur service en Italie, à Misène ou à Ravenne. Il est possible que certains d'eux aient combattu en Judée sous Hadrien[17] ou aient été envoyés rejoindre d'autres campagnes. Beaucoup de soldats sont morts en service[18], une partie est restée en Italie après la *honesta missio*[19] et d'autres soldats, assez nombreux semble-t-il sont rentrés chez eux après le service. Il s'agit de Tutius Buti f. à Dalgodeltsi[20], Tarsa, Duzi f. à Mihai Bravu[21] et très probablement de M. Aurelius Bassus[22], M. Aurelius Victor[23], M. Aurelius Statianus[24] et encore trois anonymes[25]. D'ailleurs, la formule *cui et*, suivie de l'ancien nom de pérégrin du bénéficiaire, attestée en plusieurs diplômes, indique indirectement la possibilité que le vétéran serait rentré chez lui, où il était connu non sous le nom de citoyen mais sous celui de *peregrinus*. Ce sont les cas de M. Aurelius Bassus[26], M. Aurelius Victor aussi dit Drubio[27], M. Aurelius Statianus aussi dit Apta[28] et encore d'un anonyme dont le nom du pérégrin était Zur[---][29]. Un autre militaire, libéré en 217/225 s'est trouvé en Bétique au moment de sa *honesta missio*[30]. Ainsi, on constate une forte mobilité dans le cas des militaires de la flotte : bien sûr, ils ont dû effectuer leur service en Italie. Ils ont également participé aux missions diverses, en Judée ou en Espagne et après

12 Dana 2013, 245–246. Ses arguments me semblent convaincants : dans les inscriptions entre *Thrax* (*Thracus*) et *Bessus* il n'y a pas de distinction (voir l'opinion contraire chez Tačeva 1997, 199–210 ; Tačeva 1999, 863–872).
13 RMD IV, 317 = RMD V, 457 = RGZM 54 ; AE 2001, 2165.
14 RMD V, 463.
15 RMD IV, 311.
16 RMD II, 201.
17 Selon CPL 117. Voir aussi Eck, Pangerl 2006a, 239–252 ; Eck, Pangerl 2007a, 283–290.
18 CIL X 3653, 3656, 3664, 3670 ; XI 47, 58, 103 etc.
19 AE 1988, 310; CIL X 3376, 3573: XI 82, 87 etc.
20 CIL XVI 13.
21 Chiriac, Mihailescu-Bîrliba, Matei 2004, 265–269.
22 RMD IV, 317.
23 RMD V, 463.
24 RMD IV, 311.
25 Eck, Pangerl 2014, 339–343.
26 RMD IV, 317.
27 RMD V, 463.
28 RMD IV, 311.
29 Eck, Pangerl 2014, 340–341.
30 RMD III, 201.

leur service, ils ont choisi soit de rester en Italie, soit bien de rentrer chez eux en parcourant une longue distance.

Les recrutements de la population du milieu rural de la Mésie Inférieure commencent assez tôt dans les unités auxiliaires et plus précisément dans les ailes. L'**Annexe 2** à la fin de l'article présente la fréquence des recrutements dans les ailes selon les information fournies par les sources épigraphiques. Cinq textes nous informent sur des soldats qui commencent leur service dans des unités stationnées en Syrie. Il s'agit de l'*ala Gallorum et Thracum Antiana* avec Romaesta Rescenti f., recruté en 29 en un village nommé Spiurus[31] et encore un soldat d'origine dace recruté en 126/129[32] et de l'*ala ueterana Gallica* avec trois cas en 66[33]. La première aile a été mentionnée dans la province sur plusieurs diplômes de 88 à 186, d'abord en Syrie puis en Syrie Palestine[34], tandis que la deuxième a campé en Syrie aux environs de 130 lorsqu'elle est attestée en Egypte[35]. Les soldats recrutés au milieu du Ier siècle ont commencé leur service dans l'*ala I Brittonum* en 46[36] et l'*ala I Thracum Victrix* avec deux soldats en 54[37]. La première unité a stationnée, à l'exception d'une brève période après les guerres daciques, en Pannonie[38]. La deuxième est attestée en Norique en 95 par un autre diplôme militaire[39], avant d'être transferée en Pannonie Supérieure vers 126[40].

Ici, il faut mentionner le recrutement de Cegises dans la *cohors I Thracum*[41] mais son origine de Mésie n'est pas certaine car son enrôlement en 45–49 peut être lié à la création de la province de Thrace.

Les recrutements de la population locale de Mésie Inférieure se poursuivent, en 58 un militaire dans l'*ala Siliana torquata ciuium Romanorum*[42] et 61 un soldat dans l'*ala I Thracum ueterana*[43]. Dans l'*ala Siliana*, stationnée en Germanie[44], Pannonie[45] et en Dacie Porolissensis[46] s'y sont effectués des recrutements dès la fin du Ier siècle, en 94[47] et 100[48]. Les soldats sont d'abord recrutés pour l'armée de Germanie[49] puis pour l'*exercitus Pannoniae*

31 ISM IV, 3.
32 Eck, Pangerl 2016a, 85–95.
33 RMD I, 5; Eck, Pangerl 2006b, 206–214; Eck, Pangerl 2006b, 215–218.
34 CIL XVI, 87; RMD I, 3, 60, 60; III, 160, 173; V, 329–330; RGZM 29, 41 etc.
35 CIL XVI, 3, 35, 184; RMD I, 5; III, 185 etc.
36 RMD V, 324.
37 RGZM 3; Weiß 2004, 239–246.
38 Spaul 1994, 72–73. Voir aussi RMD I, 21; II, 113; CIL XVI 112, 175, 179, 180 etc.
39 AE 2009, 993.
40 RMD IV, 236, 250; CIL XVI 76–77, 84, 96, 178 etc.
41 Eck, Cockings 2021, 285–286.
42 RMD IV, 210.
43 Eck, Pangerl 2007b, 239–251.
44 CIL XVI 23.
45 CIL XVI 30–31, 42, 47, 164.
46 CIL XVI 185: RMD I, 35, 47, 66; V, 404 etc.
47 AE 2003, 2041.
48 RMD IV, 235.
49 RMD IV, 210.

Inferioris mais ils finissent leur service en Dacie Porolissensis[50]. Le soldat recruté dans l'*ala Thracum ueterana* a effectué son service en Rhétie[51].

Trois soldats sont enrôlés la même année, en 63, dans l'*ala praetorium singularium*[52]. Ils commencent leur service lors de la campagne de Gn. Domitius Corbulo en Syrie où ils le terminent.

Le dernier quart du Ier siècle marque le recrutement de quatre soldats dans l'*ala Flauia Gaetulorum*, stationnée en Mésie sur le territoire de la future province de Mésie Inférieure[53]. Il s'agit d'un recrutement en 72[54] puis de deux en 74[55] et d'un autre en date de 74 à 85[56]. Il est important de remarquer que les recrutements locaux ont débuté à partir de cette période.

Les sources informent sur trois recrutements dans l'*ala Gallorum Flauiana* : le premier en 82[57], le deuxième en 110[58] et le troisième en 119/121[59]. L'aile a campé en Mésie Inférieure puis en Mésie Supérieure[60]. L'unité est mentionnée dans le diplôme de Cataloi daté de 92 pour l'armée de la Mésie Inférieure[61] puis dans une *constitutio* de 97 pour la même province[62]. Après avoir fait partie de l'*exercitus Moesie Inferioris* comme l'attestent les diplômes de 99[63], 105[64] et 121[65], l'aile est transférée en Mésie Supérieure probablement vers le milieu du règne d'Hadrien ce qui apparaît la première fois dans une *constitutio* de 129[66]. Les recrutements se déroulent lorsque l'aile est en Mésie Inférieure mais deux soldats finissent ce service en Mésie Supérieure. D'ailleurs, ces diplômes confirment que les recrutements locaux continueront à la fin du Ier siècle et après.

Entre les deux guerres daciques, on trouve deux militaires recrutés l'un dans l'*ala Sulpicia ciuium Romanorum*[67], l'autre dans l'*ala Thracum Herculiana*[68]. L'*ala Sulpicia* stationnait en Germanie depuis 78[69]. L'*ala Thracum Herculiana* se déplaça en Galatie et Cap-

50 AE 2003, 20142; RMD IV, 235.
51 Eck, Pangerl 2007b, 239–251.
52 RMD V, 329–331.
53 Voir Matei-Popescu 2010, avec bibliographie. Voir aussi Mihailescu-Bîrliba 2011, 89–90, avec bibliographie.
54 RMD V, 337.
55 Eck, Pangerl 2006 c, 99–100; Eck, Pangerl 2012, 295–301.
56 RMD IV, 221.
57 Eck, Pangerl 2009, 519.
58 Eck, Pangerl 2017, 233.
59 RMD V, 402.
60 Petolescu, Popescu 2004, 269–276; RMD IV, 247; V, 402, 419; RGZM 31, 37 etc. Voir aussi Spaul 1994, 115–116; Matei-Popescu, Țentea 2018, 21–23, 128–131.
61 Petolescu, Popescu 2004, 269–276.
62 RMD V, 338.
63 CIL XVI 44.
64 CIL XVI 50.
65 RMD V, 350.
66 Eck, Pangerl 2018, 226 sqq.
67 Eck, Pangerl 2010, 181–182.
68 Matei-Popescu 2007, 153–159.
69 CIL XVI 23; RGZM 9, 35 etc.

padoce[70] mais il semble qu'elle ait été transférée sous Hadrien en relation avec la guerre de Judée[71]. Il semble que notre soldat serve d'abord en Galatie puis termine son service dans la province de Syrie.

Nous disposons de 9 cas de recrutements dans l'*ala I Ulpia contariorum*, les six premiers après les guerres daciques dans le premier quart du IIe siècle[72], les trois autres au IIIe siècle[73]. L'aile a stationné en Pannonie Supérieure et en Dacie Supérieure[74]. En 112, l'unité est mentionnée en Pannonie Supérieure[75] mais en 121, elle apparaît en Dacie Supérieure[76]. À partir de 126, elle est de nouveau présente en Pannonie Supérieure[77]. L'intervalle de 120–121 à 126, lorsque l'unité campe en Dacie Supérieure, est probablement nécessité par le renforcement de la frontière dans les combats contre les Yaziges[78].

De la même période *i.* e. 115, date le recrutement d'un Thrace, Bithus Solae f., dans le *numerus equitum Illyricorum*[79]. L'aile a stationné en Dacie Inférieure et le soldat, après avoir effectué son service, rentre chez lui.

Trois militaires sont enrôlés dans l'*ala I Augusta Gallorum*[80]. Les recrutements ont eu lieu en 128 afin de renouveler ses effectifs. Les soldats, Daces du sud du Danube, bénéficient de la *honesta missio* le 26 octobre 153 avec deux autres Daces actifs dans l'*ala Gemelliana ciuium Romanorum*[81] et dans une unité inconnue[82]. Les deux ailes se trouvaient à l'époque en Tingitane[83].

L'an 133 a marqué un moment important pour les recrutements pour les unités militaires dans le contexte de la guerre de Judée contre Bar-Kochba. Les sources enregistrent quatre militaires provenant probablement du milieu rural de la Mésie Inférieure et enrôlés dans l'*ala VII Phrygum*[84]. L'aile stationne en Syrie[85] et participe certainement au conflit. De fait, trois militaires servent encore leur service en Syrie. La même année, un autre soldat a commencé son service dans l'*ala Gallorum et Bosporanorum*[86], sise alors en Dacie[87].

---

70 RGZM 7; AE 2004, 1913; 2014, 1656.
71 Voir Matei-Popescu 2007, 156, avec bibliographie.
72 RIU I, 261 (deux cas) et RMD IV, 236.
73 RIU I, 260, 262; RGZM 74.
74 Spaul 1994, 97–100; Eck, Pangerl 2008a, 281–283.
75 RMD IV, 223.
76 RMD I, 19; V, 337; Eck, Pangerl 2008a, 276–284.
77 RMD IV, 236, 250; CIL XVI 76, 96, 178 etc.
78 Eck, Pangerl 2008a, 280.
79 RMD I, 39.
80 RGZM 34; AE 2005, 1726; RMD V, 411.
81 Mugnai 2016, 243–246.
82 Weiß 2009, 246–247.
83 *Ala I Augusta Gallorum*: CIL XVI 159, 165, 181–182; RMD II, 84; III, 186, V, 409–411; RGZM 34 etc; *ala Gemelliana ciuium Romanorum*: CIL XVI 73, 159, 165–166, 171, 173, 181; RMD II, 84; V, 382, 409–410 etc.
84 RMD V, 421; Eck, Pangerl 2007a, 283–290 ; Sharankov 2009, 53–57; AE 2006, 1835.
85 CIL XVI 87, 103; RMD I, 3; III, 173; V, 329–330; RGZM 29, 41 etc.
86 CIL XVI 108.
87 CIL XVI 90; RMD II, 123, V, 384 etc.

En ce qui concerne le recrutement dans les cohortes, même si la première source en atteste un en 55, il est possible que ce phénomène ait commencé encore plus tôt en même temps que le recrutement dans les ailes (**Annexe 3**). Une seule source informe sur un recrutement dans la *cohors I Montanorum*[88]. La cohorte stationnait au moment de la *honesta missio* en Pannonie mais avant elle a agi aussi en Norique[89]. Le militaire a commencé son service en Norique puis le continue en Pannonie. Comme le diplôme a été trouvé à Klosterneuburg, il est possible qu'il soit resté en Pannonie après son service. Il faut aussi mentionner le recrutement en 55 de deux soldats[90] dans la même cohorte *IV Thracum*, campée en Germanie. En 61, Gorius Stibi f. est enrôlé dans la *cohors Musulamiorum*[91] à l'époque en Syrie et probablement à l'occasion de l'expédition arménienne de Corbulo.

Trois soldats encore d'origine thrace sont enrôlés en 65 dans la *cohors I Aquitanorum*[92] de l'armée de la Germanie[93]. Après la libération, il semble qu'au moins un militaire est resté dans la province où il a effectué son service car le diplôme a été découvert à Mogontiacum[94]. Il est possible que l'autre soldat soit rentré chez lui.

L'an 66 est marqué par le recrutement de deux soldats dans la *cohors III Thracum Syriaca*[95] et dans la *cohors I Thracum milliaria*[96]. Les deux cohortes ont stationné en Syrie et même si leur première mention date de 88[97], leur présence dans la province doit être liée de l'expédition contre les Parthes de Gn. Domitius Corbulo puis à la guerre de Judée de Vespasien. On peut donc parler d'un autre groupe de soldats recrutés dans les cohortes à avoir fait leur service en Orient.

Un autre soldat est recruté en 71 dans la *cohors VI Thracum*[98]. Avant de camper en Mésie Supérieure où le soldat reçoit sa *honesta missio*, la cohorte est installée en Germanie[99] et en Pannonie[100]. Notre militaire commence probablement son service en Germanie, le poursuit en Pannonie pour l'achever en Mésie Supérieure où il reste après sa libération, si l'on en juge du lieu de découverte du diplôme.

Les recrutements locaux ont commencé, comme on l'a vu dans les cas des ailes, le dernier quart du Ier siècle. Pour les cohortes, c'est le cas de M. Antonius Rufus, de la *cohors II Gallorum*, recruté en 74[101]. Dans la même cohorte, il faut mentionner plus tard, en 153, celui d'un Dace, Thia Timarchi f., cette fois-ci en Bretagne où la cohorte campait alors[102].

88 CIL XVI 26.
89 CIL XVI 6; RGZM 3.
90 CIL XVI 158; RGZM 4.
91 AE 1939, 126.
92 CIL XVI 36; RMD V, 333; Eck, Pangerl 2004, 259–262.
93 CIL XVI 20.
94 CIL XVI 36.
95 RMD IV, 214.
96 Eck, Pangerl 2006b, 219–221.
97 CIL XVI 35.
98 RMD I, 6.
99 CIL XIII 7502; XVI 158; RGZM 4.
100 AE 2003, 1447; CIL XVI 30–31.
101 CIL XVI 44.
102 RMD IV, 293.

La *cohors II Flauia Bessorum* est mentionnée dans l'armée de la Mésie Inférieure à partir de 92[103] mais certainement a été constituée sous Vespasien – comme d'ailleurs son nom l'indique – plus tôt, peut-être en 75, lorsqu'un soldat thrace y est recruté[104]. De toute façon, le soldat est libéré quand l'unité est encore stationnée en Mésie Inférieure.

Les sources ne mentionnent pas beaucoup de soldats dans les mêmes cohortes. Leurs informations sont importantes à l'égard des moments de recrutement et de la mobilité des militaires. Ainsi, les recrutements locaux ont continué vers la fin du Ier siècle. Tarsa Tarsae est enrôlé en 80 dans la *cohors I Tyriorum sagittariorum*[105] tandis que Hezbenus est attesté dans la même cohorte en 107, ce qui signifie qu'il a été recruté en 82. Il a commencé et fini son service lorsque la cohorte se trouvait en Mésie Inférieure[106].

Comme on l'a déjà vu, beaucoup de soldats de la region située au sud du Danube, fort probablement en Mésie Inférieure sont recrutés dans les *auxilia* romaines après les guerres daciques. Ainsi, un soldat a fait son service en Arabie, dans la *cohors VI Hispanorum*[107]. Un autre a été recruté dans la *cohors II Lingonum*[108], active en Bretagne[109]. Comme le diplôme a été trouvé en Bulgarie, on suppose que le soldat est rentré chez lui après la *honesta missio*. Un troisième militaire a fait son service en Germanie Inférieure dans la *cohors IV Thracum*[110]. Après son service, il est rentré dans sa province d'origine : son diplôme a été trouvé à Glava Panega, non loin de Montana. Enfin, Diurdanus Damanei f. est enrôlé en 106 dans la *cohors I Flauia Musulamiorum*[111] stationnée en Maurétanie Césarienne à partir de 107[112]. Plus tard, en 119, un autre Dace, Damanaeus, a été recruté dans la *cohors V Delmatarum ciuium Romanorum*[113] ayant son camp en Tingitane[114]. Le diplôme a été trouvé à Iskăr probablement dans le territoire d'Oescus, ce qui suppose que le soldat est rentré chez lui après la *honesta missio*.

Un autre recrutement local est attesté en 113 lorsque Clagissa Clagissae f. commence son service dans la *cohors II Mattiacorum*[115]. L'unité stationne en Mésie puis Mésie Inférieure de Vespasien à Marc Aurèle[116]. Notre soldat rentre à la maison après son service : le certificat de sa *honesta missio* a été trouvé près de Novae.

On a vu qu'un autre moment important pour les recrutements dans la région du Bas-Danube est représenté par les années 126–128. Les cohortes n'en font pas exception.

103 Petolescu, Popescu 2004, 269–276.
104 Eck, Pangerl 2008b, 360–361.
105 RGZM 10.
106 Eck, Pangerl 2009, 506--519; AE 2008, 1713; RGZM 1 etc.
107 Eck, Pangerl 2016b, 227–230.
108 RMD IV, 240.
109 CIL XVI 43, 69–70; RMD III, 184; IV, 293–294; V, 420 etc.
110 RMD IV, 239.
111 AE 2005, 1724.
112 CIL XVI 56.
113 RMD V, 398.
114 CIL XVI 159, 161, 165, 170, 181–182 etc.
115 CIL XVI 83.
116 Matei-Popescu 2010a, 222–224.

Un militaire est recruté en 126 dans la *cohors III Brittonum*[117] stationnée en Mésie Supérieure[118]. Deux autres font leur service dans la *cohors V uoluntariorum* à partir de 127[119]. La cohorte a son camp en Germanie Inférieure à partir du dernier quart du Ier siècle[120]. En Germanie Supérieure, toujours en 127, un soldat dont le patronyme atteste sa provenance du sud du Danube, commence son service dans la *cohors I Ligurum et Hispanorum*[121].

Un seul soldat est recruté dans la *cohors I Brittonum* en 139, Mucatralis Bithi f.[122]. L'unité a stationné à Porolissum au IIe siècle[123]. Le diplôme militaire a été trouvé à Samum ce qui signifie que le militaire n'a pas quitté la Dacie après sa libération. La cohorte a eu son camp à Samum à partir d'Hadrien[124]. En même temps, à Samum a fonctionné une *statio* de *beneficiarii consularis*[125]. Mucatralis est resté à Samum dans le *uicus militaris* constitué près du camp.

Les sources fournissent des informations sur quatre soldats recrutés en 153 dans les cohortes[126], toutes pour les troupes de Bretagne : l'un dans la *cohors I Augusta Neruiana*[127], l'autre dans la *cohors VII Thracum*[128], le troisième dans la *cohors II Gallorum*[129] déjà évoquée et le dernier, dans la *cohors I Aelia Hispanorum*[130].

Enfin, une dernière est la *cohors I Cilicum* où a été enrôlé vers la fin du Ier siècle Aurelius Ditusanus, devenu ultérieurement *strator tribuni*[131]. La cohorte fut l'une des unités les plus mobiles de Mésie Inférieure sinon la plus mobile d'entre elles comme le remarque F. Matei-Popescu[132]. En effet, un tribun de la cohorte, en collaboration avec les vexillations des légions *I Italica* et *XI Claudia*, a capturé dans la région de Montana des ours et des bisons pour une chasse impériale[133]. La cohorte est attestée à Chersonèse[134] et à Olbia, inscription datant du temps de Dèce[135]. La mobilité de la cohorte est indiquée par plusieurs textes. Un tribun a arbitré le litige entre les *Ausdecenses* et les Daces en 176–177[136]. Le texte a

117 RGZM 31.
118 CIL XVI 46; AE 2008, 1731–1735, 1738; RMD IV, 247; V, 418. Voir aussi Țentea, Matei-Popescu 2002–2003, 278 ; Matei-Popescu, Țentea 2018, 41–42.
119 AE 2004, 1911; RMD V, 408.
120 Voir dans ce sens Holder 1999, 237, 243 ; Hanel 2002, 293–296.
121 RMD IV, 274.
122 RMD I, 63.
123 Tóth 1978, 12; Piso 2004–2005; Piso 2005; pour le IIIe siècle, voir *contra* Oprean 2018, 367–370.
124 Petolescu 2002, 86–87; Isac 2003, 38–47.
125 CBI 532–536. Voir aussi France, Nelis-Clément 2014, 117–245 et surtout Piso 2019, 109–129.
126 RMD III, 184; IV, 293–294.
127 CIL XVI 51, 69; RMD III, 184; IV, 240; V, 420 etc.
128 CIL XVI 69, 82; AE 2008, 800; RMD IV, 240 etc.
129 AE 2008, 800; CIL XVI 93; RMD V, 420; CIL VII 316 etc.
130 AE 2006, 1837. Voir aussi Holder 1998, 260–261.
131 ISM IV, 187.
132 Matei-Popescu 2010b, 205.
133 AE 1987, 867.
134 CIL III 13751b.
135 AE 2004, 1289.
136 ISM IV, 82.

été largement discuté et il n'est pas utile d'en reprendre tous les détails[137]. Le conflit ne me semble pas être lié à l'invasion des Costoboces comme le pense V. Pârvan[138] car il s'est produit 7 à 8 ans plus tard. À mon avis, il s'agit d'un litige qui durait depuis un certain temps et plus probablement comme le suppose E. Popescu, était lié à la présence de Thraces dans cette région et à leurs conflits internes permanents avec les indigènes d'origine dace[139]. En tout cas, la *cohors* avait pour mission de maintenir la paix dans la zone et d'intervenir si conflits. En outre, la population de la *ciuitas Ausdecensium* est une population majoritairement thrace ; il semble qu'elle soit néanmoins assez nombreuse – voir le rang de *ciuitas peregrina* acquis par la localité. L'unité est également attestée à Tomi sous le règne de Philippe l'Arabe et a pour surnom *Philippiana*[140]. Son activité sous ce règne est complétée par les informations tirées d'un texte de Sacidava[141].

Au sujet des cohortes prétoriennes, les sources informent sur des recrutements à partir de 182 jusqu'en 232 (**Annexe 4**). Les plus nombreuses occurrences sont enregistrées pour la Ve cohorte, 9 avec des datations incluant les règnes de Caracalla et Sévère Alexandre ; pour les IIIe et IXe cohortes, 6 cas par unité, datant de Septime Sévère jusqu'à Sévère Alexandre (**Annexe 4**). Dans le cas de la Ière cohorte, on dispose de 4 occurrences tandis que pour la VIe, de 3 seulement (**Annexe 4**). Pour la IIe, VIIe et X^{e} cohorte, il n'y a que deux occurrences pour le reste de notre échantillonnage, les IVe et VIIIe cohortes n'ayant qu'une seule occurrence (**Annexe 4**). Et encore, plus de 41 occurrences proviennent de textes fragmentaires où n'est pas mentionnée la cohorte. Reconnaissons que ces données ne nous dressent pas de quelconque tableau quant à une éventuelle préférence de la part des autorités romaines pour recruter pour une cohorte ou une autre. Comme plusieurs inscriptions sont édifiées à l'occasion de la *honesta missio*, il est difficile de dire si les militaires restent à Rome après la fin de leur service ou s'ils rentrent au pays. Pourtant, certains textes fournissent des indications à ce sujet. Par exemple, un diplôme trouvé à côté de Iatrus montre que le soldat anonyme qui a reçu la *honesta missio* a fait le chemin de retour[142]. La même situation est prouvée par deux *constitutiones* trouvées dans le territoire de Nicopolis ad Istrum[143]. D'autres prétoriens sont revenus dans leur province d'origine tels qu'Aurelius Dalenis[144], Aurelius Marcus[145] et Doles, fils de Marcus.[146] Un autre prétorien, Aurelius Longinus, est mort en service mais dans sa province d'origine : les noms thraces de ses parents indiquent son *origo*. Un autre militaire, M. Aurelius Mucianus, est

137 Voir le commentaire le plus récent, avec la bibliographie, chez Emilian Popescu (ISM IV, 92, *sub numero*).
138 Pârvan 1923, 75.
139 Emilian Popescu (ISM IV, 92, *sub numero*).
140 ISM II, 345, 452.
141 ISM IV, 172.
142 RMD IV, 305.
143 CIL XVI 143; RMD II, 132.
144 ISM III, 237.
145 ISM IV, 188.
146 Narloch 2020, 282–285.

mort en service à Rome[147] tout comme Aurelius Victor[148] ou encore Aurelius Iovinus[149]. Un autre militaire d'une cohorte prétorienne est décédé en Maurétanie Césarienne vers la fin de son service[150].

Les sources concernant les *equites singulares Augusti* ne nous informent pas sur le retour des cavaliers dans la province d'origine (**Annexe 5**). Il est d'ailleurs difficile de l'affirmer d'autant que dans plusieurs cas, le lieu de découverte manque, même si on peut supposer que les diplômes militaires – car il s'agit de ce type de textes – ont été sans doute trouvés sur le territoire de la Mésie Inférieure. Ce sont les cas de M. Ulpius Valerius, originaire d'Oescus et plus probablement de son territoire, libéré en 133[151] et de C. Valerius Drigitti f. Valens qui a reçu la *honesta missio* en 223[152]. On trouve aussi des militaires morts en service à Rome, comme M. Ulpius Longinus[153], M. [---] Decimius[154] et plusieurs anonymes[155]. D'autres *equites* sont mentionnés à Rome mais ils sont soit encore en service, soit viennent de finir leur stage militaire[156]. Ainsi, il est difficile de savoir s'ils sont restés dans la capitale de l'Empire après la *honesta missio*. Pourtant, quelques textes peuvent indiquer cette situation. P. Aelius Severus, *natione Bessus* et vétéran, est mort à Rome[157]. Même si le texte ne précise pas l'unité où il a servi, sa presence dans l'*Urbs* et les noms qui suggèrent la reception du droit de cité sous Hadrien indiquent son appartenance au corps des *equites singulares*. Un autre vétéran mort à Rome, cette fois-ci certainement un *eques singularis*, se nomme M. Aurelius Optatus, *natione Thrax*[158].

3 Conclusions

On constate qu'au-delà du hasard des découvertes, les militaires provenant du milieu rural de Mésie Inférieure ont été recrutés dans tous les corps de l'armée romaine. Le même caractère fortuit des découvertes atteste le nombre le plus élevé de soldats à Rome et en Italie, mais quoiqu'il en soit cas, ils étaient très mobiles et suivaient leurs unités. Ainsi, après Rome et l'Italie, la Syrie représente le principal axe de mobilité : il s'agit de grands effectifs de recrues pendant les campagnes de Corbulo contre les Parthes et des deux guerres de Judée. De nombreux militaires provenant de Mésie Inférieure ont fait leur service dans les provinces germaniques et à partir des guerres daciques, en Bretagne. On constate aussi

147 CIL VI 2461.
148 CIL VI 2699.
149 CIL VI 2486.
150 CIL VIII 210121.
151 RMD III, 158.
152 RGZM 55.
153 CIL VI 3303.
154 CIL VI 3250.
155 Speidel 1994b, 114–116, 182–183, 216.
156 CIL VI 31146–31147, 37257, etc.
157 CIL VI 3447.
158 CIL VI 3217.

des mouvements dans les provinces voisines comme dans les Pannonies, les Dacies et la Mésie Supérieure. En ce qui concerne les recrutements locaux, l'on voit qu'ils débutent le dernier quart du Ier siècle et se poursuivent après.

Comme réponse à la question quant à l'existence d'une politique de recrutement précise diligentée par l'État romain, on remarque que d'un côté, les recrutements suivent des règles générales en Mésie Inférieure comme partout dans l'Empire et que de l'autre, la situation particulière de la province, le nombre des soldats recrutés étant très élevé par rapport aux autres provinces – du moins en l'état actuel des informations fournies par les sources dont nous disposons. Néanmoins, cela permet de confirmer pour l'instant, les qualités exceptionnelles de ces combattants et leur dévotion envers l'empereur et les commandants militaires.

Bibliographie

Chiriac, C., Mihailescu-Bîrliba, L., Matei, I. 2004. Ein neues Militärdiplom aus Moesien, ZPE 150, 265–269.

Dana, D. 2013. Les Thraces dans les diplômes militaires. Onomastique et statut des personnes, dans M.-G. Parissaki, Thrakika Zetemata 2. Aspects of the Roman Province of Thrace, Athènes, 219–269.

Eck, W., Cockings, St. 2021. Two Fragmentary Diplomas, Issued under Vespasian and Antoninus Pius, ZPE 218, 2021, 285–288.

Eck, W., Pangerl A. 2004. Neue Diplome für die Heere von Germania superior und Germania inferior, ZPE 148, 259–268.

Eck, W., Pangerl, A. 2006a. Die Konstitution für classis Misenensis aus dem Jahr 160 und der Krieg gegen Bar Kochba unter Hadrian, ZPE 155, 239–252.

Eck, W., Pangerl, A. 2006b. Syria unter Domitian und Hadrian. Neue Diplome für die Auxiliartruppen der Provinz, Chiron 36, 205–247.

Eck, W., Pangerl, A. 2006c. Neue Diplome für die Auxiliartruppen in den mösischen Provinzen von Vespasian bis Hadrian, Dacia N.S. 50, 93–108.

Eck, W., Pangerl, A. 2007a. Eine Konstitution für die Hilfstruppen von Syria Palaestina vom 6. Februar 158 n.Chr., ZPE 159, 283–290.

Eck, W., Pangerl, A. 2007b. Titus Flavius Norbanus, praefectus praetorio Domitians, als Statthalter Rätiens in einem neuen Militärdiplom, ZPE 163, 239–251.

Eck, W., Pangerl, A. 2008a. „Vater, Mutter, Schwestern, Brüder...“: 3. Akt, ZPE 166, 276–284.

Eck, W., Pangerl, A. 2008b. Moesia und seine Truppen. Neue Diplome für Moesia und Moesia superior, Chiron 38, 317–388.

Eck, W., Pangerl, A. 2009. Neue Diplome für Moesia, Moesia inferior und Moesia superior, Chiron 39, 505–589.

Eck, W., Pangerl, A. 2010. Beobachtungen zu den diplomata militaria für die Provinz Germania inferior, dans F. Naumann-Steckner, B. Päffgen, R. Thomas (éds.), Archäologie in Ost und West, Festschrift für Hansgerd Hellenkemper, Köln, 181–195.

Eck, W., Pangerl, A. 2012. Ein weiteres Diplom aus einer Konstitution für die Truppen von Moesia inferior vom 14. August 99 n. Chr., ZPE 180, 295–301.
Eck, W., Pangerl, A. 2014. Diplome für Soldaten der italischen Flotten zwischen Vespasian und Severus Alexander, dans Honesta missione. Festschrift für Barbara Pferdehirt, Mainz, 327–343.
Eck, W., Pangerl, A. 2016a. Eine Konstitution für das Heer von Syria Palaestina aus der Mitte der antoninischen Herrschaftszeit mit einem Auxiliarpräfekten Cn. Domitius Corbulo, Scripta Classica Israelica 35, 2016, 85–95.
Eck, W., Pangerl, A. 2016b. Ein Diplom für die Hilfstruppen der Provinz Arabia, ausgestellt unter Hadrian, wohl im Jahr 126, ZPE 197, 227–231.
Eck, W., Pangerl, A. 2017. Tullius Varro als Statthalter in Moesia superior in einer Konstitution des Jahres 135, ZPE 203, 227–234.
Eck, W., Pangerl, A. 2018. Neue Diplome aus der Zeit Hadrians für die beiden mösischen Provinzen, ZPE 207, 224–231.
France, J., Nelis-Clément, J. 2014. Tout en bas de l'empire. Les stationes, lieux de contrôle et de représenation du pouvoir, dans J. France, J. Nelis-Clément (éds.), La statio. Archéologie d'un lieu de pouvoir dans l'empire romain, Bordeaux, 117–145.
Hanel, N. 2002. Ein Ziegelstempel der cohors XV voluntariorum c. R. aus der tegularia transrhenana im Flottenlager Köln-Marienburg (Alteburg), ZPE 139, 293–296.
Holder, P. 1998. Auxiliary units entitled Aelia, ZPE 122, 253–263.
Holder, P. 1999. *Exercitus Pius Fidelis*: The Army of Germania Inferior in AD 89, ZPE 128, 237–250.
Isac, D. 2003. Castrul roman de la Samum-Cășeiu / The Roman Auxiliary Fort Samum-Cășeiu, Cluj-Napoca.
Matei-Popescu, F. 2007. Two Fragments of Roman Military Diplomas Discovered on the Territory of the Republic of Moldova, Dacia N. S. 51, 153–159.
Matei-Popescu, F. 2010a. The Roman Army in Moesia Inferior, Bucarest.
Matei-Popescu, F. 2010b. *Castellum Abritanorum*, Studia Antiqua et Archaeologica 16, 61–67.
Matei-Popescu, F., Țentea, O. 2018. Auxiliae Moesiae Superioris, Cluj-Napoca.
Mihailescu-Bîrliba, L. 2011. La cité romaine du Haut-Empire d'Ibida (Mésie Inférieure). Considérations historiques selon le dossier épigraphique, Studia Antiqua et Archaeologica 17, 83–143.
Mihailescu-Bîrliba. L. 2016. Observations on Local Recruiting in Lower Moesia: The Case of Troesmis, dans Al. Rubel (éd.), Die Barbaren Roms. Inklusion, Exklusion und Identität im Römischen Reich und im Barbaricum (1.-3. Jht. n. Chr.), Konstanz, 71–77.
Mugnai, N. 2016. A New Military Diploma for the Troops of Mauretania Tingitana (26 October 153), ZPE 197, 243–246.
Narloch, K. 2020. First Military Diploma from Novae, Moesia Inferior, ZPE 216, 282–285.
Oprean, C. H. 2018. The Garrison of the Roman Fort at Porolissum (Dacia). The Analysis of the Tile-Stamps, Open Archaeology 4, 365–372.
Pârvan, V. 1923. Începuturile vieții romane la gurile Dunării, Bucarest.

Petolescu, C.C. 2002. Auxilia Daciae. Contribuție la istoria militară a Daciei romane, Bucarest.

Petolescu, C.C., Popescu, A.-T. 2004. Ein neues Militärdiplom für die Provinz Moesia inferior, ZPE 148, 269–276.

Piso, I. 2004–2005. Studia Porolissensia (II), AMN 41–42/I, 283–188.

Piso, I. 2005. Die cohors III Campestris in Porolissum, dans F. Beutler (éd.), „Eine ganz normale Inschrift"... und ähnliches zum Geburtstag von Ekkehard Weber. Festschrift zum 30. April 2005, Vienne, 325–332.

Piso, I. 2019. Les *beneficiarii consularis* de Samum, dans L. Mihailescu-Bîrliba, W. Spickermann (éds.), Roman Army and Local Societies in the Limes Provinces oft the Roman Empire, Rahden (Westf.), 109–129.

Sharankov. N. 2006. A Military Diploma of 7 March 70 AD for Legio II Adiutrix, Archaeologia Bulgarica 10 (2), 37–46.

Sharankov, N. 2009. Three Roman Documents on Bronze, Archaeologia Bulgarica 13 (2), 53–72.

Spaul, J. 1994. Ala[2]. The Auxiliary Cavalry Units of the Pre-Diocletianic Imperial Roman Army, Andover.

Speidel, M.P. 1994b. Die Denkmäler der Kaiserreiter. Equites singulares Augusti, Cologne.

Tačeva 1997. The Thracian Bessi *domo et militiae*, ŽA 47, 199–210.

Tačeva 1999. Die thrakischen Bessi in der römischen Armee, dans XI. Congresso Internazionale di Epigrafia Graeca et Latina, Roma, 18–24 settembre 1997. Atti I, Rome, 863–873.

Tóth, E. 1978. Porolissum. Das Castellum in Moigrad. Ausgrabungen von A. Radnóti, 1943, Budapest.

Țentea, O., Matei-Popescu, F. 2002–2003. Alae et Cohortes Daciae et Moesiae. A review and update of J. Spaul's Ala and Cohors, AMN 39–40/I, 259–296.

Weiß, P. 2004. Zwei vollständige Konstitutionen für die Truppen in Noricum (8. Sept. 79) und Pannonia inferior (27. Sept. 154), ZPE 146, 239–254.

Weiß, P. 2009. Statthalter und Konsulndaten in neuen Militärdiplomen, ZPE 171, 231–252.

ANNEXES. Unités militaires où ont été actifs les militaires originaires du milieu rural de Mésie Inférieure

1. Les légions

Note : La source CIL III 14507 atteste des soldats originaires de Nicopolis qui appartenait au moment de leur recrutement à la province de Thrace.

No	Légion	Nombre des militaires recrutés	Date ou période de recrutement
1	*II Adiutrix*	1	44–46 (probablement dans la flotte de Ravenne)
2	*V Macedonica*	1	145–170
3	*I Italica*	2	fin du IIe s.
4	*XI Claudia*	3	fin du IIe s. – début du IIIe s., IIIe s.
5	*I Adiutrix*	1	IIIe s.
6	inconnues	1	IIIe s.

2. Les ailes

No	Aile	Nombre des militaires recrutés	Date de recrutement
1	*ala Gallorum et Thracum Antiana (ueterana Gallica)*	2	29, 126/129
2	*ala I Thracum Mauretana*	1	62
3	*ala ueterana Gallica*	2	66
4	*ala I Thracum Herculana*	1	69
5	*ala I Brittonum*	1	46
6	*ala I Thracum Victrix*	4	54, 134
7	*ala II Arauacorum*	2	IIe s., IIIe s.
8	*ala Siliana torquata ciuium Romanorum*	3	58, 94, 100

No	Aile	Nombre des militaires recrutés	Date de recrutement
9	*ala Thracum ueterana*	1	61
10	*ala praetoria singularium*	3	63
11	*ala I Flauia Gaetulorum*	4	72, 74 (2), 74/85
12	*ala Gallorum Flauiana*	3	82, 110, 119/121
13	*ala I Hispanorum*	1	95
14	*ala Sulpicia ciuium Romanorum*	1	102
15	*ala Thracum Herculiana*	1	104–109
16	*ala I Ulpia contario-rum milliaria*	10	101–125 (3), 121 (3), 215 (1), III[e] s. (3)
17	*ala Illyricorum (nu-merus Illyricorum)*	1	115
18	*ala I Asturum*	1	121
19	*ala I Augusta Gallorum*	3	128
20	*ala Gemelliana ciui-um Romanorum*	1	128
21	*ala Hispanorum Auriana*	1	132
22	*ala VII Phrygum*	4	133
23	*ala Gallorum et Bosporanorum*	1	133
24	*ala I Tungrorum*	1	134/135

3. Les cohortes

No	Cohorte	Nombre des militaires recrutés	Date ou période de recrutement
1	*cohors I Thracum*	1	45–49
2	*cohors I Montanorum*	1	55
3	*cohors IV Thracum*	2	55
4	*cohors II Thracum*	1	61
5	*cohors I Aquitanorum*	3	65
6	*cohors III Thracum Syriaca*	1	66
7	*cohors I Thracum milliaria c. R.*	2	66, 74
8	*cohors VI Thracum*	1	71
9	*cohors II Gallorum*	2	74, 153
10	*cohors Flauia Bessorum*	2	75, IIe s.
11	*coh. I. c. R. p. f.*	1	76
12	*cohors II Mattiacorum*	1	113
13	*cohors I Tyriorum sagittariorum*	2	80, 82
14	*cohors VI Hispanorum*	1	101
15	*cohors I Lingonum*	1	102
16	*cohors IV Thracum*	1	102
17	*cohors I Flauia Musulamiorum*	1	106
18	*cohors XV Delmatarum ciuium Romanorum*	1	119
19	*cohors I Bracarorum c. R.*	1	120
20	*cohors I Lusitanorum*	1	121
21	*cohors III Brittonum*	1	126

No	Cohorte	Nombre des militaires recrutés	Date ou période de recrutement
22	*cohors XV uoluntariorum*	2	127
23	*cohors I Ligurum et Hispanorum*	1	127
24	*cohors I Brittonum*	1	139
25	*cohors I Augusta Neruiana*	1	153
26	*cohors VII Thracum*	1	153
27	*cohors I Aelia Hispanorum*	1	153
28	*cohors II Sardorum*	1	IIe s
29	*cohors I Cilicum*	1	fin du IIe s.
30	*cohors II uigilum*	1	228–229

4. Les cohortes prétoriennes

Cohorte prétorienne	Nombre des militaires recrutés	Dates de recrutement
I	4	193, 212, 214, 232
II	2	182
III	6	210, 225
IV	1	225
V	9	215, 217, 225 (2)
VI	3	196, 202, 225
VII	3	206, 210, 225
VIII	1	fin du IIe s. – début du IIIe s.
IX	6	193, 209, 211, 225, 232
X	2	210
cohortes inconnues	42+	187–191, 193–194 (2), 201–209 (5), 211, 214, 225 (9), 227, 228

5. Les equites singulares Augusti

Nombre des militaires recrutés	Dates de recrutement
72+	108, 113 (2), 101–113, 114 (38), 117, 120, 101–136, 180 (4), 198

6. Les flottes impériales

Flotte	Nombre des militaires recrutés	Dates de recrutement
Misène	44	26, 27–51 (4), 44 (1), 50–75, 50–80 (4), 75–100 (2), 75–110, 93 (3), 92–112, 100–125, 132, 134
Ravenne	15	44–46 (2), 103–119, 195, 198, 199, 193–199
Non-précisée	4	116, 193–211 (2), 198–211

Ein neues Fragment der lex coloniae Ulpiae Traianae Ratiariae?

Werner Eck, Andreas Pangerl

Epigraphisch überlieferte Munizipalgesetze sind ein Phänomen, das man ganz selbstverständlich mit der südspanischen Provinz Baetica verbindet, durchaus zurecht. Denn von einigen Städten der Provinz sind umfangreiche bzw. sehr umfangreiche Teile von *leges municipales* vor allem latinischen Rechts bekannt, von vielen anderen zumindest Fragmente. Sie alle zeigen, dass solche Gesetze nicht nur als Grundlage des städtischen Lebens notwendig waren, dass sie vielmehr auch öffentlich auf Bronzetafeln den Bürgern präsentiert wurden. Antonio Caballos Rufino konnte solche öffentliche Publikation für mehr als vierzig Gemeinden nachweisen.[1] Besonders bedeutsam war die Publikation der lex Irnitana im Jahr 1986, weil von diesem Gesetz fast 70% des ursprünglichen Textes und damit auch der Großteil des inneren Aufbaus bekannt ist, weit über das hinaus, was vorher durch die lex Malacitana und die lex Salpensana bezeugt war.[2]

Dass auch die römischen oder latinischen Gemeinden in anderen Provinzen, seien es *coloniae* oder *municipia*, eine *lex* als rechtlichen Rahmen für das Zusammenleben der Bürger und *incolae* besaßen, musste man immer voraussetzen, auch wenn es dazu lange Zeit keine entsprechende bzw. als solche erkannte Dokumentation gab. Dieser Befund aber hat sich seit einiger Zeit geändert. Denn aus einer Reihe von Städten in mehreren Provinzen sind inzwischen Inschriften bekannt geworden, die, wenn auch generell in sehr fragmentarischer Form, derartige Gesetze dokumentarisch bezeugen. Die meisten dieser Dokumente wurden erst in den letzten zwei Jahrzehnten veröffentlicht bzw. in ihrem Inhalt erkannt.

Das früheste Zeugnis wurde freilich schon 1906 durch Eugen Bormann publiziert,[3] ein Fragment aus einem Stadtgesetz, das am ehesten für Lauriacum an der Donau ausgestellt wurde, auch wenn das nicht absolut sicher ist. Falls es aber von dort stammt, darf man davon ausgehen, dass Lauriacum wohl unter Caracalla als *municipium* organisiert

1 Caballos Rufino 2009, 131–172. Für Hinweise danken wir Dirk Koßmann und Florian Matei-Popescu.

2 González 1986, 147–243; EDCS-20200002; Wolf 2011.

3 Bormann 1906, 315–321; AE 1907, 100; siehe für weitere kleine Fragmente die Angaben unter EDCS-49100358.

worden ist. Das von Bormann veröffentlichte Fragment konnte wie auch einige später entdeckte Bruchstücke nach der damals schon bekannten lex Salpensana ergänzt werden.[4]

Auch zwei Bronzefragmente aus Segusio in den Alpes Cottiae waren schon seit langer Zeit publiziert, sie wurden aber erst von Michael Crawford, danach vor allem durch Cesare Letta als Teile eines Stadtgesetzes identifiziert.[5] Das Wenige, was inhaltlich erkannt werden kann, vor allem zu gerichtlichen Verfahren, steht dem, was in der *lex Irnitana* für das latinische Irni bezeugt ist, sehr nahe. Auch in Segusio hatte man wie später in Lauriacum das Grundgesetz der Stadt auf Bronzetafeln der Bevölkerung zugänglich gemacht.

Lauriacum blieb nicht die einzige Stadt im Donaubalkanraum, von der inzwischen Reste von Stadtgesetzen bekannt geworden sind. Zum einen wurde in Vindobona in Pannonia superior ein Fragment einer Bronzetafel als Teil des dortigen Stadtgesetzes wahrscheinlich gemacht, ohne dass man inhaltlich mehr daraus gewinnen konnte, als das Factum, dass die Gemeinde den Rang eines *municipium* besessen hat;[6] das war allerdings schon vorher durch eine Weiheinschrift eines Magistrats dieser Stadt bezeugt.[7]

Den wichtigsten Fund bildeten freilich zwei Bronzetafeln aus Troesmis, die bei illegalen Ausgrabungen gefunden worden waren und die nach einer langen Irrfahrt durch mehrere Länder schließlich nach Rumänien zurückgebracht werden konnten.[8] Die beiden Tafeln sind fast vollständig erhalten. Sie bieten den Text von drei Kapiteln der *lex municipii Troesmensium*, die inhaltlich, aber partiell auch in den Formulierungen der *lex* von Irni sehr ähnlich sind; allerdings sind die Ausführungen weit wortreicher und bieten konkretisierende Details, die in der lex Irnitana noch nicht enthalten sind, eine Folge der beinahe ein Jahrhundert später ausgearbeiteten Version für Troesmis. Aus dem Text ergibt sich klar, dass das Gesetz für ein römisches *municipium* bestimmt war, also anders als die spanischen Stadtgesetze sowie die *lex* für Segusio, die für Städte latinischen Rechts galten. Bezeichnend ist, dass in Kapitel 27 der Stadtverfassung von Troesmis eigens auf einige augusteische Gesetze verwiesen wird, die zum Zeitpunkt des Erlasses nur für römische Bürger galten, die somit für die Bürger in latinischen Städten, soweit sie persönlich nur Bürger latinischen Rechts waren, keine Relevanz hatten.[9]

Alle diese Gesetze waren, wenn man von der caesarischen *lex* für die *colonia Genetiva Iulia = Urso* absieht,[10] für *municipia* bestimmt gewesen, nicht jedoch für römische *coloniae*, der vom politisch-rechtlichem Prestige her gesehen höchsten Stufe von Städten in den Provinzen, die gerade auch für Legionsveteranen bestimmt waren. Doch auch für

4 Siehe AE 1953, 124; 2003, 1323. Zur Frage, ob die Fragmente nach Lauriacum gehören oder nicht, siehe vor allem B. und H. Galsterer 1971, 334–348 und Weber 1972, 181–198.

5 Crawford 1996, 483, Nr. 31; Letta 2007, 145 = AE 2007, 891; Cimarosti 2012, Nr. 60.

6 AE 2006, 1080; dazu Rafetseder 2019, 141–150 = AE 2019, 1221.

7 CIL III 4557 = EDCS-28800117: *Deor(um) Prosperitati G(aius) Marc(ius) Marcianus dec(urio) mun(icipii) Vind(obonensium), [q]uaes[t(or)], aedil(is), IIvir i(ure) [d(icundo),] praef(ectus) co[ll(egii)] fabrum, v(otum) s(olvit) l(ibens) l(aetus) m(erito).*

8 Eck 2013,199–213; Eck 2014, 75–88; Eck 2016, 33–46. Der vollständige Text bei Eck 2016, 565–606 = AE 2015, 1255.

9 AE 2015, 1255, Tafel B.

10 Crawford 1996, Nr. 25.

den Stadttyp der *colonia* ist seit Kurzem ein Stadtgesetz bezeugt. Es ist die *lex* für die *colonia Ulpia Traiana Ratiaria* in Moesia superior, die, wie schon der Name erkennen lässt, unter Traian gegründet wurde, nachdem aus dem dortigen Legionslager die Einheit, vielleicht die legio VII Claudia,[11] nach Viminacium versetzt worden war.[12] Bisher sind drei Fragmente dieser *lex* bekannt geworden, die freilich sachlich so wenig enthalten, dass daraus erneut keine Spezifika für diese Stadt gewonnen werden können. Immerhin ist in einem der Fragmente wohl ein *quaestor* genannt, ferner wird auf *divi* verwiesen und auch der Rang als *colonia* ist in zweien der Fragmente genannt, ebenso wie vor allem der Name Ratiaria.

Nun ist ein weiteres, etwas größeres beschriebenes Bronzefragment aufgetaucht, das zu diesen dreien gehören könnte. Es befindet sich in Privatbesitz, über seine Herkunft ist nichts Konkretes bekannt geworden.[13] Das Fragment ist auf allen vier Seiten abgebrochen und hat die Maße: Höhe ca. 15 cm, Breite ca. 12 cm, Dicke 5 mm; Buchstabenhöhe 7–8 mm. Das Gewicht beträgt 576 Gramm. Die Höhe und Breite entsprechen in etwa einer *tabella* eines Militärdiploms, nicht jedoch die Dicke, die bei Diplomen kaum je 1 mm übersteigt. Die Dicke von 5 mm bei diesem Fragment macht unmittelbar klar, dass der heute noch erhaltene Rest ursprünglich Teil einer weit größeren Tafel war. Dazu passt auch die Höhe der Buchstaben von 7–8 mm, die darauf verweisen, dass der Text auch noch aus einiger Distanz lesbar sein sollte. Der freie Raum zwischen den Zeilen variiert zwischen 6 und 8 mm. Trennpunkte sind nur teilweise erkennbar.

Folgender Text ist auf dem Fragment lesbar (Abb. 1):

[---]IAM COLOṆ[---]
[---] · EST · FACERE · NO[---]
[---]DVVMVIRI· QVI [---]
[---]AS · AEQVANT[---]
[---]AS CVRIAS·IN Q[---]
[---]ERTINVM IN CV[---]
[---]CES NE SVNTO QV[---]
[---]RIBVTI · DISCRIPT[---]
[---]MITIORVM CON[---]
[---]IA·I·D·PRAEERVN[---]
[---]̣PER QVOS RES P+[---]

11 Siehe Matei-Popescu, Ţentea 2018, 10.

12 Eck 2016, 538. Der vollständige Name der Kolonie in CIL III 14217: *col(onia) Ulp(ia) Traia(na) Rat(iaria)*; vgl. auch III 14500: *[col. Ulpia] Traia(na) Rat(iaria).* Dazu mit einer etwas gewagten Rekonstruktion Rafetseder 2018, 274–277. Bisher nicht in die AE übernommen.

13 Eine RFA Analyse durch R.Lehmann in München zeigte allerdings keine mit dem ersten Fragment übereinstimmende Legierung. Das muss nicht gegen die Zugehörigkeit sprechen, da man für die zahlreichen Tafeln, die für Stadtgesetze notwendig waren, nicht notwendigerweise eine gleichbleibende Mischung bei der Herstellung voraussetzen darf.

Abb. 1: Fragment eines Stadtgesetzes

Die folgenden Überlegungen, wie die Wortreste in den einzelnen Zeilen zu verstehen sein könnten, gehen davon aus, dass das Fragment auf jeden Fall zu einem Stadtgesetz gehört hat. Dafür spricht zum einen die Dicke des Fragments, die nur bei einer großen Tafel zu erwarten ist, sodann die Publikation auf Bronze, ein Material, das vornehmlich in allen lateinisch geprägten Provinzen für öffentlich ausgestellte Rechtstexte verwendet wurde. Darauf deuten weiterhin die Worte *duumviri* in Zeile 3, *curias* in Zeile 5, wohl *[co]mitiorum* in Zeile 9 und *i(ure) d(icundo) praeerunt* in Zeile 10 hin.

Zunächst ist es notwendig zu erschließen, was die Wortreste in den einzelnen Zeilen aussagen könnten:

Zeile 1: Man ist versucht, vor *colonia* einen Ortsnamen im Akkusativ Singular anzunehmen, also etwa *[Ratiar]iam coloni[am]* (dazu weiter unten). Das Problem ist dabei jedoch, dass in solchen Fällen der Name üblicherweise erst nach *colonia* angeführt wird, auch wenn es gelegentliche Ausnahmen gibt.

Zeile 2: [---]EST· FACERE · NO[---]. Nichts Spezifisches kann mit diesen Worten verbunden werden.

Zeile 3: [---]DVVMVIRI· QVI [---]. In den Stadtgesetzen wird in vielfacher Weise auf die *duumviri* verwiesen. So heißt es z. B. in der lex Irnitana rubrica 49: *duumviri qui in eo municipio nunc sunt...* oder rubrica 44: *IIviri qui in eo municipio post ha(n)c lege(m) primi erunt* ebenso in den § 22–29 in der lex Malacitana. Zum andern wird öfter auf sie als Gerichtsmagistrate hingewiesen wie in rubrica 26 und 89 der Irnitana: *IIviri, qui in eo municipio iure dicundo praeerunt.*

Zeile 4: [---]AS· AEQVANT[---]. Eine Formulierung, die eine Verbform von *aequare* einschließt, findet sich in den bisher bekannten Stadtgesetzen nicht. Wohl aber findet sich dort das Adverb *aequaliter*, so in der lex Irnitana § 44 (siehe dazu auch unten zu Zeile 8–9): danach sollen nämlich die Duumviri jährlich *decuriones conscriptosve, qui minores quam LX annorum erunt,* ***quam maxime aequaliter*** *in tres decurias distribuito.* Es ist deshalb wohl möglich, hier von einem Fehler des Graveurs auszugehen, der die beiden Buchstaben IL in *aequaliter* als ein N missverstanden hat, so dass dort das Wort zu *aequa⸢li⸣t[er]* verbessert werden darf.

Zeile 5: [---]AS CVRIAS·IN Q[---]. Nach der lex Malacitana und Irnitana werden die Bürger der Gemeinde in *curiae* gegliedert, und zwar so, dass in etwa gleich viele Bürger einer jeden *curia* angehören. Bedeutsam ist dies deswegen, weil die *curiae* auch die Stimmkörper innerhalb eines *municipium* bilden. Zu den Abstimmungen werden sie auch, wie es in der lex Malacitana und der lex Troesmensium heißt, *curiatim* aufgerufen.[14] Ebenso wird jeweils eine *curia* ausgelost, in der *incolae*, die über das latinische oder römische Bürgerrecht verfügen, bei Wahlen ihre Stimme abgeben können.[15]

Zeile 6: [---]ERTINVM IN CV[---]. Nach einem sehr kleinen Fragment eines Stadtgesetzes, das wohl einer Stadt aus dem conventus Cordubensis zuzuweisen ist, wurde offensichtlich eine *curia* bestimmt, in der die *libertini* ihre Stimme bei den Komitien abgeben konnten,[16] in ähnlicher Weise, wie das auch für die *incolae* in § 53 der lex Malacitana bestimmt wurde. Auf eine solche Regelung könnte auch hier Bezug genommen werden.

Zeile 7: [---]CES NE SVNTO QV[---]. Der Wortrest *-ces* kann im Kontext eines Stadtgesetzes nur auf *iudices* verweisen. Darüber handelt die lex Ursonensis an mehreren Stellen (§§ 95. 123), ebenso die lex Irnitana im § 86: *R(ubrica) de iudicibus legendis proponendis.* In diesem Paragraphen werden die Voraussetzungen für die Wahl als *iudex* festgelegt, ferner wird bestimmt, wie der *IIvir*, der als Gerichtsmagistrat fungiert, die Namen dieser *iudices* während seines Amtsjahres öffentlich präsentieren soll, ein Aspekt, zu dem wohl auch noch der Text in der folgenden Zeile 8 gehört.

14 Lex Malacitana § 55: *qui comitia ex h(ac) l(ege) habebit is municipes curiatim ad suffragium ferendum vocato ita ut uno vocatu omnes curias in suffragium vocet*; lex Troesmensium § 28.

15 Lex Malacitana § 53.

16 Saquete Chamizo, Iñesta Mena 2009, 293–297, hier 295 = AE 2009, 582.

Zeile 8: [---]RIBVTI · DISCRIPT[---]. Der Wortrest RIBVTI lässt sich nur mit wenigen Worten verbinden. *Tributum, distributus/m, contributus/um, attributus/um. Tributa* werden in den Stadtgesetzen von Irni (§§ 18, 63) und Malaca (§ 63) genannt, jedoch im Zusammenhang der Verpachtung von Einnahmen, worum es hier aber nicht gehen kann, jedenfalls wenn man das in Zeile 9 folgende *[co]mitiorum* berücksichtigt. Das gilt erst recht, wenn man annähme, *[t]ributi* sei hier als Genitiv Singular von *tributum* anzusehen. Auch für die Adjektiva *contributus/um, attributus/um* lässt sich kein Zusammenhang herstellen.

Sachlich am nächsten kommt den Resten der zwei Worte in dieser Zeile eine Formulierung, die sich in der Lex repetundarum aus republikanischer Zeit findet. Dort wird angeordnet, dass der Prätor, der die *quaestio* zur Untersuchung von Repetundenklagen leitet, die Richter für sein Amtsjahr bestimmen soll. Deren Namen solle er *in tabula in albo atramento script[o]s patrem tribum co[g]nomenque tributimque d[i]scriptos hab[eto].*[17] Die Namen dieser Richter sollten mit dem Vatersnamen, der Tribus und dem Cognomen angeführt werden, und zwar jeweils diejenigen zusammen, die aus derselben Tribus stammten.

Eine sehr ähnliche Formulierung findet sich erneut in der lex Irnitana in § 86, in dem die Bestellung von *iudices* in Irni durch einen der *duumviri* geregelt ist: *R(ubrica) de iudicibus legendis proponendis.* Der entscheidende Passus lautet: Der *duumvir* soll die Richter gleichmäßig auf drei *decuriae* verteilen: ... *aequalis summa[e i]n d[e]cu[rias] tres discribito, q[ui] ita iudices lec[ti] discriptive erunt*, von diesen soll der Duumvir, *qui i(ure) d(icundo) p(raeerit), praenomina, nomina, item patrum praenom[i]na et ipsorum tribus, cognomina in tabulis scripta aput tribunal suum .... [pr]oposi[ta h]a[b]eto.* Und in § 44 derselben *lex* heißt es (siehe schon oben zu Zeile 4): *R(ubrica) de decurionibus distribuendis in tres decurias quae legationibus invicem fungantur. IIviri qui in eo municipio post ha(n)c lege(m) primi erunt, item qui quoque anno, quo novam distributionem eorum, qui ex hac lege munere legationum obeundarum fungantur, fieri oportebit, iure dicundo prae(e)runt, ambo alterve primo quoque tempore decuriones conscriptosve, qui minores quam LX annorum erunt, quam maxime aequaliter in tres decurias distribuito.*

Daraus darf man schließen, dass auch in dem neuen Fragment darauf verwiesen wurde, dass die Namen wohl der Richter in einer geregelten Weise auf Stimm- oder Entscheidungseinheiten verteilt und in entsprechender Weise schriftlich fixiert sein sollten.

Zeile 9: [---]MITIORVM CON[---]. Der Wortrest [---]MITIORVM kann nur zu *[co]-mitiorum* ergänzt werden. In fast allen bisher bekannten Stadtgesetzen finden sich Bestimmungen über das, was bei Wahlen in den *comitia* beachtet werden muss. In den §§ 51–59 der lex Malacitana werden umfassend alle Regeln angeführt, die bei den Wahlen in den *comitia* zu beachten sind, etwa, wie die Namen der *candidati* präsentiert werden sollen, oder, dass im Normalfall der ältere der beiden *duumviri* die *comitia* zur Wahl der *IIviri, aediles* und *quaestores* abhalten soll. Ebenso wird angeordnet, wer an den Wahlurnen als Beobachter gegen die doppelte Abgabe von Stimmsteinen eingesetzt werden muss, was auch in § 28 der lex Troesmensium ausgeführt wird. Im vorausgehenden Pa-

17 Crawford 1996, Nr. 1 Zeile 14 und 17.

ragraphen der *lex* von Troesmis werden die augusteischen Gesetze genannt, die bei der Wahl von Magistraten und Priestern im *municipium* zu beachten sind.

Das auf *comitiorum* folgende *con[---]* könnte man mit dem Wort *convocare* oder *convocatio* verbinden; denn in § 28 der lex Troesmensium heißt es von demjenigen, der im *municipium* Wahlen abhalte: *ita ut convoc[et omnes] curia⌜s⌝ in suffragium voc[atu uno--]*; ähnliches wird in § 55 der lex von Malaga angeordnet: *qui comitia ex h(ac) l(ege) habebit is municipes curiatim ad suffragium ferendum vocato ita ut uno vocatu omnes curias in suffragium vocet.* Vom *convocare* bei einer Wahl spricht auch die lex Valeria-Aurelia des Jahres 19/20.[18]

Zeile 10: [---]IA·I·D·PRAEERVN[---]. Die Formel, dass die Duumviri in einem *municipium* die Rechtsprechung zu leiten haben, findet sich in der lex Irnitana §§ 26 und 64, ähnlich in der lex Malacitana §§ 24–28 und in der lex Villonensis § 64 in verschiedenen Formen und Abkürzungen: *IIviri qui in eo municipio iure dicundo praeerunt.* Analog darf man das *[---]ia*, in Verbindung mit der Erwähnung von *colonia* in Zeile 1, wohl zu *[in colon]ia* ergänzen, zumal vor IA am Bruchrand unten wohl noch der Rest einer senkrechten Haste zu sehen ist, der außer zu einem I nur noch zu einem N gehört haben kann. Das ergäbe dann als ergänzten Text: *[IIviri, qui in hac colo]ṇia i(ure) d(icundo) praeerun[t].*

Zeile 11: [---] P̣ER QVOS RES P+[---]. Hier dürfte etwas formuliert gewesen sein, das die *res publica* durch die *duumviri* ausführen lasse. Offen ist zunächst, welcher Buchstabe nach *res p(ublica)* folgt. Man könnte zwar vermuten, dass es sich um ein B handle, und dann PB als *p(u)b(lica)* aufzulösen sei. Doch diese Abkürzung findet sich nicht für die Wortfolge *res publica*. Vielmehr folgt auf *res p(ublica)* üblicherweise der Name der entsprechenden Gemeinde. Geht man davon aus, dass der Buchstabe am Rand ein B ist, dann findet man z.B. die *r(es) p(ublica) B(iturigum) V(iviscorum)* = Bordeaux,[19] die *r(es) p(ublica) Barbens(ium)* = Singilia Barba,[20] oder die *r(es) p(ublica) Bel(garum)* in Britannien,[21] die *res publ(ica) Banasit(ana)* in der Mauretania Tingitana[22] oder die *r(es) [p(ublica)] Ba[ss(ianorum)]* in Pannonien.[23]

Doch nach P muss kein B folgen, es kann ebenso ein Ṛ sein, wenn man P+ mit PR in Zeile 10 vergleicht. Für diese Buchstabenfolge findet sich in unserem Inschriftenmaterial *r(es) p(ublica) R(eatinorum)* in Mittelitalien[24] und die *res p(ublica) Reginensium* in der Baetica.[25] Obwohl die zuletzt angeführte Stadt aus der Provinz stammt, aus der wir die meisten Stadtgesetze kennen, kann es sich dennoch nicht um diese Stadt handeln, da nach dem Ṛ sicher kein E gestanden haben kann. Wenn der Eindruck auf dem Photo nicht

18 Crawford 1996, Nr. 37/38, 519: *itemque eq(uites) in consaeptum ex lege quam L(ucius) Valerius Messalla Volesus Cn(aeus) Cornelius Cin[na Magnus] co(n)s(ules) tulerunt suffragi ferendi caussa convocabit is uti senatores itemq(ue) equites omnium decuriar[um, quae iudiciorum public]orum gratia constitutae sunt erunt, suffragium ferant.*

19 Beispielsweise AE 2008, 892.

20 CIL II/5, 779.

21 CIL VII 1149 = RIB 2222.

22 AE 1934, 43 = IAM II 1, 104.

23 CIL III 10206.

24 CIL IX 4677a.

25 CIL II/7, 980.

täuscht, könnte noch der obere Rest eines A zu sehen sein, durchaus vergleichbar PA in Zeile 10, wo das A oben einen deutlichen Abstand zum vorausgehenden P zeigt.

Schon als das Photo und die Maßangaben des hier behandelten Fragments zugesandt wurden, ließ der erste Blick den Verdacht aufkommen, das Fragment könne zu demselben Stadtgesetz gehören wie drei andere Fragmente, die vor einigen Jahren bekannt wurden und einen kleinen Teil aus dem Stadtgesetz für die colonia Ulpia Traiana Ratiaria bezeugen.[26] Die Dicke der Fragmente zwischen 5 und 6 mm stimmt überein, ebenso die Höhe der Buchstaben zwischen 7 und 8 mm, ferner der Zeilenabstand, der zwischen 5 und 7 mm schwankt. Doch besonders das Schriftbild ist sehr ähnlich, was sich vor allem an der geschwungenen Querhaste des Buchstabens T zeigt, ebenso an dem sehr breiten N (siehe Abb. 1, 2 und bei Eck 2016, 538). Schließlich bezieht sich der Inhalt des neuen Fragments wie der drei schon publizierten Fragmente, auf eine *colonia*. Dann aber gewinnt die Beobachtung in den beiden letzten Zeilen des neuen Fragments an Bedeutung, dass dort *[IIviri, qui in hac colo]ṇia i(ure) d(icundo) praeerun[t]* genannt sind, *per quos res p(ublica) Ṛ Ạ[tiaria/tiariensium]* etwas durchführen lässt.[27]

Treffen diese Beobachtungen zu, dann darf man, wenn auch mit einem gewissen Vorbehalt, den Schluss ziehen, das hier publizierte Fragment gehöre ebenfalls zu dem schon bezeugten Stadtgesetz für die *colonia Ratiaria*. Der Inhalt des Fragments verweist auf Wahlen innerhalb der *colonia*, deren Bewohnerschaft in *curiae* gegliedert war. In diese *curiae* wurde die Bewohnerschaft möglichst gleichmäßig verteilt, vermutlich durch die ersten *duumviri*, die in der *colonia* ihr Amt ausübten. In irgendeiner Form wurde auch eine Regelung angesprochen, die das Mitwirken von *libertini* regelte, vielleicht in dem Sinn, dass sie bei der Bestimmung der *iudices* nicht berücksichtigt werden durften: *[iudi]ces ne sunto*... Dabei sollen die Namen der (wohl gleichmäßig verteilten) Bürger?/*incolae*?/*liberti*? schriftlich festgehalten werden. Wie all diese Aussagen mit den *comitia* zusammenhängen, die zusammengerufen werden, und was dabei die *duumviri* der *colonia*, die den Vorsitz beim Gericht haben, im Sinn der *res publica* durchzuführen haben, das bleibt wegen des sehr fragmentarischen Charakters des Textes unklar.

Denn vom Text fehlt sehr viel; wieviel das ist, lässt sich in etwa im Vergleich mit der lex Troesmensium wahrscheinlich machen. Dort stehen in einer Zeile ca. 50 Zeichen, hier sind zwischen 10 und 12 Zeichen erhalten, also im Vergleich zu Troesmis nur knapp 20% einer Zeile. In der lex Irnitana stehen in einer Zeile sogar etwas mehr Zeichen, im Durchschnitt mehr als 60. Würde man diese Zahl auch für die Länge der Zeilen in der *lex* für Ratiaria voraussetzen, dann wäre von den einzelnen Zeilen in dem neuen Fragment für Ratiaria etwas weniger als 16% vorhanden. All das macht dann sehr deutlich, dass alle Aussagen, die oben gemacht wurden, notwendigerweise nicht sicher sind, noch weniger der genauere Zusammenhang, der zwischen dem Inhalt der einzelnen Zeilen einst bestand. Dennoch haben wir damit einen kleinen zusätzlichen Einblick in einige strukturelle

---

26 Siehe Anm. 11.

27 In Zeile 1 muss man nicht zwingend *[Ratiar]iam colon[iam]* ergänzen; denkbar wäre auch ein Akkusativ, der auf *-iam* endete und dann der Name der colonia im Genitiv oder vielleicht auch nur *[et]iam colon[...]*. (Dankbarer Hinweis von F. Matei-Popescu).

Gegebenheiten der colonia Ratiaria. Sie war die erste kaiserzeitliche Gemeinde, von der wir wenigstens einen winzigen Teil der *lex coloniae* kennen. Nunmehr ist ein – freilich noch kleineres – epigraphisches Fragment für die colonia Ulpia Traiana Augusta Dacica Sarmizegetusa identifiziert worden, das ebenfalls zu dem, natürlich auf Bronze publizierten Stadtgesetz der ersten colonia in der neueroberten Provinz gehört haben kann.[28] Vielleicht gelingt es Ioan Piso, der jahrzehntelang die Ausgrabungen in dieser Stadt vorangetrieben hat, noch weitere Fragmente der lex coloniae Ulpiae Traianae Augustae Dacicae Sarmizegetusae zu finden. Das wäre dann das high light seiner Arbeit für diese römische Colonia.

Literaturverzeichnis

AE, L'Année épigraphique, Paris.

Beu-Dachin, E., Nemeti, S. 2019. A fragmentary bronze inscription from Colonia Dacica Sarmizegetusa, in S. Nemeti, E. Beu-Dachin, I. Nemeti, D. Dana (eds.), The Roman Provinces – Mechanisms of Integration, Cluj-Napoca, 167–177.

Bormann, E. 1906. Bronzeinschrift aus Lauriacum, JÖAI, 315–321.

Caballos Rufino, A. 2009. Publicación de documentos públicos en las ciudades del Occidente roman: el ejemplo de la Bética, in R. Haensch (ed.), Selbstdarstellung und Kommunikation. Die Veröffentlichung staatlicher Urkunden auf Stein und Bronze in der Römischen Welt, München, 131–172.

CIL, Corpus Inscriptionum Latinarum.

Cimarosti, E. 2012. Le iscrizioni di età romana sul versante italiano delle "Alpes Cottiae", SEBarc Annexos I, Barcelona.

Crawford, M.H. 1996. Roman Statutes, London.

Eck, W. 2013. La loi municipale de Troesmis: données juridiques et politiques d'une inscription récemment découverte, RD 91, 199–213.

Eck, W. 2014. Das Leben römisch gestalten. Ein Stadtgesetz für das Municipium Troesmis aus den Jahren 177–180 n.Chr., in S. Benoist, G. de Kleijn (eds.), Integration in Rome and in the Roman World, Impact of Empire 17, Leiden, 75–88.

Eck, W. 2016. Die Lex municipalis Troesmensium: Ihr rechtlicher und politisch-sozialer Kontext, in C.-G. Alexandrescu (ed.), Troesmis – A Changing Landscape. Romans and the Others in the Lower Danube Region in the First Century BC – Third Century AD. Proceedings of an International Colloquium Tulcea, 7th–10th of October 2015, Cluj-Napoca, 33–46.

Eck, W. 2016. Die lex Troesmensium: ein Stadtgesetz für ein municipium civium Romanorum. Publikation der erhaltenen Kapitel und Kommentar, ZPE 200, 565–606.

Eck, W. 2016. Fragmente eines neuen Stadtgesetzes – der lex coloniae Ulpiae Traianae Ratiariae, Athenaeum 104, 538–544.

EDCS. https://db.edcs.eu/epigr/hinweise/hinweis-en.html

28 Beu-Dachin, Nemeti 2019, 167–177.

Galsterer, B. and H. 1971. Zum Stadtrecht von Lauriacum, BJ 171, 334–348.
González, J. 1986. The lex Irnitana: a new copy of the Flavian municipal law, JRS 76, 147–243.
IAM II. M. Euzennat, J. Gascou, J. Marion 1982. Inscriptions antique du Maroc, 2: Inscriptions latines. Paris.
Letta, C. 2007. Fragmentum Segusinum. Due frammenti a lungo ignorati della *lex municipalis* di Segusio, in G. Paci (ed.), Contributi all'epigrafia d'età augustea. Actes de la XIIIe Rencontre franco-italienne sur l'épigraphie du monde romain, Tivoli, 145 -169.
Matei-Popescu, F., Ţentea, O. 2018. Auxilia Moesiae superioris. Cluj-Napoca. https://www.academia.edu/38650516/Auxilia_Moesiae_Superioris
Rafetseder, N. 2018. Die Stadtgesetzfragmente der Colonia Ulpia Traiana Ratiaria: Ein Ergänzungsversuch, ZPE 207, 274–277.
Rafetseder, N. 2019. Das Stadtgesetzfragment von Vindobona, Tyche 34, 141–151.
RIB. R. G. Collingwood, R. P. Wright 1984. Roman Inscriptions of Britain. Oxford.
Saquete Chamizo, J. C., Iñesta Mena, J. 2009. Un fragmento de ley municipal hallado en la Baeturia Turdulorum (conventus Cordubensis, provincia Baetica), ZPE 168, 293–297.
Weber, E. 1972. Die rechtliche Stellung der Zivilstadt von Lauriacum, Jahrbuch des oberösterreichischen Musealvereins 117, 181–198.
Wolf, J. G. 2011. Die Lex Irnitana: Ein römisches Stadtrecht aus Spanien, Darmstadt.

Agglomérations secondaires de Mésie supérieure

Yolande Marion, Francis Tassaux

à Ioan Piso, après plus de trente ans d'amitiés
napoco-burdigaliennes

Face aux travaux sur les capitales de cité et sur les villas, les agglomérations secondaires sont souvent les parents pauvres de la recherche. Le cas de la Mésie supérieure n'échappe pas à cette remarque, tout en montrant une profonde originalité à bien des égards. À la suite de découvertes récentes, nous voudrions tenter de cartographier ce phénomène dans la province. L'appellation "agglomérations secondaires" renvoie à une définition statutaire, celle de la hiérarchisation imposée par Rome, entre la *caput civitatis*, qui exerce son autorité sur un territoire, et les habitats groupés qui en dépendent[1]. Nous n'oublierons pas non plus que l'autonomie municipale peut s'effacer dans certains cas devant l'autorité impériale et que telle agglomération peut dépendre d'un procurateur ou d'un militaire.

A l'image de ce qui a été fait récemment en Slovénie[2], nous souhaiterions donner une vue d'ensemble de ces habitats groupés de Mésie supérieure en utilisant le vocabulaire de la géographie humaine, valable pour toutes les époques : villes, bourgs et villages. Ces entités renvoient à des critères à la fois morphologiques et fonctionnels : les bourgs ont une vocation artisanale et commerciale ; les villages abritent essentiellement une communauté de paysans ou de mineurs ou de pêcheurs, exerçant une activité primaire.

1 Cartographier des habitats groupés (fig. 1)

1.1 Les outils cartographiques de référence

Notre enquête est partie de la carte de Kiepert dans le *CIL* III[3] et de celle, hors-texte, de l'ouvrage de Mócsy[4]. Les atlas classiques, comme le Barrington[5], compte tenu de leur

1 Mangin & Tassaux 1992, 461.
2 Horvat *et al.* 2020.
3 *Tabula* IV, *Moesia et Thracia Septentrionalis*, carte hors-texte du *CIL* III, supplément 4 et 5, reprenant celle de Kiepert 1894–1910.
4 Mócsy 1974.
5 Talbert 2000.

Fig. 1: Les agglomérations secondaires de Mésie Supérieure. *Del.* Yolande MARION.

très petite échelle, ne sont pas d'un grand secours pour ce type d'habitat, mais seulement pour une vision générale du réseau des voies impériales. Pour descendre à un maillage plus fin des agglomérations, on dispose de la *Tabula Imperii Romani*, feuilles L 34 Budapest et K 34 *Naissus* et des cartes détaillées qui accompagnent les volumes des *Inscriptions de Mésie Supérieure* (*IMS*), en regrettant que toute la province n'ait pas été couverte par cette grande et belle entreprise. Enfin, nous nous sommes également appuyés sur les cartes de Slobodan Dušanić[6] et de Vladimir Petrović[7].

1.2 Les données de notre carte

– Des limites provinciales et municipales discutées
Le tracé des limites de la Mésie supérieure n'est pas toujours bien assuré et comporte des divergences selon les publications (Cartes HT de Šašel[8], les 6 volumes des *IMS*, les *TIR* et, en dernier lieu, Loma[9], Grbić[10] et Petrović[11]).

Par ailleurs, les espaces dépendants assurément, probablement ou hypothétiquement d'un chef-lieu de cité ont été mis en couleur. Ces territoires apparaissent ainsi vastes, mises à part les cités de *Viminacium* et de *Margum*. Cependant, la dizaine de points d'interrogation de notre carte rappelle toutes les incertitudes sur l'étendue de la majorité des cités – à noter une seule borne frontière connue, entre les *agri* d'*Ulpianum* et de *Scupi* – ainsi que le secteur de la Mésie nord-orientale, laissé en blanc, dont l'appartenance est incertaine entre *Horreum Margi, Ratiaria* et *Naissus*.

– Les capitales de cité sont celles de la fin du Haut-Empire : *Singidunum, Margum, Viminacium, Ratiaria, Municipium Dardanorum, Ulpianum, Scupi, Horreum Margi* et *Naissus*[12], mais la liste n'est peut-être pas complète et, par ailleurs, on n'est pas sûr de leur statut : certaines seraient restées des civitates peregrinae[13]. Cette liste est complétée au Bas-Empire par la promotion de nouvelles capitales de cité, *Aureus Mons, Romuliana* et *Remesiana* mais aussi, peut-être, *Aquae*/Prahovo, siège d'un évêché en 343. Le *municipium Cel(egerorum)*, que A. Mócsy[14] et I. Piso[15] situent en Mésie Supérieure, se trouverait en Dalmatie pour S. Loma[16] et D. Grbić Nikolić[17].

– Les agglomérations secondaires sont des villes ou des bourgs. Les quelques témoignages épigraphiques de *vici* et de *stationes* ont également été signalés. Les *mutationes* où le

6 Dušanić 2000, 350, fig. 1.
7 Petrović 2015 et 2019.
8 *ILJug* 1978 et 1986.
9 Loma 2010, 126–136 et 284–289.
10 Grbić 2019, 224–225.
11 Petrović 2019, 23–34.
12 Piso 2003, 289 et 292–293.
13 Grbić Nikolić 2018.
14 Mócsy 1974, carte HT.
15 Piso 2003, 289.
16 Loma 2010.
17 Grbić Nikolić 2018, 224.

Pèlerin de Bordeaux a changé de chevaux peuvent être des relais isolés ou bien appartenir à un habitat aggloméré[18] ; c'est pourquoi elles figurent sur la carte.
– Sur le réseau routier, on distingue les voies "impériales", principaux axes connus à la fois par les *Itinéraires*[19] et les milliaires (en dernier lieu Petrović[20], Petrović et Grbić[21]). Les autres voies sont qualifiées de "secondaires". L'ensemble des tracés repose sur les cartes des IMS et les travaux de V. Petrović[22]. Des segments de voies impériales ont été récemment découverts, ainsi à Davidovac (fouille préventive lors de la construction de l'autoroute E75 / Koridor 10[23]) et sur la voie *Ratiaria-Naissus*[24].

2 Types d'habitats groupés

2.1 Appellations antiques : les données de l'épigraphie

Seuls deux sites sont désignés officiellement comme des *vici*, l'un près de Lece : "*pro salutes suas (!) et vicanorum*" – une agglomération de mineurs, dans une zone assez isolée[25], l'autre à Vizbegovo à quelques kilomètres au nord de *Scupi*/Skopje, avec l'épitaphe d'Annaea Clementiana, faite par le *vicus Cavadinus*[26].

Deux *stationes* du *vectigal* d'Illyrie sont mentionnées dans une inscription de la province, à Lopate : *Apollonides / eorund(em) uect(igalis) Il/lyr(ici) ser(uus) (contra) sc(riptor) stat(ionis) / Lamud(- - -) quam uoue/rat (contra)sc(riptor) stat(ionis) Vizi(ani)*[27] ; il y a donc un bureau de douane en ce lieu, dont le nom commençait par *Lamud*. L'archéologie complète notre information par la présence d'un *mithraeum* et d'une grande nécropole[28]. La même inscription mentionne la *statio Vizi(ani)*, donc une autre agglomération probable mais on ne sait pas la localiser avec certitude. L'hypothèse d'une similitude avec la *mansio Vicianum* dont la localisation, elle-même, n'est pas assurée, est même carrément rejetée par la *TIR* K34, 131. Par ailleurs, une troisième station, *Aquae Bas.*, mentionnée par un *vilicus* impérial[29], se trouvait à Kuršumlijska Banja, à 12 km au sud de la *mansio* de *Ad Fines*.

18 Tassaux 2018.
19 Miller 1916, Cuntz 1929.
20 Petrović 2007.
21 Petrović & Grbić 2014.
22 Petrović 2019.
23 Petković 2016, 342.
24 Petrović, Filipović & Luka 2014.
25 *IMS*, IV, 109 ; *TIR* K34, 78.
26 *ILJug* 1978, 559 = *IMS*, VI, 86 ; *TIR* K34, 112.
27 *IMS*, VI, 212.
28 *TIR* K34, 80 ; Dragojević Josifovska 1982, 43.
29 *IMS*, IV, 104.

2.2 *Les bourgs routiers, sans autre qualification : les données des Itinéraires*

L'essentiel des toponymes susceptibles de désigner des agglomérations secondaires en Mésie supérieure, soit près d'une trentaine, provient des *Itinéraires* antiques[30]; pour une large part, ils ne sont connus que par ce type de source[31] et signalés ci-dessous d'un astérisque*. Nous en rappelons la liste en suivant les *Itinéraires.*

– Voie du Danube : *Singidunum-Ratiaria*, la route du *limes* :
mutatio Ad Sextum, Tricornium, mutatio Ad Sextum milliarem*, Aureus mons, mansio et mutatio Vinceia, Lederata, Pincum, vicus Cuppae, castrum Novae, Ad Scrofulas*, Taliata, Pontes, Transdierna, Egeta, Gerulata*, Una ou Luna*, Clevora*, Aquae, Dorticum*, Ad Malum*, Bononia.*
– *Viminacium-Naissus-Serdica-Via Militaris*
mutatio Ad Nonum, Municipium*, mansio et mutatio Iovis Pagus*, mutatio Bao*, Idimum, mutatio Ad Octavum*, mutatio Sarmatae, Praesidium Dasmini, mutatio Cametae*, Praesidium Pompei*, Gramrianae*, mutatio Rapiana*, mutatio Radices*, mutatio Ulmus*, Remesiana, mutatio Latina*, Turres** (en Thrace, *mansio* à la fois sur la *Table de Peutinger* et dans l'*Itinerarium Burdigalensis*).
– Transversale Adriatique-Danube *Lissus-Ratiaria*
Gabuleum, Theranda*, Vicianum*, Vindenae*, Ad Fines*, Hammeum*, Ad Herculem, Timacum Maius, Timacum Minus, Conbustica.*

Contrairement à d'autres provinces, l'archéologie ne nous éclaire guère pour l'instant sur ces bourgs de Mésie supérieure qui auraient une fonction purement ou essentiellement routière – mis à part les deux *Timacum, Conbustica* et la *mansio Idimum*[32].

2.3 *Les bourgs routiers avec fortifications*

Un certain nombre d'agglomérations cumulent les fonctions routière et militaire à l'intérieur de la province. Ainsi, sur la route secondaire qui suivait la vallée du Trgoviški Timok en partant de *Timacum Minus* pour rejoindre *Turres* (sur la voie *Naissus-Serdica*), on rencontre Baranica, Žukovac, Gradište, Štrbac, Donja Kamenica et Kalna[33]. En général, il s'agit de fortifications d'époque romaine et/ou protobyzantine situées sur des hauteurs dominant la route ; il est question d'un habitat et d'une nécropole au pied du fort de Baranica tandis que l'on note la présence d'une église au pied de Gradište et de Kalna. Ce sont des exemples parmi d'autres, la difficulté étant de distinguer au sein d'une abondante documentation les fortifications nées à l'époque byzantine de celles préexistantes. Nous disposons en effet de multiples vestiges pas toujours datés avec précision et de sources litté-

30 Sur le statut juridique des *mansiones*, Crogiez-Pétrequin 2009.
31 Miller 1916, Cuntz 1929, Petrović 2019.
32 Vasić & Milošević 2000.
33 P. Petrović 1995, 60–62 ; V. Petrović 2017, 135–138.

raires byzantines, avec en premier lieu Procope : par exemple pour les territoires d'*Aquae*, de *Remesiana* et de *Naissus*, celui-ci énumère 38 *castella*[34].

Dans cette catégorie peuvent entrer aussi les agglomérations dotées d'une enceinte, sans la présence avérée d'une garnison, qui caractérisent une partie de l'habitat groupé de l'*Illyricum* protobyzantin, comme le note G. Dagron : "on peut considérer comme bourg ou village toute enceinte permettant le regroupement d'une population, qu'elle soit citadine ou rurale, nombreuse ou non, rassemblée occasionnellement ou en permanence, pourvue ou non d'institutions municipales"[35]. Une bonne part d'entre elles sont des agglomérations routières, mais on constate aussi "l'extraordinaire multiplication"[36] de ce type d'habitat entre le IVe et le VIe s.

2.4 *Les bourgs et les villages miniers*

Les nombreux travaux de Slobodan Dušanić ont depuis longtemps souligné l'importance des activités minières dans la province[37], en relevant de multiples traces d'installations extractives et d'activités métallurgiques et en reconstituant à partir d'une riche documentation épigraphique[38] la complexité d'une organisation administrative et fiscale en lien avec l'armée autour de ces activités[39] ; enfin il a souligné l'hétérogénéité de la population impliquée, mêlant autochtones et immigrés aux statuts socio-juridiques et socio-économiques variés.

Qu'en est-il du statut et de la morphologie des agglomérations minières qui leur sont liées, et que S. Dušanić appelle les *vici metallorum*, qu'il traduit par *little towns*[40], en référence aux *Tables de Vipasca* (IIe s. – Portugal)[41] ? Claude Domergue montre que ces *Tables* constituent des "mosaïques juridiques", "de véritables pots-pourris de mesures juridiques et fiscales" auxquelles on ne peut donner une portée universelle[42].

Ainsi, toute agglomération minière n'a pas forcément le même statut que *Vipasca* et n'est pas systématiquement sous la gestion directe d'un procurateur impérial ; de même, il n'est pas sûr que de très vastes zones de la province fassent partie du domaine impérial, échappant à la gestion des cités, quel que soit leur statut (*colonia, municipium* ou *civitas peregrina*). Les huit ou neuf districts miniers mis en évidence par S. Dušanić[43] sont peut-être seulement des cadres fiscaux et administratifs, sans gestion des territoires sur lesquels ils exercent leur contrôle, comme en témoigne la prudence d'Alberto dalla Rosa dans son introduction de l'*Atlas Patrimonii Caesaris* (https://patrimonium.huma-num.fr/atlas/).

34 Procope, *Aedif.*, IV, p. 123, 46 et p. 124, 31, éd. Haury. Voir en particulier Băjenaru 2010 et Jęczmienowski 2013.
35 Dagron 1984, 6.
36 Bavant 2018, 76–77.
37 Dušanić 1977a et b, 1989 et 2004 avec bibliographie antérieure.
38 Dušanić 1976, 1995 et 2006.
39 Dušanić 2000.
40 Dušanić 2004, 249 et note 3.
41 Domergue 1983 ; Lazzarini 2001.
42 Domergue 1983, 178–179.
43 Dušanić 2004, 256–260.

Surtout, si l'archéologie a révélé un grand nombre de sites miniers, on dispose de peu d'éléments concrets de l'habitat des mineurs[44]. On peut tout de même citer quelques exemples précis. Dans le Kosmaj, l'agglomération fortifiée de Grad (Stojnik), riche de sept inscriptions lapidaires, a révélé l'existence de *domus* équipées d'hypocaustes et ornées de fresques[45]. Au milieu du IVe s., une basilique chrétienne y est édifiée, pavée de mosaïques portant les noms de neuf donateurs, dont un *lentiararius* (tisserand, marchand de tissus ou marchand de lentilles ?). Dans le massif de Stara Planina, Tilva Roš et Rgotsko brdo, près de Bor, offrent un paysage spécifique s'étageant sur trois niveaux : en haut, la zone d'activité métallurgique fortifiée, sur la pente, les mines de fer et, en contrebas, l'habitat et la nécropole. Ces deux agglomérations minières seraient nées à la fin du IIIe s. et ont duré tout le IVe s., voire jusqu'au milieu du Ve s.[46] La nécropole de Rgotsko brdo était connue antérieurement[47]. L'ensemble du site est repris par Pop-Lazić et ses collaborateurs[48]. Il semble que l'on retrouve cette même organisation spatiale au nord de *Municipium Dardanorum*, sur les pentes occidentales et au pied du Kopaonik avec les sites de Potok u Vrapcenvici et Rudnica[49]. A Potok, l'agglomération et un atelier de transformation du minerai se trouvent sous la protection de la forteresse de Gradina (Donji Kaznovci). Sur les versants du Radan, dans la zone de Dobra Voda, entrées de mine, activités métallurgiques et habitats s'étagent sur plus ou moins un kilomètre, également sous la protection d'une forteresse[50]. Il reste néanmoins que nous n'avons pas trouvé d'exemple de plan d'agglomération minière proprement dite plus ou moins proche des lieux d'exploitation.

On doit aussi imaginer plusieurs cas de figure possibles, comme par exemple des mines situées en montagne et qui seraient fréquentées par des mineurs se déplaçant chaque jour à plusieurs heures de marche de là. Selon l'altitude, ces sites ne pouvaient parfois être exploités qu'à la belle saison ; ainsi, dans le massif de Kopaonik, à 1800 m d'altitude et au cœur d'une zone d'extraction, l'église de saint Procope, patron des mineurs, est dans une zone inhabitable (information de Marija Marić avec qui nous avons visité le site). D'une manière générale, la présence de sanctuaires païens, puis d'églises dans des zones minières n'est pas un élément suffisant pour attester d'un habitat permanent en cet endroit comme, par exemple, dans le Kosmaj, la concentration de 6 inscriptions votives liées à un temple[51], à 2 km à l'est du bourg de Grad de Stojnik, ou encore, plus au sud dans les monts de Rudnik, à l'entrée de la mine, un temple restauré par deux *coloni*, à l'initiative d'un procurateur équestre[52].

44 Parmi les exemples récents : Stamenković 2013 et Marić 2019, au-delà des travaux de Dušanić et des *IMS*.
45 Dušanić 1976, 112–113.
46 Petković 2009, 190–191 pour Tilva Roš et 191–192 pour Rgotsko brdo.
47 Lalović & Iovanović 1981, 81.
48 Pop-Lazić *et al.* 2019, 184–185.
49 Marić 2019, 79 et carte 2, p. 78.
50 Stamenković 2013, 124.
51 *IMS* I, 90, 91, 93, 94, 111 et 113.
52 *IMS* I, 168 ; Dušanić 1999.

2.5 *Bourgs à fonction curative et religieuse dominante*

Les lieux portant le nom d'*Aquae* renvoient de toute évidence à l'exploitation de sources thermales, sites à la fois curatifs et religieux, puisqu'il s'agit d'eaux guérisseuses ou supposées telles. Elles peuvent avoir d'autres fonctions, mais c'est celle-là qui a été mise en valeur par la dénomination même de la localité, comme *Aquae*, une *mansio* entre *Viminacium* et *Ratiaria*. La vignette anonyme figurant sur la *Table de Peutinger*, juste après *Scupi*, sur la route qui mène à *Stobi* en Macédoine, pourrait correspondre à Katlanovo Banja[53], où une agglomération avec une série d'installations thermales est attestée[54]. L'archéologie donne un certain nombre de stations thermales telle Vrban (Klokot) qui abrite les vestiges d'un grand établissement utilisant des sources thermales[55]. Il est possible que les eaux de l'actuelle station thermale de Vranjska Banja, près de Vranje, aient été exploitées dès l'Antiquité ; près de ce lieu, on note des vestiges de construction, une nécropole et une forteresse[56]. De même, une petite agglomération avec sa nécropole existait autour de la station thermale de Niška Banja à 8 km à l'est de Niš[57].

L'exemple le plus documenté est Kuršumlijska banja où l'on note des vestiges de construction[58] ainsi qu'une dédicace aux Nymphes salutaires[59] et une autre qui mentionne un temple restauré par Philoxenus, esclave impérial, *vilicus stat(ionis) Aquar(um) Bas.*[60]; grâce à cette inscription, on connaît ainsi le nom antique de l'agglomération. Celle-ci se trouve à un peu plus de dix kilomètres au sud de la *mansio Ad Fines*, sur la route impériale qui s'enfonce dans la montagne en remontant la vallée de la Banjska Reka. Les fonctions routière, administrative et économique (zone minière) s'ajoutent à sa fonction curative mais c'est bien cette dernière qui est mise en valeur par le toponyme *Aquae*.

2.6 *Les agglomérations d'origine militaire aux fonctions diversifiées : bourgs ou petites villes*

Trois des agglomérations nées des camps danubiens, *Tricornium, Pincum* et *Aquae*, remplissent par la suite des fonctions variées dont celles de centre administratif et fiscal d'un district minier[61]. A cette liste, on peut ajouter *Aureus Mons*[62], qualifiée de *civitas* par le Pèlerin de Bordeaux en 333[63]. L'importance à la fois des fonctions et des vestiges d'*Aquae* et d'*Aureus Mons* permet de les désigner comme des villes secondaires.

53 Dragojević Josifovska 1982, 19.
54 TIR K 34, 68–69.
55 TIR K 34, 134.
56 TIR K 34, 17.
57 TIR K 34, 92.
58 IMS, IV, p. 18 ; TIR K 34, p. 77 ; Petrović 2019, 105–106.
59 IMS, IV, 105.
60 IMS, IV, 104.
61 Respectivement et avec bibliographie antérieure, Petrović 2019, 62–63, 75–76 et 84–88
62 Petrović 2019, 64–65.
63 *It. Burd.*, 564–565.

Les autres sites fortifiés du Danube ajoutent à leur rôle militaire des fonctions économiques et routières (et/ou portuaires[64]) comme *Vinceia, Cuppae, Novae, Ad Scrofulas, Taliata, Gerulata, Una/Luna, Egeta, Clevora, Bononia* et *Ad Malum*, ainsi que *Transdierna, Diana* et *Pontes* ; ils entrent donc dans la catégorie des bourgs, selon la hiérarchie ici proposée[65].

3 Quelques apports récents de l'archéologie.

3.1 Trois bourgs sur l'axe impérial Naissus-Ratiaria

Parmi les agglomérations secondaires les mieux, ou plutôt les moins mal connues, figurent les sites de *Timacum Maius* (Niševac), *Timacum Minus* (Ravna) et *Conbustica* (Kladorup) sur la route qui unit *Naissus* à *Ratiaria*. Toutes trois sont vraisemblablement nées lors de la mise en place du réseau routier impérial, comme autant de stations routières marquant des étapes journalières pour la *vehiculatio*. Elles ont ensuite connu un développement inégal, marquant une nette hiérarchie entre elles. Cette hiérarchie est mise en valeur entre autres dans les sources littéraires : *Conbustica* n'apparait que dans les *Itinéraires (Tabula Peutingeriana* et le Ravennate), *Timacum Maius* se rencontre dans la *Tabula Peutingeriana*, chez le Ravennate et chez Procope ; *Timacum Minus*, outre la *Table* et le Ravennate, est mentionné par Ptolémée puis par la *Notitia Dignitatum*.

L'archéologie confirme la prééminence de *Timacum Minus* dans toute la région du Timok[66]. Couvrant une superficie d'environ 30 ha, elle se compose d'une forteresse de 1,7 ha qui abritait une cohorte et d'une agglomération civile ; dans celle-ci, on a pu identifier deux établissements thermaux, trois temples, deux nécropoles et des traces d'habitats. Ses fonctions, outre celle d'étape sur l'axe majeur de *Naissus* à *Ratiaria*, sont celles du centre administratif d'une région minière, expliquant ainsi la présence d'une troupe temporaire, puis permanente à partir du milieu du IIe s. *(cohors II Aurelia Dardanorum)*. La relative abondance de la documentation épigraphique nous permet d'avoir une idée de la population militaire et civile qui l'habitait[67] ; c'est le plus gros corpus de Mésie Supérieure en dehors des chefs-lieux de cité avec 40 inscriptions civiles et 38 militaires, soit environ 220 personnes[68]. Parmi celles-ci, un décurion figurant sur une stèle funéraire pose la question d'un éventuel municipe à Ravna[69] ; P. Petrović, dans son commentaire, dit sa perplexité et propose d'y reconnaître un décurion de *Naissus* ou de *Ratiaria*[70].

64 Petrović 2019, 96.
65 Sur l'ensemble des 66 sites du *limes* recensés : Korać *et al.* 2014, carte p. 100.
66 Petrović 1995, 37–43 = *IMS*, III/2 ; Petković & Miladinović-Radmilović 2014 ; Diers 2018 ; Petrović 2019, 115–119
67 *IMS*, III/2, 1–99 ; Zotović 2012, 30–39.
68 Zotović 2012, 75–85.
69 *IMS*, III/2, 26.
70 Petrović 1995, 79.

Entre Ravna et Niš, les fouilles de V. Petrović ont révélé le bourg de *Timacum Maius* / Niševac, avec un bâtiment à hypocauste et des thermes, à faible distance de la route[71]. La découverte de briques de la *cohors I Cretum* atteste la présence de soldats de cette unité (fin Ier-début du IIe s.). La faible superficie étudiée jusqu'ici, 6 ha, ne permet pas d'évaluer davantage l'importance de ce bourg, occupé du Ier au IVe s. et situé non loin de sources thermales[72]. À 4 km plus au nord, une forteresse commandait l'entrée des gorges du Timok[73].

Notre connaissance de la troisième agglomération sur la route de *Naissus* à *Ratiaria*, *Conbustica*/Kladorop, est plus étoffée, grâce en particulier à d'importantes fouilles et à l'étude menée par Krassimira Luka sur ce site et son environnement[74]. Le bourg s'organise autour d'un camp de 1,5 ha[75] avec trois concentrations de traces d'occupation et d'inscriptions au nord et à l'ouest de celui-ci, soit au total 16 inscriptions funéraires et 8 votives. Ces données pourraient laisser penser soit à une agglomération polynucléaire, concentrant des fonctions routières, administratives[76], militaires, artisanales mais aussi agricoles, soit à un chapelet d'agglomérations très proches[77].

Au total, la route est tenue par ces trois bourgs, de caractère très différent, séparés les uns des autres par des cols, des gorges et des coupe-gorges rendant les déplacements parfois bien incertains, témoin les personnes tués par des *latrones*[78].

3.2 Deux bourgs révélés par l'archéologie préventive

– Mala Kopašnica, un bel exemple de bourg aux fonctions variées

Grâce à des fouilles préventives sur le tracé de l'autoroute E75, c'est l'une des agglomérations les mieux connues de Mésie supérieure ; elle illustre en même temps la difficulté de retrouver les vestiges de la voie aussi bien que de l'habitat, compte tenu de leur caractère extrêmement dégradé[79].

Située sur une route secondaire de *Naissus* à *Scupi*, qui suit la vallée de la Južna Morava, au sud de Leskovac, cette agglomération couvre un minimum de 20 ha et s'étend sur au moins 500 m de longueur ; la durée de son occupation révélée par le mobilier va du IIe s. au IVe s. p. C.

Elle a livré plusieurs bâtiments dont un avec hypocauste et un probable *horreum* longeant une rue. Par ailleurs, l'activité artisanale est représentée par 9 fours à céramique, ainsi que des traces du travail du verre et du métal. On a donc ici un centre de production

71 Petrović, Filipović & Milivojević 2012, 94–111 ; Petrović 2019, 109–115.
72 Petrović, Filipović & Luka 2014, 104, fig. 7.
73 Petrović, Filipović & Milivojević 2012, 94 et fig. 46.
74 Petrović, Filipović & Luka 2014, 118–123.
75 Luka 2014, 284 et 304.
76 *beneficiarii : CIL*, III, 6291= *CBI*, 582 datée de 213 p.C. et *AE*, 2010, 1394, cf. France & Nelis-Clément 2014, p. 193.
77 Four à céramique domestique : Luka 2014, 304–318 et 324–330, Tables V–XI.
78 *IMS* III/2 93, Ravna ; *AE* 1934, 209, Peć ; *CIL* III, 8242, près de *Theranda*.
79 Stamenkovic 2013, 35–36 et 147–151, n° 110a–114 ; Ivanišević & Stamenković 2014, 71 ; Ivanišević *et al.* 2016.

et de redistribution de la vallée de Leskovac au sein d'une zone minière. Une grande nécropole de 526 tombes[80] montre une population dont le niveau de richesse peut paraître parfois relativement élevé, témoin l'abondance de bijoux et d'objets en or[81]. La seule inscription retrouvée est une stèle funéraire de grande taille dédiée par L. Flavius Proculus et L. Flavius Constans à leur père[82], ce qui nous renvoie là aussi à un indice de niveau socio-économique aisé pour cette famille de citoyens romains.

– Davidovac, bourg routier

D'autres travaux sur le tracé de l'autoroute E75 ont permis de retrouver un bourg à Davidovac, à 60 km au sud de Mala Kopašnica et à 42 km au nord de Lopate, fouillé sur une longueur de 1 km, le long de la voie secondaire *Naissus-Scupi* ; il se caractérise par des thermes, de possibles *tabernae* et une nécropole (tombes à crémation du IIe–IIIe s. puis 67 tombes à inhumation datées de 350 à 450). Les premières traces d'occupation du site remontent à l'âge du Fer. Sofia Petković propose de l'identifier avec une agglomération routière[83].

4 Conclusion

Au terme de ce bilan, nécessairement incomplet, on ne peut que souligner l'importance du phénomène de l'habitat groupé, pour une part hérité de l'époque protohistorique et pour l'autre né avec le nouvel ordre romain. On s'interroge sur sa complexité, son évolution sur plus de quatre siècles, entre plaine danubienne et massifs montagneux. A travers les exemples de Mala Kopašnica et Davidovac, on a vu les progrès spectaculaires des connaissances que l'on peut attendre de l'archéologie préventive ; de même, la multiplication des prospections systématiques dans le cadre d'études microrégionales comme celles menées par Marija Marić sur la région du Kopaonik ou celle de Sonja Stamenković dans les environs de Leskovac est pleine de promesses. Enfin, l'archéologie non invasive, avec ses nouveaux outils (Lidar, drone, images satellitaires, méthodes géophysiques) suivies de vérifications sur le terrain est en train d'enrichir notre vision et laisse espérer la découverte de villages, jusqu'ici peu représentés, en raison de leur mode de construction, souvent en bois et en terre. Il y a là pour la connaissance de l'habitat et la structuration des territoires de nouvelles perspectives.

Au-delà, l'intérêt sera de mieux comprendre les périodes de transition en amont vers l'âge du Fer et en aval vers le monde protobyzantin afin de replacer l'étude de ces habitats groupés dans la longue durée.

80 Ivanišević & Stamenković 2014, 71.

81 Auparavant Jovanović 1978 ; Petrović, *IMS* IV, p. 29 et 36, note 15

82 *IMS*, IV, 116.

83 Petković 2016.

Abréviations

ILJug : Šašel, A. i J. 1978. Inscriptiones latinae quae in Iugoslavia inter annos MCMLX et MCMLXX repertae et editae sunt. Accedunt nonnullae ad annos MCMXL–MCMLX pertinentes. Situla 19. Ljubljana.
Šašel, A. i J. 1986. Inscriptiones latinae quae in Iugoslavia inter annos MCMII et MCMXL repertae et editae sunt. Situla 25. Ljubljana.
IMS : Inscriptions de la Mésie supérieure
I. Singidunum et le Nord-Ouest de la province (M. Mirković et S. Dušanić), Beograd, 1976.
II. Viminacium et Margum (M. Mirković), Beograd, 1986.
III/2. Timacum minus et la Vallée du Timok (P. Petrović), Beograd, 1995.
IV. Naissus – Remesiana – Horreum Margi (P. Petrović), Beograd, 1979.
VI. Scupi et la Région de Kumanovo (B. Dragojević Josifovska), Beograd, 1982.
TIR : Tabula Imperii Romani
TIR L 34 : Soproni, S. éd. (1968) : Aquincum-Sarmizegetusa-Sirmium, Amsterdam.
TIR K 34 : Šašel, J. éd. (1976) : Naissus. Dyrrachion. Scupi. Serdica. Thessalonike, Ljubljana.

Bibliographie

Bavant, B. 2018. Contexte historique. in B. Bavant et V. Ivanišević (éds.), Iustiniana Prima, Leskovac, 63–82 (en serbe et en français).

Dagron, G. 1984. Les villes dans l'Illyricum protobyzantin, in Villes et peuplement dans l'Illyricum protobyzantin, Rome, 1–20.

Diers, L. 2018. Timacum Minus in Moesia Superior – Centrality and Urbanism at a Roman Mining Settlement, Land 7, 126: https://doi.org/10.3390/land7040126

Domergue, C. 1983. La mine antique d'Aljustrel (Portugal) et les tables de bronze de Vipasca. Paris.

Dragojević Josifovska, B. 1982. Introduction historique, in IMS VI. Scupi et la Région de Kumanovo, Belgrade, 15–46.

Dušanić, S. 1976. Le nord-ouest de la Mésie supérieure, introduction historique, in IMS I, 95–120.

Dušanić, S. 1999. The miners' cults in Illyricum, Pallas 50, 129–139.

Dušanić, S. 2000. Army and mining in Moesia Superior, in G. Alföldy, B. Dobson, W. Eck, Kaiser, Heer und Gesellschaft in der Römischen Kaiserzeit. Gedenkschrift für Eric Birley, Stuttgart, 343–364.

Dušanić, S. 2004. Roman mining in Illyricum: historical aspects, in G. Urso (éd.), Dall'Adriatico al Danubio, L'Illirico nell'età greca e romana. Atti del convegno internazionale (Cividale del Friuli 2003), Pisa, 246–270.

Dušanić, S. 2006. Prosopographic Notes on Roman Mining in Moesia Superior: the Families of Wealthy Immigrants in the Mining Districts of Moesia Superior, Starinar 56, 85–102

Grbić-Nikolić, D. 2018. Some Considerations about the Peregrine Communities in Upper Moesia, Lucida intervalla 47, 221–234.

France, J., Nélis-Clément, J. (éds) 2014. La *statio*. Archéologie d'un lieu de pouvoir dans l'Empire romain, Bordeaux.

Horvat, J., Lazar, I. et Gaspari, A. (éds.) 2020. Manjša rimska naselja na slovenskem prostoru / Minor Roman settlements in Slovenia, Ljubljana.

Ivanišević, V. et Stamenković, S. 2014. Zaštitna arheološka iskopavanja na lokalitetima Kamenitica i Pazarište u Maloj Kopašnici, in D. Antonović, S. Golubović et V. Bikić (éds.), Arheologija u Srbiji. Projekti Arheoloskog instituta u 2012. Godini, Belgrade, 71–73.

Ivanišević, V., Stamenković, S. et Jović, S. 2016. Rimsko naselje u zanatski centar u Maloj Kopašnici. A Roman settlement and workshop Center at Mala Kopašnica, in S. Perić et A. Bulatović, Archaeological investigations along the highway route E75 (2011–2014), Belgrade, 47–69.

Jęczmienowski, E. 2013. The Fortifications of the Upper Moesian *Limes*. Topography, Forms, Garrisons, Sizes, Światowit, 10 (51) / A, 31–57.

Jovanović, A. 1978. Nakit od rimskoj Dardaniji, Belgrade.

Kiepert, H et Kiepert, R. 1894–1914. *Formae orbis antiqui*, 36 Karten im Format von 52 : 64 m mit kritischem Text und Quellenangabe zu jeder Karte. Berlin.

Korać, M., Golubović, S. Mrdić, N., Jeremić, G. Pop-Lazić S. 2014. Roman *limes* in Serbia / Rimski *limes* u Srbiji, Belgrade.

Lalović, A. et Jovanović, S. 1981. Rgotina, antičko nalazišta. Rgotina – site antique, Starinar 31, 81–86.

Lazzarini, S. 2001. Lex Metallis dicta. *Studi sulla seconda tavola di* Vipasca, Rome.

Luka, K. 2014. Tehnologični Harakteristiki na bitovata keramika ot rannorimsko vojniško žilište i kăsnoantični plastove ot *Conbustica (Combustica)* pri s. Kladorub, obština Dimovo / Technological characteristics of the pottery from Early Roman Military dwelling and Late Roman levels in *Conbustica (Combustica)* near the village of Kladorub, Dimovo Municipality, in R. Ivanov (éd.), *Ratiaria semper Floreat* I, Sofia, 284–330.

Mangin, M. et Tassaux, F. 1992. Les agglomérations secondaires de l'Aquitaine romaine, in L. Maurin (éd.), Villes et agglomérations urbaines antiques du sud-ouest de la Gaule (Bordeaux 1990), Bordeaux.

Marić, M. D. 2019. Late Roman Fortifications of the Eastern Part of the Metalla Dardanica Imperial Domain, Zbornik Instituta za Arheologiju 13, 75–89.

Miller, K. 1916. *Itineraria Romana*, Stuttgart.

Mócsy, A. 1974. Pannonia and Upper Moesia: History of the Middle Danube Provinces of the Roman Empire, London.

Petković, S. et Miladinović-Radmilović, N. 2014. Military graves from the Late Roman necropolis at Slog in Ravna – *Timacum Minus*. Vojnički grobovi sa kasnoantičke nekropole Slog u Ravni – *Timacum Minus*, Starinar 64, 87–130.

Petković, S. 2009. The Traces of Roman Metallurgy in Eastern Serbia, Journal of Mining and Metallurgy 45.2, 187–196.

Petković, S. 2016. Zaštitna arheološka istraživanja na lokalitetu Davidovac-Gradište. Preliminarni resultati. Archaeological rescue excavations at the site of Davidovac-Gradište. Preliminary results, in S. Perić et A. Bulatović (éds.), Arheološka istraživanja na autoputu E75 (2011–2014). Archaeological Investigations along the Highway Route E 75 (2011–2014), Belgrade, 301–349.

Petrović, P. 1995. *Timacum minus* et la Vallée du Timok, in IMS III/2, Belgrade.

Petrović, V. 2007. Une nouvelle borne milliaire découverte sur la voie romaine *Naissus-Lissus*, Starinar 56, 367–376.

Petrović, V. 2017. La voie romaine *Timacum Minus-Pautalia* : les contacts entre la Mésie Supérieure et la Thrace d'après les recherches archéologiques et les sources écrites, in S. Zanni (éd.), La route antique et médiévale : nouvelles approches, nouveaux outils, Actes de la table-ronde internationale (Bordeaux 2016), Bordeaux, 133–144.

Petrović, V. 2019. Les voies et agglomérations romaines au cœur des Balkans. Le cas de la Serbie, Bordeaux.

Petrović, V. et Grbić, D. 2014. Ancient *Remesiana*: a New Milestone from the Times of Severus Alexander, Journal of Ancient Topography (Rivista di Topografia Antica) 23, 95–106.

Petrović, V., Filipović, V. et Luka, K. 2014. The Roman road *Naissus-Timacum Maius-Timacum Minus-Conbustica (Combustica)-Ratiaria*, in R. Ivanov (éd.), Sofia, 97–142.

Piso, I. 2003. L'urbanisation des provinces danubiennes, in M. Reddé, L. Dubois, D. Briquel, H. Lavagne, F. Queyrel (éds.), La naissance de la ville dans l'Antiquité, Paris, 285–298. Reprint in Piso I. 2005. An der Nordgrenze des Römischen Reiches : ausgewählte Studien (1972–2003), Stuttgart, 487–506.

Pop-Lazić, S., Craft, S., Vujadinović, V. et Živić, M. 2019. *Felix Romuliana* – Gamzigrad : rekogosciranja 2017. Godine, in I. Bugarski, V. Filipović and N. Gavrilović Vitas (éds.), Arheologija u Srbiji. Projekti Arheološkog instituta u. 2017. Godini, Belgrade, 143–150.

Stamenković, S. 2013. Rimsko naseđe u Leskovačkoj kotlini. Roman legacy in the Leskovac valley, Belgrade.

Talbert, R. 2000. Barrington Atlas of the Greek and Roman World, Princeton.

Tassaux, F. 2018. En route pour Jérusalem avec l'Anonyme de Bordeaux, Tibiscum 8, 91–110.

Vasić, M., Milošević, G. 2000. *Mansio Idimum* – rimska poštanska i putna stanica kod Medveđe. Belgrade.

Zotović, R. 2012. Životno doba na tlu srbije u periodu rimske vladavine / Lifetime in the territory of Serbia during Roman rule, Užice.

Il *Barbaricum* nella Sardegna romana: omaggio al *Princeps Daciae* Ioan Piso*

Attilio Mastino

1 Per un Amico e un Maestro

L'occasione di questa nota che si inserisce in un fortunato recente filone di ricerca[1] è quella della pubblicazione degli studi in onore dell'amico e Maestro Ioan Piso, impegno al quale non ho voluto sottrarmi per la stima, l'amicizia, il debito di riconoscenza che ho contratto in tante circostanze, soprattutto per gli accesi e amichevoli confronti relativi alle dediche imperiali poste per la costituzione di una colonia (*condita colonia*), come a Sarmizegetusa in Dacia con Traiano ad opera del legato propretore *[D(ecimus) Terenti]us Scaurianus*[2] e ad Uchi Maius in Tunisia con Severo Alessandro ad opera del legato del proconsole Cesonio Lucillo[3]: con una incredibile distanza cronologica e geografica, ma insieme con l'affermarsi di analoghi riti cerimoniali e di analoghi percorsi istituzionali definiti dall'autorità romana. Oppure per gli incontri internazionali, ultimo dei quali quello per il XVI *Congressus internationalis Epigraphiae Graecae et Latinae* di Bordeaux (agosto–settembre 2022), *L'épigraphie au XXI*[e] *siècle*, dove Ioan Piso aveva discusso animatamente la mia relazione su *Geografia, geopolitica, epigrafia*. Ma tra gli incontri internazionali ai quali insieme abbiamo partecipato voglio ricordare almeno quello di Ferrara e Cento del 2009, *Roma e le province del Danubio*, Atti del I Convegno internazionale, Ferrara-Cento, 15–17 ottobre 2009, dove nelle conclusioni avevo riletto "gli aspetti religiosi dell'*epulum Iovis* nei terri-

---

* Ringrazio cordialmente Paola Ruggeri per il generoso contributo al capitolo su Diana e Silvano.

1 Vd. ora il bellissimo studio di M. Valenti, Il Barbaricum. Una periferia che si fece centro. Società, insediamento ed economia tra I e X secolo (Archeologia Barbarica 5), Mantova 2021. Naturalmente sono stato iniziato a questi temi dal mio maestro Bruno Luiselli, nei lontani anni cagliaritani, quando progettò la rivista e la collana "Romanobarbarica".

2 *CIL* III 1143 = *AE* 2013, 1339 (anni 106–117) Sarmizegetusa, *Auspiciis / [Imp(eratoris)] Caes(aris) divi Nervae f[il(ii)] / [Nervae] Traiani Augusti / [Germ(anici) Dac(ici)] condita colonia / [Ulpia Traiana Augusta] Dacica / [Sarmizegetusa] per / [D(ecimum) Terenti]um Scaurianum / [legatum] eius pro pr(aetore).*

3 *"[colonia Alexandria]na Aug(usta) Uchi Ma[i]us su[b] eius nomine auspicioqu[e]" deducta per Caesonium Lucillum Macrum c(larissimum) v(irum) partes proco(n)s(ulis) pont[ificis(?) legatu]m v(ices) adm(inistrantem?) / [arcum novu]m(?) ad ae[ter]num testimonium reciperat[ae l]ibertatis er[ex]it d(ecreto) d(ecurionum) p(ecunia) p(ublica),* Ibba 2006, 147–149 = AE 2006, 1688 = Olmo-López 2022, 579.

tori della Dacia presentati dal *Princeps Daciae* Ioan Piso con riferimento alle cerimonie imperiali che si celebravano il 23 maggio, in occasione del *tubilustrium*". In altre occasioni l'ho visto sdegnato nella difesa del patrimonio archeologico di Alburnus Maior, in assenza di interventi di tutela da parte delle autorità. Dagli anni 2000 faceva parte del Comitato internazionale che supervisionava la rivista "Epigraphica" diretta da Giancarlo Susini e poi da Angela Donati. E poi Vienna nel 2015 con la discussione sulla sua relazione (*Die Ziegelstempel als Quelle für die Geschichte der Provinz Dakien*), questione complicata dai confini nazionali di oggi e dalla mobilità delle unità militari e degli investitori privati in rete tra loro che producevano i laterizi con i bolli epigrafici: nell'occasione aveva allargato il discorso – hanno osservato gli editori Fritz Mitthof, Chiara Cenati, Livio Zerbini – alle attività agricole, alle coltivazioni, alle produzioni di olio e vino, all'allevamento, pilastri per comprendere le strategie e i processi di romanizzazione, per localizzare i centri produttivi e le vie di trasporto. Infine a Iași per la quinta Conferenza sulle province danubiane (*Romans and natives in the Danubian provinces, 1st c. BC–6th c. AD*), tra il 5 e il 9 novembre 2019, a parlare dei *carmina* della Dacia[4].

Soprattutto era stato incuriosito nel 2015 dalle mie conclusioni pubblicate nel 2021 su *L'epigrafia latina nelle province danubiane negli ultimi 15 anni (2000–2015)*[5], ricambiandomi col *Lexicon epigraphicum Daciae*, scritto con Radu Ardevan, Carmen Fenechiu, Eugenia Beu-Dachin, Ștefania Lalu (Cluj-Napoca 2016)[6]. Il nome di Ioan Piso ricorre in tutte le pagine del mio testo, partendo dal dibattito sul ruolo della geografia nella storia così come l'ha definito in occasione del Colloquio di Cluj-Napoca del settembre–ottobre 2006. Allora avevo potuto rileggere lo splendido volume degli Atti pubblicato dal Centrul de Studii Romane dell'Universitatea "Babeş-Bolyai" e del Muzeul Naţional de Istorie a Transilvaniei: un volume di sintesi che poneva il tema della flessibilità romana nella creazione di nuove province e insieme si soffermava ad analizzare aspetti specifici relativi alla storia provinciale romana[7]. E poi il tema dell'urbanizzazione[8], dei magistrati cittadini, del culto imperiale, dei *vici*, dei *pagi*[9], dei *fora*, le dediche a *Iupiter Optimus Maximus Teutanus* e *K(arnuntinus)* ad Aquincum e Carnuntum, poi Giove Dolicheno[10], i culti orientali, l'arruolamento, la costruzione degli accampamenti militari, i *castra* con le loro *canabae*, il controllo sulle regioni minerarie, la riscossione della tassa sulle eredità, l'onomastica e tanto altro. Tematiche che possono essere estese utilmente ad altre province. Soprattutto l'edizione monumentale delle IDR III/5 con le 724 iscrizioni di Apulum[11], le oltre cento

4 Piso 2023.
5 Mastino 2021.
6 A p. 91 mi aveva interessato la dedica *Genio Carthaginis* et *Genio Daciarum* di Alba Iulia, CIL III 993 = IDR III, 5, 41.
7 Piso 2008.
8 Piso 2003.
9 Il termine *pagus* sopravvive ovunque nella Sardegna moderna, vd. Guido 2006, 318, 8.2.6; Mastino 2001.
10 Anche in Sardegna, CIL X 7949, Ossi presso Turris Libisonis in età severiana.
11 Piso 2001.

iscrizioni dal *forum vetus* di Sarmizegetusa[12], i fasti provinciali[13], le altre province contigue alla Dacia, come per la sede del governatore della Mesia inferiore[14], la Pannonia, il Norico. Soprattutto emerge dalla produzione scientifica di I. Piso il ruolo gigantesco di Traiano[15] con una quantità davvero significativa di dediche: tema che ci ha sempre rimandato alla Sardegna, alla promozione istituzionale dell'antico *pagus* delle Aquae Ypsitanae nella pertica della colonia Iulia Augusta Uselis divenuto nel primo decennio del II secolo d. C. Forum Traiani in pieno *Barbaricum* oltre il fiume Tirso[16]. E poi la spedizione partica: l'imperatore Traiano potrebbe aver personalmente conosciuto l'anonimo marinaio sardo della flotta di Miseno imbarcato nella quadriere *Ops*, sepolto ad Olbia: e ciò nel 114, in occasione del viaggio in oriente verso Seleucia, prima della campagna partica (CIL XVI 60). Oggi sappiamo che l'intero equipaggio della nave, agli ordini del prefetto Quinto Marcio Turbone, ottenne allora la cittadinanza romana, forse per una diretta partecipazione alla guerra contro i Parti. Negli ultimi anni di Traiano sappiamo che il proconsole Gaio Asinio Tucuriano lastricò a Sulci nell'*insula Plumbaria* la piazza principale (CIL X 7516).

Una recente scoperta avvenuta a Posada testimonia ancor più il legame della provincia Sardinia con Traiano che il 5 maggio 102 dispone il congedo del fante *Hannibal Tabilatis f(ilius) Nur(---) Alb(---)*: possediamo il diploma col quale l'imperatore concesse la cittadinanza romana all'*ex pedite* della II coorte gemina di Liguri e Corsi nella quale erano confluiti i Sardi della I Gemina *Sardorum et Corsorum* dell'età di Domiziano, alla moglie *Iurini Tammugae filia Sordia* (*Sarda* ?), ai due figli maschi *Sabinus* e *Saturninus*, alle figlie *Tisareni*, *Bolgitta* e *Bonassoni* (non è certo che i nomi siano indeclinabili)[17]. Già i nomi soprattutto delle donne e del padre del congedato ci indirizzano verso un sostrato paleosardo davvero risalente nel tempo, per quanto il nome *Hannibal* rimandi a un contesto punico (AE 2013, 650)[18]. Gli studiosi discutono sull'abbreviazione NVR ALB: indica la provenienza da un villaggio presso il *Nur(ac) Alb(um)*, forse un nuraghe costruito con pietre di calcare chiaro; oppure meglio con Davide Faoro possiamo pensare ad un soldato originario di una *gens* locale fin qui sconosciuta, nel senso di *Nur(ritanus) Alb(---)*. Al di là della questione, che pure è di estremo interesse, assistiamo in diretta alla quasi totale smobilitazione sotto Traiano dell'esercito di occupazione in Sardegna, se si esclude la coorte *I Sardorum* costituita da ausiliari di origine locale, impegnati soprattutto nella capitale Carales e in area mineraria[19]. Il recente volume di Rosanna Arcuri approfondisce il tema del rapporto tra *Barbaricum* e provincia romana in ambiti territoriali più consueti, quelli di area renana e danubiana, nella relazione dell'impero romano con le terre oltre il *limes*, confine reale e simbolico insieme: emergono molti aspetti di carattere antropologico, le

12 Piso 2006, 211–332.
13 Piso 2013, vd. AE 2013, 1273 (il primo volume: AE 1993, 1318).
14 Piso 2014: la capitale della provincia era a Durostorum (oggi Silistra, Bulgaria).
15 Piso 2004; Piso 2014a; Piso 2017; Piso 2021. In generale vd. Piso 2014a; Tončinić, Zerbini 2021.
16 Mastino, Zucca 2012; Mastino, Zucca 2014.
17 Floris, Mastino 2019.
18 Sanciu, Pala, Sanges 2013; Ibba 2014; Faoro 2016.
19 Le Bohec 1990.

forme del potere, i riti, le attività economiche di aree caratterizzate dal nomadismo, la religione tradizionale, la cultura materiale[20].

2 I Carpi della Dacia e la magia in Sardegna

L'immigrazione di molti Carpi dal *Barbaricum* e dalla Dacia settentrionale entro l'impero e più precisamente in Pannonia nell'età di Diocleziano è stata ben studiata da P. Kovács[21]: i *Consularia Constantinopolitana* nell'anno 295 precisano: *Carporum gens universa in Romania se tradidit*[22]. Oggi conosciamo la questione meglio seguendo l'incredibile carriera di un personaggio, *Fl(avius) Maximinus*, originario del popolo dei Carpi trasferiti dai Carpazi nella *Valeria* ma alcuni ammessi dopo una sola generazione ai gradi più alti dell'impero nel corso del IV secolo, come documentano, oltre che il 28° libro delle Storie di Ammiano Marcellino (*Storie*, XXVIII, 1, 7), soprattutto i miliari stradali della Sardinia (EE VIII 781b, Sbrangatu Olbia e CIL X 8026, Nuragus, antica Valentia) che ricordano *Maximinus* come *perfectissimus* e procuratore ducenario della Sardinia, nell'età di Valentiniano I, Valente e Graziano (anni 364–367)[23]: arriviamo fino al 371 e al prestigiosissimo incarico di prefetto del pretorio per le Gallie, con l'improvvisa disgrazia e la condanna a morte nel 376 per volontà di Graziano.

L'episodio testimonia in modo sorprendente la mobilità sociale e la possibilità per una famiglia proveniente dal *Barbaricum* occupato dai Carpi di innalzarsi nell'aristocrazia della provincia e nell'impero, pur mantenendo una cultura fondata su tradizioni ancestrali legate al mondo della magia[24]: il padre del nostro, appena arrivato all'interno dell'impero, era giunto all'incarico di archivista nell'ufficio del governatore della Valeria, *tabularius praesidialis officii* probabilmente nell'età di Costanzo II. Nella sua giovinezza aveva acquisito nel *Barbaricum* la capacità di interpretare il volo e il canto degli uccelli, gli *augurales alites* e i *cantus oscinum*: proprio grazie a queste competenze ornitomantiche che gli provenivano dalla cultura barbarica di origine (carpico-gotica), aveva predetto al figlio *Maximinus* un futuro di grandi successi nella carriera, ma alla fine una morte per mano del boia.

Alle competenze magico-rituali del padre si sommavano le curiosità del figlio, alimentate in Sardegna da un mago di origine sarda e barbaricina divenuto amico del governatore tra il 364 e il 366 d.C., proprio mentre si restaurava la strada che, attraverso il piede occidentale del Gennargentu (i *Montes Insani*)[25], collegava Olbia con Carales, nell'attuale

20 Arcuri 2023.

21 Kovács 2011; vd. anche Kovács 2011a, 164–191; AE 2011, 948. Per le scorrerie dei Carpi nella provincia Dacia, vd. la dedica di *Gaius Valerius Sarapio* ad Apulum, *a Carpis liberatus* (CIL III 1054 = IDR III,5,1, 171 datata al 247–248 d.C., vd. LED 91).

22 Irmscher 1983.

23 Meloni 1958, 255, pros. 69, 1.

24 Mastino, Pinna 2008; La Fragola, Mastino, Pinna 2021. Vd. anche Pinna 2012.

25 Mastino 2005.

Barbagia: ci restano i miliari di Sbrangatu (Olbia)[26] e Valentia (Nuragus)[27]; noi pensiamo che l'amico sardo del preside fosse originario della *Barbaria* interna attraversata da questa arteria. Ammiano ricostruisce una carriera fortunata di *Maximinus* nell'età dei Flavi Valentiniano I, Valente e Graziano, inusuale per un funzionario appartenente ad una famiglia di recentissima romanizzazione. Massimino era nato a Sopianae una città della Valeria (Fünfkirchen, oggi Pécs in Ungheria)[28]: apparteneva al popolo dei Carpi, trasferiti in Pannonia da Diocleziano negli anni novanta del III secolo. Nell'età di Costanzo II, quando Massimino aveva potuto studiare le arti liberali ed iniziare a svolgere una carriera di avvocato, senza distinguersi troppo (*post mediocre studium liberalium doctrinarum defensionemque causarum ignobilem*), ma stringendo una saldissima amicizia (*sodalis et contogatus*) con quel *Festinus* di Trento che, pur provenendo da una famiglia di bassissima condizione, *ultimi sanguinis et ignoti*[29], sarebbe arrivato a governare la Siria. *Maximinus*, ancora in condizione di *vir egregius*, secondo Jones, Martindale e Morris[30] ma *vir pefectissimus* nei miliari sardi (almeno in EE VIII 781 b) avrebbe iniziato la sua carriera dopo la morte di Giuliano, nel primo o secondo anno di Valentiniano e Valente governando col titolo di *praeses* la Corsica e successivamente procuratore imperiale in Sardegna per tre anni e giungendo al culmine della carriera, nel 371, al prestigiosissimo incarico di prefetto del pretorio per le Gallie, con l'improvvisa disgrazia e condanna a morte nel 376 per volontà di Graziano (*idem Maximinus sub Gratiano intoleranter se efferens damnatorio iugulatus est ferro*)[31]. Per circa 12 anni il nostro fu tra i protagonisti sulla scena politica e tra i funzionari più vicini all'imperatore: dopo aver ricoperto l'incarico di *procurator Sardiniae* (CIL X 8026) o meglio *p(raeses)* (EE VIII 781 b), con un potere che potrebbe in realtà esser stato contemporaneamente esercitato anche sulla Corsica, il nostro fu ammesso all'ordine senatorio e il 17 novembre 366 compare come *corrector Tusciae* in una costituzione del *Codex Theodosianus*[32]; senza lasciare quest'incarico, in attesa che arrivasse il successore, fu poi dal 368 *praefectus annonae* fino al 370, secondo Ammiano iniziando allora a mostrare il suo vero carattere in una serie di processi antimagici, nei quali fu coinvolto anche il valorosissimo *comes Africae* Teodosio il vecchio, padre del futuro imperatore (XXVIII 1, 10: *relatione maligna docuit principem non nisi suppliciis acrioribus perniciosa facinora scrutari posse vel vindicari*)[33].

---

26 EE VIII 781 b.

27 CIL X 8026, vd. Floris 2009, 153.

28 Talbert 2000, 296.

29 Ammiano Marcellino, Storie, XXIX 2, 23.

30 Cfr. PLRE, I, 577 sg., Maximinus 7.

31 Massimino fu prefetto di Roma nel 370–371 e dal 371 prefetto delle Gallie fino al 376, quando fu giustiziato (Ammiano Marcellino, XXVIII, 1, 57; Simmaco, Ep. X, 2, a Graziano, nel 376: "*Ferox ille Maximinus [...] poena capitali exitia cunctorum lacrimas expiavit*"). Vd. anche: Ammiano Marcellino, XXVIII 1, 6–7, 41; XXX 3, 12 e passim. Cfr. PLRE, I, 577 sg.; Bocci s.d., 141 n. 177.

32 C.Th. IX 1, 8. Erroneamente la costituzione è riferita al 365 da Pais 1999, II, 26 e sg., n. 51 e da Bellieni 1931, 186.

33 Così S. Girolamo: *Chron., ad annum 376.*

Un passo del 28° libro delle *Storie* di Ammiano Marcellino parla dell'amicizia di Massimino con un Sardo che possedeva particolari competenze d'ordine magico, originario a quanto sostiene Camillo Bellieni delle montagne della *Barbaria* sarda[34], un vero e proprio "stregone" che non avrebbe "stimolato i suoi malefici impulsi", ma anzi avrebbe "cercato di raffrenare le passioni" di un personaggio che Ammiano rappresenta come "una belva assetata di sangue"[35]. Massimino doveva averlo incontrato in Sardegna[36], negli anni in cui, durante il regno di Valentiniano, governò l'isola, fra il 364 e il 366. Lo portò con sé anche nella Tuscia, quando ne divenne governatore nel 366, e infine a Roma, dove era stato nominato prefetto dell'annona, carica che ricoprì nel biennio 368–370[37]. Proprio a Roma si ebbe una svolta, quando Massimino giunse ad uccidere con l'inganno, *per dolosas fallacias*, il suo amico sardo.

Ma seguiamo il testo Ammiano, dove parla dei comportamenti di Massimino una volta divenuto amministratore dell'annona a Roma:

> "All'inizio procedette con prudenza, per tre motivi. In primo luogo perché gli risuonavano all'orecchio le parole pronunciate dal padre [originario del popolo dei Carpi transdanubiani], assai esperto nell'interpretazione del volo degli uccelli e del loro canto, il quale gli aveva predetto che sarebbe salito ad altissime cariche, ma sarebbe perito sotto il ferro del carnefice. In secondo luogo – e questo è quanto soprattutto ci interessa – perché aveva incontrato un sardo (*hominem Sardum*), che poi egli aveva ucciso, a quanto si diceva, con inganni, molto esperto nell'evocare anime malefiche di trapassati e nel richiedere presagi agli spiriti; finché costui restò in vita, Massimino, temendo di essere tradito, si mostrò mite e condiscendente. In terzo luogo perché, strisciando come un serpente sotterraneo in luoghi piuttosto bassi, non poteva ancora suscitare maggiori motivi di lutti"[38].

Ma la possibilità di acquisire maggior potere e di levarsi a posizioni più elevate si presentò in occasione di un'accusa di *veneficium*: Chilone e la moglie Massima chiesero al prefetto dell'Urbe Olibrio di arrestare i sospettati. Ma poiché Olibrio manifestava incertezze nella conduzione del processo a causa delle precarie condizioni di salute che ne limitavano

34 Bellieni 1931, 186.

35 Bellieni 1931, 187.

36 Anche se il testo non è chiarissimo al riguardo, perché ricorda l'*hominem Sardum* non quando scrive di Massimino come governatore della Sardegna (XXVIII, 1, 6), ma dopo che egli era arrivato a Roma come prefetto dell'annona (XXVIII, 1, 7). Solo allora ricorda che Massimino aveva incontrato un sardo (*nanctus hominem Sardum*).

37 Su tutti questi passaggi della carriera di Massimino, cfr. PLRE, I, 577 sg., Maximinus 7.

38 Ammiano Marcellino, Storie, XXVIII 1, 7: "*Primo, quod recalebant in auribus eius parentis effata, quid augurales alites vel cantus monerent oscinum, apprime callentis, ad usque sublimia regimenta <venturum>, sed periturum ferro poenali: dein, quod nanctus hominem Sardum, quem ipse postea per dolosas fallacias interemit, ut circumtulit rumor, eliciendi animulas noxias et praesagia sollicitare larvarum perquam gnarum, dum superesset, ille timens, ne proderetur, tractabilis erat et mollior; postremo, quod tamquam subterraneus serpens per humiliora reptando nondum maiore funerum excitare poterat causas*".

l'efficienza operativa, i denuncianti chiesero e ottennero che il processo fosse affidato al prefetto dell'annona, che era appunto Massimino. Costui ebbe allora modo di esprimere tutta la sua ferocia (secondo le parole dello storico); ferocia che manifestò in seguito in tutta una serie di altri processi per veneficio, per adulterio, e soprattutto per pratiche magiche, attraverso i quali (col consenso di Valentiniano I, cui aveva scritto per denunciare i vizi della città ricevendo poteri eccezionali)[39] ebbe modo di colpire soprattutto il ceto dell'aristocrazia senatoria.

La notizia di Ammiano, nella sua essenziale semplicità, ha la forza documentaria e il realismo di una scarna nota di campo, e si configura come preziosa attestazione dell'operatività in Sardegna dell'agire magico. Essa ci dice che la cultura isolana esprimeva sicuramente specialisti del sacro maturati nel contesto locale e inquadrabili nella categoria del negromante, dell'indovino e dello stregone malefico.

Sul mondo magico della Sardegna antica le fonti sono avare di notizie o, quando ne danno, lasciano insoddisfatti per diversi motivi: parlano secondo procedimenti spersonalizzati e mitizzanti (illustrano l'idea che gli altri hanno della Sardegna più che la Sardegna, e lo fanno spesso ricorrendo a stereotipi ripetitivi), oppure, quando va bene, come nel caso delle epigrafi, parlano con testi mutili non sempre facilmente ricostruibili. Questo "Sardo" amico di Massimino è una persona in carne ed ossa, della quale possiamo seguire parte dell'esistenza sino alla drammatica fine; egli rinvia ad un ambiente sociale nel quale è vissuto e nel quale sono nati e si sono esercitati i suoi saperi e i suoi poteri magici.

La notizia di Ammiano ha un pregio: passa come un lampo sull'opacità della documentazione e la illumina, permettendoci di procedere con maggiore sicurezza nel trattare gli altri dati sulla base di questo ancoraggio solido, aprendoci una finestra sul mondo magico isolano. Offre poi lo spunto per analizzare il rapporto tra potere politico e magia e per osservare il clima culturale che nel IV secolo vede il passaggio dal paganesimo al cristianesimo. Né in tutto ciò va dimenticato il filtro costituito dall'ideologia dello storico Ammiano.

Oggi conosciamo meglio la sopravvivenza in Sardegna di una serie di pratiche magiche che sembrano fondarsi su antichissime competenze e su una tradizione di conoscenze che non si può escludere vadano collegate al mondo punico ed al etrusco, se non altro per quanto riguarda il settore dell'aruspicina. A parte il sacrificio rituale dei fanciulli, l'uccisione dei vecchi ultrasettantenni e l'uso di erbe velenose (alcune provocano il "riso sardonio", la morte tra terribili sofferenze), abbiamo studiato il rito dell'incubazione per guarire dagli incubi notturni con un sonno stimolato da delle droghe (già nella Fisica di Aristotele)[40], l'interpretazione dei sogni, l'ordalia per accertare la responsabilità dei briganti e dei ladri sacrileghi, la lettura di prodigi che annunciano lo scoppio delle guerre (scudi che sudano sangue), l'idolatria e la venerazione di *ligna et lapides*, la presenza di maghi e streghe (le terribili *bitiae* dalla duplice pupilla che uccidono con lo sguardo)[41]. L'episodio che vide protagonista il governatore romano, *Flavius Maximinus*, ci fa dunque

39 Ammiano Marcellino, Storie, XXVIII 1, 8–13.

40 Mastino 2016.

41 La Fragola, Mastino, Pinna 2021.

conoscere un mago sardo che espertissimo nell'evocare anime dannate e nel trarre presagi dagli spiriti; competenze che Massimino acquisì, sommandole a quelle provenienti dalla tradizione familiare, in particolare dalla origine barbarica del padre originario del popolo transadanubiano dei Carpi; gli risuonavano le parole del padre: *parentis effata, quid augurales alites vel cantus monerent oscinum, apprime callentis, ad usque sublimia regimenta <venturum>, sed periturum ferro poenali.* Alla fine, spaventato, avrebbe ucciso con l'inganno il mago sardo. Che tali pratiche siano proseguite in Sardegna è esplicitamente testimoniato da Gregorio Magno, a proposito del chierico Paolo, accusato di celebrare nascostamente dei riti magici (*Epist.* IV, 24). Ma più in generale, Gregorio invita il vescovo di *Carales* a vigilare contro i cultori degli idoli, gli indovini e gli stregoni: una categoria di persone specializzata nelle scienze occulte[42].

3 Le variazioni dei confini del *Barbaricum*

L'esistenza di vasti territori occupati dai Barbari della Sardegna in età romana, amministrati da capi indigeni e comunque rappresentati dalle fonti come liberi ancora all'età di Cesare è ben documenta fin dalla costituzione della provincia all'indomani della prima guerra romano-cartaginese (nel 227 a.C.) e durante il *Bellum Sardum* di Hampsicora e Hostus raccontato da Livio e Silio Italico (che conosce un *Hampsagora*)[43]: nella seconda metà del I secolo a.C. Diodoro Siculo (V, 15) poteva constatare che l'oracolo di Delfi si era prodigiosamente avverato perché i discendenti del mitico Iolao arrivati in Sardegna e attaccati dai Cartaginesi si erano rifugiati nella regione montuosa (il Marghine-Goceano, il Montiferru, sicuramente anche il Gennargentu), dove costruite dimore sotterranee, si erano dedicati all'allevamento di grandi mandrie di bestiame, che fornivano un adeguato nutrimento: si cibavano perciò di latte, di formaggio e di carne. Gli Iolei (e poi gli Iliensi secondo il mito romano arrivati da Troia al seguito di Enea) si erano ritirati dalla regione pianeggiante e così non conobbero la fatica del lavoro dei campi, ma vivevano nutrendosi con abbondanza, pascolando sui monti e conducendo un'esistenza libera da pericoli: "E, pur combattendo i Cartaginesi contro di loro con forze rilevanti, a causa della difficoltà di manovra nel sottosuolo, non furono assoggettati. Alla fine, assunto il dominio i Romani, e combattuto spesso contro di loro, per questi motivi non furono piegati dalla potenza nemica"[44]. Una informazione preziosa è fornita da Pausania (X, 17, 6) a proposito dei Troiani-Iliensi del tardo mito attribuito ora al poeta Ennio: essi si congiunsero coi Greci (Iolei) che già vi si trovavano. "Ma fu impedito ai barbari di venire in battaglia con Greci e Troiani: infatti erano equivalenti in tutto l'apparato militare e il fiume Thorso che scorreva nella regione in mezzo a loro incuteva ugualmente ad entrambi il timore del guado". Se Pausania conosceva davvero la geografia della Sardegna, dovremmo collocare gli Iliensi (Iolei) in riva destra del fiume Tirso (nel Marghine-Goceano e nel Montiferru, vicino a

42 Tutto in Mastino, Pinna 2008.

43 Mastino 2016a.

44 Traduzione di Didu 2003, 173.

Cornus, capitale della regione ribellatasi sotto la guida di Hampsicora nella guerra annibalica); sulla riva sinistra vanno invece collocati i Nurritani sardi, cioè sul Gennargentu e in pieno *Barbaricum*, dunque in entrambi i casi sui *Montes Insani*, noti anche a Tolomeo. A differenza del Danubio, il grande fiume non ha svolto con continuità la funzione di *limes* tra Romani e Barbari, ma ha rappresentato il punto di riferimento costante per popolazioni diverse, spesso conflittuali tra loro.

In età Augustea assistiamo ad un'opera di riorganizzazione del territorio, quando il *Barbaricum* della Sardegna fu meglio conosciuto e articolato in *civitates* controllate da un reparto militare sotto l'autorità di un *prolegato*, poi di un *praefectus* equestre, posto a capo di una coorte ausiliaria e delle principali *civitates* della regione. I confini dell'area occupata dai Barbari non sono ben conosciuti (si è parlato di una "realtà metafisica"), anche perché variarono notevolmente nel tempo[45], si ridussero progressivamente, con linee di comunicazione legate alla transumanza[46] e con la presenza comunque dell'autorità romana che interveniva attraverso la collocazione di *termini*, di confini catastali, oltre che con l'applicazione di una rigida normativa volta a contenere il nomadismo e a promuovere la sedentarizzazione delle popolazioni dedite alla pastorizia. L'area barbaricina sembra più estesa in età bizantina se ad esempio Gregorio Magno poteva distinguere tra i cristiani della provincia bizantina e i vicini pagani dell'interno, tra *provinciales* e *barbari*[47] e, nell'ambito della stessa provincia, precisava che esistevano alcuni territori, come quello della lontana diocesi di Fausiana (al confine coi Balari), l'attuale Olbia, in cui i pagani continuavano ad essere in numero consistente: *quosdam illic paganos remanere cognovimus et ferino degentes modo Dei cultum penitus ignorare*[48]. Del resto la provincia aveva conosciuto proprio in età bizantina una riduzione territoriale fin dall'età di Giustiniano con la costruzione di *castra* fortificati, se è valida l'ipotesi di Durliat che colloca a pochi chilometri da Carales il confine con il ducato autonomo della *Barbaria* e la stazione doganale cittadina nell'età dell'imperatore Maurizio[49].

4 I *Montes Insani*

Collocati ad una latitudine di 38° a Nord dell'equatore (la stessa delle foci del fiume Temo, 15' a Sud di Capo Marrargiu, di Bosa e di Macopsisa; appena più a Nord di Cornus e di Gurulis Nova), i *Mainomena Ore* secondo Tolomeo si trovavano ad una longitudine Est rispetto alle Isole Fortunate di 31°, dunque a metà strada tra Bosa e Macopsisa[50]. Per quanto i valori numerici della *Geografia* di Tolomeo siano discutibili, soprattutto a causa

45 Sulla impossibilità di definire precisi confini per le *civitates Barbariae*, Stiglitz 2004.

46 Busonera 2022.

47 Greg. M., *Epist.* XI, 12.

48 Greg. M., *Epist.* IV, 29, cfr. Pinna 1989, 146 s.; Turtas 1992.

49 Durliat 1982.

50 Bosa in particolare è collocata, come Cornus e Gurulis Nova, a 30' ad occidente; Macopsisa 15' ad oriente, dunque più all'interno.

dell'incerta tradizione manoscritta[51], tali dati indubbiamente ci dovrebbero costringere a collocare i *Montes Insani* all'altezza della catena del Montiferru, più interna rispetto a Bosa ed a Cornus, ma più a Sud e più verso la costa rispetto a Macopsisa.

Una qualche ulteriore indicazione può essere tratta anche da Floro, che a proposito della rivolta degli *Ilienses* domata da Tiberio Sempronio Gracco nel 177–176 a. C. parla dell'*immanitas* dei *Montes Insani*, sui quali si erano rifugiati i Sardi ribelli, sicuramente gli *Ilienses*: *Sardiniam Gracchus arripuit. Sed nihil illi gentium feritas Insanorumque – nam sic vocatur – immanitas montium profuere*[52]. Tali dati collocano i *Montes Insani* a breve distanza dalle catene del Marghine o del Montiferru[53]: per il Marghine (in rapporto alla localizzazione degli *Ilienses*), sembra rilevante l'influenza esercitata dal toponimo antico sul nome di *Macopsisa-Macomisa*-Macomer-Makkumère ('la città dei Monti Pazzi'), sulla base di un processo paretimologico indagato da Giulio Paulis[54]. Al Montiferru farebbe pensare la maggiore vicinanza a Cornus, capitale della rivolta antiromana del 215 a. C. Gli studiosi sono in realtà più di recente orientati a considerare l'espressione *Montes Insani* come generica e riferita ai vari sistemi montuosi della Sardegna interna, fino al Gennargentu e più ancora fino al Monte Albo ed alla costa orientale dell'isola[55]. Ad esempio, la posizione dei *Montes Insani* all'altezza di Capo Comino era stata già suggerita da Bachisio Raimondo Motzo[56]: le caratteristiche di questi monti sono quelle indicate da Claudiano[57] per la costa orientale dell'isola, rocciosa (*scopulosa*), sconvolta da improvvisi colpi di vento sfrenato (*procax subitisque sonora flatibus*), ostile (*immitis*); Silio Italico[58] dipinge allo stesso modo il litorale della Sardegna che è posto dirimpetto alla penisola (*quae videt Italiam, saxoso torrida dorso / exercet scopulis late freta*); infine Pausania[59] fornisce molti dettagli sull'insalubrità del clima.

Si è a lungo discuso sull'*insania* dei *Montes Insani*, che sarebbe collegata da un lato all'azione sui venti ed alla nascita delle tempeste che rendevano pericolosa la navigazione e d'altro lato alla presenza di zone malariche lungo la costa[60]: secondo Michel Gras, che ha dedicato un'approfondita trattazione all'argomento[61], la denominazione allude soprattutto allo sbarramento causato dai *Montes Insani*, che impedivano ai venti settentrionali di rinfrescare la piana di Tortolì, causando in questo modo la diffusione della malaria e l'insalubrità del clima. Le difficili condizioni della navigazione lungo la costa orientale della Sardegna, l'assenza di veri e propri porti, la particolare conformazione orografica con alte falesie a picco sul mare, il succedersi di valli irregolari tagliate da fiumi e ruscelli

51 Cfr. Meloni 1986, 207 ss.
52 Flor. I, 22, 35.
53 Mastino 1993, 508 n. 195.
54 Paulis 1990, 636 ss.
55 Vd. Bonello, Mastino 1994, 157 ss.; Mastino, Ruggeri 2000; Mastino, Ruggeri 2008.
56 Motzo 1931, 385 ss.
57 *De bello Gild.* 1, 512 s.
58 *Punica*, XII, vv. 372 s.
59 X, 17, 10–11.
60 Mastino 2005.
61 Gras 1974.

spiegherebbero il ripetersi di naufragi al largo dei *Montes Insani*, specie tra Capo Comino e Capo Monte Santo: i principali episodi riguardano il console Tiberio Claudio Nerone, partito da Roma nel 202 a.C.[62]; per l'età imperiale, su questa stessa rotta dovè collocarsi la spedizione (guidata da Mascezel) inviata nel 397 da Stilicone contro il *comes Africae* Gildone, che tra l'altro aveva bloccato in precedenza i rifornimenti granari tra l'Africa, la Sardegna e la capitale: la flotta partì da *Pisae*, all'altezza dei *Montes Insani*, lungo la costa orientale dell'isola; a causa di una violenta tempesta, le navi furono disperse ed alcune trovarono rifugio a *Sulci* (l'attuale Tortolì, nell'area occupata dai *Solkitanoi* di Tolomeo), altre ad Olbia. Più tardi la flotta si ricostituì a *Carales*, ove il corpo di spedizione (oltre 5000 uomini) passò l'inverno, per poi partire per l'Africa nella primavera successiva[63]. Tale itinerario lungo la costa orientale imporrebbe la localizzazione dei *Montes Insani* di Claudiano a Capo Comino, a Nord del Golfo di Orosei, e più difficilmente a Capo Monte Santo, se la tempesta scoppiò quando la flotta si trovava a metà strada tra Olbia e Tortolì; l'identificazione con i monti tra Dorgali e Baunei, nella parte meridionale del Golfo, come ipotizzato da Michel Gras, ci porterebbe forse un po' troppo a Sud, per quanto la denominazione antica può forse essere generica e comprendere un vasto sistema orografico di monti e colline che dalla costa si spingevano all'interno verso il Gennargentu ed addirittura verso il Marghine, senza escludere neppure il Montiferru, che sembrerebbe, sulla base delle coordinate di Tolomeo, parte integrante del sistema orografico che, separando la Sardegna settentrionale da quella meridionale, tagliava tutta l'isola nel senso della latitudine.

5 La geografia urbana

La caratteristica geografia della Sardegna discende dagli sviluppi della colonizzazione fenicio-punica: è noto che l'urbanizzazione in età romana si concentra prevalentemente sulle coste, che dovevano essere ricomprese globalmente in una vasta *Romania*[64]. Gli ultimi studi hanno messo in rilievo la centralità del municipio di Carales nella Sardegna meridionale, su un territorio che toccava una linea ideale che collegava il municipio di Sulci sull'isola *Plumbaria* ad occidente e arrivava fino a Sulci-Tortolì sulla costa orientale tirrenica; all'interno di quest'area meridionale possiamo ricordare il municipio di Nora, la *civitas* sufetale di Bithia-Quiza-*Civitas Vitensium*, ancora con le istituzioni puniche a oltre tre secoli dalla distruzione di Cartagine.

Allo stesso modo la città di Tharros (probabilmente una antica colonia fondata dopo il viaggio di Cesare) era la porta di accesso per un territorio che si allargava fino ad Othoca (Santa Giusta), Neapolis (nel territorio di Guspini), e, superato ad Est il Monte Arci,

62 Liv. XXX, 39, 1–3: *ibi superantem Insanos montes multo et saevior et infestioribus locis tempestas adorta disiecit classem*; cfr. anche 27, 5 e 38, 6–7; cfr. Gras 1974; Mastino 1991, 191 ss.

63 Claud., *De bello Gild.* 1, 482 ss. (*Insanos infamat navita montes*); cfr. Rougé 1966, 95; Mastino 1991, 191 ss.

64 Irmscher 1983; Guido 2006, 33–40.

arrivava fino alla colonia augustea di Uselis e raggiungeva le Aquae Ypsitanae – Forum Traiani e la *praefectura civitatis Valentinae* (Nuragus).

La colonia triumvirale di Turris Libisonis aveva un territorio originario che in parte prendeva il nome di *Romania* e che arrivava a controllare l'*Urbs Cornus,* poi colonia; la *civitas* di *Bosa,* poi *municipium;* le *civitates* di Gurulis Vetus, oggi Padria; Gurulis Nova, Cuglieri; Macopsisa (Macomer); Tibula e Portus Tibulas; va esclusa l'esistenza di una prefettura del Porto delle Ninfe.

Il più antico insediamento romano sulla costa orientale è quello di Feronia (Posada) (IV secolo a. C.), presto soppiantato dal municipio di Olbia (Fausiana – Civita – Terranova Pausania); infine *Heraeum* (Tempio Pausania), *civitas peregrina*[65].

6 Le *civitates Barbariae*: i documenti epigrafici

La Sardegna interna era denominata *Barbaria,* un macrotoponimo romano che indicava un'area ben più estesa delle attuali Barbagie. Il toponimo *Barbaria* è documentato esclusivamente per la *Sardinia* e per la *Gallia Lugdunensis.* In quest'ultima provincia abbiamo infatti un'isola fluviale sulla Saona presso Lione, *insula Barbara*[66], corrispondente probabilmente alla *civitas Barbaria* del Martirologio Geronimiano[67]. A parte stanno i *campi Barbaricini*[68], ossia *Barbari*[69], presso *Tarracina* (odierna Terracina), nel Lazio. In Sardegna ancora in età medioevale abbracciava un territorio più vasto, che credo si spingesse sino alle porte della colonia di *Uselis,* dove è attestato il toponimo Brabaxiana < *Barbariana*[70]; ma anche ad Ozieri: casa Bavalzanis < *Barbarianus*[71]; nel linguaggio attuale, Luca Guido conosce i Barbaricini da Banari a Bortigali, da Dualchi a Olzai, da Ortueri a Samugheo, da Scano Montiferru a Paulilatino[72]. La Barbagia comprendeva l'Ogliastra, il retroterra gallurese di Olbia, la antica Barbagia di Bitti, le attuali Barbagie (da Nord verso Sud) di Ollolai, Belvì, Seulo, il Mandrolisai. Altrove, come a Perfugas, è forse rimasto il ricordo di una popolazione indigena scarsamente romanizzata, quella dei *Balari-Perfugae*[73]; ma la geografia dei popoli della Sardegna interna (inclusi nella grande

65 Seguo lo schema adottato per i capitoli XI-XV di Mastino 2024; vd. Mastino 2023.

66 Greg. Tur. *Glor. mart.* 22: *apud Insulam Barbaram monasterii Lugdunensis.* L'isola corrisponde all'odierna Ile-Barbe sulla Saona.

67 Martyrol. Hier. 17 *kal. Iul.*

68 Iord. *Rom.* 372 (*ad Campos venisset Barbaricinos*); *Get.* 309; Marcell. *Chron.* II, 104, 536, 4. Cfr. ThLL, vol. II, s.v. *Barbaricini*, col. 1731.

69 *Barbaricinus* è sinonimo di *barbarus*: GLOSS. V, 562, 32. Cfr. ThLL, vol. II, s.v. *Barbaricinus*, col. 1731.

70 Cf. Paulis 1987, XXXVIII. Il villaggio di Allai, immediatamente al di là del Tirso, si chiamava in età medioevale *Barbariana,* cf. Sella 1945, nn. 1345, 1607, 1891, 1977.

71 Paulis 1987, XXXV.

72 Vd. Guido 2006, 343, alla figura 15.

73 Paus., 10, 17, 9: il vicino popolo dei Corsi intendeva l'etnico *Balari,* come φυγάδες 'fuggitivi' (in latino *perfugae*) nel senso di 'disertori cartaginesi': l'etimologia è improbabile, ma risale ad epoca antica; vd. anche le *insulae Balarides* pesso gli Heras lutra, in Mart. Capella VI, 645; cf. Pittau 1981, 92 n. 3;

famiglia dei Sardi Pelliti perché vestiti della caratteristica *mastruca* di pelle di capra)[74], è particolarmente ricca e complessa.

La Barbagia è stata interessata solo in parte dalla colonizzazione fenicia e poi dalla presenza cartaginese che, a partire dalla fine del VI sec. a. C., ha certamente favorito la diffusione della scrittura e della cultura semitica nelle aree pianeggianti e costiere. La realtà economica e culturale della *Barbaria* interna era ben più ampia delle attuali Barbagie[75]: era collocata nelle zone montane più resistenti ma non chiuse alla romanizzazione, che hanno mantenuto consuetudini religiose preistoriche fino all'età bizantina[76]. L'insediamento interno della Sardegna fu limitato da un lato a piccoli centri agricoli di scarsa romanizzazione, su una rete di *pagi* rurali, dall'altro lato ad alcuni campi militari posti a controllo della rete stradale, almeno in età repubblicana e nei primi decenni dell'impero; per il resto, vaste aree collinari e montuose erano occupate dalle popolazioni non urbanizzate, dalle tribù bellicose della Barbagia, gli Ilienses, i Balari, i Corsi, ma anche i Galillenses o gli altri popoli enumerati dal geografo Tolomeo, distribuiti in villaggi collocati in latifondi di uso comunitario[77].

In epoca giudicale la *Barbaria* romana venne poi spacchettata tra i quattro giudicati: l'Arborea (erede della *pertica* della colonia di Tharros) arrivava ora al Mandrolisai e alle Barbagie di Ollolai e Belvì; il Regno di Gallura (erede del municipio di Olbia) comprendeva la Barbagia di Bitti e le curatorie di Orosei e Galtellì e la Barbagia di Seulo; il Giudicato di Cagliari comprendeva la curatoria d'Ogliastra. Infine il Regno del Logodoro (erede della *pertica* di Turris Libisonis) arrivava fino alla curatoria di Dore e Orotelli, ben oltre il Goceano e il corso del Tirso: si rimanda ai risultati del Convegno di Orani per l'indagine storica antica e medioevale del territorio della curatoria di Dore del 18 marzo 2000 (in particolare alle relazioni di Pier Giorgio Spanu ed Esmeralda Ughi).[78]

Se torniamo all'età di Augusto e di Tiberio, da tempo conosciamo le *civitates Barbariae*, le comunità dei villaggi e delle popolazioni della *Barbaria* : le *civitates* della *Barbaria* sarda ci erano note da un'epigrafe incisa su una tavola marmorea proveniente dall'agro di *Praeneste*, Palestrina (Roma) (CIL XIV 2954 = ILS 2684 = EDR166627 di Cecilia Ricci nel 2018)[79], probabilmente posta in onore di Tiberio qualche anno dopo la morte di Augusto dopo il 19 d. C.[80]; difficile pensare agli ultimi anni di Augusto[81].

Zucca 1997; Zucca 2003, 139 ss. (ben distinte dalle *Fossae*, ma sempre nelle Bocche di Bonifacio o sulla costa gallurese).

74 Trudu 2012. Vd. ora Mastino 2024, capitolo 6, paragrafo 8.

75 Farre 2016.

76 Conti 2019.

77 Mastino 1993; Mastino 2023a, 142 ss. e fig. 7; Sechi 1990. Vedi anche Zucca 1988; Farre 2016; Farre 2016a; Farre 2021.

78 Campus 2023, p. 133 fig. 80.

79 Bonello Lai 1993, 165–166; Ricci 2018, 212 n. 67.

80 Meloni 1958, 184; cfr. Faoro 2011, 60–64, con bibliografia precedente; Faoro 2015, 1586.

81 Taramelli 1920, 348; Taramelli 1928, 269 ss.; Le Bohec 1990, 71; Mastino 2005a, 126.

Secondo gli ultimi studi "La dedica all'imperatore suggerisce il ritorno alla pace dopo un periodo di instabilità e di disordini iniziato nel 6 d. C." [82]. C'è anche chi ha pensato ad una iscrizione votiva, con dedica posta a cura del *praefectus* provinciale[83].

L'epigrafe oggi perduta, fatta conoscere per la prima volta nella raccolta manoscritta di iscrizioni del 1489 composta da fra Giovanni Giocondo da Verona, suona così:

Sex(tus) Iulius S(puri) f(ilius) Pol(lia) Rufus,
evocatus divi Augusti,
praefectus [I] cohortis
Corsorum et civitatum
Barbariae in Sardinia.

Si tratta dell'iscrizione relativa a un personaggio altrimenti ignoto, di rango equestre, Sesto Giulio Rufo, figlio di Sesto, inscritto alla tribù Pollia e presumibilmente non originario di Praeneste, i cui cittadini erano di regola inscritti nella tribù *Menenia* o in quella *Aemilia*. Sesto Giulio Rufo, che venne mantenuto nei ranghi militari (*evocatus*) da un imperatore poi divinizzato, evidentemente Augusto, aveva gestito, probabilmente contemporaneamente, il comando (*praefectura*) della coorte I dei Corsi (da intendersi di *Corsica* piuttosto che di *Sardinia*) e la prefettura delle *civitates* della *Barbaria* in *Sardinia*. La duplice gestione di tali prefetture pare connessa al fatto che per esercitare la prefettura sulle *civitates Barbariae* fosse necessario disporre di una forza militare che fungesse da deterrente nei confronti dell'ancora vivace ribellismo dei *populi* della *Barbaria*[84]. A titolo di esempio potremmo citare i casi di altri due equestri, *L. Volcacius Primus*, che fu *praef(ectus) coh(ortis) I Noricor(um) in Pann(onia), praef(ectus) ripae Danuvi et civitatium duar(um) Boior(um) et Azalior(um)*[85] e *L. Calpurnius Fabatus, praef(ectus) cohortis VII Lusitanor(um) [et] nation(um) Getulicar(um) sex quae sunt in Numidia*[86].

Il testo ci dà notizia dell'attività della I coorte di Corsi in Sardegna poco dopo la morte di Augusto nel 14 d. C.: *Sex(tus) Iulius S(puri) f(ilius) Pol(lia) Rufus, evocatus divi Augusti, praefectus [I] cohortis Corsorum et civitatum Barbariae in Sardinia* era un ufficiale equestre che avrebbe operato nell'età di Tiberio, in rapporto al comando (*praefectura*) di un reparto originariamente doveva essere costituito in Corsica e solo in un secondo tempo trasferito sul Tirso, in riva sinistra, presso le sorgenti termali delle Aquae Ypsitanae in Barbagia[87]. Si tratterebbe di una doppia prefettura: quella di comandante di coorte e quella di prefetto delle *civitates Barbariae in Sardinia*. Solo attraverso un vero e proprio piccolo esercito

82 Faoro 2011, 55–63; Ibba 2015, 37–40.

83 Serra 2006; Serra 2006a, 298.

84 Mastino, Zucca 2011, 461.

85 CIL IX 5363 = ILS 2737. Vd. Mastino 2021, 467, 473.

86 CIL V 5267 = ILS 2721. Cfr. Saddington 1987, 268, 270 nr. 10; Zucca 1998, 138, 142 n. 30.

87 Mastino, Zucca 2011, 460 ss., con confronti sul Danubio e nella Getulia numida.

Fig. 1: Fordongianus, ILSard I 188

specializzato il prefetto poteva veramente controllare la *Barbaria,* nelle sue articolazioni cantonali, all'interno di una provincia sottoposta ad un militare subentrato al *prolegato*[88].

La localizzazione delle *civitates Barbariae* è più esattamente documentata dall'iscrizione rinvenuta nel 1920 a Fordongianus, non lungi dalle terme romane delle Aquae Ypsitanae (in riva sinistra del Tirso, dunque all'ingresso della *Barbaria*) e proveniente da un edificio monumentale (ora all'Antiquarium Arborense di Oristano)[89]. Il testo corre su tre linee (ILSard I, 188 = AE 1921, 86, cfr. AE 1971, 118)[90] (Fig. 1):

[Imp(eratori) Ti(beri) Caesa]ṛi Aug(usto) p [ont(ifici) max(imo) imp(eratori) --- co(n)s(uli) --- trib(unicia) pot(estate) ---]
[--- civ]itates Barḅ[ariae ---]
[prae]f(ẹcto) provinciạ[e Sardiniae ---].

Il testo è controverso perché si esclude la presenza di vere e proprie *urbes* nei *rura* della *Sardinia* interna: sarebbero le popolazioni rurali – raccolte insieme in un'alleanza inizialmente ostile ai Romani – a porre la dedica per iniziativa di un *praef(ectus) provinciae Sard(iniae).* L'iscrizione è posta da alcune o da tutte le *civitates Barbariae* all'imperatore, essendo governatore (*praefectus*) della *provincia Sardinia* un personaggio ignoto a causa della frammentarietà dell'iscrizione. I problemi posti dal testo sono costituiti da un lato dalla definizione di *civitates Barbariae*, dall'altro dall'identificazione dell'imperatore oggetto dell'omaggio, che è ancora una volta Tiberio più che Augusto.

Le *civitates Barbariae* rispondono assai bene a quella tipologia di *civitates* illustrate da fonti letterarie ed epigrafiche soprattutto per l'area celtica e per la Germania e corrispondenti ai "cantoni" privi di *urbes*, che non conoscevano una vera e propria organizzazione

88 Le Bohec 1990, 69–72 insiste sul carattere di discontinuità delle rivolte che avvennero in *Sardinia* tra il 6 d. C. e il 19 d. C.; *contra* Meloni 2013, 139–43.

89 Dimensioni del frammento: alt. 44 cm; largh. 92 cm; spess. 3,3 cm; alt. lettere linea 1, 12 cm; linea 2, 10 cm; linea 3, 9 cm.

90 Taramelli 1920; Pais 1999, II, 139–154, 194; Taramelli 1928, 269 ss.; Meloni 1958, 184 pros. 3; Thomasson 1972, 73–75; Zucca 1988; Zucca 1999, 44–48; Porrà 2002, 1007–1008 n. 824; Zucca 2003a, 28; Mastino 2005a, 309; Mayer 2009, 45–51; Trudu 2012; Farre 2016; Faoro 2011, 50, 60–64; Farre 2016a, 89–105; EDCS-12100474; EDR072859.

urbana[91]. Un confronto assai stringente per il testo di Fordongianus può effettuarsi con la dedica a Druso Cesare posta nel 23 d. C. dalle *[ci]vitates IIII Vallis Poenninae* (CIL XII 147 = ILS 169)[92]. Come osservato da Theodor Mommsen, le quattro *civitates* della *Vallis Poennina* devono identificarsi con le *gentes alpinae* degli *Uberi*, *Nantuates*, *Seduni* e *Varagri*[93], vinte da Augusto[94]. Le principali *civitates*, come quella degli *Helvetii*, secondo Cesare, erano suddivise in *pagi*, ossia estensioni territoriali definite (4 *pagi* per gli *Helvetii*) con centri fortificati (12 *oppida*) e villaggi (400 *vici*)[95]. Possiamo ipotizzare che la dottrina giuridica romana in età augustea poté utilizzare anche per la *Sardinia* l'ambigua nomenclatura di *civitas*, non nella consueta accezione di organizzazione dei *cives* di una *urbs* provvista di *territorium*, bensì in quella recenziore di cantone di *populi* barbari, privi di *urbs*, con eventuale suddivisione in *pagi*, cui facevano capo *vici* piuttosto che *oppida*, per noi del tutto sconosciuti nella *Barbaria* del I secolo d. C. I problemi posti dal testo sono numerosi, partendo dalla definizione di *civitates Barbariae*, che rispondono assai bene ad una particolare tipologia di *civitates* che conosciamo specialmente in area celtica. Quali e quante fossero le *civitates* della *Barbaria* ci è ignoto, ma un criterio di similitudine ci porta a credere che esse venissero denominate dai *populi* che le componevano, sicché è probabile che una delle *civitates* della *Barbaria* fosse quella dei *Celes(itani)*, estesa a partire dalla fonte di Turunele di Fonni in direzione occidentale, così come si annoverassero nell'ambito delle *civitates Barbariae* la *civitas Cusin(itanorum)*, documentata in direzione orientale (CIL X 7889)[96], e forse anche la *civitas Nurr(itanorum)*, attestata nel cippo di Procalzos di Orotelli presso le sorgenti termali di Oddini (EE VII 729)[97]. Un confronto con le *civitates* alpine ci induce a ritenere che le *civitates* della *Barbaria* non fossero numerosissime, anche se la documentazione epigrafica potrà in futuro contribuire all'arricchimento degli etnici dei *populi* delle varie *civitates*, ma anche degli etnici dei *vici*, in cui si aggregavano le diverse componenti dei *populi* delle *civitates*. Nulla, dunque, vieta di considerare che allorquando nel 6 d. C. Augusto, a causa dei disordini provocati dai briganti[98], prese in carico la *Sardinia*, fino ad allora retta da un *proconsul* come provincia senatoria, vi inviasse un *prolegato* dell'ordine equestre sino al termine delle operazioni militari, durate dal 6 d. C. a qualche

91 De Ruggiero 1900, 258–259.

92 *[D]ruso Caesari / [Ti.] Augusti f., Divi Augusti / nepoti, /Divi Iulii pronep(oti), / [a]uguri, pontif(ici), quaestori / [f]lamini Augustali, / co(n)s(uli) II, / [t]ribunicia potestate II, / [ci]vitates IIII Vallis / Poenninae.*

93 CIL V 7817 = Plin. *nat.* III, 20, 136–137.

94 CIL XII, p. 20 (Th. Mommsen).

95 Caes. *b.g.* I, 5, 12. Cfr. De Ruggiero 1900, 259.

96 Farre 2016, 91–93, n. FON002.

97 Farre 2016, 126 s., n. OROT001.

98 „In questi stessi tempi [ossia nel 6 d. C.] si verificarono numerosi fatti d'armi. Infatti i briganti (*lestai*) compivano tanto frequentemente delle scorrerie, che per alcuni anni la Sardegna, anziché avere per il suo governo un senatore, venne affidata a degli *stratiotai* tratti dall'ordine equestre" (Dio Cass. 55, 28, 1).

anno più tardi. In tale occasione Augusto o meglio negli anni successivi Tiberio sarebbe stato celebrato dalle *civitates Barbariae* sottomesse con l'iscrizione sopra ricordata[99].

Noi ignoriamo a quale tipo di unità militare appartenessero i soldati inviati in Sardegna, ma non escluderemmo che Augusto avesse provveduto a una leva di soldati *Lusitani*, inquadrati in coorti ausiliarie, di cui una destinata in *Sardinia*, l'altra nella *provincia Cyrenarum*[100], nella quale i torbidi causati dalla guerra marmarica avevano suggerito ad Augusto di assumere il controllo diretto della provincia inviandovi un *prolegato*[101] alle dirette dipendenze del principe[102], dunque un equestre militare di carriera, che poteva essere il comandante supremo delle unità militari nell'isola, ciascuna delle quali retta dal proprio comandante.

Se tali forze fossero state le coorti ausiliarie e non, come vogliono alcuni storici, dei legionari[103], *Sex. Iulius Sex. f. Pol(lia tribu) Rufus* poté essere il responsabile dell'unità della coorte I dei Corsi, probabilmente quingenaria, dotata cioè di 500 effettivi, e, in contemporanea, il prefetto delle *civitates Barbariae*.

L'attività di Augusto e di Tiberio si concentrò soprattutto in direzione della *Barbaria*: tra il 6 e il 14 d.C. dovette essere costituito ad Austis (una fondazione augustea)[104] un presidio militare della *cohors Lusitan(orum)* e uno stanziamento civile legato ai familiari dei soldati ed eventualmente ai veterani cui fossero state fatte assegnazioni di terre: nel cuore della *Barbaria*, è attestato un *Isasus, Chilonis f(ilius) Niclinus, tubicin* [*sic*], *ex coho(rte) Lusitan(a)* (CIL X 7884), dunque un Lusitano, come dichiarato esplicitamente dal suo nome (legato secondo Yann Le Bohec a *Fabius Isas*, noto a *Mirobriga*, Santiago do Cacém a Sud di Lisbona in una dedica ad Esculapio effettuata in esecuzione del testamento di un medico originario dalla vicina Pax Iulia)[105], trombettiere di una coorte lusitana[106]. Il nostro, documentato dal suo epitafio, si rivela forse un veterano che aveva meritato trentun *stipendia*, iniziando la sua milizia proprio in età augustea. Ancorché l'epitafio di *Isasus* sia l'unico *titulus* militare di Austis, l'attestazione nello stesso centro di un *Caturo*[107], dal nome sicuramente lusitano, e la dedica alla dea lusitana *A(tecina) T(urobrigensis)*, posta da un *Serbulus* (CIL X 7557) probabilmente nel santuario delle acque salutari delle vicine Aquae Ypsitanae, ci rendono certi dello stanziamento di effettivi della *cohors Lusitana*

99 Taramelli 1928; Le Bohec 1990, 69–72, sulle rivolte che avvennero in *Sardinia* tra il 6 d.C. e il 19 d.C.; *contra* Meloni 2013, 139–143. La posizione assunta da Davide Faoro è innovativa sulla questione: Faoro 2017.

100 Gasperini 1967, 174, n. 34.

101 Laronde 1988, 1020–1021.

102 Meloni 2013, 140. Vd. ora Faoro 2011, 50, 60–64.

103 Le Bohec 1990, 22, nota 4 ricorda diversi casi di prolegati che in età augustea hanno il comando di truppe ausiliarie e non di legionari: CIL III 605; CIL V 3334; CIL XI 1331.

104 Su Austis cfr. Fiorelli 1887; Taramelli 1931, 55 nr. 11; Lilliu 1947, 45 s., n. 26; Rowland 1981, 16. Sulla documentazione epigrafica cfr. Mastino 1976; Ruggeri 1987–1992; Rowland 1994–1995.

105 CIL II 21 = AE 2017, 576.

106 Le Bohec 1990, 30–32.

107 AE 1978, 376, cfr. Zucca 1984, 245, nota 54; Rowland 1994–1995. Il quadro delle attestazioni è in Ruggeri 1987–1992.

Fig. 2: Fonni, CVSIN, CIL X 7889
(Collezione Attilio Mastino)

ad Austis agli inizi del I secolo d.C. Ad Austis, come desumiamo dal toponimo odierno, che continua il medievale *Agustis* e il latino **Augustis*[108], presumibilmente nel sito della distrutta chiesa di Sant'Agostino, fu costituito l'insediamento denominato *Augustis* in locativo ovvero *Augusti*. In Africa e più precisamente a Milev, nella Numidia cirtense (Algeria), conosciamo un ausiliario al comando di dieci soldati arrivato dalla Sardegna, forse da Austis nel I secolo d.C., *Optatus Sadecis f(ilius) decurio co(ho)rti(s) Lusitana(e),* sicuramente un *Sardus*[109]; il reparto di Lusitani sarebbe stato trasferito da Austis a Milev in occasione della rivolta di Tacfarinas[110].

Sembra dunque evidente che durante i primi Giulio Claudii in Barbagia non era ancora comparso un gruppo dirigente filo-romano, se il governo ed il controllo militare del territorio era affidato non più ai capi locali (i *principes*) ricordati da Livio durante la guerra annibalica[111], ma ad un prefetto equestre comandante di un reparto militare ausiliario di 500 Corsi (con sede alle Aquae Ypsitanae) qualche decennio dopo di Lusitani stanziati ad Austis. Del resto la toponomastica sarda ha conservato il ricordo della *Barbaria* romana, dato che il toponimo Barbagia – nelle sue articolazioni territoriali – è ancora oggi utilizzato per indicare l'area della Sardegna interna.

7 Le *civitates Barbariae* : la localizzazione

Possiamo tentare un elenco di alcuni dei *populi* della *Barbaria*. Plinio il vecchio preferiva utilizzare il temine *populus* per indicare gli *Ilienses*, così come i *Balari* e i *Corsi*: *celeberrimi in ea [Sardinia] populorum Ilienses, Balari, Corsi,* più famosi tra tutti gli altri popoli della Sardegna, perché fin dai primi decenni dell'occupazione romana del porto di Olbia

108 Pittau 1970, 35 ss; Paulis 1986, p. XXXIII; Meloni 2013, 511.

109 AE 1929, 169; vd. Mastino 1995, 33. Per Austis, vd. Le Bohec 1990, 109, a proposito di CIL X 7884.

110 Michel 2010, 180.

111 Hampsicora era il *primus* tra *i principes* della Sardegna, *qui tum auctoritate atque opibus longe primus erat*, vd. Mastino 2016a, 26.

Fig. 3: Fonni, CELES, CIL X 7889 (Collezione Attilio Mastino)

hanno resistito già nella seconda metà del III secolo a.C. e poi nei secoli successivi all'avanzata delle legioni romane lungo la linea che, passando per il Monte Acuto, lasciava a Nord i Corsi della Gallura settentrionale, a Occidente i Balari del Logudoro, a Sud gli *Ilienses* che dalla Campeda arrivavano al Marghine-Goceano in destra Tirso[112]. Livio ridimensiona alquanto la pericolosità di questi popoli, XXI, 16, 4: *Sardos Corsosque et Histros atque Illyros lacessisse magis quam exercuisse Romana arma*.

Nella Geografia di Tolomeo (*Geogr.* 3, 3, 1–8) si ricordano otto popoli legati a *poleis* e undici insediati (*katéchontes*) da Nord a Sud in Sardegna. Escludiamo in questa sede i *Kórsioi*, e i popoli costieri come i *Roubrensioi* da avvicinare ai *Rubr(enses)* di Custodia Rubriensis-Barisardo (apparentemente un sito fortificato, *Custodia* presso le rocce rosse di Arbatax): un cippo terminale ricorda i *Rubr(enses)* proprio a Barisardo al confine con gli *Altic(ienses)* (ILSard I 184); i *Karénsioi*, da collegare a Fanum Carisi (oggi Irgoli), vanno confrontati coi *Cares(ii)* del diploma del soldato della II coorte Gemina di Liguri e Corsi rinvenuto a Dorgali (CIL XVI 40) e gli immigrati dalla Sicilia, *i Sikouléńsioi* o dall'Etruria gli *Aisaronénsioi.*

Allora ci rimarrebbbero alcuni popoli non tutti di localizzazione certa:

- i *Korakénsioi*,
- i *Kounousitanoì,* che collochiamo a Sorabile (Fonni), al confine con i *Kelsitanoì,* vedi i CUSIN di CIL X 7889 (Fig. 2)
- i *Kelsitanoì,* che collochiamo a Sorabile (Fonni), al confine con i *Kounousitanoì,* vedi i CELES di CIL X 7889 (Fig. 3)
- i *Korpikénsioi*,
- i *Rouakénsioi*,
- gli *Skapitanoì*,
- gli *Aichilénsioi* (i Sardi Pelliti), vicini a Cornus.

112 Mastino 2021a.

Se guardiamo al complesso della documentazione escludendo gli etnici urbani ed i popoli costieri (*Eutichiani*, immigrati dalla Magna Grecia, *Muthonenses Numisiarum*, *Uddadhaddar(itani) Numisiarum*, entrambi immigrati dal Nord Africa[113], i *[---]rarri(tani) [Nu]misiaru[m]*, *Giddilitani*, ecc. del territorio di Cornus; si sono citati in Ogliastra i *Rubr(enses)*; si aggiungano i vicini i *Fifenses* del diploma del marinaio sardo della flotta di Miseno rinvenuto a Tortolì – CIL XVI 79[114], possiamo collocare in *Barbaria*, con riferimento alla denominazione di un centro abitato, un *vicus* o un *pagus*:

– gli *Ypsitani*, da Aquae Ypsitanae, un *vicus* entro un territorio paganico della colonia di Uselis, prima della nascita nel III d.C. di Forum Traiani, Fordongianus[115];
– i *Lesitani* da Lesa e dalle Aquae Lesitanae (San Saturnino di Benetutti-Bultei nella prima vallata del Tirso);
– i *Sorabenses* per Sorabile nella *Barbaria* interna (Fonni) (AE 1992, 891)[116].

Veri e propri popoli sarebbero allora:

– i *Barbaricini* della *Barbaria* (forse organizzati in piccole comunità semi-urbane dotate comunque di una qualche struttura politico-sociale): ancora nel VI secolo d.C. si confrontavano col comandante militare, il *dux Sardiniae*, collocato *iuxta montes ubi Barbaricini videntur sedere* (*Cod. Iust.*, I, 27, 2, 3)[117].
– i *Nurr(enses)* o *Nurr(itani)* di Orotelli, ultra Thyrsum vanno anch'essi all'interno della vasta definizione di *civitates Barbariae*: da Nuoro dovevano arrivare alla riva sinistra del Tirso[118], dove guardavano al Marghine e al Goceano, sede degli Ilienses[119]. Il popolo barbaricino ha fornito le reclute per la coorte prima di Nurritani che, assieme alla coorte II di Sardi combatteva nel II secolo d.C. in Numidia e in Mauretania (attuale Algeria)[120]. Il collegamento con il culto dell'Ercole Nouritano della Sicilia occidentale (promosso dai Frentani nel II secolo a.C. a Lilibeo) è assolutamente plausibile[121], così come il collegamento con Nora e con Nure nella Nurra, sempre dalla radice della parola nuraghe[122]. A parete gli *Ilii* di Molaria (AE 1993, 849), va presa in considerazione la recente interpretazione di Davide Faoro dell'espressione NVR ALB del diploma di Posada del 102 d.C. (che abbiamo fin qui inteso come toponimo collegato ad un nuraghe bianco)[123] e che invece

113 Mastino 2014.
114 Per le popolazioni del Sulcis (con lo spostamento dalla costa orientale a Vallermosa dei *Fifenses*), vd. Corda 2018, 151–153.
115 Per il territorio della *colonia Iulia Augusta Uselis*, vd. Usai, Zucca 1981–1985; Mastino, Zucca 2007, 94–101.
116 Per il *nemus Sorabense*, vd. Gasperini 1992, 575–577.
117 Serra 2006a.
118 Per i *Nurritani* della Sardegna, vd. Bonello Lai 1993, 175–177; Mastino 1995, 32; Faoro 2016.
119 Mastino 2005.
120 Laporte 1989, 37.
121 Vd. Ampolo 2016; Mastino, Abrignani 2021.
122 Wagner 1957, II, 177 ss. s.v. nuráke.
123 Per il diploma di Posada (con il toponimo o l'etnico NVR ALB), vd. Sanciu, Pala, Sanges 2013; Ibba 2014.

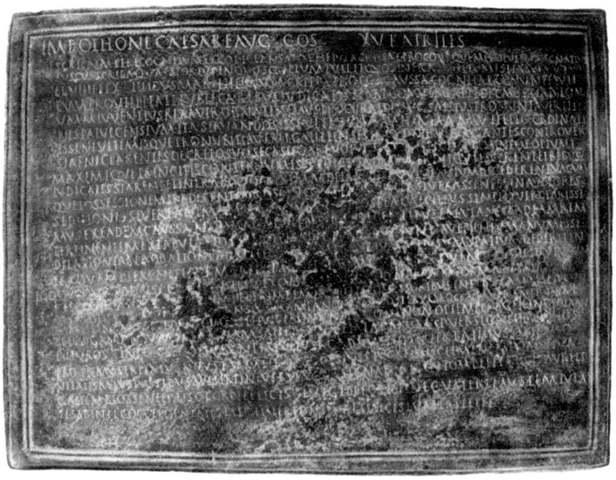

Fig. 4: La Tavola di Esterzili, CIL X 7852

potrebbe in ipotesi riferirsi da un lato alla *gens* di appartenenza [non *natio*] del veterano Hannibal *Nur(ritanus)* oppure *Nur(rensis)*, dall'altro lato, il secondo *Alb(---)* potrebbe indicare "la *civitas*, da intendersi come un gruppo più limitato all'interno della prima": del resto è vero che nei diplomi militari la menzione del luogo d'origine è di solito preceduta dalla provincia e seguita dal *vicus* o dal *pagus* per i soldati provenienti da aree rurali: viceversa è più abituale il riferimento all'etnico di afferenza (nel nostro caso allora *Nurritanus*), seguito dal *pagus*[124]: la questione resta indubbiamente misteriosa.

– i *Galillenses*: è opportuno citare la Tavola di Esterzili, un documento in bronzo conservato al Museo Nazionale Sanna di Sassari (Fig. 4), che ci fa conoscere la controversia che si trascina tra la fine del II secolo a.C. e la metà del I secolo d.C. (più precisamente fino all'età di Otone nel 69 d.C.) tra i *Galillenses* sardi (Gerrei) ed i contigui *Patulcenses* campani (che gli ultimi studi condotti da Nadia Canu collocano proprio ad Esterzili)[125]. Essi sono da avvicinare ai *Patulcii* di Gurulis Nova (Cuglieri) e sembrano insediati da Marco Cecilio Metello attorno al 115 a.C. sulle terre in passato occupate dagli autoctoni *Galillenses*[126]. Che i sardi fossero pastori ed i campani agricoltori è un'ipotesi molto probabile (per quanto vanamente contrastata da alcuni), se pensiamo alle frasi di Diodoro Siculo, che

124 Faoro 2016, 247–249.

125 Per la Tavola di Esterzili, Mastino 1993a; in particolare sulla localizzazione dei *Patulcenses Campani*, vd. Bonello Lai 1993, corretta ora da Canu 2016; Canu 2018 (che propende per identificare il luogo del ritrovamento della tavola di bronzo, all'interno di una fattoria romana con il *vicus* dei *Patulcenses*): del resto è certo che il documento fu rilasciato alla parte che ha vinto la causa, gli attori del processo, i *Patulcenses*; non certo ai convenuti perdenti, i *Galillenses*. Il fatto che il ritrovamento sia avvenuto ad Esterzili, (se si esclude una razzia che può aver spostato la tavola di bronzo) rende possibile che le sedi dei *Patulcenses* si trovassero proprio a Corte Luccetta di Esterzili.

126 Bonello Lai 1981; Bonello Lai 1993a.

poteva constatare come ancora al tempo di Cesare la feracità delle "amenissime pianure iolee" attirò successivamente la cupida attenzione di molti popoli: pensando ai Sardi (ma più precisamente ai discendenti di Eracle) egli afferma che rifugiatisi nella regione montana e abitando in dimore sotterranee da loro costruite e in gallerie, si dedicarono alla pastorizia, nutrendosi di latte, formaggio e carne e facendo a meno del grano. Seppero così conservare quella libertà che, ai Tespiadi, era stata effettivamente assicurata, in eterno, da Apollo.

– Al Campidano orientale ci porta la localizzazione, recentemente proposta, a Barumini, dei *Barsanes*[127]; in epoca più tarda un cippo di confine separava i *Maltamonenses* dai contigui *Semilitenses* a Sanluri, nelle terre del *clarissimus Cens(orius) Secundinus* e della *h(onestissima) f(emina) Quarta*, ricordati sui cippi terminali che erano stati strappati (*ebulsi*, da *evellere*) e nuovamente collocati con l'impiego di monumentali blocchi monolitici (EE VIII 719)[128].

– Di minore importanza sembrano i *Martenses* di Biora (Serri) (CIL X 7858), forse appartenenti ad una sodalità ed i *Moddol(itani)*, contadini insediati sul *fundus* di *Villasor* (ILSard I 168).

– Molto incerta la localizzazione degli *Aconites*, dei *Parates* e dei *Sossinates* (Logudoro) di Strabone (5, 2,7).

8 Gli Ypsitani di Fordongianus e i popoli di Austis: il controllo militare tramite ausiliari Corsi e Lusitani

Torniamo così al *pagus* degli Ypsitani sul fiume Tirso, nella parte più settentrionale della colonia Iulia Augusta Uselis, prima della nascita del Forum Traiani, scorporato dalla pertica della colonia sotto Traiano, nel punto terminale dei due tronchi della strada centrale sarda, *a Turre* ed *a Karalibus*: le Aquae Ypsitanae sono le acque calde dove si praticava un antico culto medico di Esculapio e delle Ninfe salutari. Il *vicus* relativo, al centro del *pagus*, era gestito da *magistri* (del *vicus* o del *pagus*), all'interno del territorio della colonia di Uselis, che però non avevano *iurisdictio*. Gli Hypsitani in epoca tarda diventano *Forotraianenses*, dopo la decurtazione del territorio della colonia Uselis e la costituzione del *Forum* nel III d. C., che arriva a comprendere il villaggio vicino alle sorgenti termali, dove si svolgevano le pratiche di *sanatio*; successivo è il passaggio di Forum Traiani alla condizione di *civitas* in età severiana e poi probabilmente di municipio. Per Cesare Letta "i centri più cospicui, costituiti a capoluogo dei *pagi*" dovevano essere i *vici*, veri e propri villaggi, che costituivano i poli di attrazione della popolazione rurale, ai quali facevano capo i *fundi*, cioè secondo Raimondo Zucca "i fondi rustici con gli edifizi necessari per la economia rurale e con gli immobili" (la *villa* e le modeste abitazioni dei servi, se non comprese nella *villa*) e gli *agri* (terreni sprovvisti di costruzioni rurali)[129].

---

127 Corda, Piras 2009.

128 Per i *Maltamonenses* ed i *Semilitenses*, vd. Pais 1999, II, 86; Bonello Lai 1993, 179–184.

129 Per i *vici* e i *pagi* in Italia, vd. Letta 1993, 35 s.; per la funzione aggregativa dei santuari rurali, Letta 1992 (si veda in particolare 117 e n. 45 con l'elenco di ben 24 santuari paganici di Giove e di 20 santuari di Ercole).

Il caso di Austis, sede probabilmente di un reparto di Lusitani (CIL X 7884; ILSard I 218), conserva evidente la testimonianza di una profonda penetrazione militare romana in Barbagia già nell'età di Augusto, sulle falde occidentali del Gennargentu: collegata con Ad Medias (Abbasanta), come testimonia un miliario del prolegato Tito Pompeo Proculo (EE VIII 742), Austis ricorda in piena area barbaricina il nome del primo imperatore, così come Forum Traiani conserva, sempre sul Tirso, il ricordo di un provvedimento costituzionale di Traiano[130]. L'insediamento religioso di Sorabile ai piedi del Monte Spada a quasi mille metri di altitudine e ad esempio l'abitato di Sant'Efisio di Orune, per quanto riferibile ad una fase tarda dell'impero, ci consentono di documentare l'opera di profondissima penetrazione romana nella Barbagia sarda, anche sul piano religioso, culturale e linguistico: dagli studi più recenti lo scenario già della prima età imperiale appare dunque notevolmente mutato rispetto agli ultimi secoli della repubblica, quando ai presidi militari si affiancarono abitati rurali ed insediamenti stabili, che testimoniano un'intensa romanizzazione anche delle zone interne dell'isola, per quanto esposte ai *latrocinia* delle popolazioni non urbanizzate; il sottoporsi dei *Galillenses* al giudizio dei governatori romani nella capitale Carales è stato interpretato come un indizio di un nuovo rapporto tra l'autorità romana e le popolazioni locali, che continuavano comunque a rimanere ostili agli immigrati italici. Nel complesso si tende oggi a studiare meglio le fasi di un processo che si sviluppò nel tempo, con profonde trasformazioni ed articolazioni locali, al di là delle esemplificazioni un poco ideologiche e di superficie.

9 L'onomastica paleosarda nel *Barbaricum*

Nella Sardegna interna l'uso del nome unico d'origine indigena portato da "stranieri in patria" privi della cittadinanza è ampiamente documentato per tutta l'età imperiale e oltre: una categoria importante all'interno del materiale onomastico è quella dei nomi unici o rarissimi, testimoniati in Sardegna per la prima volta o che comunque hanno pochi paralleli fuori dall'isola: si tratta probabilmente di nomi indigeni (o punici), che persistevano in età romana: l'elenco è davvero impressionante e in questa sede possiamno solo fare qualche esempio, con nomi forse declinati in dativo o in genitivo, oppure indeclinabili o femminili in *-i*, come a suo tempo supposto da Lidio Gasperini.

Bascio Losonis (filius) (CIL X 7870, Busachi)
Belsa Cariti (filia) (ILSard I 196, Forum Traiani)
Beviranus (CIL X 7873, Busachi)
Bolcia (CIL X 7871, Busachi)
Caritus-Karitus-Charitus (AE 1992, 889, Borore)
Curadro (CIL XVI 72, Ilbono)
Curelo Nercaụ(nis filia) (ILSard I 212, Sedilo)

130 Mastino, Zucca 2012, 31–50; Mastino, Zucca 2014.

Disanirius Torceri f(ilius) (CIL X 7872, Busachi)
Foronto (AE 1992, 881, Sedilo)
Gauga Targuroionis f(ilius) (CIL X 7874/5, Busachi)
Gins-ora (EE VIII 730, Macomer)
Gocaras Nercaunis (filius) (AE 1993, 846, Allai)
Ietoccor Torceri filius (AE 1993, 842, Busachi)[131]
Miaricora Turi (filia) (AE 1993, 839, Busachi)
Mislius Cora[---] (ILSard. I 176, Usellus) *Nercadau* (CIL X 7888, Austis)
Nercadau (AE 1992, 887, Aidomaggiore; vd. AE 1993, 846, Allai; ILSard I 209, Samugheo; ILSard I 212 e AE 1992, 885, Sedilo)
Nispeni (AE 1992, 888, Borore; cd. AE 1996, 821 Olbia)
Nispellus figlio di *Pipedio,* Ula Tirso (Zucca 1999, 64), gli ultimi due da collegare con la giudicale *Nispella*[132]
Tarcisius (figlio) di *Tarincius* (Zucca 1999, 64)
Tarcutius e *Tarsalia* del diploma di *Caius Tarcutius Hospitalis,* figlio di *Tarsalia,* originario di Carales in Sardegna, da Seulo (CIL XVI 127)[133]
Tarpalaris (CIL XVI, 79, Tortolì)
Tarsinnius (AE 1993, 837, Busachi)[134]
Tartalasso (ELSard, p. 655 B 101 f, Tertenia)
Tertellus padre di *Urseccur* (ELSard, p. 638 nr. B 127, Tertenia)
Torbenius Kariti (filius) (CIL X 7876, Busachi), vedi ad Ula Tirso *L(ucius) Valerius Torbenius Iunior* (AE 2003, 820)
Torcerius, padre di *Disanirius* (CIL X 7872, Busachi)
Turus Torveni (filius) (AE 1993, 840, Busachi)
Tunila del popolo dei *Caresii* o dei *Carensi* (CIL XVI 40, Dorgali)
Ursaris Tornalis (filius) (CIL XVI 9, Anela)
Urseccur figlio di *Tertellus* (ELSard, p. 638 nr. B 127, Tertenia)
Urseti Nercauni(s) (AE 1992, 887, Aidomaggiore)
Urseti Nispenini (AE 1992, 888, Borore)[135]
Tubmar (CIL X 7878, Samugheo), *ecc.*[136].

Il diploma di Posada, recentemente scoperto ci fa conoscere i seguenti nomi unici che ci arrivano dal sostrato paleosardo: *Bolgitta, Bonassonis, Iuri* o *Iurinis Tammugae filia Sordia* (difficilmente *Sarda*), *Tabilatis* oppure *Tabilas, Tisarenis* o *Tisare*[137]. E lasciamo da parte in questa sede l'onomastica documentata dalle *tabellae defixionum*, come a Nulvi

131 Il nome continuò ad essere utilizzato in età medioevale dall'aristocrazia giudicale, Mastino 2001a, 60.
132 Mastino 2001a, 59–60; Mastino 2005a, 530–531.
133 Il dativo è scioltro come nominativo da Farre 2016, 154, SEU002.
134 Ibba 2006a, 21 s. nn. 111 e 114.
135 Vd. *Ursa* CIL X 7657; *Ursinus*: CIL X 7935.
136 Floris 2021.
137 Sanciu, Pala, Sanges 2013.

(AE 1992, 911), Orosei (ELSard, p. 639 B 128–129), Olbia (AE 2017, 545), per non parlare degli *ostraka* come quello di Neapolis (AE 2007, 690) oppure delle invocazioni a *Salamàzaza* in greco come a Cornus (AE 2005, 687)[138].

I documenti presentati, alcuni recentissimi, ci dicono quali possibilità enormi abbiamo di ricostruire l'onomastica di sostrato paleosardo barbaricino negli anni futuri.

10 Gli dei del bosco: Diana e Silvano, la *Barbaria* e l'economia della selva

In piena *Barbaria,* l'area dove sorge l'attuale Fonni nella Barbagia di Ollollai in epoca romana era scarsamente urbanizzata e coperta da fitti boschi: essa era resa raggiungibile da una strada interna denominata *aliud iter ab Ulbia Caralis* che toccava, sul versante occidentale, il Gennargentu a novecento metri di altezza. Qui nell'antica *Sorabile* (oggi Sorovile alla periferia di Fonni) un bosco, il *Nemus Sorabense*, assunse caratteristiche simili a quelle dei boschi sacri della Penisola e del *limes* renano-danubiano, divenendo un luogo di culto e di devozione capace di "federare" o di rappresentare un punto di incontro a livello religioso per le popolazioni del luogo, unite nella venerazione a Diana e Silvano. In questo senso si dispone di una testimonianza puntuale risalente con tutta probabilità alla seconda metà del II secolo d. C. che fornisce informazioni sul toponimo *nemus Sorabense* ma anche sulle divinità oggetto del culto, Diana e Silvano, entrambe collegate con funzioni simili ma diversificate ai boschi, alla vegetazione, alla natura selvaggia (AE 1992, 891)[139]. Si tratta di una dedica posta dal procuratore e prefetto della provincia *C. Ulpius Severus*: presso Sorabile (Fonni) esisteva dunque un bosco sacro, il *nemus Sorabense* dove si tributava, forse presso un sacello, un culto per una dea e un dio che parevano ben adattarsi alla morfologia del territorio, alle sue caratteristiche economiche e culturali e al suo popolamento (Fig. 5). Pur se non si ha certezza che il luogo di culto all'interno del *nemus Sorabense* fosse erede di una tradizione religiosa più antica – presso il Monte Spada, difatti, sorgeva un antico santuario nuragico – pare possibile che qui convergessero, nelle occasioni rituali, le *civitates* sarde confinanti dei *Celes(itani)* e dei *Cusin(itani)*, note anche da Tolomeo, unite nella venerazione per Diana e per Silvano, protettori della natura incolta e selvaggia.

Le popolazioni delle due *civitates*, separate da una linea catastale – come attesta, insieme ad altri, il cippo di confine rinvenuto a Turunele (Fonni), immediatamente ad Est del lago Govossai, inscritto sulle due facce a separare i *Celes(...)* e i *Cusin(...)* -, vivevano nel cuore del territorio delle *civitates Barbariae* (CIL X 7889). L'economia di questi luoghi oltre che dalla pastorizia, dall'allevamento del bestiame e dai derivati dal latte, il formaggio anzitutto, doveva reggersi sulla cosiddetta "economia della selva", ben nota per essere stata oggetto ormai in anni lontani, di approfondimenti relativi ad alcune aree dell'Italia meridionale[140]. Si è ipotizzato che *Sorabile* fosse una *statio*, fondata in epoca traianea, alla quale andrebbero riferiti alcuni resti archeologici scoperti già dall'Ottocento; questo contesto

138 Agus 2002; La Fragola, Mastino, Pinna 2021.
139 Vd. già Taramelli 1929.
140 Giardina 1997.

insediativo e funzionale alla penetrazione romana della *Barbaria* nel II secolo d. C., unito a ritrovamenti monetali, ha fatto supporre contatti tra *negotiatores* e abitanti delle *civitates Barbariae* e nello specifico dei *Celes(itani)* e dei *Cusin(itani)*. All'interno di un quadro di tal genere si comprende ancor meglio la devozione per Diana e Silvano presso il *nemus Sorabense*. La Diana venerata a Roma era di origine latina, protettrice della lingua latina, una dea lunare che, prima della costruzione di un tempio a lei dedicato sull'Aventino a Roma promossa da Servio Tullio, ebbe il proprio culto nell'epiclesi *Diana Nemorensis* presso il bosco di Nemi, ad Aricia, celebrato dal *rex nemorensis*, il re-schiavo-sacerdote, la cui successione avveniva attraverso un omicidio rituale da parte di un pretendente più giovane: in questa veste Diana possedeva caratteristiche simili alle grandi dee mediterranee[141]; la dea venne successivamente inserita nel sistema di relazioni religiose romane e affiancata ad altre divinità apparentemente eccentriche rispetto ai suoi contenuti religiosi (Vortumno, Fortuna Equestre, le Camene, Castore e Polluce, Eracle Vincitore) come attestano diversi calendari festivi nel giorno tradizionalmente dedicato ai riti di Diana, il 13 agosto[142]. Silvano veniva assimilato con Fauno, il dio rappresentato nudo, espressione della natura selvaggia e primordiale e dell'*ager Romanus* non ancora soggetto alle procedure di divisione del suolo attraverso la centuriazione, sebbene Silvano fosse anche il dio della campagna coltivata, protettore dei contadini e "inventore" dei cippi di confine a separazione delle singole proprietà[143]. Il culto di Silvano-Fauno tra la fine del I secolo d. C. e l'età di Traiano ebbe una diffusione notevole in alcune province dell'impero come quelle dalmate e danubiane e oggi si può affermare anche in Sardegna. Proprio Traiano attraverso i suoi governatori sviluppò un importante processo di urbanizzazione in Sardegna con la creazione di Forum Traiani presso le antiche Aquae Ypsitanae, nel territorio degli Ypsitani e delle *civitates Barbariae*[144]. A proposito delle province dalmate ad esempio si ritiene che il culto di Silvano fosse utilizzato come manifestazione d'identità di alcuni gruppi locali non urbanizzati che arrivavano ad integrare le tradizioni locali con la declinazione romana di Silvano-Fauno ai fini dell'inclusione di quegli stessi gruppi nel mondo "globale" dell'impero[145]. In Dacia e nelle province danubiane furono le successive campagne di Traiano tra il 101–102 e il 105–106, in particolare quest'ultima, a favorire l'introduzione del culto di Diana e Silvano in ambito militare, con profili del tutto romani senza risentire di fenomeni assimilativi[146].

---

141 Champeaux 2002, 37.

142 Sabatucci 1988, 327.

143 Per un profilo generale su Silvano: Dorcey 1992; Evangelisti, Ricci 2022. Il lavoro di Cecilia Ricci e Silvia Evangelisti mostra un profilo di Silvano simile a quello del Silvano sardo, sebbene l'associazione con Diana sia esclusa da quell'orizzonte territoriale e il dio risulti associato a *Liber pater* e ad *Hercules*; Silvano pare conformarsi alle caratteristiche dei paesaggi e avere prerogative legate alla natura, all'economia della selva e in parte all'allevamento del bestiame. Cecilia Ricci aggiorna criticamente, rispetto al materiale oggetto di studio, alcune conclusioni di Dorcey.

144 Trudu 2012a.

145 Dzino 2012.

146 Per limitarci alla Dacia: CIL III 1154 = 7775 = IDR III, 5,1 349, Apulum dopo il 211 (dedica effettuata da un decurione *Silvano Silvestri et Dianae*); AE 1913, 54, Negrilești tra il 171 e il 250 (*Dian(a)e et*

In Sardegna uno studio recente ha valorizzato il tema della lunga durata del culto di Silvano presente nell'isola e in particolare a Sorabile, che traspare nei suoi continuatori romanzi a partire da *Silvana/Selvana*, la strega vampiro (*sùrbile*), temibile per gli infanti o i bambini nei primi anni di vita, alla quale si rivolgevano scongiuri che dovevano essere recitati dalle madri[147]. Di essi rimane attestazione in alcuni paesi sardi come Siligo e Siniscola – per l'Ottocento e gli anni quaranta del secolo scorso – in formule ritmiche di scongiuro. *Silvana/ Selvana* avrebbe assorbito la fisionomia del *Silvanus* notturno e dai tratti spaventosi, più vicino agli dei funzionali arcaici della religione romana, soprattutto per quanto riguarda l'assimilazione con Fauno, tant'è che Agostino lo considera immondo al pari di altre divinità della medesima sorta e pericoloso per la pudicizia delle donne con le quali avrebbe avuto la capacità di unirsi carnalmente (*civ.* 15, 23)[148]; il contatto con le Diane (in logudorese Janas, alcune *maistas, magistrae*) appare del resto molto significativo[149]. Timidamente avanziamo il sospetto che situazioni analoghe siano conosciute anche nella Transilvania dacica. Resta da studiare il capitolo relativo alle guaritrici con specifiche competenze magico-curative relative alla *sanatio*, ottenuta attraverso pozioni preparate con erbe del bosco[150], una pratica ben descritta dagli antropologi ancora nella Sardegna moderna[151].

11 Altri culti nel *Barbaricum*

La presenza di Giove-*Iupiter* in Sardegna rimonta al periodo successivo all'occupazione romana. Da Bidonì nel Barigadu in vetta al Monti Onnarìu, sulla riva sinistra del Tirso, proviene un importante documento epigrafico che riporta una dedica a Giove. Qui dovette sorgere un tempio intitolato al dio capitolino di cui ad oggi rimangono visibili solo le fondazioni, come testimonia un altare collocato nell'area antistante il luogo di culto, secondo la comune disposizione dei templi romani. L'altare di forma parallelepipeda utilizzato dal sacerdote per i sacrifici reca due iscrizioni incise sui lati brevi il cui testo conferma la dedica del luogo di culto a Giove: *dei Iovis* da intendersi come *(ara) dei Iovis*. Si è ipotizzato che la costruzione di questo luogo di culto sulla sommità del Monti Onnarìu e dunque in una posizione di confine tra i territori barbaricini e l'area romanizzata, avesse una funzione di controllo e di affermazione del potere politico romano, forse a seguito di una vittoria e di un trionfo (AE 1998, 673)[152]. Questa ipotesi appare maggiormente fonda-

Silvano sacrum, dedica effettuata da un decurione *ex singulari consularis*). Separatamente conosciamo un centinaio di dediche a Silvano in Dacia e quasi altrettante a Diana.

147 Respinge l'ipotesi di Terracini (Terracini 1936, 16) di un collegamento tra Sorabile e *sùrbile* Wagner II 1957, 448 s.

148 Strinna 2022.

149 Strinna 2012. Per il "riuso" degli ipogei funerari preistorici, vd. ad es. Gasperetti, Carenti 2012.

150 Paulis 1991.

151 Solo a titolo di esempio: Nappi 2023.

152 Salvi, Sanna 2006. Vedi inoltre Zucca 1999, 44–46; Fadda, Muscas 2002, 26–27; Zucca 2004, 140–145; Farre 2016, 49–51 n. BID003 e 119–120, n. LAC002. Vedi infine per la documentazione epigrafica di età repubblicana, Zucca 1996, 1450 ss.

ta rispetto a quella che, sulla base del confronto del graffito su frammento di ceramica con la scritta *Iovi* proveniente dal santuario talaiotico di Son Oms (Palma di Maiorca), ha portato a pensare che i Romani nelle Baleari e in Sardegna avessero reinterpretato il culto di una divinità tauromorfa identificandola con Giove[153]. Più specificamente alle operazioni militari della fine del II secolo a. C. andrebbe riferita la dedica sul monte di Santa Sofia di Laconi nella *Barbaria*: il testo riguarderebbe la spedizione del propretore Tito Albucio, il quale celebrò in *Sardinia* forse nel 106 a. C. un vero e proprio trionfo sui Sardi (Cicerone, *de prov. cons.* 7, 15; *in Pisonem* 92)[154].

Le Ninfe, connesse all'utilizzo delle acque salutari, dominarono il panorama religioso e cultuale dell'antica *Barbaria,* lì dove era insediato il popolo degli Ypsitani da cui presero il nome le Aquae Ypsitanae (Tolomeo). Le *acque calidae*, sgorgavano presso l'attuale area di Caddas, al di là del Tirso, dove nel 111 d. C. fu istituito il *Forum Traiani* (attuale Fordongianus)[155]: accanto alle Ninfe veniva venerato Esculapio.

Sempre presso le Aquae Ypsitanae, già alla metà del I sec. d. C., prima della costituzione del *Forum Traiani*, per motivazioni di carattere militare e strategico, condizionato dalla presenza delle *civitates Barbariae* (ILSard I, 188), si era sviluppato un popolamento composito, condizionato dalla presenza di truppe, la *cohors I Corsorum* e di personale servile o libertino probabilmente a disposizione dei militari come più tardi sarebbe accaduto con liberti e liberte al servizio dei governatori dell'isola. Ad es. *Valeria Modesta*, liberta del governatore della Sardegna in età severiana *M. Valerius Optatus*, pose una dedica alle Ninfe (EDR181204)[156]. Questo comparto territoriale era poi un nodo della via *a Turre* che dalle Aquae Ypsitanae si diramava a nord est verso Austis (*Augustis*) e a sud est verso Usellus (*Uselis*).

Per le ragioni sin qui esposte, si può ritenere che sia interpretabile come frutto di presenze e influenze straniere, anche la dedica incisa su una stele in trachite posta da *Serbulus*, oggi custodita al Museo di Cagliari, che si ipotizza provenga da Fordongianus (CIL X 7557)[157]. La dedica abbreviata (*D. S. A. T.*) è rivolta alla *Dea Sancta A(tecina)* o *A(tegina)* o *A(degina) Turobrigensis* (di Turobriga in Portogallo)[158], una divinità straniera proveniente dall'area iberico-lusitana, interpretata come Proserpina – dea della notte, della luna e delle fonti (il timpano della stele è decorato con un crescente lunare tra due astri) – come pure in rapporto alle acque termali e con poteri risanatori.

153 Zucca 1998; Zucca 1999, 44–46; Farre 2016, 49–51 n. BID003.
154 AE 2002, 621 = Murru, Zucca 2002; Zucca 2003a, 24–26; Farre 2016, 119–120 n. LAC002.
155 Mastino, Zucca 2012.
156 Mastino, Zucca 2021.
157 Farre 2016, 98–100 n. FOR003.
158 Rojas Gutiérez 2016.

Bibliografia

Agus, A. 2002. Le pratiche divinatorie e i riti magici nelle insulae del Mare Sardum nell'antichità, in P. G. Spanu (a cura di), Insulae Christi. Il cristianesimo primitivo in Sardegna, Corsica e Baleari, Oristano, 29–36.

Ampolo, C. 2016. Il culto di Ercole a Lilibeo: un nuovo documento dei rapporti tra genti e culture diverse nella Sicilia occidentale, Mare internum 8, 21–38.

Arcuri, R. 2023. Poteri al confine. Filarchi giudici re tra Impero romano e Barbaricum, Biblioteca Tardoantica 14, Bari.

Bellieni, C. 1931. La Sardegna e i Sardi nella civiltà del mondo antico, vol. II, Cagliari.

Bocci, St. s. d., Ammiano Marcellino, XXVIII e XXIX, problemi storici e storiografici, Università degli studi di Roma tre, Dottorato di ricerca in civiltà e tradizione greca e romana, XXIV ciclo, tutor Leandro Polverini, Roma.

Bonello Lai, M. 1981. Sulla localizzazione delle sedi di Galillenses e Patulcenses Campani, StudSard 25, 29–42.

Bonello Lai, M. 1993. Il territorio dei *populi* e delle *civitates* indigene in Sardegna, in Mastino 1993a, 157–184.

Bonello Lai, M. 1993a. Sulla localizzazione delle sedi dei Galillenses e Patulcenses Campani, in Mastino 1993a, 49–61.

Bonello, M., Mastino, A. 1994. Il territorio di Siniscola in età romana, in E. Espa (a cura di), Siniscola dalle origini ai nostri giorni, Ozieri, 157–218.

Busonera, R. 2022. A nos ponere in caminu. L'impatto della transumanza nel sistema viario della Sardegna romana, in M. L. Marchi, G. Forte, D. Gangale Risoleo, I. Raimondo (a cura di), Landscape 2, una sintesi di elementi diacronici. Crisi e resilienza nel mondo antico, Venosa, 65–70.

Campus, F. R. 2023. Le vie di comunicazione: le strade e i ponti, in S. Cisci, R. Martorelli, G. Serreli, Banco di Sardegna (a cura di), Il tempo dei Giudicati. La Sardegna medievale dal X al XV secolo d. C., Ilisso, Nuoro, 131–139.

Canu, N. 2016. Tra Sarcidano e Barbagia. Spunti sulla romanizzazione in una zona di transizione, in S. De Vincenzo, C. Blasetti Fantauzzi (a cura di), Il processo di romanizzazione della provincia Sardinia et Corsica. Atti del Convegno Internazionale di Studi, Cuglieri (OR) 26–28 marzo 2015, Roma, 275–291.

Canu, N. 2012–2013 (2018). Esterzili. L'insediamento romano di Corte Luccetta in rapporto alla Tavola di Esterzili, Erentzias II, 458–460.

Champeaux, J. 2002. La religione dei Romani, Bologna (ed. italiana).

Conti, J. A. 2019. Romània e Barbària. Alcune considerazioni in merito al limes antibarbaricino, Otium 6, 1–41.

Corda, A. M. 2018. La romanizzazione delle aree produttive: Vallermosa, in D. Artizzu et alii, Leggere le fonti, interpretare il paesaggio, Cagliari, 141–166.

Corda, A. M., Piras, A. 2009. Alcune note sulla geografia umana della *Provincia Sardinia*, Theologica & Historica XVIII, 259–271.

De Ruggiero, E. 1900. Civitas, DE II/1, 255–267.

Didu, I. 2003. I Greci e la Sardegna, Il Mito e la Storia, Cagliari.

Dorcey, P. 1992. The Cult of Silvanus. A Study in Roman Folk Religion, Leiden – New York – Köln.

Durliat, J. 1982. Taxes sur l'entrée des marchandises dans la cité de Carales-Cagliari à l'époque byzantine (582–602), DOP 36, 1–14.

Dzino, D. 2012. The cult of Silvanus: rethinking provincial identities in Roman Dalmatia, VAMZ 45, 261–279.

Evangelisti, S., Ricci, C. 2022. Laribus (Augustis), Silvano Sacrum. Una ricognizione delle attestazioni epigrafiche del culto nell'Italia meridionale, in G. M. Annoscia, F. Camia, D. Nonnis (a cura di), Scrittura epigrafica e sacro in Italia dall'antichità al Medioevo. Luoghi, oggetti e frequentazioni. Atti del workshop internazionale (Scienze dell'Antichità, 28, 3), Roma, 255–275.

Fadda, L., Muscas, R. 2002. Bonacattu Deligia, Bidonì. Memorie del territorio, Ghilarza.

Faoro, D. 2011. Praefectus, procurator, praeses. Genesi delle cariche presidiali equestri nell'Alto impero Romano, Milano – Firenze.

Faoro, D. 2015. L'imperatore come *proconsul* di *Sardinia*, L'Africa romana XX, 1585–1591.

Faoro, D. 2016. In margine all'indicazione d'origine Nur(---) Alb(---) in un diploma dalla Sardegna, ZPE 211, 247–249.

Faoro, D. 2017. Pro legato, Klio 99, 1, 226–237.

Farre, C. 2016. Geografia epigrafica delle aree interne della Provincia Sardinia, Ortacesus.

Farre, C. 2016a. Alcune considerazioni sulla Barbaria: definizione, percezione e dinamiche di romanizzazione nella Sardegna interna, in S. De Vincenzo, C. Blasetti Fantauzzi (a cura di), Il processo di romanizzazione della provincia Sardinia et Corsica, Roma, 89–105.

Farre, C. 2021. L'epigrafia delle aree interne, in R. Carboni, A. M. Corda, M. Giuman (a cura di), Il tempo dei Romani. La Sardegna dal III secolo a. C. al V secolo d. C., Nuoro, 294–298.

Fiorelli, G. 1887. Austis, NSA, 336.

Floris, P. 2009. Nota sul centro romano di Valentia in Sardegna, Epigraphica 71, 133–160.

Floris, P. 2021. Breve rassegna dell'onomastica paleosarda della Sardegna, in F. Doria et al. (a cura di), Sardegna isola megalitica. Dai menhir ai nuraghi: storie di pietra nel cuore del Mediterraneo, Milano, 175–181.

Floris, P., Mastino, A. 2019. Traiano e la Sardegna, in L. Zerbini (ed.), Traiano: L'optimus princeps (Ferrara, 29–30 settembre 2017), Treviso, 121–153.

Gasperetti, G., Carenti, G. 2012. Un complesso ipogeo nell'agro di Romana (SS). Problematiche e ipotesi di ricerca, L'Africa Romana XIX, 2689–2704.

Gasperini, L. 1967. Le epigrafi, in S. Stucchi, Cirene 1957–1966. Un decennio di attività della Missione Archeologica Italiana a Cirene, Tripoli, 165–180.

Gasperini, L. 1992. Ricerche epigrafiche in Sardegna (II), L'Africa Romana IX, 571–593.

Giardina, A. 1997. Allevamento ed economia della selva in Italia meridionale (cap. III), in L'Italia romana. Storie di un'identità incompiuta, Bari, 139–192.

Gras, M. 1974. Les Montes Insani de la Sardaigne, in Littérature gréco-romaine et géographie historique: mélanges offerts à Roger Dion, Paris, 349–366.

Guido, L. 2006. Romania vs. Barbaria. Aspekte der Romanisierung Sardiniens (Berichte aus der Geschichtswissenschaft D61), Aachen.

Ibba, A. 2006. In M. Khanoussi, A. Mastino (ed.), Uchi Maius II. Le iscrizioni, Sassari.

Ibba, A. 2006a. Integrazione e resistenza nella provincia Sardiniae: Forum Traiani e il territorio circostante, in A. Ibba (a cura di), Scholia epigraphica, saggi di storia, epigrafia e archeologia romana, Ortacesus, 11–37.

Ibba, A. 2014. Il diploma di Posada: spunti di riflessione sulla Sardinia all'alba del II secolo d. C., Epigraphica LXXVI, 1–2, 209–229.

Ibba, A. 2015. Processi di "romanizzazione" nella Sardinia repubblicana e alto-imperiale (III A. C. – II D. C.), in L. Mihailescu-Bîrliba (a cura di), Colonization and Romanization in Moesia Inferior. Premises of a contrastive approach, Kaiserslautern und Mehlingen, 11–76.

Irmscher, J. 1983. Sulle origini del concetto di Romania, in Atti del III Seminario internazionale di studi storici "Da Roma alla terza Roma", 21–23 Aprile 1983, II, Roma, 421–429.

Kovács, P. 2011. A karpok beletepitése Pannoniába, in P. Kovács, B. Fehér, Á. Szabó (edd.), Közlemények, tanulmányok, előszók (Studia Epigraphica Pannonica III), Budapest, 31–38.

Kovács, P. 2011a. Fontes Pannoniae Antiquae in aetate Tetrarcharum I, Budapest.

La Fragola, A., Mastino, A., Pinna, T. 2021. Defixiones, maledizioni e pratiche magiche nella Sardinia e nella Corsica tardoantiche, in F. Marco Simón, F. Pina Polo, J. Remesal Rodriguez (eds.), Enemistad y odio en el mundo antiguo, Collecció Instrumenta 74, Zaragoza, 183–240.

Laporte, J.-P. 1989. Rapidum. Le camp de la cohorte des Sardes en Maurétanie Césarienne, Sassari.

Laronde, A. 1988. La Cyrénaïque romaine, des origines à la fin des Sévères (96 av. J.-C. – 235 ap. J.-C.), ANRW, II, 10, 1006–1064.

Le Bohec, Y. 1990. La Sardaigne et l'armée romaine sous l'Haut-Empire, Sassari.

Letta, C. 1992. I santuari rurali nell'Italia centro-appenninica: valori religiosi e funzione aggregativa, MEFRA 104, 1, 109–124.

Letta, C. 1993. L'epigrafia pubblica di *vici* e *pagi* nella *Regio IV*: imitazione del modello urbano e peculiarità del villaggio, in A. Calbi, A. Donati, G. Poma (a cura di), L'epigrafia del villaggio (Epigrafia e Antichità 12). Atti del Colloquio Borghesi (Forlì, 27–30 settembre 1990), Faenza, 33–48.

Lilliu, G. 1947. Per la topografia di Biora-Serri-Nuoro, StudSard 7, 29–103.

Mastino, A. 1976. Un'Iscrizione funeraria inedita proveniente da Aùstis (Nuoro), ASS 30, 51–53.

Mastino, A. 1991. Le fonti letterarie ed epigrafiche, in G. Camassa, S. Fasce (a cura di), Idea e realtà del viaggio. Il viaggio nel mondo antico, Genova, 191–244.

Mastino, A. 1993. Analfabetismo e resistenza: geografia epigrafica della Sardegna, in A. Calbi, A. Donati, G. Poma (a cura di), L'epigrafia del villaggio (Epigrafia e Antichità 12), Faenza, 457–536.

Mastino, A. (a cura di) 1993a. La Tavola di Esterzili. Il conflitto tra pastori e contadini nella Barbaria sarda. Convegno di studi (Esterzili, 13 giugno 1992), Sassari.

Mastino, A. 1995. Le relazioni tra Africa e Sardegna in età romana, ASS 38, 11–82.

Mastino, A. 2001. Rustica plebs id est pagi in provincia Sardinia: il santuario rurale dei Pagani Uneritani in Marmilla, in S.M. Bianchetti (ed.), Poikilma. Studi in onore di M.R. Cataudella in occasione del 60° compleanno, Firenze, 781–814.
Mastino, A. 2001a. La romanità della società giudicale in Sardegna: il Condaghe di San Pietro di Silki, in Atti del Convegno Nazionale "La civiltà giudicale in Sardegna nei secoli XI–XIII. Fonti e documenti scritti", Sassari, 23–61.
Mastino, A. 2005. I Montes Insani e gli Ilienses della Sardegna interna: Montiferru, Marghine o Gennargentu ?, in G.P. Mele (a cura di), Santu Lussurgiu. Dalle origini alla Grande Guerra. I. Ambiente e storia, Nuoro, 137–139.
Mastino, A. (a cura di) 2005a. Storia della Sardegna antica, Nuoro.
Mastino, A. 2014. Tradizione, modernità, fonti classiche, in M. Madau, Mamuthones e Issohadores. Maschere e riti di Mamoiada, identità della Sardegna, Associazione culturale Atzeni, Nuoro, 161–170.
Mastino, A. 2016. Aristotele e la natura del tempo: la pratica del sonno terapeutico davanti agli eroi della Sardegna, in M. Torelli (a cura di), Giornata di studio "I riti della morte e del culto di Monte Prama – Cabras" (Roma, 21 gennaio 2015). Atti dei Convegni Lincei 303, Roma, 151–178.
Mastino, A. 2016a. Cornus e il *Bellum Sardum* di *Hampsicora* e *Hostus*, storia o mito? Processo a Tito Livio, in S. De Vincenzo, C. Blasetti Fantauzzi (a cura di), Il processo di romanizzazione della provincia Sardinia et Corsica. Atti del convegno internazionale di studi (Cuglieri OR, 26–28 marzo 2015), Roma, 15–67.
Mastino, A. 2021. L'epigrafia latina nelle province danubiane negli ultimi 15 anni (2000–2015), in F. Mitthof, C. Cenati, L. Zerbini (eds.), Ad ripam fluminis Danuvi: Papers of the 3rd International Conference on the Roman Danubian Provinces. Vienna, 11th–14th November 2015 (Tyche Suplementband 11), Wien, 431–506.
Mastino, A. 2021a. La natio Sarda e le sue articolazioni territoriali: i popoli della Sardegna, in R. Carboni, A.M. Corda, M. Giuman (a cura di), Il tempo dei Romani. La Sardegna dal III secolo a.C. al V secolo d.C., Nuoro, 26–33.
Mastino, A. 2023. Le assegnazioni di *praedia* e *metalla* nella *Sardinia* di età repubblicana: da Gaio Gracco ad Ottaviano passando per Mario e Silla. L'evoluzione verso il latifondo senatorio ed imperiale e le eredità giudicali, in Roma e le province tra integrazione e dissenso, Università degli Studi di Milano – Giurisprudenza, in c.s.
Mastino, A. 2023a. Geografia, Geopolitica, Epigrafia. Conference de l'AIEGL, Bordeaux 31 agosto 2022, in L'épigraphie au XXIe siècle, Bordeaux, in c.s.
Mastino, A. 2024. Storia della Sardegna romana fino a Costantino, Cagliari, in c.s.
Mastino, A., Abrignani, A. 2021. Ancora il circuito Africa, Sicilia, Sardegna, sotto il segno di Melqart-Ercole e Astarte-Venere: il fanum salutifero dedicato Hercolei Nouritano a Lilibeo, Sicilia antiqua XVIII, 135–144.
Mastino, A., Pinna, T. 2008. Negromanzia, divinazione, malefici nel passaggio tra paganesimo e cristianesimo in Sardegna: gli strani amici del preside Flavio Massimino, in F. Cenerini, P. Ruggeri (edd.), Epigrafia romana in Sardegna. Atti del I Convegno di studio, Sant'Antioco, 14–15 luglio 2007 (Incontri insulari I), Roma, 41–83.

Mastino, A., Ruggeri, P. 2000. La romanizzazione dell'Ogliastra, in M. G. Meloni, S. Nocco (a cura di), Ogliastra. Identità storica di una Provincia. Atti del Convegno di studi, Jerzu-Lanusei-Arzana-Tortolì 23–25 gennaio 1997, Senorbì, 151–189.
Mastino, A., Ruggeri, P. 2008. La romanizzazione dell'Ogliastra, in AA.VV., Ogliastra. Antica cultura – nuova provincia. Storia e società, I. La storia, Ortacesus, 45–63.
Mastino, A., Zucca, R. 2007. Le proprietà imperiali della *Sardinia*, in D. Pupillo (a cura di), Le proprietà imperiali nell'Italia romana. Economia, produzione, amministrazione, Firenze, 93–124.
Mastino, A., Zucca, R. 2011. Urbes et rura. Città e campagna nel territorio oristanese in età romana, in P. G. Spanu, R. Zucca (a cura di), Oristano e il suo territorio. 1. Dalla preistoria all'alto Medioevo, Roma, 411–601.
Mastino, A., Zucca, R. 2012. La constitutio del Forum Traiani in Sardinia nel III a. C., JAT XXII, 31–50.
Mastino, A., Zucca, R. 2014. L. Cossonius L. f. Stell(atina tribu) Gallus Vecilius Crispinus Mansuanius Marcellinus Numisius Sabinus pro consule provinciae Sardiniae e la constitutio del Forum Traiani, Gerión 32, 199–223.
Mastino, A., Zucca, R. 2021. M. Valerius Optatus proc(urator), in S. Antolini, S. M. Marengo, Pro merito laborum. Miscellanea epigrafica per Gianfranco Paci (Ichnia 16), Tivoli, 417–440.
Mayer, M. 2009. Las civitates Barbariae: una prueba de la realidad de la organización territorial de Sardinia bajo Tiberio, in A. Mastino, P. G. Spanu, R. Zucca (a cura di), Naves plenis velis euntes, Roma, 43–51.
Meloni, P. 1958. L'amministrazione della Sardegna da Augusto all'invasione vandalica, Roma.
Meloni, P. 1986. La geografia della Sardegna in Tolomeo (Geogr. III, 3, 1–8), NBAS 3, 207–250.
Meloni, P. 2013. La Sardegna romana, Nuoro.
Michel, F. 2010. De l'union des îles à leur séparation. L'organisation administrative de la Corse et de la Sardaigne au Ier siècle, Conimbriga XLIX, 161–181.
Motzo, B. R. 1931. La posizione dei Montes Insani della Sardegna, in: Atti del II Congresso Nazionale di Studi Romani, I, Roma, 379–387.
Murru, G., Zucca, R. 2002. Frammenti epigrafici repubblicani da Laconi (Sardinia), Epigraphica 64, 213–223.
Nappi, R. 2023. Guaritrici sarde tra medicina, magia e inquisizione, Lecce.
Olmo-López, R. 2022. L'intervention du proconsul d'Afrique et des légats dans la pertica des Carthaginois de Trajan aux Sévères, in La pertica des Carthaginois, de la consitution au démembrement (Ier siècle av. J.-C., – IIIe siècle ap. J.-C.), AHAC 1, 563–587.
Pais, E. 1999. Storia della Sardegna e della Corsica durante il dominio romano, a cura di A. Mastino, Nuoro (prima edizione Roma 1923).
Paulis, G. 1987. I nomi di luogo della Sardegna, I, Sassari.
Paulis, G. 1990. Sopravvivenze della lingua punica in Sardegna, L'Africa Romana VII, 599–639.
Paulis, G. 1991. Le piante dei Punici, dei Romani e dei Sardi, L'Africa Romana VIII, 827–854.
Pinna, T. 1989. Gregorio Magno e la Sardegna, Cagliari.

Pinna, T. 2012. Il mondo magico isolano: Ammiano Marcellino e altre fonti, in Il sacro, il diavolo e la magia popolare. Religiosità, riti e superstizioni nella storia millenaria della Sardegna (Clio 7), Sassari, 37–66.

Piso, I. 2001. Inscriptions d'Apulum, Inscriptions de la Dacie romaine III/5 (Mémoires de l'Académie des Inscriptions et Belles-Lettres 24), Paris.

Piso, I. 2003. L'urbanisation des provinces danubiennes, in M. Reddé et al. (edd.), La naissance de la ville dans l'antiquité (De l'archéologie à l'histoire), Paris, 285–298.

Piso, I. 2004. Zu den Fasten Dakiens unter Trajan, in H. Heftner, K. Tomaschitz (edd.), Ad fontes! Festschrift für Gerhard Dobesch zum fünfundsechzigsten Geburtstag am 15. September 2004, Wien, 515–518.

Piso, I. (ed.). 2006. Le forum vetus de Sarmizegetusa I, Bucureşti.

Piso, I. (ed.). 2008. Die römischen Provinzen. Begriff und Gründung (Colloquium Cluj-Napoca, 28. September – 1.Oktober 2006), Cluj-Napoca.

Piso, I. 2013. Fasti provinciae Daciae II: Die ritterlichen Amtsträger (Antiquitas I 60), Bonn.

Piso, I. 2014. Le siège du gouverneur de Mésie inférieure, in V. Cojocaru, A. Coşkun, M. Dana (edd.), Interconnectivity in the Mediterranean and Pontic World during the Hellenistic and Roman Periods, Cluj-Napoca, 489–504.

Piso, I. 2014a. Die Trajansfora: politische Botschaft, in I. Piso, R. Varga (edd.), Trajan und seine Städte (Colloquium Cluj-Napoca, 29. September – 2. Oktober 2013), Cluj-Napoca, 255–273.

Piso, I. 2017. Colonia Dacica Sarmizegetusa, short introduction; The forum of Trajan (forum vetus); The forum of Antoninus Pius (forum novum) and the Capitol, in O. Ţentea, Al. Raţiu (edd.), The exhibition Sarmizegetusa – the beginning of the Roman Dacia, Bucureşti 2017, 14–37.

Piso, I. 2021. Deux inscriptions rupestres d'Arulis sur l'Euphrate et la supposée participation de la Legio IIII Flavia Felix à l'expédition parthique de Trajan, in K. Balbuza, M. Duch, Z. Kaczmarek, K. Królczyk, A. Tatarkiewicz (edd.), Antiquitas Aeterna. Classical Studies Dedicated to Leszek Mrozewicz on His 70th Birthday, Wiesbaden, 339–344.

Piso, I. 2023. La Dacie poétique (I), in L. Mihailescu-Bîrliba, I. Piso (eds.), Romans and Natives in the Danubian Provinces (1st–6th C. AD), Philippika 173, Wiesbaden, 309–324.

Pittau, M. 1970. Lingua e civiltà della Sardegna, Cagliari.

Pittau, M. 1981. La lingua dei Sardi nuragici e degli Etruschi, Sassari.

Porrà, F. (a cura di). 2002. Catalogo P.E.T.R.A.E. delle iscrizioni latine della Sardegna: versione preliminare, Cagliari.

Ricci, C. 2018. Security in Roman Times. Rome, Italy and the Emperor, London – New York.

Rojas Gutiérrez, R. 2016. Ataecina, un análisis de la continuidad de los cultos locales o indígenas en la Hispania romana, Ligustinus 5, 8–25.

Rougé, J. 1966. Recherches sur l'organisation du commerce maritime en Méditerranée sous l'empire romain, Paris.

Rowland, R.J. jr. 1973. Onomastic Remarks on Roman Sardinia, "Names', XXI, 2, 82–101.
Rowland, R.J. jr. 1981. I ritrovamenti romani in Sardegna, Roma.
Rowland, R.J. jr. 1994–1995. Caturo, not Caturon(i?)us, BeitrNamForsch 29–30, 355–357.
Ruggeri, P. 1987–1992. Aùstis: l'epitafio di Cn(aeus) Coruncanius Faustinus, NBAS 4, 159–169.
Sabbatucci, D. 1988. La religione di Roma antica, dal calendario festivo all'ordine cosmico, Milano 1988.
Saddington, D.B. 1987. Military praefecti with administrative functions, in Actes du IXe Congrès international d'Épigraphie Grecque et Latine, Sofia, 268–274.
Salvi, D., Sanna, A.L. 2006. Il *Templum Iovis* nella collina di Onnarìu a Bidonì (Oristano), Quaderni 21 (2004) 119–135.
Sanciu, A., Pala, P., Sanges, M. 2013. Un nuovo diploma militare dalla Sardegna, ZPE 186, 301–306.
Sechi, A. 1990. Cultura scritta e territorio nella Sardegna romana, L'Africa Romana VII, 641–654.
Sella, P. 1945. Rationes decimarum Italiae nei secoli XIII e XIV. Sardinia, Città del Vaticano.
Serra, P.B. 2006. Popolazioni rurali di ambito tardoromano e altomedievale in Sardegna, L'Africa Romana XVI, 1279–1305.
Serra, P.B., 2006a. I Barbaricini di Gregorio Magno, in L. Casula, G. Mele, A. Piras (a cura di), Per longa maris intervalla. Gregorio Magno e l'Occidente mediterraneo fra tardoantico e alto medioevo. Atti del convegno internazionale di studi (Cagliari 17–18 dicembre 2004), Cagliari, 289–361.
Stiglitz, A. 2004. Confini e frontiere nella Sardegna punica e romana: critica all'immaginario geografico, L'Africa Romana XV, 805–817.
Strinna, G. 2012. Le fate eredi di Diana. La magistra e le sue sociae, in S.M. Barillari (a cura di), Fate, madri-amanti-streghe. Atti del XVII Convegno internazionale (Genova – Rocca Grimalda, 16–18 settembre 2011), Alessandria, 273–289.
Strinna, G. 2022. Una sopravvivenza sarda di Silvano e un passo di Varrone, L'immagine riflessa XXX, 2, 43–64.
Talbert, R.A. (ed.). 2000. Barrington Atlas of the Greek and Roman World I, Princeton – Oxford.
Taramelli, A. 1920. Fordongianus. Inscrizione romana di età augustea rinvenuta presso le terme di "Forum Traiani", NSA 17, 347–352.
Taramelli, A. 1928. Un omaggio delle civitates Barbariae di Sardegna ad Augusto, in: Atti del I Congresso nazionale di studi romani, Roma, 269–276.
Taramelli, A. 1929. Fonni (Nuoro). Iscrizione votiva a Silvano, della foresta Sorrabense, rinvenuta entro l'abitato, NSA, 319–323.
Taramelli, A. 1931. Edizione Archeologica della Carta d'Italia al 100.000. Foglio 207. Nuoro, Firenze.
Terracini, B. 1936. Gli studi lingustici sulla Sardegna preromana, Roma.

Thomasson, B.E. 1972. Zur Verwaltungsgeschichte der Provinz Sardinia (Eranos 70), Uppsala – København.
Tončinić, D., Zerbini, L. (edd.). 2021. Traian and the Danubian Provinces. The Political, Economic and Religious Life in the Danubian Provinces. Proceedings of the 4th International Conference on the Roman Danubian Provinces (Zagreb, 15th–17th November 2017), Zagreb.
Trudu, E. 2012. Civitates, latrunculi mastrucati? Alcune note sulla romanizzazione della Barbaria, L'Africa romana XIX, 2645–2659.
Trudu, E. 2012a. Sacrum Barbariae: attestazioni cultuali nelle aree interne della Sardegna in epoca romana, in S. Angiolillo, M. Giuman, C. Pilo (a cura di), MEIXIS. Dinamiche di stratificazione culturale nella periferia greca e romana (Archaeologica, 169), Roma, 217–236.
Turtas, R. 1992. Rapporti tra Africa e Sardegna nell'epistolario di Gregorio Magno (590–604), L'Africa Romana II, 691–710.
Usai, E., Zucca, R. 1981–1985 (a. 1986). Colonia Iulia Augusta Uselis, StudSard XXVI, 303–342.
Wagner, M.L. 1957–1964. Dizionario etimologico sardo, Heidelberg, I (1960), II (1957), III (1964 – compilato da R.G. Urciolo).
Zucca, R. 1984. Una nuova iscrizione relativa alla cohors I Sardorum (contributo alla storia delle milizie ausiliarie romane in Sardegna), Epigraphica 46, 237–246.
Zucca, R. 1988. Le civitates Barbariae e l'occupazione militare della Sardegna: aspetti e confronti con l'Africa, L'Africa Romana V, 349–373.
Zucca, R. 1996. Inscriptiones latinae liberae rei publicae Africae, Sardiniae et Corsicae, L'Africa Romana XI, 1425–1489.
Zucca, R. 1997. Βαλιαρίδες Τυρρενικαῖ νῆσοι, Miscellanea greca e romana XXI, 355–365.
Zucca, R. 1998. Insulae Baliares. Le isole Baleari sotto il dominio romano, Roma.
Zucca, R. 1998a. Un altare rupestre di Iuppiter nella Barbaria sarda, L'Africa Romana XII, 1205–1211.
Zucca, R. 1999. Ula Tirso. Un centro della Barbaria sarda, Dolianova.
Zucca, R. 2003. Insulae Sardiniae et Corsicae. Le isole minori della Sardegna e della Corsica nell'antichità. Roma.
Zucca, R. 2003a. Neoneli – Leunelli. Dalla civitas Barbariae all'età contemporanea, Bolotana.
Zucca, R. 2004. Sufetes Africae et Sardiniae: studi storici e geografici sul Mediterraneo antico, Roma.

Deux fondations urbaines de l'empereur Trajan: *Municipium Ulpium Traianum Tropaeum* et *Colonia Ulpia Traiana Augusta Dacica Sarmizegetusa*

Constantin C. Petolescu*

Tel qu'on sait, l'empereur Trajan a affronté à l'hiver de 101/102 une grande invasion barbare (Daces, Sarmates, Bures) en Mésie Inférieure. Il est probable que les Daces et leurs alliés ont utilisé la même voie d'invasion qu'à l'époque de Domitien[1]. Pour commémorer la victoire contre les envahisseurs et souligner que la double offense – celle de 85/86, et celle de 101/102 – contre le peuple romain a été vengée, l'empereur Trajan ordonna l'érection du grand trophée[2], dont l'inscription inaugurale porte l'invocation à *Mars Ultor*[3]. On peut même croire qu'il s'agit de la conception du grand architecte Apollodore de Damas.

Selon Gr. Tocilescu, le trophée a été inauguré le 1er août 109 : l'année est certaine de par le numéro de la puissance tribunicienne de Trajan; la date du 1er août a été acceptée par comparaison avec celle de l'inauguration du temple de Mars Ultor, en 2 av. J.-C.[4].

Parallèlement à la construction de l'imposant trophée, s'est constitué un important établissement civil[5], dénommé également *Tropaeum* et qui accéda au statut municipal[6]. Plus récemment, on a reconsidéré une inscription découverte déjà par Gr. Tocilescu mais restée longtemps inédite; il en résulte que le premier municipe romain de la Mésie Inférieure est l'oeuvre de l'empereur Trajan : *[municipium] Traianum Tropaeum*[7]. Ainsi s'avère juste l'opinion d'Eugen Bormann[8] et Brigitte Galsterer-Kroll[9], selon lesquels l'inscription

* Institut d'Archéologie « Vasile Pârvan» , Bucarest; ccpetolescu@yahoo.fr.

1 Petolescu 2016, 72 sqq.

2 Voir Tocilescu 1895. Voir encore Alexandrescu-Vianu 2021, 159–175; Petolescu 2021, 177–193; Matei-Popescu 2021, 195–210.

3 ISM IV, 5 (= CIL III, 12467).

4 Tocilescu 1895, 127.

5 Le petit fragment d'inscription ISM IV, 6 peut provenir de la porte de la cité fondée par l'empereur Trajan.

6 Voir à ce-propos: Popescu 2013, 127–144 (= Popescu 2015, 182–199).

7 L'inscription a été publiée par Popescu 1964, 191–192 (= AE, 1964, 2510) ; voir récemment Popescu 2013, 131–133 (= Popescu 2015, 1890, n° 2); ISM IV, 11.

8 *Apud* Benndorf 1896, 184–185, n° 5.

9 Galsterer-Kroll 1972, 77, 92, 98, 123, n° 137.

dédiée en 116 à l'empereur Trajan par les *Traianenses Tropaeenses* (il s'agit probablement d'une base de statue)[10] indique comme auteurs de la dédicace les citoyens du municipe de Tropaeum. L'indication du topique du municipe romain apparaît aussi dans cinq autres inscriptions d'Adamclissi[11].

Outre les inscriptions présentées, le nom de la ville antique est mentionné aussi dans quatre inscriptions d'Adamclissi: dans une dédicace faite à *Nept(unus) Aug(ustus)* par une *vexil(latio) leg(ionis) I Ital(icae) M(oesicae) et V Ma(cedonicae) D(acicae) Tropa[e]i (agens)*[12]; dans l'inscription attestant la reconstruction des murailles de la *Tropeensium civitas* au temps des empereurs Constantin le Grand et Licinius[13]; dans deux inscriptions grecques dédiées à Héra Basilissa[14] et à Poseidon[15] par la πόλις Τροπεισίων, remerciant pour la découverte de l'eau. Toujours en tant que πόλις Τροπεισίων apparaît dans l'inscription de Thyatire (en Lydie)[16], indiquant les fonctions d'un officier équestre, T. Antonius Cl. Alfenus Arignotus, qui accomplit quelques charges en tant que λογιστὴς – – – τῆς [Ἰσ]τριανῶν πόλεως καὶ Τροπησίων etc.

Ce toponyme est ainsi attesté jusqu'à la fin de l'Antiquité[17]: Τρόπαιον (Hierocles, *Synekdemos*, 637, 8; Theophylactos Simokattes, *Histoires*, I, 8; *Notitia episcopatuum* de De Boor[18]; Constantinus Porphyrogenitus, *De administrando imperio*, [47] 1, 58–60).

Il résulte de la présentation des inscriptions et des sources narratives, que le nom de l'habitat civil fondé auprès du complexe triomphal d'Adamclissi était *Tropaeum*[19]; la dénomination Tropaeum *Traiani*, utilisée encore par les historiens et les épigraphistes, est iréelle et artificielle, crée par Grigore Tocilescu[20] et Eugen Bormann[21].

Donc, la ville avait reçu ce rang quelques années auparavant[22]: au plus tard en 114, quand l'empereur se trouvait déjà à Antioche; ou éventuellement en 113, avant son départ de Rome pour la guerre contre les Parthes. Mais il est plus probable que Tropaeum ait reçu le rang municipal en même temps que l'inauguration du trophée, en 109.

---

10 ISM IV, 9 (= CIL III, 12470)

11 ISM IV, 12 (= CIL III, 14214, 2): *mu[n(icipium) Tro]p(aeum)*, 13 (= 12461 = 7484; ILS, 7183; AE 1964, 253): *ordo spl[endi]dissima* (!) *mun[ic(ipii)] Trop(aei)*, 40: *dec(urio) m(unicipii) T(ropaei)*, 61 (= CIL III, 14214, 6): *duumvira[lis m]unic(ipii) Trop(aei)*, 62 b (= CIL III 12473): *bis IIviral(is) munic(ipii) Trop(aei)*.

12 ISM IV, 26 (= CIL III, 14433; ILS, 9118)

13 ISM IV, 16 (= CIL III, 13734; ILS, 8938).

14 ISM IV, 24 (= AE 1976, 625; AE 2011, 1139).

15 ISM IV, 25 (= AE 2009, 1206; AE 2011, 1139).

16 IDRE II, 383 (= AE 1995, 1450; AE 1996, 1446).

17 Voir *Fontes historiae Daco-Romanae*, II, Bucarest, 1970, passim.

18 De Boor, 1891, 532; voir aussi Darouzès, 1981, 651 (*apud* Em. Popescu).

19 Attention: toutes les sources antiques (narratives et épigraphiques) attestent de la forme *Tropaeum* : remarque de Petolescu 2006, 103–108 (étude reprise dans Petolescu 2007, 169); Petolescu 2014, 77–84); observation retenue par Em. Popescu, dans ISM, IV, p. 95 [*ad* n° 9]).

20 Voir Tocilescu 1895, 27.

21 E. Bormann, *apud* Benndorf 1896, 184–185.

22 Voir l'opinion d'Eugen Bormann et Brigitte Galsterer-Kroll (*supra*, notes 8–9).

À l'occasion de la fondation du municipe de *Tropaeum*, on constitua son premier *ordo decurionum* avec ses magistrats, ayant entre autres la mission d'accomplir les cérémonies annuelles visant la commémoraison des *fortissimi viri*[23] qui s'étaient sacrifiés pour la patrie en 85/86 et 101/102[24].

Nous trouvons encore un bon parallèle dans la fondation de la *Colonia Ulpia Traiana Augusta Dacica Sarmizegetusa* en 109 ou 110, tel qu'il résulte d'une importante inscription: *Divinis auspiciis Imp(eratoris) Caesaris divi N(ervae) f(ilii) Nervae Traiani Augusti Germanici Dacici condita Colonia Ulpia Traiana Augusta Dacica per D(ecimum) Terentium Scaurianum, leg(atum) eius pro pr(aetore)*[25].

Aussi, suivant le modèle des colonies romaines, les magistrats suprêmes du municipe de Tropaeum étaient appelés *duumviri*[26].

En conclusion: il est possible que les deux villes aient été créées simultanément par l'empereur Trajan; l'acte a été précédé de l'octroi d'une *lex municipii Ulpii Traiani Tropaei (Tropaeensium)*, respectivement *lex Coloniae Ulpiae Traianae Augustae Dacicae Sarmizegetusae (Sarmizegetusensium)*.

Bibliographie

Alexandrescu-Vianu, M. 2021. Y-a-t-il une narration sur le trophée d'Adamclissi? dans G. Castellvi, F. Matei-Popescu, M. Gallinier (éds.), Actes du colloque international Trophées et Monuments de victoire romains. 21–23 octobre 2015, Université de Perpignan, Bucarest-Perpignan, 159–175.

Benndorf, O. 1896. Adamklissi, Archäologisch-Epigraphische Mitteilungen aus Österreich-Ungarn 10, 181–204.

Darouzès, J. 1981. Notitia episcopatuum ecclesiae Constantinopolitanae, Paris.

23 Voir ISM IV, 8 (= CIL III, 14214).

24 Nous apprenons de l'*Histoire romaine* de Dion Cassius (LXVIII, 8, 2) que l'empereur Trajan, après la bataille de Tapae, extrêmement sanglante, « ordonna d'élever un autel en l'honneur de ses soldats morts dans la bataille, et de leur offrir tous les ans des sacrifices funèbres ». Selon Vulpe 1964, 211–223, cette narration ferait référence aux combats d'Adamclissi, en Dobroudja, où l'on a érigé le célèbre trophée. Bien que cette identification semble inacceptable, l'opinion du grand historien reste valable, à savoir que la cité civile a été fondée « dans le même cadre commémoratif ». En absence d'une garnison militaire, la mission d'organiser ces cérémonies revenait au conseil municipal de la cité *(ordo decurionum)* et à ses magistrats.

25 CIL III, 1443 ; voir Wolff 1976, 99–118 (= AE 1976, 570; IDR III/2, 1). Voir encore: Etienne, Piso, Diaconescu 2002–2003, 88 (note 86, lecture de I. Piso) : *Divinis auspiciis Imp(eratoris) Caesaris divi N(ervae) f(ilii) Nervae Traiani Augusti Germanici Dacici condita Colonia Ulpia Traiana Augusta Dacica per D(ecimum) Terentium Scaurianum, leg(atum) eius pro pr(aetore)*; Piso 1998, 276, n° 212 (= AE 1998, 1084 et AE 2007, 1203).

26 ISM IV, 11 (= AE 1964, 25), *IIviri q(uin)q(uennales)*; 12 (= CIL III, 14214, 2) *IIvir(i)*; 13 (= CIL III, 12461 = 7484; ILS, 7183; AE 1964, 253) *d[uu]mveros* (!); 20 (= CIL III, 12465) *IIv(iri) q(uin)q(ennales)*; 61 (= CIL III, 14214, 6) *duumvir*; 62 (= CIL III, 12473) *IIviral(is) iterum IIvir, bis IIviral(is)*.

De Boor, C. 1891. Nachträge zu den Notitia episcopatuum, II, Zeitschrift für Kirchengeschichte 12, 520–534.

Etienne, R., Piso, I., Diaconescu, A. 2002–2003. Les fouilles du *forum vetus* de Sarmizegetusa. Rapport général, Acta Musei Napocensis 39–40, 59–153.

Galsterer-Kroll, B. 1972. Untersuchungen zu den Beinamen der Städte des Imperium Romanum, Epigraphische Studien 9, 44–145.

Matei-Popescu, F. 2021. Municipium Tropaeum: histoire et institutions, dans G. Castellvi, F. Matei-Popescu, M. Gallinier (éds.), Actes du colloque international Trophées et Monuments de victoire romains. 21–23 octobre 2015, Université de Perpignan, Bucarest-Perpignan, 195–210.

Petolescu, C.C. 2006. Politica urbană a împăratului Hadrian la Dunărea de Jos, Argesis 15, 103–108.

Petolescu, C.C. 2014, Tropaeum. Complexul comemorativ de la Adamclisi şi oraşul roman, Academica 24, 77–84.

Petolescu, C.C. 2016. Decebal, regele dacilor[2], Bucarest.

Petolescu, C.C. 2021. *Tropaeum*. Le complexe commémoratif et la ville romaine (Moesia Inferior), dans G. Castellvi, F. Matei-Popescu, M. Gallinier (éds.), Actes du colloque international Trophées et Monuments de victoire romains. 21–23 octobre 2015, Université de Perpignan, Bucarest-Perpignan, 177–193.

Petolescu. C.C. 2007. Politica urbană a împăratului Hadrian la Dunărea de Jos, dans Contribuţii la istoria Daciei romane, 91–98.

Piso, I. 1998. Apulum, dans Gr. Arbore-Popescu (éd.), Traiano. ai confini del Impero, Milan, 276.

Popescu, E. 1964. Epigraphische Beiträge zur Geschichte der Stadt Tropaeum Traiani, Studii Clasice 6, 185–203.

Popescu, E. 2013. Municipium Tropaeum, Dacia, N.S. 57, 127–144.

Popescu, E. 2015. *Municipium Tropaeum*, dans C.C. Petolescu, M. Galinier, F. Matei-Popescu (éds.), Colonne Trajane et trophées romains. Actes du Colloque franco-roumain « Études sur la Colonne Trajane. 1900 ans depuis l'inauguration (113–2013) » Bucarest, 28–29 octobre 2013, Bucarest, 182–199.

Tocilescu, G. 1895. Monumentul de la Adamklissi Tropaeum Traiani (en collaboration avec O. Benndorf et G. Nieman), Vienne.

Vulpe, R. 1964. Dion Cassius et la campagne de Trajan en Mésie Inférieure, Studii Clasice 6, 205–232.

Wolff, H. 1976. Miscellanea Dacica (II), Acta Musei Napocensis 13, 99–118.

Un possible Jupiter Thrace à Ulpiana (Mésie Supérieure)

Radu Ardevan, Raffaele d'Amato

Les recherches archéologiques entreprises en 1958–1959 sur le site archéologique d'Ulpiana en Dardanie, dans la province de Mésie supérieure[1] (aujourd'hui localité de Gračanica/ Graçanicë dans la région du Kosovo), ont également permis la découverte d'une inscription votive. Signalée depuis 1969[2], la pièce a été publiée en 1980 par Zef Mirdita avec la lecture suivante[3]:

> *I(ovi) O(ptimo) M(aximo) / Melcid / Ael(ius) Octa/vianus / vet(eranus) cum / suis v(otum) p(osuit).*

La seule ambiguïté dans la lecture étaient les lettres MELCID à la ligne 2. Sans proposer de complément, l'auteur estimait qu'elles devraient cacher le nom d'une divinité locale, apparaissant ici dans l'*interpretatio Romana*. Il remarquait également que cette épithète de Jupiter n'était plus attestée nulle part[4]; la datation proposée était très large, IIe–IIIe siècles apr. J.-C. Dans cette variante, l'inscription a ensuite été reprise[5].

Mais des réserves sur cette interprétation sont vite apparues. Dès 1984, l'opinion était formulée qu'en fait les lettres CID de la ligne 2 de l'inscription pouvaient se lire *Cid(onius)*, de sorte qu'elles exprimeraient pour Iupiter Melanus, en latin, l'épithète divine Κυδώνιος, dérivée du nom d'une localité de Crète, célèbre pour le temple de Zeus[6]. Plus tard, Maja Parović-Pešikan a développé l'argument dans le même sens: le passage controversé abrégerait une épithète supplémentaire du dieu suprême, dans la pose de Jupiter Melanus – pose

1 Parović-Pešikan 1981, 70. La ville romaine s'est développée à partir d'un centre minier (*metalla Ulpiana*) et est devenue *municipium Ulpianum* vers le milieu du IIe siècle apr. J.-C.; elle n'est désignée comme *Ulpiana* que durant le Bas-Empire (Mócsy 1974, 131, 133; Hoxhaj 2000, 95–96, 101–102).

2 Čerškov 1969, 65; Mócsy 1970, 84; probablement la pièce signalée brièvement dans ILJug II 523.

3 Mirdita 1980, 186, nº 2.

4 On invoquait l'absence d'une telle épithète de Jupiter chez Roscher II, 750-754. Il n'y a rien de similaire parmi les épithètes de Zeus non plus (Roscher VI, 638–643).

5 Mirdita 1981, 251, nº 236 (35); AE 1981, 725; Parović-Pešikan 1981, 70.

6 Peja 1984, 59-60.

Fig. 1: L'inscription AE 1981, 725, dessin (après ArhKosovo 1998, 307)

attestée à Ulpiana[7]. Et les lettres CID de la ligne 2 de l'inscription dont nous parlons étaient completées *Cid(iessus)* – l'équivalent latin de Κιδυήσσος, donc comme épithète d'un Jupiter Melanus, mais dérivé du nom d'une petite ville de la Phrygie occidentale (Κιδήσσος)[8]. La présence d'un point séparateur sur la pierre, entre les groupes de lettres MEL et CID, était invoquée aussi pour cette lecture[9]. L'auteur rassemblait également une série de preuves de la présence de colons de l'Asie Mineure occidentale, notamment de Phrygie, dans la région de la Dardanie romaine[10]. Ulpiana était un centre minier cosmopolite, l'explication proposée semblait donc convaincante[11]. En effet, la lecture proposée fut acceptée et l'inscription fut citée à plusieurs reprises[12] avec cette complétion: *I(ovi) O(ptimo) M(aximo) / Mel(ano) Cid(iesso).*

À cette occasion, M. Parović-Pešikan a cité une autre inscription aussi, provenant également d'Ulpiana et avec un texte similaire; le dieu suprême portait les mêmes épithètes, complétées de la même manière[13]. Nous avons un dessin publié pour cette pièce (voir Fig. 1)[14]. Sa lecture se présentait comme suit:

7 ILJug II 531a = AE 1972, 501; Parović-Pešikan 1990, 608–610, 611 (n°s 15–18). Voir aussi AE 1990, 859: *I(ovi) O(ptimo) M(aximo) / Mel(ano) Asclep(ia)/des ex v(oto) pa(terno) / ara(m) posui(t).*

8 Parović-Pešikan 1990, 607. Un tel attribut peut effectivement dériver d'une série d'anthroponymes de l'ouest de la province d'Asie (Zgusta 1964, 228, § 602, 1–5), ainsi que de certaines toponymes du même espace (Zgusta 1984, carte 169).

9 Parović-Pešikan 1990, 609.

10 Parović-Pešikan 1990, 607, 610–613.

11 Voir aussi Gavrilović Vitas 2021, 118–119.

12 HD-005464; Ferri 1997, 126, no. 47; Hoxhaj 2000, 170, no. 4; Bošković-Robert 2006, 99, n° 115; Gavrilović Vitas 2021, 242, n° 2; EDCS-09100863. Il faut faire mention que nous n'avons trouvé aucune photographie de l'inscription.

13 Parović-Pešikan 1990, 611, no. 18; initialement publiée par Peja 1984, 59. Voir également: Bošković-Robert 2006, 100, n. 635; Gavrilović Vitas 2021, 242, n° 4; EDCS-81000042.

14 Nous profitons de cette occasion pour exprimer nos remerciements à Mme N. Gavrilović Vitas de Belgrade, qui nous l'a aimablement fourni.

> *I(ovi) O(ptimo) M(aximo) / Mel(ano) Cid(iesso) / M(arcus) Aur(elius) Oc/tavius / ex voto.*

Il existe donc deux témoignages épigraphiques sur cette pose inhabituelle de Jupiter dans la région de l'ancienne Ulpiana. Nous pensons qu'une troisième inscription avec le même théonyme[15] est en réalité le résultat d'une confusion; seul le très bref avis de l'ILJ 523 est cité pour cela, il pourrait donc faire référence à l'une ou l'autre des deux mentionnés ci-dessus.

Mais la lecture proposée est-elle vraiment correcte? Nous exprimons une certaine réserve, en raison du caractère singulier en Europe de l'épithète proposée, *Cid(iessus)*. La séparation des lettres MEL de CID par un point n'est pas un argument décisif pour cette lecture, puisque de nombreux cas de points séparateurs mal placés sont connus dans l'épigraphie latine[16]; par exemple, même à Ulpiana, dans une inscription pour *I. O. M. Melanus* le point de séparation, qui aurait été nécessaire, entre les lettres I et O de la ligne 1 fait défaut[17]. Ainsi les lettres en question pouvaient aussi être lues MELCID, comme dans les premières publications.

Cependant, cette formulation fait penser à une inscription funéraire de Drobeta (province de la Dacie supérieure), connue depuis longtemps[18]; le vétéran légionnaire décédé s'appelle C. Iulius Melcidianus. Le *cognomen* est pour l'instant une apparition unique, du moins dans les provinces européennes de l'Empire romain[19]. Il fut considéré, hypothétiquement, d'origine thrace, dérivé du nom Μελγίς[20]. Les recherches récentes ont confirmé ce point de vue: ce nom thrace féminin assez rare est présent chez les Thraces occidentaux[21]. De plus, il convient de noter que sur la pierre de Drobeta, partiellement endommagée, le nom peut avoir été orthographié *Melgidianus*[22], plus proche de la forme Μελγίς – telle que lue par I. I. Russu[23] et C. C. Petolescu[24].

On peut donc être sûr qu'il existait ce nom de forme romaine, dérivé d'un nom thrace, même si l'on ne connaît toujours pas le pendant masculin de la forme originale. Son porteur aura eu une origine thrace, même si assez éloignée[25].

À la lumière de ces constatations, la lecture la plus probable des lettres MELCID sur les deux inscriptions discutées maintenant se présente autrement. Elles pourraient être

15 Signalée dans EDCS-10000537. Les travaux récents consacrés au thème (Bošković-Robert 2006 ; Gavrilović Vitas 2021) ne la prennent pas en compte.
16 Cagnat 1898, 29.
17 Parović-Pešikan 1990, 609, fig. 2 (l'observation nous appartient).
18 CIL III 14216^{6}; IDR II, 41.
19 OPEL III, 73 (l'ortographe *Melchidianus* est fausse).
20 Mateescu 1923, 109; Russu 1967, 91.
21 Dana 2014, 212, 438, 455.
22 Voir IDR II, fig. 41.
23 Russu 1967, 91.
24 Dans IDR II, 41 la transcription est *Melcidianus*, mais dans le commentaire connexe apparaît *Melgidianus*.
25 La dérivation onomastique se fait à la manière romaine et dot avoir eu lieu dans un milieu romanisé.

l'abréviation d'une épithète du dieu suprême, une épithète thrace. Faute de sources plus explicites, nous ne pouvons pas restituer sa forme correcte, mais nous pouvons nous attendre à des formes telles que *Melcidas, Melcidus, Melcidis* etc. Il s'agit plutôt d'une forme courte, connue et facilement reconnaissable par les adorateurs du dieu, même abrégée. Et le dieu en question devait être une divinité thrace, locale ou régionale, identifiée à la divinité romaine suprême par un processus d'*interpretatio Romana*[26].

Bien entendu, aujourd'hui nous ne pouvons pas connaître la sémantique d'un nom comme Μελγίς en langue thrace. Mais il est fort probable que sa racine exprimât une certaine qualité du dieu suprême. De cette épithète divine, un anthroponyme dérivé sera formé plus tard – comme dans de nombreux cas – éventuellement avec la transformation de la consonne G en C.

L'apparition à Ulpiana d'un tel Jupiter thrace n'aurait rien de surprenant. Toute la région de Dardanie, bien que illyrienne en majorité, présente d'importantes implantations thraces, visibles épigraphiquement aussi[27]. On y retrouve également des divinités d'origine thrace[28]. Par ailleurs, dans l'espace thracophone apparaissent fréquemment des divinités aux noms locaux, peu répandus[29].

Nous n'avons aucun élément certain d'une datation plus précise des deux monuments épigraphiques. Le nom d'Aelius du dédicataire, vétéran d'une troupe inconnue, suggère une date ultérieure au règne d'Hadrien; mais l'absence du *praenomen* conforte plutôt le placement de l'inscription dans la première moitié du IIIe siècle apr. J.-C., et les autres traits caractéristiques du monument (dédicace votive à caractère personnel, nom romain, divinité exotique) correspondent aux tendances générales de la même période[30]. La dédicace de M. Aurelius Octavius peut également être datée de la même manière; il n'a aucun lien avec l'armée et pourrait être un citoyen de date récente, grâce à la *Constitutio Antoniniana*.

Abréviations bibliographiques

Périodiques et collections

AE =	L'Année Épigraphique, Paris.
AMN =	Acta Musei Napocensis, Cluj-Napoca.
AV =	Arheološki Vestnik, Ljubljana.
BHR =	Bulgarian Historical Review, Sofia.
CIL =	Corpus Inscriptionum Latinarum, Berlin.

26 Pour ce problème, voir: Ando 2005; Häussler 2008, 15–19.

27 Hoxhaj 2000, 20–21; Dana 2014, XXXIII, LXXIV-LXXVIII, LXXXII-LXXXIII. Des opinions plus anciennes considéraient les Dardaniens comme un peuple thrace (Mócsy 1974, 27, 65).

28 Mócsy 1974, 253–254.

29 Voir par exemple: Georgiev 1975; Tačeva-Hitova 1978.

30 Mócsy 1974, 248–249, 253–256.

ClassPhil = Classical Philology, Chicago.
ED = Ephemeris Dacoromana, București – Roma.
EDCS = Epigraphisches Datenbank Clauss-Slaby http://db.edcs.eu/epigr/epi.php?s_sprache=en (consultée au 20 Février 2024).
GMKM = Glasnik Muzeja Kosova i Metohje, Priština.
HD = Epigraphisches Datenbank Heidelberg https://edh-www.adw.uni-heidelberg.de/home (consultée au 22 Février 2024).
IDR = I. I. Russu (ed.), Inscripțiile Daciei romane, București.
ILJug = A. Šašel, J. Šašel, Inscriptiones Latinae quae in Iugoslavia ... repertae et editae sunt, Ljubljana, I (1963), II (1978), III (1986).
LB = Linguistique Balkanique, Sofia.
OPEL = B. Lőrincz, Onomasticon provinciarum Europae Latinarum, I^2 (Budapest, 2005, avec Á. Szabó), II (Wien, 1999), III (Wien, 2000), IV (Wien, 2002).
Roscher = W. H. Roscher, Ausführliches Lexikon der griechischen und römischen Mythologie, Leipzig, I (1884) – VI (1924–1937).
Starinar = Starinar. Arheološki Institut u Beogradu, Beograd.

Livres et études

Ando, C. 2005. Interpretatio Romana, ClassPhil 100/1, 41-51.
ArhKosovo 1998. Arheološko blago Kosova i Metohije: od neolita do ranog sredneg veka. Katalog, Beograd.
Bošković-Robert, A. 2006. Le culte de Jupiter en Mésie supérieure, Paris (non vidimus).
Cagnat, R. 1898. Cours d'épigraphie latine, Paris, IIIe édition.
Čerškov, E. 1969. Rimljani na Kosovu i Metohiji, Beograd.
Dana, D. 2014. Onomasticon Thracicum. Répertoire des noms indigènes de Thrace, Macédoine orientale, Mésies, Dacie et Bithynie, Athènes.
Ferri, N. 1997. Monumentet ushtarake të periudhës romake në Mezi të Epërme, Prishtinë (thèse de doctorat manuscrite – non vidimus).
Gavrilović Vitas, N. 2021. Ex Asia et Syria: Oriental Religions in the Roman Central Balkans, Oxford.
Georgiev, Vl. 1975. Die thrakischen Götternamen: ein Beitrag zur Religion der alten Thraker, LB 18, 5–56.
Häussler, R. 2008. Signes de la "romanisation" à travers l'épigraphie: possibilités d'interprétation et problèmes méthodologiques, in R. Häussler (éd.), Romanisation et épigraphie. Études interdisciplinaires sur l'acculturation et l'identité dans l'Empire romain, Montagnac, 9–30.
Hoxhaj, E. 2000. Untersuchungen zur Geschichte des Kosova in der Römerzeit. Militär, Städte, Gesellschaft und Bevölkerung, Wien, 2000 (thèse de doctorat manuscrite; nous remercions également le Prof. Dr. Ekkehard Weber, son responsable scientifique, qui nous l'a fait connaître).
Mateescu, G. G. 1923. I Traci nelle epigrafi di Roma, ED 1, 57–290.
Mirdita, Z. 1980. Novitates epigraphicae e Dardania collectae, AV 31, 186–198.

Mirdita, Z. 1981. Antroponimia e Dardanisë në kohën romake (Die Anthroponymie der Dardanien zur Römerzeit), Prishtinë.
Mócsy, A. 1970. Gesellschaft und Romanisation in der römischen Provinz Moesia Superior, Budapest – Amsterdam.
Mócsy, A. 1974. Pannonia and Upper Moesia. A History of the Middle Danube Provinces of the Roman Empire, London – Boston.
Parović-Pešikan, M. 1981. Antička Ulpiana prema dosadašnim istraživanima, Starinar 32, 57–74.
Parović-Pešikan, M. 1990. Novi spomenik Jupitera Melana iz Ulpijane, AV 41, 607–616.
Peja, F. 1984. Jedan zanimljiv natpis sa Ulpiane, GMKM 13–14, 59–62 (non vidimus).
Russu, I.I. 1967. Tracii în Dacia romană, AMN 4, 85–105.
Tačeva-Hitova, M. 1978. Über die Götterepitheta in den griechischen Inschriften aus Moesia inferior und Thracia, BHR 3, 52–65.
Zgusta, L. 1964. Kleinasiatische Personennamen, Prag.
Zgusta, L. 1984. Kleinasiatische Ortsnamen, Heidelberg.

Mogionibus: the foundation and territory of the city

Ádám Szabó*

Ioan Piso octogenario l. a.

In three of my previous works, I have provided information on the city's existence, administrative and inscriptional details, and archaeological remains. I have also referenced prior research in the field. Additionally, I have observed that the Azalian tribe in northeastern Pannonia was divided into at least two groups based on the city names and personal names derived from them: the Mogetians (*Mogetiones*) and the Mogiuses (*Mogiones*).[1] The south-western part of the civitas Azaliorum was under the control of the Mogetians as they founded the municipium of Mogetiana there. The north-eastern part was under the control of the Mogiuses as they founded the municipium of Mogionibus there. The legionary camp of Brigetio, along with its *canabae* and associated area, the *prata* or *regio* (see below), was situated between the two from the north-northwest. This text focuses solely on the eastern part of the *civitas Azaliorum*, specifically the territory of the Mogiuses (*Mogiones*), the *municipium* Mogionibus, and its corresponding territory. These sources provide insight into the eastern half of the *civitas*. The extent of the city's territory can be approximated through internal sources, diplomas, and stone inscriptions that mention Azalus soldiers and leaders. External sources can be approached based on the sources for the Boii, Eravisci, and Brigetio, which are external indicators of the boundaries of the civitas. These sources can be compared with known provincial administrative data and field conditions, supplemented by environmental and archaeological studies.[2] The inscriptions documenting the city found in the area covered by the *civitas Azaliorum* can be used to attempt to define the urban territory, expanding on the data for the *civitas*.

The issue of territory, which is also connected to the date of the city's foundation, pertains to the *civitates* established in the undivided territory of Pannonia, including

* Ádám Sándor Nagyernyei Szabó: Ludovika University of Public Services, Roman State- and Provincial Administration Workshop, Budapest – Hungarian National Museum, Department of Archaeology, Budapest.

1 Szabó 2018, 129–209; Szabó 2022, 163–167; Szabó 2024. Previous studies: Kovács 2003, 277–306; Tóth 2003, 307–330; Mráv 2008, 105–155 with the full older literature.

2 Cf. on the subject: Bödőcs, Kovács 2011, 20–25.

the civitas Azaliorum, as well as to the provinces of Pannonia Inferior and Pannonia Superior created in the divided territory of Pannonia in 106/107, and to the boundary modification of 214.[3]

During the period of undivided Pannonia, the civitas Azaliorum (Asaliorum) was located in the eastern Pannonian territory, in a narrowing zone to the northeast to the Danube bend and Solva (Esztergom)[4], bordering the *civitas Eraviscorum* from the east-southeast[5], the *civitas Boiorum* from the west[6], the *ripa* and *prata* from the north[7], and Lake Balaton (Pelso) from the south. The maps in the volumes I and II of Fontes Pannoniae Antiquae[8] illustrate the territorial division of Pannonia to the best of today's knowledge, based on the extant source data.[9]

The earliest inscription documented the vicinity of civitas Boiorum and civitas Azaliorum:

1. Picenum, Italia Regio V. (Fermo / Firmum Picenum). Dated 65–80.
CIL 9 5363 = ILS 2737 = RHP 396 = Grbić 2014, 105 = Epigraphica 2016, 59 = FPA II, 68–69. (Cf. also fragment CIL 9 5364, with identical text. See also Grbić 2014, 306–308.)
L(ucio) Volcacio Q(uinti) f(ilio) | Vel(ina tribu) Primo | praef(ecto) coh(ortis) I Noricor(um) | in Pann(onia) praef(ecto) ripae | Danuvi(i) et civitatium | duar(um) Boior(um) et Azalior(um) | trib(uno) milit(um) leg(ionis) V | Macedonicae in | Moesia praef(ecto) alae I | Pannonior(um) in Africa | IIviro quinq(uennali) | flamini divorum | omnium p(atrono) c(oloniae) | ex testamento eius | posita | M(arco) Accio Seneca | [...] Manlio Planta | IIvir(is) quinq(uennalibus) | l(ocus) dat(us) dec(reto) dec(urionum).

The area was incorporated into Pannonia Superior after the division of Pannonia in 106/107. It was situated in the eastern-northeastern region of the province. Two municipiums, Mogetiana and Mogionibus, were established in the civitas area, likely around the same time between 117 and 138 during the reign of Hadrian, as indicated by inscriptions from the 2nd and 3rd centuries. At least one of the municipiums had Latin right. A change in administrative system may also imply a change in legal status.

---

3 Cf. Fitz 1994, 971–977; Szabó 2000, 85–109; Kovács FPA II. 2004, 178–179; Kovács FPA IV. 2007, 168–169; Kovács 2015, 287–288.

4 Cf. Grbić 2014, 173–292. and 204–222. See also Fehér - Kovács FPA II, 2004/2005 map, for this the map by Grbić 2014, 207 as well. The FPA map covers a larger area for the whole area of the civitas based on auctor sources and inscription material. Grbić's map shows a slightly different area in the eastern part of the civitas, based on the inscribed sources, than the area presented in this communication. For the Pannonian civitates see also Nagy 2003, 439–464 and Kovács 2013.

5 Cf. Grbić 2014, 235–264.

6 Cf. Grbić 2014, 276–284.

7 Cf. Visy 2001 (=2003), 37–53.

8 Fehér, Kovács, FPA I-II. 2004 (hungarian version) és 2005 (english version), map appendices at the end of both volumes.

9 Cf. also in principle Kovács 2013, 131–154.

Mogionibus was situated on the northeastern border of Pannonia Superior, with its centre located in present-day Környe (Komárom-Esztergom County, Hungary). In 214, the boundary was modified, placing the territory of Mogionibus within the administrative boundaries of the province of Pannonia Inferior, where it remained until 258–260.[10]

Between its foundation and 214, the city's territory was bordered to the east-southeast by the provincial boundary of Pannonia Inferior and the west-northwest border of the coinciding Aquincum territory. To the north, it was bordered by the ripa and the prata militaris, and to the northwest-west by the legionary camp of Brigetio, its canabae and their territory (*regio*[11]). To the west-southwest, it was bordered by Mogetiana, in a narrower band. Between 214 and 258–260, the territory of the municipium of the Mogiones was bordered by Brigetio to the west-north-west and Mogetiana to the west-south-west. It was also bordered by the *ripa* to the north and by the territory of Aquincum to the east-south-east.

The inscriptions containing the name of the city provide a more precise delimitation of its territory, found on the edges or periphery of the area. The inscriptions discovered in the western area, which feature the name of the town abbreviated as M, can only be attributed to either Mogetiana or Mogionibus based on their location, unless additional information is provided in the text. The inscriptions pertaining to the city's territory are supplemented by texts, inscriptions, and diplomas related to the *civitas Azaliorum* and the *Azali*, which indicate the *Azalus* territory prior to the city's establishment. The *Azalus* area's boundaries are determined by the horizons of the inscriptions that mention the *Eravisci* to the east and the *Boii* to the west.[12] For the latter, please refer to the above text Nr. 1, which alone mentions the common boundary of the two civitates. The other known inscriptions document the western boundary of the *civitas Boiorum*[13], which may

10 Cf. Szabó 2018, 129–209.

11 Cf. AE 1944, 103 = RIU 663 = AE 1950, 105 and Borhy, Számadó 2008, 118–119 (inde AE 2008, 1086) a *centurio regionarius* from 210 AD, and a *beneficiarius tribuni militum* et *coregionarius* from the legio I Adiutrix of Brigetio. For an overview of the regio question see Árpád Szabó 1955, 217–132. The traditional notion of *regio*, with its religious background, may also correspond to the rectangular shape of the part of the Mogionibus territory towards Brigetio, as outlined here, within the concept of regio associated with the legio.

12 Cf. most recently Grbić 2014, 235–265 – for specific issues of the civitas Eraviscorum, with earlier literature see. Kovács 1998, 278–295. Inscriptions from near the border: Diósd: RIU 1347 = Ep. Pann 3, p. 26 = Grbić 2014, 137 = AE 1969/70, 493 (cf. AE 2004, 1133) = TitAq 1753 (B. Fehér), gravestone from the 2nd century: *Alorix | Bassi f(ilius) decu|rio Erav|iscus ann(orum) | XXXV h(ic) s(itus) e(st) | f(ilius?) p(atri?) p(ientissimo?).* (I also think that decurio can be taken in a military sense.) Tárnok: RMD 3, 152 = RMD 4, 228 = RMD 5, 345 = RHP 16 = Grbić 2014, 171 = AE 1994, 1480 = AE 2002, 1728, military diploma issued by Traianus in 114 *Advesioni Matici f(ilio) Erav(isco)* and through him *Suttae Touconis fil(iae) ux(ori) ei(us) Erav(iscae)* also citizenship.

13 Cf. the diploma issued to *Ti. Claudio Secundi f(ilio) Masculo Boio ex Pannon(ia)* in 145 by Antoninus Pius, Scherrer 2008, 149–159 = AE 2008, 1111 = Grbić 2014, 204. The last mention of the civitas so far. Deducting the length of service of the soldier conscripted from the civitas Boiorum, the dated of conscription is 120 AD.

have existed until the 120s, to the east-southeast of Carnuntum.[14] According to auctor sources, the eastern border of the civitas Boiorum was formed by the river Rába. Therefore, the Azalus area originally extended westwards to the Rába. Its north-western corner was near the Danube estuary of the Rába at Győr (Arrabona).[15] After the settlement of *legio I Adiutrix* in Brigetio in the 80s[16], the camp, the *canabae* and the fertile eastern territory of the Kisalföld (regio, later municipium and then *colonia* of Brigetio) were wedged from the north into the territory of the *civitas Azaliorum*. Based on the Vászoly[17] inscription and the environmental geography, it is possible that the Brigetio area extended at least as far as the foothills of the mountain range along the northern shore of Lake Balaton, and possibly even somewhat into the mountains. This suggests a potential connection between the territories of Mogetiana and Mogionibus in the southern half of the area between the Danube and Lake Balaton, including the Balaton highlands (Balatonfelvidék) and the Bakony region. The relationship between the Azalus territory and the Roman city is worth examining to determine if the creation of a city with a specific number of inhabitants resulted in the immediate organization of the civitas territory into an urban territory. This process may have been gradual as the inhabitants of the area progressed in their acquisition of citizenship. A diploma from Aquincum, dated 167, was given to Oxetio Naevionis f(ilio) Erav(isco).[18] By deducting 25 or more years of service, we can obtain dates of 142 or slightly earlier. This exceeds by more than a decade the date of foundation of the Aquincum municipium, which was founded in the 120s. This is also in accordance with the existence of vici organised into *pagi* of indigenous tradition[19] in the territory, after the foundation of the *municipium* of Aquincum, and probably elsewhere in the province and the empire[20].

---

14 See Grbić 2014, 278 - considers the year of the diploma as the last mention of the civitas - which is true for the year of its issuance, but not for the last year of the existence of the civitas. Inscriptions, e.g.: CIL 3, 14359,23 = CSIR Ö 1 3, 314 = Schober 171 = AEA 2006, 4 = AEA 2013/14, 18 = AE 1900, 66 = AEA 2016/17, 36 = AEA 2016/17, 74 = AEA 2016/17, 76 = AEA 2020/21, 44, dated on the 2nd half of the first century, f.p. Bruckneudorf (Carnuntum terr.): *Belatusa Cau|ti l(iberta) Boius pos|uit an(n)oru(m) XXX | hic sita | [est].*; Hild 157 = Grbić 2014, 197 = AEA 2005, 75 = AEA 2006, 7a = AEA 2007, 26 = AEA 2007, 77 = AEA 2008, 7 = AEA 2008, 40 = AEA 2008, 65 = AEA 2013/14, 18 = AE 1951, 64 = AE 1999, 1251 = AE 2003, 1285 = AEA 2016/17, 23, dated ont he first third of the 2nd century, f.p. Bruckneudorf (Carnuntum terr.): *M(arcus) Coc[c]eius | Caupianus pr(inceps) | c(ivitatis) B(oiorum) v(ivus) f(ecit) sibi et | Cocceiae Dago|vassae coniugi | anno[r]um LV - - - - - -*; CIL 3 4594 = CIL 3 11311 = CSIR Ö 1 3, 336 = Mander 629 = Schober 276 = Grbić 2014, 200 = AEA 2001/02, 40 = AEA 2008, 40 = AEA 2016/17, 23 = AEA 2016/17, 36, dated on the third third of the first century, f.p. Ebreichsdorf (Carnuntum terr.): *Ariomanus | Iliati f(ilius) Boi(us) | annorum | XV | h(ic) s(itus) e(st) | pater posuit.*

15 Cf. Fehér, Kovács FPA I. 2004, 59–60.

16 Cf. Lőrincz 2000, 151–158.

17 Vászoly, RIU S (TRH, Kovács P.) 78 = AE 2003, 1376: *[- - - dec(urioni)] m(unicipii) M(ogetianae) du[umviro - - -].*

18 CIL 16 123 = CIL 3 p. 888 (p. 1992) = RHP 33 = Grbić 2014, 184.

19 Cf. Kovács 1999, 114–115; Mráv – Ottományi 2005, 71–118.; Kovács 2013, 136; Ottományi 2014, 97–142.

20 Cf. Kovács 2013, 131–154; Bíró 2017; for an outlook on the topic see also e.g. Hanel, Schucany 1999.

The city's name appears in several inscriptions, with the most significant being the grave-stele from Tokod (below No. 23) in the northeast, the Bakonycsernye-Inotapuszta diploma (below No. 20) in the south, and the grave-stele from Almasfüzítő (below No. 22) in the northwest. The stele from Tokod includes the city's name with the abbreviation M, and the site confirms that the only possible resolution of M is Mogionibus. The letter M of the inscription found in the area of Almásfüzítő is suggested to be resolved as Mogionibus. This is because it was found east of Brigetio and lies roughly in line with Környe to the north, which forms the centre of the city. Additionally, this regional link is supported by the Általér river, which originates below Császár and flows through Környe before flowing into the Danube between Almásfüzítő and Dunaalmás. The inscriptions known as Mog(ionibus) or M(ogionibus), found along the lines connecting the three mentioned sites or slightly beyond them, clarify the boundaries of the territory.

Inscriptions from known sites in east-northeastern Pannonia that mention Azalians

Inscriptions in stone

2. Esztergom (Solva). Dated 51–70.
AE 1937, 138 = RIU 790 = Mander 617 = Grbić 2014, 109.
Solva | Iucundi | princ(ipis) Azali(orum) f(ilia) | ann(orum) IIX | pater pos(u)it.

3. Esztergom – Bánom (Solva). Dated 71–100.
AE 1997, 1261 = RIU S, 117 = RHP 139 = Mander 618 = Klio 1997, 180 = Grbić 2014, 110.
Dis Manib(us) sacrum || Asper | eq(ues) alae | Hisp(anorum) I | Aurian(ae) | Iucondo Talal|ni f(ilius) [[principi]] civ|itatis Azalior|um patri vivo et | ------

4. Sárisáp. Dated, third third of the first century / 2. century[21].
Schober 152 = RIU 769 = Grbić 2014, 114 (cf. AE 2014, 1047).
Aicca Cansali f(ilia) | Asalia an(n)oru|m XL Racio uxo|ris suae titulum | pos(u)it.

The erectors of the altar CIL III 4292 = RIU 405 = Grbić 111, f.p. Brigetio: *I(ovi) O(ptimo) M(aximo) s(acrum) | Aurel(ii) Vega|bius(?) et Valentis | principis.* may have been Azalian principes, the text, however, does not include a ethnonym and because of its location, does not provide any information on the territory.

21 On a linguistic basis, the fact that *anorum* instead of *annorum* and *posit* instead of *posuit* are given, does not make the dating more precise, cf. Fehér 2007, 378 *nn* general, *i* instead of *ui* phenomenon 336–369 is not discussed in terms of chronology.

Military diplomas[22]

5. Csabdi. Dated 146.
CIL 16 178 = AE 1947, 135 = AE 1949, 83 = RHP 44 = Grbić 2014, 118.
Imp(erator) Caes(ar) divi Hadriani f(ilius) divi Traiani | Parth(ici) n(epos) divi Nervae pron(epos) T(itus) Aelius Ha|drian(us) Antoninus Aug(ustus) | Pius ... Viatori Romani f(ilio) Asalo ...
The soldier, counting at least 25 years of service *(„quinis et vicenis pluribusve stipendi(i)s")*, was recruited in 121.

6. Regöly. Dated 148. (A diploma mentioning an Eraviscus person was also found here.[23] The geographical location of the site indicates that it was neither part of the civitas Azaliorum nor of the towns founded on it.)
CIL 16 180 = AE 1947, 37 = RMD 4, 272 = ZPE 203, 250 = RHP 25 = Grbić 2014, 119 = AE 2017, 1188.
Imp(erator) Caes(ar) divi Hadriani f(ilius) divi Traiani | Parth(ici) nepos d[i]vi Nervae pron(epos) T(itus) Aelius | Hadrianus Antoninus Aug(ustus) Pius ... Fusco Luci f(ilio) Azalo ...
The soldier, counting at least 25 years of service *(„quinis et vicenis pluribusve stipendi(i)s")*, was recruited in 123.

7. Kisbér/Ászár. Dated 148.
CIL 3 p. 1985 = AE 1890, 159 = AE 1891, 167 = CIL 16, 96 = ILS 2005 = RHP 45 = Grbić 2014, 120.
Imp(erator) Caes(ar) divi Hadr(iani) f(ilius) divi Traian(i) Part(hici) n(epos) | divi Nerv(ae) pronep(os) T(itus) Aelius Hadr(ianus) Anton(inus) | Aug(ustus) Pius ... Attae Nivionis f(ilio) Azalo ...
The soldier, counting at least 25 years of service *(„quinis et vicenis pluribusve stipendi(i)s")*, was recruited in 123.

8. Komárom (Brigetio). Dated 149. (For geographical and historical reasons, the site was neither part of the civitas Asaliorum after the establishment of legio I Adiutrix, nor of the towns founded on it.)
CIL 16 97 = CIL 3 p. 1986 (p. 2212) = RHP 46 = Grbić 2014, 121.

---

22 Komárom (Brigetio), CIL 3, p. 2212 = AE 2008, 75 = CIL 16, 49 = Grbić 2014, 115 = Brit. Rom 4,11, military diploma, issued in 105: *[Imp(erator) Caesar divi Nervae f(ilius) Nerva Traianus Augustus Germanicus Dacicus ... Lucconi Treni f(ilio) Dobunn(o) | et Tutulae Breuci filiae uxori eius Azal(ae) | et Simili f(ilio) eius ...* as the wife's name is in the ethnonym, it does not carry any information on the dated of recruitment from the Azalus area.

23 Military diploma: CIL 16 179 = RHP 24 = Grbić 2014, 179 = AE 1944, 102 = AE 1947, 30, military diploma issued by Hadrian *Reidomaro Siuppi f(ilio) Eravisc(o)* in 148 AD., f.p. Regöly.

Imp(erator) Caes(ar) divi Hadriani f(ilius) divi Traiani / Parth(ici) n(epos) divi Nerv(ae) pron(epos) T(itus) Aelius / Hadrianus Antoninus Aug(ustus) Pius ... Dasmeno Festi f(ilio) Azalo ...
The soldier, counting at least 25 years of service *(„quinis et vicenis pluribusve stipendi(i)s")*, was recruited in 124.

9. Komárom (Brigetio). Dated 150. (For geographical and historical reasons, the site was neither part of the civitas Asaliorum after the establishment of legio I Adiutrix, nor of the towns founded on it.)
CIL 3 p. 2213 (p. 2328,204) = AE 1894, 3 = ILS 9056 = CIL 16, 99 = RHP 47 = Grbić 2014, 122.
Imp(erator) Caes(ar) divi Hadriani f(ilius) divi Traian(i) Parth(ici) / nep(os) divi Ner(vae) pron(epos) T(itus) Aelius Hadrianus / Antoninus Aug(ustus) Pius ... [V]ictori Liccai(!) f(ilio) Azalo ...
The soldier, counting at least 25 years of service *(„quinis et vicenis pluribusve stipendi(i)s")*, was recruited in 125.

10. Őskü. Dated 154.
CIL 16 104 = CIL 3 p. 881 (p. 1988) = RHP 48 = Grbić 2014, 125.
Imp(erator) Caesar divi Hadriani f(ilius) divi Tra/iani Parthici nep(os) divi Nervae pr(onepos)/ T(itus) Aelius Hadrianus Antoninus Aug(ustus) / Pius ... Ursioni Busturonis f(ilio) Azalo ...
The soldier, counting at least 25 years of service *(„quinis et vicenis pluribusve stipendi(i)s")*, was recruited in 129.

11. Győr, near to (Arrabona). Dated 161.
RMD 5 430 = RMM 43 = Grbić 2014, 126 = AE 2001, 1640.
Imp(erator) Caes(ar) divi Hadriani f(ilius) divi Traiani Parthi|ci nep(os) divi Nervae pronep(os) T(itus) Aelius Hadri|anus Antoninus Aug(ustus) Pius ... Nigro Siusi f(ilio) Azalo ...
The soldier, counting at least 25 years of service *(„quinis et vicenis pluribusve stipendi(i)s")*, was recruited in 161.

12a–d. Four diplomas are still known to have been issued to soldiers of Azalus origin, but they are from an unknown location.[24] Although their chronology falls between 110 and 142, it does not impact the conclusions that can be drawn from the chronology of the previous diplomas. However, knowledge of their location would provide clarity regarding the conclusions drawn about the area.

24 AD 110: ZPE 176, 221 = Grbić 2014, 116 = AE 2011, 1790 = AE 2018, 1367 = ILD 2, 806; AD 112: RMD 4, 223 = RMM 15 = RHP 510 = Grbić 2014, 117 = AE 1997, 1782; AD 134: RMD 4, 250 = RMM 26 = Grbić 2014, 93 = AE 2006, 77; AD 142: ZPE 191, 272 = AE 2014, 1640 = AE 2015, 1118 = EpRom 2014, 61 n.1 = ILD 2, 823.

The civitas Azaliorum's area, as defined by auctor sources and the sites of stone inscriptions and diplomas, delineates the territory on which the city was founded and its boundaries were established. The soldiers' place of origin is listed as the name of their tribe rather than the name of their municipality in the diplomas above. This implies that they were recruited from the civitas Azaliorum, registered as such, and discharged with this place of origin. During the period between recruitment and discharge, a settlement of urban rank was established in the soldier's tribal territory within the civitas. However, this settlement could not be included in the soldier's personal registration as it was not his birthplace or origin within the city or urban territory. The town of his birth, established in the meantime, could also not be listed as his place of origin. It is important to note that settlements established during this period did not serve as proof of registration. By counting back from the latest known date of the civitas Azaliorum as the place of origin to the date of recruitment at least 25 years earlier, and comparing this with the known tribus of the municipium during the imperial period of its foundation, it is possible to determine roughly the date of the city's foundation based on the date of the latest known diploma.

The Sergia tribus and the Aelia pseudotribus show a Hadrianic foundation[25] (cf. below Nos. 16., 19., 20.), which is confirmed by some of the personal names known from the area, which I will summarize in the following study. Of all the currently countable diplomas related to this area, the soldier who received the diploma issued in 161 from a site near Győr (cf. above No. 10.) was recruited from the *civitas Azaliorum* in 136 AD, after at least 25 years of service. Based on the Győr diploma, it can be assumed that the *civitas Azaliorum* was urbanized, and urban territories were established no later than 136. There is no evidence of continuing service. According to the Tribus, the founding of the municipia of the *Mogiones* or of the *Mogetiones* was done on Hadrian's orders during the years 138 onwards. According to the *tribus*, the founding of the municipia of the *Mogiones* or of the *Mogetiones* was done on Hadrian's orders during the years 138 onwards. Therefore, the narrower time frame for their establishment is between 136 and 138, as opposed to the previously suggested period of 120s (Carnuntum, Aquincum, Mursa) for Hadrian's policy of founding cities in Pannonia. This period also coincides with the governorship of L. Aelius Caesar over both Pannonia from 136–137.[26] Among the well-managed military and civil affairs of the heir to the throne appointed by Hadrian by adoption (cf. HA v. Hadr. 23,11–13; v. Aeli 3,1–2), the foundation of two small towns in inner Pannonia may have been included. It is not possible to confirm, but the appearance of Aelia pseudotribus[27], introduced in the period alongside the Hadrianic Sergia tribus, may be linked to it, occurring in two of the city citizens, as opposed to the Hadrianic Sergia tribus documented in one example. For the foundation of the city, L. Aelius Caesar not only had the title of Caesar (after 19. July 136), i.e. the dignity and authority of a pretender to the throne, but was also invested with the office of consul by the emperor in 136 and in 137 as well. In 137,

25 On Hadrian's urban policy, cf. Boatwright 1999. For Pannonia cf. Mráv 2003, 125–137.

26 Cf. Fitz 1993, 475–477 no. 283 – L. Aelius Caesar. See Piso 1994, 198–200. The period is discussed in detail in Kovács FPA II. 2004, 183–191.

27 Forni 1985, 5. It also occurs in Aquincum, cf. TitAq 510 and CIL 8 2826 for Aquincum.

he served as consul and then proconsul. The latter position was essential for governing and commanding the provincial or two-provincial army. The XVdecemvir sacris faciundis high priest title was helpful in introducing the cult of Antinous in Carnuntum. However, this topic is not relevant to the current discussion of territories. L. Aelius Caesar's mandate covered both Pannonia, indicating that he had to address issues that impacted both provinces. These included civil affairs too, which was confirmed by the person and office of C. Claudius Maximus *iuridicus pr(o) pr(aetore) utriusque Pannoniae*, who was also assigned to both provinces.[28] The municipalisation of the territory of Azali (civitas Azaliorum) is a valid issue in civil affairs. It is important to maintain a clear and logical structure when discussing these issues. Specifically, the separation of the territory of the military region of Brigetio from the territory of the new municipality, the arrangement of the territory of Mogetiana in relation to the two previous ones, and the delimitation of its western and northern borders are important considerations. The statue of Hadrian, known by his inscription from Győr (Arrabona)[29], was erected in the area where the Rába (Arrabo) flows into the Danube. It was placed on the former border between the civitas Boiorum and the civitas Azaliorum. This may be related to the territorial division and change of status outlined here.

The territorial arrangement, which includes the foundation of the municipium of Mogiones (Mogionibus), can be dated to between February 136 and December 137 at the latest. This is supported by the diploma near Győr dated 8 February 161 and the presence of L. Aelius Caesar in Pannonia from 137 onwards. However, the *municipium Aelium Mogionensium* (Mogionibus) was founded in 137 AD under the proconsular authority (*imperium*) of L. Aelius Caesar, which covered both Pannonia, and the office of C. Claudius Maximus *iuridicus pr(o) pr(aetore)*, who was also assigned to him and had two provincial (*utriusque Pannoniae*) jurisdictions.

It may be questioned whether the foundation of the two towns in the civitas area should be dated at the same time. Based on current knowledge, the administrative systems of Mogetiana and Mogionibus were different, with Mogetiana being administered by duumvirs and Mogionibus by quattuorvirs. This may suggest different founding dates and/or statuses for the two cities. It is also possible that the administrative system of the civitas Azaliorum, as evidenced by the diplomas, existed in the territory not occupied by the previously founded city until the next city was established. Similarly, it is uncertain whether the disappearance of certain civitas institutions was immediate in the newly established municipium territories. Diplomas issued to Azalus soldiers cover the entire civitas area. Therefore, the date of issuance of the foundations falling within the area of one of the later cities can be directly verified in theory. Thus, the diplomas that fall within the probable territory of the municipium of the *Mogiones* would provide a more direct basis

28 Fitz 1993, 483–485 no. 287 – Claudius Maximus. See also RIU 1499.

29 Győr (Arrabona), CIL 3 4366 = ILS 319 = RIU 251, dated 137: *Imp(eratori) Caes(ari) | Traiano | Hadriano | Aug(usto) p(atri) p(atriae) trib(unicia) pot(estate) | XXI co(n)s(uli) III imp(eratori) II | L(ucius) Aelius Caes(ar) f(ilius) | trib(unicia) potes(tate) co(n)s(ul) II | proco(n)s(ul) XVvir | sacris faciund(is).*

for the foundation of *municipium Mogionibus*, while those falling outside it to the west-south-west would provide more data for the foundation of Mogetiana. Based on this, the Győr diploma could potentially be related to the western part of the civitas. The last data concerning the eastern part of the civitas, mentioning them, is found in the diploma of Öskü issued in 154 AD (see above No. 10). Using the diploma of Öskü and taking into account the year of recruitment of the soldier, the date of foundation of the municipium of Mogiones would be 129/130 AD. The incorporation of the camp and canabae of Brigetio, along with their respective territories (*regio*), into the *civitas Azaliorum* offers a plausible explanation for the establishment of two distinct Azalus ethnic towns. These towns were situated in close proximity to each other, with their borders only touching the mountainous area of the Balaton highlands, in the strip between Lake Balaton and the Brigetio region. At the same time, the complexity of territorial planning supports the greater probability that the fate of the three contiguous areas was arranged simultaneously. This, according to the above, based on the data of the Győr diploma and the commissions of L. Aelius Caesar and C. Claudius Maximus for both Pannonia, could therefore, once again emphasized, be in 137 AD.

A similar case also occured in 213: in autumn 213, Svetrius Sabinus, a friend of Caracalla, was given the task of organizing the territorial arrangement for both Pannonia, which was enforced from 214. Sabinus, a former legio commander who had previously held the rank of praetor, was given the rank and authority of *iudex vice Caesaris* (deputy emperor for legal affairs) to carry out this mission. In the same year, Brigetio and Mogionibus were included in Pannonia Inferior. By 214, Svetrius Sabinus was given the title of *consul ordinarius*, along with the dignities of *pontifex* and *augur*. He also had a statue of Caracalla erected in Aquincum, the seat of Pannonia Inferior. Aquincum had just become a consular province, probably towards the end of 213, and Svetrius Sabinus completed the inscription in 214, indicating his new dignities.[30] The administrative systems of the two ethnic Azalus cities may have been influenced by the area's particularities and social differences, resulting in different legal statuses. For instance, one city may have been founded as a municipum under Latin law, while the other as a municipum under Roman law, which could be reflected in their administrative systems.

Inscriptions containing the city name Mog(ionibus) / M(ogionibus)[31]

From the west and south-west, the urban territory can be verified by the presence of inscriptions attesting to the existence of Mogetiana: CIL 3 4338 = CIL 3 11043 = RIU 697, Brigetio (Komárom): *Moge(tiana)*; CIL 3 10993 = RIU 642, Ad Statuas (Ács-Vaspuszta): Moget(iana), and RIU S (TRH, Kovács P.) 78 = AE 2003, 1376, Vászoly: *[- - - dec(urioni)] m(unicipii) M(ogetianae) du[umviro - - -]*.

30 Cf. Szabó 2000, 85–109.

31 Cf. Szabó 2022, 163–167 and Szabó 2024.

As discussed here, the legionary camp and canabae of Brigetio, and its territory (regio) south of the Danube, fell between the territories of Mogionibus and Mogetiana, and above the latter. The northern band of the Brigetio area (camp and canabae) along the Danube, as described above, can be placed between Almásfüzítő-Neszmély – Odiavum/Azaum (in the east) and Ács Vaspuszta – Ad Statuas[32] (in the west), and this may be the narrowest part of the area, from where it widened out to the south-southwest and south-southeast. The inscriptions that have been found in the immediate settlement area of Brigetio, whether documenting Azali, Mogionibus or Mogetiana, cannot be included in the question of territory. Neither is there an inscription referring to the inhabitants of Brigetio, known from the castle of Tata[33], nor, finally, inscriptions relating to Brigetio itself, which have been found in the urban area of Brigetio since the beginning of the 3rd century[34].

The municipium and colonia of Brigetio likely had a large and fertile agricultural and forested area in the lowlands and Lake Balaton uplands, possibly extending as far west as the Rába (Arrabo) and south to the northern border of the territory of Mogetiana. The territories of Mogetiana and Mogionibus were primarily located in the Bakony, along the Kisbér-Bakonycsernye-Öskü line in a north-south direction. The territory of Mogetiana extended west-southwest between the northern coast of Lake Balaton and the military region of Brigetio. It also extended between the southern border of the territory of the municipium, then colonia of Brigetio.[35]

32 For the place see Gabler 1989. The inscription CIL 3 10993 = RIU 642 Moget(iana) from Ács-Vaspuszta does not allow to determine its relation to the territories of Brigetio and Mogetiana.

33 Tata, CIL 3 4281 = RIU 693 (cf. AE 1944, 117) = AE 2003, 1377, dated ont he first half of the 3rd century: *Modiasio Lucio et Aureliae | Valentinae soc(e)ris pientis|simis et Modiasiae Luciae | coniugi karissimae quae | vixit ann(os) XXV Aurel(ius) | Ant□h‘iochianus <d=F>ec(urio)* vel *Aug(ustalis) mun(icipii) | Brig(etionis) fac(iendum) c(uravit).*

34 Cf. e.g. Kisigmánd (Brigetio), AE 2006, 1043 = L. Borhy 2006, 38, dated on the first half of the 3rd century: - - - - - -| *[- - - harus]pex(?) | [- - -] dec(urio) | [mun(icipii) Br]ig(etionensium) c(urator) c(ivium) R(omanorum) | [- - -]s fil(ius) et h(eres) | [- - - mon(umentum?)] magnum | f(aciendum) c(uravit).*; Kisigmánd (Brigetio), RIU 651, kelt. 3. sz. eleje: - - - - - - | *[- - -]i Ex|[tricati(?)] dec(urionis) | [mun(icipii) Br]ig(etionis) c(uratoris) c(ivium) R(omanorum) | [- - -]s fil(ius) et h(eres) | [monum(entum)] magnum | f(aciendum) c(uravit).* etc.

35 See also e.g. Gabler 1993–1994, 149–155 and Gabler 1994, 377–419 with the earlier literature.

Mog(ionibus)[36]

13. Környe: *mun. M[o]g(ionibus).*

14. Környe: *[mun.] Mog(ionibus).*

15. Környe: *[[ordo Mog(ionibus)]].*

16. Környe / Tagyospuszta: *Serg(ia tribu) Mog(ionibus).*

17. Tata: *Mog[ionibus].*

18. Császár: *mun. Mog(ionibus).*

19. Császár: *Aelia (tribu) Mo|g(ionibus)*

20. Inotapuszta-Bakonycsernye: *Ael(ia tribu) Mogionibus.*

21. From outside the territory, from Aquincum (Budapest III): CIL 3 15166; TitAq 698; Szabó 2018, 149 Bizi: mun. Mog(ionibus), so this cannot be evaluated in terms of the border of the territory of Mogionibus.

M(ogionibus)[37]

22. Almásfüzítő-Neszmély (*Azaum/Odiavum*): *m(unicipium) M(ogionibus).* Based on the location of the site, the resolution can only be M(ogionibus).

23. Tokod (*Gardellaca / Cardabiaca*): *m(unicipium) M(ogionibus).* Based on the location of the site, the resolution can only be M(ogionibus).

Finally, there is also a fragmentary diploma of Császár (refer to above Nos. 18–19), issued in 222 to a soldier serving in the urban cohort of Rome. The soldier's name has not been

36 **13.** RIU 674; AE 1944, 104; EDCS9900276; Szabó 2018, 191–192 KO19#. **14.** RIU S (TRH), 111; AE 2003, 1376; EDCS27900187; Szabó 2018, 130–201 KO4#. **15.** RIU S (TRH), 110; AE 2003, 1375 (Mráv Zs.); EDCS30100965 = EDCS27900186. **16.** Kovács P. – Lőrincz B. 2010, 284 29 = AE 2010, 1258, Szabó 2018, 130–201 Kieg2#. **17.** Kisné Cseh – Kovács 2021, 57–70. = Kisné Cseh – Kovács, 2022, 241–252. **18.** CIL 3 15188; RIU 657; MNM Lapidarium Nr. 148, HD37713; Lupa 8080; Szabó 2018, 130–201 Kieg1#. **19.** Császár: CIL III 15188/4; RIU 660; CBI 276; EDCS-30301329; Szabó 2024 Appendix 16. **20.** Visy 1999, 575–584, 816–823; RMD 4, 303; AE 2002, 1182 (cf. AE 2017, 36; AE 2018,1284). **21.** CIL 3 15166; TitAq 698; Szabó 2018, 149 Bizi.

37 **22.** IPSSTA 33; RIU 707; RHP 201; EDCS 09900287; Szabó 2024 Appendix 15. **23.** RIU 763; Mander 2013, 625; Prohászka 2005, 13 (cf. AE 2005, 1197); HD038298; EDCS9900324; Lupa 3286; Szabó 2018, 120 TV3#.

preserved, but the site and date of issue suggest that he may have originated from Mogionibus,[38] like C. Iulius Passar (see Nr. 20.). Passar who was he was a Roman citizen, he served as a praetorian for 16 years. If he was recruited with Mogionibus origo, it would have been in 190, unless he had already been transferred to the praetorian guard as an active soldier. The earliest mention of the town's name in the form Mogionibus would be 190. If he was actively elevated to the praetorian guard as a legionary, for example by Septimius Severus in 193,[39] then, given his discharge in 206, his recruitment would have been in 186. Based on the probable date of the city's foundation in 137 AD and the short 50-year period before its assumed 186-year recruitment, it is possible that the author's grandfather was one of the first citizens to participate in the founding of the town and was enlisted in the Aelia *pseudotribus*.

Summary: the borders of the territory (Fig. 1.)

The boundary between Pannonia Superior and Pannonia Inferior, which was in place until 214, can be easily located between Csabdi and Bicske (Lusomana?). The Bicske sarcophagus was created by a magistrate and priest from Aquincum[40], while the diploma issued to the Azalus soldier from Csabdi (refer to above No. 5) has already been mentioned. The tomb fragment at Mány[41] located towards the north-east, was likely created by a magistrate of Aquincum and high priest of Pannonia inferior during the early Severan period. This suggests that the provincial border may have extended slightly further north from Mány, through Piliscsév in the Danube bend, and possibly reaching the Danube below Visegrád (Pone Navata) at Dunabogdány (Cirpi).

The territory[42] has the following reference points: the north-western corner could have been at Odiavum/Azaum (see above No. 22), and the western corner at Kisbér/Ászár (see above No. 7). These two points cannot be connected by a direct line because Szákszend is located a few kilometres away. Szákszend is opposite the Császár, which marks a secure territorial point (see Nos. 18–19). An altar was erected in Szákszend by the *legatus* of Pannonia Inferior between 130/131–133.[43] The presence of the *legatus* may have been

---

38 RMD 5, 460 = AE 2000, 1203 = AE 2011, 51.

39 Cf. e.g. Birley 1971, 89–107. See also Cenati 2023, 258–260 Nr. C5., Roma, saec. 3 in.: Mogi(- - -) = Szabó 2024: Mogi(onibus), with the previous full literature.

40 Bicske (Lusomana?), CIL 3 3368 = RIU 1356 = Ep. Pann 3, p. 26 (inde AE 2002, 1176), cf. AE 2004, 1133 and AE 2006, 1088 (Á. Szabó) = TitAq 1721 (B. Lőrincz), dated from 194 until the first third of the 3rd century: *D(is) M(anibus) || Ulpiae Antonillae quon(dam) Ulpi | Candidiani |(centurionis) filia(e) T(itus) Ael(ius) Verinus | dec(urio) col(oniae) Aq(uincensium) flame<n=M> du(u)mvir|alis sacerdos urbis Romae | coniugi pientissimae <q=O>uae | vixit annis XXIIII.*

41 Agócs, Lencsés, Szabó Er. 2021, 11–17.

42 Cf. also MRT 5.

43 Szákszend (Brigetio terr.), CIL 3 4356 = CIL 3 11077 = RIU 649 = AEA 2020/21, 26, dated 130/131–133 (cf. Lőrincz B. FPA II. english, 149, hungarian 199 and AE 1937, 213): *Nymph[is] | sacr(um) | L(ucius) Attius | Macro | leg(atus) Aug(usti)* and Szákszend (Brigetio terr.) CIL 3 4355 = RIU 654, dat-

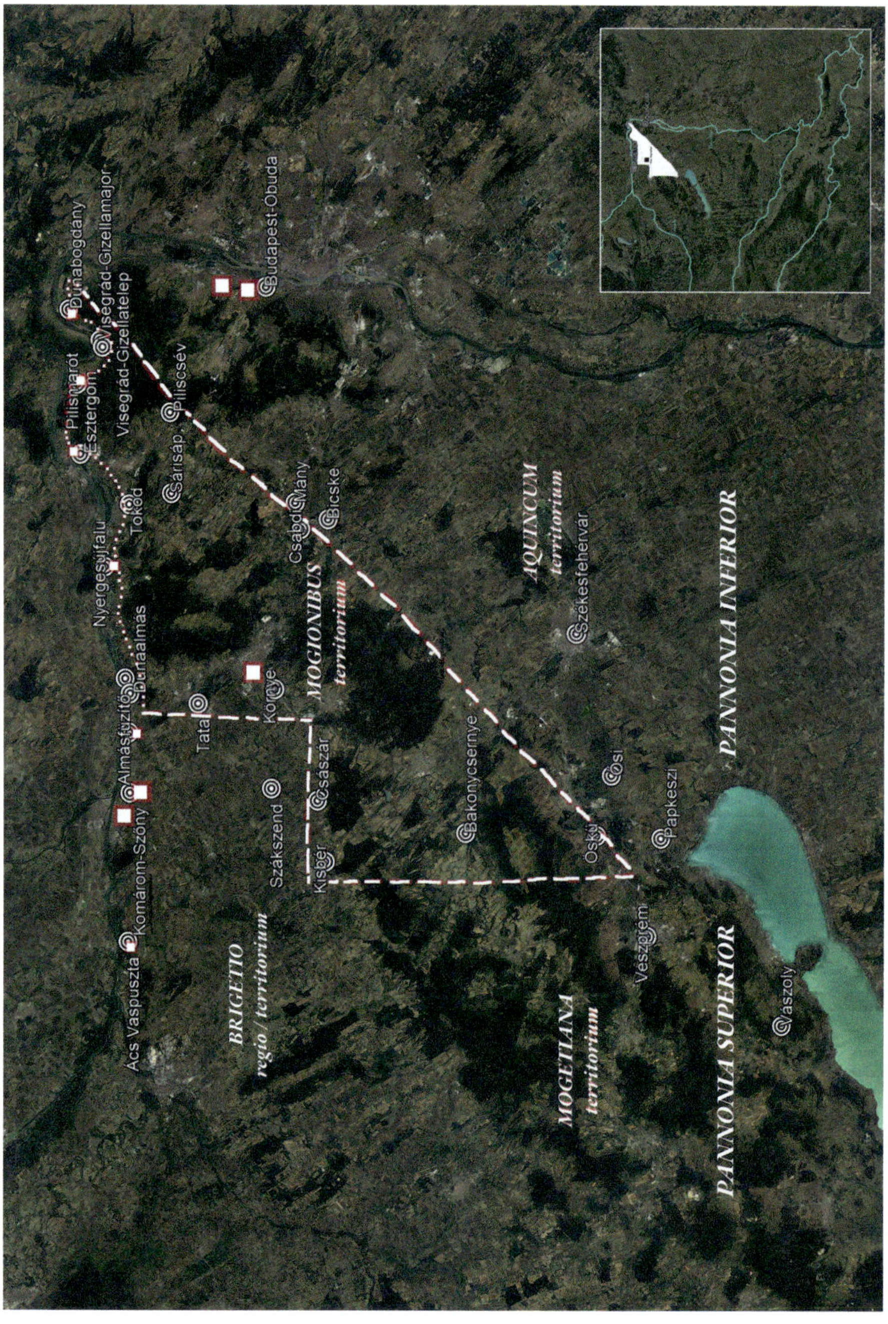

Fig. 1: The boundaries, location and size of the territory of Municipium Mogionibus in Pannonia, and the sites discussed in the text (Drawn by Á. Szabó using GoogleEarth).

primarily due to the legio, while the decurio clearly indicates an eastern point of Brigetio's 3rd century territory, opposite the territory of *Mogionibus*. The Szákszend inscriptions align the north-western margin of the territory of *Mogionibus* with the valley of the small river Által ér. Without them, a straight line could be drawn between Almásfüzitő and Kisbér/Ászár, which would then be parallel to the southern border of the territory. The Általér river originates from Császár and flows in a southeasterly direction until it reaches Mór and Pusztavám, where it turns sharply to the north-northwest. It then flows between Almásfüzitő and Dunaalmás before joining the Danube. The language used is clear, concise, and objective, with a formal register and precise word choice. The sentence structure and logical flow of information are well-maintained. No changes in content have been made. The small river, which was navigable during the Roman era, flows through Környe (cf. Nos 13–16) and Tata (cf. No 17). Therefore, the associated landscape naturally falls within the territory of the *municipium Mogionibus*, which is centred on Környe. This fact can be proven from archaeological and epigraphic points of view. The southwestern corner of Mogionibus' territory may have been at Öskü (see above No. 10). Bakonycsernye-Inotapuszta is located between Kisbér/Ászár and Öskü (see above No. 20). In the area of Papkeszi and Ősi, a few kilometres below Öskü, two Pannonia Inferior inscriptions are known, one dated 197 and the other probably from before 214 AD.[44] The northeastern corner of *Mogionibus'* territory was situated in the Danube bend, below the Visegrád region, which was a significant strategic point at Cirpi (Dunabogdány), according to the provincial border until 214. At this point, the Danube is reached by a straight border line that can be extended from Piliscsev (see below). The direction of this line is parallel to the course of the Danube meander below Visegrád (Pone Navata) in the area.

Its northern boundary was the Danube and the part below the military area of the Danube camps[45] and their vici: Almásfüzitő-Neszmély (Odiavum/Azaum), Nyergesújfalu (Crumerum), north of Tokod (Gardellaca/Cardabiaca) then Esztergom (Solva), from where two inscriptions with Azalus ethnonyms are known (cf. Nos. 2–3 above) and Pilismarót (Ad Herculem), already in the Danube bend, representing a small eastern band between Visegrád (Pone Navata) and Dunabogdány (Cirpi). Above Cirpi, on the inscriptions of Visegrád-Gizellatelep, there are also indigenous Azalus names.[46]

---

ed on the first half of the 3rd century: *Bonae* ❦ | *Fortunae* ❦ | *M(arcus) Septimius* | *Valentinus* | *dec(urio) Brig(etionis)* | *ex voto.*

44 Papkeszi, CSIR U 8, 123 = RIU 1419 = Ep. Pann. 3, 36 = AE 1976, 553 = AE 1994, 1390 (cf. AE 2004, 1133) = TitAq 1926 (B. Lőrincz), dated 197: *T(itus) Fl(avius) T(iti) fil(ius) Qu(i)r(ina) Ius<t=I>inus* | *vet(eranus) leg(ionis) II Ad(iutricis) dom(o) Sirm(io)* | *ann(orum) LXX sibi et Iuliae* | *Optatae coniugi* | *vivae{s* ❦ *f(aciendum) c(uravit) d(ecreto) d(ecurionum?)* | *Lat<e=F>ran(o) et Rufino co(n)s(ulibus).* and Ősi, RIU S (TRH Kovács P.), 70 = ZPE 179, 273 = AE 2002, 1210 = AE 2011, 1018 = TitAq 1854 (G. Alföldy – P. Kovács), dated first half of the 3rd century: *------* | *[e]t Q(uinto) Vi[---]|niano [---]* | *col(oniae) Sep(timiae) [Aq(uincensium) ---]* | *col(legii?) T(ito) Vi[---]* | *Victori[no --- fili]|is eius E[---]* | *[V]ir(ius) Merc[---]* | *[---]S[---]* | *------.*

45 On this cf. Lőrincz 2001, 78, 83, 93, 96 and Visy 2001, 37–53.

46 For inscriptions of the region see RIU 3, including e.g. 802 (Pilismarót) and Kovács, Lőrincz 2010, 277–287, and Kovács, Lőrincz 2011, 64–99.

In the area, the road next to the ripa and the Limes road diverge, the latter leading from the Öregárok of Táti through Tokod (Gardellaca/Cardabiaca) to Piliscsév[47]. The site may have been important first as a provincial border point, and later only as a Limes-road location, also according to the milestones found there, complemented by an altar dedicated earlier by the provincial governor for the welfare of Caracalla or Elagabalus.[48] The question may arise as to whether Mogionibus' territory to the north extended only as far as the *Limes* road. However, the status of the provincial or military road was not linked to the territory; it simply passed through it. The forts along the ripa and their vici could not belong to the municipium as they were built in the military area, and this strip of land cannot be counted as part of the city's territory.[49] The inscription of Almásfüzítő (above No. 22) by a decurion of Mogionibus, a former soldier, is noteworthy for its indication of a connection between the veteran and the fort/vicus. However, it does not prove that the vicus of Azaum/Odiavum belonged to the territory of Mogionibus. The territory towards the ripa extended only to the edge of the military zone. However, the territory of Tokod (Cardabiaca/Gardellaca) was included in the region, despite the lack of evidence for an early imperial military presence. A fortress was constructed during the late imperial period under different administrative conditions.

The southern border of the territory coincides with the common border of Pannonia Superior and Pannonia Inferior. The border is marked from west to east by the following places: Öskü, Csabdi, Piliscsév, Dunabogdány. Bicske, located a few kilometres below Csabdi, has long been identified as an area belonging to Pannonia Inferior before 214 (cf. e.g. TitAq 1721 l.c.). More recently, the nearby Mány is also very likely to have been part of Pannonia Inferior.[50] The borders of the territory to the northwest and southwest run parallel to the north-south course of the Danube, while the east-west border between them is parallel to the east-west course of the Danube. The use of parallel lines indicates that the river was also utilized as a reference system for surveying and demarcating the territory, potentially for its centuriation as well. The mensors did not solely rely on the western foothills of the Vértes and the valley of the Általér to establish the boundaries of the territory. The territory's southern border extends northeastward along the southern

47 Ld. See DLP 2011, 65–73 and Visy 2001 (=2003), 42.

48 Piliscsév, CIL 3 3637 = RIU 800 (cf. AE 2000, 1185), dated 214–217 or 218–222 (W. Eck): *Iovi Optimo M[ax(imo)] | Neptuno Serap[idi] | pro salut[e et] victor[ia] | et perpetuitate | [I]mp(eratoris) Caesaris | [M(arci) A]urel(i) ◻Antonini◻ | [Pii] Felicis Aug(usti) | [L(ucius) Al]fenus Avitianus | [leg(atus)] eius pr(o) pr(aetore) | prov(inciae) Pann(oniae) inf(erioris).*; CIL 3 4634, kelt. 244–249: *Imp(eratori) Caes(ari) | M(arco) Iul(io) Philippo | P(io) F(elici) Invicto Aug(usto) | Part(h)ico maximo | pontifici maximo | trib(uniciae) potestatis | p(atri) p(atriae) proco(n)s(uli) a Br(i)g(etione) | m(ilia) p(assuum) XXXIII.*; CIL 3 4633, kelt dated 286–310: *Imp(eratori) Caesari | M(arco) Aur(elio) Val(erio) Maxi|miano P(io) F(elici) Aug(usto) | pontifici max|[imo - - -] | - - - - - -;* CIL 3 4632, kelt. dated 287–310: *Imp(erator) Caesar | [- - -]us Maximi|anus [- - -]ER[- - -] | Aug(ustus) P(ius) F(elix) p(ontifex) m(aximus) | trib(unicia) p[ot(estate) - - -] co(n)s(ul) | p(ater) p(atriae) | m(ilia) p(assuum) XXXII.*

49 On this question see e.g. Kovács 1999.

50 Cf. Agócs, Lencsés, Szabó Er. 2021, 11–21. See also the comments of P. Kovács and Á. Szabó, in SEP 15, in print.

foothills of the Bakony Mountains, then continues along the southern foothills of the Vértes Mountains, and finally reaches the Pilis Mountains, where it meets the Danube River at Dunabogdány. The urban centre of the municipalised region in the Környe area and the area of Tata are the most significant locations within the territory. A milestone marking the Roman road and two inscriptions documenting the city, one of which was erected by the quattuorvir and flamen of the city, are located in the Császár area (cf. Nos. 13–19).[51] The terrain of the *municipium Mogionibus* was predominantly hilly and mountainous, suggesting that animal husbandry may have been a more significant economic activity than agriculture.

The borders of the territory were drawn based on existing data, with some adjustments made to account for the terrain, such as mountain tops and watercourses. It is possible that the real borders of the territory consist of straight lines with different directions. This is particularly evident for the southern territorial border, which coincides with the provincial border, and for the western border sections. In the north-western border sections, the plain terrain of the eastern Kisalföld may have provided the opportunity to measure straight borders in either north-south or east-west directions. The northern border of the territory was predetermined and could only be oriented towards the Danube and the area of the riverside fortresses and *vici*. Border lines that are close to a straight line also made it easier to measure the area, the *centuriatio*.[52] The *municipium*, or urban centre, was situated at the heart of the territory, along the area's axes between the borders (refer to Fig. 1).

In following researches, I will cover various sites, inscriptions, and significant archaeological discoveries within the territory.

Bibliography

Agócs N., Lencsés Zs., Szabó Er. 2021. Egy tartományi főpap felirata Mányról, Alba Regia, 49, 11–21.

Birley, A. E. 1971. Septimius Severus. The African Emperor, London-New York.

Bíró, Sz. 2017. Die zivilen Vici in Pannonien, Monographien des RGZM Bd. 131., Mainz.

Boatwright, M. T. 1999. Hadrian and the Cities of the Roman Empire, Princeton.

Borhy L., Számadó E. 2008. Feliratok egy késő római kőladasírból a brigetiói Gerhát temetőből, SEP 1, Budapest, 115–132.

Borhy, L. 2006. Vezető Komárom város római kori kőemlékeihez, Komárom.

Bödőcs A., Kovács G. 2011. A római kori birtokrendszer kialakítása és tájformáló hatása Pannoniában, Geodézia és kartográfia 63, 2011/3, 20–25.

CBI. Schallmayer, E., Eibl, K., Ott, J., Preuss, G., Wittkopf, E. 1990. Der römische Weihebezirk von Osterburken I: Corpus der griechischen und lateinischen Beneficiarier-Inschriften des Römischen Reiches, Stuttgart.

51 Szabó 2022, 175.

52 Thanks also here to Péter Kovács for his observations.

Cenati, C. 2023. Miles in urbe. Identità e autorappresentazione nelle iscrizioni dei soldati di origine danubiana e balcanica a Roma, Roma.

DLP. Visy, Zs. (ed.-szerk.). 2011. A Danube Limes Program régészeti kutatásai 2008–2011 között / The Danube Limes Project Archaeological research between 2008–2011, Pécs.

Ep. Pann. Alföldy, G. 2004. Epigraphica Pannonica III, Specimina Nova Universitatis Quinqueecclesiensis 18, 1–48.

Fehér B. 2007. Pannonia latin nyelvtörténete, Budapest.

Fitz, J. 1993. Die Verwaltung Pannoniens in der Römerzeit vol. II., Budapest.

Fitz, J. 1994. Die Verwaltung Pannoniens in der Römerzeit vol. III., Budapest.

Forni, G. 1985. Le tribù Romane. III.1. Le Pseudo-tribù Roma, 5.

FPA. Kovács, P., Fehér, B. (eds.). 2004-. Fontes Pannoniae Antiquae I–VII (II.: 2004; IV. 2007), Budapest.

Gabler, D. 1989. The Roman fort at Ács-Vaspuszta on the Danubian limes, BAR IS 531, Oxford.

Gabler, D. 1993–1994. A Balatontól északra lévő terület római kori településtörténetének néhány kérdése, Veszprém Megyei Múzeumok Közleményei 19–20, 149–155.

Gabler, D. 1994. Die ländliche Besiedlung Oberpannoniens, in Bender, H., Wolff, H. (Hrsg.), Ländliche Besiedlung und Landwirtschaft in den Rhein-Donau-Provinzen des Römischen Reiches, Passauer Universitätschriften zur Archäologie, Espelkakmp, 377–419.

Galli, M. 2012. Il culto e le immagini di Antinoo, in M. Sapelli Ragni (cura): Antinoo. Il fascino della bellezza. Catalogo della mostra (Tivoli, 4 aprile-4 novembre 2012), Roma, 38–63.

Grbić, D. 2014. Tribal Communities in Illyricum. Pre-urban Administrative Structures in the Roman Provinces between the Adriatic and the Danube (first–third centuries), Belgrade.

Hanel, N., Schucany, C. (eds.). 1999. Colonia – municipium – vicus: Struktur und Entwicklung städtischer Siedlungen in Noricum, Rätien und Obergermanien. Beiträge der Arbeitsgemeinschaft ‚Römische Archäologie' bei der Tagung des West- und Süddeutschen Verbandes der Altertumsforschung in Wien 21.–23.5.1997, BAR International Series 783, Oxford.

Hild, F. 1968. Supplementum epigraphicum zu CIL III: das pannonische Niederösterreich, Burgenland und Wien 1902–1968, Wien.

Kovács P., Kisné Cseh J. 2021. Egy római mérföldkő Tatáról és a Capita Viarum Pannoniában, in Kovács P., Szabó Á. (szerk.): SEP, 12, Budapest, 57–70.

Kovács, P., Kisné Cseh, J. 2022. A Roman milestone from Tata and the capita viarum in Pannonia, in: Budai Ballogh, T., Láng, O., Vámos, P. (eds.), Aquincum aeternum. Studia in honorem Paula Zsidi. Aquincum Nostrum II.9., Budapest, 241–252.

Kovács, P., Lőrincz, B. 2010. Neue römische Inschriften aus Komitat Komárom-Esztergom, ZPE, 174, 277–287.

Kovács P., Lőrincz B. 2011. Új római feliratok Komárom-Esztergom megyéből II., SEP, 3, 64–99.

Kovács, P. 1998. Civitas Eraviscorum. Antaeus, 24–25, 278–295.

Kovács P. 1999. Vicus és Castellum kapcsolata az Alsó-Pannoniai Limes mentén, PPKE-BTK Sorozat: Studia Classica, Piliscsaba.

Kovács, P. 2003. Mogetiana und sein Territorium, in Szabó, Á., Tóth, E. (Hrsg.), Pannonica. Provincialia et archaeologia. Studia sollemnia Eugenio Fitz octogenario dedicata. LibArch, 1, 277–306.

Kovács, P. 2013.Territoria, pagi and vici in Pannonia, in Eck, W., Fehér, B., Kovács, P. (Hrsg.), Studia Epigraphica in memoriam Géza Alföldy, Antiquitas Reihe, 1 Bd. 61. Bonn, 131–154.

Kovács, P. 2015. Admistrative changes in Pannonia under Diocletian and Constantine, in: Zerbini, L. (a cura di): Culti e religiosità nelle province Danubiane. Atti del II Convegno Internazionale Ferrara 20–22 Novembre 2013. Pubblicazione del LAD Laboratorio di studi e ricerche sulle Antiche province Danubiane Università degli Studi di Ferrara, Dipartimento di Studi Umanistici II. Bologna, 287–298.

Lőrincz, B. 2000. Legio I Adiutrix, in: Le Bohec, Y. (éd.): Les légions de Rome sous le Haut-Empire, 151–158.

B. Lőrincz. 2001. Die römischen Hilfstruppen in Pannonien während der Prinzipatszeit. Teil I: Die Inschriften. O. Harl (Hrsg.): Wiener Archäologische Studien 3, Wien. (= RHP)

Mander, J. 2013. Portraits of children on Roman funerary monuments, Cambridge.

MNM Lapidarium. Nagy, M. 2007. Lapidárium. A Magyar Nemzeti Múzeum régészeti kiállításának vezetője: Római kőtár, Budapest. (= 2013 english version)

Mráv, Zs. 2003. Kaiserliche Bautätigkeit zur Zeit Hadrians in den Städten Pannoniens. Acta Antiqua Academiae Scientiarum Hungarica, 43, 125–137.

Mráv Zs. 2008. A pannoniai városok közösségi szoborállításai. Philippus Arabs szoborbázisa Környéről, Esztergom Megyei Múzeumok Közleményei, 12 (2006–2008), 105–155.

Mráv Zs., Ottományi K. 2005. A pagus Herculius és vicusainak Terra Mater oltára Budaörsről, Specimina Nova Universitatis Quinqueecclesiensis, 19, 71–118.

MRT 5. Horváth I. H., Kelemen M., Torma I. 1979. Magyarország Régészeti Topográfiája 5: Komárom megye régészeti topográfiája, Esztergomi és dorogi járás, Budapest.

Nagy, M. 2003. Die Beziehung der im Siedlungsgebiet der Urbevölkerungsgruppen entstandenen Civitates und Munizipii, in Szabó, Á., Tóth, E. (Hrsg.). Bölcske. Römische Inschriften und Funde. LibArch, 2, Budapest, 439–464.

Peachin, M. 1996. Iudex Vice Caesaris: Deputy Emperors and the Administration of Justice During the Principate, Stuttgart.

Piso, I. 1994. Zur Tätigkeit des L. Aelius Caesar in Pannonien, Carnuntum Jahrbuch, 198–200.

Prohászka, P. 2005. Tokod a rómaiak korában – Tokod in der Zeit der Römer,Tokod.

Šašel Kos, M. 2009. Antinous in Upper Moesia – The Introduction of a New Cult, in: M. G. Angeli Bertinelli, Donati A. (eds.), Opinione pubblica e forme di comunicazione a Roma: il linguaggio dell'epigrafia. Faenza, 177–188.

Scherrer, P. 2008. Bau und Brand - Aspekte der Holznutzung im römischen Aelium Cetium, Römisches Österreich. Jahresschrift der österreichischen Gesellschaft für Archäologie, 31, 149–159.

Schober, A. 1923. Die römischen Grabsteine von Noricum und Pannonien, Wien.
Szabó, Á. 2000. Svetrius Sabinus c.v. "újabb" felirata Pannoniából. – Das „neuere" Inschrift des Svetrius Sabinus c.v. aus Pannonien, Folia Archaeologica, 48, 85–109.
Szabó Á. 2018. 'Quaestiones Valerianae'. A belső valeriai katonai objektumok szervezési kérdései, az erődök szpólia-adatai és az újabb környei kutatások (Organisational problems of the inner military establishments in Valeria ripensis, the spolia data of the inner forts and the latest research in Környe). LibArch Ser. nova, Supplementum 3. Budapest.
Szabó, Á. 2022. Source data for municipium Aelium Mogionibus (Környe, Komárom-Esztergom County, Hungary), Acta Archaeologica Academiae Scientiarum Hungaricae, 73.2, 163–167.
Szabó, Á. 2024. Municipium Aelium Mogionibus: On the question of the name of the city on the basis of the Bakonycsernye-Inotapuszta military diploma, in Bîrliba, L. (ed.), Vol. Mensa Rotunda Epigraphica, Iaşi, 2022 sept. 20–21. s.a.
Szabó Ár. 1995. Roma Quadrata, Antik Tanulmányok / Studia Antiqua, 2.4, 217–232.
Tóth, E. 2003. Zur Frage der Stadt Mogetiana, in Szabó, Á., Tóth, E. (Hrsg.), Pannonica. Provincialia et archaeologia. Studia sollemnia Eugenio Fitz octogenario dedicata. LibArch, 1, 307–330.
Visy, Zs. 1999. Severus et Antoninus C. Iulio Passari, in Vaday, A. (ed.), Pannonia and beyond. Studies in honour of László Barkóczi. Antaeus, 24. Budapest, 575–584, 816–823.
Visy Zs. 2001. A ripa Pannonica Magyarországon, Budapest (= Visy, Zs. 2003. The Ripa Pannonica in Hungary, Budapest).

Q. Marcius Turbo

Ekkehard Weber

Zu den nicht wenigen Dingen, die den Jubilar mit Wien verbinden, gehört auch eine Ehreninschrift für Q. Marcius Turbo Fronto Publicius Severus, die mit vielen anderen im 18. Jh. durch den adeligen Infanterieoffizier Giuseppe Ariosti aus dem Raum der dakischen Provinzhauptstadt *Sarmizegetusa* nach Wien gebracht worden ist, weil dieser das besondere Interesse Kaiser Karls VI. für römische epigraphische Altertümer kannte. Ariosti hielt sich im Stab des Prinzen Eugen im – damals österreichischen – Siebenbürgen auf, während dieser die Befestigungsarbeiten der Stadt im Bereich des alten Römerlagers *Apulum* – Karlsburg, jetzt Alba Iulia – gegen die Türken leitete. Viele der bei dieser Gele-

Abb. 1: Die Inschrift des Q. Marcius Turbo in der Nationalbibliothek in Wien (copyright Ekkehard Weber)

genheit gefundenen Inschriften oder solche aus der Umgebung, auch aus dem Raum von *Sarmizegetusa*, sind damals nach Wien gebracht worden.[1]

> CIL III 1462; ILS 1324; IDR 3.2, 96; Beutler – Weber 23 Nr. 7 mit weiterer Literatur; Lupa.at/6731 (Abb. 1).
> *Q. Marcio Turboni Frontoni Publicio Severo praef(ecto) praet(orio) Imp(eratoris) Caesaris Traiani Hadriani Augusti p(atris) p(atriae) colon(ia) Ulp(ia) Traian(a) Aug(usta) [Dac]ica Sarmizegetus(a).*

Es ist aber nicht die einzige Inschrift, die uns von ihm erhalten ist, ganz abgesehen davon, dass dieser Mann wegen seiner Bedeutung auch in der antiken und modernen Literatur schon vielfach Beachtung gefunden hat.[2] Weitgehend gleichlautend ist eine zweite Inschrift aus Dakien, die in *Tibiscum* – Caransebeş gefunden wurde, aber wohl ebenso aus *Sarmizegetusa* stammt:

> CIL III 1551 (p. 1417); IDR 3.1, 131; Lupa.at/15197.
> *Q(uinto) Marcio Turb[oni] Frontoni Publicio Severo praef(ecto) praet(orio) Imp(eratoris) Caes(aris) Aelii Traiani Hadriani Augusti p(atris) p(atriae) colon(ia) Ul⸢p⸣(ia) Traian(a) Aug(usta) Dacica Sarmizegetus(a).*

Im Folgenden soll versucht werden, aus der literarischen und epigraphischen Überlieferung einige der entscheidenden Stationen in der Karriere dieses Mannes nachzuzeichnen.[3] Die vermutlich älteste und eher zufällige Nachricht, die wir haben, stammt aus der Grabinschrift eines Soldaten der *legio II Adiutrix* aus *Aquincum* – Budapest:

> CIL III 14349; TitAq 2, 588; Lupa.at/2706.
> *C(aius) Castricius C(ai filius) O⸢u⸣f(entina) Victor Como mil(es) leg(ionis) II Ad(iutricis) (centuria) M(arci) Turbonis an(norum) XXXVIII stip(endiorum) XIIII h(ic) s(itus) e(st) L(ucius) Lucilius fr(ater) et he(res) posuit p(ro) p(ietate).*

Aus seiner weiteren Karriere wird klar, dass dieser Zenturio Marc(i)us Turbo kein schlichter Truppenoffizier aus dem Mannschaftsstand war, sondern diese Funktion nur der ers-

---

1 Über die Geschichte und Schicksale dieser Sammlung, die sich heute im Stiegenhaus der Österreichischen Nationalbibliothek in Wien befindet, ist schon mehrfach gehandelt worden; zuletzt (kurz) Beutler, Weber (Hrsg.) 2005, 8–9.

2 Diese Belege und die Literaturzitate, die im Folgenden nur teilweise angeführt werden können, sind sorgfältig zusammengestellt von Petersen 1970, 188–190 Nr. 249, und in der sehr ausführlichen Behandlung dieses Mannes von Piso 2013, bes. 67–109. Älter und teilweise abweichend Dobó 1968, 46–48 Nr. 31.

3 Eine vollständige Biografie zu geben ist hier nicht beabsichtigt; siehe dazu neben Piso und dem oben angeführten PIR-Zitat (und der dort jeweils angegebenen Literatur) nur die Behandlung in den Standard-Handbüchern von Stein 1930, 1597–1600; Hanslik 1979, 1005 und Eck 1999, 865, jeweils mit weiterer Literatur.

te Schritt in einer, wie sich zeigen wird, vor allem militärischen Laufbahn eines Mannes aus dem Ritterstand gewesen ist. So scheint eine Ehreninschrift aus *Tibur* – Tivoli die für eine solche Laufbahn vorgesehene zweite Funktion als *primus pilus* zu enthalten und zugleich den Nachweis, dass er in den großen Feldzügen Trajans die seinem Rang entsprechenden militärischen Auszeichnungen erhalten hat:

> *[Q.] Marcio [C. f. Tro(mentina)] Turb[oni Fro]ntoni Pub[licio Severo] [p(rimo) p(ilo) bi]s donis do[nato bello Dacico et Part]hico ...*

Soweit aber seine Verwendung als Truppenoffizier. Eine Inschrift aus *Kyrrhos* – Nebi Huri, Syrien, nennt neben diesem zweiten Primipilat eine Reihe von höheren militärischen Kommandofunktionen, aber auch zivilen Ämtern – und ein Detail zu seiner Herkunft:

> AE 1955, 225.
> *[Q. Marcio] C. fil. Tro(mentina) Frontoni Turboni Publicio Severo domo Epidauro p(rimo) p(ilo) bis praef(ecto) vehic(ulorum) trib(uno) coh(ortis) VII vigil(um) trib(uno) equ(itum) sin[g(ularium)] Aug(usti) trib(uno cohortis ..?) pr[ae]t(oriae) proc(uratori) Ludi magni praef(ecto) class[is] pr(aetoriae) Misenensis P. Va[le]rius P. f. Qui[r(ina) Va]lens o[b m]eritis.*[4]

Auch ein bemerkenswertes Militärdiplom aus Sardinien zeigt, dass er im Jahr 114 Kommandant der Flotte von Misenum war:

> CIL XVI 60 (p. 215)
> Der Kaiser Trajan verleiht die üblichen Privilegien hier offenbar ausschließlich den Mannschaften *qui naviga[verunt in qua]driere Ope*[5] *et [militaverunt in] classe praetor[ia Misenensi] sub Q. Marcio Tu[rbone ...*

Noch im selben Jahr finden wir ihn aber an einem ganz anderen Kriegsschauplatz:

> Eusebius, Kirchengeschichte 4, 2, 1–4 (gekürzt; vgl. Rufinus, Hist. eccl. 4, 2, 3–4)):
> Ἤδη γοῦν τοῦ αὐτοκράτορος εἰς ἐνιαυτὸν ὀκτωκαιδέκατον ἐλαύνοντος, αὖθις Ἰουδαίων κίνησις ἐπαναστᾶσα πάμπολυ πλῆθος αὐτῶν διαφθείρει. ἔν τε γὰρ Ἀλεξανδρείαι καὶ τῇ λοιπῇ Αἰγύπτῳ καὶ προσέτι κατὰ Κυρήνην, ὥσπερ ὑπὸ πνεύματος δεινοῦ τινος καὶ στασιώδους ἀναρριπισθέντες, ὥρμηντο πρὸς τοὺς συνοίκους Ἕλληνας στασιάζειν ...

---

4 Eine detaillierte Behandlung dieser einzelnen Funktionen kann hier entfallen; wesentlich ist, dass wir hier erfahren, dass er aus *Epidaurum* – Zavtat in Dalmatien (Kroatien) stammte. Die ranghöchste Funktion ist zweifellos die des Flottenpräfekten von Misenum. Nur: was er als ein solcher während des Feldzuges in Syrien zu tun hatte, ist ein wenig unklar. Ich halte es daher für möglich, dass er erst jetzt – unter Beibehaltung seines Ranges – formell seinen zweiten Primipilat abdiente (und als solcher die *dona militaria* erhielt).

5 Dass es dieses Schiff war, das den Kaiser nach Syrien brachte, ist wegen dieser besonderen Betonung vermutet worden.

οἱ κατὰ Κυρήνην τὴν χώραν τῆς Αἰγύπτου λεηλατοῦντες καὶ τοὺς ἐν αὐτῇ νομοὺς φθείροντες διετέλουν, ἡγουμένου αὐτῶν Λουκούα· ἐφ› οὓς ὁ αὐτοκράτωρ ἔπεμψεν Μάρκιον Τούρβωνα σὺν δυνάμει πεζῇ τε καὶ ναυτικῇ, ἔτι δὲ καὶ ἱππικῇ. ὃ δὲ πολλαῖς μάχαις οὐκ ὀλίγῳ τε χρόνῳ τὸν πρὸς αὐτοὺς διαπονήσας πόλεμον, πολλὰς μυριάδας Ἰουδαίων, οὐ μόνον τῶν ἀπὸ Κυρήνης, ἀλλὰ καὶ τῶν ἀπ› Αἰγύπτου συναιρομένων Λουκούᾳ τῷ βασιλεῖ αὐτῶν, ἀναιρεῖ.
„Als der Kaiser (Trajan) das 18. Jahr seiner Regierung angetreten hatte (114 n. Chr.), verursachten die Juden einen neuen Aufstand[6], der einen hohen Blutzoll von ihnen forderte. In Alexandria und ebenso im übrigen Ägypten und auch in Kyrene begannen sie, von einem bösen, aufrührerischen Geist ergriffen, gegen ihre griechischen Mitbürger vorzugehen ... Die Juden in Kyrene fuhren, obwohl sie von den alexandrinischen Juden dann keine militärische Unterstützung mehr zu erwarten hatten, fort, unter Führung des Lukuas (Lukas ?)[7] Ägypten zu plündern und seine Fluren zu verwüsten. Der Kaiser entsandte daher gegen sie Marcius Turbo mit Fußsoldaten, Kriegsschiffen und auch Reiterei. Dieser führte einen langwierigen Krieg mit zahlreichen Gefechten und tötete tausende Juden nicht nur von Kyrene, sondern auch ägyptische Juden, die sich ihrem „König“ Lukuas angeschlossen hatten“.

Vielleicht schon während des Aufenthalts Hadrians in Pannonien[8], spätestens aber während des Partherfeldzugs Trajans, als sich die Nachfolge schon abzuzeichnen begann, scheint sich eine nähere Beziehung ergeben zu haben:

HA Hadrian 4, 2:
Qua quidem tempestate utebatur Hadrianus amicitia Sosi Papi et Platori Nepotis ex senatorio ordine, ex equestri autem Attiani, tutoris quondam sui, et Liviani <et> Turbonis.
„Zu dieser Zeit stand Hadrian in einem freundschaftlichen Verhältnis zu den Senatoren Sosius Papus (Q. Sosius Senecio ?) und (A.) Platorius Nepos, aber ebenso zu (P. Acilius) Attianus, der einst sein Vormund gewesen war, zu (Ti. Claudius) Livianus und (Q. Marcius) Turbo aus dem Ritterstand“.[9]

Der Regierungsantritt Hadrians vollzog sich bekanntlich nicht ganz problemlos, weil sich dieser zunächst möglicher – vermuteter oder wirklicher – Konkurrenten entledigen musste. Zu diesen gehörte auch der Berberfürst Lusius Quietus, der noch während des jüdischen Aufstandes eine willkommene Hilfe gewesen war:

6 Es ist der in der Literatur sogenannte Diasporaaufstand; dazu Timothy D. Barnes, Trajan and the Jews, in: Journal of Jewish Studies 40, 1989, 145–162.

7 Dio 68, 32, 1 nennt diesen Führer Andrias oder Andreas.

8 Vielfach wird vermutet, dass sich eine nähere Bekanntschaft (und Freundschaft) schon während der Tätigkeit Hadrians als Tribun eben dieser *legio II Adiutrix* in Pannonien ergeben habe.

9 Alle drei bekleideten, teilweise als Vorgänger des Q. Marcius Turbo, das Amt des *praefectus praetorio.*

HA Hadrian 5, 8:
Lusium Quietum sublatis gentibus Mauris, quos regebat, quia suspectus imperio fuerat, exarmavit Marcio Turbone Iudaeis compressis ad deprimendum tumultum Mauretaniae destinato.
„Lusius Quietus, der für das Reich eine Gefahr darzustellen schien,[10] stellte er (Hadrian) militärisch kalt, indem er ihm die einheimischen Truppenkontingente der Mauren, über die er herrschte, entzog und Marcius Turbo nach Niederschlagung des Judenaufstandes mit der Unterdrückung der Unruhen in Mauretanien beauftragte".

Hadrian hält sich jenseits der Donau auf, wo feindlicher Einfälle wegen seine Anwesenheit erforderlich schien. Allerdings geht er bald wegen der angedeuteten Probleme nach Rom, und jetzt wird Turbo gleichsam Statthalter dieser eigentlich „senatorischen" Provinzen:

HA Hadrian 6, 6–7 und 7, 3:
Audito dein tumultu Sarmatarum et Roxolanorum praemissis exercitibus Moesiam petit. Marcium Turbonem post Mauretaniam praefecturae infulis ornatum Pannoniae Daciaeque ad tempus praefecit.
Unde statim Hadrianus ad refellendam tristissimam de se opinionem, quod occidi passus est uno tempore quattuor consulares, Romam venit Dacia Turboni credita titulo Aegyptiacae praefecturae, quo plus auctoritatis haberet, ornato.
„Auf die Nachricht von den durch Sarmaten und Roxolanen verursachten Unruhen schickte er (Hadrian) die Armee voraus und begab sich nach Moesien. Marcius Turbo, der nach Mauretanien die Auszeichnungen eines Präfekten[11] erhalten hatte, machte er angesichts der augenblicklichen Situation zum Statthalter von Pannonien und Dakien.
Von dort begab sich Hadrian sofort nach Rom, um dem so unerfreulichen Gerede entgegenzutreten, das ihn betraf, weil er zugelassen hätte, dass zugleich vier ehemalige Konsuln liquidiert würden. Dabei überließ er Dakien dem Turbo, der mit dem Titel eines Präfekten von Ägypten (?) ausgezeichnet wurde, um ihm mehr Autorität zu verleihen".

Nun ist die Historia Augusta, was Detailangaben betrifft oder die Chronologie, bekanntlich nicht sehr verlässlich, und so ist es auch eher wahrscheinlich, dass mit der Präfektur, die ihm höhere Autorität verleihen sollte, tatsächlich bereits die Funktion eines *praefectus*

10 Die gängigen Übersetzungen bieten hier „weil er verdächtigt wurde, nach der Herrschaft zu streben" (oder Ähnliches), was zwar dem Sinn nach richtig sein mag, mir aber über den lateinischen Wortlaut hinauszugehen scheint.

11 „*Infulis ornatum*" ist vermutlich ein Anachronismus nach der Amtstracht der Bischöfe in der Spätantike; Ernst Hohl u.a., Historia Augusta, Band I, Zürich – München 1976, 379; dass damit auf eine formell noch immer beibehaltene Ehrenfunktion als *praefectus Aegypti* angespielt werde, vermutet Stein 1930, 1600.

praetorio gemeint war.[12] Das zeigen die oben angeführten Inschriften, und zudem wird er als Befehlshaber der in diesen Provinzen stationierten Truppen auch durch Militärdiplome bestätigt, wenn seine Kommandobefugnis auch nicht die eines formellen „Statthalters“, eines *legatus Augusti*, sondern eben die des *praefectus praetorio* war.[13] Als *praefectus praetorio* erscheint er schließlich auch auf einer Ehreninschrift aus Nordafrika.[14]

Aus diesen Inschriften und den literarischen Zeugnissen ergibt sich ein eindrucksvolles Bild dieses bedeutenden Mannes, der als Offizier mit einer vorgezeichneten Karriere begonnen und schließlich als *praefectus praetorio* die höchste – und einflussreichste – militärische Kommandofunktion erreicht hat, die einem Mann aus dem Ritterstand möglich war – weitaus bedeutender als selbst ein hochrangiges Armeekommando, wie es üblicherweise den Senatoren vorbehalten war, oder die Statthalterschaft in einer Großprovinz. Wie wir aber gesehen haben, hat es bei ihm auch an solchen nicht gefehlt.

Vielleicht sollte hier kurz auf die Funktion des *praefectus praetorio* eingegangen werden, wobei sich ein generelles Bild, das auf alle diese Amtsträger anwendbar wäre, vermutlich gar nicht zeichnen lässt. Zu sehr waren diese nach Charakter und Fähigkeiten verschieden, zu sehr von ihrer Aufgabenstellung und dem Freiraum abhängig, der ihnen vom jeweiligen Kaiser eingeräumt wurde.[15] Zunächst ist es das Kommando über die in Rom stationierte kaiserliche Garde, eine Elitetruppe jedenfalls der Theorie nach, und damit verbunden die Obsorge für die Sicherheit des Kaisers. Das muss, obwohl es nie ausdrücklich gesagt wird, zwangsläufig auch die Oberaufsicht über eine Art Geheimdienst mit sich gebracht haben, der regierungsfeindliche Bestrebungen rechtzeitig aufdecken und vereiteln sollte. Das bedingte in hohem Maß das Vertrauen des Kaisers, brachte aber eine ebenso große Machtfülle mit sich, die unter Umständen sogar dem Kaiser selbst gefährlich werden konnte.[16] Um diese Gefahr gering zu halten, wurde das Amt immer wieder mit zwei Personen besetzt, die sich gegenseitig kontrollieren sollten. Im Fall des Q. Marcius Turbo war dies jedenfalls in den Anfangsjahren neben dem noch zu nennenden Ser. Sulpicius Similis und anderen auch C. Septicius Clarus, der Sueton zu seinen Kaiser-

12 Für eine Statthalterschaft von Ägypten (und deren Beibehaltung auch noch in Dacien) werden mitunter staatsrechtliche Argumente bemüht; anders aber auch schon Ioan Piso, Fasti provinciae Daciae I, Die senatorischen Amtsträger (Antiquitas 1, 43, Bonn 1993), 31.

13 RMD 1, 21 und RMD 5, 351. Dass zu seinem Kommandobereich auch Moesia inferior gehört hat, zeigt die Ehreninschrift eines seiner Freigelassenen: Eck 1993, 247–255, wo er ebenfalls als ἔπαρχος πραιτώριος bezeichnet wird.

14 AE 1913, 164.

15 Änderungen im Verlauf einer historischen Entwicklung werden hier bewusst ausgeblendet. So sind unter den Severern die *praefecti praetorio* (zusätzlich) die obersten Rechtsberater des Kaisers – die bedeutendsten römischen Juristen finden wir unter ihnen –, und wieder eine andere Funktion erhalten sie ab der Tetrarchie. Dass die *praefecti praetorio* auch schon früher Rechtsprechungsbefugnisse hatten, zeigt, falls die hier am Ende ausgeschriebene Anekdote kein Anachronismus aus seiner Gegenwart ist, Cassius Dio 69, 18, 3.

16 Dies ist jedenfalls schon bei P. Aelius Seianus unter Tiberius befürchtet worden; dass in autoritären Herrschaftsformen frühere Geheimdienstchefs zu mächtig und eines Staatsstreichs verdächtigt wurden (Beria) oder tatsächlich zu Staatspräsidenten aufstiegen (Putin), können wir bis in die Gegenwart sehen.

biographien und Plinius zu seiner Briefsammlung angeregt haben soll. 122 oder 123 verlor er – wie Sueton – sein Amt im Zuge einer seltsamen Palastintrige um die Kaiserin Vibia Sabina.[17] Danach scheint Turbo allein amtiert zu haben.

Eine schöne Charakteristik des Q. Marcius Turbo und seiner Dienstauffassung bietet Cassius Dio 69, 18:

> Γεγόνασι δὲ καὶ ἄλλοι τότε ἄριστοι ἄνδρες, ὧν ἐπιφανέστατοι Τούρβων τε καὶ Σίμιλις ἤστην, οἳ καὶ ἀνδριᾶσιν ἐτιμήθησαν, Τούρβων μὲν στρατηγικώτατος ἀνήρ, ὃς καὶ ἔπαρχος γεγονώς, εἶτ' οὖν ἄρχων τῶν δορθφόρων, οὔτε τι ὑπερήφανον ἔπραξεν, ἀλλ' ὡς εἷς τῶν πολλῶν διεβίω. τά τε γὰρ ἄλλα καὶ τὴν ἡμέραν πᾶσαν πρὸς τῷ βασιλείῳ διέτριβε, καὶ πολλάκις καὶ πρὸ μέσων νυκτῶν πρὸς αὐτὸ ᾔει, ὅτε τινὲς ἄλλων καθεύδειν ἤρχοντο. ἀμέλει καὶ Κορνήλιος Φρόντων ὁ τὰ πρῶτα τῶν τότε Ῥωμαίων ἐν δίκαις φερόμενος, ἑσπέρας ποτὲ βαθείας ἀπὸ δείπνου οἴκαδε ἐπανιών, καὶ μαθὼν παρά τινος ᾧ συνηγορήσειν ὑπέσχετο δικάζειν αὐτὸν ἤδη, ἔν τε τῇ στολῇ τῇ δειπνίτδι, ὥσπερ εἶχεν, ἐς τὸ δικαστήριον αὐτοῦ ἐσῆλθε καὶ ἠσπάσατο, οὔτι γε τῷ ἑωθινῷ προσρήματι τῷ χαῖρε, ἀλλὰ τῷ ἑσπερινῷ τῷ ὑγίαινε χρησάμενος. οἴκοι δὲ ὁ Τούρβων οὔποτε ἡμέρας οὐδε νοσήσας, ὤφθη, ἀλλὰ καὶ πρὸς τὸν Ἀδριανὸν συμβουλεύοντα αὐτῷ ἀτρεμῆσαι εἶπεν ὅτι τὸν ἔπαρχον ἑστῶτα ἀποθνήσκειν δεῖ.
>
> „Es gab damals auch andere tüchtige Männer, unter denen die hervorragendsten Turbo und (Ser. Sulpicius) Similis[18] waren, die auch durch Statuen geehrt wurden. Turbo war ein Mann von größter militärischer Erfahrung, der Präfekt oder eben Kommandant der Garde geworden war. Er zeigte weder Dekadenz noch Selbstüberschätzung, sondern lebte wie viele andere auch. Unter anderem verbrachte er den ganzen Tag im Kaiserpalast und blieb dort oft bis Mitternacht, wenn viele andere sich schon niederzulegen begonnen hatten. Unvermeidlich (berichtet über ihn) auch Cornelius Fronto[19], der damals für einen der Bedeutendsten unter den Rechtsgelehrten der Römer gehalten wurde. Als er einmal spätabends von einem Gastmahl nachhause ging, erfuhr er von einem Mann, dem er zugesagt hatte, ihn vor Gericht zu vertreten, dass er (Turbo) schon rechtspreche. Noch in seinem formellen „Dinner Jackett" für das Gastmahl ging er, wie er war, in dessen Gerichtssaal, und begrüßte ihn nicht mit dem üblichen Morgengruß „Sei gegrüßt", sondern mit dem Abendgruß „Leb' wohl".[20] Während des Tages hielt sich Turbo niemals zuhause auf, auch nicht, wenn er krank war; und einmal sagte er zu Hadrian, der ihm riet, sich doch Ruhe zu gönnen, „für den Prätorianerpräfekten gehört es sich, in den Stiefeln zu sterben".

---

17 *Quod apud Sabinam uxorem in usu eius familiarius se tunc egerant, quam reverentia domus aulicae postulabat*; HA Hadrian 11, 3; vgl. ebd. 15, 2.

18 Eine Zeitlang gemeinsam mit Marcius Turbo Prätorianerpräfekt und offenbar von noch höherer Autorität, legte er seine Funktion bald nieder und zog sich ins Privatleben zurück. Cassius Dio hat ihm den gleich folgenden Abschnitt 69, 19 gewidmet.

19 Fronto erwähnt ihn auch in einem seiner Briefe; van den Hout 1954, 157, 23.

20 Dio gibt hier offenbar griechisch die üblichen lateinischen Grußformeln „Salve" und „Vale" wieder.

Literaturverzeichnis

Barnes, T. D. 1989. Trajan and the Jews, Journal of Jewish Studies 40, 145–162.
Beutler, F., Weber, E. (Hrsg.) 2005. Die römischen Inschriften der Österreichischen Nationalbibliothek, Wien.
Dobó, A. 1968. Die Verwaltung der römischen Provinz Pannonien von Augustus bis Diocletianus, Amsterdam.
Eck, W. 1993. Q. Marcius Turbo in Niedermösien, in K. Dietz u.a. (Hg.), Klassisches Altertum, Spätantike und frühes Christentum. Adolf Lippold zum 65. Geburtstag, Würzburg 1993, 247–255.
Eck, W. 1999. Q. Marcius Turbo, Der Neue Pauly 7, Leiden, 865.
Hanslik, R. 1969. Marcius II.6., Der Kleine Pauly 3, Stuttgart, 1005.
Petersen, L. 1970. Q. Marcius Turbo, PIR V/1, Berlin, 188–190.
Piso, I. 2013. Fasti provinciae Daciae II, Die ritterlichen Amtsträger, Bonn.
Stein, A. 1930. Q. Marcius Turbo Gallonius Fronto Publicius Severus Iulius Priscus 107), Feldherr und Freund Hadrians, RE 14/2, Stuttgart, 1597–1600.
van den Hout, M. P. J. 1954. M. Cornelii Frontonis epistolae, Leiden.

A Note on a Military Diploma Discovered at *Porolissum* (RMD IV, 248)

Dan-Augustin Deac

I have had the privilege and honour of working with Professor Ioan Piso for several years now. During this time, I discovered a great scholar, genuinely and constantly preoccupied with the Roman world, relentlessly working to uncover its secrets. I have learned a lot from him over the years while deciphering together Roman era inscriptions in the field and in museums. This paper focuses on the text of a military diploma discovered by chance at *Porolissum*, specifically on the *origo* and the patronymic of the recipient. By this, I hope to bring a modest contribution to the knowledge of military diplomas from Roman Dacia, thus also honouring the lifelong scientific achievements of Professor Ioan Piso.[1]

In 1993 workers dug a pit for a water basin near the archaeological base of the site from *Porolissum*, located on the southern slopes of the "Bisericuța" hill (fig. 1).[2] While digging the pit, the workers found a fragmentary military diploma, which is the subject of this paper. Its dimensions are 6.7 × 6 × 0.075 cm, the height of the letters is approx. 0.35 cm, it weighs 17.141 grams and it is housed by the Zalău History and Art County Museum, without an inventory number. On the extrinsecus, one can observe two parallel demarcation lines on the right side, incised at a distance of 0.1 and 0.5 cm from the right edge and one such line on the bottom, 0.1 cm from the lower edge (fig. 2–3).

The diploma was published several times, initially by Nicolae Gudea, with an improved reading by Constantin C. Petolescu, and subsequently by Margaret Roxan and Paul Holder in the *Roman Military Diplomas* series.[3] Furthermore, Holder advances a

1 This work was supported by a grant of the Ministry of Research, Innovation and Digitization, CNCS – UEFISCDI, project number PN-III-P1–1.1-TE-2021–0165, within PNCDI III.

2 In the area of the OL sector of the civilian settlement adjacent to the Pomet hill auxiliary fort, two other fragments of military diplomas were found, one issued for Hamasaeus, son of Alapatha, who fought among the *Palmyreni sagittarii*, being discharged on June 29th AD 120 (CIL XVI, 68; AE 1925, 76; AE 1935, 3; IDR I, 6 and latest AE 2019, 1334) and one issued for Aprio, son of Limen+[---] who was discharged from *cohors II Augusta Nervia Pacensis Brittonum milliaria*, dated cca. AD 138–142 (Dana, Deac 2018, 276–278, no. 2 = AE 2018, 1325). The rest of the military diplomas known from *Porolissum* were discovered in the auxiliary fort of the Pomet hill.

3 Gudea 1995, 77–80, no. II, p. 85–86, fig. 4–5 (drawing); Petolescu 1996, 407–408, no. 685; AE 1995, 1283; AE 1996, 1275; RMD IV, 248; ILD I, 30; RMD V, p. 701–702; Piso 2013, 115, *4*.

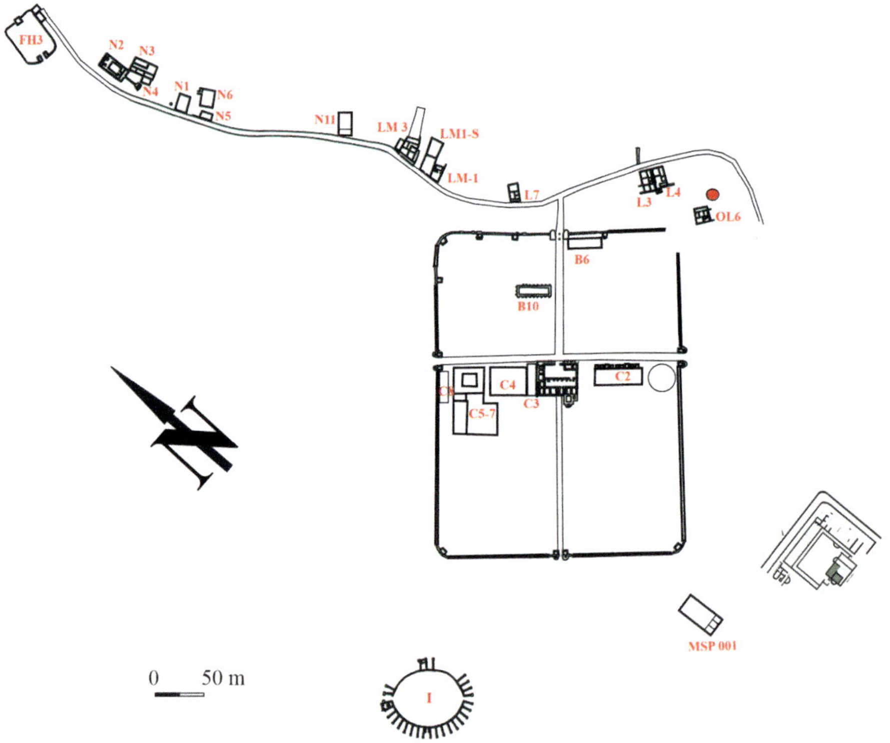

Fig. 1: Plan of *Porolissum* and the location of the discovery marked by a red dot (author)

new dating, between November 14th and December 1st AD 135.[4] However, although it had been analysed so many times, the diploma was previously never published with a photographic illustration. It preserves the lower right side of the *tabella I* intus and the right side of the *tabella I* extrinsecus. Based on a new examination, some further improvements of the text are made in the following, primarily regarding the *origo* and possible patronymic identification.

Tab. I extr.:

[--]
[ET SVNT IN DACIA POR]**Ọ̣L SVB FL ITALICO**
[---------------------------------- S]**Ṭ̣IP EME DIM HON**
[MISS QVOR NOM SVB]**Ṣ̣CR SVNT IPS LIB**

4 RMD V, p. 701.

Fig. 2: Photo of the *tabella I* intus of the diploma (author)

[POSTERISQ EOR CIVIT DEDIT ET C]**ON CVM VXORỊ**[B]
[QVAS TVNC HAB CVM EST CI]**Ṿ IIS DAT AVT SỊ** [QVI]
[CAELIBES ESSENT CVM IIS QVAS POST D]**ṾX DVMTAX̣**[AT]
[--]

Tab. I intus:

[---]
[DATA AVT SI QVI CAELIBES E]**ṢẸṆṬ CṾṂ Ị**[S QVAS]
[POSTEA DVX DVMTAXAT] **SINGVLIS SINGVLAṢ**
[AD------------------------------]+ **K DEC**
[P RVTILIO FABIANO CN].**PAPIRIO AELIANO COS**
[----------------------------------] **CR CVI PRAEST**
[----------------------------------]**VPER NOVIOMAG**
[----------------------------------]**ITE**
[----------------------------------]**LLADI F DẠṚ**[D]
[----------------------------------]**O F EIṾ**[S]
[----------------------------------]**O F** [EIVS]
[DESCRIPT ET RECOG]**NIT EX TABṾ**[LA AENEA]
[QVAE FIXA EST RO]**MAE IN MṾ**[RO POST]
[TEMPL DIVI AV]**G AD MINẸ**[VAM]

Fig. 3: Photo of the *tabella I* extrinsecus of the diploma (author)

[Imp(erator) Caesar, divi Traiani Parthic(i) f(ilius), divi Nervae nepos, Traianus Hadrianus Aug(ustus), pont(ifex) max(imus), trib(unicia) pot(estate) XIX, co(n)s(ul) III, p(ater) p(atriae),] [equitib(us) et peditib(us), qui militaver(unt) in alis --- et cohortibus --- quae appellantur --- et sunt in Dacia Por]ọl(issensis) sub Fl(avio) Italico [quinis et vicenis plurib(usve) aut *quinq(ue) et vigint(ti) s]ṭip(endis) eme(ritis) dim(issis) hon(esta) [miss(ione), quor(um) nom(ina) sub]ṣcr(ipta) sunt, ips(is) lib[eris posterisq(ue) eor(um) civit(atem) dedit et c]on(ubium) cum uxorịb(us) [quas tunc hab(uissent), cum est ci] ṿ(itas) iis dat(a), aut sị[qui caelibes es]ṣẹṇṭ cụṃ ị[s quas post(ea) d]ụx(issent) dumtaẋ [at] singuli singulaṣ.*
[a(nte) d(iem) ---]+ k(alendas) Dec(embres) [P. Rutilio Fabiano, Cn.] Ṗapirio Aeliano co(n)s(ulibus) [---] c(ivium) R(omanorum), cui praest [--- S]uper Noviomag(o) [ex ped- aut *equ]ite [---]lladi f(ilio) Dạṛ[d(ano)] [et ---]o f(ilio) eiụ[s et ---]o f(ilio) eius. Descript(um) et recog]nit(um) ex tabụ[la aenea quae fixa est Ro]mae in mụ[ro post templ(um) divi Au]g(usti) ad Minẹ[vam].*[5]

Little is known about the praesidial procurator Titus Flavius Italicus before he took command of the province. He was identified with a homonymous prefect of the *ala I Vlpia*

5 The text is reproduced here from RMD V, p. 701–702 with modifications made by the author.

Contariorum milliaria civium Romanorum who consecrated an altar to Diana at *Arrabona*, in Pannonia Superior.[6] His fourth *militia* was to date at the latest during the years AD 125–128,[7] perhaps even earlier. A diploma of unknown provenance attests him as the praesidial procurator of Dacia Porolissensis as early as the period when Hadrian held the *tribunicia potestas* for the fifteenth time, namely the period spanning from December 10th 130 to December 9th AD 131.[8] A recently published military diploma discovered in the area of the *principia* of the Pomet Hill auxiliary fort from *Porolissum* dates to the 15th or 16th of April AD 131, which makes it the earliest secured date of Flavius Italicus' governorship of Dacia Porolissensis.[9] Other military diplomas attest him in the meantime in this office.[10] The diploma under analysis acknowledges the latest known date of Flavius Italicus as a praesidial procurator of Dacia Porolissensis in between November 14th and December 9th AD 135,[11] but his office might have lasted until the end of that year.[12] What stands out is the unusual amount of time spent in this office by Flavius Italicus, from early AD 131 to late AD 135, although, at least in theory, these procuratorships must have lasted approximately from two to three years.[13] Unfortunately, the reasons behind this long period evade us for now.

Nothing much can be said regarding the military unit. The identification of the unit rests on the epithet *c(ivium) R(omanorum)* and the candidates include *ala Siliana* and *cohors I Vlpia Brittonum milliaria* (which most authors favour)[14] or several *cohortes*, es-

---

6 CIL III 4362; RIU I, 243; Lőrincz 2001, 187, no. 95; Piso 2013, 114, no. 74, *1*. For the debate regarding the career of Italicus, see Faoro 2011, 294–295, no. 2 with references; Piso 2013, 116–117 with references. If we are dealing with the same individual, the altar from *Arrabona* dates from the first half of the 120's AD.

7 Piso 2013, 117. Previously, B. Lőrincz proposed AD 130–132. Davide Faoro on the other hand suggests that the individual from *Arrabona* is a homonymous successor (son or nephew) of the procurator of Dacia (Faoro 2011, 295, n. 323).

8 Weiß 2002, 248–251, no. 5; AE 2002, 1745; Petolescu 2003–2005, 354, no. 981; RMD V, 378; ILD I, 29; Faoro 2011, 294, 2/a; Piso 2013, 114–115, no. 75, *2*; Petolescu 2021, 34 and 185.

9 Opreanu, Lăzărescu 2020, 297–298 with references for the discussion on the dating; AE 2020, 1023.

10 IDR I, 11 with references; RMD I, 35; Faoro 2011, 294, 2/b; Piso 2013, 115, *3*; Dana 2017 with references; Petolescu 2021, 34 (Gherla, Dacia Porolissensis, 2nd July, AD 133); Eck, Pangerl 2015, 239–240, no. 2; AE 2015, 1894; Petolescu 2018, 279, 280, no. 1946; Petolescu 2021, 34 (unknown provenance, AD 133/134).

11 Another diploma mentioning this Equestrian ranked governor is Eck, MacDonald, Pangerl 2002–2003, 38–41, no. 3; AE 2003, 2043; Petolescu 2003–2005, 354–355, no. 982; Piso 2013, 115, *5*; Petolescu 2021, 34 (unknown provenance, AD 135).

12 This assertion is made because the consular pair is attested on December 31st AD 135 in military diplomas issued for the units from Mauretania Tingitana (see further RMD V, 382 and Weiß 2007, 249–250 = AE 2007, 1778). See also the discussion in Opreanu, Lăzărescu 2020, 298.

13 Piso 2013, 10, with references.

14 *Cf.* note 10. For *cohors I Brittonum milliaria* see latest Petolescu 2021, 190–193, no. 25. *Ala Siliana* is the only military unit bearing this epithet in the diploma closer in date to the one currently analysed, taking into consideration the ones where the names of the military units can be read; for this unit, see latest Petolescu 2021, 174–176, no. 15.

Fig. 4: Detail of the *tabella I* extrinsecus of the diploma where the patronymic can partially be read (author)

Fig. 5: Detail of the *tabella I* extrinsecus of the diploma where the patronymic can partially be read. H-RTI, Luminance Unsharp Masking (author)

pecially *cohortes milliariae.*[15] Its commander, [---] Super, is otherwise unknown but we are informed that he originates from *Vlpia Noviomagus Batavorum*, as first observed by Constantin C. Petolescu back in 1996.[16]

The H-RTI (*Highlight Reflectance Transformation Imaging*) method helps improve the text to a certain extent.

---

15 M. Roxan and P. Holder in RMD IV, 248 reject an identification with an *ala* and question as well the identification with *cohors I Brittonum milliaria*. *Cf.* Petolescu 2021, *passim*, for the possible *cohortes*.

16 *Cf.* note 3.

Fig. 6: Detail of the *tabella I* extrinsecus of the diploma where the patronymic can partially be read. H-RTI, Normals Visualisation (author)

N. Gudea proposed the reading of the patronymic as [---]alladi, identifying a lower right side of the right stroke of A. However, the H-RTI method does not reveal any traces of this letter (as what N. Gudea saw was a damaged area of the surface), which leaves us with two possible readings (fig. 4–6). Naturally, one solution could be that offered by N. Gudea, [Pa]lladi, which refers to the *cognomen* of Greek origin, Palladius, encountered sporadically in Dalmatia and the Gallic provinces,[17] while its Greek version occurs before the fourth century only rarely in Athens.[18] Secondly, one can advance the reading as [He] lladi; this Greek origin *cognomen* – Helladius – is even more rarely attested in the European provinces in Latin, namely once in Dalmatia.[19] In regard to the *origo* which follows the filiation, most authors followed the solution offered initially by Nicolae Gudea, namely DV[---] or just simply D[---].[20] However, the H-RTI method improves the reading here as well. After D, the upper sides of two letters can be read, the first one being A. It is followed by a letter from which one can distinguish the upper side of a vertical stroke which connects to the right, at a ninety-degree angle, with a horizontal, slightly curved one. This situation rules out, for example, the identification of this letter with C or L, i. e. *Dạç[o]* or *Dạḷ[m(atae)]*. Accordingly, the best solution for interpreting this letter is R, meaning the word should be read as *Dạṛ[d(ano)]* (fig. 7–9).

RMD IV 247 lists Vannus, son of Timens, a Dardanian, recruited into *ala I Claudia nova miscellanea* and discharged on September 9th AD 132 or 133, when the unit was part

17 OPEL III 121.
18 LGPN II, 356.
19 OPEL II 176.
20 RMD V, p. 702.

Fig. 7: Detail of the *tabella I* extrinsecus of the diploma where the *origo* can be read (author)

Fig. 8: Detail of the *tabella I* extrinsecus of the diploma where the *origo* can be read. H-RTI Luminance Unsharp Masking (author)

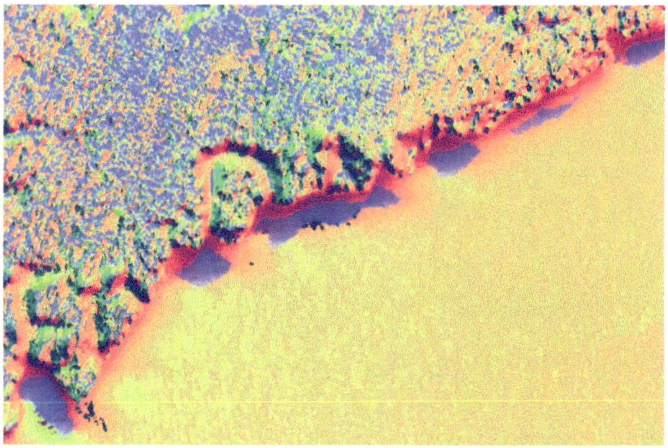

Fig. 9: Detail of the *tabella I* extrinsecus. H-RTI, Normals Visualisation (author)

of the armies of Moesia Superior.[21] At the time of the recruitment, *ala I Claudia nova miscellanea* was stationed for a short while in Dacia, subsequently participating in Trajan's Parthian expedition and then returning to Moesia Superior.[22] The pieces of information extracted from both this diploma and the one from *Porolissum* suggest that there was a recruitment taking place among the Dardanians for military units stationed in the Danube region after the end of the Second Dacian War.

To conclude, the H-RTI method with different visualization options which has been applied on the surface of this military diploma has improved the reading of the text in some critical areas. First, it questions the previous readings of the patronymic, although a definite solution cannot be offered. But, most importantly, it reveals the ethnic background with which the recipient identified himself, namely Dardanian, which triggering some wider implications regarding the recruitment taking place among them at the beginning of the 2nd century AD.

Abbreviations

IDR I	I. I. Russu, Inscripţiile Daciei romane I, Bucharest 1975.
ILD I	C. C. Petolescu, Inscripţii latine din Dacia (ILD), Bucharest 2005.
LGPN II	P. M. Fraser, E. Matthews, A Lexicon of Greek Personal Names, volume II. Attica, Oxford 1994.
OPEL II	B. Lőrincz, Onomasticon Provinciarum Europae Latinarum, Vienna 1999.
OPEL III	B. Lőrincz, Onomasticon Provinciarum Europae Latinarum, Vienna 2000.
RIU I	L. Barkóczi, A. Mócsy, Die römischen Inschriften Ungarns (RIU), Budapest 1972.
RMD I	M. Roxan, Roman Military Diplomas 1954–1977, London 1978.
RMD IV	M. Roxan, P. Holder, Roman Military Diplomas IV, London 2003.
RMD V	P. Holder, Roman Military Diplomas V, London 2006.

Bibliography

Dana, D. 2010. Corrections, restitutions et suggestions onomastiques dans quelques diplômes militaires, Cahiers du Centre Gustave Glotz 21, 35–62.

Dana, D. 2017. A Hitherto Unrecognised Cornovian on a Roman Military Diploma (*RMD* I, 35), Britannia 48, 9–20.

Dana, D., Deac, D. 2018. D. Dana, D. Deac, Un diplôme militaire fragmentaire du règne d'Hadrien découvert à Romita (Dacie Porolissensis) et relecture du diplôme *RMD* I 40 (*Porolissum*), ZPE 208, 273–278.

21 AE 2003, 1378; RMD IV 247; RMD V, p. 701. For the onomastic suggestions, see Dana 2010, 47, no. 17, who stresses upon the Illyrian origin of the names.

22 Matei-Popescu, Ţentea 2018, 20; Petolescu 2021, 65–66, no. 10.

Eck, W. MacDonald, D. Pangerl, A. 2002–2003. Neue Militärdiplome für die Auxiliartruppen von Unterpannonien und die dakischen Provinzen aus Hadrianischer Zeit, ActaMN 39–40 [2004], 25–50.

Eck, W. Pangerl, A. 2015. Eine Konstitution für die Truppen von Dacia inferior vom 16. Juni 123 unter dem Präsidialprokurator Cocceius Naso und weitere diplomata militaria, ZPE 195, 231–242.

Faoro, D. 2011. *Praefectus, procurator, praeses*. Genesi delle cariche presidiali equestri nell'Alto Impero Romano, Milan.

Gudea, N. 1995. Despre fragmente de diplome militare "revăzute" sau mai nou descoperite la Porolissum, ActaMP 19, 73–88.

Lőrincz, B. 2001. Die römischen Hilfstruppen in Pannonien während der Prinzipatszeit, Vienna.

Matei-Popescu, F. Țentea, O. 2018. Auxilia Moesiae Superioris, Cluj-Napoca.

Opreanu, C.H., Lăzărescu, V.-A. 2020. A New Military Diploma Recently Found at Porolissum (Dacia Porolissensis), EN 30, 295–308.

Petolescu, C.C. 1996. Cronica epigrafică a României (XIV-XV, 1994–1995), SCIVA 47, 4, 401–419.

Petolescu, C.C. 2003–2005. Cronica epigrafică a României (XXI-XXIV, 2001–2004), SCIVA 54–56, 337–396.

Petolescu, C.C. 2018. Cronica epigrafică a României (XXXVII, 2017), SCIVA 69, 1–4, 269–286.

Petolescu, C.C. 2021. Armata romană din Dacia, Bucharest.

Piso, I. 2013. Fasti provinciae Daciae. II. Die ritterlichen Amtsträger, Bonn.

Weiß, P. 2002. Neue Diplome für Soldaten des Exercitus Dacicus, ZPE 141, 241–251.

Weiß, P. 2007. P. Weiß, Weitere Militärdiplome für Soldaten in Mauretania Tingitana aus dem Balkanraum, ZPE 162, 249–256.

Graffiti from the House of the Centurion in Novae*

Piotr Dyczek**

Archaeologists from the Antiquity of Southeastern Europe Research Center of the University of Warsaw have been exploring a sector of the ancient Roman army camp at Novae located east of the *principia* since 2011 (Fig. 1).[1] The sector was chosen for exploration because it was believed, based on an analysis of the plan of the *castrum* as a whole, that the barracks of the first cohors of the I Italica legion could be found in this area. Exploration confirmed this supposition and more: timber-and-earth remains discovered in the lower-lying layers[2] were linked to the VIII Augusta legion which is known to have come to Novae about 45 CE.[3] The remains belonged to timber-built double barracks and a house identified as the locum of a centurion of most probably the I cohors of this legion.

When the I Italica replaced the VIII Augusta at Novae in 69, a large stone building was constructed in place of the wooden barracks. It was composed of different rooms grouped around a central courtyard, which had a small pool at the center. The south wing was occupied by a bathhouse with floors laid with *tegulae* or mortared. Semicircular borders lay on the floor alongside the walls. A fine white plaster covered the walls; in some instances the walls were also painted red. Traces of floral ornaments in green and red on the white plaster background have been preserved in some places. The building appears to have been refurbished at least twice: once about 80 CE, after a strong earthquake had laid waste to the architecture, and the second time at the beginning of the 3rd century CE. During the second renovation the original wall paintings were given a secondary coat of poorer-quality cream-colored plaster. Fragments of the original plaster were preserved in some places even up to a meter high. Graffiti, all of them damaged to some extent, were found on three of the original walls (Fig 2).[4] Two of these are of particular interest: one is a representation of a boar and the other of a sailing ship.

A small-sized image of a boar, 7 cm × 4 cm, was rendered on the south wall of the south portico. (Fig. 2, 1 and Fig 3). The drawing is schematic but leaves no doubt as to the

* The resources for the implementation of the project were allotted by the National Science Center, Poland, by decision DEC 2018/31/B/HS3/02593

** ORCID 0000-0001-7011-524X

1 Dyczek 2018, 27–71.

2 Dyczek 2015, 530–536; Genčeva 2002; Sarnowski 1985, 153–160; Ziomecki 1981, 25.

3 Dyczek 2019, 115–126.

4 Płóciennik, Żelazowski 2011, 77–84.

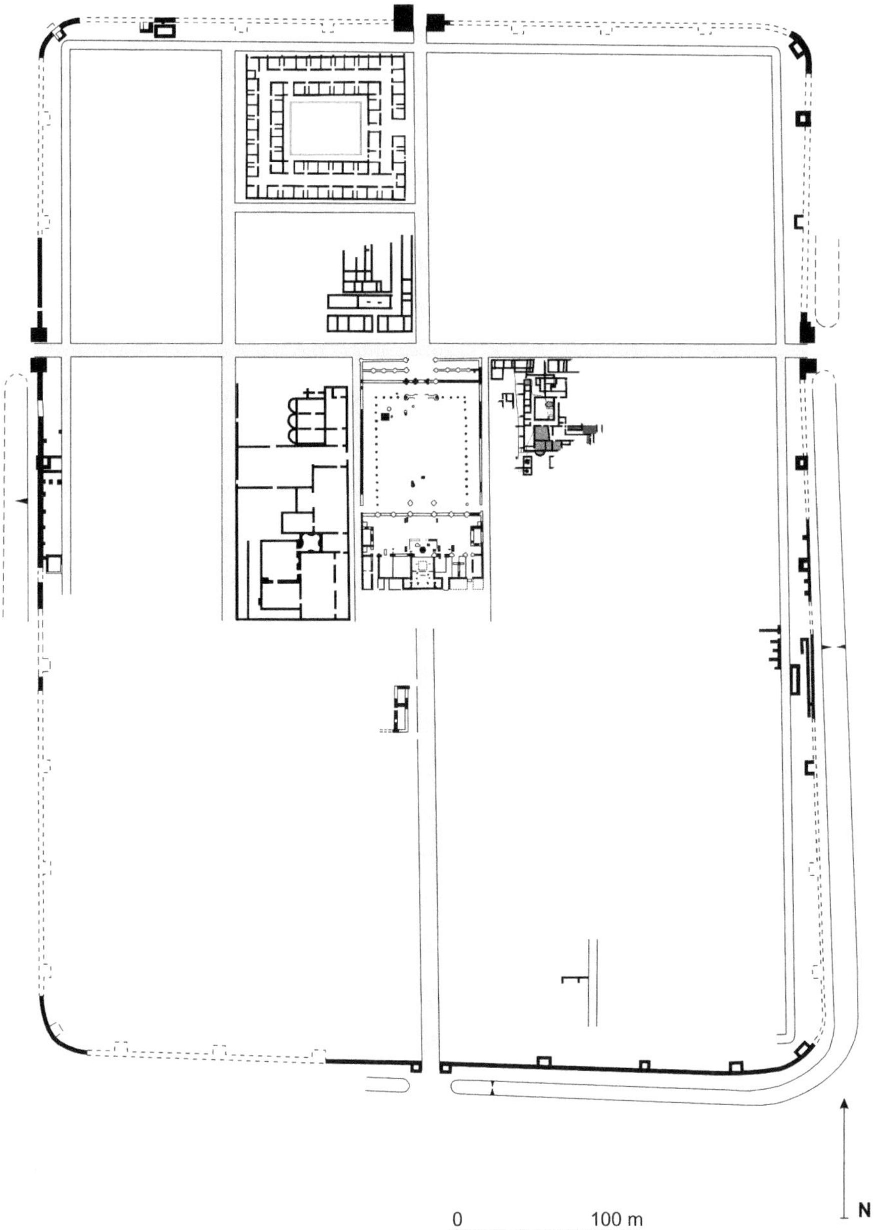

Fig. 1: Novae Legionary Fortress I–III AD, P. Dyczek, B. Wojciechowski

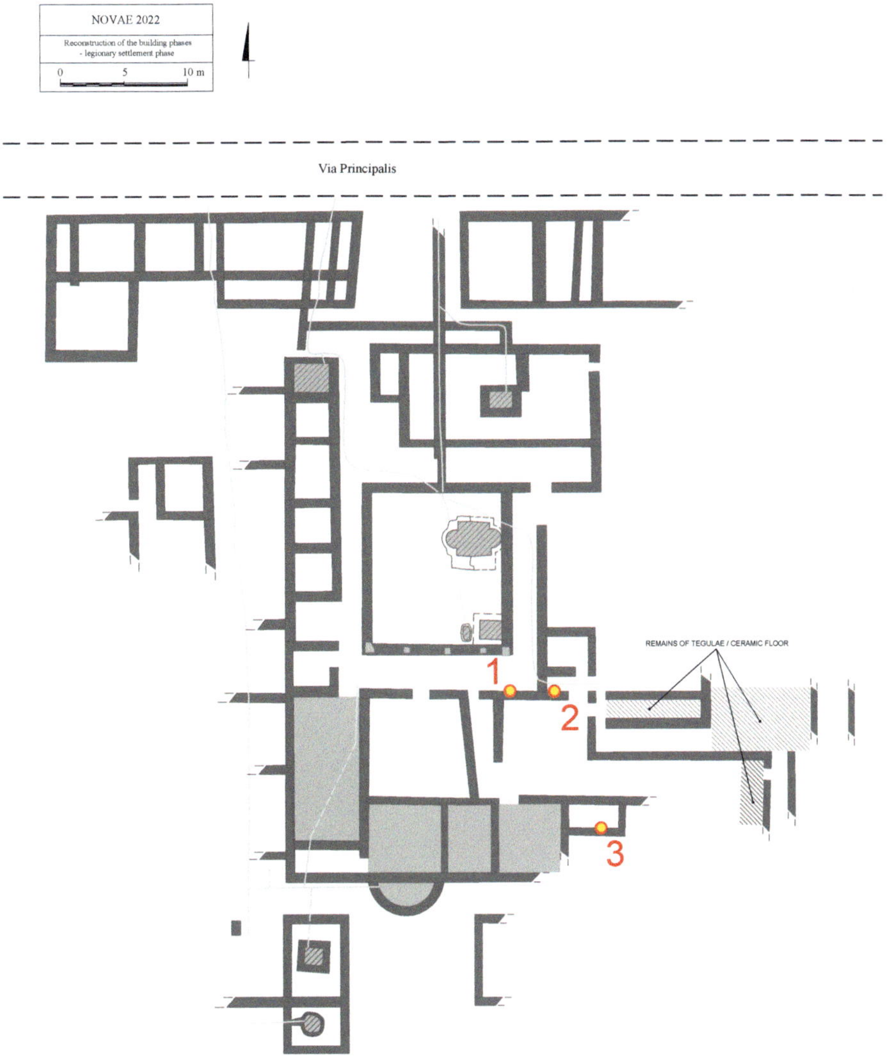

Fig. 2: Plan of the building in section XII marked with places where graffiti were discovered, P. Dyczek, B. Wojciechowski

author's intent. The animal is pictured motionless, its mouth slightly open, the hair on its back bristling, the tail raised. It looks ready to charge. Lacking the boar's characteristic sabers, it could well be a sow. Some engraved lines at the edge of the fragment cannot be interpreted. Considering that the boar was a symbol of the I Italica, this representation in such a context could well have been imbued with a deeper meaning.

Fig. 3 a, b: Representation of a wild boar, P. Dyczek, W. Maszewska

Images of boars are actually quite common in ancient art from different periods, including tribal depictions, for example, among the Picts, the Germanic and Nordic tribes, but also in Chinese, Hindu or American Indian cultures. They are part of European heraldry and appear in city and state coats-of-arms. The animal is not represented in European cave art, but there is an image of a Sulawesi warty pig (*Sus celebensis*) known from the Indonesian island of Celebes.[5]

From time immemorial, judging by what the written sources reveal, the boar has been associated with strength, a capacity to adapt to different, perhaps even harsh conditions, protection of offspring, intrepidness and determination, wisdom and vitality. Despite its relatively small size, it was a threat to man. Putting down a boar was proof of a man's courage and a mark of glory. Its importance as a symbol already in the Bronze Age is attested indirectly by the well-known Mycenaean helmets made of boar's sabers (*The Iliad*

5 Brumm *et al.* 2021, 3–6, Figs. 2, 3.

Fig. 4 a, b: Representation of the ship with inscriptions, P. Dyczek. W. Maszewska

10, 260–265, see helmets from Elateia, Dendra). It merits note in this context that the boar was one of the symbols of the Greek god of war Ares. In Greek mythology, capturing the Erymanthian boar was one of the labors of Herakles. In turn, Meleager hunted and killed the Calydonian boar that the enraged Artemis sent down on the land of his father Oineus. In another cultural context, the killing/death of a boar portended the end of winter and the coming of spring, making it thus a symbol of the good forces. Christianity first identified the forces of evil with the boar, using the image of this animal to represent heretics and the devil himself.

So deeply rooted was the symbol in ancient tradition that it was chosen as the emblem of three of the Roman legions: I Italica, X Fretensis and XX Valeria Victrix. In the case of the I Italica legion, the boar could have been a reference to the place of origin of the unit, which was formed by the Emperor Nero out of Italics originating from Campania, a region which had the boar among its symbols. A reference of this kind would not have been exceptional. The Legio X Fretensis had three other emblems beside the boar: a bull, a sailing ship and the god Neptune. The bull symbolized Venus and the Julian family, thus referring to the origins of the legion's founder, Octavius Augustus. Both the ship and

Fig. 5: Model of a Roman liburna, W. Maszewska

Neptune were iconographic allusions to the legion's victorious battles at Naulochos and Actium. In turn, the boar as an emblem of the XX Valeria Victrix highlighted the prowess of the soldiers of this "Victorious" legion.

The image from Novae may have thus been merely an expression of the author's pride in having perhaps killed a boar, symbolically confirming the legion's prowess. It was certainly not just an artistic rendering of an ordinary boar hunt for alimentary purposes, but was imbued with a deeper sense. However, archaeo-zoological analyses of faunal remains discovered in the excavations at Novae have revealed no bones of boar.[6] A few boar sabers reworked into pendants/amulets are the sole exception. One is entitled to assume that "hunting" boar could have been part of military training rather than a way of procuring extra food.

Even though osteological material is modest at best, we can be sure that boars were encountered in the wild around Novae in Roman times. According to archaeo-botanical studies, the oak forests in the region would have offered a ready supply of acorns for these animals to forage on in this period.[7]

The other graffito of interest, 24 cm by 18 cm in size, appears at first glance to be nothing but disorderly lines (Fig. 2, 3 and Fig. 4). RTI photographs of the image enabled three elements to be distinguished: two sets of thin engraved lines running one horizontally and the other crossing at right angle, plus three inscriptions. Straight striations on the

6 Gręzak, Lasota-Moskalewska, 1998, 203–209; Gręzak, Piątkowska- 2000, 99–105; Gręzak, Piątkowska-Małecka 2007, 39–44; Ninov, 2003, 231–239.

7 Jankowska, Kozakiewicz 2022, 119–125; Dyczek 2019 a, 66–64.

Fig. 6: The image of a liburna on the stamp of the legio I Italica, J. Recław

surface are due to the fine-grained plaster being smoothed while still wet. These lines were useful in determining the orientation of the graffito. A closer look at the scratched elements suggested a representation of a ship, most likely a *liburna*: one can trace the rounded form of the hull, the raised and curving prow, a large schematically drawn rudder and oars, and the mast rigging (Fig. 5).

Images of merchant ships as well as warships are known from both Greek and Roman culture. A rich collection, dated to the 6th century BC, can be found engraved on rocks in southern Attica. Added to these engravings are inscriptions naming the type of ship.[8] Representations of this kind left by the Romans are equally common. They appear on mosaics, in reliefs, wall painting and graffiti. The fullest set – 25 different kinds of ships – is to be seen on a mosaic floor from the 3rd century CE discovered in 1895 in Althiburus (Tunisia). The vessels are depicted in detail and each is designated with its name in either Latin or Greek.[9] The names coincide with those on a list included by Aulus Gellius in his *Noctes Atticae*, a work from the 2nd-century CE. Another interesting find was a large-sized graffito of a Roman *corbita*, discovered in 1980 in the ruins of a Gallo-Roman house, the so-called Villa Viély, in the town of Cucuron. The image was engraved on a plastered wall that was painted red.[10] These two representations of Roman ships, rendered with different artistic techniques, are the most interesting for the subject at hand, but the catalog is of course much longer.[11] Notwithstanding, few of these images are sufficiently detailed to contribute more information to the discussion.

8 van de Moortel, Langdom 1917, 1–24.
9 Duval 1949, 119–149.
10 Pomey, 1993, 149.
11 Pomey 1993, 150–163.

The *liburna* recognized in the image from Novae takes its name after Liburnia, a region on the eastern coast of the Adriatic, between the rivers Raša, Zrmanja and Krka (*Arsia*, *Tedanius*, *Titius*).[12] The tribes living there designed a kind of universal ship that served them for sea, cabotage and river navigation, all in one. Its maneuverability made it also a great pirate ship. The Romans improved the design after conquering Liburnia and incorporating it into the province of Dalmatia. They used it for both civil and military purposes. In the latter case, they added a battering ram, protection against missiles[13] and an additional row of oars.[14] There were *liburnae* of different sizes depending on needs.[15] In effect, the *liburna* was the mainstay, next to the *hemiola*, of the provincial fleet, the *Classis Moesiaca* which operated in the part of the limes on the Lower Danube,[16] from the Iron Gates to Crimea (from 41 CE).[17]

The river port of the Roman period in Novae has not been located despite efforts in this direction.[18] Owing to riverbank erosion, it is likely that the remains of the harbor are now underwater. The logic of site topography, supported by depictions on the Column of Trajan,[19] suggests that it was situated at the bottom of the escarpment on which the fortress was built. Indirect evidence of a harbor is also provided by the image of a *liburna* pictured beyond all doubt as one of the devices on the Legio I Italica stamps (Fig. 6).[20] In Tadeusz Sarnowski's preliminary typology,[21] stamps of this type are dated provisionally to the first half of the 2nd century CE.[22]

Inscriptions are also extremely interesting. Three of these are Roman names: *ROMNUS*, *RUFINUS*, *RUNTICUS* (read differently prior to the RTI photo images).[23] It is not clear how to interpret these names in the context of the ship representation, but the two do seem to be contemporary. Could they be the names of some of the crew (perhaps commanders) of the pictured ship? The second type of inscription has been interpreted in different ways. Pictured on the hull are the Roman numerals V and IX. They could also be the letters VX (mistaken for XV) recorded before the R in the name of ROMNVS, or it could be an abbreviation from the word *vexillarius* referring to his rank. The last part – DV or VD – is also unclear. DV is more likely and assuming it is an abbreviation, it could be a reference to *duumvirii navales*, that is, a repair crew. In that case, the three Romans named in the graffito could have been members of this crew. The numerals ren-

12 Zaninović 1988, 43–67.
13 Morrison, Coates 1996, 170, 317.
14 Gabriel 2007, 36–43.
15 Morrison, Coates 1996, 171; Casson 1971, 14.
16 Cleere 1977, 110.
17 Webster, Elton 1998, 162–165.
18 Sarnowski, Trynkowski 1986, 536–541.
19 Dyczek 2016, 95–110.
20 Božilova 1988, 27–30.
21 Sarnowski 1983, pl. VI.
22 Duch 2017, 105, fig. 5.
23 Dyczek 2018, 65.

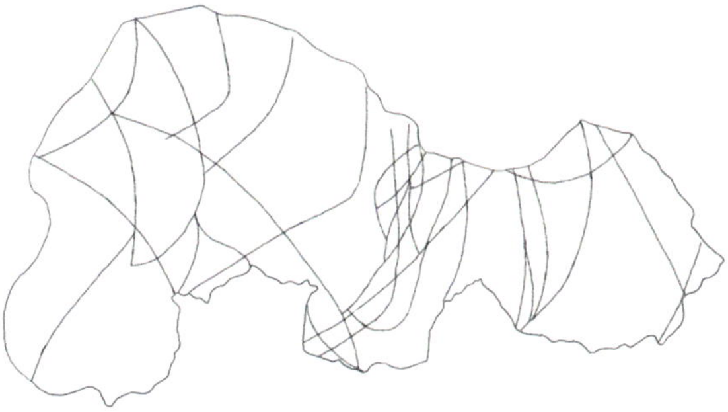

Fig. 7 a, b: "Geometric graffito", K. Narloch, W. Maszewska

dered in images of ship appear to hold significance. They can be found in the graffito from Cucuron. Could they refer to the number of sailors or perhaps legionaries in the crew?

The third graffito, 19 X 11 cm, could have been part of a larger composition (Fig. 2, 1 and Fig. 7). It consists of apparently haphazard curved lines, but the intent in the arrangement is clear – a representation of waves which could even be part of another scene with a ship, although this is pure speculation.

The three graffiti appear to be separate compositions, which were probably more extended seeing that the lines extend beyond the preserved edges of the individual fragments. They come most certainly from different times even if they cannot be dated precisely. Taking into consideration the state of preservation of the fragments, and the kind of engraving and the background plaster on the wall, it seems that the ship graffito was the earliest – it dates to the first half of the 2nd century CE. The boar drawing came later, in the second half of the 2nd century CE, and the latest is the set of disorderly lines assigned to the end of the 2nd or beginning of the 3rd century CE. Whatever the image, the representations seem to have held significance apparently not only for their makers. Considering their position on the walls of the architectural complex as a whole, they could have been well visible to all either living in this building or just passing through it.

The symbolism of ships is quite elaborate naturally. Many theories exist linking these representations with various aspects of material and spiritual culture.[24] In the case of Novae it is most likely, however, a reflection of everyday life and duties of the legionaries rather than being just a symbol.

The three graffiti from Novae are so far the most complete discovered compositions, but it does not mean they were the only ones. Single lines and difficult to interpret geometric motifs have been discerned on many fragments of plaster from different buildings. The habit of covering walls with graffiti has a long tradition and although these are hardly masterpieces of drawing, they supply information regardless of how valuable it is. Linking them is a need for expression that makes their makers less anonymous in modern eyes.

Bibliography

Batović, Š. 2005. Liburnska kultura. Matica Hrvatska i Arheološki muzej Zadar, Zadar.

Božilova, V. 1988. Izobraženija na korab vărhu moneti, tuhli I keramidi, Numizmatika, 27–30.

Casson, L. 1971. Statki i żeglarstwo w starożytnym świecie. Princeton, NJ.

Cleere, H. 1977. The Classis Britannica, in D. E. Johnstone (ed.), The Saxon shore, 16–19.

Dyczek, P. 2015. Wooden barracks of the First Cohort of the legio VIII Augusta from Novae (Moesia Inferior), in Limes XXIII. Proceedings of the 23rd International Congress of Roman Frontier Studies, Ingolstadt, 530–536.

Dyczek, P. 2016. Image of the castrum of the I Italica on the Column of Trajan: Fiction or archaeological reality?, in A. Panaite, R. Cîrjan, C. Căpiţă (eds.), Moesica et Christiana. Studies in Honour of Professor Alexandru Barnea, Brăila, 95–110.

Dyczek, P., 2018. Novae – Western Sector (Section XII), 2011–2018. Preliminary report on the excavations of the Center for Research on the Antiquity of Southeastern Europe, University of Warsaw, Novensia 29, 27–71.

Dyczek, P. 2019. Discovering the history of the VIII Augusta legion in Novae, in G. I. Farkas, R. Neményi, M. Szabó (eds.), Visy 75. Artificem commendat opus. Studia in honorem Zsolt Visy, Pécs, 115–126.

Dyczek, P. 2019. a Novae and its natural environment in the 1st c. AD and beginning of the 2nd c. AD, in: J. Mellnerová Šuteková, M. Bačá, P. Pavúk (eds.), Salve Edvarde! A Toast to the Jubilee of Professor E. Kreković, (= Studia Archaeologica et Mediaevalia 12), Bratislava, 55–64.

Duch, M. 2017. Stamps on the bricks and tiles from Novae. Outline of chronology, Novensia 28, 99–119.

Duval P.-M. 1949. La forme des navires romains d'après la mosaïque d'Althiburus, Mélanges d'archéologie et d'histoire, 61, 1949, 119–149.

24 Panou *et al.* 2022, 13.

Gabriel, R. A. 2007. Rzymska marynarka wojenna: władcy Morza Śródziemnego, Historia wojskowości 29 *(9)*, 36–43.

Genčeva, E. 2002. Părvijat voenen lager v Nove, provincija Mizija, Sofia-Warszawa.

Gręzak, A., Lasota-Moskalewska, A. 1998. Szczątki zwierzęce z *principia* w Novae z I w.n.e., Novensia 11, 203–209.

Gręzak, A., Piątkowska-Małecka, J. 2000. Szczątki zwierzęce z *principia* w Novae z IV w.n.e., Novensia 12, 99–105.

Gręzak, A., Piątkowska-Małecka, J., 2007. Szczątki zwierzęce z *principia* w Novae z I w.n.e. Drugi zespół, Novensia 17, 39–44.

Ninov, L. 2003. Animal Bones from *mithraeum* at Novae, Novensia 14, 231–239.

Jankowska, A., Kozakiewicz, P. 2011. Identyfikacja węgli drzewnych i odcisku drewna w opus caementitium z Novae (Moesia Inferior), Novensia 11, 119–125.

Morrison, J. S., Coates, J. F. 1996. Greckie i rzymskie okręty wojenne 399–30 p.n.e., Oxford.

Płóciennik, T., Żelazowski J. 2011. Erotic graffito on the Roman brick from Novae (Moesia Inferior), Novensia 22, 77–84.

Pomey, P. 1993. Le navire de Cucuron. Un graffito décoratif, Archaeonautica 11, 149–163.

Sarnowski, T. 1981 (1983). Die Zigelstempel aus Novae, I: Systematik und Typologie, Archeologia 34, 17–61.

Sarnowski, T. 1983 (1985). Wschodni bok twierdzy legionowej (Ha XXVI) Sondaże, Novae – Sektor Zachodni, Archeologia 34, 153–160.

Sarnowski, T., Trynkowski, J. 1983. Legio I Italica – Liburna – Danuvius, in Studien zu der Militärgrenzen Roms ,Vorträge des 13. Internationalen Limeskongress, Aalen, Stuttgart, 536–541.

van de Moortel A., Langdon M. K. 2017. Archaic Ship Graffiti from Sourthern Attica, Greece: typology and preliminary constectual analysis, The International Journal of Nautical Archaeology, 1–24.

Webster, G. Elton, H. 1998. Armia Cesarstwa Rzymskiego z I i II wieku, Norman.

Zaninović, M. 1988. Liburnia Militaris, Opusc. Archeol. 13, 43–67.

Ziomecki, J. 1983 (1985). Novae – Sektor Zachodni, 1981, Archeologia 34, 162–164.

Du Danube à l'Afrique: retour sur la mystérieuse escadre de Maurétanie

Michel Reddé

Pour Ioan Piso, qui a consacré tant d'études à la frontière nord de l'Empire romain[1], le déplacement des unités militaires vers ce front mais aussi depuis l'espace danubien vers d'autres secteurs qui avaient besoin de renforts ne connaît pas de secrets. La manière dont s'effectuaient ces mouvements de troupes, notamment par mer, reste en revanche assez mal connue. C'est dans cette perspective que je voudrais revenir sur un thème que j'avais déjà abordé[2] mais que la multiplication récente des sources épigraphiques invite à revoir, celui de la présence d'une éventuelle escadre régulière à Césarée de Maurétanie.

Depuis E. Ferrero, à la fin du 19e siècle, la plupart des savants qui se sont intéressés aux flottes romaines ont postulé l'existence d'un détachement conjoint et permanent des flottes d'Égypte et de Syrie dans la capitale de la Césarienne[3]. Pour C. G. Starr, cette présence remontait même à la fondation provinciale. Cette opinion n'était fondée, en réalité, que sur un très petit nombre de sources épigraphiques provenant de Cherchel même, et dont la chronologie n'est pas homogène. La plus ancienne est sans doute l'inscription CIL VIII, 21025, pierre tombale d'un triérarque de la *classis Augusta Alexandrina*. Le nom de cet homme – Ti. Claudius Eros –, son statut d'affranchi impérial et la dédicace au datif permettent de situer cet homme sous Claude ou Néron[4]. Vient probablement ensuite une autre épitaphe dédiée par son épouse à un marin de la flotte de Syrie[5]. Dans la mesure où la création de celle-ci n'est sans doute pas antérieure au règne de Vespasien, au plus tôt, voire à celui de Trajan[6], sans parler de la formule dédicatoire employée (DMS), une datation avant la fin du Ier siècle, au mieux, est évidemment exclue. La troisième inscription semble

1 Piso 2005.

2 Reddé 1986, 244–248 ; 561–567.

3 Ferrero 1881; 1882; 1884; Cagnat 1912 ; Courtois 1939, 33–35 ; Starr 1941, 117–118 ; Kienast 1966, 97–103.

4 CIL VIII, 21025 : *Ti(berio) Claudio Aug(usti) lib(erto) Eroti / trierarcho liburnae Ni/li exacto classis Aug(ustae) / Alexandrinae L(ucius) Iuli/us C(ai) f(ilius) Fab(ia) Saturninus et M(arcus) / Antonius Heracla trier(archus) / heredes eius fecerunt* (Cherchel).

5 CIL VIII, 9385 : *D(is) M(anibus) s(acrum) / Lucia Petronia fe/cit Crescenti Silvani / militi classis Syriacae / marito suo bene merenti* (Cherchel).

6 Reddé 1986, 237; 493.

en revanche parler en faveur de la thèse traditionnelle défendue par C. G. Starr[7]. Elle nous révèle en effet le cursus de P. Aelius Marcianus qui, après ses différentes milices, a été *praepositus classis Syriacae et Augustae*, avant de finir sa carrière au commandement de la flotte de Mésie. Il s'agit peut-être d'un Africain revenu à Cherchel, car il doit sa dédicace à un cavalier de l'ala II Thracum, stationnée en Césarienne, dont le défunt avait été préfet. H.-G. Pflaum plaçait ce cursus sous le règne d'Antonin[8]. Le titre de *praepositus* implique un commandement extraordinaire des deux flottes de Syrie et d'Égypte, peut-être pour l'une de ces campagnes militaires en terre d'Afrique dont les exemples abondent au milieu du 2e siècle. Nous y reviendrons. Enfin, une quatrième inscription de Cherchel mentionne encore un commandant des flottes (*praepositus classibus*) que, par analogie avec l'épitaphe de P. Aelius Marcianus, on identifie généralement comme celles de Syrie et d'Égypte, bien que d'autres solutions soient possibles[9]. Ce poste est occupé par un officier qui dédie la pierre à Ti. Claudius Priscianus, procurateur de Césarienne vers 175[10], ce qui permet de situer chronologiquement cette mention des flottes présentes à Cherchel. Aucune de ces inscriptions, étalées sur un bon siècle, ne permet, à elle seule, de conclure à l'existence à Césarée d'une escadre permanente, composée de détachements des deux flottes de Syrie et d'Égypte, surtout dès le milieu du 1er siècle. Les autres textes épigraphiques découverts à Cherchel ne vont pas non plus dans ce sens : CIL VIII, 9379 mentionne un *scr[i]ba classis liburna Aug.*, que l'on développera plus volontiers en *Aug(ustus)* qu'en *Aug(usta)*, qui n'est jamais attesté comme nom de navire[11]. L'inscription n'a de toute manière rien à voir avec la flotte d'Égypte[12] ; différentes épitaphes mentionnent des marins, officiers ou soldats, mais pas leurs unités et peuvent renvoyer à n'importe quelle escadre[13].

---

7 CIL VIII, 9358 = AE 1987, 827 : *P(ublio) Aelio P(ubli) fil(io) Palati/na Marciano / praef(ecto) coh(ortis) I Augustae / Bracarum / praeposito n(umeri) Illyricorum / trib(uno) coh(ortis) Ael(iae) expeditae / praef(ecto) al(ae) Aug(ustae) II Thracum / praeposito al(ae) Gemin(ae) / [[Seba[sten(ae)]] / praeposito classis / Syriacae et Augustae / praef(ecto) classis Moesiaticae / C(aius) Caesius Marcellus / veter(anus) ex dec(urione) / al(ae) II Thracum* (Cherchel).

8 Pflaum 1960–1961, n° 125.

9 CIL VIII, 9363 : *Ti(berio) Cl(audio) Prisciano / proc(uratori) Aug(usti) / proc(uratori) provinciae / Pannoniae / superioris / proc(uratori) regni Norici / proc(uratori) XX(vicesimae) hereditatium / proc(uratori) provinciae / Q[- -]N[- - -]io/rius Severus / praef(ectus) coh(ortis) / Sigambro/rum praepo/situs clas/sibus* (Cherchel).

10 Pflaum 1960–1961, n° 175.

11 Reddé 1986, 665–672.

12 CIL VIII, 9379 : *D(is) M(anibus) / Insteius Victorinus scr[i]/ba classis liburna Aug(ustus) / vix(it) an(nos) XLV h(ic) s(itus) e(st) s(it) t(ibi) t(erra) l(evis) Trebia / Mustia heres coniugi faciun/dum curavit* (Cherchel)

13 CIL VIII, 21017 : *D(is) M(anibus) s(acrum) / Antonio Avito / militi ex n(atione) Sur/orum vixit an(nos) / XXI militavit / an(nos) VI Antonius / Karus duplicar/ius classis fra/tri bene meren/ti fecit pio* ; CIL VIII, 21032 : *D(is) M(anibus) / Gargiliae Honoratae Salditanae vix[it - - -] / annos sine crimine ullo vivite morta[les moneo mors] / omnibus instat discite qui legitis ego [dolens feci] / Herennius Rogatus ses<q=C>u(i)plicarius cla[ssis - - -] / maritae meae dignae et meritae Gargi[lia terra] / tibi levis sit* ; CIL VIII, 9386 = 9562 = 21042 : *Magius Maxim(u)s / [(centurio) c]lassicus vix(it) an(nis) / LX mensibus II et / Rogata Fabricia / Proc(u)li f(ilia) Caesarie(n)s(is) / Max[i]mi \|(centurionis) uxor / [- - - h(ic)] s(iti) s(unt) [- - -] / [Magius] Max[im]us / [sibi et] con[iugi(?) - - -]ri* ; CIL VIII, 9392 = 20946 : *Ob*

Trois documents papyrologiques latins sont parfois évoqués pour mettre en évidence les relations de la *classis Alexandrina* avec Césarée, sans qu'il soit possible d'être toujours assuré de l'identité de cette ville. Le premier (CPL 128) mentionne un soldat (?) anonyme d'une liburne de la flotte égyptienne dans un reçu signé à Césarée au cours du second siècle, mais on n'a pas d'indication permettant de préciser le lieu ; le second (CPL 210) est un document relatif à une dot. Il met en scène un certain C. Valerius Gemellus, *mil(es) classis Aug(ustae) Alexandrinae, libyrni Dracontis*, et il a été acté dans la colonie de Césarée. Dans ce document rédigé en latin, les témoins signent en grec, les sommes sont exprimées en drachmes, de sorte qu'il n'est pas du tout certain, à mon sens, que la rédaction du contrat ait eu lieu en Césarienne. Il est en effet très possible que l'opinio communis selon laquelle la flotte d'Égypte avait une base permanente dans cette province ait jouée dans l'identification topographique de la ville. Le troisième document m'a été signalé par Hélène Cuvigny : il s'agit d'une inscription funéraire écrite à l'encre en grec sur un cartonnage de momie. Elle met en scène un certain Lucius Dexius Herculeianus[14], qui a rendu les devoirs funèbres à son épouse Valeria Marci filia Ingenua, citoyenne romaine originaire de Césarée de Maurétanie[15]. La provenance géographique de la trouvaille (l'Égypte) peut faire du dédicant un marin de la flotte d'Alexandrie, mais la conclusion ne s'impose pas absolument et aucune indication militaire n'est mentionnée. En l'occurrence, le document méritait d'être signalé.

Que l'ancienne capitale de Juba ait été un port d'escale militaire régulière sous l'Empire ne fait évidemment aucun doute. Les inscriptions de *classici* sont trop nombreuses pour qu'on ne puisse l'admettre. On connaît l'étude qu'a consacrée M. P. Speidel[16] à l'envoi de nouvelles recrues constituées par un contingent de 1000 *Iuniores Bessi* à destination des diverses unités de Tingitane, sans doute sous les Sévères. Or c'est à Cherchel qu'est mort le commandant de cette troupe, lors d'une escale dans ce port, ce qui prouve au passage que celui-ci assurait aussi le transit vers la province voisine[17]. Différentes inscriptions d'unités légionnaires venues de Pannonie mais non strictement datées, ont d'ailleurs été découvertes à Cherchel, comme l'avait aussi relevé M. P. Speidel[18]. Les autres ports de

---

memoriam / mariti sui Val(eri) Si/lvani tr(i)erarchi / Celia Monnata cupulam super/stitem rogus eius / vixit an(nos) XLI m(enses) V d(ies) X ; AE 1976, 744 : *[- - -] / Iulius Germanus mil(es) / classis contubernali suo / m(erenti) f(ecit).*

14 Λούκιος Δέξιος Ἡρκουλῃειανός. Le premier éditeur y voyait un natif d'Herculanum, donc un Italien (Sijpesteijn 1978).

15 SEG XXVIII 1536 (TM 24941). D'après l'emploi des épithètes laudatives, Jean Bingen datait le document du 1er s. (Bingen 2005, 148). L'interponction entre les mots aux lignes 1–4 suggère également une datation haute.

16 Speidel 1977b.

17 CIL VIII, 20945 = 9381 : *D(is) M(anibus) s(acrum) Sex(tus) Iul(ius) Iulianus / ex Germania superiore / tribunus n(umeri) Syrorum M(a)l/vensium hic sepultus est / dum deducit iuniores Bessos / (mille) in Tingitana(m) provinci(a)m / qui vixit annis XXXXV cui / monumentum fecit / Iul(ius) Ingenuus frater / et heres curante / Sacimatho / liberto eiusdem / defuncti.*

18 Speidel 1977b. CIL VIII, 9376; 9382; 21049; 21057.

l'ouest de la province, Cartenna[19], Portus Magnus[20] ont joué le même rôle. On trouve aussi des éléments venus de Mésie dans cette dernière ville[21]. Une vexillation de l'*ala Augusta* envoyée du Norique est attestée à Fedjana, au sud de Cherchel, sans doute sous Antonin[22], mais on trouve encore l'*ala Ulpia contariorum* à Portus Magnus ou à Tipasa, qui a vu aussi passer l'*ala Cannanefatium*[23]. Dans tous les cas, il s'agissait de détachements et non d'unités entières, comme l'a bien montré M. P. Speidel[24].

Plusieurs diplômes militaires permettent de replacer certains de ces mouvements de troupes dans un contexte chronologique précis. On mentionnera tout d'abord la libération, le 20 septembre 104, de soldats de la garnison de Tingitane et de *classici*, associés à ce contingent pendant la préfecture de L. Plotius Grypus[25]. C'est, en l'état actuel d'une documentation en perpétuelle évolution, la première fois qu'on voit des marins associés à des auxiliaires en Tingitane, une province qui ne comprenait normalement aucune escadre. En 107 sont libérées des troupes de l'armée de Césarienne ainsi que des *classici* dans un document provenant de Cherchel même[26]. On retrouve sous Hadrien, entre 128 et 131, une composition similaire associant des marins aux auxiliaires de la même garnison dans un texte publié par P. Weiss (2002)[27]. Le diplôme RGZM 34, de 153, fait figurer des soldats de la flotte dans une constitution destinée à la garnison de Tingitane[28]. Trois autres diplômes de la même année, qui mentionnent explicitement des *classici*, peuvent en outre être restitués d'après le libellé du précédent[29]. Enfin, un texte fragmentaire provenant de Mésie inférieure nous oblige à considérer que cette situation existait déjà en 144[30].

Ce n'est pas dire, pour autant, que toutes les constitutions attestent une libération de marins sous le règne d'Antonin, puisque, par exemple, le fameux diplôme de Brigetio, daté de 150, et qui fait allusion à une expédition en Césarienne ne les mentionne pas[31] ; il en va de même pour celui du 24 septembre 151[32]. Le même cas se présente encore dans un document de 152 publié par W. Eck et A. Pangerl[33]. La même année ou l'année suivante, les renforts mentionnés dans un autre diplôme incluent aussi, pour la première fois, des éléments venus de Bretagne en sus des éléments tirés de Mésie inférieure, mis, cette fois,

19 CIL VIII, 2357; 9653.
20 CIL VIII, 9761.
21 CIL VIII, 972.
22 AE 1975, 951. Voir Speidel 1975.
23 CIL VIII, 21620; 9291; AE 1951, 265. La liste n'est sans doute pas exhaustive. Pour une mise au point récente sur ces unités, voir Le Bohec 2015 et Laporte 2016.
24 Speidel 1977b.
25 Eck, Gradel 2021.
26 CIL XVI, 56 = CIL VIII, 20978 (Benseddik 1982, n° 35).
27 AE 2002, 1753 = RMD V, 377.
28 Les remarques de W. Eck dans la recension de la publication des diplômes du RGZM (Bon. Jahrb. 206, 2006, 353–354) n'ont pas abordé cette question.
29 RMD V, 409 ; 410 ; 411.
30 AE 2004, 1924 = RMD V, 398 = RGZM 34, 102.
31 CIL XVI, 99.
32 RGZM 32.
33 Eck, Pangerl 2018.

à disposition du préfet de Tingitane. Là non plus les marins ne sont pas mentionnés, pas plus que dans le diplôme daté de 156, réétudié par P. Holder[34].

Que conclure de cette longue énumération ?

On se gardera tout d'abord de rapprocher systématiquement tous ces textes des célèbres révoltes Maures survenues sous le règne d'Antonin, dont le volumineux dossier historiographique n'a pas besoin ici d'un feuillet supplémentaire[35] : la chronologie des documents examinés montre en effet que la libération de *classici* et d'unités ou de recrues venues des provinces danubiennes s'est faite en 104, en 107, entre 128 et 131, en 144, en 153 dans des conditions similaires. Si celles de 153 peuvent sans doute être rattachées aux soulèvements attestés sous le règne d'Antonin, et dont la chronologie exacte est toujours débattue, il n'en va évidemment pas de même pour les autres. En revanche, la présence de marins dans la garnison de Tingitane pourrait être plus significative.

Ce n'est pourtant pas une raison suffisante, à mon avis, pour chercher à localiser une base navale inédite dans cette province. Les marins libérés dans les diplômes que nous avons cités ont toute chance d'être des recrues envoyées en renfort, sans que leur unité d'origine soit impliquée en tant que telle. M. P. Speidel[36] avait en effet montré, de manière convaincante, que les hommes envoyés depuis le front pannonien ne voyageaient pas en corps constitués, ce qui aurait probablement déstabilisé le front danubien ; ils étaient extraits des différentes unités installées sur le *limes* et affectés à leur arrivée par le procurateur provincial. M. P. Speidel a été suivi sur ce point par M. Christol[37] puis, plus récemment, par W. Eck, P. Holder et A. Pangerl[38]. On ne voit pas pourquoi il n'en aurait pas été de même des marins qui accompagnaient ces auxiliaires. Mais l'inscription des *Iuniores Bessi* montre en même temps que, si la destination finale des renforts était bien la garnison de Tingitane, le convoi passait par le port de Césarée puisque c'est là que le commandant de l'expédition est mort. Voilà qui nous ramène à la composition possible de l'« escadre de Maurétanie ».

Il n'est pas sans intérêt de rappeler, à ce moment du raisonnement, que les deux seules inscriptions mentionnant des détachements groupés de plusieurs escadres apparaissent l'une sous Antonin, avec P. Aelius Marcianus, *praepositus classis Syriacae et Augustae*, l'autre sous Marc-Aurèle, avec un *praepositus* de flottes anonymes, et non dès la création provinciale. Il n'est donc pas exclu de penser que ces groupements tactiques étaient provisoires et non permanents, liés à une situation qui pouvait être temporairement troublée. On peut songer, à cette occasion, aux opérations menées sous Antonin et son successeur ;

---

34 Eck, Holder, Pangerl 2016.
35 En dernier lieu, voir les bonnes analyses de Hamdoune 2018 et de Matei-Popescu 2021.
36 Speidel 1977a.
37 Christol 1981.
38 Eck, Holder, Pangerl 2016.

de ce point de vue, la réflexion déjà ancienne conduite par J. Baradez[39] sur les autres ports de la côte de la Césarienne occidentale (Portus Magnus, Cartenna, Tipasa) où ont été retrouvées des épitaphes de légionnaires venus de Pannonie retrouve quelque crédibilité, bien que toutes ne soient sans doute pas homogènes chronologiquement et ne puissent être systématiquement reliées aux révoltes des Maures sous Antonin, comme l'avait fait remarquer R. Rebuffat[40]. Mais les critiques de ce dernier à la thèse « coloniale » de J. Baradez mériteraient aussi d'être réexaminées. Quant aux incursions en Bétique de ces tribus, sous Marc-Aurèle, elles auraient pu nécessiter une présence navale renforcée sur la côte rifaine, mais ce n'est là, bien entendu, qu'une hypothèse finalement mal étayée[41]. Il est donc possible que, vers le milieu du 2e siècle, le port de Cherchel ait accueilli non pas une escadre permanente constituée sur le modèle des autres flottes provinciales, mais un détachement constitué ad hoc, sous commandement d'un *praepositus* temporaire et non d'un préfet. D'une manière générale, néanmoins, la documentation épigraphique actuellement disponible semble montrer que Césarée constituait le principal port de destination pour les troupes qui gagnaient la Césarienne occidentale et la Tingitane intérieure.

Mais ce mouvement n'était pas à sens unique et il fallait bien que les troupes repartent un jour vers le *limes* danubien. G. Di Vita-Évrard[42] a ainsi publié une épitaphe de Cherchel qui montre le passage dans ce port d'un vétéran de la *legio II adiutrix* revenu dans son pays et mort à Césarée entre le 14 février et le 15 mars 169[43]. La carte des Africains enrôlés dans les légions de Pannonie, majoritairement originaires de proconsulaire ou de Numidie, ne plaide pas, néanmoins, pour un rôle particulier du port de Cherchel dans ces déplacements qui concernaient plutôt l'est de la province[44]. En revanche, le dossier des *Mauri gentiles* envoyés sur le front danubien offre d'intéressants développements. Réétudiant les trois diplômes dans lesquels ils sont mentionnés[45], et auxquels est récemment venu s'ajouter un quatrième document[46], M. Christol a rappelé les origines de cette levée[47]. Il s'agissait probablement de soldats recrutés au sein des tribus révoltées et qu'on envoyait en Dacie supérieure, accompagnés de vexillaires détachés des armées d'Afrique et de Césarienne et chargés de les encadrer. Sans revenir ici sur tous les problèmes juridiques posés

39 Baradez 1954.

40 Rebuffat 1974.

41 La bibliographie est considérable et il n'est pas question de la mentionner ici. On se référera pour l'essentiel à Alföldy 1985 et à son étude de l'inscription de Liria, avec les réserves de Le Roux 2000, 453.

42 Di Vita-Évrard 1994b.

43 AE 1993, 1783 : *D(is) M(anibus) s(acrum) / [- - -] Firmo, Tub(usuctu ?) ex vet(erano) leg(ionis) II / [Ad]iu(tricis), vix(it) ann(is) LXXX, def(uncto) / [- - -] Mart(iis* vel *ias) Caes(area), Sossio Prisco / [et A]pollinare co(n)s(ulibus), pr(ovincia) CXXX, / [et Fi]rm(a)e fil(iae) virg(ini), v(ixit) a(nnis) X, def(unctae) / [- - -] isd(em) co(n)s(ulibus), ead(em) pr(ovincia), Per/[- - -a- - -]sca coni(ugi) b(ene) m(erenti).*

44 Di Vita-Évrard 1994a. Voir aussi Le Bohec 1989, 508–514. Comme l'avait déjà souligné G. Di Vita, l'enquête mériterait sans doute d'être poursuivie.

45 AE 2014, 1639, de 146 ; AE 2007, 1763, de 152 ; CIL XVI, 108, de 158.

46 Holder 2022, 283, n° 5, de 152. Il faudrait bien entendu se demander pourquoi ces vexillaires de Maurétanie césarienne sont renvoyés en Dacie supérieure avec les *Mauri Gentiles* au moment de la révolte maure, alors que l'on envoie des renforts en Afrique depuis le limes danubien.

47 Christol 2020.

par ces diplômes[48], il suffira de rappeler que tous ces mouvements de troupes entre le front danubien et l'Afrique nécessitaient un dispositif portuaire dont Cherchel était l'élément principal et la marine le vecteur essentiel.

La manière dont s'effectuaient ces déplacements entre la frontière septentrionale de l'Empire et les rivages sud de la Méditerranée n'est pas très bien documentée dans nos sources mais on dispose malgré tout de quelques éléments de réflexion. Peu après la mort de Germanicus, écrit Tacite dans les Annales III, 9, *Piso, Delmatico mari tramisso relictisque apud Anconam navibus, per Picenum ac mox Flaminiam viam adsequitur legionem, quae e Pannonia in Urbem, dein praesidio Africae ducebatur.* Ce passage est important car il décrit, de manière assez exceptionnelle, l'itinéraire des troupes entre le limes danubien et la rive sud de la Méditerranée. Celles-ci évitaient en effet de contourner toute l'Italie par mer —un voyage dangereux et plus long— mais transitaient par Rome même. Ce passage par la capitale de l'Empire est encore attesté grâce à une inscription qu'y a laissée, au second siècle, un décurion de l'*Ala Atectorigiana*, appartenant à l'armée de Mésie, en souvenir de son épouse[49]. M. P. Speidel, qui a attiré l'attention sur ce texte, considère que cette femme[50], originaire de Césarienne, est morte à l'occasion d'un transfert de l'unité entre l'Afrique et le front Danubien, une hypothèse vraisemblable[51]. D'Ostie s'offraient différentes routes maritimes possibles, probablement via la Sardaigne, où est connu un port d'escale de la flotte de Misène[52].

Ces transferts de troupes s'effectuaient régulièrement à bord de bâtiments appartenant aux escadres militaires[53]. Un vaisseau long ponté pouvait accueillir un nombre important de soldats, comme le montre l'histoire de la marine militaire à l'époque républicaine, où les exemples sont nombreux. Pendant les guerres civiles, c'était la norme. César fit par exemple traverser la mer à six légions en les embarquant sur des galères au début de la guerre d'Afrique; seuls les cavaliers voyagèrent avec leurs chevaux sur des bâtiments de commerce pour d'évidentes raisons de place[54]. Naturellement, on choisissait toujours le trajet le plus court, en l'occurrence le détroit de Sicile, sans réussir forcément à éviter tous les dangers et les mauvaises fortunes de mer. C'est probablement ce type de pratique, toujours en usage sous l'Empire, qui fit de Salone un port de transit entre l'Adriatique et le front oriental, raison pour laquelle on retrouve des escales militaires des flottes prétoriennes à Athènes ou Éphèse[55] : la vie militaire imposait en permanence des transferts de front à front, donc l'usage de la voie maritime. À Césarée de Maurétanie aussi on avait be-

48 Outre l'article de M. Christol, déjà cité, on pourra voir aussi Le Roux 1986.

49 CIL VI, 33032 : Rome : *D(is) M(anibus) / Ulpia Danae / ex Mauretania / Caesariensi v(ixit) a(nnos) XXIIX / C(aius) Valerius Maximus / decurio alae Atectorigi/arse (sic!) exercitus Moesiae / inferioris coniugi / [pi]entissimae fecit.*

50 Speidel 1977b.

51 La date de l'inscription ne peut être précisée davantage, l'unité en question étant présente en Mésie tout au long du second siècle.

52 Reddé 1986, 205–207.

53 Reddé 1986, 370–399.

54 César, B.Afr. II, 1.

55 Reddé 2001.

soin de bateaux pour ces tâches ordinaires de logistique : ainsi peuvent s'expliquer la présence de la flotte d'Égypte ou celle de Syrie, après sa création, même si nos sources sur les transferts entre la Césarienne et l'Orient sont moins abondantes que celles qui concernent le limes danubien. Pendant les campagnes importantes, comme celles d'Antonin contre les Maures, on pouvait laisser sur place un dispositif semi-permanent, sous l'autorité d'un *praepositus*, sans avoir à créer une escadre nouvelle.[56]

Bibliographie

Alföldy G. 1985. Bellum Mauricum, Chiron 15, 87–105 (= MAVORS III, 463–481).

Baradez J. 1954. Les nouvelles fouilles de Tipasa et les opérations d'Antonin le Pieux en Maurétanie, Libyca II, 89–147.

Benseddik N. 1982. Les troupes auxiliaires de l'armée romaine en Maurétanie Césarienne sous le Haut-Empire, Alger.

Bingen J. 2005. Pages d'épigraphie grecque II, Bruxelles.

Cagnat R. 1912. L'armée romaine d'Afrique, Paris.

Christol M. 1981. L'armée des provinces pannoniennes et la pacification des révoltes maures sous Antonin le Pieux, Antiquités Africaines 17, 133–141.

Christol M. 2020. Conflits, tensions et recrutements : les Mauri Gentiles, Antiquités Africaines 56, 293–301.

Courtois Ch. 1939. Les politiques navales de l'Empire romain, Revue historique, 17–47 et 225–259.

Di Vita-Évrard G. 1994a. Légionnaires africains en Pannonie au IIe s. ap. J.C, in G. Hajnóczi (ed.), La Pannonia e l'Impero Romano. Atti del convegno internazionale "La Pannonia e l'Impero romano". Academia d'Ungheria e l'Istituto Austriaco di Cultura (Roma, 13–16 gennaio 1994), Rome, 97–114.

Di Vita-Évrard G. 1994b. L'ère de Maurétanie : une nouvelle attestation, L'Africa Romana 10–3, 1061–1070.

Eck W., Holder P., Pangerl A. 2016. Eine Konstitution aus dem Jahr 152 oder 153 für niedermösische und britannische Truppen, abgeordnet nach Mauretania Tingitana, mit einem Appendix von Paul Holder, ZPE 199, 187–201.

Eck W., Pangerl A. 2018. Eine Konstitution für abgeordnete Truppen aus vier Provinzen aus dem Jahr 152, ZPE 208, 229–236.

Eck W., Gradel I. 2021. Eine Konstitution für das Heer von Mauretania Tingitana vom 20. September 104 n. Chr., ZPE 219, 248–255.

Ferrero E. 1881. Iscrizioni classiarie dell'Africa. Atti della Reale Accademia delle scienze di Torino 17, 88–93.

Ferrero E. 1882. Inscriptions de l'Afrique relatives à la flotte, Bulletin épigraphique II, 157–162.

56 Nous avons eu connaissance trop tard de l'article de Matei-Popescu 2021 que nous a gentiment communiqué son auteur et dont nous n'avons pu intégrer toutes les conclusions dans cette contribution.

Ferrero E. 1884. La marine militaire de l'Afrique romaine. Bulletin trimestriel des Antiquités Africaines 2, 157–181.

Hamdoune C. 2018. Ad Fines Africae Romanae. Les mondes tribaux dans les provinces maurétaniennes. Scripta Antiqua 111, Ausonius Éditions, Bordeaux.

Holder P. 2022. Some Roman military diploma fragments found in Ukraine, in W. Eck, F. Santangelo, and K. Vössing (eds.), Emperor, Army, and Society. Studies in Roman Imperial History for Anthony Birley, Bonn, 275–288.

Kienast D. 1966. Untersuchungen zu den Kriegsflotten der römischen Kaiserzeit, Bonn.

Laporte J.-P. 2016. Notes sur l'armée romaine de Maurétanie césarienne de 40 à 455, in C. Wolff, P. Faure (éds.), Les auxiliaires de l'armée romaine. Des alliés aux fédérés, CEROR 51, Paris, 379–408.

Le Bohec Y. 1989. La troisième légion Auguste, Paris.

Le Bohec Y. 2015. La stratégie de Rome en Maurétanie césarienne sous le Principat, Ikosim 4, 39–50.

Le Roux P. 1986. Les diplômes militaires et l'évolution de l'armée romaine de Claude à Septime Sévère : auxilia, numeri et nationes, in W. Eck, H. Wolff (eds.), Heer und Integrationspolitik: die römischen Militärdiplome als historische Quelle, Köln, Böhlau, Passauer historische Forschungen 2, 347–374.

Le Roux P. 2000. Armée et société en Hispania sous l'Empire, in G. Alföldy, B. Dobson, W. Eck (eds.), Kaiser, Heer und Gesellschaft in der römischen Kaiserzeit : Gedenkschrift für Eric Birley, Habes 31, Stuttgart, 261–278.

Matei-Popescu F. 2021. Auxiliary Units from the European Provinces in the Moorish War of Antoninus Pius, in S. Cristea, C. Timoc, E.C. De Sena (eds.), Africa, Egypt and the Danubian Provinces of the Roman Empire, BAR S 3010, Oxford, 5–16.

Pflaum H.-G. 1960–1961. Les carrières procuratoriennes équestres sous le Haut-Empire romain, Paris.

Piso I. 2005. An der Nordgrenze des Römischen Reiches. Ausgewählte Studien (1972–2003), Habes 41, Stuttgart.

Rebuffat R. 1974. Enceintes urbaines et insécurité en Maurétanie Tingitane, MEFRA 86–1, 501–522.

Reddé M. 1986. Mare Nostrum. Les infrastructures, le dispositif et l'histoire de la marine militaire sous l'Empire romain, BEFAR 260, Rome.

Reddé M. 2001. Le rôle militaire des ports de l'Adriatique sous le Haut-Empire, in Cl. Zaccaria (ed.), Strutture portuali e rotte maritime nell'Adriatico di età romana, Antichità Altoadriatiche XVLI, 43–54 (= Legiones, provincias, classes. Morceaux choisis par l'auteur, Bordeaux, 2022, 43–52 ; on line una-editions.fr).

Sijpesteijn P.J. 1978. An unpublished Greek Funeral Inscription, Mnemosyne 31–4, 416–420.

Speidel M.P. 1975. Africa and Rome : Continuous Resistance ? (a Vexillation of the Norican Ala Augusta in Mauretania), Proceedings of the African Classical Association 13, 36–38 (= MAVORS I, 337–339).

Speidel M.P. 1977a. Pannonian Troops in the Moorish War of Antoninus Pius, in Acta International Limes Congress, Budapest, 129–135 (= MAVORS I, 211–215).

Speidel M.P. 1977b. A thousand Thracian Recruits for Mauretania Tingitana, Antiquités Africaines 11, 167–173 (= MAVORS I, 341–347).
Starr C.G. 1941. The Roman imperial navy, 31 BC-AD 324, Cambridge.
Weiss P. 2002. Ausgewählte neue Militärdiplome. Seltene Provinzen (Africa, Mauretania Caesarensis), späte Urkunden für Praetorianer (Caracalla, Philippus), Chiron 32, 491–544.

Honouring the emperor in the personal *nomen* nomenclature

Ivo Topalilov*

It is now well established that the imperial cult as the essential in the Roman empire finds its manifestation in almost every aspect of the life of the Roman citizens – public or private. Thus, along with the construction or adaptation of temples and shrines, public buildings and complexes such as for example central main square (agora, forum), but also the central market, basilica, city-hall, baths, triumphal or honorary arch etc., and other openair spaces, all of this attested by archaeology, local and central coin issues as well as epigraphic monuments, it is to be found also in private *domus* and *villae* by votives, statues, images etc. It is not the purpose here to present all its manifestations in public and private life, but rather to deal with one aspect that can be attributed to both public and private life, viz. the nomenclature of the Roman citizens, and especially those with military milieu. Indeed, one would point out the use of the imperial *nomina* that is to be found in the personal name nomenclature of many of the new citizens as *praenomen* and *nomen*. And this may be so for example in the cases with the *equites singulares Augusti* who received the name of the emperor on their recruitment in the cavalry without receiving citizenship yet.[1] This may be also so with the auxiliary soldiers when receiving *honesta missio* or granting Roman citizenship of the heirs, and not in the nomenclature of the sailors, although serving in the praetorian fleets – either in Misenum or Ravenna.[2] Subsequently, there are not a few cases when the imperial names are passed on to the first-born son of these new Roman citizens and further on, which resulted the numerous cases of citizens with same imperial names attested in inscriptions dated the 3rd century reveal. Undoubtedly, in this way they would fit more easily into the *Pax Romana* than by retaining their fully peregrine names, although used as cognomens in order to complete the *tria nomina* requirement. The early recruits in Thrace provide an approximate date for this change which opened the possibility of receiving also the imperor's *nomina*. Thus, based on the available for now sources it was not until the reign of Trajan when the full use of

* Institute of Balkan Studies and Centre of Thracology "Prof. Alexander Fol" - Bulgarian Academy of Sciences,

1 Speidel 1994, 10–11. See on the status of the sailors – Starr 1993, 66–74; Kienast 1966, 26–29; Reddé 1986, 526.

2 Salomies 1996, 174.

the *tria nomina* is detected in the nomenclature of a Thracian auxiliary soldier. This was C. Iulius C. f. Valens Tralles, who was an *eques* of *cohors III Gallorum* and on 19 July 114 when discharged he also received the Roman *tria nomina*.[3] Consequently veterans like P. Aelius Bassus, nat(ione) Bessus, Claudia Apris[4] and of P. Aelius Avitus, Traianopoli, natione Trax appeared.[5]

I believe, however, that there is another possibility in the *nomen* nomenclature of honouring the emperor who granted Roman citizenship to someone, his father or grandfather and thereby provided a greater opportunity for career advancement and a better life in the province and likely at Rome itself. It deals with one of the main components of the name nomenclature, which is the tribal affiliation. Thus, according to *lex Iulia municipalis* every citizen's nomenclature should include *nomina, praenomina,* the names of *patres* or *patronus,* tribal designation, and *cognomina*.[6] The new Roman citizens (*cives novi*) until the reign of Hadrian should have been traditionally enlisted in emperor's tribe on discharge, although the military diplomas issued for the Thracian auxiliary veterans missed the tribe affiliation and even the *tria nomina* to the contrary to the cases with the Thracian aristocrats of 1st century, the so-called *strategoi*.[7] Given these diplomas, it is very tempting to conclude that not all of the *cives novi* were enlisted in the emperor's tribe, especially in the auxiliary in the second half of 1st c. In the time of Hadrian, however, the traditional tribe system seems to had lost its importance and functions and therefore abandoned, and in order to meet the requirements of *lex Iulia municipalis* especially for the soldiers in Rome, but not only, the so-called 'pseudo-tribe' was invented. In fact, this was not something new as we could point out the earlier 'tribes' *Iulia* and *Claudia* by which Caesar and then Tiberius and Claudius extended the social base of their imperial authority in contrast to the traditional tribe system.[8] Indeed, Augustus with *Fabia*,[9] Flavian emperors with *Quirina*, Trajan with *Papiria* and Hadrian with *Sergia* returned to the traditional tribe system, but the decline of this institution opened the way of the pseudo-tribes in the nomen nomenclature of Roman citizens. According to the established practice the new Roman citizens received the epithet in the city-title which is the *nomen gentilicium* of the emperor who promoted most recently the *civitas* in rang.[10] In the cases with the citizens

3 On the diploma – see Roxan, Paunov 1997, 269–279.

4 CIL 6, 3177.

5 CIL 6, 3176.

6 CIL 12, 593: quae municipia, coloniae, praefecturae c(iuium) R(omanorum) in Italia sunt erunt, quei in eis municipieis, colon[i]eis, / praefectureis maximum mag(istratum) maxim[a]mue potestatem ibei habebit, tum cum censor aliusue / quis mag(istratus) Romae populi censum aget, is diebus LX proxumeis quibus sciet Romae c[e]nsum populi / agi, omnium municipium, colonorum, suorum queique eius praefecturae erunt q(uei) c(iues) R(omanei) erunt censum / ag[i]to eorumque nomina, praenomina, patres aut patronos, tribus, cognomina et quot annos quisque eorum habe[bi]t et rationem pecuniae ex formula census quae Romae ab eo qui tum censum / populi acturus erit proposita erit a[b] ieis iurateis accipito.

7 See for this Topalilov 2017, 125–138.

8 On *Iulia* and *Claudia* – see Forni 1985, 3–12, 29–32.

9 See Lassère 2005, 119.

10 See Forni 1985.

originated from the Roman colonies and *municipia*, although some exceptions, this rule was followed as a whole. It was, however, another matter with the Thracians who enter the Praetorian Guards after 193 with Septimius Severus's reform. The prevailing number of them originated from the *civitates stipendiariae*, with just few from colonia Claudia Aprensis. The lack of any epithet in the title of these *civitates* allowed the veterans to undertake an initiative in choosing a tribe, in this case a pseudo-tribe in their nomenclature. Consequently, the epigraphic monuments reveal variety of imperial names used such as Ulpia, Flavia, Aelia, Iulia and Claudia, with the first two mostly repeated. It is not rarely the cases with several imperial *gentilicia* used by veterans from the same town.[11] It was in these cases, where, I believe, honouring of the emperor may be observed. For example, a small group of citizens may be attested in the epigraphic sources dated particularly later to the second half of 2nd century – first decades of 3rd century with the resemblance of their *praenomen* which is the emperor's gentilicium names and the pseudo-tribe. Some examples such as this of P. Ael. P. f. Aelia (tribu) Pacatus Scupis (CIL 6, 533 = ILS 2088) and T. Ae. T. f. Ael(ia tribu) Titianus Pauta(lia) (CIL 6, 32624 c 26) are very telling and have already been discussed. In both cases, it is obvious that the use of this very pseudo-tribe is a personal choice and had nothing to do with the epithet in the respective city-title, or some initiative such as construction of curtain wall, emperor's visits or even re-establishment.[12] These examples, however, are not the only ones, and I would like to add some more in this article. They are as follows:

- P. Aelius P. f. Ael. Sept. Romulus Aquinq(o) (CIL 6, 1057–1058/31234)
- M. Aur. M. f. Aur. Dalutius Cibal(is) (CIL 6, 2833–32542, b 9)
- M. Aur. [M. f. Aur]el. Daezius Cibal(is) (CIL 6, 2833–32542b 12)
- M. Aur. M. f. Aur. Dassianus Cibal(is) (CIL 6, 2833–32542b 17)
- M. Aur. M. f. Aur. Dolea Cibal(is) (CIL 6, 2835–32542, d 6)

Indeed, this type of cases are not numerous, and some of them may be accepted as a pure mistake by the benefactor or stone cutter as suggested for the case with T. Aelius Titianus from Pautalia who chose *Aelia*,[13] but it is highly improbable that all of the cases of this kind would be mistaken. I believe that the resemblance between the imperial *praenomen* and *nomen* of T. Aelius Hadrianus and *Ael(ia tribu)* should not be regarded accidentally as it is not an isolated example. The case P. Aelius P. f. Ael. Sept. Romulus Aquinq(o) is even more cogent. He was a centurion of the fifth cohort of vigilantes known from the inscription on the base of statue for Caracalla set up in Rome, dated to 210 and whose inscription should be developed as *P(ublius) Aelius P(ubli) f(ilius) Ael(ia) Sept(imia) Romulus Aquinq(o)* rather than *P(ublius) Aelius P(ubli) f(ilius) Ael(ia) Sept(imius) Romulus Aquin<q>(o)*.[14] A few words ahead are needed.

---

11 See most recently in Topalilov 2018, 151–154.
12 See Topalilov 2018, 153.
13 Геров 1960, 106, note 2.
14 Cenati 2023, 256–257, C 2.

It is now established that among the Hadrianic *municipia* in Pannonia was municipium Aelium Aquincum, which was inhabited with natives who owned their citizenship to Trajan or Hadrian.[15] Probably in the year 194 Aquincum was promoted to the rank of *colonia* becoming *colonia Septimia*.[16] It seems that the grandfather of P. Aelius Romulus, given the absence of his tribe affiliation to *Sergia*, did not belong to the aristocracy and therefore he did not enter the *ordo* of the *municipia*.[17] Even if he was, and therefore present an isolated case, the possible strict control in Rome over the nomen nomenclature did not enable his eventual tribe affiliation to be transferred to the *nomen* nomenclature of his heirs as it might be in the provinces. Nonetheless, what interests is the mention of two tribe affiliations.

The two tribes affiliation used in P. Aelius Romulus' nomenclature is not an isolated case. Indeed, such type of cases are rare, but nonetheless they existed. A similar case is that of the eques singularis Dextrianus in whose tombstone set in Rome his *origo* is mentioned as *Ael. [Sept. Aquin]ci.*[18]

Of great importance for our study are the cases with the numerous *M. Aurelii* who are listed in the *laterculi Praetorianorum*, originating from Cibalae. Thus, according to A. Mócsy with their cognomina revealing intense Dacianization these *M. Aurelii* should be regarded are heirs of this group of Cotini that settled under Marcus Aurelius in the territory of Cibalae and which under the Severans entered the legions, and some of them – the praetorian guard as we can observe from the laterculi.[19] Cibalae was among these Hadrianic municipia, which developed from *civitas peregrina* and whose decurions were most probably natives who acquired citizenship.[20] Later, during the time of the Severans Cibalae become colony.[21] The case with the pseudo-tribe and its connection with Cibalae has been discussed by A. Moscy who concludes that *Aurelia* can hardly be accepted as indication of a promotion under Marcus Aurelius.[22] So, the question was why these praetorians used *Aurelia* instead of possible *Aelia* or *Septimia* especially given the date of the inscription, 8 June 223, which offers the possibility of two pseudo-tribes as it was mostly in the rest of the examples from the province? I believe that the answer lies on the presumption that by this act the praetorians honoured the emperor who gave their fathers the Roman citizenship, possibly *latifundia* in the marshy region of the *Hiulca palus* and high rank into the municipal society of Cibalae. We can hardly find such well attested in the epigraphy example of this type and therefore they may serve as *par excellence* for this type of study. It should be underlined that *Aurelia tribu* did not gain much acceptance in

---

15 CIL 3, 10418; Mócsy 2014, 141–142.
16 Mócsy 2014, 218.
17 For the constitution of the *ordo* of municipium Aelium Aquincum from the aristocracy of *civitas peregrina* – see Mocsy 2014, 144.
18 AE 1954, 77.
19 Mócsy 2014, 248.
20 Mócsy 2014, 142, 152.
21 Mócsy 2014, 225; CIL 3, 14038.
22 Mócsy 2014, 390, n. 60.

the *nomen* nomenclature in the province although the physical appearance of the emperor Marcus Aurelius in the region.

These examples, which do not include all known similar ones, and whose number will, no doubt, increase in time, in my opinion unequivocally reveal the emperor's veneration in one of the most important and personal specificities of each individual in the Roman Empire, namely, the *origo*, an immutable element alongside the *tria nomina*. Through the use of the imperial genitive as a pseudo-tribe, however, not only is the emperor honoured as the one who gave Roman citizenship and therefore the opportunity for privilege and a better life within *Pax Romana*, but in fact the origin of the individual Roman are linked to the emperor. Belonging to his own *gens*, he belonged to the *gens* of the emperor; honouring his ancestors, he honoured the emperor. The social base of the emperor and his heirs was in the system of patronage: the emperor was the patron and the rests – his clients.

Indeed, the use of two tribes in the *nomen* onomastics was a practice although not widely spread practice. The epigraphic reveals the use of at least two models when the *full origo* is presented, *i.e.* with the full city-title: the mixture of two traditional tribes or of tribe and pseudo-tribe.[23] The case with P. Aelius Romulus belongs to the latter, while this of M. Titius Proculus to the former. The case of M. Titius Proculus is of particular interest. He was *trib(unus) mil(itum) leg(ionis) IIII F(laviae) F(elicis)* who died in Pontes where his tombstone was found, and he was also former *praef(ectus) coh(ortis) I Alpinor(um)*. His full nomenclature is M. Titius M. f. Quir. Proculus Fabia Roma[24] and most probably he died somewhere between 105–131.[25] His *gens* belonged to *Quirina*, and Rome is mentioned with one of the most popular tribes of the city – *Fabia*. Already C. Grotefend had noted the popularity enjoyed by the tribe *Fabia* in imperial Rome, suggesting that it was a consequence of the expansion of the city into the *pomerium*.[26] J.-M. Lassère allows for another interpretation, related to the fact that this was the tribe in which the colonies in the time of Augustus in the eastern provinces of the empire were ascribed to,[27] allowing for a closer relationship between the first *princeps* and *Fabia* to be concluded. Probably for this reason the tribe was subsequently favoured,[28] and given the basic reconstruction of Rome under Augustus, but also his authority, the appearance of *Fabia Roma* is a logical consequence. Given the discussed so far examples with the deliberate use of the pseudo-tribe, one would suspect that the model of mixture of two pseudo-tribes may also be expected.

It seems, however, that this is not the only kind of honouring the emperor by the tribe affiliation in the *nomen* nomenclature. A group of *P. Aelii* of various civic and religious rank in Apulum may provide a good example for this. Among these *P. Aelii* were P. Aelius Marcellus, *vir egregius*,[29] P. Aelius Silvanus, who was *IIvir(alis) et sa/cerd(otalis) [co]l(oniae)*

23 The examples with tribe and pseudo-tribe and cited in Forni 1985, 40–42.

24 AE 2003, 1530.

25 Matei-Popescu & Tentea 2018, 32–33.

26 Grotefend 1863, 75.

27 Lassère 2005, 119.

28 Stoev 2019, 408, 410.

29 CIL 3, 1180 = CIL 3, 7795 (= IDR-03-05-02, 442 = IDRE-01, 121)(193–235): P(ublio) Ael(io) P(ubli) f(ilio) P[a]p(iria) Marcello / v(iro) e(gregio) p(rimo) p(ilo) ex praef(ecto) leg(ionis) VII /

A[p(ulensis)] as well as *eques Romanum*,[30] P. Aelius Genialis, who a *decurio* and pontifex of the colony,[31] and P. Aelius Strenus, who held the office of *sacerdotes*, and various civic ones in *colonia* Sarmizegetusa, *colonia* Apulum and *colonia* Drobeta.[32] The date of these tombstones is the time of Septimius Severus at earliest. In order to reveal their importance for our study, a few words are needed in advance.

It is now established that after the second Dacian war (AD 105–106), Apulum became the garrison of the 13th Gemina legion with a civilian settlement, the *canabae legionis*, which in the first half of the 2nd century AD was a *pagus* of the colonia Ulpia Traiana Sarmizegetusa. Under Marcus Aurelius the *canabae* were promoted to *municipium Aurelium Apulum/ municipium Aurelium Apulense* and with the military and administrative reforms undertaken the consular governor of *Dacia Apulensis* started to reside at Apulum in the *praetorium consularis*. Since that time it was also the place for the reunion of the province assembly (*concilium trium Daciarum*). Most probably in the time of Commodus, the *municipium* became *colonia Aurelia Apulensis*.

From the time of Septimius Severus another civilian settlement of the legionary fort become *municipium Septimium Apulense*, and coexisted with the *colonia Aurelia*. In around middle of the 3rd century it was promoted to the rank of *colonia* as *colonia nova Apulensis*.[33]

It should be emphasized that due to its late establishment, the colonial elite of Apulum was not enrolled into the emperor's tribe and therefore no specific tribe's identity linked with Apulum would be clearly established in this way. Given this, and also the existing practice of preserving the original tribe by the settlers, several original Roman tribes can be found in grave epitaphs in Apulum such as *Fabia*,[34] *Collina*,[35] *Vellina*,[36] *Galeria*,[37]

Cl(audiae) et I Adiut(ricis) s[u]bprin / cipe peregr(inorum) |(centurioni) frum[ent(ario)] / sacer(doti) Lauren[t(ium) Lavi]/niae(!) patr(ono) [rerum publi] / car(um) Fu[lgin(iatium) Foro Fla] / min(ensium) [itemq(ue) Iguvinor(um)] / [.

30 CIL 3, 1207 (= IDR-3-5-2, 483)(201–275): P(ublio) Ael(io) P(ubli) f(ilio) Pap(iria) / Silvano / IIvir(ali) et sa/cerd(otali) [co]l(oniae) A[p(ulensis)] / eq(uiti) R(omano) e(gregiae) m(emoriae) v(iro) / Fabia Lucil/la e(gregiae) m(emoriae) v(iri) filia / mater coll(egiorum) / fabr(um) et cent(onariorum) / coloniae s(upra) s(criptae) / socero sui / amantissi/mo.

31 CIL 3, 1208 (= IDR-03-05-02, 440)(201–230): P(ublio) Ael(io) P(ubli) fil(io) Pap(iria) / Geniali dec(urioni) / et pontifici / col(oniae) Apul(ensis) pa/tron(o) coll(egii) / cent(onariorum) P(ublius) Ael(ius) / Euthymus / libert(us).

32 CIL 3, 1209 (= IDR-03-05-02, 443)(222–275): P(ublio) Ael(io) P(ubli) fil(io) Pap(iria) / Strenuo eq(uo) / p(ublico) sacerd(oti) arae / Aug(usti) auguri et / IIviral(i) col(oniae) / Sarm(izegetusae) augur(i) / col(oniae) Apul(ensis) dec(urioni) / col(oniae) Drob(etensis) pat/ron(o) collegior(um) / fabr(um) cento/nar(iorum) et naut/ar(um) conduc(tori) pas/cui salinar(um) / et commer/cior(um) Rufinus / eius.

33 Găzdac, Alföldy-Găzdac, Suciu 2009, 1–2.

34 IDR-03-05-01, 270; 271.

35 IDR-03-05-01, 140.

36 IDR-03-05-01, 166: Vel{l}(ina) Aq(uileia).

37 CIL 3, 1158 (= IDR-03-05-01, 366): Galer(ia) Clunia.

Crustumina,[38] *Sulpicia*,[39] *Sergia*,[40] and of course *Papiria*. No doubt, the number of tribes would have to be reduced if we assume that not all military men who served in the 13th Legion subsequently accepted to enter the civil community of Apulum or other urban communities such as for example that of *colonia Saemizegetusa*. The persons discussed here, however, with one exception –P. Aelius Marcellus were undoubtedly members of the colonial elite. Unsurprisingly, they are among those mentioned in Grotefend's study on the distribution of Roman tribes in the empire in the section on Apulum.[41] It must be emphasized that our examples are not the only attested representatives with the *Papiria* tribe,[42] nor are they the earliest which is the case with C. Cervonius Sabinus who was a decurio of *mun*[*i*][*c*]*ipi*(*i*) *Apul*(*ensis*) dated between 161–180.[43] However, they are distinguished from the rest of the *Papiria* examples by their *nomina*, which clearly contradict the practice with tribe's affiliation. So, for example, with certain conventions, we can accept the belonging of C. Antonius Valentinus or C. Cervonius Sabinus to the tribe *Papiria*, but this can hardly be applied to those *P. Aelii* considered here. Thus, according to the established onomastic practices, the imperial name can be given to *equites singulares Augusti* when enlisted in the Guard, without, however, being granted with immediate citizenship[44] and therefore tribe affiliation. This was done upon their *honesta missio*. If this is so, it would seem that ours *P. Aelii* are heirs of Roman soldiers who served in the emperor's horse guard and were enlisted in the time of the emperor Hadrian. Normally, even if they retired under Hadrian, they would be enlisted in the emperor's tribe *Sergia* and not *Papiria*. Of course, this is with the proviso that the tribal system still existed at the time. So, the question which arises is why these *P. Aelii* used *Papiria* instead of *Sergia* in their *nomen* nomenclature?

I believe there are two possibilities to explain this fact. The first concerns the time when this phenomenon began, namely – the beginning of the 3rd century, judging by the earliest date proposed for the inscriptions of P. Aelius Silvanus and P. Aelius Genialis. This was the time of Septimius Severus' eastern campaign against the Parthians, but it was also the time of the emperor's blind following of the actions of *Optimus Maximus* during his campaign some 80 years earlier. A. Birley shows this clearly. Thus, after initial success, the emperor decided to attack the enemies by a fleet which moved down on the Euphrates probably in late September toward Babylon and then by crossing the Tigris to reach the once great city of Seleucia. Across the river was Ctesiphon, the royal city, which after minimal Parthian resistance and king's escaped was sacked and plundered. On 28 January 198 Septimius proclaimed himself as 'Parthicus Maximus' which was the title Trajan had first held. Birley links this with the exact centenary of Trajan's accession and therefore Septi-

38 Grotefend 1863, 134.

39 CIL 3, 1196 (= IDR-03-05-02, 574): Sulp(icia) Antiq(uaria).

40 CIL 3, 1200 (= IDR-03-05-02, 601).

41 Grotefend 1863, 134.

42 CIL 03, 1198 (= IDR-03-05-02, 596); CIL 3, 1481 (= IDR-03-02, 120 = IDR-03-05-02, 582); CIL 3, 7804 (= IDR-03-05-02, 495); CIL 3, 7805 (= IDR-03-05-02, 446); AE 2007, 1199.

43 CIL 3, 7805 (= IDR-03-05-02, 446).

44 See note 2.

mius Severus was now the equal of the 'best of emperors', whose great-greatgrandson he claimed to be.[45] Unsurprisingly, the Trajanic *gentilicium* received wide acceptance among the veterans listed with *origo* form *civitas peregrina* used as pseudo-tribe in the *laterculi praetorianorum* set in Rome at the end of 2nd – first decade of 3rd c. Furthermore, a connection with *Optimus Maximus*, albeit a fictitious one, would have given more prestige to the new Roman citizens, especially these who originated from *civitas peregrina*. The praetorians from Thrace give a good deal of information for this, causing what is called in the Bulgarian historiography 'Trajanic cities' and in some cases controversies with other type of sources. Therefore, it is very tempting to see the aforementioned *P. Aelii* among those who acted in such way and given their specific Hadrianic names, the only possible way to do that was via the tribe affiliation, especially considering the fact that the tribal system at the time no longer existed and the control over the use of tribes in the nomenclature in the provinces was not particularly strict. By establishing, although illusory, a connection with *Optimus Princeps* based on his reputation, but also on the Septimius Severus's desires and deeds, these *P. Aelii* tried to receive more prestige and possible privileges in the provincial elite of *Dacia Apulensis* as Apulum was the seat of the consular governor of the province and the place for the province assembly.

The second possible explanation which concerns the incursion of *Papiria* in the *nomen* nomenclature of the colonial elite of Apulum does not contradict the proposed connection between Septimius Severus and Trajan, but rather offers another way to reveal the mechanism of choosing the tribe affiliation among the members of the Apulum elite.

It is assumed that the tombstone of C. Sentius Flaccus reveals that the future *municipium Aurelium Apulum* was initially a *pagus* of the *colonia Ulpia Traiana Sarmizegetusa* as he was a *decurio coloniae Daciae Sarmizegetusae*.[46] This could not be accepted as a crucial argument, as C. Sentius Flaccus is not the only attested person in Apulum who held high civic office at *colonia Sarmizegetusa*; numerous inscriptions provide more examples from the beginning of the colonial life in Apulum and ever earlier until 275.[47] Rather, it is the dedication for the legate P. Furius Saturninus by *col(onia) Dac(ica) Sarmiz(egetusa)* of 161–162 found in Apulum,[48] i.e. of pre-municipal Apulum, that may be considered in this case. Nonetheless, a tied link between the colonial elites of both *colonia Sarmizegetusa* and *colonia Aurelia* may be observed with common members as well, mostly from Apulum to *colonia Ulpia Trai(ana) Aug(usta) Dacic(a) Sarmiz(egetusa) metrop(olis)*. The aforementioned P. Aelius Strenus was one of them as he was also 'eq(uo) p(ublico) sacerd(oti) arae Aug(usti) auguri et IIviral(i) col(oniae) Sarm(izegetusae)'. His names allow the assumption that his great – grandfather although granted with Roman citizenship and onomastic under Hadrian, might had settled in *colonia Sarmizegetusa* and enrolled in the colony's tribe *Papiria*. This enables P. Aelius Strenus to use without hindrance *Pa-*

45 Birley 1999, 129–130.
46 Găzdac, Alföldy-Găzdac & Suciu 2009, 2.
47 CIL 3, 972; 973; 1060; 1141; 1198; 1209; IDR-03-05-01, 29 etc.
48 CIL 3, 1177: P(ublio) Furio / Saturnino / leg(ato) Aug(usti) pr(o) pr(aetore) / co(n)s(uli) / col(onia) Dac(ica) Sarmiz(egetusa) / praesidi / dignissimo.

piria in his nomenclature. The epigraphic reveals that he was not the sole example of this. By use of *Papiria* he claimed his belonging to the elite of the oldest colony in Dacia, its metropolis, which was the most prestigious than anything else in Dacia. Thus, according to the funeral epithet of P. Aelius Strenus and others, Apulum was after Sarmizegetusa, followed by Drobeta.

It was not, however, the same case with the other *P. Aelii* considered in Apulum who did not held any high office in *colonia Dacica*. Given the fact that they belonged to *colonia Aurelia*, they may use the Apulum's birth which was at that time under the administrative jurisdiction of Sarmizegetusa to establish, although illusory, a link with the metropolis and hence – the metropolitan society and claimed the origin of their *gentes* from the Dacian *metropolis*. The use of *Papiria* that was the tribe of the oldest colony in Dacia was the logical manifestation of these aspirations and a significant mark in each *nomen*.

Considering the treatment of Apulum's birth in this aspect, the *Papiria* affiliation besides indication of the affiliation with *colonia Dacica*, may also help in establishing first lineages in the Apulum elite and therefore reveal their *gentes* as the oldest, whose settling/establishment was under the jurisdiction of *colonia Dacica*.

To sum up, although we may avoid the possibility by which the use of *Papiria* in the third century was simply copying by the local aristocracy of the capital's nomenclature as a sign of greater prestige and authority, the beginning of this phenomenon in Apulum started at the time when the emperor Septimius Severus himself proclaimed his equality with Trajan. Therefore, the *Papiria* affiliation may connect in one way or another the *origo* of some of the *gentes* of the high Apulum society with *colonia Dacica* and with *Optimus Maximus*, but it also allowed the provincial aristocracy to show their loyalty to Septimius Severus, the new 'Parthicus Maximus', and join the emperor's world.

The two cases considered in this short study reveal that in the second half of the second to the first half of the third century the tribal affiliation, although officially abandoned, did not entirely lose its significance. Moreover, the examples reveal that its use in personal name nomenclature can be interpreted as a distinguishing mark in society associated with higher status and belonging to *Pax Romana*. Their use, however, allows the individual to emphasize his or her belonging to traditional Roman society. K. Stoev even assumes that through it an old Roman status is emphasized, connected also with the use of land under *ius Italicum*.[49]

At the same time, however, the use of the tribal affiliation makes it possible to connect the beginnings of the lineages of the *cives novi* with a particular emperor. The examples offered here are twofold: on the one hand, it is the honouring of the emperor who incorporated the Roman citizen's lineage to *Pax Romana* through the granting of Roman citizenship and names, and on the other hand, the testimony of loyalty to the ruling emperor following his ambitions. These examples, though few in number, reveal different aspects of a seemingly conventional part of the Roman onomastic formula, which is also used as an identify-marker of the individual and/or his *gens*. However, it also allows to reveal in a

49 Стоев 2017, 62.

peculiar form the veneration of the imperial cult, which opens up new possibilities for the study of its spread in a mixed social and personal context.

Bibliography

Birley, A. 1999. Septimius Severus. The African emperor, London–New York.

Cenati, C. 2023. MILES IN VRBE. Identità e autorappresentazione nelle iscrizioni dei soldati di origine danubiana e balcanica a Roma, Roma.

Forni, G. 1985. Le tribù romaine. III. 1. Le pseudo-tribù, Roma.

Găzdac, C., Alföldy-Găzdac, A., Suciu, V. 2009. Apulum, vol. V, Cluj-Napoca.

Grotefend, C.L. 1863. Imperium Romanum Tributim discriptum. Die geographische Vertheilung der römischen Tribus im ganzen Römischen Reiche, Hannover.

Kienast, D. 1966. Untersuchungen zu den Kriegsflotten der römischen Kaiserzeit, Bonn.

Lassère, J.-M. 2005. Manuel d'èpigraphie romaine I. L'individu – La cité, Paris.

Matei-Popescu, F., Ţentea, O. 2018. *Auxilia Moesiae Superioris,* Cluj-Napoca.

Mócsy, A. 2014. Pannonia and Upper Moesia. A History of the Middle Danube Provinces of the Roman Empire, London.

Reddé, M. 1986. Mare nostrum: les infrastructures, le dispositif et l'histoire de la marine militaire sous l'Empire romain, Rome.

Roxan, M., Paunov, E. 1997. The Earliest Extant Diploma of Thrace, A.D. 114 (= RMD I 14), Zeitschrift für Papyrologie und Epigraphik 119, 269–279.

Salomies, O. 1996. Observations on some names of sailors serving in the fleets of Misenum and Ravenna, Arctos 30, 167–186.

Speidel, M. 1994. Die Denkmäler der Kaiserreiter. Equites singulares Augusti, Köln.

Starr, Ch. 1993. The Roman imperial navy, 31 B.C.–A.D. 324, Chicago.

Topalilov. I. 2017. A Note on the nomenclature of the Thracian veterans, Studia Antiqua et Archaeologica 23(1), 125–138.

Topalilov, I. 2018. Thracian Veterans and the Pseudo-tribes, in L. Vagalinski, M. Raycheva, D. Boteva, N Sharankov (eds) Proceedings of the First International Roman and Late Antique Thrace Conference "Cities, Territories and Identities" (Plovdiv, 3rd–7th October 2016). Bulletin of the National Archaeological Institute 44, 151–160.

Геров, Б. (1960). Проучвания върху западнотракийските земи през римско време, ч. 1, Годишник на Софийския университет, Филологически факултет 54/3, 153–407.

Стоев, К. (2017). Да бъдеш римлянин в Мизия. Антропонимия и просопография на романизираното население в Горна и Долна Мизия (I–III век) ,София.

Стоев, К. (2019) '*DOMO HERACLEA, FABIA TRIBU.* Военни от Хераклея (Синтика?) в легионите и градските войски на Рим, Thracia 24, 404–417.

A dedication for Mars from the site of *ala I Batavorum*

Rada Varga, George Bounegru*

This article presents a new epigraphic find from Războieni-Cetate (Alba County, RO), the seat of *ala I Batavorum milliaria* from Roman Dacia.

The fortress of the *ala* is situated 50 km north of the legionary fort of *Apulum*/Alba Iulia, headquarters of the *legio XIII Gemina*, and in the immediate proximity of the salt mines from *Salinae*/Ocna Mureş.[1] (Fig. 1) In 168, *legio V Macedonica* was quartered at *Potaissa*/Turda,[2] placing the *ala* at relatively equal distance between the two legionary stations of the province.

The ancient name of the settlement is not known for a fact; an inscription from *Apamea* (Syria),[3] dated during the first half of the 3rd century AD, states that Aelius Verecundinus was *natus in Dacia ad Vatabos.* It is generally believed that the place mentioned in the inscription is the settlement of Războieni,[4] but, lacking any additional epigraphic information, this assertion could be challenged.

During the last few years, the site has been systematically excavated. The enterprise offered numerous data regarding its planimetry,[5] pottery production and imports,[6] epigraphy[7] and numismatics,[8] many of them already published or in print. The main conclusions drawn so far from the geophysical surveys and archaeological excavations point towards a large and rich settlement, evolved around the fortress and influenced by the wealth as well as the cultural preferences of the militaries from the *ala*.

---

* Work on this article was supported by a grant of the Ministry of Research, Innovation and Digitization, CNCS – UEFISCDI, project number PN-III-P1-1.1-TE-2021-0165, within PNCDI III.

1 Oltean 2007, 39, 182; Mihailescu-Bîrliba 2018; Mihailescu-Bîrliba, Asăndulesei 2019, 31–33.

2 Ritterling 1925, 1572–5; Piso 2005, 119.

3 AE 1993, 1577.

4 Petolescu 2002, 65.

5 Mischka, Rubel, Varga 2018.

6 Rusu-Bolindeţ, Onofrei 2010; Varga, Crizbăşan 2019; Bounegru, Varga 2020, 221–232.

7 Piso, Varga 2018; Rubel, Varga 2021.

8 Ardevan, Varga 2010; Găzdac, Bounegru, Varga 2020.

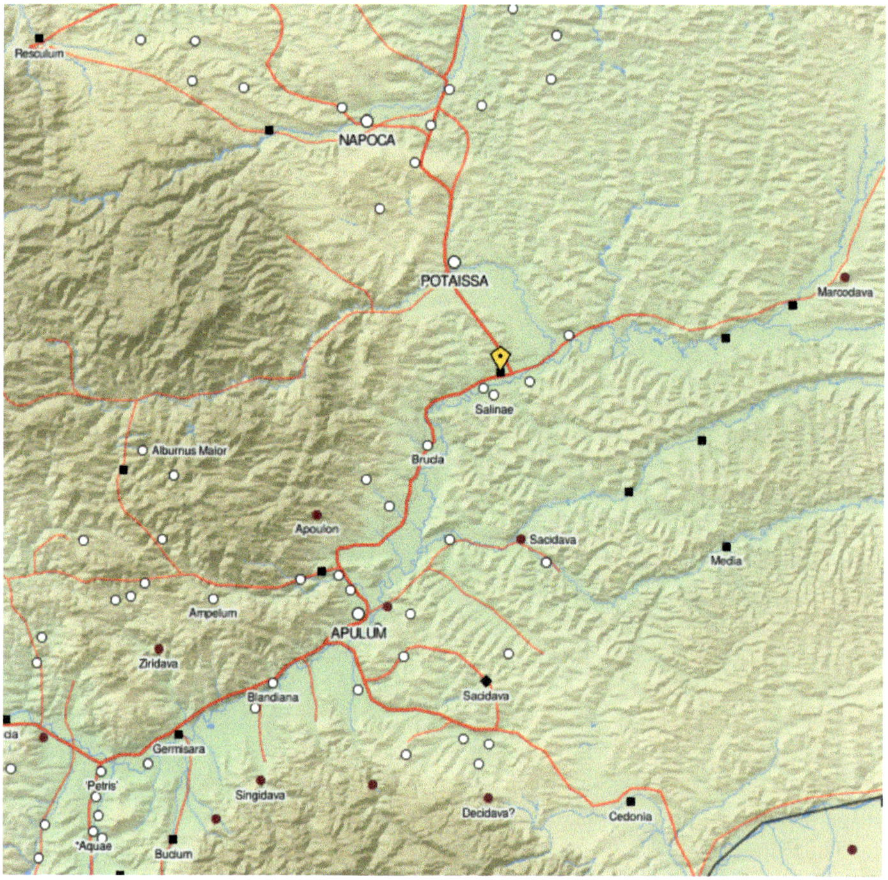

Fig. 1: Map of the area, highlighting the location of Războieni-Cetate (from https://imperium.ahlfeldt.se/)

The altar and its dedicators

The inscription we are dealing with was, unfortunately, discovered without an archaeological context. More precisely, we found it in the courtyard of a villager, who wasn't the primary discoverer, but obtained it from another inhabitant of the village. Allegedly, the discovery place is somewhere in the south-west region of the modern village, in an area which doesn't benefit from geo-physical investigations. In addition, we are in an impossibility to verify the source, as well as if this place of discovery was a secondary location for the altar (as it is highly probable), or not.

The monument is a votive dedication, carved in the local, rather poor quality, limestone. Stylistically, it is very simple, without any artistic qualities (Fig. 2), and small in size:

height = 57,5 cm;
width = 25,5 cm;
depth = 21,5 cm;
inscription field = 27,6 × 20,2 cm.

The dimensions of the letters are: 4,6 cm (1st & 2nd rows), 3,5 cm (3rd & 4th rows) and 1,5 cm (5th row).

Though not an esthetical masterpiece, the letters are well carved, in a very regular and attentive manner.

The text is also a simple one:

MARTI
IVL LIBER
ET SEPTIMI
NVS DD
[VS] LM

The epigraphic text displays a few particularities, namely separation dots after *Iul(ii)*, *et* and *Septiminus*, and ligatures for ET and TI from *Septiminus*.

Given the presence of the conjunction *et*, we assume that we are dealing with two men with the same *nomen* dedicating the altar together. They were most probably father and son or siblings, but of course the possibility of a freedman and his *patronus* cannot be completely excluded. The name of the two men most probably are Iulius Liberius[9] and Iulius Septiminus. We don't fully discard the possibility of the *cognomen* pertaining solely to the first man, but it seems unlikely that the second was not a citizen or didn't want to display his *nomen* as well.

The names, though not spectacular, are interesting in themselves. First, one must note a particularity of Batavian onomastics: as their material culture is remarkably unspecific, their onomastics is also generally Latin. Liberius is not a common name, but has a few attestations throughout Roman Europe.[10] What's remarkable is the fact that two of its European occurrences come from Germania Inferior: one from the Belgica area (modern day Rheder),[11] and one precisely form *Ulpia Noviomagus Batavorum*, the homeland of the *Batavi*,[12] (although in this case we are dealing with a *nomen*, not a *cognomen* as in the occurrence from Belgica). These attestations also support opting for this particular name and not a different form of onomastic completion. Septiminus, a derivative form of Sep-

9 Other attested *nomina* which could be abbreviated as Liber- are Liberalinius, Liberarinius, Libertius (OPEL III, 25).

10 AE 1984, 460 (Lusitania); CIL XIII 7672 (Germania Superior); CIL II 2997 (Hispania). The variation Liberinus,-a is also attested in Hispania (ILER 9417; CIL II 3301), Aquitania (CIL XIII 1246), Narbonensis (CIL XII 549).

11 CIL XIII 7920a.

12 AE 2007, 1024.

Fig. 2: The altar for Mars discovered at Războieni

timius, is frequent in Europe and the Empire in general.[13] One of its attestations comes from Germania Inferior (Bonna, more exactly),[14] but as it is not a rare name at all, we don't consider this detail to be of crucial importance.

In Dacia, both these names appear in a few instances, Septiminius (with the feminine variation) on three monuments,[15] and Liberius possibly in two instances.[16]

The god

The dedication is for Mars, a popular deity in Dacia, revered in martial contexts, as well as an official god.[17] It appears either alone,[18] or associated with Iupiter and other gods.[19] He is also revered in syncretic forms, such as Mars Gradivus,[20] Toutaticus,[21] or Singilis.[22] The attestations don't have a pattern, they show up in urban, as well as rural sites, civilian, as well as military, northern and central Dacia alike. While not comparable to Iupiter or Silvanus quantitatively, Mars is also one of the main presences on gemstones decorations.[23] In glyptic, there appears to be a general preference for martial deities: Minerva is in her armour, Venus is *Victrix*, and Mars is a constant presence.

The stone epigraphy of Războieni is not particularly rich or peculiar, thus we will only mention the other two most important votive dedications: Aurelius Occon Thus, Aurelius Occon Quetianus,[24] bearing a Celtic *cognomen*[25] along a Latin one, dedicates for Epona[26] – goddess of horses, fit to be revered at the location of an *ala*. Another man attested on site, but most probably not serving in the *ala* (as we assume military status would have been recorded on stone), is Flavius (H)adrianus. This particular case is very interesting, as we find him on a 3rd century AD dedication to Hercules Magusanus.[27] The Lower Germanic deity was exported to Dacia by the auxiliary troops. Just like Liberius

13 OPEL IV, 69: Dalmatia (CIL II 2524; CIL III 9028), Hispania (CIL II/5, 1163), Belgica (CIL XIII 11835), Pannonia Inferior (AE 1937, 194), Moesia Superior (IMS I 34) etc.
14 AE 1977, 576.
15 CIL III 7666 (Napoca), CIL III 1471 (Sarmizegetusa; both masculine and feminine forms are worn by members of a family), CIL III 927 (Potaissa).
16 CIL III 867 (Napoca), IDR III/5, 579 (Apulum; solely *Libe* is readable of the name).
17 For Mars in Dacia, see Nemeti 2019, 141–146.
18 CIL III 793; CIL III 6273; CIL III 12577; IDR III/1, 271; AE 1930, 12; AE 1998, 1078; CIL III 948; CIL III 897 (*amicus et consentiens*); AE 1982, 834 (*Augustus*); CIL III 1433 (*Augustus*); AE 1912, 74 (*Augustus*); CIL III 1099 (*conservator*).
19 AE 1903, 217; CIL III 1080; CIL III 1098, 1–2; AE 1934, 11; AE 1998, 1100; CIL III 1600.
20 CIL III 1619; IDR III/2, 241.
21 AE 2004, 1204.
22 AE 1983, 829.
23 Bărbulescu 2003, 158.
24 OPEL III, 109 (Occo and Occus).
25 Holder 1962, 825.
26 Băluţă 1990, 83–85.
27 Roymans 2004, 235–250; Rubel, Varga 2021.

and Septiminius, these dedicators are not explicitly connected to the troop, but the gods they revere imply a certain association with the *ala*.

Final remarks

Coming from a settlement without numerous conserved epigraphic sources, the dedication we are publishing here adds to our knowledge of the site of the *ala Batavorum*, its society and culture, as well as to the bigger picture of religious life in province Dacia.

Bibliography

Ardevan, R., Varga, R. 2010. Descoperiri monetare antice la Războieni (jud. Alba), BHAUT 12, 183–199.
Băluță, C.L. 1990. Relief votiv dedicat Eponei descoperit la Războieni-Cetate, SCIVA 41, 1, 83–85.
Bărbulescu, M. 2003. Interferențe spirituale în Dacia romană, Cluj-Napoca.
Bounegru, G., Varga, R. 2020. Two face pots from the vicus of Războieni-Cetate (Alba County), in S. Nemeti, E. Beu-Dachin, I. Nemeti, D. Dana (eds.), The Roman provinces. Mechanisms of integration, Cluj-Napoca, 221–232.
Găzdac, C., Bounegru, G., Varga, R. 2020. Paying and saving in gold in the Roman army. The aureus of Vespasian from Războieni-Cetate and the evidence of gold coins in Roman Dacia (Romania), JAHA 7, 2, 94–102.
Holder, A. 1896–1914. Alt-Celtischer Sprachsatz, vol. I, II, III, Leipzig.
Mihailescu-Bîrliba, L. 2018. The importance of salt exploitation in Roman Dacia. The case of Ocna Mureș (*Salinae*), JAHA 5, 4, 32–36.
Mihailescu-Bîrliba, L., Asăndulesei, A. 2019. Roman army and salt exploitation in Dacia, JAHA 6, 3, 27–48.
Mischka, C., Rubel, A., Varga, R. 2018. Das Lager der *ala I Batavorum milliaria* und sein *vicus* in Războieni-Cetate (Kreis Alba/RO). AK 48, 3, 377–402.
Nemeti, S. 2019. Le syncrétisme religieux en Dacie romainne, Cluj-Napoca.
Oltean, I. 2007. Dacia: Landscape, Colonisation, Romanisation, London – New York.
Petolescu, C.C. 2002. Auxilia Daciae. Contribuție la istoria militară a Daciei romane, București.
Piso, I. 2005. An der Nordgrenze des Römischen Reiches. Ausgewählte Studien (1972–2003), Stuttgart.
Piso I., Varga, R. 2018. Les éstampilles militaires de Razboieni-Cetate, AMP 41, 263–290.
Ritterling, E. 1925. Legio. Bestand, Verteilung und kriegerische Betätigung der Legionen des stehenden Heeres von Augustus bis Diocletian, RE XII, 2 (1925), 1329–1829.
Roymans, N. 2004. Ethnic Identity and Imperial Power. The Batavians in the Early Roman Empire, Amsterdam.

Rubel, A., Varga, R. 2021. Hercules Magusanus im Lager der *ala I Batavorum milliaria* in Războieni-Cetate (Kreis Alba, Rumänien), Germania 99, 2021, 107–132.

Rusu-Bolindeţ, V., Onofrei, C. 2010. Date noi privind activitatea militară şi cultura materială a alei *I Batavorum* de la Războieni-Cetate, in V. Rusu-Bolindet, T. Sălăgean, R. Varga (eds.), Studia archaeologica et historica in honorem magistri Dorin Alicu, Cluj-Napoca, 401–447.

Varga, R., Crizbăşan, C. 2019. The impact of the Batavian auxiliaries on the community at Războieni-Cetate (Alba County). Case study: the ceramic artefacts, in L. Mihailescu-Bîrliba, W. Spickermann (eds.), Roman Army and Local Society in the Limes Provinces of the Roman Empire. Papers of an International Conference, Iaşi, June 4th–6th, 2018, Rhaden / Westf., 139–162.

Carmina for the Nymphs in the Danubian provinces*

Chiara Cenati, Csaba Szabó, Ernő Szabó

1 Introduction

"The poets say that the Nymphai (Nymphs) live for a great number of years, but are not altogether exempt from death".[1] It was a common knowledge in classical antiquity, that water springs (hot and cold) were protected and populated by the Nymphai, the Nymphs, as well as other elements of the natural landscape, such as trees, rivers and the sea.[2] Nymphs in Greek and Roman mythology represent archaic, primordial divine agents in direct interaction and messenger role between the human and divine worlds.[3] They are often in interpersonal connection with the human world, especially in bucolic, natural landscapes, often – although not only – as helpers and interpersonal agents in natural and imaginary spaces of religious communication.[4] Nymphs are also associated as secondary divine agents in fertility and magical practices, as the case of Anna Perenna shows.[5]

They are often represented as elegant, young female figures represented in the intimate moment of bathing and changing their clothes or holding the symbols of their natural environment, symbols of the local, often reappropriated and mythicized spaces of springs, caves and rivers (reeds, lilies).[6] Nymphs are associated with Neptunus, Silvanus, Pan, Hercules, Diana, Apollo, Aesculapius, Bacchus-Dionysus, Jupiter but also with river and

---

* This project has received funding from the European Research Council (ERC) under the European Union's Horizon 2020 research and innovation programme (grant agreement No. 832874 – MAPPOLA). We would like to thank the colleagues Bruna Kuntić-Makvić and Ante Rendić-Miočević from the Archaeological Museum in Zagreb and Spomenka Vlahović of the Regional Museum of Varaždinske Toplice for allowing us to perform an autopsy and document the inscriptions from Aquae Iasae.

1 Pausanias, *Description of Greece* 10. 31. 10 (trans. Jones).

2 Hom. *Hymn. Aphr.*, 256, Plin. *HN* 36.26, Verg. *Aeneid* 8.314–318: *"haec nemora indigenae Fauni Nymphaeque tenebant gensque virum truncis et duro robore nata, quis neque mos neque cultus erat, nec iungere tauros aut componere opes norant aut parcere parto, sed rami atque asper victu venatus alebat."* See also: Campbell 2012, 133–134; Armstrong 2019, 28–29.

3 On the parthenogenesis and archaic nature of Nymphs, see Rigoglioso 2009, 89–90.

4 On the Greek cult of the Nymphs, see Larson 2001. On the Roman aspects and appropriation of natural landscapes in urban context: Wright 2019.

5 Piranomonte 2009; Blennow 2019.

6 Halm-Tisseran and Siebert 1997, 894, nos. 27 and 29.

sea-divinities of indigenous origin, therefore their divine network and religious functionality need to be interpreted always as glocal phenomena.[7] The glocal cult of the Nymphs presumes a strong emphasis on local, often pre-Roman cults or reinvented local traditions shaped by canonical literary and iconographic traditions of the Hellenistic and Roman world.[8] Nymphs represent the living power and personalised *numen* of the Roman ecological landscape, as eco-religious *genii,* who serve the living dialogue between the natural landscape, its elementary sources (especially water) and the human world.[9] Nymphs are often individualised, having their own personal myths and religious narratives used in space sacralisation, transformation and manipulation of the natural environment[10] and political-genealogical legitimisation of royal families, mythical heroes, ethnic and urban communities or even divine figures.[11]

Nymphs are not only personifications of rivers, healing springs, spirits of caves and archaic divine figures of the Golden Age of Gaia, a pre-human phase of Earth, but divine representations of the strong *numen* of nature, as living and transformative agents in the daily life of the ancients.[12] Nymphs, associated with the transformative power of nature, are among the strongest cognitive entities in religious communication. The direct, physiological effects of the springs and waters (rivers, lakes, sea) associated the Nymphs with healing and apotropaic aspects too.[13] This might be the reason, why recent studies are focusing more intensively on the cognitive aspects of the Nymphs and their sacralised spaces, with a special emphasis on the impact of the natural environment and its elements on human religious behaviour, interpreted as space-related divine agents of episodic memory and embodied religion.[14]

The cults of the Nymphs are well attested in the Danubian provinces too, where several hot and cold springs were transformed into healing sanctuaries and bath complexes, which served not only as thirdspaces (imagined spaces of religious communication) of individuals, but also as spaces of embodied religion and examples of monumentalisation in natural environments. The rich individual and group-identities and their religious interferences attested in these spaces will be discussed through the epigraphic material discovered in some of the healing sanctuaries and other contexts too.

7 A comprehensive catalogue of groups and individual Nymphs from the Greek mythology is collected here: https://www.theoi.com/greek-mythology/nymphs.html. Last accessed: 1.10.2023. The cult of the Nymphs and their associated pantheon in provincial context created an even larger variety of cults. There is no comprehensive, empire-scale study of the cult of Nymphs in the Roman Empire. For comprehensive, regional studies see Lhote-Birot 2004; Oppermann 2014; Bassani 2014; Dalmon 2016.

8 Hedreen 1994. On religious glocalism in the Roman Empire see Van Alten 2017; Szabó 2022, 20–22.

9 Eidinow 2023 on the cognitive aspects of the cults of the Nymphs, as ecological agents in ritual space.

10 Sporn 2015; Häussler and Chiai 2020.

11 Larson 2001, 194.

12 Häussler and Chiai 2020, 3.

13 Sineux 2006; Bassani and Fusco 2019.

14 Fabiano 2013; Larson 2019; Misic 2022, 158, with a rich bibliography on contemporary cognitive religious studies on antiquity. See also: Eidinow et al. 2022.

2 Hot springs and the Nymphs in the Danubian provinces

Springs and natural sources of water are well-attested spaces of religious communication already in the pre-Roman, Bronze Age period.[15] The healing aspects of thermal waters – named recently as "medical geology" – was discovered naturally by human communities probably long before these spaces where transformed, sacralised and monumentalised into building complexes of shrines, baths and domestic or representative spaces.[16] Bronze Age deposits in waters and thermal springs reflect also the repetitive and transgenerational use of such sites.[17] The transgenerational aspect and inconsistency of the deposits suggest that these sites had no organised religious control (priests, institutions, centralised spaces of religion) in the pre-Roman period, although such claim cannot be proved or contested neither.[18]

The Danube area (from Bavaria to the Danube delta) is a geologically and hydrologically rich and extremely diverse area,[19] where several natural thermal springs are attested and used already in the pre-Roman period.[20] The biggest challenge of field archaeology and religious studies is to identify the sources of pre-Roman use and sacralisation of thermal springs, as many of the Roman sites had no pre-Roman phase or it is hard to attest them.[21]

Before a short overview of the thermal springs and healing sanctuaries of the Danubian provinces, it is useful to have a terminological clarification. The notion of healing shrines and sanctuaries are now a canonised category in the literature of Roman religion,[22] however not all of them can be associated with a natural cavity or thermal springs: in several cases of Asklepieia, the water source of the sanctuary is artificially arranged, or it is related to a brook or river.[23] Healing sanctuaries are strictly related to medical care and health-providing divine and human agency, especially Asclepius and Hygieia, but several other divinities (Apollo, Serapis, Jupiter Dolichenus, Glykon) had similar aspects too.[24] These are not usually related to thermal springs, although in presence of such natural resources, these functionalities of the space had multiple religious aspects.[25] Not all healing sanctuaries within the Roman Empire are thermal springs, but almost all springs had medical and heal-

15 See the case study of Sardinia and Anatolia: Køllund 1997, 230; Bryce 2009, 214.
16 Komatina 2004, 158.
17 On the Obi Pramen bronze deposit in thermal spring see Dvorjetski 2007, 95; Osanna 2015; Metzner-Nebelsick 2023, 250.
18 Bassani and Fusco 2019, 3.
19 Brilly 2010.
20 A comprehensive analysis of the thermal springs in the Danubian area is not yet published. A similar attempt was published for the Mediterranean: Dvorjetski 2007, 53–83.
21 On the issue of continuity and discontinuity in sacralised spaces of the region see Gleirscher 2015; Szabó 2022, 27–88.
22 Petridou 2016.
23 Szabó 2018, 68–75, on the Asklepieia of Roman Dacia.
24 Szabó 2018, 75–77.
25 Bassani and Fusco 2019, 5.

ing aspects.[26] The notions therefore need to be strictly separated and our paper will focus especially on the monumentalised cases of thermal springs associated with the Nymphs.[27]

The Danubian area is very rich in thermal springs and represents one of the major resources of space sacralisation, religious and leisure-mobilities (short and long-term mobilities as well).[28] These sites were studied in regional surveys, focusing on traditional, provincial limits, although the religious and touristic impact of the thermal springs were far beyond the provincial borders. The case studies of Pannonia (especially Pannonia inferior) were analysed by Klára Póczy, Zoltán Kádár, Szilvia Horváth, Hedwig Kenner and many others.[29] In the latest catalogue of thermal springs and baths in Pannonia, 50 case studies are mentioned, however many of these sites are only presumed, based on occasional finds.[30] Thermal springs of Moesia superior and Dacia were discussed only shortly in articles focusing on local or regional case studies of baths, healing sanctuaries and the cult of the Nymphs.[31] Not all these sites are related to the cult of the Nymphs (and not all the epigraphic or figurative monuments of the Nymphs are related to thermal springs), however their role is predominant in the religious landscape of these case studies.

During the Principate, the major thermal springs were monumentalised and transformed into complex, multifunctional sanctuaries.[32] Their natural, healing geology was transformed into a sacralised space and an architectural atmosphere aiming to control the forces of nature and religious communication as well. In seven provinces (Raetia, Noricum, Pannonia inferior, Pannonia superior, Moesia superior, Moesia inferior, Dacia) there were circa 80 inscriptions dedicated to the Nymphs, most of them in Pannonia superior (42) and Dacia (20).[33] In both provinces, the monumentalised and complex healing centres of thermal springs represent the largest concentrations of epigraphic dedications. Similarly to the Asklepieia, epigraphic habit in healing sites and thermal springs represent a monumentalisation of an "episodic memory" of religious experience and a visual and textual narrative of a highly individualised, and embodied religious experience.[34] A special source of these monumentalised spaces and narrative memorialisations of embodied experiences are the verse inscriptions dedicated to the Nymphs.

26 Dvorjetski 2007, 95–105. Not all thermal springs had however, medical specialists.

27 For a comprehensive analysis of the Asklepieia see Renberg 2017.

28 Szabó 2020.

29 Kenner 1978; Póczy 1980; Kádár 1981; Kádár 1989; Póczy 1998; Kádár 1999; Kiss 2003; Horváth 2015; Mráv 2017; Horváth and Kiss 2018; Horváth and Kiss 2019; Pochmarski and Handy 2020.

30 Horváth and Kiss 2018, 128, fig. 2. See also Kiss 2003.

31 Ghinescu 1998; Varga 2005; Nemeti 2006; Nemeti 2010; Fodorean 2012; Janković 2012; Szabó 2018, 145–154.

32 On the notion of complex sanctuaries see also Raja 2015.

33 Szabó 2022, 231.

34 Szabó 2018, 73–75; Misic 2022.

3 The epigraphic evidence

If we have a closer look at the epigraphic evidence related to the Nymphs in the seven provinces mentioned above, we immediately notice a quite variegated panorama. As we have seen, the distribution of the inscriptions is irregular, with a major concentration in Dacia, while other provinces are completely lacking attestations. Among all thermal springs in the Danubian provinces, just few have returned a consistent epigraphic corpus. Four simple *ex voto* to the Nymphae Augustae come from the thermal springs of Rimske Toplice, in the territory of Celeia.[35] Only one inscription was found *statio aquarum Bas(---)*, today Banja, an altar to the Nymphae Salutares raised by the *pontifex* Catius Celer together with his family.[36] One collective dedication is attested in Baden bei Wien (see below). In this scattered panorama two sanctuaries emerge because of their importance in the respective provinces and because of the large number of votive inscriptions and other votive monuments that have been found: Germisara in Dacia and Aquae Iasae in Pannonia superior. Both will be addressed separately in Section 4.

The circumstances of the dedications also vary a lot: not all inscriptions for the Nymphs are in fact connected to healing sanctuaries, and, in turn, the Nymphs are not the only deities worshipped in healing sanctuaries. Nymphs can be worshipped in contexts that are not related to the presence of hot springs and appear in natural places like lakes and rivers, which they inhabit as protective deities. Especially in Noricum the cult of the Nymphs seems to be often connected to water, lakes and streams.[37] The link of the cult to natural places is made explicit in one inscription from Savaria, in Pannonia superior (*Nymphis quae in nemore sunt*).[38]

Roman sanctuaries were never strictly devoted to the cult of only one deity, even if there is always a prevailing cult. Therefore, in thermal centres Nymphs were worshipped next to other healing gods, like in Aqua Herculis (Băile Herculane), where the main cult

---

35 CIL III 5146 = ILLPRON 1841: *Nymphis / Aug(ustis) / Fructus / Q(uinti) Sabini Verani / c(onductoris) p(ublici) p(ortorii) ser(vus) vilic(us) / posuit*; CIL III 5147 = ILLPRON 1842: *Nymphis / Aug(ustis) / Matius / Finitus / v(otum) s(olvit) l(ibens) m(erito)*; CIL III 5148 = ILLPRON 1843: *Nymphis / Aug(ustis) sacr(um) / C(aius) Veponius / Phoebus et / Felix eius / v(otum) s(olverunt) l(ibentes) m(erito)*; CIL III 11688 = ILLPRON 1953: *Nymphis / Aug(ustis) sacr(um) / Appuleius / Finiti / v(otum) s(olvit) l(ibens) m(erito).*

36 CIL III 8167 = CIL III 8168 = CIL III 14548 = IMS IV 105: *Nymphis / Salutaribus / [- - -] Catius Cele[r] / [p]ontifex{s} [- - -] / [L]ucilla co(n)iug(e) / [et] Lucio et Sex{s}to / filiis.* This together with the dedication by a soldier in Viminacium (see below) and a third inscription from Ulpiana (ILJug III 1431: *Nym[phis] / L(ucius) Titov[ius - - -] / Pro[- - -] / v(otum) s(olvit) [l(ibens) m(erito)]*) are the only epigraphic attestations of the cult of the Nymphs in Moesia superior.

37 ILLPRON 35: *Fontanis / Nymphis / P(ublius) Cornel(ius) / Diadume/nus et Iul(ia) / Threpte v(otum) s(olverunt) / lib(entes) mer(ito)* (Berg im Drautal); ILLPRON 1164: *Nimp(h)is (!) G(eminis) / sac(rum) G(aius) (!) Annius Iu/venalis v(otum) s(olvit) l(ibens) m(erito)* (Donnersbach Au); CIL III 11802 = ILLPRON 850: *[N]ymphi[s - - -] / Pri[- - -] / T(itus) Fl(avius) Magis[ter - - -] / T(itus) Fl(avius) [- - -]* (Gottweig, Stift).

38 CIL III 6478: *Nymphis / quae in nemore / sunt arulam / T(itus) Pomponius Atticus / Numini / Adiut(rici) devot(am) / d(e)d(icavit).*

was the one of Hercules Invictus, attested on several inscriptions found in Ad Mediam (Mehadia).[39] The Nymphs are here epigraphically completely absent, even if they might have been worshipped through votive statues.[40] The situation is not dissimilar in Aquae (Cioroiul Nou), where no votive monument is dedicated to the Nymphs.[41]

Among the dedicators the presence of urban élites and soldiers, especially officials of the Roman army up to the provincial governors is consistent, and especially in Imperial time when the cult of the Nymphs seems to acquire a political role. In inscriptions these are often addressed with the epithet of *Augustae* and invoked in *ex voto* for the emperor's health.[42] Monuments set up by soldiers, which are not directly connected to thermal springs can be detected for example in Aquincum[43] and Viminacium.[44] In Madara (Moesia inferior) a monument is dedicated by a *centurio* of the legio I Italica,[45] while in Crumerum (Pannonia superior), an inscription to Neptunus and the Nymphs *pro salute* of the emperor is set up by the praefect of the *cohors V Lucensium*.[46] The cult of the Nymphs seems to be one of the favourite of the provincial governors, perhaps because of their healing properties.[47] In Crumerum we find a dedication to the *Nymphae medicae* by the *legatus Augusti pro praetore* C. Iulius Commodus Orfitianus (AD 168–170),[48] which has probably to be related to the group of altars found in Brigetio and dedicated by *legati Augusti legionis*.[49] In Tihău (Dacia Porolissensis), fort of the *cohors I Cannanefatium*, a collective dedication to the Nymphae Augustae was very likely raised collectively by the soldiers of the same unit under the governor Claudius or Flavius Postumus.[50]

39 CIL III 1563–1573. Bărbulescu 1977; Popescu 2004, 195–196.

40 Nemeti 2010.

41 Popescu 2004, 196 on Aquae; Schäfer 2009, 188–189.

42 See the cases quoted above (nt. 36) and below in the discussion, e.g. ILD I 326, 761; Ferjančić et al. 2017.

43 CIL III 3489 = TitAq I 292 [Á. Szabó]: *Nimphis (!) / sacrum / Iul(ius) Pusinio / imm(unis) leg(ionis) II / [A]d(iutricis) p(iae) f(idelis) v(otum) l(ibens) m(erito).*

44 Ferjančić et al. 2017: *Nymphas (!) / Aug(ustas) P(ublius) An(tonius?) / MARCELEO / vat(eranus) (!) leg(ionis) VII Cl(audiae) / v(otum) s(olvit).*

45 AE 2010, 1424: *[N]ymp[h]is / Tib(erius) C[l(audius)] D[- - -] / cen[turio leg(ionis)] / I Ita[l(icae)].*

46 CIL III 3662 = RIU III 751 = AE 1995, 1274: *Neptuno / et Nymphis / pro salute Imp(eratoris) / Caes(aris) M(arci) Au/rel(i) Aug(usti) Anto/nius Iulianus / praef(ectus) coh(ortis) V Lu[c]e(nsium) / posuit.* On the *cohors V Lucensium* in Crumerum see Lőrincz 2010.

47 Várhelyi 2010, 143–144.

48 CIL III 10595 = RIU III 752: *Nymphis / Medicis / sacrum / C(aius) Iulius Commodu[s] / Orfitianus / leg(atus) Aug(usti) pr(o) pr(aetore) v(otum) s(olvit) l(ibens) m(erito).* For the side-reliefs of the altar see Agócs et al. 2023, 45–46, fig. 4.

49 CIL III 4356 = CIL III 11077 = RIU III 649: *Nymph[is] / sacr(um) / L(ucius) Attius / Macro / leg(atus) Aug(usti)*; CIL III 10961 = RIU III 686: *Nymph[is] / [s]acrum / L(ucius) Eg[nat(ius)] / [Victor] / [leg(atus) Augg(ustorum)]*; RIU III 709: *Nymphis / sacrum / L(ucius) Aurelius / Gallus / leg(atus) Aug(usti).*

50 ILD I 761 = AE 1977, 666 = AE 1978, 678 (AD 211–212): *[N]ymphis / Augg(ustorum duorum) / pro sal(ute) / domin[[n(orum)]] / [n[[n(ostrorum)]] dedic(ante) / [F]l(avio) / Postu/[m]o co(n)s(ulare).* Cf. Piso 1993, 168–169, no. 37.

The three inscriptions from Vindobona are clearly not related to hot springs, but to the Danube, as an essential waterway for military logistics.[51] One inscription in particular, dated to AD 268, mentions the Nymphs together with other water and local divinities like Neptunus, Salacea and Acaunus and is collectively dedicated by the *vexillarii* of different legions.[52]

The presence of baths nearby auxiliary forts is a constant. It is therefore not surprising at all that the presence of the Roman army enhanced the development of thermal stations which might have had also a sanctuarial function. As we have seen, the cult of the Nymphs in military contexts was also very popular, perhaps because these were the recipients of collective *vota* for the health of the emperors. An example for this specific circumstance can be found in the thermal station of Baden, close to Vindobona, where the legio XV Apollinaris set up a dedication to the Nymphs.[53] Soldiers from a nearby auxiliary fort were also the most assiduous visitors of the thermal station of Germisara, where they appear at least in one dedication as a group (see Section 4.1).

4 Germisara and Aquae Iasae: verse inscriptions for the Nymphs

Votive verse inscriptions are in general very rare. This pattern can be recognised also in the case of the inscriptions to the Nymphs in the Danubian provinces. In fact, among all votive inscriptions verse inscriptions are singular and unique cases and they appear in the two largest sanctuaries of Germisara and Aquae Iasae. In the following paragraphs the main topics addressed in the texts are explored and compared with the literary works circulating at the time. The monuments and their dedicators are also studied in the contexts of the local and regional epigraphic production.

4.1 Germisara

Germisara is the sanctuary that offers the richest dossier of inscriptions after Aquae Iasae. Here a natural cavity created by the water became with the time a small lake thanks to the erosion. Caves all around were used for leaving offerings and perhaps for healing sleep,

---

51 CIL III 4556 = CSIR Ö I.1, 17: *[Apollini et Nymphi]s sac(rum) Claudia Attuia / [pro salute sua et] suorum Ulpiorum Sec/[- - - so]ror(is) et Augurini mil(itis) leg(ionis) X G(eminae) et / [- - - liben]tes m(erito)*; CIL III 4563 = CIL III 13496: *Nymphi[s] / sacrum / T(itus) Vettius / Rufus / (centurio) leg(ionis) XIII[I] / G(eminae) M[- - -]*; CIL III 14359,27 = ILS 9268 = CSIR Ö I.1, 18 = AE 2011, 1007: *[I(ovi)] O(ptimo) M(aximo) Neptuno [Aug(usto)] / [S]alaceae Nimph[is (!) Flu]/[v]io Acauno dis [deab]/[us] q(ue) omnib(us) v[exill(arii) leg(ionis)] / [VI]II Aug(ustae) sub c[ura - - -] / A[u]re[li] Secun[di (?) (centurionis)] / [p]r(aepositi) tra(ns)lati a le[g(ione) X G(emina) VII] / [P(ia)] V[II] F(ideli) in leg(ionem) I[I Italicam] / [[[Gallienam VII P(iam) VII F(idelem)]] / Aurel(io) Monta[no] / [v(ices)] a(gente) leg(ati) l[e]g(ionis) s(upra) s(criptae) [- - - Sa]/t[u]rn[i]n[o - - -] / [e]t Aurel(io) [- - -] / [-]NAVMA[- - -] / eq(uitum) f[ec(erunt) Mariniano et] / Paterno co(n)[s(ulibus) - - -] / [- - -] Maias.*

52 Alföldy 2011.

53 AE 1907, 142: *Nymp[his] / le[g(io) XV] / Ap[oll(inaris)] / feci[t]*. Cf. Mosser 2003, no. 206.

while a sacred area was reserved to votive monuments, mainly for the Nymphs and Diana. The sanctuary was situated in the vicinity of the fort of the *numerus peditum singularium Britannicianorum*, in Cigmău. The high frequentation of the sanctuary by soldiers may be one of the reasons behind the numerous inscriptions, but its crucial geographic position also contributed to the popularity of the site. Germisara is located on the left side of the Via Traiana, the major commercial and "political" highway of the province, which connected the edges of the empire with Rome.[54] The toponym of the site is not Latin, it has a pre-Roman etymology (which with no doubt means "hot waters"), which suggest that the site was known and used by Dacians before the conquest of the kingdom by Trajan.[55] Despite its obvious pre-Roman etymology, the site shows no clear, archaeological evidence for the pre-Roman religious activities and the monumentalisation and transformation of the site before the 2nd century AD. The transformation of the site and the natural cavity occurred after AD 106 in several phases: small, rectangular buildings with religious functionality and public bath-complex instalments were established, manipulating and radically modifying the natural environment.[56] If there were visible traces of pre-Roman religious activity, those were probably completely destroyed and modified by Roman interventions.

Very simple *ex voto* monuments are dedicated by soldiers and officers of the *numerus* as well of Dacian legions. These are for example the *tribunus numeri singularium Britannicianorum* T. Fabius Aquileiensis,[57] the *signifer* of the same unit, P. Aelius Marcellinus, who escaped a situation that endangered his life,[58] or the *optio* of the legio XIII Gemina M. Aurelius Mossianus[59]. Connected to the cult of the Nymphs in Germisara seems to be also the inscription set up by the legionary *centurio* of the legio XIII Gemina C. Iulius Iulianus, which was found in Micia.[60] Out of the fourteen inscriptions dedicated to the Nymphs[61]

54 Fodorean 2012.

55 Szabó 2018, 145–154; Varga 2019, 337.

56 Rusu and Pescaru 1993; Pescaru-Rusu and Alicu 2000, 67; Schäfer 2009; Ardevan and Cociş 2014.

57 ILD I 329 = AE 1992, 1487: *Nymphis / T(itus) Fab(ius) Aqui/leiensis / trib(unus) n(umeri) s(ingularium) B(ritannicianorum).*

58 CIL III 1396 = ILS 2630 = IDR III/3 243: *Nymphis / sanctissimis / P(ublius) Aelius Marce/llinus signifer / et quaestor n(umeri) Brit(tannicianorum) / mortis periculo li/ber(atus) v(otum) s(olvit) l(ibens) m(erito) / Imp(eratore) Comm(odo) Aug(usto) / Felice V et Glabrione / II co(n)s(ulibus).*

59 ILD III 319 = AE 1993, 1341 = AE 2015, 1187: *Nymphis / sanctissi/mis M(arcus) Aur(elius) / Mossianus / opti(o) I leg(ionis) / XIII Gem(inae) / v(otum) s(olvit) l(ibens) m(erito).*

60 CIL III 7858 = IDR III/3 115: *Nymphis / C(aius) Iul(ius) Iu/lianus (centurio) / leg(ionis) XIII / G(eminae) v(otum) s(olvit).*

61 CIL III 940 = IDR III/3 241 = AE 1971, 386a; CIL III 1395 = CLE 864 = IDR III/3 239; CIL III 1396 = ILS 2630 = IDR III/3 243: CIL III 1397 = IDR III/3 242; CIL III 7882 = IDR III/3 240; ILD I 319 = AE 1993, 1341 = AE 2015, 1187; ILD I 323 = AE 1992, 1481; ILD I 324 =AE 1992, 1482; ILD I 325 = AE 1992, 1483 = AE 2016, 1338; ILD I 326 = AE 1992, 1484; ILD I 327 = AE 1992, 1485; ILD I 328 = AE 1992, 1486; ILD I 329 = AE 1992, 1487; AE 2015, 1186. A dactylic rhythm can be also identified in the votive inscription by M. Aurelius Theodotus, healed three times by the Nymphs (ILD 326 = AE 1992, 1484 = CLE 2965 bis: *Nymphi[s] sanctis / August(is) simul et / tibi Sancta(e) Deana(e) (!) / Fontiq(ue) vestro / re(t)tulit sua vo/ta libens salu/ti ter refirmatus /*

two are in verses. One is the famous bilingual verse inscription published by I. Piso in 2015 and revised by A. Melero Bellido and Hernández Pérez in 2020.[62]

The verse inscription which can be dated to AD 183–185, when L. Vespronius Candidus Sallustius Sabinianus was the governor of the III Daciae,[63] contains a dedication to the Nymphs in the form of a hymn. The dedication was set up in the sanctuary by a *centurio* of the legio V Macedonica, C. Sentius Iustinus, on behalf of the *milites* of the *numerus Britannicianorum*, who apparently renewed collectively as a unit annual votes to the patron deity/deities of the sacred springs (ll. 3–5: *miles Brittannicus sollemnia annua ducit / ex voto efferens solvitque vota priora / temporis excessi et rusum suscipit ipse*). The regular cadence of this vote might be related to some military religious calendar, which includes the worship of healing gods, probably also in relation with *vota pro salute Imperatoris*.[64]

---

aquis Germis(ensibus?) / M(arcus) Aur(elius) Theodo/tus v(otum) s(olvit) l(ibens) m(erito) Imp(eratore) / Comm(odo) [Fe]lice c(onsule) VI VIII Kal(endas) / Com(modas), cf. Piso 2015, 65 and Piso 2023, 317, but this could only be accidental.

62 AE 2015, 1186; Melero Bellido and Hernández Pérez 2020 = CLE 2689 ter: *Sunt Getici fontes divina Nympha creati, / cui formonsus ager vicinus Germisarae est, / cui miles Brittannicus sollemnia annua ducit / ex voto referens solvitque vota priora / temporis excessi et rusum suscipit ipse, / cui cristatus apex procumbit vortice summo. / Hinc undas miles convenas videre solens, / unde et pumice[us fons et li]quor inde salutis / excipiunt [- - -] / virtus [- - -] / [- - -] / [- - -]que voverat portam / [- - -] praepositus hunc tibi [- - -] / [- - -]re cingeris vite comati / [- - -]o nata dono circumdata uvis; / te precor Odrysia donum terrena recondas.* / Νῦμφαι Γερμισαρῶν ὕπ+++ γὰρ ἀπέφυνα[ν]·/ νῆμα τόσον προνοίᾳ θεοῦ Ἀσκληπίειε δῶρα / ἃ κλῄζουσιν βροτοὶ ἄνδρες θεραπείᾳ χρησάμενοί πε[ρ] / ἐλθόντες κυλλοὶ ὀρθοποδοῦντες δαὶ ἱκανόν, / εὐξάμενοι πάλιν ἦλθον πανακέῃ δῶρα φερόντες, / λουτροῖσιν χρηστοῖσιν ἀγαλλόμενοι χαρι<σ>τήρια / δῶκαν, κηπαίᾳ θύρᾳ [φερ]όντες πότιμον ὕδωρ·/ Ἄρτεμι δέ πη κυναγέτει καρπήσια δῶρα / [μι]κρὸ[ν] εὐξάμενοι ἀπέδωκαν τάς τε ἑορτὰς / σήρανγ[ι] θυσίας καὶ ἐπανῆλθαν ὁ[δ]ὸν ἑαυτῶν. / Εἰ οὖς τείνεις, Βριττανεικῶν / ἡγήτωρ τὸνδε ἀνέθηκεν / ὕπνον λαμπροτάτου ἐπὶ Καν/δίδου ἀρχῆς. / *C(aius) Sentius Iustinus, (centurio) l(e)g(ionis) / V Mac(edonicae), agens per terr(itorium) Lucanum.* Transl. adapted from Chaniotis 2018: The Getic sources were created by the divine Nymph; her land is adjacent to Germisara. A Britannic soldier performs for them the annual rites, in fulfilment of his vow. While he fulfills the earlier vows of time past, he makes yet another one. He bows his helmet, decorated with tuft. From here the soldier is used to see waves flowing together, from where a source born from the porous rock and salubrious water take out… virtue… You (i.e. the image of the Nymph) are crowned with grapevine. … I beg you, Odrysia, to hold my present fixed in the ground. The Nymphs of Germisara bring sleep (?) from their nature. Such a thread (of fate) is a present of Asklepios through the providence of the god. This is what the mortals say, after they have used the cure, coming walking with a stoop and leaving walking straight. They returned, having made a vow, bringing presents from the healing goddess, enjoying the good baths, they gave thanksgiving gifts, bringing drinking water through the gate of the garden. But to Artemis, the huntress, they brought fruit. After they prayed for a long time, they rendered the celebrations as is due and the sacrifices in the cave and returned to their journey. If you come close, the commander of the Britannic soldiers has raised this Hypnos under the government of the illustrious Candidus. C. Sentius Iustinus, centurio of the legio V Macedonica, operating in the Lucan territory.

63 PIR^2 V 439.

64 On military calendars and festivities see Herz 1975.

As Nymphs usually appear in a plurality, the mention of only one Nymph in the Latin part of the inscription (l. 1: *Sunt Getici fontes divina Nympha creati*)[65] might point to one specific divinity, who could be identified with Diana or a pre-Roman goddess. This second hypothesis is also supported by what seems to be an epithet of the Nymph (l. 16: *te precor Odrysia*),[66] which points to the survival of a local cult or a case study of an appropriation of a Thracian ethnic name or Thracian Nymph.[67] To this cult might have belonged the Celtic (or reinvented Roman) tradition of donating golden plaques in water, some of which are inscribed with the names of the dedicators.[68] However, the ritual described in the inscription was not limited to the cult of the Nymphs: offerings were made also to Diana and to the healing god Asclepius. In the Greek half of the verse inscription the healing aspects of the dreams (and possibly, a reference to the ritual of the *incubatio*) is reflected in the mention of a monument to Hypnos (ll. 28–29: ἡγήτωρ τὸνδε ἀνέθηκεν / ὕπνον)[69] and is perhaps already introduced at l. 17.[70] This might have taken places in the caves, where also the offerings were laid. The role of the water in the cult and ritual is also addressed many times throughout the poem (l. 7: *undas*; l. 8: *liquor*; l. 23: πότιμον ὕδωρ). Despite some spelling mistakes, the 32 hexameters, especially the Latin ones, contain several literary references, mainly to Ovid, Vergil and to the epigrammatic Latin poetry.[71] These create a unique text with a strong literary character, which is hard to assign to a specific epigraphic category.[72]

We know another verse inscription from Germisara, which is dedicated by a certain Bassus.[73] As we have observed for Germisara and will observe also for Aquae Iasae (Section 4.2), votive inscriptions in the main area of the sanctuary are mostly dedicated by members of the élites or military officers. The Bassus who commissioned this verse

65 In the Greek text, however, the Nymphs are invoked in plural (Νῦμφαι Γερμισαρῶν).

66 Piso 2015, 61; On Odrysia instead of Odrysta see Dana 2015.

67 Szabó 2018, 145–154.

68 Piso 1993. One of them in particular reveals the Dacian origin of the dedicator: ILD I 325: *Nymfis (!) Deci/balus Lu/ci posuit*, cf. Nemeti 2010 and Piso 2015, 51. See also: Nemeti 2013 and Varga 2019 on the possible traces of the religion of the Dacians.

69 The word ὕμνον, suggested in Dana 2015, which would make more sense in this context is not readable on the stone, while the Π is very clear (autopsy C. Cenati, July 2021).

70 Among Greek and Roman gods the practice of *incubatio* was specific of Asclepius and practiced in Asklepieia. According to Renberg 2006 the identification of incubation structures in healing sanctuaries in the West depends from a misinterpretation of the archaeological and epigraphical evidence. Even the dedication of a statue to Hypnos, as in this case, would be part of the cult of Asclepius, without implying any overnight sleep in the sanctuary (Renberg 2006, 127). On the relation of Asclepius and the healing aspects of the dreams see Szabó 2008.

71 See for a complete analysis Melero Bellido and Hernández Pérez 2020.

72 Piso 2015, 64–65.

73 CIL III 1395 = CLE 864 = IDR III/3, 239: *[Hanc ti]bi marmoreo caesam de monte d[icavit], / regina undarum Nympha, decus nemoru[m], / [vo]to damnasti perfecto quem prece Bassus / moenitae propter moenia Germisarae.* Transl.: This altar cut from a marble mountain dedicated to you, Nymph, queen of the waters, ornament of the forests, Bassus, whom you obliged (to set it up) according to his prayer, once his vote had been fulfilled, next to the walls of the fortified Germisara. See also Piso 2023, 316–317, according to whom Bassus doesn't belong to any élite.

inscription was therefore not a *peregrinus*, but a citizen, who perhaps had some military role. He might have been an officer, perhaps the *tribunus* of the *numerus singularium Britannicianorum*, as he mentions the walls of the fortified Germisara (*moenitae propter moenia Germisarae*), or even a provincial governor.[74] This last hypothesis cannot be excluded as dedications by provincial governors in these contexts seem to be very common. Two epigraphic monuments to the Nymphs are raised in the sanctuary by the governor M. Statius Priscus (AD 156–158),[75] one *ex voto* with a private character,[76] one official dedication *pro salute* of the emperor Antoninus Pius.[77] However, other provincial governors also visited Germisara and set up dedications to other deities.[78] Whether an army officer or a governor, it is possible that Bassus, like M. Statius Priscus, had set up in Germisara more than one inscription. The one in verses, where he expresses only his *cognomen*, must have stood next to another one, perhaps more official, where the full name was written, accompanied by his rank.

The inscription itself is a simple dedication for the accomplishment of a vote. The elegiac couplets show a verse line correspondence and other small touches that reveal the accuracy of the short composition: the last words of the two hemiepes of the first pentameter rhyme (*undarum / nemorum*), while the corresponding two in the second pentameter show and assonance (*propter / Germisarae*). The poet also plays with etymologies in the last verse (*moenitae / moenia*).

The parallels between this and the previous inscription are so many that we have to take into account a reciprocal influence of the texts.[79] In both inscriptions only one Nymph is mentioned (*divina Nympha / regina undarum Nympha*).[80] The expression *moenitae propter moenia Germisarae*, a clear reference to the auxiliary fort, finds a parallel in *ager vicinus Germisarae*.[81] Finally, in both texts similar lexical choices can be highlighted (*undas / undarum*, *precor / prece*).

The hint in both verse inscription to the military unit in Cigmău and to its fort testifies to the strong link between this sanctuary and the military. This famous thermal

74 Perhaps Iulius Bassus, *legatus Augusti pro praetore Daciae superioris* between AD 135 and 139 (Piso 1993, 53–54, no. 9). C. Iulius Quadratus Bassus governor in AD 117 (Piso 1993, 23–41, no. 4) has to be excluded.

75 Piso 1993, 66–73, no. 16. According to Popescu 2004, 119 Priscus inaugurated the thermal complex in Germisara.

76 CIL III 7882 = IDR III/3 240: *Nymphis / M(arcus) Stati[u]s / Priscus / legatus / Aug(usti) pr(o) pr(aetore) / v(otum) s(olvit) l(ibens) m(erito).*

77 CIL III 940 = IDR III/3 241 = AE 1971, 386a: *Nymphis Aug(ustis) / pro salute / Imp(eratoris) Caes(aris) Titi / Ael(i) Hadr(iani) Anto/nini Aug(usti) Pii p(atris) p(atriae) / M(arcus) Statius Pris/cus leg(atus) Aug(usti) p[r(o) pr(aetore)] / v(otum) s(olvit) l(ibens) m(erito).*

78 Nemeti 2010, 380, nt. 14.

79 On the reciprocal influence of verse inscriptions in a close context see Cenati forthcoming.

80 See also Piso 2015, 49.

81 Piso 2015, 65; Melero Bellido and Hernández Pérez 2020, 434.

complex had turned into a place of self-representation,[82] where to the thermal, religious and military functions[83] a political role can also be added.

4.2 *Aquae Iasae*

The territory originally inhabited by the tribe of the *Iasi*, in Pannonia superior, is characterised by the presence of circa 25 thermal springs,[84] but from none of them we have evidence of dedications to the Nymphs, neither from the sanctuary of Aquae Balissae, where the remains of the Roman thermal structures are connected to the main cult of Silvanus.[85] At the centre of this territory, Aquae Iasae is the sanctuary that offers the richest dossier of inscriptions for the Nymphs in the Danubian provinces, some of which are still unpublished.[86] The Nymphs were the main (but not the only) deities worshipped here and like in Germisara their cult must have been the evolution of a pre-Roman cult.[87] Administratively Aquae Iasae was part of the Colonia Ulpia Traiana Poetovio,[88] which had financed some of the renovations of the sanctuary, like the construction of a Nymphaeum above the spring.[89] Like Germisara, this became a place of self-representation which attracted influential members of the urban élites, especially those of Poetovio,[90] members

82 On this see also Schäfer 2009.

83 Popescu 2004, 196.

84 Schejbal 2004, 103.

85 Nevertheless, the cult of a female deity connected to the water cannot be excluded and has survived in the medieval cult of the Holy Mary close to springs (Schejbal 2004, 108–111).

86 CIL III 4117 = ILJug I 57 = Lučić 2014, no. 12; CIL III 4118 = ILS 96 = Lučić 2014, no. 5; CIL III 4119 = Lučić 2014, no. 10; CIL III 10891 = Lučić 2014, no. 8; CIL III 10892 = Lučić 2014, no. 13; CIL III 10893 = ILS 3865 = Lučić 2014, no. 9 = Lučić 2014, no. 16 = AE 1938, 156; CLEPann 19 = Lučić 2014, no. 1; Kušan Špalj 2017, no. 76, 79, 80, 81, 87, 88; ILJug II 1170 = Lučić 2014, no. 7; ILJug II 1171a = Lučić 2014, no. 2; ILJug II 1171b = Lučić 2014, no. 3; ILJug II 1171c = Lučić 2014, no. 4; Kušan Špalj 2017, 292–294 = AE 2014, 1049 = AE 2017, 1143; Lučić 2014, no. 14 = AE 2013, 1209 = Kušan Špalj 2017, no. 29.

87 See AE 1985, 714: *Nymphae Iasae.*

88 Aquae Iasae has never been a *municipium* (Rendić-Miočević 1992).

89 Lučić 2014, 187.

90 Kušan Špalj 2017, no. 79: *Nymphis / Aug(ustis) sacr(um) / C(aius) Valerius / P(h)osphorus / Aug(ustalis) c(oloniae) U(lpiae) T(raianae) P(oetovionensis) / pro salute sua / et suorum / v(otum) s(olvit) l(ibens) m(erito)*; CIL III 891 = Lučić 2014, no. 8: *Nymphis / Salutarib(us) / Aug(ustis) sac(rum) / Iul(ius) Maximu[s] / dec(urio) muni[c(ipii)] / - - - - - -*; Kušan Špalj 2017, no. 76: *Fortunae / Iasonianae / Nymphis Salu(taribus) / ceterisq(ue) dis dea/busq(ue) quor[um] / tutel{l}a est / C(aius) Iul(ius) Victorinus / dec(urio) m(unicipii) VIIvir fl(amen) vot(o) / susc(e)pt(o) pro civ(itatibus) Va(rciani?) et N/ES(?) pecu(nia) p(rivata?) p(ro) s(alute) fratr(i) / suo [suo]rumque / [- - -] dedidit.* One collective inscription is dedicated by the *collegium iuventutis*, likely of Poetovio (AE 1938, 156 = Lučić 2014, no. 16: *Dianae et / Nymphis / sacr(um) / collegium / iuventutis / v(otum) s(olvit) l(ibens) m(erito)*). On these *collegia* see Kleijwegt 1994.

of the entourage of the *conductores publici portorii Illyrici*[91] or clerks of the *vectigal Illyrici*,[92] both offices with seat in Poetovio,[93] as well as military high officers and provincial governors. The importance of the sanctuary increased during the whole imperial time and reached the highest point when the emperor Constantine commissioned the renovation of the porticoes and their decoration.[94]

The military presence in Aquae Iasae is clear, nevertheless, simple soldiers setting up dedications for the Nymphs are actually few, exactly like in Germisara: a *speculator* of the legio XIV Gemina[95] and a *beneficiarius consularis*.[96] Another *beneficiarius* might be a C. Petronius Optatus, who dedicates a monument to Iuno, Minerva, Apollo and only at last the Nymphs.[97] A collective monument to the Nymphae Salutares might have been set up by a group of soldiers.[98] All other dedicators that are linked to the army are actually high officers and ultimately provincial governors, among whom the sanctuary was popular in imperial times.[99] The first of them is M. Fabius Fabullus, governor of Africa under Nero and then *legatus* of the legio XIII Gemina in Poetovio,[100] then M. Rutilius Lupus,

---

91 Kušan Špalj 2017, no. 80: *Nymphis Aug(ustis) sac(rum) / Verus T(iti) Iuli / Ianuari cond(uctoris) / p(ortorii) p(ublici) Illyr(ici) servos (!) / ex privatis / vot(um) sol(vit) / Mess(ius?) fecit.* On T. Iulius Ianuarius see Ørsted 1985, 321–324.

92 AE 1985, 714 = Lučić 2014, no. 6: *Nymphis / Iasis / Fl(avius) Herm/adion cir(citor) / vec(tigalis) Illy(rici) et / Ul(pia) Piste ei(us?) / cum Avito et / Suriaco / f(iliis) phialam / arg(enteam) p(ondo) II d(ono) d(ederunt).* See Ørsted 1985, 299–301.

93 Clerks of the *portorium* were also dedicating monuments to the Nymphs in Rimske Toplice, in the territory of Celeia (see above).

94 CIL III 4121 = ILS 704 = Lučić 2014, no. 30 = Kušan Špalj 2017, no. 1: *Imp(erator) Caes(ar) Fl(avius) Val(erius) Constantinus Pius Felix maximus Aug(ustus) / Aquas Iasas olim vi{i} ignis consumptas cum porticibus / et omnib(us) ornamentis ad pristinam faciem restituit / provisione etiam pietatis su(a)e nundinas / die Solis perpeti anno constituit / curante Val(erio) Catullino v(iro) p(erfectissimo) p(raeside) p(rovinciae) P(annoniae) p(rimae) super(ioris).*

95 Kušan Špalj 2017, 285: *Apolli[ni] / Dianae [et (?)] / Nymph[is] / L(ucius) Arrius / Florentin[u]s / speculator / leg(ionis) XIIII Gemi(nae).*

96 Lučić 2014, no. 11 = AE 2013, 1208: *Nymphis Aug(ustis) Ael(ius) / Victorinus / b(ene)f(iciarius) co(n)s(ularis) et / Lucilia / coniunx / v(otum) s(olverunt) l(ibentes) m(erito).*

97 Kušan Špalj 2017, 288 = AE 2017, 1142: *Iunoni R(eginae) et / Minerva[e] / Apollini / et Nymphi[s] / C(aius) Petr[onius (?) / Opta[tus (?)] / be[- - -] / - - - - - -.* The reading might also be *b(ene)f(iciarius)* according to Kušan Špalj 2017, 288.

98 Lučić 2014, no. 14 + Lučić 2014, no. 29 = AE 2013, 1209: *Nymp(his) / Aug(ustis) / Salutarib(us) / collatores / pec(unia) sua fec(erunt) / Imp(eratore) d(omino) n(ostro) / Gordiano / Aug(usto) / et Aviola / co(n)s(ulibus) / pr(idie) Nonas / Octobres / Val(erius) Vitalinus / Val(erius) Crispinianus // - - - - - - / La[- - -] / Iul(ius) [- - -] / Aureli(us) Ur[- - -] / Aureli(us) Dub[- - -] / Aureli(us) Fortun[atus - - -] // - - - - - - / Aur(elius) M[- - -] // Au[- - -] / Au[- - -] / La[- - -] / Au[- - -] / Cas[- - -] / Sta[- - -] / Aur[- - -] / Aur(elius) V[- - -] / Ces[- - -] / Va[- - -] / A[- - -] / Iu[- - -] / Do[- - -] / St[- - -] / Vi[- - -] / Au[- - -] / Aur(elius) Victorinus / Iul(ius) Euprorius / Aur(elius) A[-]cuspis / Aur(elius) Aquila / Aur(elius?) Marnusia / Aur(elius) Antonius / Aur(elius) Lucianus.*

99 As observed also by Kušan Špalj 2017, 256.

100 CIL III 4118 = ILS 996 = Lučić 2014, no. 5: *M(arcus) Fabius / Fabullus / trib(unus) militum / leg(ionis) XIII Gem(inae) / leg(atus) Aug(usti) provinc(iae) / Africae pr(o) pr(aetore) / leg(atus) Aug(usti) leg(ionis) XIII Gem(inae) / sacr(um) Nymp(his).* This Fabius Fabullus (PIR² F 32) can be identified

legatus of the legio XIII Gemina[101] and finally L. Dasumius Tullius Tuscus, governor of Pannonia superior at the beginning of the reign of Marcus Aurelius and Lucius Verus,[102] who ordered a monument on his behalf to the city of Poetovio.[103] Like in Germisara, the presence of *legati legionis* is not limited to the cult of the Nymphs: L. Alfenus Avitianus, for example, raises a monument with a relief depicting Aesculapius, Hygia and Telesphorus for the health of Caracalla, before becoming governor of the province Arabia.[104]

Among the dedications to the Nymphs in Aquae Iasae some fragments of marble slabs preserve texts in verses. The fragments seem to belong to at least five different monuments. All fragments present a stylistic, thematic and palaeographic[105] uniformity which prove that they were part of the same artistic plan. They were probably displayed on the walls of the *porticus* surrounding the warm water basin after the renovation of the complex under Constantine. These poems celebrated, as pieces of art, the medical properties of thermal water and the Nymphs protecting the place, decorating Constantinian complex exactly like the statues that perhaps embellished the baths and the sanctuary.

As only one of these fragments had been published at the time of the writing of this paper, we will limit our analysis to a general comment, waiting to be able to present a more detailed interpretation and commentary to the inscriptions.[106] The first published text is very fragmentary.[107] It is written in a iambic rhythm and contains all the main topics

---

with the Fabius Fabullus, *legatus legionis V (Alaudae)* in AD 69 (PIR² F 30), who killed Galba (Plut. *Galba* 27).

101 CIL III 10893 = ILS 3865 = Lučić 2014, no. 9: *Nymphas Salutares / M(arcus) Rutilius Lupus tr(ibunus) mil(itum) / leg(ionis) XXII q(uaestor) tr(ibunus) pl(ebis) / leg(atus) Aug(usti) leg(ionis) XIII Gem(inae).*

102 PIR² D 16.

103 CIL III 4117 = ILJug I 357 = Lučić 2014, no. 12: *Nymphis Aug(ustis) sacr(um) / res publica Poet(ovionensis) mandante / L(ucio) Tullio Tusco leg(ato) Augg(ustorum duorum) / pr(o) pr(aetore) curante T(ito) Gem(i)nio Ru/fino proc(uratore) Augg(ustorum duorum).*

104 Kušan Špalj 2017, 285, no. 69: *Pro salute et victoriis / Imperatoris Caesaris / M(arci) Aurelli Antonini / Pii Felicis Augusti // L(ucius) Alfenus Avitianus leg(atus) leg(ionis) X Gemin(ae) / Antoninianae P(iae) F(idelis) praes(es) prov(inciae) Arab(iae) / devotus Numini maiestatique eius.* See Eck 2022.

105 See for example the shape of the Ls.

106 Pictures of the unedited fragments have been published in Kuntić-Makvić et al. 2012. Since then the texts have been transcribed in several epigraphic databases. We have decided to reproduce all the unpublished texts as they are reported in the epigraphic database EDH, making only major changes which resulted from the autopsy of May 2023. The texts as they appear here have therefore to be considered as working transcriptions. A new edition by the same authors of this paper is in preparation. There, corrections and new readings, as well as an English translation for each text, will be provided and the inscriptions will be described and analysed more extensively. After the conclusion of this paper, the inscriptions have been included in the new CLE volume (CLE IV by P. Cugusi). One of them has been edited by Prontera 2023. Both these new editions, which are based on the transcriptions accessible in the online epigraphic databases, will be addressed and discussed in the forthcoming publication.

107 AIJ 470 = CLEPann 19 = Lučić 2014, no. 1: CLE 2597 *- - - - - - / [- - -] cursu perpeti / [- - - v]olatu similis / [- - - famam] secutus nobilem / [- - - qua]m credebam repperi / [dis]cordant ignea / [- - -] flamma persona / [- - -] morbo luitur / [- - -]u corpus est / [- - -] viscera / [- - - N]ympha est / [- - -]mo uri[- - -] / - - - - - -* Transl. Lučić 2014: ... uninterrupted pace ... like the wind ... ... having followed

which can be found also in the other *carmina*: i) the description of the hot water moving under the earth and coming to the surface (*cursu perpeti, volatu similis*), ii) the stress put on the high temperature of the water (*ignea, flamma, uri[- - -]*), iii) the curative properties of the thermal spring (*morbo, corpus, viscera*) and iv) the reference to a single Nymph, divine guardian of the water source, like in Germisara (*Nympha est*).

The longest fragment,[108] still unpublished, was composed in hexameters. Each hexameter occupies a line. Although being the longest one, this does not contain any reference to the Nymphs, who could nevertheless have been mentioned in the lost part of the text. The main theme that finds place in this long poetic fragment is the water flowing from the spring and its temperature, in a long description rich of literary references, especially to the Silvae of Statius[109] and to Ovid.[110] The topic of the burning water flowing from natural springs, connected to the Nymphs, was common and used in other literary contexts too, for example to introduce the topic of the flame of love.[111] A hint to the curative properties of this water seems to be given by the word *medicamina*. Similarities can be traced also with the two inscriptions from Germisara where the Nymph is called *regina undarum*. In this inscription there are several references to the waves and the word *unda* appears three times. As we cannot assume a direct intertextuality between the inscriptions in Germisara and the ones in Aquae Iasae, these common traits must depend from the same literary models (see section 4.3).[112]

---

the widely-known rumour ... ... for which I believed uncovered ... ... inciting the flaming ... ... the fire of persons ... ... punished by illness ... ... the body is ... ... abdomen ... ... Nymph is ...

108 Kuntić-Makvić et al. 2012, A1-A2 in the picture = HD075058 = CLE 2598: *Candentes vernantur aquae quas lucid[- - -] / unda pari(e)tem aulosque solis dat gentibus aes[- - -] / quis neque quod satis est utendo vincere +[- - -] / nam postrema novis renovant primordia +[- - -] / et fessis augent sensus iuvantque laborem [- - -] / pabula sunt me(m)bris (?) caelestia dona per ign[e - - -] / quis s[e]ntit lux alma parens medicamina unam [- - -] / atque (?) cadente freto nullis fornacibus ae[- - -] / caeditur acceptisqu(e) incendit balnea plagis / dumque solum rursus percussum flamma calesc[- - -] / evomit ad supera flagrantem protinus undam [- - -] / daedala quam tribuit ardentis flumine lympha / et nobis Elysios tribuit Titania fontes / naturae hic fervet opus ubi gurgite multo / crispificas movet ignis aquas adque ardorem [- - -] / fluctibus erectis non se capit(e) unda prob[- - -] / quitquit (!) enim residet alto de flumine [- - -] / ignibus ad caelum rursus propellitur +[- - -] / sic fit ut adsiduis incursibus lymph[a - - -] / adque indefessis servet so+[- - -] / hic qui tranquillo vit[- - -] / [m]ortales fusos / [- - -]pit++[- - -]*

109 Stat. *Silv.* I, 5, 23–28 on the Nymphs: *mihi, quae Latium septenaque culmina, nymphae, / incolitis Thybrimque novis attollitis undis, / quas praeceps Anien atque exceptura natatus / Virgo iuvat Marsasque nives et frigora ducens / Marcia, praecelsis quarum vaga molibus unda / crescit et innumero pendens transmittitur arcu*; Stat. *Silv.* I, 5, 48: *propellitur unda* (cf. l. 18: *ad caelum rursus propellitur*); on the hot water and the Nymphs see Stat. *Silv.* I, 3, 43–47: *an quae graminea suscepta crepidine fumant / balnea et impositum ripis algentibus ignem? / quaque vaporiferis iunctus fornacibus amnis / ridet anhelantes uicino flumine nymphas?*

110 Ov. *Met.* 3, 173: *Dumque ibi perluitur solita Titania lympha* (cf. l. 13: *et nobis Elysios tribuit Titania fontes*).

111 AE 1987, 655e = CLEHisp 90a = Hernández Pérez 2007, no. 1: *Nympharum latices / alios restinguitis / ignis me tamen at (!) / fontes acrior urit / [a]mor.* On the literary link between hot water and love see Busch 1999, 542–551.

112 See references to Statius nt. 109.

Two smaller fragments containing few words seem to have the same content, describing the environment of the springs.[113] The third longer fragment gives the impression of belonging to the same decorative project, nevertheless the tone is completely different, as well as the layout. The text is disposed on two columns, the first one of which is almost completely lost.[114] The iambic trimeters, unusual for the time, contain a reference to the hot water in the first lines (*fertur flumine / rotanti sese igneo / caloris vasto inpetu*) and then the words of somebody who is speaking in the first person and expresses his wish to stay in Aquae Iasae.

4.3 *Verse inscriptions and literary models*

The common traits between literary standards and votive inscriptions in verses and their intertextuality are so strong that the inscriptions which originally had a religious function, turn into, occasionally very long, literary texts. It is hard to assign the inscription by C. Sentius Iustinus, in Germisara, to a specific epigraphic category, as it is not properly a votive inscription, nor a prayer, nor a hymn.[115] The same might be said for the bigger fragment from Aquae Iasae, where the long description of the water is closer to a literary text than to an inscription, and for one of the most significant verse inscriptions for the Nymphs, a monument from Aquae Flavianae (El Hamma), a thermal station in Numidia, which is related to a stay of the dedicator in Dacia. In the trochaic verses he lists all his main fulfilments, which include the defeat of the Dacians during Trajan's campaigns, the triumph, the promotion to *primus pilus* and, at last, having seen the Nymphs naked, perhaps after his visit at Aquae Flavianae.[116] The *topos* of seeing a female divinity taking the bath naked is common in literature.[117] The playful literary reference is very clear and

113 Kuntić-Makvić et al. 2012, A3 in the picture = HD075058 = CLE 2598: *[- - -]ANS[- - -] / [- - -] +is stamina s[- - -] / [- - -]ios terris signa [- - -] / [- - -]m lucis naturae d[- - -] / [- - -] camporum [- - -] / [- - -]t depicto [- - -] / [- - -]+++[- - -]* Kuntić-Makvić et al. 2012, C in the picture = HD075060 = CLE 3040: *- - - - - - / [- - - ae]therio[s - - -] / [- - -]eris liq[- - -] / [- - -] num duo +[- - -] / [- - -]t actu fove[- - -] / [- - -] anis (!) amoen[- - -] / [- - -] egris (!) medi[- - -] / [- - - a]mnis hic ho[- - -] / [- - -]llum odore[- - -] / [- - -]es in plen[- - -] / [- - -]ENAPRO[- - -] / [- - -] caeli[- - -] / - - - - - -*

114 Kuntić-Makvić et al. 2012, B1-B2 in the picture = HD075059 = CLE 2599: *[- - -]ebit / [- - -]lli / [- - -]s / [- - -]ore // [- - -] balsamo / [- - -]d permanent / [- - -]ste in Nymphis est / [- - - liq]uore fons scatit / crispo n[- - -] fertur flumine / rotanti sese igneo / caloris vasto impetu / fatis qui natus prosperis / et lucis filo splendido / mundumque hospes contigit / huc destinatus advenit / o si liceret iudici / ut quies esset libera / his sempiternis uterer / quis meto nulla nascitur / Hoc radius libens dixerim / cui pacatum non omen est / amore magno huc veni / gravique abscessu desero.*

115 See Piso 2015.

116 IDRE II 456 = CLEAfr II 101: *[O]ptavi Dacos tenere caesos tenui / [opt]avi in sella pacis residere sedi / [o]ptavi claros sequi triumphos factum / optavi primi commoda plena pili hab[ui] / optavi nudas videre Nymphas vidi.*

117 See for example Catull. *Carm.* 64; Callim. *Hymn* 5 (On the bath of Pallas). For the *topos* of the Nymphs in the epigrammatic poetry on baths see Busch 1999, 303–306 and in particular *Ep. Bob.* 58, for a close parallel: in *Aquas Maternas / has Amor incendit lymphas, cum ludere Nymphis / iussit in his nudas pulchra Venus Charitas.*

it seems to be the principal communicative aim of the poet, so that the function of the inscription, perhaps a votive one, vanishes.

Literary references in verse inscriptions also allow to trace some analogies between verse inscriptions from natural springs and those from baths. One example for the Danubian provinces comes from Singidunum, where Aelius Tertius commemorates his own construction of baths for the veterans of the legio IV Flavia.[118] The personification of the spring water that supplies the bath, speaking in the first person, sets it close to a divinity, giving some kind of solemnity to the whole composition (*Alma lavacrorum de saxis decido lympha*). The lingering on the image of the flowing water, coming to the surface from the stones (*cadunt iam fonte liquores*) is common with the longest fragment from Aquae Iasae (and perhaps with Germisara, if the reading of l. 8 is correct). If there the figurative device focuses on the temperature of the water, here the main sensorial sphere is sound, with the use of *raucisonus*[119] at the opening of a verse, which closely reminds the compound adjective *crispificus* of Aquae Iasae. Regarding the lexical choices, in both inscriptions the word *lympha* is used to indicate the water: the alliteration between the word *Nympha* and *lympha* can be a reason behind this frequent lexical choice.[120] The literary imagery that links Nymphs and hot springs is anyway so strong, that the word Nympha in poetry is used as a synonym for hot spring at least in one Greek inscription from Italy.[121] Finally, in all these inscriptions the spring is described as a *locus amoenus*: in Singidunum the baths are defined *laeti loci*; in Germisara the *ager* is *formonsus* and in Aquae Iasae (perhaps) the landscape is *amoenus*.

5 Outlook and research perspectives

The evidence of votive inscriptions for the Nymphs in the Danubian provinces is very scattered and diverse. Inscriptions for the Nymphs come from thermal sites, natural plac-

118 CIL III 6306 = CIL III 8153 = CLE 273 = ILJug I 20 = IMS I 48: *Alma lavacrorum de sa[xis deci]do lympha / Et sunt ex lapide perfecta[e balnea]e pulchrae / Laetis inque locis natus la[cus. Haec] tamen ipsis / Tunc cum sospes erat coniux s[acravit] in usum / Emeritis quondam Alexandr[i] nomine dignae. / Raucisoni lapidoso cadunt [iam fo]nte liquores. / Tam laudati operis dominus ve[- - -] et auctor / In suae memoriam voluit con[secrare] maritae. / Ut tamen et lector nomen cog[nosce]re possis, / Singulae declarant exordia l[itter]ae primae: / Aelia cum Tertia subole de coniuge [cas]ta / Ael(ius) Tertius.* Transl. adapted from Marcovich 1984: I, the clear spring Water, nurturer of every bath, fall down from these rocks, so that a beautiful bath, made of stone, could be built, and a pond could rise in this delightful landscape. This was once consecrated by a husband, when his wife was still alive, for the use of the veterans belonging to the legion worthy of the name of Alexander (Severus). Hear the hoarse-resounding clear water falling from its rocky spring! The renowned donor and builder of this highly praised construction wanted to dedicate it to the memory of his wife. And in order that you too, reader, may learn his name, the first letter of each verse, the beginnings, will tell you: Ael(ius) Tertius, with Aelia Tertia, daughter of his chaste spouse.

119 Cf. AL 377, a poem on baths: *Murmure raucisono fornacibus aestuat ardor.* On the sensorium in verse inscriptions see Cenati et al. 2022.

120 See also Busch 1999, 359.

121 CIG III 5956 = IG XI 889: πόντῳ καί Νύμφαις Κύπριδα καί Βρομίωι, cf. Busch 1999, 346–348.

es or can be connected with waterways. Dedicators of the monuments are mainly soldiers, who appear in a few cases in collective dedications, high ranking officers of the army, members of the urban élites and provincial governors. The largest groups of inscriptions cluster in the sanctuaries of Germisara and Aquae Iasae and it is from these two sanctuaries that we have the only evidence of epigraphic poems.[122] Perhaps, the singing nature of Nymphs contributed to the tradition of addressing these water divinities with *carmina*.[123] The intense, personal religious experience in the baths was one of the few, intensive, bodily and highly cognitive experiences in religious context available for larger groups in the Roman Empire. The, often long, *carmina* dedicated to the Nymphs in the public and visible areas of the sanctuaries are testimonies of religious experiences, the materialised form of the embodied epiphany the visitors often had. Nymphs are direct and active agents in religious communication in these cases, the *carmina* are textual (and often visual, figurative) summaries of communication between the divine and human agency. The tradition of Nymphs both in the case of Germisara and Aquae Iasae seems to be pre-Roman (as the name of the settlements and some of the epigraphic and archaeological evidence suggest). In Roman times, these sites are monumentalised, but the forms of religious communication are continued and diversified: throwing gold tablets in water and dedicating *carmina* can be interpreted as a monumentalised, Romanised form of old, perhaps pre-Roman religious communication, where bronze and organic material were dedicated to the local Nymphs followed by songs and chants (soundscape).[124]

The main themes of the *carmina* include detailed descriptions of the flowing water, of its temperature and healing properties. The officiality and striving for self-representation of prose inscriptions fade in these texts, which show very strong common traits with literary poetic compositions in what we can define a cultural appropriation of the religious communication. The literary character of these *carmina* can be recognised not only in the many literary references, which turn the inscriptions into proper literary compositions, but also in the use of iambo-trochaic verses, very unusual in the popular epigraphic poetry of the second, third and fourth century. Beside the clear influence of literary models which can be extended to verse inscriptions from baths, epigraphic *carmina*[125] seem to influence each other in closed contexts as well, like the *area sacra* of Germisara.

These first introductory and general observations on the inscriptions for the Nymphs in the Danubian provinces, in which the *carmina* find their small but important place, is meant to be a starting and not an arrival point. A new edition of the bilingual inscription from Germisara as well as the forthcoming first edition of the *carmina* from Aquae Iasae

---

122 The number of verse inscriptions seems to be proportional to the total material. See for example the verse inscriptions from Tomis, Salona or the necropolis of the *equites singulares Augusti* in Rome (Cenati forthcoming).

123 Larson 2001, 269.

124 E. Urciuoli named this process as the "citification" of religion in the countryside: Rüpke and Urciuoli 2023.

125 See Cenati forthcoming.

with a linguistic and historical commentary will certainly allow to deepen and move the discussion on *carmina* for the Nymphs forward.

Abbreviations

AE: L'Année Epigraphique, 1888–.
AIJ: V. Hoffiller, B. Saria, Antike Inschriften aus Jugoslawien. Zagreb 1938.
CIG: Corpus Inscriptionum Graecarum. Berolini 1828–1877.
CIL: Corpus Inscriptionum Latinarum. Berolini 1863–.
CLE: Carmina Latina epigraphica. Leipzig 1895–1897, 1926, 2023.
CLEAfr II: P. Cugusi, Carmina Latina Epigraphica Africarum provinciarum post Buechelerianam collectionem editam reperta cognita. Faenza 2014.
CLEHisp: P. Cugusi, Carmina Latina Epigraphica Hispanica post Buechelerianam collectionem editam reperta cognita. Faenza 2012.
CLEPann: P. Cugusi, M. T. Sblendorio Cugusi, Carmina latina epigraphica Pannonica. Bologna 2007.
CSIR Ö I.1: A. Neumann, Die Skulpturen des Stadtgebiets von Vindobona. Wien 1967.
IDRE: C. C. Peteolescu, Inscriptiones Daciae Romanae. Inscriptiones extra fines Daciae repertae Graecae et Latinae (saec. I.II.III). Inscriptions de la Dacie romaine. Inscriptions externes concernant l'histoire de la Dacie (I^{e}–IIIe siècles). Bucureşti 1996, 2000.
IG: Inscriptiones Graecae. Berolini 1903-
ILD: C. C. Petolescu, Inscripţii latine din Dacia. Bucureşti 2005.
ILJug: A. Šašel, J. Šašel, Inscriptiones Latinae quae in Iugoslavia inter annos … et … repertae et editae sunt. Ljubljana 1963–1986.
ILLPRON: M. Hainzmann, P. Schubert, Inscriptionum lapidariarum Latinarum provinciae Norici usque ad annum MCMLXXXIV repertarum indices. Berlin 1986–.
ILS: H. Dessau, Inscriptiones Latinae selectae. Berolini 1892–1916.
IMS: Inscriptions de la Mésie Supérieure. Beograd 1976-
PIR^{2}: E. Groag, A. Stein et al., Prosopographia Imperii Romani Saeculi I, II, III. Berlin 1933–2017.
RIU: Die römischen Inschriften Ung.arns. Budapest, Amsterdam 1972–.
TitAq: Tituli Aquincenses. Budapest 2009–2011.

Bibliography

Agócs, N., Mosoni, M., Szabó, E. 2023. Új római oltár Győrből, Arrabona 61, 43–57.
Alföldy, G. 2011. Eine umstrittene Altarinschrift aus Vindobona, Tyche 26, 1–22.
Ardevan, R., Cociş, S. 2014. Drei weitere goldene Votivplättchen aus Dakien, in A.-R. Barboş, V. Iliescu, D. Nedu (eds.), Graecia, Roma, Barbaricum. In memoriam Vasile Lica, Galaţi, 315–327.
Armstrong, R. 2019. Vergil's green thoughts : plants, humans, and the divine. Oxford–New York.
Bărbulescu, M. 1977. Cultul lui Hercules în Dacia romană, Acta Musei Napocensis 14, 173–189.
Bassani, M. 2014. I santuari e i luoghi di culto presso le sorgenti termominerali, in M. Annibaletto, M. Bassani, F. Ghedini (eds.), Cura, preghiera e benessere. Le stazioni curative termominerali nell'Italia romana, Padova, 143–160.
Bassani, M., Fusco, U. 2019. Methodological Aspects, in M. Bassani, M. Bolder-Boos, U. Fusco (eds.), Rethinking the concept of "healing settlements": water, cults, constructions and contexts in the ancient world: Roman archaeology conference 2016: proceedings of the Session of study (nr. 27), Sapienza University, Aula "Partenone", 17th March 2016, Oxford, 3–7.
Blennow, A. 2019. Instability and Permanence in Ceremonial Epigraphy: The Example of Anna Perenna, in G. McIntyre, S. McCallum (eds.), Uncovering Anna Perenna : a focused study of Roman myth and culture, London; New York; Oxford; New Delhi; Sydney, 94–110.
Brilly, M. (ed.) 2010. Hydrological Processes of the Danube River Basin : Perspectives from the Danubian Countries. Dordrecht; Heidelberg; London; New York.
Bryce, T. 2009. The Routledge handbook of the peoples and places of ancient Western Asia : from the early Bronze Age to the fall of the Persian Empire. London.
Busch, S. 1999. Versvs balnearum: die antike Dichtung über Bäder und Baden im römischen Reich. Stuttgart; Leipzig.
Campbell, B. 2012. Rivers and the power of ancient Rome. Chapel Hill, NC.
Cenati, C. (forthcoming). Poetry from the limes: The verse inscriptions of the soldiers serving in Rome, in D. Massimo, C. Ricci (eds.), City of Strangers: archaeological and epigraphic perspectives on foreigners in ancient Rome, Roma.
Cenati, C., González Berdús, V., Kruschwitz, P. 2022. When poetry comes to its senses: inscribed Roman verse and the human sensorium, in E. H. Cousins (ed.), Dynamic Epigraphy: New Approaches to Inscriptions, Oxford, 143–176.
Chaniotis, A. 2018. Epigraphic Bulletin for Greek Religion 2015 (EBGR 2015), Kernos. Revue internationale et pluridisciplinaire de religion grecque antique 31, 167–219.
Dalmon, S. 2016. Espaces et lieux de culte des nymphes en Grèce ancienne [thèse de doctorat]. Paris.
Dana, D. 2015. Hymne bilingue aux Nymphes de Germisara, Epigraphica Romana 2015_35_005 [http://www.epigraphica-romana.fr/notice/view?notice=3251] (Last accessed: 1.10.2023)

Dvorjetski, E. 2007. Leisure, Pleasure and Healing: Spa Culture and Medicine in Ancient Eastern Mediterranean. Leiden ; Boston.

Eck, W. 2022. L. Alfenus Avitianus, Senator und Statthalter unter Caracalla und Elagabal. EDCS-J 25, 07/2022, DOI:10.36204/edcsj-025-202207

Eidinow, E. 2023. I-Thou-Nymph: a relational approach to ancient Greek religious devotion, Religion 53:1, 24–42.

Eidinow, E., Geertz, A.W., Deeley, Q., North, J. 2022. Introduction, in E. Eidinow, A.W. Geertz, J. North (eds.), Cognitive approaches to ancient religious experience, Cambridge-New York; Port Melbourne; New Delhi; Singapore, 1–16.

Fabiano, D. 2013. La nympholepsie entre religion et paysage, in P. Borgeaud, D. Fabiano (éds.), Perception et construction du divin dans l'Antiquité, Genève, 165–195.

Ferjančić, S., Korać, M., Ricl, M. 2017. New Greek and Latin Inscriptions from Viminacium, Zeitschrift für Papyrologie und Epigraphik 203, 235–249.

Fodorean, F. 2012. Tourism or health necessities? "Spa" vignettes in Tabula Peutingeriana. Travelling Ad Aquas: thermal water resources in Roman Dacia, Ephemeris Napocensis 22, 211–221.

Ghinescu, I. 1998. Cultul nimfelor în Dacia romană, Ephemeris Napocensis 8, 123–144.

Gleirscher, P. 2015. Vorrömerzeitliche Naturheiligtümer und die Frage ihres Fortwirkens in die Römerzeit. Fallbeispiele aus dem Ostalpenraum, in K. Sporn, S. Ladstätter, M. Kerschner (eds.), Natur – Kult – Raum : Akten des internationalen Kolloquiums, Paris–Lodron–Universität Salzburg, 20. – 22. Jänner 2012, Wien, 127–151.

Halm-Tisseran, M., Siebert, G. 1997. Nymphai, in Lexicon iconographicum mythologiae classicae : (LIMC) 8. Thespiades – Zodiacus et supplementum Abila – Thersites, Zürich, 891–902.

Häussler, R., Chiai, G.F. 2020. Interpreting Sacred Landscapes: towards a cross-cultural approach, in R. Häussler, G.F. Chiai (eds.), Sacred landscapes in antiquity : creation, manipulation, transformation, Oxford; Haverton; Philadelphia, 1–13.

Hedreen, G. 1994. Silens, Nymphs, and Maenads, The Journal of Hellenic Studies 114, 47–69.

Hernández Pérez, R. 2007. Los "tituli picti" métricos de la Cueva Negra de Fortuna (Murcia), Epigraphica: periodico internazionale di epigrafia 69, 287–320.

Herz, P. 1975. Untersuchungen zum Festkalender der Römischen Kaiserzeit nach datierten Weih- und Ehreninschriften [Dissertation]. Mainz.

Horváth, S. 2015. Pannoniai gyógyfürdők, in S. Horváth, M. Tóth (eds.), A fürdőélet és egészségturizmus a Dunántúlon az ókortól napjainkig című konferencia tanulmánykötete: A Kaposváron 2013. október 15-én megrendezett Fürdőélet és egészségturizmus a Dunántúlon az ókortól napjainkig című konferencia tanulmányai, Kaposvár, 21–32.

Horváth, S., Kiss, M. 2019. Pannoniai fürdőkalauz. Kaposvár–Pécs.

Horváth, S., Kiss, M. 2018. Pannoniai fürdőkalauz – Római fürdőkultúra, gyógyfürdők Pannoniában Beharangozó, in M. Varga, J. Szentpéteri (eds.), Két világ határán. Természet- és társadalomtudományi tanulmányok a 70 éves Költő László tiszteletére, Kaposvár, 123–132.

Janković, M.A. 2012. The social role of Roman baths in the province of Moesia Superior, in M. Żuchowska (ed.), The Archaeology of Water Supply, Oxford, 27–39.
Kádár, Z. 1999. Asklépios-Aesculapius világa a Kárpát-medencében, in K. Kerényi (ed.), Az isteni orvos. Tanulmányok Asklépiosról és kultuszhelyeiről, Budapest, 67–75.
Kádár, Z. 1989. Der Kult der Heilgötter in Pannonien und den übrigen Donauprovinzen, in W. Haase (ed.), Aufstieg und Niedergang der römischen Welt (ANRW) Band 18/2. Teilband Religion (Heidentum: Die religiösen Verhältnisse in den Provinzen [Forts.]), Berlin; Boston, 1038–1061.
Kádár, Z. 1981. Gyógyító istenségek tisztelete Pannóniában topográfiai adatok tükrében, Orvostörténeti Közlemények 93–96, 63–78.
Kenner, H. 1978. Nymphenverehrung der Austria Romana, in G. Schwarz, E. Pochmarski (eds.), Classica et Provincialia. Festschrift Erna Diez, Graz, 97–113.
Kiss, M. 2003. „Nymphis medicis" Gyógyfürdők Pannóniában, in L. G. Szabó, D. Vargha (eds.), Emlékkönyv Baranyai Aurél gyógyszerész születésének centenáriumára: Gyógyszerésztörténeti tanulmányok, Pécs, 123–146.
Kleijwegt, M. 1994. Iuvenes and Roman imperial society, Acta Classica 37, 79–102.
Køllund, M.G. 1997. Urbanization in Nuragic Sardinia – Why Not?, in H.D. Andersen, H.W. Horsnæs, S. Houby-Nielsen, A. Rathje (eds.), Urbanization in the Mediterranean in the 9th to 6th centuries BC, Copenhagen, 229–242.
Komatina, M.M. 2004. Medical Geology : Effects of Geological Environments on Human Health. Amsterdam.
Kuntić-Makvić, B., Rendić-Miočević, A., Šegvić, M., Krajcar, I. 2012. Integracija i vizualna prezentacija ulomaka monumentalnog metričkog natpisa iz V. Toplica, in J. Balen, H. Potrebica (eds.), Arheologija varaždinskog kraja i srednjeg Podravlja: znanstveni skup, Varaždin, 11.-15. listopada 2010, Zagreb, 285–295.
Kušan Špalj, D. 2017. Aquae Iasae – new discoveries in the Roman sanctuary – with special regard to the cults of Apollo, Asclepius and Serapis, Vjesnik Arheološkog muzeja u Zagrebu 50:1, 255–308.
Larson, J. 2019. Nature Gods, Nymphs and the Cognitive Science of Religion, in T.S. Scheer (ed.), Natur – Mythos – Religion im antiken Griechenland, Stuttgart, 71–85.
Larson, J. 2001. Greek nymphs: myth, cult, lore. New York.
Lhote-Birot, M.-C. 2004. Les nymphes en Gaule Narbonnaise et dans les Trois Gaules, Latomus 63:1, 58–69.
Lőrincz, B. 2010. Ein Ziegelstempel der Cohors V Callaecorum Lucensium aus Crumerum, Acta Classica Universitatis Scientiarum Debreceniensis 46, 79–81.
Lučić, L. 2014. The Roman inscriptions from Varaždinske Toplice, Vjesnik Arheološkog muzeja u Zagrebu 46:1, 185–255.
Marcovich, M. 1984. CIL III 6306 = 8153 (Singidunum) Revisited, Zeitschrift für Papyrologie und Epigraphik 56, 231–236.
Melero Bellido, A., Hernández Pérez, R. 2020. Nueva lectura de una inscripción votiva bilingüe de las termas de Germísara (Dacia superior), Fortunatae 332, 427–448.
Metzner-Nebelsick, C. 2023. Central Europe, in C. Haselgrove, K. Rebay-Salisbury, P.S. Wells (eds.), The Oxford Handbook of the European Iron Age, Oxford, 217–273.

Misic, B. 2022. Worship of the Nymphs at Aquae Iasae (Roman Pannonia Superior): Cognition, Ritual, and Sacred Space, in M. Henig, J. Lundock (eds.), Water in the Roman world : engineering, trade, religion and daily life, Oxford, 157–174.
Mosser, M. 2003. Die Steindenkmäler der legio XV Apollinaris. Wien.
Mráv, Zs. 2017. Considerations on the archaeological and natural contexts of cult places and sanctuaries in the Pannonian provinces, Carnuntum Jahrbuch 2016, 101–108.
Nemeti, I. 2006. Nudas Nymphas vidi... Imaginarul religios şi războaiele dacice, in E. Teodor, O. Ţentea (eds.), Dacia Augusti Provincia. Crearea Provinciei. Actele simpozionului desfăşurat în 13–14 octombrie 2006 la Muzeul Naţional de Istorie a României, Bucureşti, 299–303.
Nemeti, I. 2010. Germisara – the Waters and the Nymphs, in V. Rusu-Bolindeţ, T. Sălăgean, R. Varga (eds.), Studia archaeologica et historica in honorem Magistri Dorin Alicu, Cluj-Napoca, 377–389.
Nemeti, S. 2013. La religione dei Daci in età romana, in M. Taufer (ed.), Sguardi interdisciplinari sulla religiosità dei Geto-Daci, Freiburg, 137–155.
Oppermann, M. 2014. Nymphenkult im Ostbalkanraum zwischen Donau und Rhodopen während der Römerzeit, Il Mar Nero. Annali di archeologia e storia 8, 249–275.
Ørsted, P. 1985. Roman imperial economy and romanization: a study in Roman imperial administration and the public lease system in the Danubian provinces from the first to the third century A.D. Copenhagen.
Osanna, M. 2015. Zwischen Quellen und Gebirgsbaechen: Wasser in lukanischen Heiligtuemern, in K. Sporn, S. Ladstätter, M. Kerschner (eds.), Natur – Kult – Raum : Akten des internationalen Kolloquiums, Paris-Lodron-Universität Salzburg, 20.–22. Jänner 2012, Wien, 267–280.
Pescaru-Rusu, A., Alicu, D. 2000. Templele romane din Dacia. Deva.
Petridou, G. 2016. Healing Shrines, in G.L. Irby (ed.), A Companion to Science, Technology, and Medicine in Ancient Greece and Rome. Volume I., Chichester, 434–449.
Piranomonte, M. 2009. Anna Perenna a dieci anni dalla scoperta : un riepilogo e un aggiornamento, MHNH : Revista Internacional de Investigación sobre Magia y Astrología Antiguas 9, 251–264.
Piso, I. 2023. La Dacie poétique (I), in L. Mihailescu-Bîrliba, I. Piso (eds.), Romans and Natives in the Danubian Provinces (1st–6th c. AD), Wiesbaden, 309–324.
Piso, I. 2015. Ein Gebet für die Nymphen aus Germisara, Acta Musei Napocensis 52:1, 47–68.
Piso, I. 1993. Fasti provinciae Daciae 1. Die senatorischen Amtsträger. Bonn.
Pochmarski, E., Handy, M. 2020. Zur Nymphenverehrung in Noricum und Pannonien, in S. Petković, N. Gavrilovic Vitas (eds.), Ancient Cults in Balkans through archaeological findings and iconography, Belgrade, 37–65.
Póczy, K. 1998. Healing Deities, in J. Fitz (ed.), Religions and cults in Pannonia. Exhibition at Székesfehérvár, Csók István Gallery 15 May – 30 September 1996, Székesfehérvár, 33–36.
Póczy, K. 1980. Közművek a római kori Magyarországon. Budapest.
Popescu, M.-F. 2004. La religion dans l'armée romaine de Dacie. Bucureşti.

Prontera, A. 2023. Un carmen epigraphicum da Varaždinske Toplice (Croatia), Epigraphica 85, 383–392.

Raja, R. 2015. Complex sanctuaries in the Roman period, in R. Raja, J. Rüpke (eds.), A companion to the archaeology of religion in the ancient world, Chichester, 307–319.

Renberg, G.H. 2017. Where dreams may come : incubation sanctuaries in the Greco-Roman world. Leiden; Boston.

Renberg, G.H. 2006. Was incubation practiced in the Roman West?, Archiv für Religionsgeschichte 8, 105–147.

Rendić-Miočević, D. 1992. On the epigraphic heritage of Aquae Iasae and the pecularities of its cult dedications, Vjesnik Arheološkog muzeja u Zagrebu 24–25:1, 67–76.

Rigoglioso, M. 2009. The cult of divine birth in ancient Greece. New York.

Rüpke, J., Urciuoli, E.R. 2023. Urban religion beyond the city: theory and practice of a specific constellation of religious geography-making, Religion 53:2, 289–313.

Rusu, A., Pescaru, E. 1993. Germisara daco-romaine, in D. Alicu, H. Bögli (éds.), Politique édilitaire dans les provinces de l'empire romain. Colloque roumano-suisse, Deva 21–26 octobre 1991, Cluj-Napoca, 201–213.

Schäfer, A. 2009. Die Sorge um sich: Die Heil- und Quellheiligtümer von Germisara, Aquae und Ad Mediam in Dakien, in H. Cancik, J. Rüpke (eds.), Die Religion des Imperium Romanum: Koine und Konfrontationen, Tübingen, 181–198.

Schejbal, B. 2004. Municipium Iasorum (Aquae Balissae), in M. Šašel Kos, P. Scherrer (eds.), The autonomous towns of Noricum and Pannonia = Die autonomen Städte in Noricum und Pannonien. Pannonia II, Ljubljana, 99–129.

Sineux, P. 2006. Asklépios, les Nymphes et Achéloos : réflexions sur une association cultuelle, Kentron – Revue pluridisciplinaire du monde antique 22, 177–198.

Sporn, K. 2015. Natur – Kult – Raum. Eine Einführung in Methode und Inhalt, in K. Sporn, S. Ladstätter, M. Kerschner (eds.), Natur – Kult – Raum : Akten des internationalen Kolloquiums, Paris-Lodron-Universität Salzburg, 20.–22. Jänner 2012, Wien, 339–356.

Szabó, Á. 2008. Aesculapius és az álom általi gyógyítás Daciában, in G. Németh (ed.), A gyógyító számok : források és tanulmányok a számok szerepéről az antik gyógyászatban, Szeged, 97–108.

Szabó, Cs. 2022. Roman religion in the Danubian provinces : space sacralisation and religious communication during the Principate (1st–3rd century AD). Oxford–Philadelphia.

Szabó, Cs. 2020. Pilgrimage and Healing Sanctuaries in the Danubian Provinces, Studia Universitatis Cibiniensis. Series Historica 17, 83–97.

Szabó, Cs. 2018. Sanctuaries in Roman Dacia. Materiality and Religious Experience. Oxford.

van Alten, D.C.D. 2017. Glocalization and Religious Communication in the Roman Empire: Two Case Studies to Reconsider the Local and the Global in Religious Material Culture, Religions 8, 1–20.

Varga, R. 2005. Locuri de cult ale zeilor taumaturgi în Dacia romană, Chronos. Revistă de Istorie 3, 5–8.

Varga, T. 2019. Te religion of the Dacians in the Roman Empire, in S. Nemeti, D. Dana (eds.), The Dacians in the Roman Empire: provincial constructions, Cluj-Napoca, 327–350.
Várhelyi, Z. 2010. The religion of senators in the Roman Empire: power and the beyond. Cambridge.
Wright, D.J. 2019. Anna, Water and Her Imminent Deification in Aeneid 4, in G. McIntyre, S. McCallum (eds.), Uncovering Anna Perenna: a focused study of Roman myth and culture, London; New York; Oxford; New Delhi; Sydney, 71–82.

Women of Roman Dacia (Re-)Centred: Roman Verse Inscriptions between Macro-History and Micro-Narrative*

Peter Kruschwitz, Denisa Murzea

1 What Dacia Wants, Dacia Gets

In the context of the Roman military fort of Micia, situated by village of Mintia, in the Veţel commune of the county of Hunedoara, Transylvania,[1] a substantial funerary monument comprising some fourteen lines of inscribed Latin text is preserved in the floor of the local reformed church (Fig. 1). Its text, dated between the late second and early third century A. D., reads and translates as follows:[2]

D(is) M(anibus).
Aelia Hygia vixit
annos XVIII.
Ael(ius) Valent[inus dec(urio) (?)]
col(oniae) Apul(ensis) fl(amen)
libertae et coniugi
gratae,

* This project has received funding from the European Research Council (ERC) under the European Union's Horizon 2020 research and innovation programme (grant agreement No. 832874 – MAPPOLA). – We thank all museums, collections, and institutions that hold the monuments and objects under consideration in this article for kindly and generously granting Team MAPPOLA permission to access, study, document, and publish these monuments.

1 Further on Roman Micia see Andriţoiu 2003, 181–202, Andriţoiu 2006, and Barbu, Simion 2020, 231–258. Cf. also https://ran.cimec.ro/?codran=91991.01 (last accessed: December 2023).

2 The object in question is a fragmentary andesite stele, measuring 155 × 80 cm. The letter height of the inscription varies from 3.5 to 4.5 cm. The upper part of the monument is severely damaged so that its original relief is missing. The stone is also broken into two fragments, with l. 4 and 5 of the inscription destroyed almost entirely. The text of the inscription is centred in its alignment, and it is placed inside a frame measuring 93.5 × 60 cm. Metrical lines are separated by punctuation; further on the metrical design of the piece cf. Cenati, Gangoly, González Berdús, Hobel, Kruschwitz, Murzea, Tasso 2021, 18–19.

Fig. 1: Detail of the inscription. Photo: C. Cenati

quam tempus durum
rapuit familiam-
quae simul. Dacia te
voluit, possedit
Micia secum. Have,
puella, multum adque
in aevum vale.

To the Spirits of the Departed.

Aelia Hygia lived 18 years. Aelius Valentinus, decurion (?) of the colonia (Aurelia) Apulensis and flamen, (*sc.* erected this monument) for his freedwoman and dear wife, whom a hard time snatched away, and at the same time the family. Dacia wanted you, Micia holds you. Greetings, girl, many times and forever farewell.

(CIL III 7868 = CLE 1558 = IDR III 3.159)

The text constitutes the funerary commemoration of a woman called Aelia Hygia, who had died at the young age of just eighteen. It was carried out by one Aelius Valentinus, (most likely) decurion of the colonia Aurelia Apulensis and flamen, in honour of the young woman who had initially been his slave (she is referred to as a *liberta* at the time of her death: l. 6) and who had subsequently become his wife (*coniugi*, l. 6). Following the customary dedication to the *Di Manes* (l. 1), the text is divided in a prose *praescriptum* containing the names and relevant information of both the deceased and the commemorator (ll. 2–7), and a poetic part with an overall dactylic rhythm (ll. 8–14), which reflects on a general (though not generic) level on the circumstances of Aelia Hygia's death and burial before wishing her a final, eternal farewell.

There are numerous, perfectly legitimate ways to approach this remarkable document, and, perhaps unsurprisingly, it has been quoted and used in a range of studies concerning local and provincial history, military history, and, of course, social history, especially with a focus on the lived experience of Roman Dacia.[3] What all these approaches have in common, however, is that they follow the inherent narrative perspective of the text, *viz.* the perspective of Aelius Valentinus, the individual who commemorated his late wife by means of the present monument. This is not an epistemological problem as such, but it certainly is not the only way to read and approach this document, either, especially as it virtually eclipses the lived experience of the very individual whose death was used as a profoundly and genuinely sad, though perhaps ultimately also welcome, opportunity for the commemorator to self-represent and self-promote in a public space. Certainly, one may adduce this piece as powerful evidence for the dangers and hardships experienced by those men who served the Roman (civic or military) establishment at its north-eastern frontiers, or as a document to the difficulty of making family plans and building meaningful connections during a life of service in the context of Roman army settlements, always in danger and potentially on the move. In doing so, however, one does not only perpetuate a (valid, but not *exclusively* valid) male perspective on the lived experience in Roman Dacia (and the Roman Empire, more generally): one also, by extension, subscribes to a historical narrative that places a male experience at its centre and renders the lives and experiences of women mere screens and mirrors onto which male experiences can be projected.[4]

Aspects of female lives and identities in the geographical and historical context of Roman Dacia, especially with a view to the epigraphic record, have received a certain amount of scholarly attention over the last years.[5] Predominantly, relevant studies have, following established tradition in the field, carried out extensive research into quantifi-

3 See Studniczka 1884, 47 n. 13, Münsterberg, Oehler 1902, 129, Téglás 1910, 499, Ardevan 1998, 397 n. 267, Ciongradi 2007, 192 S/M 9, and Sămărghițan 2003, 180–181, n. 12. Cf. also http://lupa.at/11797 (last accessed: December 2023), Andrițoiu 2006, 164–167, and Cenati, Gangoly, González Berdús, Hobel, Kruschwitz, Murzea, Tasso 2021, 18–19.

4 In this paper, we use the terms 'male' and 'female' to indicate biological sex, as palpable from individuals' nomenclature, not as terms denoting gender identity, as we lack sufficient information in our evidence that would allow any meaningful conclusions.

5 See, e.g., Stănescu 2004, 5–14, Brancato 2006, 349–368, and Byros 2011.

able data and drawn their conclusions in the areas of social, religious, and cultural history based on such datasets. What is conspicuously absent from these approaches, however, is the attempt to recentre the research around Dacia's female population, meaning that the knowledge and understanding that has been amassed may very well be regarded a history *of* women in Roman Dacia, but is not a narrative of the history of Roman Dacia *through* members of its female population: Dacia may have wanted, and Micia may have kept Aelia Hygia in its possession, but it has effectively merely buried and thus silenced her.

An important corrective in the field of gender and women's studies, in such circumstances, may be found in what one might call 'ego documents', i.e. documents that provide not only first-hand, but also first-person accounts of historical relevance – historical documents with micro-narratives that, under these circumstances, enshrine and transmit a significantly richer diversity of voices beyond the dominant ones that have resulted in the narrative(s) of macro-history.[6] This approach, when it comes to Roman History, is, however, only of limited use due to a very limited supply of documents that may be regarded as ego documents of women. And even where documents purport to be authored by women, there is often (unjustified, yet undeniable) prejudice as to whether female authorship can be ascertained with sufficient certainty: a level of scepticism and scrutiny that texts pretending to be of male authorship do not receive even to a remotely similar extent.[7]

Given this conundrum, a second, somewhat more challenging method might usefully be introduced to the field, namely that of critical fabulation. This method, introducing methodical forms of story-telling and (to an extent speculative) narration to fill the gaps of canonised historical accounts, was initially developed by Saidiya Hartman with a view to overcome the (perceived) silence of archival and other written sources regarding aspects of African-American slavery in the United States.[8]

More recently, Deborah Kamen and Sarah Levin-Richardson have proposed, with considerable merit and potential to our mind, to apply this methodology to the study of Greco-Roman sexual slavery and its traces in the epigraphical record.[9] But matters need not stop there, of course, and even the field of gender studies is likely to benefit from it when it comes to the extraction of micro-narratives and micro-histories from a cluster of historical sources that do not constitute ego documents (or that, while constituting actual ego documents, remain of debated authorship and authenticity due to paradigmatic objections, founded and unfounded).

Returning to the specific case of the inscription for Aelia Hygia, what would it mean then to readjust the centre of attention away from the male commemorator to the female honorand? First and foremost, perhaps, it would give us the story of a young woman of uncertain, though arguably not local, geographical origin. Her birth name is unknown – it may or may not have been Hygia, 'Health'. At some point in her life, Hygia arrived in Micia and became the possession of one Aelius Valentinus, councillor and priest at Apu-

6 See, for example, Petersen 2021, 11–28.
7 Cf. Kruschwitz 2023, 169 (with bibliography).
8 See Hartman 2008, 1–14.
9 See Kamen, Levin-Richardson 2022, 201–221.

lum. Whether she arrived in conjunction with Valentinus (who may have been an arrival from another part of the empire, subsequently serving the community that developed and existed around the strategically important auxiliary fort of Micia), or whether she (or her parents) already were in the area, is unknown. What is clear, however, is that Valentinus took fancy to her, freed her, and made her his 'dear wife' (*coniugi* | *gratae*, ll. 6–7): a feeling that may or may not have been mutual, considering that, as a slave her liberty and well-being very much depended on being at her owner's disposal and on being compliant with his wishes. There is a good chance that she bore Valentinus' child, as the inscription mentions that during hardship (*tempus durum*, l. 8), arguably the result of acts of war and / or diseases in the area,[10] both Hygia, by now Aelia Hygia, and the *familia* (l. 9) was snatched away by fate. What for Valentinus clearly was a devastating traumatic experience, for Hygia thus may not have been much more than the end of a life under continued coercion.

Valentinus claims that Dacia and Micia obtained what they desired, taking his dear wife from him.[11] Whether Hygia wanted to be in Micia, in Dacia, and with Valentinus, however, will remain a mystery. What is perfectly clear, however, is that Hygia's fate was by no means unique – and that she represents just one point on a wide spectrum of lived experiences of female slaves-turned-wives of Roman officials in the area – lived experiences of individuals whose fate was not merely one of prevented self-determination, but most notably one of being turned into a means of male self-representation in order to be seen as faithful, dutiful, compassionate, and betrayed by an unjust ill fate, prevented from living in a state of happiness at the expense of the freedom of another human being.

2 'Wife Material'

The phrase 'wife material', though undoubtedly representative of a certain and not altogether uncommon (and by no means exclusively male) way of thinking about partnership, has to be one of the most loathsome and demeaning colloquial expressions in the English language, as it not only would seem to imply a form of vertical ordering of the sexes, but also because it dehumanises women, turning half of humanity into a commodity, a resource readily available to be exploited for the benefit of the other half. Whether Valentinus thought of Hygia as 'wife material', cannot be known, of course: their relationship may have been one of ardent, mutual love, support, and unbridled passion just as much as it may have been one of coercive convenience[12] or even one formed to avoid a notion of shame, on the side of Valentinus, deriving from being seen as having fathered a child with a slave.

What makes the monument for Hygia especially ambivalent is, of course, the matter of authorship – the monument and its texts clearly represent the perspective of the politi-

10 F. Bücheler, *CLE* ad loc. thought that this was a reference to armed conflicts with the Marcomanni.

11 A similar idea would appear to exist in IDR III 2.400 The identity, specifically the sex, of the deceased in that case remains unclear, however.

12 Further on this matter see Huemoeller 2020, 123–139.

Fig. 2: Sarcophagus for Ael. Iulius Iulianus.
©Muzeul Romanaţiului Caracal (inv. 1135). Photo: Sabin Popovici

cally exposed and publicly visible husband. The desire to link oneself in funerary inscriptions, in the public eye and always with a clear view to matters of self-representation, to one's spouse is not an exclusively male trait, of course. There are a number of documents from Roman Dacia that, as (arguable: see above!) ego documents, narrate matters from a female perspective, and in that function they, too, would – at first glance, at least – appear to depict female existences as extensions of male, and providers of couple, happiness.

One such example is the inscription of one Valeria Gemellina for her deceased husband Aelius Iulius Iulianus from Romula, near the village of Reşca in the Oltenia region of modern-day Romania, situated by the limes Alutanus, in the province of Dacia inferior/Malvensis. The monument was discovered in 1952, near the Drumul lui Traian, a Roman road, south-east of the city walls.[13] Inscribed in a *tabula ansata* on the long side of a substantial sarcophagus (see fig. 2), the text, datable (like the inscription for Hygia) to the early third century A.D., reads and translates as follows:[14]

13 Tudor 1978, 178, fig. 178.
14 See further on this piece e.g. Cugusi 1996, 259–261, and CLENovo p. 79.

in ansis:

D(is) M(anibus).

in tabula:

Ael(io) Iul(io) Iuliano dec(urioni) quaestoric(io)
aedilic(io) col(oniae) Romul(ensis) Valeria Ge-
mellina marito b(ene) m(erenti) p(osuit).
Coniugi pro meritis quondam karissimo coniunx
hanc Iuliano domum flendo fabricavi perennem
frigida qua membra possint requiescere morti.
quattuor hic denos vixit sine culpa per annos
et sua perfunctus vidit cum gloria honores.
ecce Gemellina pietate ducta marito
struxi dolens digno sedem cum liberis una
inter pampinea virgulta et gramina laeta
umbra super rami virides ubi densa ministrant.
qui legis hos versus opta leve terra viator.

To the Spirits of the Departed.

For Aelius Iulius Iulianus, decurion, one-time quaestor and edile of the colony of Romula: Valeria Gemellina has erected (*sc.* this monument) for her very deserving husband.

To my husband, once my dearest for his achievements, I, the wife, have built this eternal dwelling, for Iulianus, in tears, so that your cold limbs might find rest in death. He lived for ten times four years, without reproach, and upon his death he looked back on his distinctions combined with his acclaim. Behold: I, Gemellina, led by dutifulness and in pain, erected a resting place for my worthy husband, together with the children, amidst the vines and grass in abundance, where green branches provide dense shade. You, wayfarer, who read these lines, wish (*sc.* him) a light earth (*sc.* resting upon him).

(IDR II 357 = AE 1957.334 = AE 2003.1528 adn. = CLE 2690)

The text consists of three distinctive parts, namely, once again, the customary dedication to the *Di Manes* (l. 1 – inscribed around the main part of the text, namely in the winged handles of the *tabula ansata*), a prose *praescriptum* with the names and functions of the deceased and the dedicant (ll. 2–4), and finally a poem, inscribed in smaller, more densely written letters than the *praescriptum*, celebrating the deceased husband and family of Valeria Gemellina in dactylic hexameters (ll. 5–14).

Whereas in the previous instance it may have been somewhat more obvious how an attempt to (re-)centre the female lived experience could work, the same matter may not be equally obvious in the case of a text that is, in fact, an ego document (or, at the very least, pretends to be one). The starting point here must be, however, that funerary texts are written typically with a purpose and with an audience in mind – a purpose for the living, and an audience contemporary to the lives of those left behind, if (maybe) with a view to address the next generations (though, with some wishful thinking, conceptualising them as 'eternity').

Looking at the text more closely then, one cannot but acknowledge the difficult predicament in which Valeria Gemellina would appear to have found herself following her husband's demise. In better times, Valeria Gemellina was the matron of a family in which she was married to a dignitary of the local community as well as a proud mother of two or more children – an elevated and exposed position that came with a certain level of pride that is still palpable from the dimensions and design of the sarcophagus itself. This (arguably) ideal world for her was not to last, however, as her husband died at an early age of forty: the sarcophagus, provided by the mourning wife together with her children (*cum liberis una*, l. 11) lays him to rest. Thus Valeria Gemellina suddenly found herself in a situation in which her current existence, and especially her own status as it was derived from her husband's, together with any potential ambitions for the future, began to crumble and fade.

All of this may already seem devastating on a personal and psychological level first and foremost, but the implications are significantly more wide-ranging, as well as potentially more threatening, than that: the text does not make it clear what personal and family-related connections Valeria Gemellina – or her deceased husband – had in this area (or anywhere else, for that matter). As the children's social status remains unmentioned, it is possible that they were either still fairly young or at least not yet in a position to advertise their own achievements for the benefit of the mother. With that, the obvious question is: following the departure of the present provider for the family's livelihood, how would Valeria Gemellina, suddenly a widower, be able to support and sustain herself – and potentially the children? – in a system that did not have any central provisions for the elderly?[15]

Re-reading the text from that point of view, one cannot help but see the way in which Valeria Gemellina talks about her relationship to her deceased husband, and in which she self-represents, in a somewhat different light: the text, poetically combining expressions of dutifulness and devotion to her husband (*vulgo pietas*) with highly sensuous references to temperature and light and shade, most of all perhaps, paints a picture of Valeria Gemellina as a loyal, trustworthy, and (apart from her mourning, as required by duty) restrained lady and mother who seemingly chooses to stay out of the limelight of public visibility that her former husband enjoyed. She self-represents as the pillar of strength behind her husband, even in the face of adverse fate. In doing so, however, her own name and perception are closely linked to her deceased husband's reputation and distinction, and thus she subtly inscribed herself into the roll of honour of the *colonia*, as a permanent member of the elite by association, and an educated, cultured one, as the poetic language and imagery of the poem implies.

15 This aspect may also have been the leading element in the narrative of another verse inscription from Roman Dacia, namely ILD 592 = AE 1976.580, on which see below, section 4.

Precisely this is, of course, what the view that funerary inscriptions are written for the living, and for contemporary audiences, entails of course: those who wished to pay their respect to Iulius Iulianus as their former civic leader would now always also encounter, and remember, the devoted widowed wife (and her children).

Whether this strategy paid off for Valeria Gemellina in real terms, is impossible to say. That this was the strategy behind the design of the text nonetheless, by contrast, is rather obvious – a strategy born from the need to secure one's own social and economic survival when a fundamental pillar of support that one had cultivated throughout one's life broke away and disappeared.

A second example that merits a closer look from this point of view, datable to the second or early third centuries A. D., was discovered at Sarmizegetusa. The inscription, now lost, was recorded, and may be translated, as follows:

D(is) M(anibus).
Hic pietatis honos,
haec sunt pia dona
mariti, cui multum
dilecta fui ego Mar-
cellina, pro merita:
cernis que (!) mihi
solus coniux
Aelius coque (!) post
obitum memor
amoris dicat.

To the Spirits of the Departed.

This is recognition of dutifulness, these are the dutiful gifts of a husband to whom I truly was much loved, I, Marcellina, for my merits: you behold what my only husband, Aelius, dedicates to me in memory of this love even after my demise.

(CIL III 1537 (cf. p. 1407) = CLE 597 = IDR III 2.430)

The text consists of a verse inscription in a dactylic rhythm (ll. 2–11), preceded by the customary dedication to the *Di Manes* (l. 1).[16] The text, in a first-person narrative from the perspective of the deceased, celebrates one Marcellina, wife of one Aelius, without revealing much, if any, information about the identity of either one of them.

This inscription introduces a third communicative scenario after the two that we already encountered, (i) a widower commemorating his former (ex-slave and subsequent) wife in his own voice and (ii) a widow commemorating her former husband in her own voice. Here, (iii), a widower commemorates his former wife in a text that purports to speak with the voice of the deceased wife herself. Unlike the previous example (ii), though introducing the

16 Further on this piece see Cenati, Murzea, González Berdús 2023, 149–150.

female speaker in the first person, this piece is not an ego document – the female voice has no agency of its own, but is the imagination of the husband, or, in other words, it is what he wanted her to say and repeat in perpetuity. The text asserts that Marcellina deserved this monument, it is a badge of honour in recognition of her dutifulness (*pietatis honos*, l. 2), in fact an ἀντίδοσις of dutifulness (*pia dona* | *mariti*, ll. 3–4) – and (for that reason?) Marcellina was much loved:[17] a love that was merited (*pro merita*, l. 6), a love that remained unforgotten (*memor* | *amoris*, ll. 10–11) even after her departure (*coque post* | *obitum*, ll. 9–10).

While the text reveals much about the value system of Aelius, a value system firmly based on loyalty and obsequiousness, it says virtually nothing meaningful about Marcellina – not even that she adhered to his principles, as we can only be sure that this is how Aelius wanted her (and himself as well as his relationship) to be seen in the public sphere of funerary commemoration, but not that this represents factual truth. (It may well have done so, of course.)

This is where any attempt to de-centre the narrative, and to re-centre it around the woman who was commemorated here, must quickly reach its limits. At the same time, it is not altogether hopeless. A first question might be: who were these individuals? There is very little to proceed on, of course. Yet, the name Aelius firmly points in the direction of someone who was (or, possibly, whose ancestors were) given Roman citizenship after completing their military service. An army career may perfectly well have been the background of this particular Aelius at Sarmizegetusa. Unlike in the first example that was discussed, i.e. that of Aelia Hygia, the female name Marcellina does not at all point to the servile or libertine sphere – it is the name of a freeborn Roman woman, arguably her *cognomen* rather than her sole name.

Whether Marcellina already lived locally when she met and married Aelius, or whether she moved to Sarmizegetusa and met Aelius there, or whether they had already met elsewhere, cannot be known. At any rate, Marcellina's social status was potentially somewhat higher than that of her husband, and with that she entered into a relationship from which she emerged as a dutiful wife, a traditional *univira* (*solus coniux*, l. 8), entirely devoted to, and focused on, her husband's (social, if not private) happiness, continuing to provide him with the potential for favourable self-promotion in the funerary sphere.

If the same values and principles that Aelius chose to commemorate on Marcellina's tombstone also characterised their relationship during the time they had together, one would have to imagine that Marcellina's main purpose in life had become to serve her husband, to earn his good will, to work for his love and favour, and to be the wife to be proud of. Yet, it is also interesting to note what the inscription does not say: though otherwise wordy, the text does not mention the amount of time they spent together, it does not mention any children, and it does not mention that, though Marcellina remained an *univira*, that Aelius would stay unmarried and sad for the remainder of his life. If this is anything to go by, one might be tempted to infer that Marcellina died at a relatively young

17 Note the first-person subject pronoun in a Wackernagel position, *fui ego*, shifting emphasis on the semantic (rather than tense- or person-related) aspect of the verb *esse*: she (truly) was loved. Further on the uses of the clitic subject pronoun in Latin see, for example, Adams 1994 and, more recently, Kruschwitz, Coombe 2016 (with further bibliography).

age, and that the relationship remained childless. Thus, all that remained for Aelius to praise were the *pietas*, the *merita*, and the *amor*.[18]

3 Mother Dacia: Poetry Majestic Tells the Time of a Great Empire…

An additional step in the reduction of adult female human beings to their being part of the societal construct that is marriage, i.e. to their being wives (dependent of husbands), is the emphasis on their reproductive facilities and, more importantly still in this framework, achievements – the customary and topical funerary celebration, and fetishisation, of successful motherhood (from any child's birth to the mother's demise). In the texts that have been discussed so far, motherhood only played a minor part, largely due to the fact that the individuals mentioned in these pieces would seem to have died even before they were able to give birth: the exception to this was Valeria Gemellina, above (section 2), who, together with her children, survived her husband.

Celebration of motherhood is not altogether absent from Roman Dacia, however, and it features especially prominently in an inscription that was discovered in the context of the Roman auxiliary fort at Gherla (in the county of Cluj). The piece, datable to the second or third centuries A.D., appears to be lost, but it was read and edited by Gábor Finály (fig. 3).[19] The inscription, whose top part was lost to damage, has been described as a plaque, and it comprised a text of four hexameters followed by a prosaic formula.[20] The text has been edited, and may be translated, as follows:

\- - - - - -
Perpetuam fama[m maternae]
gloriae semper pro[sequi]-
tur nurus. pietate nati fr[e]-
quentant. Vixisti grate,
c[onvi]vio celebrantur ami-
ci. aeternumq(ue) vale nobis pi-
entissima mater. v(otum) l(ibens) r(eddiderunt?).

… The eternal fame of your [maternal?] reputation is continually deemed worthy of emulation by your daughter-in-law. Your children visit you frequently in filial dutifulness. You lived gracefully. Your friends celebrate you with a (funeral) banquet. An everlasting farewell from us, most dutiful mother.

They kept their promise willingly.

(CLE 1976)

18 A similar case may have been the fragmentary piece that is IDR III 5.02, 471; cf. Ciongradi 2007, 186, S/A 100.

19 Finály 1902, 336–338.

20 Further on the metrical scheme see Sămărghițan 2003, 173–174, n. 4.

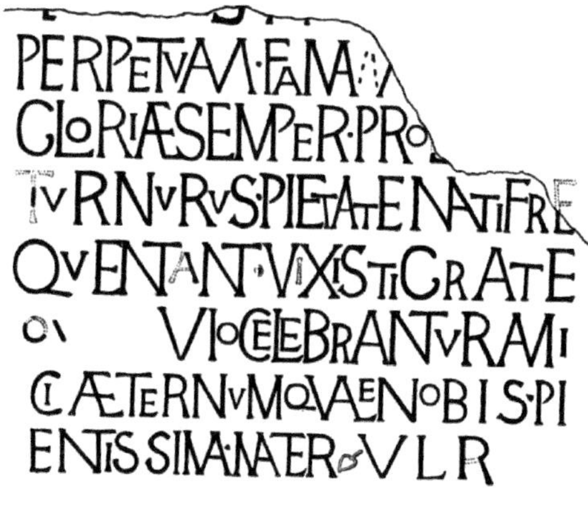

Fig. 3: Exemplum provided by Finály 1902, 337

The text, albeit fragmentary and without any surviving mention of personal names that would allow us to identify and understand the social and economic background of the individuals involved, is a funerary inscription for a woman who had died when at least one of their (all male?) offspring had already entered marriage, as reference to a *nurus*, a daughter-in-law (but not to, for example, a daughter with own children or any such ambitions / hopes) in l. 3 shows. Whether or not the father of the children (whose plurality is implied by *nobis* in l. 6, which need not be understood, *a priori*, as a poetic plural) was still alive by the time the unnamed mother died, is unclear, and, perhaps, even unlikely, for the monument would appear to have been procured by the children who bid their final farewell in ll. 6–7. In quick sequence, short sentences commemorate the *mater*, alternating between references to her life and conduct ((i) and (iii)) and to her commemoration after her departure ((ii) and (iv)), prior to the farewell: (i) she continues to be the perpetual role model of her daughter-in-law, (ii) her grave is visited regularly, (iii) her life was worthy of praise, and (iv) she is celebrated in due ceremony.

Whereas reference to motherhood in ll. 6–7 is clear (*pi|entissima mater*, 'most dutiful mother'), the adjective *maternae* is restored in the first line of the (partly) surviving text: *perpetuam fama[m maternae] | gloriae semper pro[sequi]|tur nurus*, 'the eternal fame of your [maternal?] reputation is continually deemed worthy of emulation by your daughter-in-law'. Though not altogether certain, of course, this supplement is eminently plausible, not as a matter of any romanticism based on traditional family values, but, more importantly, as it contrasts meaningfully the reference to a female family member for whom the *perpetua fama ... gloriae* of the deceased would have been able to serve as a paradigm. Proven achievement resulted in the deceased mother's reputation, and thus in something that was considered to provide guidance both within and beyond the family's bloodline.

The text does not reveal much, of course, about the life and actual achievements and deeds of the commemorated individual – it is not an ego document by any means, and it does not provide any female perspective on the lived experience. Rather, it is the celebration of an idealised and cherished mother by her – presumably all male (see above) – offspring (assuming that the father / husband) was no longer involved in the creation of this memorial. With that in mind, however, it is certainly possible to de-centre the narrative: whether or not the text and its kind words about the *mater* contain any element of truth, it certainly comprises a strict male instruction to at least one female who, unusual for such texts, has been introduced (at least for us) completely out of the blue, namely the *nurus*, who now found herself in the family's leading generation, dependent on one of the *mater*'s sons. For her, the need to live up to the fabled mother-in-law's reputation, her *perpetua fama ... gloriae*, arguably in the field of *materna gloria*, were from this point on literally set in stone, visible to one and all.

It is unclear whether the *mater* had any noteworthy level of liberty and agency in arranging her life – she may have had, but she also simply may have had to live the life that a traditionally minded, male-led family considered worthy. What is clear, though, is that, at least on the basis of the public-facing image created here, the *nurus* had significantly less scope to set, and room to manoeuver to interpret, her own values in life: her publicly inscribed role was to live up to the expectations rooted in a male interpretation of an idealised mother's example. Her lived reality may well have been less rigid – the value framework that governed her life, however, was clearly a strict one, and the firm belief in *pietas* and *gratia* as guidelines for family conduct is palpable throughout.[21]

4 Won't Somebody *Please* Think of the Children?

Already the epitaph of Valeria Gemellina[22] had brought up the matter of parents at a more advanced age, whose social (and economic) situation, in the event of widowhood, might take a turn for the worse, potentially heading into an uncertain and insecure future of old age, under new guardianship, in a system in which social security for the elderly was most commonly administered through family provisions. This implies in turn, of course, that any investment in raising a child was simultaneously an investment in one's own peace of mind for the future. This economic implication must not be mistaken, of course, for an otherwise distant relationship between parents and their children – this relationship was never purely functional and purpose-driven, but generally, as far as the inscriptions may assist us in our understanding, one characterised by deep affection, love, and care. In turn, in the event of child loss (especially at an early stage of a child's life), the emotional trauma and despair of parents, and of mothers in particular, can often be felt. This is certainly the case in the following piece (fig. 4), also from Gherla (in the county Cluj), an inscription on a fragmented limestone plaque, datable to the late second or early third century A.D. The text reads and translates as follows:

---

21 *Pietas* is a common *Leitmotiv* in poetic funerary inscriptions, of course – note, especially, also from Roman Dacia, CIL III 12552 = IDR III 4.216 = CLE 1780 = CLE 2073.

22 See above, section 2 (with nt. 14).

Fig. 4: Epitaph for Aelia Ingenua. © MNIT (inv. 2669) Photo: V. González Berdús

Ael(ia) Ingenua F[- - -]-
inis Iris. Hic iac[et - - -]
sub terra mis[era (?) - - -]
alita es in ann[is - - -]
plus fata veta[runt - - -]
iam nulla est [- - -]
parentes mater [- - -]

Aelia Ingenua F... Iris.

Here she lies . . . under the earth, wretched, . . . you were nourished for . . . years: the Fate disallowed a greater number . . . now you are not . . . the parents . . . the mother ...

(ILD 592 = AE 1976.580 = CLE 2693)

Celebrating a life cut short, this text appears to commemorate one Aelia Ingenua, who, in an oft-observed reversal of fate, died before her parents, presumably at a very young age. And while the parents' pain is inscribed, and audible loud and clear, one cannot but notice the remarkable emphasis on *alita* (l. 4), 'nourished', as an important aspect – and clearly one of the very few memorable things to say about a child who would seem to have died prior to any achievements that would have been more noteworthy than their being sustained and fed by their parents. At the same time, of course, this piece, too, allows us at least a very minor glimpse into the lived realities of women in Roman Dacia, both at the age of motherhood and into the early stages of childhood.

Somewhat more useful, when considering the lived experience of women in Roman Dacia in re-centred narratives, is the case of Aemilia Plotia, commemorated in a monument from Apulum (Alba Iulia), dated to the first half of the third century A. D. The text of the monument (now lost) has been edited, and may be translated, thus:

D(is) M(anibus).
Quinque hic
annorum aetatis
conditur infans.
Aemilius Hermes
hanc generavit,
matris de nomine
dixit Plotia(m). pa-
tris praenomine
Aemilia vixit
rapu[it] quam
mors in limin[e]
vitae.

To the Spirits of the Departed.
Here lies buried an infant of five years. Aemilius Hermes begot her. He called her Plotia, after her mother's name. She lived with her father's *praenomen,* Aemilia, she, whom death snatched away on the very threshold to life.

(CIL III 1228 = IDR III 5.2.489 = CLE 567)

Notionally, this inscription is the funerary commemoration of a girl called Aemilia Plotia, who died at the young age of five. Following the customary dedication to the Manes (l. 1), a dactylic poem (ll. 2–13),[23] in an impersonal voice, reveals only a very small number of pieces of information about the girl, namely (i) her age (ll. 1–4), (ii) the somewhat convoluted history of her name (ll. 5–10), and (iii) the information that death came at a very young age (ll. 11–13). In doing so, however, the author of the poem managed to say virtually nothing about the girl herself (which is obviously a challenge in the funerary commemoration of very young children, as they have not achieved much that would be worthy of any extensive narrative in the public eye), and it does not expand on the cause of death, either. Instead, the parents take centre stage, structurally, when it comes to the explanation of the name Aemilia Plotia, named, as it would appear, Plotia after her mother, and Aemilia after the father – a father, Aemilius Hermes, whose name suggests that he had endured slavery at an earlier stage in his life, while his daughter was born free.

23 Further on this piece see Sămărghițan 2003, 174, n. 5.

The status of Plotia, the mother, cannot be ascertained on the basis of the information provided in the text.

With two female lives mentioned, or at least alluded to, in this text, attempts to re-centre the narrative away from the impersonal (though – arguably at least – effectively paternal) voice enshrined in this piece must decide which of these two lives subsequently ought to occupy the central position.

Plotia, the mother, remains even more obscure than her ill-fated daughter. Her origin and status remain unknown. She had at least one child with Aemilius Hermes, a former slave, and – as the narrative of the inscription suggests – it was the couple's (or just the father's?) decision to perpetuate, if not honour, the mother's (onomastic, familial) history by incorporating her *nomen gentile* in the name of the daughter: not an altogether uncommon move by any means, yet one that is interesting due to the space that this inscription devotes to mentioning it, presenting it as a deliberate and conscious act of the father. Whether this might be read as an indication of the respect that Aemilius Hermes had for Plotia, or whether it was purely a strategic or customary decision for the benefit of the daughter, remains unknown.

Aemilia Plotia, the daughter, in turn, is marginally less obscure a character as a result of the text's presentation, even though it hardly would seem to say anything at all about her. Born free, the daughter of a former slave and a mother of unclear status, both arguably (and the father most certainly) not of local origin, she thus was the offspring of a couple with only very limited footing in the society of Apulum, on the (wide) margins of Apulum's society rather than anywhere near the centre of the local elites. The proudest aspect of her life, as commemorated in this memorial, was the parents' ability to choose her name, and to make her a true combination of two familial strands. Apart from that, her parents – even as she had already turned five – choose to describe her as an *infans*, as a child of very young age (though certainly already able to speak to some extent, unlike the term *infans* might suggest, etymologically, in other contexts). Her father is presented as an active decision maker – he sired her (*generavit*), he named her (*dixit*) – all Aemilia Plotia had to do was to live (*vixit*), which she managed to do until an even more powerful force of nature, Fate, stepped in to steal her away from the living (*rapu[it]*).

What remains unclear, of course, is what the parents had hoped for, and would have allowed, Aemilia Plotia to do had she been able to cross the threshold of life from being an *infans* to childhood, youth, and even adulthood. What levels of self-determination and agency might she have been permitted within her family (and beyond)? However optimistic or sceptical one might be in this regard, it is obvious that the parents, or at least the father, thought that the *limen vitae* was an important gateway for Aemilia Plotia to cross – she failed fully to enter a world in which something that is called life, beyond the mere carrying of one's parents' names, was even possible.

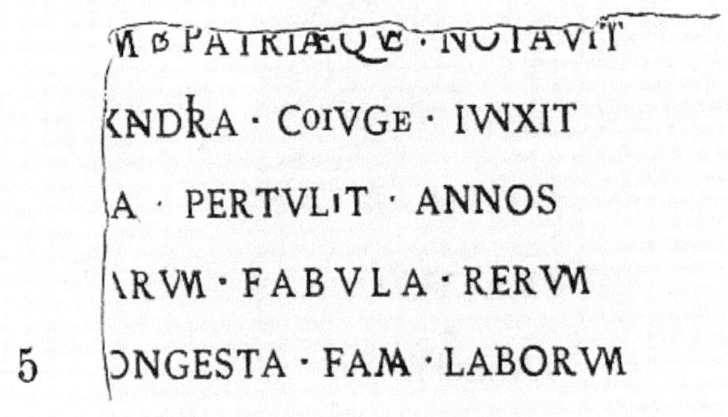

Fig. 5: Exemplum provided by Torma 1882, 119, n. 62

5 Here Today, Gone Tomorrow

The extraordinary world and journey of life that might open up in front of one's eyes once a foot is set through that door defined by the *limen vitae* for women in Roman Dacia is recorded in two further inscriptions that must be mentioned here. The first one, inscribed on a white marble plaque, was discovered in the vicinity of the Roman fort of Tibiscum. The monument itself is lost, but its text, dated to the second or third century A.D., has been recorded (as well as – very tentatively – supplemented),[24] and may be translated, as follows:

\- - - - - -
[quem Nilotica ripa suu]m patriaque notavit
[ingenioque et Ale]xandria co(n)iuge iunxit,
[quacum nihil questus trigint]a pertulit annos.
[iamque levis pereat van]arum fabula rerum
[permaneat modo re c]ongesta fama laborum.

… [whom the bank of the Nile] has marked as its possession, by fatherland [and talent: what is more,] he married in Alexandria, a wife [with whom, without complaints, he lived for thirty] years. [May that inconsequential] tale of [meaningless] matters [die out already, may only that] acclaim of hard work, [based on what has been] achieved, [persist.]

(CIL III 8002 = CLE 482 = IDR III 1.174)

24 The text was first recorded by C. Torma without any reconstructions or corrections. Note, for example, the variant edition of *patriaeque* instead of *patriaque*. F. Buecheler, CLE ad loc. proposed a reconstruction of the text, with two variants for vv. 4–5, namely *[vana relicta modo est mag]narum fabula rerum / [paruaque fortuna] congesta fama laborum*. We provide the supplement already proposed in CIL III.

It is impossible, of course, to build any far-reaching conclusions upon a text that is highly fragmentary and problematic in its restoration (see above fig. 5), not least since a substantial amount of potentially interesting and relevant information has been supplied in this (and other) attempts to provide a readable text. Focusing on the recorded part of the inscription alone, one may still make a number of observations: (i) someone has been noted (for?) their fatherland, (ii) someone got married in a place ending in -xandria, (iii) someone spent a number of years, (iv) reference is made to a somewhat farcical tale of matters, and (v) there is the reputation accumulated by hard work. Based on that, as well as on the assumption that (Egyptian) [Ale]xandria is the only meaningful restoration and interpretation of the fragmented word of l. 2, one may very well imagine that an individual who either was Egyptian or had made that place their home, physically and / or otherwise, got married to a partner there with whom they spent an unknown (but long) period of time, toiling hard – for which their reputation was hoped to persist even after any inane chatter had died down. To identify the honoured individual behind this inscription as male may seem vastly more likely, but is not strictly speaking necessary.

If – and this is not an insignificant 'if' – one accepts these premises, then, in a second step, it is, of course, possible to build, with all necessary caveats, a small narrative around an (unnamed) female: a woman – from, or at least dwelling in, Egyptian Alexandria at some point in her life – was married by a man, closely linked to Egypt himself, whom she would seem to have followed to Dacia (for reasons unknown). Their marriage lasted for a substantial period of time (arguably for some thirty years), and it may very well have been described as harmonious – at least, as the supplement suggests, to the effect that no complaints were raised. (Not that such aspects, if not applicable, would otherwise have been mentioned in a funerary inscription…!) The surviving text does not give any clear indication whether it commemorated the husband or the wife. Attempts to restore the text all seem to presuppose that it was the male rather than the female who was commemorated here, which is certainly possible (but not the only way to read the fragment). If one wishes to follow that logic, the widow, remembering her late husband, would seem to have followed the same strategy as Valeria Gemellina, representing herself as without reproach, faithful, and reliable, arguably for the same reasons as Valeria Gemellina (hypothetically, though not necessarily, for the same reasons, too).[25]

More importantly, however, and regardless of the configuration of individuals honoured and mentioned in this piece, the inscription would seem to tell a remarkable tale of love and conduct and long-distance mobility in Roman Dacia – taking us to a social substrate of female migrants, whose roots lead into regions far remote from the place where they lived (and potentially died). What this means for their ability, following the death of their partner, to re-establish and integrate themselves into local networks (even linguistically, but, given that the text is written in Latin rather than Greek, still almost certainly culturally), is a question that is both of crucial importance and, once again, impossible to answer, of course.

25 See above, section 2.

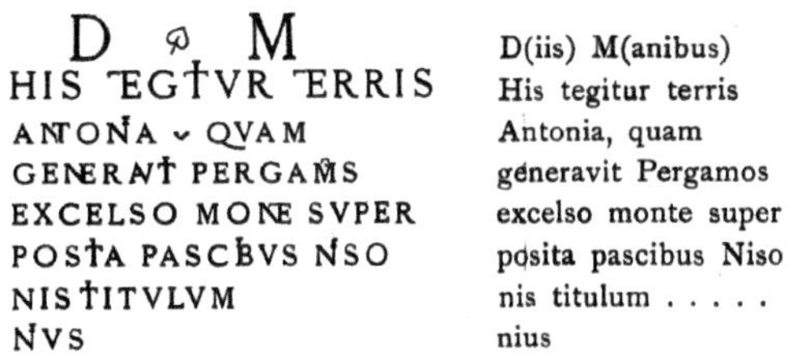

D ⚘ M	D(iis) M(anibus)
HIS TEGTVR TERRIS	His tegitur terris
ANTONA ˅ QVAM	Antonia, quam
GENERAT PERGAMS	generavit Pergamos
EXCELSO MONE SVPER	excelso monte super
POSTA PASCBVS NSO	posita pascibus Niso
NIS TITVLVM	nis titulum . . . . .
NVS	nius

Fig. 6: Exemplum provided by Jánó 1912, 405

A second piece that speaks to the issue of female mobility and female migration into Roman Dacia was discovered at Grădişte, in the vicinity of Sarmizegetusa. The monument, a marble plaque, is now lost, but its text, datable to the second or third century A. D., has been recorded (fig. 6), and may be translated, thus:

D(is) M(anibus).
His tegitur terris
Antonia quam
generavit Pergamos
excelso monte super-
posita pascibus inso-
nis titulum [Anto]-
nius [- - -]
\- - - - - -

To the Spirits of the Departed.

Antonia, whom Pergamon, situated on top of a towering mountain, begat, is covered in this soil: in the soundless pastures, Antonius (*sc.* set up) the inscription ...

(IDR III 2.382 = CLE 2112 = AE 1914.108)

The text opens with a customary dedication to the Manes, after which a dactylic poem follows (ll. 2–8).[26] It commemorates one Antonia, arguably remembered by one [Anto]-nius, whose relationship with the deceased is unclear. They both may have been freed by the same owner, as a couple, just as much as they may have been related with a view to their bloodline. The poem creates a stark contrast between mountainous Pergamon, in the Roman province of Asia, Antonia's place of origin, and Grădişte, in the valleys of Hunedoara county, Antonia's final resting place – from the top of the world (*excelso monte super|posita*) to (under) the eerily silent pastures of provincial Dacia, so to speak. Perga-

26 Further on this poem see Sămărghiţan 2003, 179, n. 10 and Cenati, Murzea, González Berdús 2023, 151–152.

mon itself takes up the role of Antonia's birth parents,[27] while Antonius takes it upon himself to commemorate her, as she is enveloped by soil at Sarmizegetusa, thus breaking the silence at least in writing.

Much like the pastures of Sarmizegetusa, Antonia remains *insona*, without as much as a peep, in this inscription, as well as she remains without any agency of her own: she is covered (in the passive voice), she was born (in the active voice, though with Pergamon as the subject), and she was commemorated – of course – by someone else. At the same time, even these few words are testimony to a life that, once role of the female at the heart of this memorial is shifted from being its passive object of someone else's narrative to representing its active protagonist, reports a life of considerable transformations – the life of an individual who, for reasons unknown (though slavery may arguably have been an element of it), was an alien migrant, displaced from her native Pergamon, to the proximity of the provincial capital of Roman Dacia near the north-eastern frontier of the Roman Empire. In that, her lived experience may not have been altogether different from that of Aelia Hygia (above, section 1). For Antonia, however, it is significantly more difficult to imagine the social and ethnic networks in which she was involved after her relocation, and the fact that she is commemorated by an individual of the same *nomen gentile*, but without indication of any obvious familial ties, does not suggest that she found herself in any elevated social or economic position at Sarmizegetusa, even if a substantial presence of individuals from Asia Minor, most notably with roots in Palmyra, is, of course, well attested in this area.[28]

6 An Outlook

Given the small size of our sample of evidence presented here, resulting from the relatively small body of evidence overall that constituted Roman verse inscriptions from Dacia, it is unsurprising that the number of themes and issues emerging from these texts remains limited. This pessimistic observation must not distract from the more positive insight that thus at least *some* of the issues that defined and characterised the lived experience(s) of women in Roman Dacia may be identified and somewhat better understood.

A first aspect of relevance, as witnessed in several texts, is the question of social dependence and (relative lack of) autonomy. In this regard, a broad and complex spectrum of dependence emerges through the close reading of the verse inscriptions. The most traditional approach would involve a division between *familia-* and *gens-*based relations, i.e.

27 Replacing the mention of actual parenthood with that of the region whence one hails is not an uncommon theme in *carmina epigraphica*; cf., for example, CLE 407, 479, CLEHisp 82, CLEMoes 40, and Zarker 59. Further on the matter more generally see Cugusi 1996, 199–221 and Arena, Bitto 2006, 1021–1042.

28 For the presence of Lucii Antonii in Sarmizegetusa see Piso 2001, 363–370 = Piso 2005, 459–466; for the presence of Palmyrenes see Bianchi 1987, 87–95 and e.g. Piso, Țentea 2022, 277–284, moreover also Dirven 1999, 157–189 and Smith 2013, 163–174.

forms of dependency that are defined by a woman's relation to a father, a husband, or other family members (including their children) on the one hand or, where and when slavery is involved, by her position in relation to a *dominus* (during slavery) or patron (following manumission). In reality, these divisions sometimes become blurred, e.g. in the case of Aelia Hygia, where the former owner and patron then became the husband. Description of such (conventional and unsurprising, and moreover: absolutely ubiquitous) legal forms of dependency, with its repercussions in socio-economic terms, do not fully capture the realities of the lived experience, however, as the analysis of the texts demonstrates. Already the case of Aelia Hygia (section 1) unfolds the complexities: this woman experienced consecutive phases of dependency in her life, even with the same individual at a key position, from slavery to marriage to her very own funerary commemoration, all accompanied by what the widowed husband then describes as 'tough times' (*tempus durum*). In other instances, such as that of Valeria Gemellina (section 2) we encounter a woman, from the exact opposite of the social spectrum, whose entire life had (seemingly voluntarily) been fashioned around her continuous dependency, but whose plans may well have come to nothing after her husband died before her at a reasonably early stage in his life – leaving her in a situation in which she then had to remind the public of her former social standing in conjunction with a clear need (rather than desire) to self-promote her own public persona and her good character (as well as that of their children).

Beyond that, we encounter a complex mixture of individuals, not only socially, but also ethnically – members of local elites such as Valeria Gemellina (section 2) alongside migrants who may have come voluntarily (such as the unnamed woman from Alexandria, section 5) or coercively (in addition to the aforementioned Aelia Hygia, one must consider e.g. Antonia, section 5). Finally, we encounter a complex set of networks into which these women were, or hoped to be, involved – socially, economically, legally, ethnically.

An especially interesting problem in this context is, of course, the question of linguistic networks: several of the women mentioned here, certainly including both of those mentioned in section 5, come from a geographical context in which Greek would have been the lingua franca. At the same time, they feature in Latin inscriptions in contexts in which Latin is the common (official) language. What impact would this have had on their daily lives and their ability to function within their spaces and domains in society? How did it aid, or impede, their independence in relation to other members of their families and networks? How did it allow them, as well as their relatives of similar background, or individuals sharing the same fate, to take part in life in their community (or communities)?

A second – seemingly divergent, in reality, though, closely related – matter of importance that emerges from the evidence is the issue of normative ethics regulating female life experiences. An especially prominent characteristic in this regard, by no means restricted to Roman Dacia of course, is the celebration of *pietas*, which can be noted in a number of pieces that were discussed here. Rather more noteworthy, however, is a comparatively conservative frame of mind that can be detected in more than one item when it comes to 'traditional Roman values' that needed advertising in the public sphere. This is not to say that Dacia is special in that regard – the contrary is true: Dacia shows patterns similar to what can be seen elsewhere. What is noteworthy, however, is how there is no celebration of individuality, of strong and independent personalities, or other female success. In other words, while a traditional set of values persists, more progressive forms are not (yet) attested.

A conspicuous absence in the Dacian inscriptions is the relative celebration, or rather objectification, of the female body and mind. None of the inscriptions adduced in the present context focus on the female body's appearance, features, or functionalities, regardless of their being written from a male or female perspective, and regardless of the age of the females mentioned. This extends to the matter of social or professional achievement (which, to some extent, but not exclusively, may be related to the social spectrum covered by this type of evidence). The only – trite and obvious – aspect that comes through in a small number of pieces is the ability to bear children.

A final issue palpable in the Roman verse inscriptions of Dacia is the matter of female mobility and (voluntary as well as involuntary) displacement. The evidence of the Roman verse inscriptions, though certainly not representative of the complex population of Roman Dacia as a whole, represents a great level of mobility, which only to a certain extent would seem to attest to an autonomous decision to embark on such a relocation. Most, if not all, of the displaced women that we see in these inscriptions moved because of their relative alignment to male individuals, who, in turn, would seem to have been driven into this area for professional reasons. In other words: Dacia may have 'wanted' Aelia Hygia, as her funerary inscription says, but what we do not know, and may even doubt to an extent, is whether that feeling was mutual. When it comes to matters of displacement, however, the important questions that need to be asked include, but are not limited to, those regarding (i) their ability to maintain any meaningful connection and communication with their kinfolk in their respective places of origin, (ii) their ability to make new connections and integrate themselves into local networks (linguistic, religious, social, economic, otherwise) at their (temporary or final) destination, (iii) their ability to construct, express, and assert their complex identity in their everyday lives. And finally, as with every journey, in the event of displacement, too, we must, of course, consider that there were not only points of departure and arrival, but also the entire (potentially rather convoluted and dreadful) experience in between.

We began our considerations with the observation of a conspicuous absence in research on Roman Dacia (and, to an extent, on Roman History more broadly): we may, over decades and centuries now, have assembled and curated our knowledge and understanding of a history *of* women in Roman Dacia, but effectively failed to consider how a narrative of the history of Roman Dacia *through* members of its female population might have looked. We proposed to address this matter, to an extent and as a first remedial step, through the extraction of micro-narratives and micro-histories from a cluster of historical sources that do not commonly feature prominently in historical research, namely the Roman verse inscriptions – be they 'ego documents' or, in many cases, simply documents that, through re-centring of narrative foci, might, at least to an extent, be used in their stead. It would be misguided to think, not least when considering the overall sample size, that this method is designed to re-write Roman Dacian History. In fact, the cases we considered may not even speak for all women of Roman Dacia – they remain anecdotal evidence. As such, however, they are still *evidence* – and they constitute a body of evidence that even larger-scale statistical approaches cannot, and must not, override: these lived experiences cannot, and must not, be invalidated by the production of datasets that, based on statistical analysis, want to suggest what actual female experiences in Roman Dacia looked like. If anything, such datasets may be designed to provide some historical background – the backdrop of the stage that was life in Roman Dacia, in which the individuals considered here were able to manage – and live – their own lives (as well as that of their families).

Bibliography

Adams, J. N. 1994. Wackernagel's law and the position of unstressed personal pronouns in Classical Latin. Transactions of the Philological Society, 92, 103–178.

Andrițoiu, I. 2003. Istoricul cercetărilor privitoare la aşezarea şi fortificația romană de la Micia, Sargetia 31, 181–202.

Andrițoiu, I. 2006. Necropolele Miciei, Timişoara.

Ardevan, R. 1998. Viața municipală în Dacia romană, Timişoara.

Arena, M., Bitto, I. 2006. Il motivo della morte in terra straniera nei CLE bücheleriani, in A. Akerraz, P. Ruggeri, A. Siraj, C. Vismara (eds.), L'Africa romana. Mobilità delle persone e dei popoli, dinamiche migratorie, emigrazioni ed immigrazioni nelle province occidentali dell'Impero romano. Atti del XVI convegno di studio Rabat, 15–19 dicembre 2004, Rome, 1021–1042.

Barbu, M.G., Simion, M. 2020. Castrul Micia. 1. Stadiul cercetărilor, ArcheoVest 8, 231–258.

Bianchi, L. 1987. I Palmyreni in Dacia: Comunità e tradizioni religiose, Dialoghi di Archeologia 5/1, 87–95.

Brancato, N.G. 2006. Mulieres Daciae Romanae (le donne della Dacia sulla base della documentazione epigrafica), in L. Mihăilescu-Bîrliba, O. Bounegru (eds.), Studia Historiae et Religionis Daco-Romanae in honorem Silvii Sanie, Bucharest, 349–368.

Byros, G. 2011. Reconstructing identities in Roman Dacia: Evidence from Religion, (Diss.) Yale University, 2011.

Cenati, C., Gangoly, A., González Berdús, V., Hobel, T., Kruschwitz, P., Murzea, D., Tasso, M. 2021. Depeșe poetice de pe Limesul Dacic, Limes. Frontierele Imperiului Roman în România 10, 15–20.

Cenati, C., Murzea, D., González Berdús, V. 2023. Sounds from Sarmizegetusa: Poetry and Performance in the Province of Dacia, AMN 60/I, 139–159.

CLENuovo = Cugusi, P. 2007. Per un nuovo "Corpus" dei "Carmina latina epigraphica". Memorie / Classe di Scienze Morali, Storiche e Filologiche, Accademia Nazionale dei Lincei Ser. 9, Vol. 22, Fasc. 1.

Cugusi, P. 1996. Aspetti letterari dei Carmina Latina Epigraphica, II edizione, Bologna.

Ciongradi, C. 2007. Grabmonument und sozialer Status in Oberdakien, Cluj-Napoca.

Dirven, L. 1999. The Palmyrenes of Dura-Europos. A Study of Religious Interaction in Roman Syria, (Religions in the Graeco-Roman World 138), Boston.
Finály, G. 1902. Egy Szamosujvári római feliratról, Archaeologiai Értesítő 22, 336–338.
Hartman, S. 2008. Venus in Two Acts, Small Axe, vol. 12 no. 2, 1–14.
Huemoeller, K. P. D. 2020. Freedom in Marriage? Manumission for Marriage in the Roman World, Journal of Roman Studies 110, 123–139.
Jánó, B. 1912. Római emlékek Hunyadvármegyében, Archaeologiai Értesítő 32, 49–57; 393–411.
Kamen, D., Levin-Richardson, S. 2022. Epigraphy and Critical Fabulation: Imagining Narratives of Greco-Roman Sexual Slavery, in E. Cousins (ed.), Dynamic Epigraphy: New Approaches to Inscriptions, Oxford, 201–221.
Kruschwitz, P., Coombe, C. 2016. I, Claudian: the syntactical and metrical alignment of ego in Claudian and his epic predecessors, Journal of Latin Linguistics, vol. 15, no. 1, 73–115.
Kruschwitz, P. 2023. „Diese Verslein hat Proficentius hervorgebracht“: Überlegungen zum Konzept der Autor*innenschaft mit besonderem Blick auf die lateinischen Versinschriften, in N. Glaubitz, K. Wesselmann (eds.), Plurale Autorschaft. Formen der Zusammenarbeit in Schriftkultur, Kunst und Literatur, Literatur in Wissenschaft und Unterricht, neue Folge 2, 155–185.
Münsterberg, R., Oehler, J. 1902. Antike Denkmäler in Siebenbürgen, Jahreshefte des Österreichischen Archäologischen Institutes in Wien, 5, 93–136.
Petersen, L. 2021. Pompeian Women and the Making of a Material History, in B. Longfellow, M. Swetnam-Burland, (eds.) Women's Lives, Women's Voices: Roman Material Culture and Female Agency in the Bay of Naples. New York, USA, 11–28.
Piso, I. 1993. Fasti provinciae Daciae I. Die senatorischen Amtsträger, Bonn.
Piso, I. 2001. De nouveau sur les Lucii Antonii de Sarmizegetusa, in V. Crişan, G. Florea, G. Gheorghiu, E. Iaroslavschi, L. Suciu (eds.), Studii de istorie antică. Omagiu profesorului Ioan Glodariu, Cluj-Napoca, 363–370 = Piso 2005, 459–466.
Piso, I. 2005. An der Nordgrenze des Römischen Reiches. Ausgewählte Studien (1972–2003), Stuttgart.
Piso, I., Țentea, O., 2022. Der Palmyrener P. Aelius Theimes, Duumviralis der Colonia Dacica Sarmizegetusa, ZPE 223, 277–284.
Sămărghițan, A., 2003. Poezia funerară în Dacia, in M. Bărbulescu (ed.), Funeraria Dacoromana. Arheologia funerară a Daciei romane, Cluj-Napoca, 170–195.
Smith II, A. M., 2013. Roman Palmyra: Identity, Community, and State Formation, New York.
Stănescu, A. 2004. Idealul stoic feminin reflectat în inscripțiile din Dacia romană, Țara Bârsei 3, 5–14.
Studniczka, F. 1884. Mithraeen und andere Denkmäler aus Dakien (Fortsetzung), Archäologisch-Epigraphische Mitteilungen aus Österreich-Ungarn 8, 34–51.
Téglás, G. 1910. Neue Beiträge zur Inschriftenkunde Dakiens, Klio 10, 495–505.
Torma, C. 1882, Inschriften aus Dacia, Moesia superior und Pannonia inferior, Archäologisch-Epigraphische Mitteilungen aus Österreich-Ungarn 6, 97–145.
Tudor, D. 1978. Oltenia romană[4] , Bucureşti.

La Colonna di Marco Aurelio e l'esercito romano ai tempi di Marco Aurelio e Commodo

Livio Zerbini

Tutti gli imperatori romani si ripromettevano durante il loro principato di dare vita a un articolato programma di lavori pubblici a Roma, in Italia e nelle province, a cominciare da Augusto, che, come ricorda il biografo latino Svetonio, "si vantava di lasciare una Roma di marmo dopo averla ricevuta di mattoni[1]".

Incidere in maniera significativa dal punto di vista architettonico e urbanistico sul volto di Roma avrebbe infatti generato un unanime consenso presso il popolo romano, anche per gli indubbi benefici economici derivanti dalla costruzione di molte opere pubbliche, che garantivano maggiori opportunità occupazionali in tutti i settori produttivi.

Molti imperatori durante il loro principato furono però costretti, a causa delle ristrettezze finanziarie del momento, ad abbandonare gli ambiziosi progetti urbanistico-architettonici che avevano pensato di realizzare, per concentrarsi invece su quei pochi interventi edilizi improcrastinabili e che venivano maggiormente richiesti dal popolo romano.

Una situazione simile avvenne anche nel caso di Commodo, il quale dovette fare i conti con una situazione economica a dir poco complessa, a causa delle guerre marcomanniche prima e della peste antonina poi, tanto che a ben vedere sono poche le opere pubbliche che vennero commissionate dall'imperatore, dal momento che vi erano priorità ben più urgenti da affrontare.

Il biografo della *Storia Augusta* a questo proposito ricorda che "Delle sue opere pubbliche, ad eccezione delle terme che Cleandro aveva costruito in suo nome, non ne resta alcuna. Ma il senato ebbe a far cancellare il suo nome che egli aveva fatto incidere su opere non sue. Non portò neppure a compimento le opere iniziate dal padre[2]".

Sappiamo per certo dalle fonti antiche che l'imperatore Commodo fece costruire il Tempio al divo Marco Aurelio, costruito nelle vicinanze della Colonna di Marco Aurelio e che si trovava nel luogo dove ora sorge Palazzo Wedeking, e che realizzò un grandioso

1 Svetonio, *Vite dei Cesari, Augusto*, 28, 3.

2 *Storia Augusta, Vita di Commodo*, 17, 5–7: *Opera eius praeter lavacrum, quod Cleander nomine ipsius fecerat, nulla exstant. Sed nomen eius alienis operibus incisum senatus erasit. Nec patris autem sui opera perfecit.*

complesso termale, le *Thermae Commodianae* appunto[3], ma nulla di più, perché non abbiamo altre notizie di grandi costruzioni edificate durante il suo principato.

In ragione di ciò il più importante monumento che venne eretto durante il principato di Commodo, e ancor oggi visibile a Roma in Piazza Colonna, è senza dubbio la Colonna di Marco Aurelio, la cui struttura richiama chiaramente la Colonna Traiana, voluta dall'imperatore Traiano per celebrare la conquista della Dacia del re Decebalo[4].

Iniziata nell'anno 176 d. C. dall'imperatore Marco Aurelio, la Colonna venne portata a compimento nel 192 d. C. da Commodo per onorare il padre per le vittoriose campagne militari condotte contro i Marcomanni, i Quadi e i Sarmati sul Danubio[5]. Il monumento equiparava di fatto l'imperatore Marco Aurelio a Traiano.

La Colonna di Marco Aurelio, la cui collocazione è quella originale, avvalora la fortuna che ebbe con la dinastia degli Antonini il tipo architettonico della colonna coclide. Oltre infatti alla Colonna Traiana e alla Colonna di Marco Aurelio, tra il 161 e il 162 d. C. venne innalzata nel Campo Marzio anche la Colonna di Antonino Pio, di cui è rimasta solamente la base, conservata nei Musei Vaticani, fatta erigere in onore dell'imperatore e di sua moglie Faustina Maggiore dai suoi successori Marco Aurelio e Lucio Vero. Ma la sorte ha voluto che giungessero intatte sino ai giorni nostri la Colonna Traiana e la Colonna di Marco Aurelio.

La Colonna di Marco Aurelio è alta 29,617 metri (pari a cento piedi romani), che diventano 42 se si considera anche la base, ed è costituita da ventisette grandi blocchi di marmo lunense, il cui diametro varia da 3,80 a 3,65 metri, pertanto con una leggera rastrematura del monumento verso l'alto. La Colonna di Marco Aurelio misura all'incirca due metri in più rispetto al modello rappresentato dalla Colonna Traiana.

Il monumento è ben conservato, a eccezione del suo basamento, i cui fregi andarono distrutti durante il restauro voluto nell'anno 1589 da papa Sisto V. Sulla base della colonna venne quindi apposta un'iscrizione in latino che ricorda l'intervento del papa e riporta l'errata dedica all'imperatore Antonino Pio: «Sisto Quinto, Pontefice Massimo, questa colonna coclide dedicata all'imperatore Antonino, miseramente deteriorata e rovinata, restituì alla forma originaria. Nell'anno del Signore 1589, nell'anno IV del suo pontificato[6]».

---

3 *Storia Augusta, Vita di Commodo*, 17, 5.

4 Sulla Colonna Traiana si veda: Rossi 1971. *Trajan's Column and the Dacian Wars, London*; Coarelli 1999. *La Colonna Traiana, Roma*; Settis, La Regina, Agosti, Farinella 1988. *La Colonna Traiana, Torino*; Bianchi Bandinellli 2003. *Il Maestro delle imprese di Traiano, Milano*; Zerbini 2021. *Traiano, Roma*, pp. 152–156.

5 Sugli anni in cui venne realizzata la Colonna di Marco Aurelio si rimanda a *ILS* 5920, in cui si può evincere che nell'agosto-settembre del 193 d. C. i lavori erano ancora in corso o terminati da poco. Sulla datazione della Colonna si veda anche Morris 1952. *The Dating of the Column of Marcus Maurelius, Journal of the Warburg and Courtauld Institutes 15*, 33–47. Sulla Colonna di Marco Aurelio: Depeyrot 2010. *La colonne de Marc Aurèle. II. Iconographie, Wetteren*; Depeyrot, G. 2011. *Les Légions face aux Barbares. La colonne de Marc Aurèle Paris.*

6 *Sixtus V Pont. Max. / columnam hanc / coclidem Imp. / Antonino dicatam / misere laceram / ruinosamq. primae / formae restituit / A. MDLXXXIX Pont. IV.*

La statua di bronzo dell'imperatore Marco Aurelio, posta sulla sommità della colonna, andò invece perduta nel corso del Medioevo e sostituita poi con quella di san Paolo da papa Sisto V.

La Colonna di Marco Aurelio come detto trae ovviamente ispirazione dalla Colonna Traiana, ma si differenzia da quest'ultima in quanto i rilievi che avvolgono il fusto e che ripercorrono i momenti salienti della guerra contro i Marcomanni, i Quadi e i Sarmati non sono hanno *stricto sensu* un ordine cronologico e le scene si raggruppano per così dire in due sezioni: la prima che racconta gli episodi bellici relativi al periodo che va dal 168 al 172 d. C.; la seconda che riguarda gli anni dal 173 al 174 d. C.

Il racconto che accompagna la Colonna di Marco Aurelio si struttura dunque in modo completamente differente rispetto alla Colonna Traiana. Il solo elemento ripetitivo, la cui presenza potrebbe indicare una successione cronologica, è costituito dalla presenza dell'imperatore Marco Aurelio. È pertanto la presenza dell'imperatore che ritma l'ordine di successione degli avvenimenti bellici[7].

Ma, al di là delle evidenti affinità tipologiche, nello stile dei rilievi si notano delle palesi differenze, dovute ai mutamenti intercorsi nell'arco di poco più di sessant'anni nella concezione artistica, nel senso che dallo stile classico della Colonna Traiana si era passati a un registro compositivo più semplice e quindi meno raffinato.

Anche la rappresentazione della figura dell'imperatore è decisamente mutata, mentre Traiano nella Colonna Traiana viene raffigurato di profilo e come un uomo tra gli uomini o meglio come un generale tra i suoi soldati, Marco Aurelio è ritratto invece frontalmente, a dimostrazione di come si stava ormai affermando il concetto della maestà divina dell'imperatore, tipico delle monarchie orientali, che poi prevarrà nel corso del III secolo d. C.

Molte scene della Colonna di Marco Aurelio raffigurano lo stato maggiore dell'imperatore; quest'ultimo è generalmente accompagnato da due generali: uno dei quali dovrebbe essere Pompeiano, tra i più importanti e valenti comandanti di Marco Aurelio e marito della figlia Lucilla; l'altro potrebbe essere Pertinace, il futuro imperatore.

Nella Colonna Traiana l'imperatore Traiano appare come un generale invincibile e la conquista della Dacia mostra chiaramente la forza di Roma e del suo esercito dopo la ripresa della politica espansionistica.

Nella Colonna di Marco Aurelio si percepisce invece un'atmosfera decisamente diversa, in cui Roma sembra aver perduto le certezze dell'età traianea e non sembra più così invincibile come un tempo, tanto che la vittoria dell'esercito romano si deve in alcuni momenti non all'abilità dei generali, bensì ad eventi miracolosi, del resto ampiamente sottolineati nei rilievi, come nel caso del miracolo del fulmine e della pioggia, che dissetò i soldati romani che stavano morendo di sete e che trascinò via i nemici in trombe d'acqua.

Con la Colonna di Marco Aurelio per la prima volta nell'arte romana si avverte un senso di incertezza e di inquietudine, che permea tutti quanti i rilievi e che si farà ancor più manifesto negli anni a venire.

---

7 A questo si veda: Depeyrot 2011. *Les Légions face aux Barbares. La colonne de Marc Aurèle*, cit., p. 13.

La Colonna di Marco Aurelio, al di là dell'importante valore storico, rappresenta una preziosa testimonianza sulle armi e sull'equipaggiamento dei soldati romani durante il principato di Marco Aurelio e quello di Commodo.

I rilievi della Colonna di Marco Aurelio, oltre a raccontare le vicende salienti delle guerre marcomanniche combattute dall'imperatore Marco Aurelio, rappresentano infatti in un certo senso le pagine di un vero e proprio album sull'equipaggiamento militare dei soldati, anche se la valenza delle raffigurazioni non deve essere sempre assunta con un valore paradigmatico, in considerazione del loro intento propagandistico, ma va ponderata con la dovuta attenzione, in quanto è probabile, in alcuni casi, che nell'ambito dell'armamento a disposizione si dovette tener conto della necessità di scegliere, ai fini della rappresentazione, quello che meglio contraddistingueva il soldato romano rispetto al nemico.

Nella Colonna di Marco Aurelio il legionario romano presenta ancora il tipico armamento della prima età imperiale, con innovazioni proprie del periodo degli Antonini.

La principale arma da getto era ancora il *pilum*, almeno sino alla fine del II secolo[8]. Accanto a questi giavellotti vi era la pesante *lonchês* o *lancea* e l'*hasta*, la tipica arma da botta del soldato romano, con la sua punta in ferro (*cuspis*)[9], che nella colonna istoriata si vede ben rappresentata nelle mani dei legionari dell'imperatore Marco Aurelio.

In particolare la Colonna di Marco Aurelio mostra in più occasioni come le lance romane dell'età tardo Antonina avessero sezione romboidale. Le punte di lancia di questo tipo erano massicce, con una scanalatura media di notevole entità.

Un esempio di tali lance, attribuibile cronologicamente al II secolo d. C., proviene da *Ulpia Traiana Sarmigezetusa*, la metropoli della Dacia romana. La lunghezza di alcuni esemplari potrebbe agevolare l'identificazione di queste lance con quelle dei *kontophoroi* menzionati da Arriano[10].

La lunghezza della lancia variava a seconda della specialità dei reparti e del loro uso in battaglia. Nella Colonna di Marco Aurelio si può notare infatti come i *milites gregarii* usassero in battaglia, nel combattimento corpo a corpo, sia esemplari più lunghi sia lance senza puntali all'estremità inferiore.

La presenza di un puntale (*spiculum*) all'estremità inferiore della lancia, vale a dire di un rinforzo metallico della parte terminale dell'*hasta*, è ben documentato in quel periodo dall'archeologia, nonostante sia scarsamente visibile sui monumenti figurativi dell'età di Marco Aurelio.

Il *gladius*, l'arma da fianco del *miles Romanus* più celebre dell'Antichità, viene rappresentata sui monumenti di età Antonina portata usualmente al fianco destro dei soldati e a quello sinistro degli ufficiali e dei comandanti superiori.

8 D'Amato, Sumner 2009, *Arms and Armour of the Imperial Roman Soldier. From Marius to Commodus, 112 BC–AD 192*, London, pp. 67 sgg.

9 D'Amato, Sumner 2009, *Arms and Armour of the Imperial Roman Soldier*, cit., p. 73.

10 Arriano, *Schieramento contro gli Alani*, 12.

Come si vede nella famosa scena che la Colonna di Marco Aurelio dedica al miracolo della pioggia, la tipologia del gladio è decisamente quella di tipo Pompei, che dalla seconda metà del I secolo d. C. aveva iniziato gradualmente a rimpiazzare quelle precedenti.

Tuttavia alcuni esemplari di questo periodo, come il *gladius* di Svilengrad, che appartiene a una sepoltura dell'età di Commodo, o il gladio di Komtiní, dello stesso periodo, mostrano quell'allungamento della lama che gradatamente porterà all'adozione della lunga *spatha* da parte della fanteria romana[11].

Tali tipologie di spade non sono solo visibili sulla Colonna di Marco Aurelio, ma anche su altri monumenti celebrativi dell'età di Marco Aurelio e di Commodo, come il fregio di Chiusi, che rappresenta probabilmente una battaglia tra Romani e Iazigi.

Su questi monumenti figurativi il gladio viene portato attraverso un balteo sospeso sulla spalla sinistra, che sembra in quel periodo essere la regola.

L'equipaggiamento difensivo dell'età tardo Antonina è ben documentato sia archeologicamente che iconograficamente.

Gli elmi raffigurati sulla Colonna di Marco Aurelio e sul sarcofago del Portonaccio sono sia del tipo pseudo-attico, con un frontone difensivo a diadema, sia di tipo Weisenau, che trova riscontro in un esemplare proveniente da Theilenhofen[12]. Molti di questi elmi, di entrambi i tipi, sono rappresentati con una cresta forgiata ad anello, mentre altri hanno piume inserite sulla sommità. Alcuni elmi presentano decorazioni in rilievo, che sugli originali erano probabilmente in metallo sbalzato.

Questi tipi erano portati anche dalla cavalleria, che nel fregio di Chiusi mostra l'uso in battaglia di elmi a maschera, con capelli veri attaccati alla calotta dell'elmo, come quelli ritrovati a *Noviomagus*, (l'attuale Nijmegen, in Olanda), sul *limes* renano.

La Colonna di Marco Aurelio mostra chiaramente come le corazze (*loricae*) della tarda età Antonina sono quelle ben documentate nella cultura materiale romana: la *lorica conserta hamis* (la corazza a maglie di ferro, che più comunemente è chiamata *hamata*),[13] la *squamata* (la corazza a scaglie)[14] e la *lorica segmentata* (la corazza a bande di metallo o di cuoio che cingono il corpo del legionario).

Tutte e tre le tipologie di corazze sono state trovate in frammenti di diverse proporzioni e dimensioni in diversi luoghi che furono teatro delle guerre marcomanniche, e in particolare a *Carnuntum* e ad *Aquincum*, che con *Vindobona*, dove morì l'imperatore Marco Aurelio, furono la base delle operazioni militari di contrattacco romano contro i Quadi e i Marcomanni e le altre tribù germaniche, nonché il quartier generale dell'imperatore.

Un esempio quasi integro di corazza segmentata, che presenta alcune caratteristiche evolutive rispetto a quelle precedenti, è venuto alla luce a Stillfried, in Austria, attribuibile cronologicamente proprio all'età di Marco Aurelio e in un'area che fu interessata dalle guerre marcomanniche.

11 D'Amato, Sumner 2009, *Arms and Armour of the Imperial Roman Soldier*, cit., p. 87.

12 D'Amato, Sumner 2009, *Arms and Armour of the Imperial Roman Soldier*, cit., p. 120 e figg. 57, 59, 63, 65, 114.

13 Virgilio, *Eneide*, III, 467.

14 D'Amato, Sumner 2009, *Arms and Armour of the Imperial Roman Soldier*, cit., p. 124.

Sebbene questa corazza fosse prevalentemente in ferro, non mancava l'uso di tipologie in cuoio, indossate dai cavalieri nel sarcofago romano del Portonaccio[15], che raffigura probabilmente una *vexillatio* della legione *IIII Flavia* in un combattimento contro i barbari.

I monumenti figurativi mostrano come tutti e tre i tipi di corazza venissero portati sopra un giustacuore in cuoio o in feltro, con tutta probabilità il *subarmalis* o la *globa* delle fonti tarde, che emergeva con linguette al di sotto della corazza, alla vita e sulle spalle. Le estremità inferiori e i bordi delle corazze a cotta di maglia sono spesso foggiati in maniera triangolare.

La corazza muscolare (*stadios* o *thorax stadion*) in bronzo, ferro o cuoio era riservata ai comandanti militari, agli ufficiali superiori, ai centurioni e forse anche agli *optiones*[16].

Nei monumenti vengono raffigurati anche schinieri (*ocreae*), come per esempio quelli sul sarcofago romano Amendola, conservato ai Musei Capitolini, che rappresenta, in uno stile simile a quello del Portonaccio, una battaglia tra Romani e Barbari. La forma di questi schinieri riproduce la foggia di quelli ritrovati in siti archeologici di età posteriore, come quelli rinvenuti nel campo militare di Künzing.

Lo *scutum* del legionario assume una forma prevalentemente ovale, come attestano anche i monumenti di età Severiana e gli scavi di *Dura-Europos*, benché databili cinquant'anni dopo l'età di Commodo. Gli scudi vengono sbalzati con fregi (*deigmata*) che rappresentano gli emblemi delle legioni.

Tuttavia lo scudo poligonale tipico del legionario della prima età imperiale non scompare del tutto e viene raffigurato sulla Colonna di Marco Aurelio accanto a quello ovale, anche se con minore frequenza. Gli scudi della cavalleria erano di forma ovale o circolare, come nel periodo traianeo.

I monumenti figurativi dell'età di Commodo ci forniscono anche molte informazioni sull'abbigliamento dei soldati romani: l'uso di *tunicae* a maniche corte (ma spesso frangiate all'estremità), di *bracae* lunghe poco sotto il ginocchio (*femoralia* o *foeminalia*), di calzature chiodate che seguivano o lo stile delle vecchie *caligae*, nella forma di *carbatinae*, oppure erano stivaletti chiusi al collo del piede (*calcei*).

Molto diffuso nell'età tardo Antonina era ancora il fazzoletto di lana annodato intorno al collo del legionario, il *focale* o *maphorion*, che, oltre a servire ad attutire il peso

---

15 Questo importante sarcofago romano apparteneva presumibilmente a un importante generale dell'imperatore Marco Aurelio, che si batté nelle guerre marcomanniche; si è supposto che si trattasse di *Aulus Iulius Pompilius Piso Titus Vibius Laevilius Quadratus Berenicianus*, che militò al servizio di Marco Aurelio al comando della cavalleria nella guerra contro i Marcomanni nel 172–175 d.C. (*CIL* VIII 2582). Lo stile del sarcofago del Portonaccio è indubbiamente legato agli artisti che realizzarono la Colonna di Marco Aurelio.

16 La corazza muscolare veniva chiamata θώραξ στάδιος o στατός (*thorax stadios* o *statos*), perché se posta sul terreno con il bordo inferiore rimaneva eretta. In ragione della sua solidità la corazza muscolare veniva addirittura usata come sedia. Pausania, che scrive al tempo di Antonino Pio, descrive un esempio in bronzo di queste corazze, dipinto nel Tempio di Delfi (*Periegesi della Grecia*, 10, 27, 2). Per esempi di corazze muscolari del periodo si veda per esempio la statua loricata di Pertinace, nella sua qualità di *praeses Daciae*, in *habitu militari*, ad *Apulum*, l'odierna Alba Iulia, in Romania.

e la sfregatura dell'armatura attorno al collo, poteva essere impiegato anche in altri usi pratici[17].

I monumenti raffigurano anche molto bene le tre tipologie di mantello dell'esercito romano: il *paludamentum* dei generali e degli imperatori, il *sagum* dei centurioni e dei *milites gregarii*[18] e il mantello da viaggio dei soldati, vale a dire la *paenula*.

Non mancano inoltre le rappresentazioni del simbolo della *militia armata*, il *cingulum militiae* o *balteus*, ben documentata in ambito danubiano.

Le tipologie di cinture militari di questo periodo cambiano completamente rispetto ai tipi precedenti di età Flavia e Traianea e la maggior parte degli elementi della cintura incorporano ora elementi bronzei con decorazione aperta, che mostra forti tracce di influenze decorative celtiche.

Altri tipi di placche mostrano una decorazione a smalto del tipo "millefiori" e alcuni elementi della cintura, visibili anche sulla Colonna di Marco Aurelio, mostrano baltei a linguetta, pendenti da cinghiette verticali inserite nella parte frontale, come sulla Colonna Traiana.

Non mancano poi le raffigurazioni degli stendardi delle legioni e degli *auxilia*, come *aquilae*, *vexilla* e *signa*, e per la prima volta sono attestati come stendardi delle truppe romane i *dracones*, come nel sarcofago romano del Portonaccio, che i Romani conobbero per la prima volta combattendo contro i Daci del re Decebalo.

La scena LXXVIII della Colonna di Marco Aurelio ci mostra infine anche gli ausiliari orientali dell'esercito romano, con i reparti di arcieri dal berretto frigio e la cavalleria con *vexilla* e lance.

Questo contributo è comunque l'anticipazione di un lavoro più approfondito che a breve intraprenderò sulla Colonna di Marco Aurelio, attraverso una diretta visione autoptica dei rilievi, un monumento che non ha avuto l'attenzione che gli studiosi hanno rivolto alla Colonna Traiana e che proprio in ragione di questo merita di essere ulteriormente studiato per meglio comprenderne l'importante valenza storica.

Bibliografia

Arriano, Schieramento contro gli Alani, a cura di S. Belfiore, Roma 2012.
Storia Augusta, a cura di F. Roncoroni, Milano 1972.
Svetonio, Vite dei Cesari, traduttore F. Dessì, Milano 1982.
Virgilio, Eneide, a cura di E. Paratore, Milano 1978.

Bianchi Bandinellli, R. 2003. Il Maestro delle imprese di Traiano, Milano.
Coarelli, F. 1999. La Colonna Traiana, Roma.
Settis, S., La Regina, A., Agosti, G., Farinella, V. 1988. La Colonna Traiana, Torino.

17 D'Amato, Sumner 2009, *Arms and Armour of the Imperial Roman Soldier*, cit., pp. 90, 220.
18 D'Amato, Sumner 2009, *Arms and Armour of the Imperial Roman Soldier*, cit., p. 206.

D'Amato, R., Sumner, G. 2009, Arms and Armour of the Imperial Roman Soldier. From Marius to Commodus, 112 BC–AD 192, London.
Depeyrot, G. 2010. La colonne de Marc Aurèle. II. Iconographie, Wetteren.
Depeyrot, G. 2011. Les Légions face aux Barbares. La colonne de Marc Aurèle, Paris.
Morris, J. 1952. The Dating of the Column of Marcus Aurelius, Journal of the Warburg and Courtauld Institutes 15, 33–47.
Rossi, L. 1971. Trajan's Column and the Dacian Wars, London.
Zerbini, L. 2021. Traiano, Roma.

A new *praefectus* and *patronus* of the *collegium centonariorum* of the *colonia Aurelia Apulensis*

Florian Matei-Popescu, Radu Ota, Darius Groza*

Introduction

An important archaeological site of the Roman Dacia is overlapped by the nowadays Partoş neighbourhood, Alba Iulia (Romania), namely a Roman civilian settlement, developed on the right side of the river Mureş, immediately after the making of the province of Dacia in AD 106. From the administrative point of view, it is highly possible that the settlement could have been a *pagus* of the *colonia Ulpia Traiana Dacica Sarmizegetusa*, or a simple civilian *vicus* emerged at a *leuga* distance from the fortress of the legion XIII Gemina, located in the area of the future medieval and modern centre of Alba Iulia (underneath of the so-called Vauban fortification). This civilian settlement received the municipal grant during the reign of Marcus Aurelius, *municipium Aurelium Apulense*, being further raised at the colonial status by Commodus, *colonia Aurelia Apulensis*.[1] In an inscription dated to AD 252–253, the *colonia* is attested as *Chrysopolis*,[2] another proof of its continuous development during the late Antonine and Severan periods. At its maximum extension, *colonia Aurelia Apulensis* covered almost 75 ha (1500 × 500 m)[3] being by far the most important economic and political centre of the Dacian provinces.

Adalbert Cserni, the first custodian and director of the Alba Iulia Museum, uncovered, in 1911–1912, an impressive building with thirteen rooms, in the north-western part of the Roman city, which housed a bone and horn carving workshop, together with a ceramic production centre.[4]

During the 1988–1994 archaeological seasons, a team of archaeologists from Cluj-Napoca (I. Piso, A. Diaconescu, I. Bogdan-Cătăniciu) and Alba Iulia (V. Moga and R. Ciobanu) highlighted all the phases of the city ramparts, along with the foundations

* Vasile Pârvan Institute of Archaeology, Bucharest; florian.matei@gmail.com; The National Union Museum, Alba Iulia; raduota2@gmail.com; Total Business Land, Alba Iulia; grozadarius@gmail.com

1 For a short historical overview see Diaconescu, Piso 1993, 67–70 and Ardevan 1998, 45–49.

2 AE 1989, 628 = IDR III/5. 432.

3 Diaconescu, Piso 1993, 67–70; Ardevan 1998, 47.

4 Cserni 1912, 282, fig. II; Anghel 2023, 236.

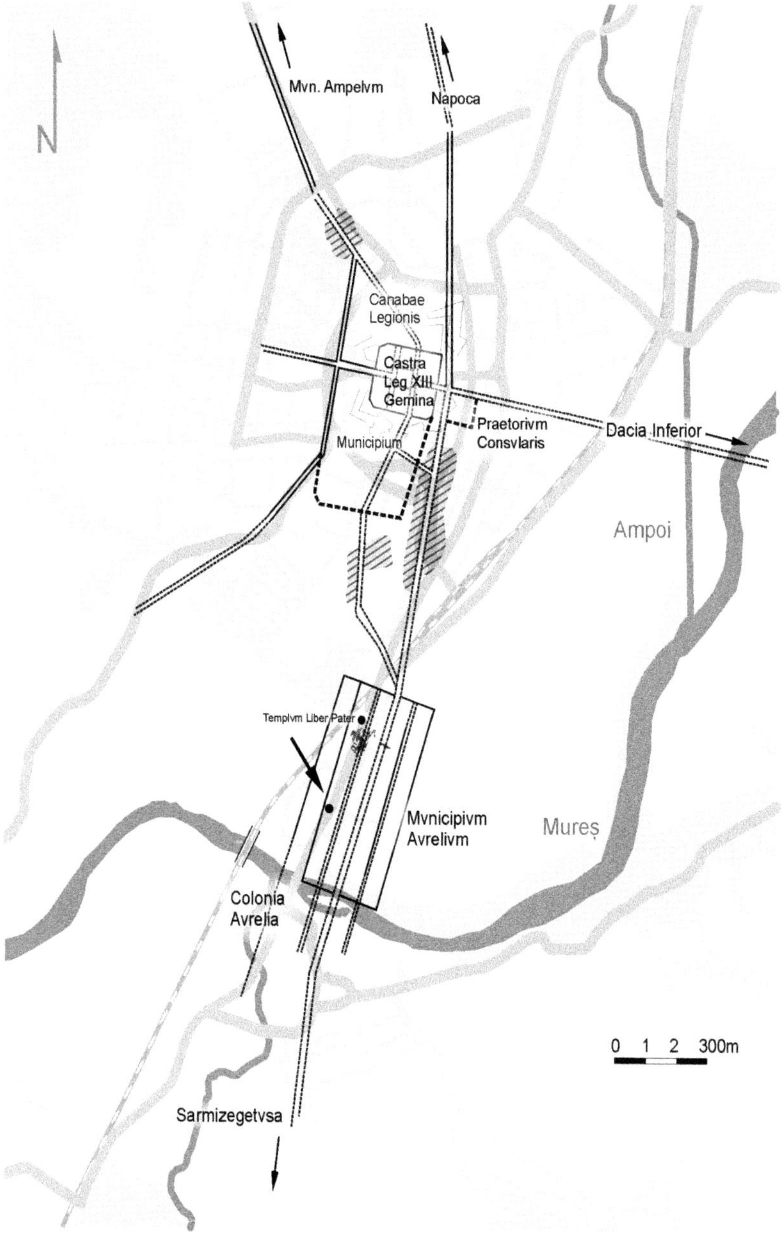

Fig. 1: The general layout plan of Apulum during the Roman period (*castra legionis, canabae legionis, municipium Septimium Apulense, praetorium consularis, municipium Aurelium Apulense / colonia Aurelia Apulensis*) and the place of the discovery (Darius Groza, based on the layout plan published by Matei-Popescu, Țentea 2017, 166, fig. 4)

of a building from the *forum* and one of the main roads of the city, the *cardo maximus*, oriented NNE-SSV.[5] During the 1989–1992 and 1998–2003 archaeological seasons, the sanctuary of Liber Pater has been excavated, by A. Diaconescu and further on together with I. Haynes (Birkback College, University of London) and A. Schäfer (Winckelmann Institut, Humboldt-Universität zu Berlin).[6]

All these excavations and public works carried out in nowadays Alba Iulia led at the discovery of Roman period inscriptions, enriching thus an important epigraphic heritage, collected and published more than two decades ago by Ioan Piso. It is therefore more than appropriate to publish a newly discovered inscription into a volume to honour his 80th birthday and his outstanding achievement in the field of the epigraphy, history and archaeology of the Roman Empire.

The context of the discovery

In the spring of 2023, a fragmentary inscribed limestone slab was discovered during the archaeological supervision of the reparation works of the roadway and changing of sewage and of the water, gas and electrical power facilities on the 74 Regimentul 5 Vânători str., at a depth of 0.60–0.70 m from the level of the nowadays repaired roadway. The place of the discovery is located in the south-central area of the Roman city, not far from the presumed location of the *forum*. The context had been previously destroyed by excavations carried out for the sewage system almost one decade ago. The discovery itself has been therefore fortunate, taking into account that the inscription has been found in the filling ditch of the contemporary sewage. It is worth mentioning that the honorific inscription for Volusianus, dated to AD 252–253 (*cos. II, trib. pot. II*),[7] in which *colonia Aurelia Apulensis* bears the name *Chrysopolis*, had been discovered in the proximity, in the courtyard of the no. 156 house on that street.[8]

The inscription

The lower half of a limestone slab, the bottom is partially damaged and, judging by the text of the inscription, it seems like that only the margin and the left-hand corner is missing. The right and left margins, although little damaged (especially the right-hand one), are preserved and only the upper part of the slab is entirely missing.

Height: 0.50 m; length: 0.40 m; thickness: 0.16 m. The letters are 0.054–0.051 m high. For the inscription's alignment guide-lines are used. In the l. 4, O is cut smaller into the

5 Diaconescu, Piso 1993, 67–81; Bogdan-Cătăniciu 2000, 109–139; Moga, Ciobanu, Drîmbărean 2000, 141–202.

6 Diaconescu 2019, 49.

7 Kienast, Eck, Heil 2017, 201.

8 AE 1989, 628 = IDR III/5. 432; Petolescu 2000, 213.

Fig. 2: The inscribed limestone slab: the drawing and the photo (Darius Groza)

C letter, another proof that the right-hand margin is preserved. Most of the words are divided by *interpunctiones*. The letters are elegantly cut, which could indicate a date in the late Antonine or early Severan period.

- - - - - - - - -
praefectus·et
patronus co[l]-
legi·centona-
riorum·eidem·col-
legio·d(onum)·d(edit).

The inscription was set by an unknown prefect and patron of the guild of the textile dealers that made a gift to the members of the guild. It is highly probable that he had paid for a construction or a decoration in the meeting place of the guild and the slab was fixed on the walls of that meeting place.

Collegium centonariorum coloniae Aureliae Apulensis

The guild of the textile dealers is already attested in *colonia Aurelia Apulensis* by several inscriptions. Thus, a honorific inscription was set for the imperial house by the governor of the three Dacian provinces, Lucius Pomponius Liberalis, in AD 202/203–205,[9] with the occasion of the erection by the guild itself of the meeting place (*schola*),[10] decorated with gable (*aetoma*).[11] Another inscription attests Fabia Lucilla, *mater collegiorum fabr(um) et*

9 Piso 1993, 161–162, no. 34.

10 *Schola* could have been in fact an entire compound, see Goffaux 2011, 48: "par une sorte de convention tacite, la terminologie moderne a consacré le vocable de schola dans le sens d'«édifice collégial» pour désigner avant tout les édifices complexes bien connus, par exemple, à Ostie. On désigne par là des sortes de maisons très vastes, souvent organisées autour d'un plan axial, et composées d'une salle de réunion, d'une cour centrale et de nombreuses dépendances"; and Goffaux 2012, 199: "le terme même de *schola* est souvent employé abusivement, de manière générique, pour désigner l'ensemble des édifices collégiaux, alors qu'il ne renvoie sans doute qu'à la seule salle de réunion du collège, éventuellement (mais pas obligatoirement) intégrée au sein des édifices collégiaux".

11 CIL III 1174 = ILS 7255a = IDR III/5. 425 = Liu 2009, 332, no. 2: *Pro salute Augg[g(ustorum)] / L(uci) Sept(imi) Severi Pii Pert(inacis) et M(arci) / Aur(eli) Antonini Impp(eratorum) ⟦et P(ubli)⟧ Sept(imi) / ⟦Getae Caes(aris)⟧ coll(egium) centona/rior(um) scholam cum aetoma / pecunia sua fecit dedicante / L(ucio) Pomp(onio) Liberale co(n)s(ulari) Dac(iarum) III*; Goffaux 2011, 66. The meeting place of the *collegium fabrum* was also decorated with a *aetoma*, CIL III 1212 = ILS 7255 = IDR III/5. 444: *M(arcus) Aurel(ius) / Chrestus / ob hono/rem patro/nat(us) coll(egii) / fabr(um) col(oniae) / Apul(ensis) ad ex/(s)truction(em) / aetomae / ded(it) HS n(ummum) VI(milia)*; Liu 2009, 157–158; Ciambelli 2022, taking into account that the word itself is rarely attested in the Latin epigraphy, highlights the competition among the two *collegia* of having the most lavish meeting place: "provando così a ricostruire l'ordine sequenziale dei fatti, possiamo supporre che i centonarii nel finanziare la costruzione della loro sede tra il 202 e il 205 d.C. scelsero di integrarne la struttura con

cent(onariorum), who raised a funerary inscription to her father in law, former *duumvir* and *sacerdos* of the *colonia Aurelia Apulensis*, P. Aelius Silvanus.[12]

An honorific inscription was raised at the beginning of the 3rd century AD for Publius Aelius Genialis, patron of the guild, former *decurio* and *pontifex* of the *colonia Aurelia Apulensis*, by his freedman, Euthymus.[13]

Finally, an honorific inscription was set for Publius Aelius Strenuus, *sacerdos arae Augusti*, *augur* and former *duumvir* of the *colonia Ulpia Traiana Dacica Sarmizegetusa*, *augur* of the *colonia Aurelia Apulensis* and *decurio* of the *colonia Septimia Drobetensis*, patron of the guilds of the craftsmen, textile dealers and ship-owners and farmer of the salt mines, pastures and of the trade activities, by his slave, Rufinus.[14]

If we agree that the slab recorded some works performed at the *schola* of the guild, then this activity could be dated after the moment of the erection of that *schola*, therefore after AD 202/203–205, in the last years of Septimius Severus' reign or during the reign of Caracalla.

In a Roman city, the *collegia* of the *fabri* and *dendrophori*, both of them mentioned together in one inscription from the *colonia Aurelia Apulensis*,[15] built alongside the *collegium centonariorum* the so-called *tria collegia*.[16] At Apulum, the *collegium nautarum* (probably the owners of the ships navigating on the Mureş River[17]) must be added, as

---

un fastigio triangolare. Questo elemento architettonico era motivo di orgoglio per l'associazione tanto da essere stato menzionato fieramente addirittura nella placca commemorativa (*scholam cum aetoma*). La sede dei fabri, invece, preesistente a quella dei centonari per l'antichità del collegio, ne era sprovvista. Questi ultimi, dunque, per non mostrarsi inferiori ai centonarii, si sarebbero attivati per apportare tale miglioria riuscendo a provocare la liberalità del loro neo-patrono Cresto che decise di finanziarne la costruzione".

12 CIL III 1207 = IDR III/5. 483 = Liu 2009, 332, no. 3: *P(ublio) Ael(io) P(ubli) f(ilio) Pap(iria) / Silvano / IIvir(ali) et sa/cerd(otali) [co]l(oniae) A[p(ulensis)] / eq(uiti) R(omano) e(gregiae) m(emoriae) v(iro) / Fabia Lucil/la e(gregiae) m(emoriae) v(iri) filia / mater coll(egiorum) / fabr(um) et cent(onariorum) / coloniae s(upra) s(criptae) / socero sui / amantissi/mo.*

13 CIL III 1208 = IDR III/5. 440 = Liu 2009, 333, no. 4: *P(ublio) Ael(io) P(ubli) fil(io) Pap(iria) / Geniali dec(urioni) / et pontifici / col(oniae) Apul(ensis) pa/tron(o) coll(egii) / cent(onariorum) P(ublius) Ael(ius) / Euthymus / libert(us).*

14 CIL III 1209 = ILS 7147 = IDR III/5. 443 = Liu 2009, 333, no. 5: *P(ublio) Ael(io) P(ubli) fil(io) Pap(iria) / Strenuo eq(uo) / p(ublico) sacerd(oti) arae / Aug(usti) auguri et / IIviral(i) col(oniae) / Sarm(izegetusae) augur(i) / col(oniae) Apul(ensis) dec(urioni) / col(oniae) Drob(etensis) pat/ron(o) collegior(um) / fabr(um) cento/nar(iorum) et naut/ar(um) conduc(tori) pas/cui salinar(um) / et commer/cior(um) Rufinus / eius*; Liu 2009, 159 and 229.

15 CIL III 1217 = IDR III/5. 599: *Verzoviae Sa/turninae [e]q(uitis) R(omani) f(iliae) / C(aius) Numm(ius) Certus / eq(ues) R(omanus) augur col(oniae) / Apul(ensis) patr(onus) coll(egiorum) / fab(rum) et dendr(ophororum) col(oniae) / s(upra) s(criptae) suadente ad/fectione ma/tri*; Ardevan 2018.

16 Verboven 2012, 20; see also Liu 2009, 51–54, who argues against this common assumption, stretching the importance of the local contexts and the cultic aspect of *dendrophori*, bound together with the worship of Magna Mater/Cybele (54): "in other words, the cultic aspects of the *dendrophori* seem to have been the determining factor in their formation and spread. It is precisely this feature that separates this type of organization from the *collegia fabrum* and the *collegia centonariorum*. Lumping all these *collegia* together only obscures their origins and peculiar places in Roman society".

17 Petolescu 2014, 262, assumes that *collegium nautarum* belonged to Drobeta and not to Apulum.

they appeared all together in the honorary inscription of P. Aelius Strenuus (see above). *Collegium fabrum* was the most populated guild in the *colonia Aurelia Apulensis*, being divided in at least eleven *decuriae*.[18] Another *collegium fabrum* is attested in the *municipium Septimium Apulense*, too.[19] There are no available sources on the inner structure of the *collegium centonariorum* of the *colonia Aurelia Apulensis*, but one can also think that it was divided in *decuriae*, of 22–25 persons each,[20] and they are led by a *praefectus*, according to this inscription. Many members of the local or provincial elite acted, from time to time, as *patroni*. An inscription mentioned a *mater* (see above), which implies that from time to time there was also a *pater* of that *collegium*. Their presence indirectly speaks about the cultic organisation of the guild, related with some unknown god or goddess or with more than one deity.

The title of *praefectus collegii centonariorum* is attested only seven times in the Latin epigraphy of the western provinces of the Roman Empire.[21] It is up to this moment still unclear it was an honorific title, like *patronus*, or the *praefecti* led the guilds.[22] Since our unknown person was in the same time *praefectus* and *patronus*,[23] one can argue that probably the first title was related with the hierarchy of the *collegium*, while the second was merely an honorary one. Therefore, as it has been already highlighted, using the title of *praefectus* for the person who led *collegium centonariorum* was a regional custom in areas as Pannonia, Dalmatia and the northern part of Italy (Aquileia).[24]

Together with the *fabri*, the *centonarii* have been regarded as fire brigades in the Western provinces of the Roman Empire, although there was no proof to back such assumption.[25] They were producers and textile dealers, an activity of higher importance for the Roman society, bound together into a corporation to look after their economic and social interests, first of all to preserve their monopoly on those activities.[26] Their presence at Apulum could be connected with the sheep-farming in the Dacian highlands, but as it has been already highlighted, the easy access to wool is not the only reason of developing of the textile industry and of the guild related to it: "[T]he production mode, urbanization, scale of demands and production, and other stimuli including governmental promotion through legal infrastructure combine to provide the answer."[27] The presence of

18 CIL III 1043 = IDR III/5. 147: *I(ovi) O(ptimo) M(aximo) / pro salute Im[p(eratoris)] / et coll(egii) fabr[um] / Tib(erius) Iul(ius) Bubal[us] / ex dec(uria) XI / d(onum) d(edit).*

19 CIL III 1051 = ILS 7144 = IDR III/5. 164 (AD 205).

20 Liu 2009, 131, provides this number in relation with the seventeen attested *decuriae* in Ravenna (CIL XI 125 = ILS 8242 = Liu 2009, 358, no. 107). Taking into account that at least eleven *decuriae* are attested for the *collegium fabrum*, thus approximatively 250–300 members, we can guess, that the *decuriae* of the *collegium centonariorum* are fewer.

21 For the religious activities of the *collegia centonariorum* see Liu 2009, 252–255.

22 Liu 2009, 155.

23 For the patronage related to various *collegia* in *colonia Aurelia Apulensis* see Liu 2009, 243–244, together with *Chart* 6.2.

24 Liu 2009, 156.

25 Liu 2009, 1–11 and 159–160, with the older bibliography.

26 Liu 2009, 63: "theoretically, *centonarius* may mean either a user or a maker/dealer of *cento*".

27 Liu 2009, 82.

the legion XIII Gemina also at Apulum could have gave an input to this activity,[28] many textile producers and dealers would have been active in the area long before granting the municipal and, then, the colonial rights to the civil settlement from Partoş. When the city was founded, they simply merged together to form a *collegium*, under the higher patronage of the *consularis III Daciarum*, as we can assume, based on the inscription mentioning the erection of the *schola* (see above).

Conclusions

The inscribed limestone slab was probably fixed on the walls of the meeting place of the *collegium centonariorum* of the *colonia Aurelia Apulensis* to honour a local benefactor, who acted both as *praefectus* and *patronus*. He was without any doubts a member of the local elite. As the text of the inscription implies, he made a donation to the members of the *collegium* and we can assume that he had probably built something in the area of the meeting place or simply decorated it. Unfortunately, both the name and the exact donation remained obscure to us, being mentioned in the missing part of the inscription. If we are right in assuming that his donation was related with the *schola* of the *collegium*, than the inscription could date from the period immediately after the erection of that *schola* in AD 202/203–205, during the last years of Septimius Severus' reign or during the reign of Caracalla.

Abbreviations

AE.	*L'Année Épigraphique*, Paris 1888–
CIL.	*Corpus Inscriptionum Latinarum*, Berlin, 1863–
IDR III/5.	I. Piso, *Inscriptiones Daciae Romanae. III/5. Inscriptions d'Apulum*, Paris, 2001.
ILS.	H. Dessau, *Inscriptiones Latinae Selectae*, I–III, Berlin, 1892–1916.

28 Liu 2009, 125 and 158: "[T]he *collegium centonariorum* of Apulum may have been possibly created on the initiative of the government. The need for this *collegium* perhaps arose from the increased necessity to secure supplies of clothing to the legion (*XIII Gemina*) stationed there as well as the other Danubian legions".

Bibliography

Anghel, D. G. 2023. Olăritul la Apulum – ateliere, inventar tehnologic și produsele ceramice specifice. Apulum, 60/1, 235–297.

Ardevan, R. 1998. Viața municipală în Dacia romană, Timișoara.

Ardevan, R. 2018. La famille de Verzovia Saturnina, in M. Popescu, I. Achim, F. Matei-Popescu (eds.), La Dacie et l'Empire Romain. Mélanges d'épigraphie et d'archéologie offerts à Constantin C. Petolescu, Bucharest, 127–133.

Bogdan-Cătăniciu, I. 2000. Territoire civil et militaire à Apulum, in H. Ciugudean, V. Moga (eds.), Army and Urban Development in the Danubian Provinces of the Roman Empire, Bibliotheca Musei Apulensis, XV, Alba Iulia, 109–139.

Ciambelli, S. 2022. La mia schola è più bella della tua. Rivalità tra i fabri e i centonarii della colonia Aurelia Apulensis (inizio III sec. d. C.), MEFRA 134.2, 501–509.

Cserni, A. 1912. Jelentés a Colonia Apulensis területéten végzett Asatáskról, Múzeumi és Könyvtári Értesitö, 6, 106–114, 257–283.

Diaconescu, A. 2019. Sanctuarul lui Liber Pater de la Apulum/Sanctuary of Liber Pater from Apulum, in A. Timofan, A. Diaconescu (eds.), Pantheon 3D, IV, Dionysos – Bacchus – Liber Pater, Cluj-Napoca, 49–51.

Diaconescu, A., Piso, I. 1993. Apulum, in D. Alicu, H. Boegli (eds.), La politique édilitaire dans les provinces de l'Empire romain (Actes du 1er Colloque roumano-suisse, Deva 1991), Cluj-Napoca, 67–81.

Goffaux, B. 2011. *Schola*: vocabulaire et architecture collégiale sous le Haut-Empire en Occident, REA, 113.1, 47–67.

Goffaux, B. 2012. À la recherche des édifices collégiaux hispaniques, in M. Dondin-Payre, N. Tran (eds.), *Collegia*. Le phénomène associatif dans l'Occident romain, Bordeaux, 199–219.

Kienast, D., Eck, W., Heil, M. 2017. Römische Kaisertabelle. Grundzüge einer römischen Kaiserchronologie: 6. überarbeitete Auflage, Darmstadt.

Liu, J. 2009. *Collegia Centonariorum*: The Guilds of Textile Dealers in the Roman West, Leiden–Boston.

Matei-Popescu, F., Țentea, O. 2017. I primi insediamenti romani nella Dacia: il contributo dell'esercito, in Traiano. Costruire l'Impero, creare l'Europa, Rome, 163–168.

Moga, V., Ciobanu, R., Drîmbărean, M. 2000. Recherchés archéologiques à Partoș (*municipium Aurelium Apulense* et *colonia Aurelia Apulensis*), in H. Ciugudean, V. Moga (eds.), Army and Urban Development in the Danubian Provinces of the Roman Empire, Bibliotheca Musei Apulensis, XV, Alba Iulia, 141–202.

Petolescu, C. C. 2000. Dacia și Imperiul Roman. De la Burebista până la sfârșitul Antichității, Bucharest.

Petolescu, C. C. 2014. Dacia. Un mileniu de istorie, Bucharest.

Piso, I. 1993. Fasti provinciae Daciae I. Die senatorischen Amtsträger, Bonn.

Verboven, K. 2012. Les collèges et la romanisation dans les provinces occidentales, in M. Dondin-Payre, N. Tran (eds.), *Collegia*. Le phénomène associatif dans l'Occident romain, Bordeaux, 13–46.

The Meaning of "*conductor commerciorum*" in Dacia during the Third Century AD. A Hypothesis

Coriolan Horaţiu Opreanu

A famous 19th century found inscription from Apulum[1] is enumerating the positions and honors held by the Roman knight P. Aelius Strenuus along his political career in Dacia. The most interesting and little researched of his public offices is that of "*conductor pascui, salinar(um) et commercior(um)*". A conductor was in Roman Imperial period a lessee who perceived tax (*vectigal*) in the name of the imperial tax administration from the free peasants[2]. The *vectigal* perceived was sent to the imperial fisc, the owner which leased the income to the conductor. But obviously the lessee, after paying the debt, which was owed to the state, had to earn something for himself. It means that he was free to sell the produces from the land leased. Coming back to the text of the inscription the first land leased were the pastures. At first sight the main commodity which was possibly offered to the market was the hay necessary for cattle's food during the winter. But at the same time pastures were used to pasture herds or flocks of sheep in the warm season. We have little data concerning the usage of pastures in antiquity in Dacia. The only scholar who dealt with this topic was D. Benea[3]. She was suggesting the possibility of connection between pastures mentioned in the Latin inscriptions from Dacia and the transhumance well attested in Italy and in other provinces of the Roman Empire. In this respect she agreed with the hypothesis that the transhumance was practiced by the shepherds across the frontiers of the province, even barbarians' flocks entering possible temporarily inside the province's pastures. Tight linked with the pastures were the salt mines (*salinae)* leased to the same *conductores*[4]. In our opinion there is obviously a connection with the breeding as the same lessees were dealing with the pastures and salt. The inscriptions mentioning "*conductores pascui et salinarum*" were dated in the 2nd century[5]. The fourth inscription mentioning the same *conductor*, P. Aelius Marius, comes from Porolissum. The authors

1 CIL III 1209=ILS 7147=IDR III/5 443.
2 Piso 2004–2005, 181.
3 Benea 2010.
4 For Dacia's salt mines, see Wollmann 1996 and for the organization of salt extraction, see Benea 2007.
5 The best epigraphically recorded conductor is P. Aelius Marius whose activity was dated in the 2nd century, see Dana, Zăgreanu 2013, 31.

pointed out that the inscriptions recording such characters were found not only around the salt mines, but also in customs stations, where the trade with the barbarians existed[6].

The only *conductor* attested as "*conductor pascui salinarum et commerciorum*" was P. Aelius Strenuus. The question is why was added "*commercia*" to the leased categories and what was the meaning of "*commercia*"? The explanations that "*conductor commerciorum*" was incidental being only once recorded, or that it meant the right of the *conductor* to sell the products of pastures and salt mines[7] are weak. As we have shown, the position of the *conductores* as lessees offered them the right to sell the products and was not necessary to add the right of trading. Furthermore, for most of the *conductores* the inscriptions do not mention "*commercia*" beside pastures and salt mines. The only difference between P. Aelius Strenuus and the other *conductores* is the chronology; he lived in the 3rd century, probably in Severian period[8]. The epigraphical text contains, in our opinion, taking into consideration the above-mentioned observations, three distinct objects which were leased by P. Aelius Strenuus. We must admit that if there is a connection between pastures and salt mines, the third added, "*commercia*", must be also in relation with the other two. In this respect it is probable that by "*commercia*" we must understand a new category of resources leased by the Imperial fisc to the conductores only in the 3rd century. But "*commercia*" is also recorded in an inscription found in the temple[9] dedicated to the *Genius* of the *publicum portorium* from Illyricum at Porolissum[10]. The temple (or, maybe the *sacellum*[11]) was built at the end of the paved main Imperial Roman Road which crossed the province and in the very neighborhood of the customs milecastle[12] from Porolissum. Here is the text of the inscription:

PRO SALVTE
ET VICTORIA
IMP(eratoris) CAES(aris) [M(arci)
Aur(elii) antonini
Commodi p(ii) fel(icis)]
AVG(usti) N(ostri) RESTITV
TORI(s) COMMERC(iorum)
ET GENIO P(ublici) P(ortorii) ILLY
RICI CL(audius) XENOPHON
PROC(urator) AVG(usti) N(ostri) PER
MARCION(em) ET POL(ionem) VIL(icos)

6 Dana, Zăgreanu 2013, 31.
7 Petolescu 2010, 255, footnote 716.
8 IDR III/5 443.
9 Piso, Opreanu, Deac 2016.
10 Opreanu 2021, 234.
11 Opreanu 2021, 233.
12 Opreanu 2023.

The inscription was inaugurated in Commodus time, probably between AD 185–187[13]. After Commodus' death on 31 December 192 he suffered "*damnatio memoriae*" and his name was erased from inscriptions. This action happened at Porolissum either. Erasing only that part of the condemned emperor's name which represented his identity was a usual practice, so a statue base, or an altar can be reused and assigned to another emperor. In the case of Commodus' name, the commonest change in his inscriptions' text was the erasing of the name Commodus and of the epithet *Felix*, so the name let over being identical with that of Marcus Aurelius[14]. While this rule was followed in the case of an inscription found in the same room of the temple[15], in the inscription we are dealing with was erased also the name *M(arci) Aurel(ii) Antonini*, so the identification with Marcus Aurelius was not possible anymore. The effect for those who were reading the text in Antiquity was the update of the inscription with the new emperor, Septimius Severus, even not directly named:

PRO SALVTE
ET VICTORIA
IMP(eratoris) CAES(aris)
AVG(usti) N(ostri) RESTITV
TORI(s) COMMERC(iorum)
...

In our opinion the main reason for this unique situation was the Commodus' title "*restitutor commerciorum*". That means this title was not compatible with Marcus Aurelius, because he cut that reality named "*commercia*" and Commodus restituted it after the end of the wars. But the title also fitted with the new emperor Septimius Severus, probably because he continued Commodus' policy in this field, maybe even improved it. But what was the meaning of this title, only once attested in Latin epigraphy due to the inscription from Porolissum? By "*commercia*" it is possible to understand all the trading articles, or trade seen as juridical transaction of merchandise and maybe the exchanges over the frontier[16]. But another hypothesis was advanced. "*Commercium*" also had some more precise meanings in Roman law terms. It offered to foreigners the legal personal, or collective right to buy, or sell goods on Roman soil under the frame of the diplomatic agreements. As part of the Empire's relations with the barbarian tribes across the frontier, by a sliding of sense "*commercium*" became the place where this legal right was performed and where the legal exchanges have taken place[17]. The finding of the inscription at Porolissum in the temple of the customs station proves that "*restitutor commerciorum*" was closely related with the trade with Barbaricum. Ancient literary sources mention that Roman

13 For discussion of chronology see, Opreanu 2020, 80.
14 Højte 2005, 58–59.
15 Opreanu 2021, 228–230.
16 Piso 2013, 194.
17 Moatti 2011; Opreanu 2021, 80–81.

diplomacy used the trading right during the Marcomannic wars, forbidding, or allowing different barbarian tribes to attend Roman frontier's "commercia"[18]. "*Commercium*" was a marketplace on the Roman frontier, where barbarians from outside the Empire were periodically allowed to trade with the Romans. The best epigraphic confirmation for our interpretation comes from a 4th century AD inscription from Solva (Hungary), on Pannonia's frontier. The inscription dated AD 371 records the name and function of a *burgus* built on the left bank of the Danube in Barbaricum: "*burgum cui nomen commercium qua causa et factus est*"[19]. The role of the *burgus* was to shelter and supervising a market where barbarians were trading with the Romans[20]. A "*commercium*" across Solva was supposed to existed also in the 2nd- 3rd centuries[21]. Beside the epigraphic evidence above presented, at Porolissum a unique archaeological excavation succeeded in 2013 to identify such a marketplace[22]. It was an area in the vicinity of the customs station and of the frontier watch towers. The only archaeological structures recorded were a few pits, several post-holes, and stick-holes without a definite arrangement in the plan. But the 129 Roman coins and 43 brooches, mostly of barbarian type, as well as more than 300 iron hobnails were in contrast with the poor constructive structures. At the same time the density of the artefacts indicates an area intensively used by people. No contour of any dwelling was recorded. The archaeological contexts identified represent traces of some temporary, light wooden structures, like stalls, or pits for temporary short time shelters for goods. All these taken together determined us to conclude it is about a periodical marketplace on the Roman frontier of Dacia, one of the "*commercia*" mentioned in the written sources.

In the case of a "*conductor commerciorum*", as P. Aelius Strenuus was named in the inscription from Apulum, who leased from the Roman state some incomes are more reasonable to consider that the term "*commercia*" was referring to these periodical marketplaces from Dacia's frontiers, a decision taken probably by Septimius Severus. The recording of the "*conductores pascui et salinarum*" from the 2nd century in the frontier's main military stations (including in Porolissum), most of them known as customs points suggests their activity was at least partially linked with the trade across the frontier with Barbaricum. In this frame it is a reasonable hypothesis to suppose that in the Severian period, a peace period, the increasing of the trade with the regions outside the Empire, made Roman authorities to lease to the *conductores* also the frontier marketplaces, the *commercia*. If our hypothesis is correct, it means that hay and salt was also sold in the *commercia* to the barbarians, both goods being vital for surviving of their herds and flocks during the winter. On the other side, barbarians living in the interaction zones over the Roman frontier and attended the frontier marketplaces were using Roman coins, being at least partially integrated in the Roman market type economy.

---

18 Cassius Dio 71, 11; 15.

19 RIU 771.

20 Poulter 2014, 40.

21 Stoklas 2019, 187, Fig. 1.

22 Opreanu, Lăzărescu 2015.

Bibliography

Benea, D. 2007. Cu privire la administrarea salinelor din Dacia romană, Analele Banatului, S.N. 15, 41–46.
Benea, D. 2010. Organizarea păşunilor în Dacia romană şi importanţa lor pentru economia provinciei, Bibliotheca Historica et Archaeologica Universitatis Timisiensis 12, 45–74.
Dana, D., Zăgreanu, R. 2013. Deux dédicaces latines inédites de Porolissum (Dacie romaine), Tyche 28, 27–35.
Højte, J., M. 2005. Roman Imperial Statue Bases from Augustus to Commodus, Aarhus-Oxford.
Moatti, C. 2011. La mobilité négociée dans l'Empire romain tardif: le cas de marchands etrangers, in Le relazioni internazionali nell alto medioevo. Settimane di studio della Fondazione Centro Italiano di studi sull'alto Medioevo, 58, Spoleto, 8–12 aprile 2010, Spoleto, 159–188.
Opreanu, C., H. 2020. Commodus restitutor commerciorum. The Role of Palmyrene Trading Community at Porolissum, Ephemeris Napocensis 30, 79–100.
Opreanu, C., H. 2021. Revisiting Three Inscription of Commodus at Porolissum, in L. Mihailescu-Bîrliba, I. Dumitrache (eds.), Persevera lucere. Studia in memoriam Octaviani Bounegru, Wiesbaden, 225–235.
Opreanu, C., H. 2023. Barbarians from Dacia's Northern Frontier: Enemies, or Trading Partners? Daily Life Sequences at Porolissum, in L. Mihăilescu-Bîrliba, I. Piso (eds.), Romans and Natives in the Danubian Provinces (1st–6th C. AD), Wiesbaden, 307–322.
Opreanu, C., H., Lăzărescu, V., A., 2015. A Roman Frontier Marketplace at Porolissum in the Light of Numismatic Evidence. Contribution to the Roman Limes Economy, Cluj-Napoca/Zalău.
Petolescu, C., C. 2010. Dacia. Un mileniu de istorie, Bucureşti.
Piso, I. 2004–2005. Un nouveau conductor salinarum en Dacie, Acta Musei Napocensis 41–42/1, 179–182
Piso, I. 2013. Fasti Provinciae Daciae II. Die ritterlichen Amtsträger, Bonn.
Piso, I., Opreanu, C.H., Deac, D. 2016. Das Heiligtum der Zollstation von Porolissum, Zeitschrift für Papyrology und Epigraphik 200, 544–549.
Poulter, A. 2014. Illyricum and Thrace from Valentinian I to Theodosius II. The Radical Transformation of the Danubian Provinces, in I. Jacobs (Ed.), Production and Prosperity in the Theodosian Period, Leuven-Walpole, 27–68.
Stoklas, B. 2019. Der Einfluss der Markomannenkriege auf die Zirkulation der römischen Münzen in Mitteldonaugebiet in der 2. Hälfte des 2. Jahrhunderts-aktuelle Forschungen, in M. Karkowski, B. Komoróczy P. Trebsche (Hrsg.), Auf der Spuren der Barbaren-archäologisch, historisch, numismatisch, Brno, 185–194.
Wollman, V. 1996. Mineritul metalifer, extragerea sării şi carierele de piatră în Dacia romană. Der Erzbergbau, die Salzgewinnung und die Steinbrüche im römischen Dakien, Cluj-Napoca.

Some Notes on a Roman Funerary Inscription From County Veszprém (TRH 70 = Tit. Aq. IV, 1854)

Péter Kovács

During the works of the supplement volume of the series *Die römischen Inschriften Ungarns* (RIU) in 2002, Sylvia Palágyi drew my attention to an unpublished Roman grave stela wihout provenance and inventory number in the collection of the Lapidarium at Baláca (County Veszprém). I published[1] and identified the funerary inscription hypothetically with the find from Ősi that was mentioned (but the inscription was not published) by Jenő Fitz in volume 6 of the RIU, mentioned as lost (RIU 1418). Later, Géza Alföldy attempted to correct my reading in one of his last publications.[2] We also prepared the Latin scheda of the inscription for the series *Tituli Aquincenses* based on his interpretation. *Pietatis causa*, I did not want to correct his text and this scheda was published in 2020 (Tit. Aq. IV, 1854). On the other hand, several colleagues followed Alföldy's version in the ZPE and visioned further unfounded theories, therefore I must deal with the grave stela again in this paper as the works of a new volume of the Roman inscriptions of County Somogy, Veszprém and Zala has begun. I do not intend to iterate every single detail of my publication in 2002, therefore I will deal with the provenance and the problems of the restoration of the funerary text.

The right part of the inscription field of a stela from limestone remained, below broken, above cut during the secondary use (Fig. 1). During this use, the frame of the epigraphic field was totally levelled, and the carefully carved letters are also damaged, worn, partly they can hardly be read. I described and drew the inscription in 2002 at Baláca. The photo published here was taken by Dénes Józsa.

Height.: 92, width.: 40, depth: 26 cm. Letter height: 5–5,5 cm. InvNr.: ?

Literature: Kovács 2002, 213–216 (AE 2002, 1210); TRH 70; Alföldy 2011, 271–278 (AE 2011, 1018); Tit. Aq. IV, 1854 (G. Alföldy – P. Kovács). – Cf. Alföldy 2004, 25, 41 n. 11.

1 Kovács 2002, 213–216; TRH 70.

2 Alföldy 2011, 271–278.

Fig. 1: The Roman tombstone from County Veszprém (photo: Dénes Józsa)

The provenance

As I mentioned, I identified hypothetically the funerary stela with the inscription from Ősi that was not found by Fitz in the museum of Veszprém in 1990s. Somehow, my earlier idea has now become a certainty, but this is obviously erroneous. The find from Ősi received an inventory number and was mentioned in the *Archaeological Topography of Hungary* (66.163.1).[3] The problem is that I did not find any inventory number on the new find. Because of this fact, the identification must remain only a possibility, that is why I edited the stela in the *Tituli Aquinceses* with unknown provenance from County Veszprém.

Fig. 2: The inscription (drawing by Péter Kovács)

The interpretation of the inscription

I published the inscription earlier with the following reading and interpreted the gravestone as erected by the mother of the family to her two sons (one of them was the magistrate of a Roman colony, most probably Aquincum) (Fig. 2):

- - - - -
[e]t Q(uinto) Vi[- - -]
niano [- - -]
col(oniae) Sep(timiae) [Aq(uincensium) - - -]
col(legii) T(ito) Vi[- - -]
Victori[no - - - fil]-
is eius E[- - -]
[mat]er or *[Val]er(ia) Merc* or *-o[- - -]*
[---]+S[- - -].

Later, Alföldy attempted to correct my restoration and gave the following plausible interpretation that the stela was erected by the father to his wife and his two sons (Fig 3):

3 Éri, Kelemen, Németh, Torma 1969, 158 Nr. 36.

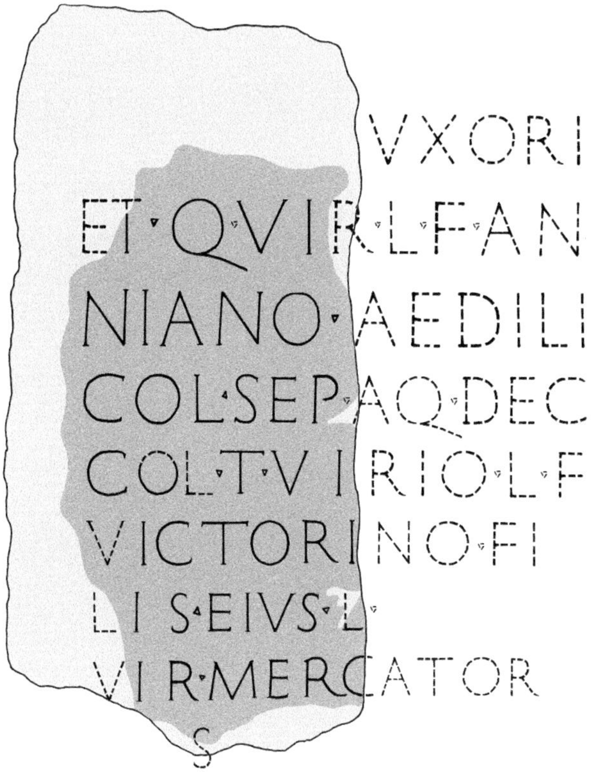

Fig. 3: The restoration of Géza Alföldy

- - - - - -
[- - - uxori]
[e]t Q(uinto) Vi[rio L(uci) f(ilio) An?]-
niano [aedili]
col(oniae) Sep(timiae) [Aq(uincensium) dec(urioni)]
col(oniae), T(ito) Vi[rio L(uci) f(ilio)]
Victori[no fi]-
[l]is eius L(ucius) [- - -]
[V]ir(ius) Merc[ator]
[- - -]S[- - -]
- - - - - -?

Furthermore, Alföldy saw in line 6 a letter I instead of E, so he restored the gentile name of the family as Virius and identified the father with L. Virius L. fil. Mercator who as the *sacerdos* of the deities erected the altar from Tác to the Dii Magni (*pro salute templensium*) (Tit. Aq. 1928).

However, there are serious problems with the latter interpretation:

1. The first and most serious problem is that Alföldy read I instead of E based only on the photo sent by me (and he could not personally study the stela because of his unexpected death in November 2011). Following an iterated epigraphic autopsy, I must repeat that the first letter in line 6 was clearly an E (Fig. 4), so the gentile name of Mer+[---] could not be Virius! One could assume a typo i>e that occurs several times in the Pannonian inscriptions, but in the inscription no vulgar Latin phenomenon can be observed and the gentilicium of the two sons was clearly VI[---]. Based on this fact it cannot be ruled out that the members of the family were Virii, but other *gentilicia* with beginning VI- must be considered as well: e.g. Vibii, Victorii (in the repertorium of Solin and Salomies the gentile names beginning with VI- are enumerated in six pages, some of them are frequent in Pannonia too[4]). Similarly, there are several cognomina beginning with MERC or MERO, Mercator is only one of the many possibilities (e.g. Mercator and his derivatives, Mercurius, Meroe).[5]

Fig. 4: The beginning of line 6

Alföldy attempted to solve the problem of the distance between the praenomen L and the gentile name and he argued that Virius Mercator would have had another gentilicium. The problem is that this second gentile name is not attested in the inscription from Tác either where Mercator used his full name with the *filiatio*. The problem could have been solved if one would restore the letters ER in line 6 as the *tribus Ser(gia)* as colonia Septimia Aquincum (Carnuntum cannot be excluded either) belonged to this tribe as a Hadrianic municipium.[6] This means that the father's name should be restored as L. Vir(ius) L. fil. Ser. Mercator. However, we must also rule out this possibility as at the end of line 5 cannot be read as an L, because the horizontal upper stroke of an E or rather a ligature ET can clearly be seen (Fig. 5).

2. It is also clear that my earlier interpretation did not clarify sufficiently the relationship of the family members mentioned in the epitaph, but based on these observations, Alföldy's restoration was not the correct one either. The first two members mentioned in the stela were obviously the sons of the family (the former one was Quintus Vi[---][7],

4 Solin, Salomies 1994, 206–212.
5 Solin, Salomies 1994, 362.
6 Forni 1956, 14–15.
7 The gentile name Vibius is the most frequent among the names beginning with VI- in Pannonia inferior: OPEL IV, 165–166.

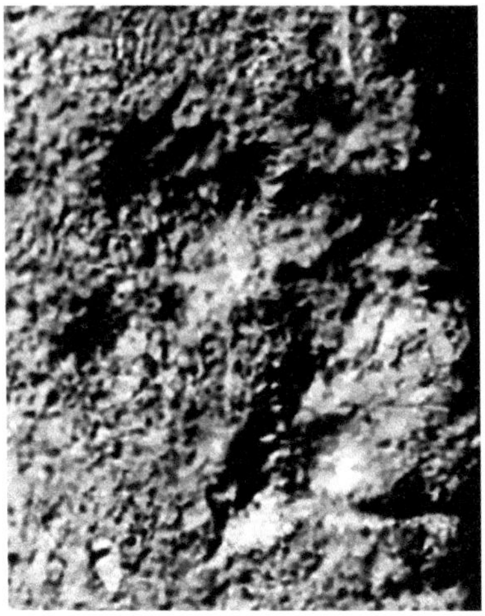

Fig. 5: The end of line 5

but his cognomen can only hypothetically be restored as Annianus). Because of the hyphen *et*, one or more deceased persons are surely missing at the beginning of the epitaph. One of the brothers was a magistrate of Aquincum; his offices could have been enumerated in chronological order as suggested, but he also could have several magistrates at the same time as I suggested, that means he could have been a decurion (or higher ranking magistrate) of Aquincum, but he could have been a magistrate in of the municipal *collegia* as well. It depends on how one expands the abbreviation COL. The question can hardly be solved because of the lack of other evidence. Based on another *et* in line 5, the enumeration of the dead family members must have been continued. Based on the different gentile name in line 6, she must have been identified with the mother of the sons. As Alföldy's restoration is incorrect (he calculated with approx. five missing letters) it must remain unclear how many letters are missing at the end of the lines. If it is fewer than five, my earlier restoration becomes the most plausible one and she was probably a *Valer(ia)*, but there are several other possibilities.[8] In this case, the cognomen of the second son cannot be restored as Victorinus, but he was a Victor (this cognomen is several times attested in Pannonia inferior too). The mother can probably be called Mercatilla (attested in Brigetio: RIU 506). As the age was not mentioned in the remained part of the epitaph, it can be supposed that at least the children were still alive when the grave stela war erected to them. In the last line, the father's name must have been mentioned, but it cannot be excluded that his name was mentioned first in the missing beginning of the inscription (obviously with adjective *vivus*). This phenomenon occurs several times in Pannonia inferior as well (in the *ager Aquincensis*: Tit. Aq. 1593, 1601, 1618, 1632, 1682, 1687, 1702, 1926, 1949). In this case, line 7 may have ended as follows: *coniugi (eius) et sibi vivus posuit* (*fecit*) or with a similar formula. The remained letters S+ in line 7 cannot surely be restored (perhaps *si[bi]*). It can be supposed it is more plausible that grave stela was erected when one of family members died (e.g. the eldest son or daughter who was mentioned in the missing part of the epitaph). Naturally, in this case the father's name was mentioned at the end of the epitaph in line 7 (and one or two lines are missing). This question must remain unsolved.

Based on these arguments, the funerary text did not mention L. Virius Mercator and the text can be restored in two ways as follows:

8 Solin, Salomies 1994, 262–263.

- - - - - -
[e]t Q(uinto) Vi[- - -]
niano [- - -]
col(oniae) Sep(timiae) [Aq(uincensium) - - -]
col(oniae) or *col(legii) T(ito) Vi[- - -]*
Victori[no? fil]-
is eius et [- - -]
[- - -]er Merc[- - -]
[- - -]+S[- - -].
- - - - - -

or

Victori [fil]-
is eius et [Va-]
[l]er(iae) Merc[- - -] or *-o[- - -]*
[- - -]+S+[- - -]
- - - - - -

Bibliography

Alföldy, G. 2004, Epigraphica Pannonica III. Inschriften aus dem Gebiet der Eravisker und vom Territorium von Aquincum, SpecNova 18, 1–48.

Alföldy, G. 2011. Eine führende Familie der Kolonie von Aquincum, ZPE 179, 271–278.

Éri, I., Kelemen, M., Németh, P., Torma, I. 1969. Magyarország Régészeti Topográfiája 2. A veszprémi járás. Budapest.

Forni, G. 1956. Die römischen Tribus in Pannonien, CJ, 13–22.

Kovács, P. 2002. Újabb római feliratos emlék Veszprém megyéből – Neuere römerzeitliche Inschrift im Komitat Veszprém, Balácai Közlemények 7, 213–216.

Kovács, P. 2005. Tituli Romani in Hungaria reperti, Budapest – Bonn.

Solin, H., Salomies, O. 1994. Repertorium nominum gentilium et cognominum Latinorum. Hildesheim – Zürich – New York, editio nova.

Die norischen Meilensteine des Maximinius Thrax: Zum Stellenwert fehlerhafter Inschriftenformulare

Manfred Hainzmann

Die epigraphische Hinterlassenschaft aus der nur dreijährigen Herrschaftsperiode des Maximinus Thrax ist unverhältnismäßig hoch. Dies vor allem aufgrund des überragenden Anteiles an Meilensteinen.[1] In Norikum kamen bisher sechs Stück ans Licht (Tabelle 1). Drei hatten ihren Standort im (nachmaligen) Ufernorikum (M2, 5, 6) und ebenso viele in Binnennorikum (M1, 3, 4).

Tabelle 1

Nr.	Fundort / municipium	EDCS	HD	lupa.at	CIL
M 1	Brestanica / **Celeia**	27900359	039629 (2014-11-13, Gräf)	vacat	III 11316; XVII/4, 135; XVII/4, p. 126
M 2	Salzburg / **Iuvavum**	14400453	039520 (2014-07-01, Feraudi)	12983 (F)	XVII/4, 91; XVII/4, p. 125
M 3	Stranice / **Celeia**	14501020	039596 (2014-07-01, Feraudi)	vacat	III 5741; XVII/4, 129
M 4	Stranice / **Celeia**	14501021	0395965 (2014-07-01, Feraudi)	6720 (F)	III 5742; XVII/4, 128
M 5	Tulln / **Cetium**	14400351	011264 (2014-06-06, Gräf)	11404 (F)	XVII/4, 76; XVII/4, p. 125
M 6	Wels / **Ovilava**	27900328	035502 (2013-04-10, Gräf)	3191 (F)	III 14110; XVII/4, 82; XVII/4, p. 125

1 Nach dem letzten Suchergebnis bei *EDCS* (vom 29. September 2023) waren es genau 200.

1 Zur konkreten Fragestellung

Angesichts der längst erfolgten Edition dieser Steindenkmäler mag es zunächst befremdlich anmuten, ihnen erneut Aufmerksamkeit zu widmen. Verständlich wird das erst, wenn man den Fokus auf die Siegestitulatur des „ersten Soldatenkaisers" richtet, die in der Forschung zu unterschiedlichen Zeitansätzen geführt hat. Im Mittelpunkt stand dabei die Frage, ob der *Germanicus*-Titel bereits im Jahre 235 oder doch erst 236 angenommen wurde und mit welcher imperatorischen Akklamation er zu verknüpfen sei.[2] Welchen Stellenwert diese Problematik besitzt, zeigen die beiden erst kürzlich erschienenen Aufsätze von Rainer Wiegels und Reinhard Wolters.[3] Letzterer hat nun dafür alle Münzemissionen ausgewertet[4] und sie den übrigen Quellengattungen – darunter die Meilensteine – gegenüber gestellt. Das Resultat seiner erschöpfenden Vergleichsanalysen enthält zwei Thesen:[5]

1. Maximinus' Sieg über die Germanen wurde erst im Sommer 236 erfochten und der Titel *Germanicus* ab Herbst (nach Bestätigung durch den Senat natürlich) in die offizielle Kaisertitulatur übernommen.
2. Selbiger *Germanicus*-Siegesbeiname sei „mit einer gewissen Wahrscheinlichkeit mit der dritten imperatorischen Akklamation zu verbinden".

Beide Urteile sind allerdings nicht von gleicher Tragfähigkeit. Während die *Constitutio Maximiniana I* (*a. d. VII Id. Ian.* 236)[6] wie auch die Münzlegenden (inklusive Münzbilder) des Jahres 236 Wolters Datierungsansatz zu bestätigen scheinen, bleibt das Junktim des Siegesbeinamens mit *IMP III* fragwürdig. Und es sind ausgerechnet zwei Meilensteine[7] (darunter der aus dem norischen Brestanica stammende M-1), die in diesem Zusammenhang (nebst anderen Inschriften) nochmals auf den Prüfstand gestellt werden sollen. Dabei gilt es, einen besonderen Umstand nicht aus den Augen zu verlieren: Die Meilensteinformulare generell folgen keiner strikten Norm, sind oft fehlerhaft und daher – im Gegensatz etwa zu den Titulaturen der Militärdiplome und Münzumschriften – vielfach unzuverlässige Quellenzeugnisse.[8]

1.1 *Constitutio Maximiniana I–IV*

Wie aus den Angaben in Tabelle 2 ersichtlich, enthalten zwar auch die Meilensteininschriften jene Komponenten, die (oft aber nicht immer) für die Feinchronologie als aussagekräftig erscheinen. Deshalb seien hier den einzelnen Datierungsparametern jene vier

2 Für eine Frühdatierung sprachen sich u.a. Stylow 1974, 520f., Lehmann 2018, 182 Anm. 262, Haegemans 2010, 62–65, Pearson 2016, 92f. und Moosbauer 2018, 105 aus.
3 Wiegels 2023 und Wolters 2023.
4 Wolters 2023, 242.
5 Wolters 2023, 242–243 mit einer abschließenden chronologischen Übersicht.
6 Siehe Anm. 11.
7 Genau darauf berufen sich auch die in Anm. 2 genannten Autoren.
8 Darauf hat natürlich auch Wolters in Kapitel 3 mehrfach hingewiesen.

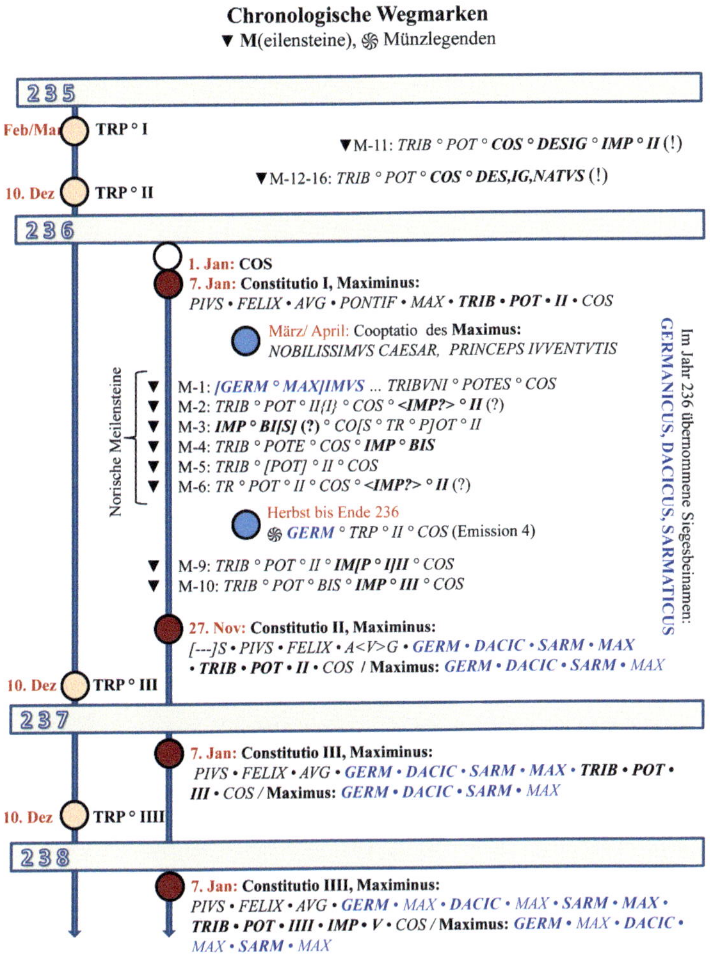

Grafik 1: Feinchronologie

Diplomformulare[9] vorangestellt, die sich in der kontextuellen Gegenüberstellung mit den übrigen dokumentarischen Quellen als sichere Anhaltspunkte, ja sogar als Richtschnur für unsere Problemstellung eignen:[10]

9 Genauer gesagt, der Wortlaut des ersten Paragraphen, der den Kaiser als Privilegienstifter mit all seinen offiziellen Titeln ausweist. Dazu ausführlich in meinem Tagungsbeitrag zum Göttinger Kolloquium „Maximinus Thrax in seiner Zeit" – veranstaltet von der Forschungskommission „Imperium und Barbaricum" an der Akademie der Wissenschaften zu Göttingen (28.-30. Juni 2023). Das Erscheinen der Tagungsakten ist für 2024 zu erwarten.

10 Siehe auch die in Tabelle 2 verzeichneten Parameter.

Constitutio I (7. Jänner 236)[11]
IMP • CAES • C • IVLIVS • VERVS • ***MAXIMINVS*** *• PIVS • FELIX • AVG • PONTIF • MAX •* ***TRIB • POT • II • COS*** *• P • P • PROC*

Constitutio II (27. November 236, RMD V, 471b)
IMP • CAES • C • IVLIVS • VERVS • ***MAX[•]S*** *• PIVS • FELIX •* ***A<V>G • GERM • DACIC • SARM • MAX [•]AX*** *• TRIB {B}• POT • II • COS • P • P • PROC • ET • C • IVLIV[•] •* ***MAXIM{IN}VS • GERM • DACIC • SARM • MAX • N[•]ES***

Constitutio III (7. Jänner 237)[12]
IMP • CAES • C • IVLIVS • VERVS • ***MAXIMINVS*** *• PIVS • FELIX • AVG •* ***GERM • DACIC • SARM • MAX*** *• PONTIF • MAX •* ***TRIB • POT • III • COS*** *• P • P • PROC • ET • C • IVLIVS • VERVS •* ***MAXIMVS • GERM • DACIC • SARM • MAX • NOBILISSIMVS • CAESAR***

Constitutio IV (7. Jänner 238)[13]
IMP • CAES • C • IVLIVS • VERVS • ***MAXIMINVS*** *• PIVS • FEL• AVG •* ***GERM • MAX • DACIC • MAX • SARM • MAX*** *• PONT • MAX •* ***TR • POT • IIII • IMP • V • COS*** *• P • P • PROC • ET • C • IVLIVS • VERVS •* ***MAXIMVS • GERM • MAX • DACIC • MAX • SARM • MAX • NOBILISSIMVS • CAES***

1.2 *Die Datierungsparameter*[14] (Tabelle 2, im Anhang)

Um aus den Kaisertitulaturen eine einigermaßen sichere chronologischen Abfolge ihres Erscheinens zu rekonstruieren, bedarf es einer Aufschlüsselung der darin enthaltenen Komponenten. In einer solchen Übersicht inkludiert sein muss auch die Nennung der beiden (kaiserlichen) Bezugspersonen samt ihren Epitheta. Laut unserem Verzeichnis ergibt das insgesamt 16 Parameter:

(P1) *Maximinus et Maximus*: Was die gemeinsame Nennung von Kaiser und Sohn angeht, so gibt das erste Konstitutionsformular den 7. Jänner 236 als Terminus-postquem vor. Relativchronologisch lässt sich dies dank der Zusatztitel des Maximus (P6+7) auf den Zeitraum ab März/April 236 begrenzen. Den frühesten dokumentarischen Nachweis für das gemeinsame Auftreten attestiert ein Papyrus vom 16. Mai 236.[15]

---

11 *RMD*-I, Nr. 77.

12 *RMD*-III, Nr. 198; zum Formular der übrigen Zeugnisse siehe meinen Tagungsbeitrag.

13 Eck 2022, 227–230.

14 Dass diese von Fall zu Fall einen unterschiedlichen Wortlaut haben, spielt für die Datierungsproblematik an sich keine Rolle.

15 P.Rein II 91 <http://papyri.info/ddbdp/p. rein;2;91>. – Wolters, 2023, Anm. 62.

(P2) *Pius Felix*: Diese beiden Epitheta gehören zum Standardrepertoire; die Münzlegenden kennen allerdings nur das erste.

(P3) *pater patriae*: Dieser Ehrentitel ist bis auf die Münzprägung durchgehend belegt.

(P4) *invictus*: Das die Sieghaftigkeit des Kaisers zum Ausdruck bringende Epitheton bleibt in den Diplomformularen sowie in den Münzlegenden unberücksichtigt und findet sich auch nicht in allen Meilensteinformularen.

(P5) *pontifex maximus*: Diese Angabe fehlt im norischen M-6 wie auch auf dem unterpannonischen Meilenstein M-14 sowie in der stadtrömischen Ehreninschrift M-16.

(P6) *nobilissimus Caesar* und **(P7)** *princeps iuventutis*: erscheinen auf den Münzen (ersteres ohne Attribut *nobilissimus*) ab Herbst 236,[16] sind in den stadtrömischen *fasti sodalium* jedoch bereits für das Frühjahr nachweisbar. Demnach wurde Maximus vermutlich im März (vielleicht am *dies imperii* seines Vaters) zum *princeps iuventutis* und zum *Caesar* ernannt.[17]

(P8) *Germanici maximi* – vergleichbar dem *Augusti Germanici* im Medaillon vom Jahresanfang 238[18] begegnet dieser plurale Titel nur auf M-1 und in Verbindung mit

(P9) *domini indulgentissimi*. Auch diese Bezeichnung für Kaiser und Sohn bleibt auf die norischen Zeugnisse beschränkt.

(P10) *Germanicus* (mit/ ohne *maximus*). Der unbestritten erste der drei Siegesbeinamen findet sich ab dem zweiten Konstitutionsformular, das uns folglich mit dem 27. November 236 den Terminus-ante-quem für die Annahme dieses Titels liefert. In den Münzlegenden (Emission 4)[19] erscheint der *Germanicus*-Beiname erst im Herbst des Jahres 236 und sollte daher auch nicht viel früher in die dokumentarischen Quellen übernommen worden sein:

MAXIMINVS • PIVS • AVG • ***GERM*** *• PM • TRP • II • COS • PP*
MAXIMVS • CAES • ***GERM*** *• PRINC • IVVENTVTIS*

Als Datierungskriterium für die unterschiedlichen Meilensteinformulare bildet die hier anzutreffende Kombination von *GERM* + *TRP II* + *COS* eine sichere Orientierung. Während die beiden später erworbenen Beinamen

(P11) *Dacicus* und **(P12)** *Sarmaticus* in den Münzlegenden und auch in den sechs norischen Meilensteinformularen nicht dokumentiert sind, attestiert M-1 immerhin den *[Germ(anicus) max]imus*. Dass dieser Tatbestand trotz der auch bei zahlreichen anderen Meilensteinen (in Tab. 2, M-7+8) vorhandenen Evidenz der Siegerbeinamen zu kontroversen Interpretationen Anlass gegeben hat, liegt nur an den mit ihm

16 Beide Titel erscheinen erstmals ab der 3. Emission/1 (Allram 1989, 70–71) und auf einem AE-Medaillon (Wolters 2023,229, mit Anm. 40).

17 *CIL* VI 2001 = *EDCS*-18200407 = *EDR121925* und *CIL* VI 2009 = *EDCS*-18100824. Dazu ausführlich in meinem Tagungsbeitrag. – Zu Datierungsansatz Wolters, 2023, 235 mit weiterer Literatur in Anm. 63.

18 Wolters 2023, 230.

19 Wolters 2023, 229.

vergesellschafteten drei weiteren Komponenten (P13–14+16)[20] und ihren zum Teil fehlerhaften Einträgen:

(P13) *tribunicia potestate* (mit und ohne Iteration) ist dabei ebenso fixer Bestandteil der Formulare wie

(P14) *consul*, nur dass bei Letzterem auch in den norischen Miliaria (M-2+6) zweimal die irrige Iterationszahl *II* hinzu kommt. Maximinus hat bekanntlich nur einmal (im Jahr 236) den Konsulat bekleidet.

(P15) *proconsul*: Fehlt überraschender Weise nur auf dem unterpannonischen Formular von M-14, und das wohl irrtümlich.

(P16) Das *IMP* (*I–VII*) erweist sich, da bei den Münzlegenden generell ohne Evidenz, in der Gegenüberstellung mit den Konstitutionsformularen als der Schlüsselbegriff für unseren – nur durch die Meilensteinbefunde evozierten[21] (!) – Diskussionsgegenstand.

2 Germanicus maximus: *IMP II* (235?) vs. *IMP III* (236?).

2.1 *Die Militärdiplome*

Was die Verknüpfung des ersten Siegesbeinamens mit den (bisher) dafür in Verbindung gesetzten imperatorischen Akklamationen (II vs. III) betrifft, so bilden die vier oben zitierten Konstitutionsformulare den Grundstein für unsere Revision, wobei der vierten Konstitution vom 7. Jänner 238 mit dem dort verankerten *IMP V* (!) als Terminus-ante-quem eine besondere Aussagekraft beizumessen ist. Wenn nämlich die stadtrömische Kanzlei hierin die fünfte siegreiche Beendigung eines Feldzuges verkündet und diese Zählung den Tatsachen entspricht,[22] so folgt daraus schlüssig, dass *IMP II-IV* mit jenen Akklamationen im Einklang stehen, die zur Verleihung der drei Siegestitel an Maximinus Thrax (und seines Sohnes) Anlass gegeben haben.[23] Schon aus der zweiten Konstitution ist abzuleiten, dass alle drei Siegesbeinamen vor dem 27. November 236 angenommen wurden, und zwar in der dort ausgewiesenen Reihenfolge: *Germanicus*, *Dacicus* und *Sarmaticus*.[24] Das passt weitestgehend zum chronologischen Verlauf der militärischen Geschehnisse, die das kaiserliche Heer vorerst in Germanien und danach an der unteren Donau zum Einsatz brachten.[25] Dass dem Führen eines Siegesbeinamens jeweils eine gezählte imperatorische Akklamation zugrunde lag,[26] wird an vielen Formularen augenscheinlich.

20 Wolters 2023, 232–235.

21 Deshalb bei Wolters im Titel seines Aufsatzes die Formulierung:„Numismatik vs. Epigraphik".

22 Soweit mir bekannt, wurde sie von niemandem in Frage gestellt.

23 Wie schon Wolters hervorhebt, sind demnach jene Zeugnisse, die bereits für die zweite und dritte Akklamation alle drei Siegestitel führen, fehlerhaft – Wolters 2023, 233 mit Anm. 53.

24 So auch Wolters 2023, 243.

25 Wolters 2023, Kapitel 1 und 6.

26 Wolters 2023, 233 als Arbeitshypothese, und mit dem Zugeständnis, dass unter dieser Prämisse „GERMANICVS ab IMP II möglich" wäre.

2.2 *Die Meilensteine* (vgl. Tabelle 2+3, im Anhang)

2.2.1 Belege außerhalb Noricums

Die chronologische Abfolge von *IMP II* → *GERM*, *IMP III* → *DACIC* und *IMP IIII* → *SARM* (bis Herbst 236) erfährt außerdem durch jene Inschriften eine Bestätigung, deren Formulare nebst den drei Beinamen auch ein *IMP IIII* enthalten. Das sind die beiden Meilensteine M-7 aus der Baetica[27] und M-8 aus Unterpannonien[28]:

> **(M-7)** *[Imp(erator) Caesar] | [C(aius)] Verus [Maximinus] Pius | [F]el(ix) [Au] g(ustus) pontifex ma|ximus [Germanicus maximus D]aci[c]us ma|ximus Sarmatic|us [maximus tri]b(unicia)* ***potest(ate) III imp(erator) | IIII*** *co(n)s(ul) p(ater) p(atriae) pro|co(n)s(ul) [et] C(aius) I[u]l(ius) Verus Ma|ximus nobilissimus | Caes(ar) Germanicus | maximus [Sarmaticus maximus D]aci[c]us ma|ximus [fi]lius Imp(eratoris) Cae|s[a]ris Aug(usti) restitue|runt*

> **(M-8)** *Imp(erator) Caes(ar) | G(aius!) Iul(ius) Verus [[Maxi[minus]]] | P(ius) F(elix) Aug(ustus) pont(ifex) m(aximus)* ***trib(unicia)*** **p[ot(estate)]** | *[---* ***i]mp(erator) IIII*** *co(n)s(ul) proco(n)s(ul) p(ater) p(atriae) et | [G(aius!) Iul(ius)] Verus [[Maximus]] | nobil(issimus) Caes(ar) filio (!) Aug(usti) n(ostri) | Dacici Ger(manici) Sarmat[ici(?)] | maximis (!) [---] | ab Aq(uinco) m(ilia) p(assuum) XCVII*

Mit *IMP IIII* waren somit alle bekannten Sieges-Titel erreicht.[29] Wie das *TRIB POT II* im zweiten Konstitutionsformular zu erkennen gibt, müssen die Siegesbeinamen vor dem 27. November 236 angenommen worden sein. Dies steht auch im Einklang mit dem *TRIB POT II* und *TRIB POT BIS* zweier Meilensteinformulare aus Unterpannonien.[30]

Kommen wir nun zu jenem Testimonium, dessen Komponenten bis heute für die kontroversen Datierungen verantwortlich sind, zum sardinischen Meilenstein (M-11),[31] mit seiner bislang singulären Kombination von *TRIB POT* + *COS DESIG* + *IMP II*.

---

27 *CIL* II, 4693 = *EDCS*-21700397.

28 *CIL* III, 3732 = *EDCS*-28701261. Die inkorrekte Reihenfolge der Beinamen bleibt irrelelvant.

29 Nach Wolters 2023, 233 erst mit IMP V.

30 (M-9-Tab. 2) *AE* 1998, 1060 = *EDCS*-12000858: *Impp(eratores) C[aess(ares)] | G(aius!) Iul(ius) Ver[u]s Ma[xi]|minus P(ius) F(elix) Aug(ustus) p(ontifex) max(imus) |* ***trib(unicia) pot(estate) II*** *im[p(erator) I]II* (!) *co(n)s(ul) | proco(n)sul p(ater) p(atriae) et G(aius!) Iul(ius) | Verus Maximus | nobil(issimus) Caes(ar) fili<us=O> Aug(usti) | n(ostri) Dacici Germ(anici) Sar|matici maximi | ab Aq(uinco) | m(ilia) p(assuum) CVII.* (M-10-Tab. 2) CIL III, 3736 = EDCS-28701281: *Imp(erator) Caes(ar) | C(aius) Iul(ius) Verus Maxim|inus P(ius) <F=E>(elix) Aug(ustus) p(ontifex) m(aximus)* ***trib(unicia) pot(estate) | bis*** *imp(erator) III* (!) *co(n)s(ul) proco(n)s(ul) | p(ater) p(atriae) et C(aius) Iul(ius) Verus Maxi|mus nobilissimus | Caes(ar) fil(ius) Aug(usti) n(ostri) Daci|ci German(ici) Sar(matici) Imp(eratores) | maximi | ab Aq(uinco) m(ilia) p(assuum) | CLX.* Die imperatorische Akklamation III erweist sich angesichts des postulierten *IMP IIII* → *Dacicus* in beiden Formularen als fehlerhaft.

31 *EDCS*-09401432 = *AE* 1973, 276 = *AE* 1977, 346 und mit detaillierter Beschreibung (samt Umzeichnung) bei Stylow 1974, 515–517.

[M(ilia)] p(assuum) CXXII | [I]mp(eratori) Caes(ari) C(aio) Iulio | Vero Maximino | Pio Felici Aug(usto) pont(ifici) | max(imo) ***trib(unicia) pot(estate) co(n)s(uli) | desig(nato) imp(eratori) II*** *p(atri) p(atriae) pro|co(n)s(uli) bia(m)* (!) *qu(a)e duc(it) a Karalib(us) Olbiae | ve[t]ust(ate) corrumpta(m) | restituit curant(e) | C(aio) F(abio?) Fabiano | [pr]a[e]f(ecto) prov(inciae) Sard(iniae) | proc(uratore) suo v(iro) e(gregio)*

Die Kohärenz dieses Formulars ist nur dann aufrecht zu erhalten, wenn es als erwiesen gilt, dass die hier bezeugte zweite imperatorische Akklamation mit dem großen Germanensieg im Jahre 235 verbunden werden kann. Und davon geht zumindest Stylow aus. Für die *tribunicia potestas* möchte er eine „Zählung parallel zu den Kalenderjahren" nicht ausschließen. Da darüber keine Sicherheit besteht, verweise ich durch Klammerzusatz (scil. I / II) auf den traditionellen Wechsel am 10. Dezember. So dann auch bei den übrigen hier vorgestellten Meilensteinformularen (M-1+4 sowie M-11–18), bei denen die Iteration ebenfalls fehlt. Im Abgleich des *TRIB POT + COS DESIG + IMP II* mit den übrigen dokumentarischen Quellen offenbaren sich folgende Ungereimtheiten:

a) Die kaiserliche Münzstätte verkündet erst ein halbes wenn nicht sogar ein ganzes Jahr später (vom Sommer 235 bis zum Sommer 236) die *VICTORIA GERMANICA* (Emission 3/II) und setzt (knapp) danach (Emission 4) den *Germanicus*-Beinamen in Umlauf.

b) Weitere vier Meilensteine (M-12–15, Alpes maritimae 2, Pannonia inferior 2) des sowie eine stadtrömische Ehreninschrift (M-16) für Maximinus aus dem Jahre 235 kennen ebenfalls keinen Hinweis auf *IMP II*:

(M-12) *CIL* XVI/2, 2: IMP CAES C IVLIVS VERVS MAXIMINVS PIVS FELIX INVICTVS AVG
P M ***TRIB [pot]*** *P P PROC* ***COS [design]ATVS***

(M-13) *CIL* XVI/2, 4: IMP CAES C IVLIVS VERVS MAXIMINVS PIVS FELIX INVICTVS AVG
PONT MAX P P ***TRIB POT*** *PROC* ***COS DESIGNATVS***

(M-14) *CIL* III 10645: IMP CAES C IVL VERVS MAXIMINVS P F AVG
TRIB POT *P P* ***COS DESIG***

(M-15) *CIL* III 6465: IMP CAES C IVLIVS VERVS MAXIMINVS P F AVG
P M ***TRIB POT COS DES*** *P P PROCOS*

(16) *CIL* XI 4177: IMP CAES C IVLIO VERO MAXI[min]O PIO F[e]LI[ci] AVG
TRIB POTEST *[p p]* ***COS DESIG***

Das könnte daran liegen, dass die Inschriften vor der zweiten imperatorischen Akklamation angefertigt wurden und deckt sich mit dem Inhalt der

c) ersten Konstitution (datiert auf den 7. Jänner 236), die davon gleichfalls keine Notiz nimmt! Und dies, obwohl Constitutio IV (am 7. Jänner 238) mit *IMP V* eine titellose Akklamation[32] kennt. Gewiss lassen sich dafür mehrere Erklärungen vorbringen, je nachdem, welchem historischem Werdegang man hinsichtlich des Germanensieges zu folgen geneigt ist. Dass *IMP II* dem stadtrömischen Büro entgangen wäre oder dies zu vermelden übersehen wurde, ist eher unwahrscheinlich. Mit Blick auf das Gesamtbild der dokumentarischen Quellen, insbesondere auf die Fehleranfälligkeit der Meilensteinformulare, plädiere ich deshalb für eine Streichung des Attributs „*DESIG*" in der Konsulatsangabe. Damit wäre eine direkte Anbindung an die norischen Zeugnisse M-1 und M-4 und deren Feinchronologie möglich.

2.2.2 In Noricum

M-1: Brestanica / Celeia [Datierung: ab Sommer 236]

In den nachfolgenden Minuskelumschriften der sechs Meilensteine stehen die signifikanten Datierungsparameter (ausgenommen P1) in Fettdruck. Als zusätzliche Diakritika zum Einsatz kommen:

[a]abc = Eigene Neulesung oder Neuinterpretation (siehe dazu im kritischen Apparat).

> *[Im]p(erator) Caes(ar) G(aius!) Iulius [Verus] | [M]aximinus Pius Fel[ix* ***Germ(anicus)] | [max]imus*** *Aug(ustus) pontife[x maxim(us)] | [p(ater) p(atriae)]* ***tribuni(cia) potes(tate)*** (scil. *II)* ***co(n)s(ul)*** *[pro]\|[co(n)]s(ul)* ***imp(erator) bis*** *et G(aius!) Iulius [Verus] | [Max]imus* ***nobilissimus [Caes(ar)] | [princ(eps) iuvent] u{s}tis*** (!) *dom<i>ni* (!) *in<d>u[lgen]\|[tissimi]* ***G⌜e⌝rma(nici)*** (!) ***max(imi)*** *a Ce[leia] | m(ilia) p(assuum) XXXV*
>
> App. crit.:
>
> v. 4: *(*scil. *II)* – um Kohärenz zwischen den Datierungsparametern herzustellen! Die *CIL*-Editoren kommentieren den Wegfall der Zählung nicht.
>
> v7: *inv[icti Aug(usti) fil(ius)]* → *RINMS* anstelle des *indulgentissimi Garmanici*; diese Lesart kennt keine Parallele und wurde auch schon von anderen (*CIL* XVII, *EDCS* und *HD*) korrigiert.
>
> v. 8: *Garma(nici)* pro *Germa(nici)* → *EDCS*, *HD*, *RINMS* ohne Korrekturzeichen; das Foto bei *RINSM* (p. 179) gibt eindeutig ein "A" wieder!

Da keine Notwendigkeit besteht, *TRIBVNI POTES* ohne immer auf das erste Jahr zu beziehen, erweisen sich die chronologischen Parameter als stimmig. Das *IMP BIS* mit daran gekoppeltem *Germanicus*-Beinamen[33] und *TRP II* stehen dabei für ein weiteres

32 Auch wenn damit keine konkreten Ereignisse verknüpfbar wären, so gehörten auch IMP VI und VII zur selben Kategorie.

33 Er nimmt hier die Stelle des in M2+4–6 bezeugten *INVICTVS* ein, das dort die Sieghaftigkeit des Kaisers zum Ausdruck bringt, die übrigens auch in der Münzprägung bereits ab 235 mit *VICTORIA AVGVSTI* gepriesen wird. Wiegels 2023, 114, Anm. 22 und Wolters 2023, 227.

singuläres Formular. Die beiden letztgenannten Komponenten decken sich aber mit den Münzlegenden.[34]

M-2: Salzburg / Iuvavum [Datierung: März bis Sommer 236]

Imp(erator) Caes(ar) G(aius!) Iul(ius) | Verus Maximinus P(ius) F(elix) | Invict(us) Aug(ustus) pont(ifex) maximus | ***trib(unicia) pot(estate) II{I} co(n)s(ul) ª<imp(erator)?> II*** *p(ater) p(atriae) pro|co(n)s(ul) et G(aius!) Iul(ius) Verus Maximus |* ***nobiliss(imus) Caes(ar) princ(eps) iuvent(utis)*** *| domini indulgent(issimi) pontes | refecerunt et vias munierunt | et miliaria restituerunt | m(ille) p(assuum) I*

App. crit.:

v. 4: *COS {II}* fehlerhafte Iteration; *CIL* XVII „errore lapicidae"!

M-3: Stranice / Celeia [Datierung: ab März bis Sommer 236]

[--- M]aximinus | [------] | ***imp(erator) ªbi[s (?) ---]*** *| [---]S[---] | [---]I[---] | [m]axi(mus)* ***co(n)[s(ul) tr(ibunicia) p]ot(estate) II*** *p[ro]co(n)s(ul) [--- ªm(ilia) ªp(assuum)] | XI*

App. crit.:

v. 3: *BI[--- → EDCS, HD, ILLPRON*;

v. 6: Hier sollte die Entfernungsangabe vermerkt gewesen sein, womöglich gemeinsam mit dem munizipalen Ausgangspunkt – *a Celeia*.

Das Formular als solches bleibt aufgrund der abweichenden Positionierung einzelner Komponenten rätselhaft.

M-4: Stranice / Celeia [Datierung: 236 (März bis Sommer)]

Imp(erator) Caes(ar) G(aius!) Iul(ius) | Verus Maximinus | P(ius) Feli(x) Invictus | Aug(ustus) pont(ifex) maxi(mus) | p(ater) p(atriae) ***trib(unicia) pote(state)*** (scil. *II)* ***co(n)s(ul)*** *| pro co(n)s(ule)* ***imp(erator) bis*** *| et G(aius!) Iul(ius) Verus | Max[i]mus |* ª[nobiliss(imus) ªCaes(ar) ªprinceps ªiuventutis?] | *[------]*

App. crit.:

v. 8: *Max[i]mus → EDCS, HD*, nach der Umzeichnung fehlen hier die Buchstaben „XI".

v. 9: Die Lücke kann mit den beiden Titeln ergänzt werden.

M-5: Tulln / Cetium [Datierung: März-bis Sommer 236]

[Imp(erator)] Caes(ar) | G(aius!) Iul(ius) Verus | ªMaximinus | P(ius) F(elix) Invictus Aug(ustus) [pon]\tifex (!) *max(imus)* ***trib(unicia) [pot(estate)] | II co(n)s(ul)*** *p(ater) p(atriae) proco(n)s(ul) [et] | G(aius!) Iul(ius) Verus Maxi[mus] |* ***nobilis(simus) Caes(ar) prin[ceps] | iu(v)entutis*** (!) *dd(omini-duo) ªindulg[en(tissimi)] | pontes ref`e´cerunt [vias] | munierunt milia[ria] | restituerunt | a Ceti(o) m(ilia) p(assuum) XXII[---]*

App. crit.:

v. 5/6: *pontifix* pro *pontifex*.

34 Wolters, 2023, 235–236.

M-6: Wels / Ovilava [Datierung: März bis Sommer 236]

Imp(erator) Caesar C(aius) Iul(ius) | Verus Maximinus | Pius Felix Invictus | Auc(ustus!) ***tr(ibunicia) pot(estate) II co(n)s(ul)*** ª***<imp(erator)?> II*** *p(ater) p(atriae) | proco(n)s(ul) et C(aius) Iul(ius) Verus | Maximus* ***nobilissim|us Caes(ar) princeps iuve|ntutis*** *domini indul|gentissimo* (!) *pontes | refecerunt et | vias munierunt et | miliaria restituer|unt | m(ille) p(assuum) I*

App. crit.:

v. 4: *COS II* – Iteration irrig; *CIL* XVII „errore lapicidae".

v. 8–9: *indulgentissimo* pro *indulgentissimi*.

Dass die norischen Meilensteine M-1–6 in das Jahr 236 (bis auf M-2 wohl schon ab März/April) gehören, dafür sprechen die Zusatztitel des Maximus (P6+7). Bei M-4 darf man – analog zu M-1 – der *TRIB POTE* ebenfalls ein (scil. *II*) hinzufügen. Eine Verschreibung stellen die beiden *COS II* in M-2+6 dar. Gut möglich, dass dort von einem *COS <IMP> II* auszugehen ist,[35] Die negative Evidenz des *Germanicus*-Titels[36] in den Zeugnissen M-2+4-6 (vor allem bei M-4 mit *IMP BIS*) schlüssig zu begründen, bleibt – wollte man dahinter nicht eine fehlerhafte Auslassung sehen – ein schwieriges Unterfangen. Die Formulare dürften alle aus jenem Zeitraum stammen, wo der Siegerbeiname noch keine Bestätigung durch den Senat erfahren hatte, also von April bis Sommer 236. Ganz aus dem Rahmen fällt M-2 mit seinem *TRIB POT III* ohne Siegerbeinamen, zumal die Übernahme aller drei Titel für dieses Jahr als gesichert gilt. Ich plädiere daher für eine Korrektur der Iteration auf *II{I}*. Bemerkenswert ist ferner, dass M-6 ohne *pontifex maximus* erscheint, welcher Tatbestand auch bei zwei außernorischen Formularen (M-14+16) gegeben ist.

3 Schlussbewertung

Die sich aus den verschiedenen Quellenzeugnissen ergebende, verwirrende Gemengelage von fehlerhaften (vor allem bei den Iterationszahlen), unvollständigen wie stimmigen Angaben erschwert die Rekonstruktion eines auch den literarischen Berichten entsprechenden Gesamtbildes bezüglich des großen Germanensieges von Maximinus Thrax. Wenig verwunderlich, wenn man bedenkt, dass für die Meilensteine kein fixes Regelwerk dahingehend bestanden hat, welche der einzelnen Titulatur-Komponenten jeweils zu berücksichtigen waren.[37] Und so vermitteln sie – aufs Ganze gesehen – den Eindruck der Beliebigkeit. Das mit der Langzeitchronologie (Wechsel der Truppen nach Sirmium erst im Winter 236/37)[38] übereinstimmende Junktim von *IMP II* und dem nachträglichen Sieges-

35 Wolters 2023, 236, Anm. 72.

36 Auch bei M2 dürfte man bereits alle drei Siegerbeinamen erwarten.

37 Anders als bei den Münzumschriften war dies bei den Meilensteinen sicher keine Frage des benötigten Platzes. Von möglichen durch die Steinmetzen verursachten Schreibfehlern ist gleichfalls auszugehen.

38 Wolters 2023, 226 inkl. Anm. 22+23 (mit den kontrastierenden anderen Sichtweisen in der Forschungsliteratur).

Titel *Germanicus maximus* erklärt zwar einzelne Formulare für inkohärent, zeigt andererseits aber auch, dass hier die epigraphischen Zeugnisse mit den numismatischen Befunden mehrfach konform gehen. Das „*consul designatus*" des sardinischen Formulars (M-11) als unumstößliches Indiz für eine (titellose?) Akklamation aus dem Jahr 235[39] zu verankern, erfährt durch die hier zur Diskussion gestellten Inschriften keine Stütze.

Abkürzungen

EDCS	Epigraphik-Datenbank Clauss-Slaby <www.manfredclauss.de>
HD	Epigraphische Datenbank Heidelberg <https://edh.ub.uni-heidelberg.de>
lupa.at	F. und O. Harl, <http://lupa.at> (Bilddatenbank zu antiken Steindenkmälern)
RINMS	Šašel Kos 1997

Literaturverzeichnis

Allram, M. 1989. Die Münzprägung des Kaisers Maximinus Thrax (235 / 238),.

Eck, W. 2022. Ein Diplom aus dem Jahr 238 für einen Prätorianer aus Anchialis, ZPE 223, 227–230.

Haegemans, K. 2010. Imperial Authority and Dissent. The Roman Empire in AD 235–238, Leuven.

Kienast, D. Eck, W., Heil, M. 2017 Römische Kaisertabelle, Darmstadt (6. Aufl.).

Lehmann, G.A. 2018. Imperium und Barbaricum. Neue Befunde und Erkenntnisse zu den römisch germanischen Auseinandersetzungen im nordwestlichen Raum – von der augusteischen Okkupationsphase bis zum Germanien-Zug des Maximinus Thrax (235 n.Chr.), Wien (2. Aufl.).

Moosbauer, G. 2018. Die vergessene Römerschlacht. Der sensationelle Fund am Harzhorn, München.

Pearson, P.N. Maximinus Thrax: From Common Soldier to Emperor of Rome, South Yorkshire.

Šašel Kos, M. 1997. The Roman Inscriptions in the National Museum of Slovenia, Ljubljana.

Stylow. A.U. 1974. Ein neuer Meilenstein des Maximinus Thrax in Sardinien und die Straße Karales-Olbia, Chiron 4, 515–532.

Wiegels, R. 2023. Memoria. Vom gefeierten zum ausgelöschten und entehrenden Erinnern an den Imperator Maximinus Thrax, in: Frankfurter elektronische Rundschau zur Altertumskunde 49, 108–126 <*http://www.fera-journal.eu*>.

Wolters, R. 2023. Numismatik vs. Epigraphik? Zur Chronologie des Maximinus Thrax als Herrscher und der große Sieg über die Germanen, ZPE 226, 3, 223–248.

39 Kienast/ Eck/ Heil 2017, 176 und zuletzt Wolters, 2023, 243.

Tabelle 2: Datierungsparameter und ihre Evidenzen

	(A) **Maximinus** (B) **Maximus**	(A) Pius Felix	(A) pater patriae	(A) invictus	(A) pontifex maximus	(B) nobil. Caesar	(B) princ. Iuvent.	(A+B) **Germanici max.**	(A+B) domini indulg.	**Germanicus**	Dacicus	Sarmaticus	TRIB POT	COS	PROCOS	IMP
P(arameter) →	**P1**	**P2**	**P3**	**P4**	**P5**	**P6**	**P7**	**P8**	**P9**	**P10**	**P11**	**P12**	**P13**	**P14**	**P15**	**P16**
								Constitutiones								
I (7. Jan 236)	A	•	•		•								II	•	•	
II (7. Jan 237)	AB	•	•		•	•				A•B	A•B	A•B	III	•	•	
III (7. Jan 238)	AB	•	•		•	•				A•B	A•B	A•B	IIII	•	•	V
								Norische Meilensteine anno 236								
M **1** ab Sommer	AB(n)	•	[•]		•	•	•	•	•	A•			• (sc.II)	•	•	BIS
M **4** März – Som	AB(n)	•	•	•	•	[•]	[•]		[?]				• (sc.II)	•	•	BIS
M **3** ab März	[AB?] (n)	[?]	[?]	[?]	[?]	[?]	[?]	[?]	[?]	[?]			II	•	•	BI[S?]
M **5** März – Som	AB(n)	•	•	•	•	•	•		•				II	•	•	
M **6** März – Som	AB(n)	•	•	•	(!)	•	•		•				II	{II{	•	
M **2** 236	AB(n)	•	•	•	•	•	•		•				II{I}	{II{	•	

Meilensteine mit Siegestitulatur

M-7 =Baet, 236/7	AB(n)	•	•		•	•				A•B	A•B	A•B	III	•	•	IIII
M-8 =PanI, 236/7	AB(n)	•	•		•	•				A•	A•	A•	[---]	•	•	IIII
M-9 =PanI, 236	AB(n)	•	•		•	•				A•	A•	A•	II	•	•	⸢III⸣
M-10 =PanI, 236	AB(n)	•	•		•	•				A•	A•	A•	BIS	•	•	⸢III⸣

Meilensteine anno 235

M-11 =Sard	A(d)	•	•		•								• (sc.I / II)	⸢DES⸣	•	II
M-12 =AlpM	A(n)	•	•	•	•								[• (sc.I/ II)]	DES	•	
M-13 =AlpM	A(n)	•	•	•	•								• (sc.I / II)	DES	•	
M-14 =PanI	A(n)	•	•		(!)								• (sc.I / II)	DES	(!)	
M-15 =PanI	A(n)	•	•		•								• (sc.I / II)	DES	•	
16 =Roma (tit-hon)	A(d)	•	[•]		(!)								• (sc.I / II)	DES	•	

	Münzen und/ oder Medaillone															
ab 235(I) – IIII													•			
ab 1.Jan 236														•		
ab 235		PIVS														
ab Herbst 236	A, B									A•B						
ab 235					•											
nur Herbst 236						•										
nur Herbst – E.236							•									
Anfang 238	AB							•								

Legende: ⁅NN⁆ irrig / inkohärent, (d) = Dativ, (n) = Nominativ, DES(ignatus)

Tabelle 3: Chronologische Übersicht über die richtungsweisenden Formulare

235: 25. März	□	**Maximinus** → *TRP* (Cooptatio)
April? – Ende	□	**Maximinus** → *TRP* (Emission 2)
vor 10. Dez	▼	**Maximinus** → *TRP + COS ¿DESIG¿ + IMP II* (→M-11)
10.Dez		(Wechsel zu → TRP II)
236: 1. Jan		**Maximinus** → TRP II + COS
7. Jan	□	*Constitutio Maximiniana I*
		Maximinus → *TRP II + COS* (als t.p. q. für IMP II)
Jan – Sommer	□	**Maximinus** → *TRP II + COS* (Emission 3/I+II)
März/ April	□	**Maximus** → *CAES* (Cooptatio 1)
	□	**Maximus** → *CAES + [PRINC] IVVENTVTIS* (Cooptatio 2)
16. Mai (als t.a.q.)	□	erste offizielle gemeinsame Nennung von **Maximinus** et **Maximus** (P. Rein)
Sommer	□	*VICTORIA GERMANICA* (Emission 3/II)
Spätsommer – Herbst	▼	**Maximinus** → *[GERM MAX]IMVS + TRP* (scil. *II) + COS + IMP BIS* (!) et
		Maximus → *NOBILISSIMVS [CAES] + [PRINC IVENT]VTIS* (→M-1)
Herbst bis Ende	□	**Maximus** → *CAES* (AE-Medaillon)
	□	**Maximinus** → *GERM + TRP II + COS* (Emission 4)
	□	**Maximus** → *CAES + GERM + PRINC IVENTVTIS* (Emission 4)
Herbst – 9. Dez	▼	**Maximinus** → *TRP II + IMP ¿III¿ + COS* et **Maximus** → *NOBILISSIMVS CAES filius*
		Aug. n. DACICI GERMANICI SARMATICI MAXIMI (→M-9+10)
10.Dez		(Wechsel zu → TRP III)
ab 10. Dez	▼	**Maximinus** → *[GERMANICVS MAXIMVS + D]ACI[C]VS MAXIMVS +SARMATICVS*
(als t.a.q. für die		*o*
Siegesbeinamen sowie		**Maximus** → *NOBILISSIMVS CAES + GERMANICVS MAXIMVS + [SARMATICVS*
als t.p. q. für *IMP V*)		*MAXIMVS + D]ACI[C]VS MAXIMVS* (M-7)

	▼	**Maximinus** → *TRP [---] + IMP IIII + COS* et
		Maximus → *NOBIL CAES + filius Aug. n. DACICI + GERM + SARMAT[ICI] MAXIMIS*
		(→M-8)
237: 7. Jan	□	*Constitutio Maximiniana II*
		Maximinus → ***GERM*** *+ DACIC + SARM MAX +TRP III + COS et*
		Maximus → *GERM + DACIC + SARM MAX + NOBILISSIMVS CAES*
		(als t.a.q. für die Sieges-Beinamen und t.p. q. für *IMP V*)
(als t.a.q. für *IMP IIII*)	▼	**Maximinus** → *TRP III + IMP V* (an die 15 ▼ mit den 3 Sieges-Bn für Kaiser + Sohn)
10.Dez		(Wechsel zu → TRP IIII)
238: 7. Jan	□	*Constitutio Maximiniana III* (mit IMP V als titellose Akklamation!)
(als t.a.q. für *IMP V*)		**Maximinus** → *GERM MAX + DACIC MAX + SARM MAX +TRP IIII + IMP V + COS* et
		Maximus → *GERM MAX+ DACIC MAX+ SARM MAX + NOBILISSIMVS CAES*

Legende: (□) Konstitution, (□) Fasti sodalium (▼) Meilenstein, (□) Münzen und Medaillons (Datierung nach Wolters bzw. Alram), (□) Papyri; t.a./p. q = Terminus-ante/ post-quem; ⌇IMP⌇ = fehlerhaft / inkohärent

Honorific Inscriptions for Philippus and Philippus Iunior in Inlăceni/Énlaka

Zsolt Visy

The excavation from *porta praetoria* of the *castellum* from Énlaka/Inlăceni in 2022 was carried out in the same way as before, under the supervision of the Molnár István Museum in Székelykeresztúr, according to the contract, with the permission of the *Ministerul Culturii, Direcția Patrimoniu Cultural,* as well as on the basis of an agreement and permit with the affected landowners.[1]

It was not the first excavation at the *porta praetoria*. The north gate tower and a section of the *via praetoria* has been excavated by Zoltán Székely in 1947.[2] The tower proved to be 4 × 5 m, the width of its wall 1,6 m (front side) and 1 m (inside). There were newer excavations in the castellum in 1950, made by a research team lead by Mihail Macrea.[3] Fragments of two inscriptions were found in the threshold of the *porta pratoria*,[4] originating from the 3rd century.[5] (Fig. 1)

In 2022, a section of the wall, the ditch, and part of the north gate tower of the *porta praetoria* were excavated.[6] (Fig. 2) It was built in 149 without gate towers or with non-identifiable inner towers, as the partly protruding towers were erected only at the time of repairing and renovation, at the beginning of the 3rd century, on the site of demolished sections of the wall adjacent to the gate.[7] Three sections of the wall of the 4.5 m wide gate tower[8] were excavated. On the south side of the gate tower, part of the *via praetoria* was unearthed. According to the previous excavations, the gate was twofold, with a square

1 The financing of the research program was provided by MOL and two donations from Unicons RL, Székelykeresztúr and Fresh-Color RL, for a three-week period (17 July and 5 August 2022). I am grateful for every support and also to the scientific collaborators of the excavation: the archaeologist Katalin Sidó, the restorer Rita Visy-Késmárky, and archaeology students Bence Ábrahám and Simonetta Göblyös.

2 Székely 1956, 33.

3 Macrea *et al.* 1951, 304–306. – The research in Inlăceni was made by Zoltán Székely and István Molnár.

4 Gudea 1979, 161–162: „un prag sau un zid de blocare", fig. 12.1.

5 Gudea 1979, 201, no. 5–6.

6 Visy 2022, forthcoming.

7 Visy 2021c, 121–124; cf. Visy 1977, 12; Visy 2003, 76.

8 Székely 1956, 33: 4 × 5 m; Gudea 1979, 162: 4,20 × 5,80 m.

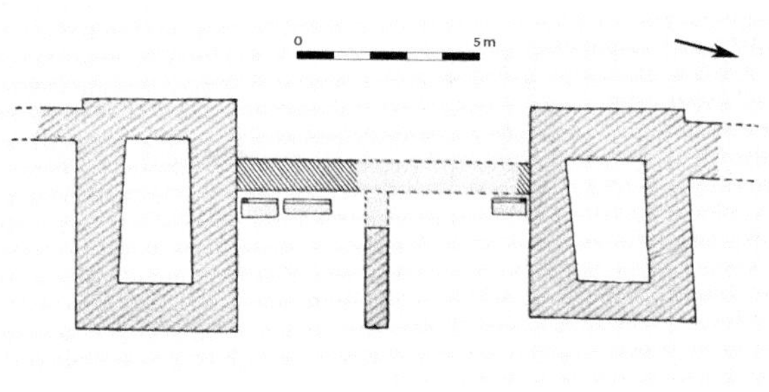

Fig. 1: The *porta praetoria*, excavated in 1950 – Gudea 1979, fig. 12.1

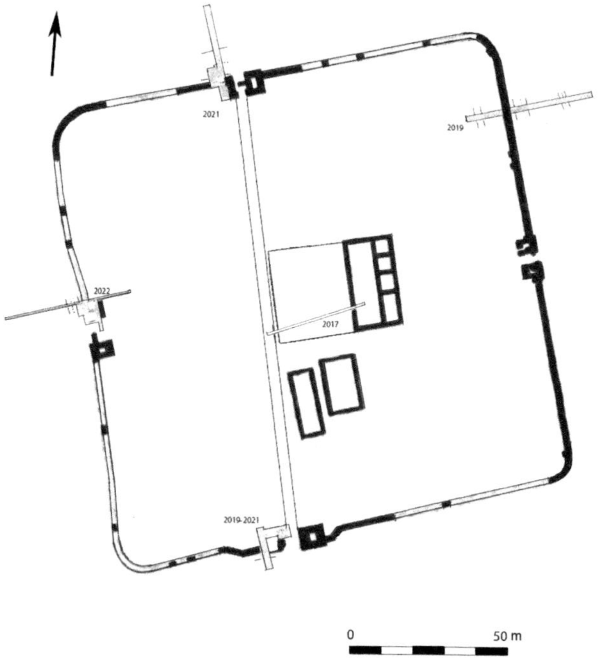

Fig. 2: The state of the research of the *castellum* at Inlăceni/Énlaka in 2022 using the map of Gudea 1979, fig. 12.1

wall in the middle dividing the exit road into two lanes.[9] The pillar unearthed at the end of the excavation stood in the midway of the double gate, and the width of the *via praetoria* can be determined. The excavated section is 3.5 m wide, so the total width, including the pillar, was 7.5 m, which is the same as in the observations made earlier at Énlaka/

9 Gudea 1979, 162. – Fig 5, fig. 12.1.

Fig. 3: The wall of the *castellum* and the northern gate tower of the *porta praetoria*

Inlăceni and elsewhere. After removing the stone rubble, it was possible to excavate the protective trench, which had three periods. The first one belonged to the earth-and-timber fort, the second one to the stone fort built in 149, and the third one to the renovated fort with protruding towers from the beginning of the 3rd century.[10] (Fig. 3)

The two inscriptions found in the gate opening of the *porta praetoria* and used as threshold, with holes for the gate-hinges, were mentioned by Macrea, but published by Gudea.[11] He described them as honorific inscriptions erected by the *cohors IIII Hispanorum* for Caracalla and for another unknown emperor. The inscriptions were published again by I.I. Russu.[12] He took over the descriptions of Gudea with slight differences: no. 265: Honorific altar for Caracalla with traces of *damnatio memoriae*[13] no. 269: honorific altar probably for Philippus Arabs and his co-ruler son, both inscriptions having been dedicated to two emperors. The first inscription was also discussed by R. Ardevan.[14] According to him it could be the basis for a statue and was dedicated to Philippus Arabs and Philippus Iunior:

10 Visy 2022, forthcoming.

11 Macrea *et al.* 1951, 305; Gudea 1979, 201, pl. XXVI/3, XXVII/1; XXVI/3, XXVII/3.

12 IDR III/4, 265 and 269.

13 The inscription could not be dedicated to Caracalla, because he did not suffer *damnatio memoriae*, see Kienast, Eck, Heil 2017, 157.

14 Ardevan 2018, 533–542; Abb. 3.

Fig. 4: IDR III/4, 265
according to R. Ardevan

[I]mp(eratori) Ca[es(ari) [[M(arco) Iul(io)
Philippo]] pio]
felici [Aug(usto) tr(ibunicia) p(otestate)
I]III co[(n)s(uli) proco(n)s(uli) p(atri) p(atriae)]
[[et M(arco) Iul(io) Philippo
iun(iori)]] [i]m[p(eratori) co(n)s(uli) coh(ors)
I]II[I] His[pan(orum) eq(uitata)]
[[Philippiana]]
[n]umin[i et ma/i]estati [eor(um) d(evota)]
fec[it per? ......]
[........]

It was right stating that Caracalla had not been punished with *damnatio memoriae*, and according to it the inscription had been erected for another emperor(s), but we should consider some other facts as well. The broken inscription is in bad condition, partly because the abolition of the name and the usage as threshold, but against these facts it is clear that the only letter in the 6th row cannot be an M, because both other M-s have vertical *hastae*. Another issue is that there is another, very similar inscribed slab, no. 269. Their dimensions are almost the same, 95 × 22 × 14 cm and 96 × 26 × 30 cm. The form of the letters speaks for the same stone-cutter. Also the fact that they were used secondarily in the same place corroborate the possibility that originally there stood in close vicinity to each other. Ardevan's opinion that no. 265 was a base for an emperor statue is quite right, but as it was – according to him – dedicated for two emperors, the statues of Philippus and his son should have stood on it – however it is impossible.

As both inscriptions can be evaluated as bases for emperor statues, one has to find the right interpretation for the inscriptions. Both texts are quite similar, partly the same, and both were dedicated to two emperors: *[n]umin[i et ma/i]estati [eor(um)]* (no. 265) and *[n]umini [et / maie/sta]ti eoru[m]* (no. 269). The solution can be that they were prepared for the statues of Philippus Arabs and for Philippus Iunior, with the father's name on one, and with the son's name on the other stone. If it is so, the reading of Ardevan must be modified, no. 265 being dedicated either to the father or the son.

Such cases are known from the 3rd century. Let us mention the basis of Trebonianus Gallus in Intercisa or that of Volusianus in Lussonium in Pannonia from the year 252.[15] These inscriptions mentioned only one emperor each, but at the end of the text there can be read *numini maiestatique eorum*. The monuments had to be made separately, because on the top of the bases only one emperor-statue could be placed. The two inscriptions at Énlaka/Inlăceni were then dedicated to Philippus Arabs and Philippus Iunior, and they served with their honorific inscriptions as bases for the statues of the two emperors. The question is, how their texts should be extended and interpreted.

The inscribed area of the bases is in very bad condition. The erasing of the names and of some parts of the titles was made efficiently, so that sometimes also the height of the rows is almost indeterminable. Earlier the height of the letters was given as 4,5 cm and 4 cm,[16] but the height of the rows was different. The actual heights of the rows in IDR III/4, 265 are: 68 mm (1st row), 60 mm (2nd row), 51 mm (3th–8th rows), 42 mm (9th–11th rows). The actual heights of the rows in IDR III/4, 269 are: 68 mm (1st row), 58 mm (2nd-4th rows), 48 mm (5th–6th rows), 45 mm (7th–9th rows), 42 mm (10th–11th rows). It is quite evident that these very similar data also speak for a common action.

Accepting and stating that the emperors in question are the two Philippi, also the dating of the dedications is evident: *[tribu/nici]ae po[te/statis] IIII*, the year 247 AD. Regarding the known dedications to Philippus and Philippus Iunior (there are only common dedications on milestones for them, no such parallel dedications like that in Énlaka/Inlăceni), and taking into account the most plausible analogies, especially a military diploma from the same year,[17] one can try to reconstruct both inscriptions. Considering the analogies, and the proposals of Russu and Ardevan,[18] the inscriptions of the twin bases erected for Philippus and Philippus Iunior in AD 247 can be interpreted and extended as follows:

15 Intercisa: Visy 1988, 149; Visy, 2021a, 35, no. 2008; Lussonium: Visy 1989, 385–397 = Visy 2021b, I, 127–138.

16 Russu in IDR III/4, 209, 211.

17 CIL XVI 152 = CIL III 896 (p. 2003) = CIL X 3335 = AE 2002, 59 = AE 2016, 26; EDCS-12300356 – AD 28.12.247. Napoli: *Imp(erator) Caes(ar) M(arcus) Iulius Philippus Pius Felix Aug(ustus) / pontif(ex) max(imus) trib(unicia) pot(estate) IIII co(n)s(ul) III des(ignatus) p(ater) p(atriae) proc(onsul) et / Imp(erator) Caes(ar) M(arcus) Iulius Philippus Pius Felix Aug(ustus) / pont(ifex) max(imus) tr(ibunicia) pot(estate) IIII co(n)s(ul) designat(us) p(ater) p(atriae).*

18 Russu in IDR III/4, 209–212; Ardevan 2018, 535–537, with fig. 3.

Fig. 5: photo of IDR III/4, 265

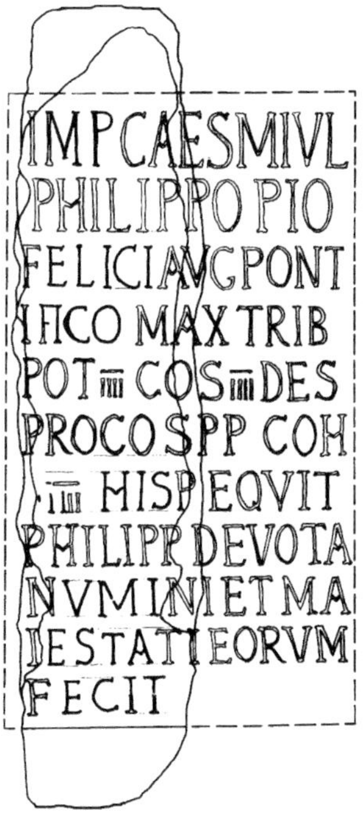

Fig. 6: reconstructed text of IDR III/4, 265

IDR III/4, 265 PHILIPPVS

IMP CAE[S M IVL
[[PHILIPPO PIO]]]
FELICI [AVG PONT
I]FICO [MAX TRIB sic!
POT IIII COS IIII DES
PROCOS P P COH]
IIII HISP [EQVIT
[[PHILIPP]] DEVOTA]
NVMIN[I ET MA
I]ESTATI [EORVM]
FECIT

Imp(eratori) Cae[s(ari) M(arco) Iul(io)] / [[Philippo pio]]] / felici [Aug(usto) pont/i]fico (sic!) [max(imo) trib(uniciae) / pot(estatis) IIII / co(n)s(uli) IIII des(ignato) / proco(n)-s(uli) p(atri) p(atriae) coh(ors)] / IIII Hisp(anorum) [equit(ata) / [[Philipp(iana)]] de-vota] / numin[i et ma]/iestati [eorum] / fecit.

The inscription reconstructed like this is the most probable solution of the text, but as the letters are missing in a great portion, the reconstructed text is only the most likely one. It was made based on a new photo, which shows the surface of the stone quite good.[19] I could not see all rests of letters like Ardevan, also the l. 12, so I left it out. Instead, I see there the lower edge of the inscribed area.

Following the proposed fourth, designated consulship of Philippus, the basis could be made and erected at the end of 247.

Russu thought that the remaining part of the inscription is approximatively the middle section of the stone slab. However, it is more plausible that the beginnings of the rows

19 I thank for the photos of the inscriptions to István Vári, Molnár István Museum, Székelykeresztúr/Cristuru Secuiesc.

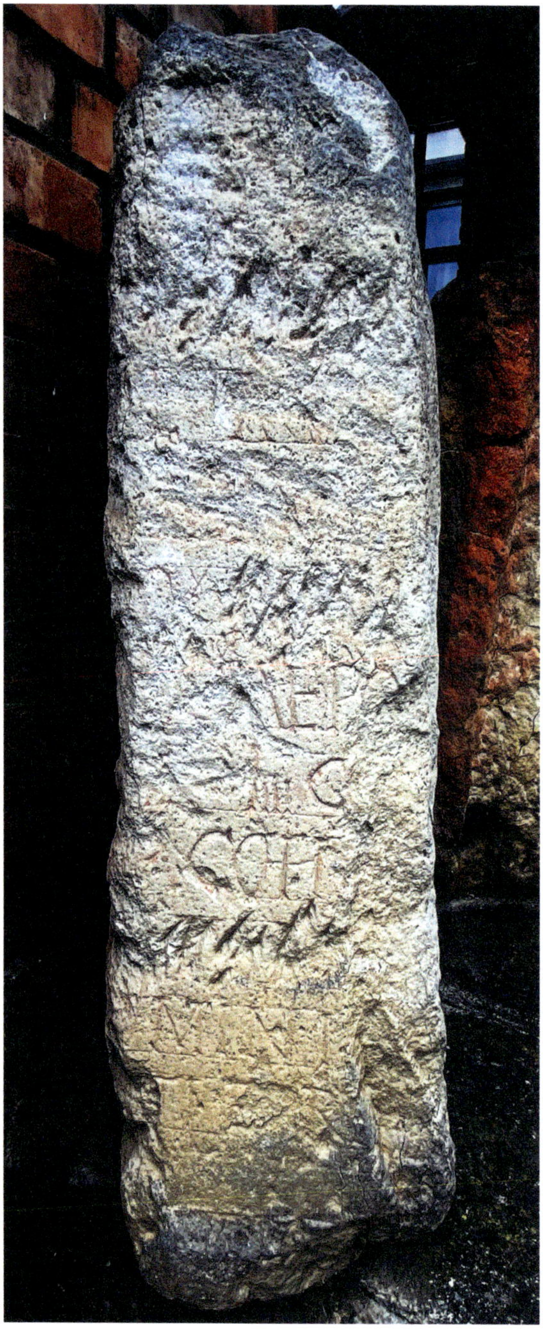

Fig. 7: photo of IDR III/4, 269

are visible here, as *numini* could stand at the beginning of the row. The full form of *tribuniciae potestatis* gives clues for writing also other words in full[20].

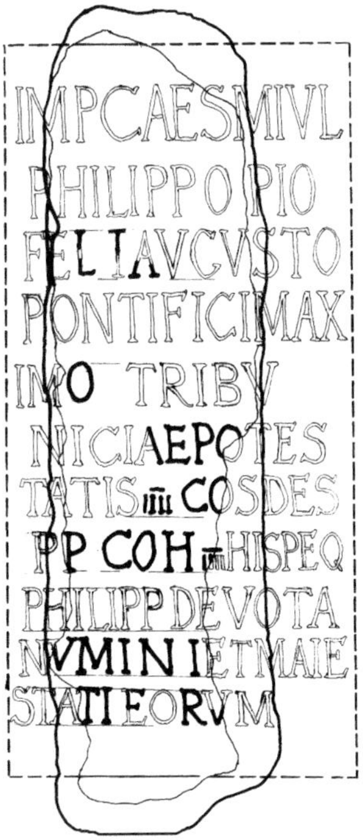

Fig. 8: restored text of IDR III/4, 269

IDR III/4, 269 PHILIPPVS IVNIOR

IMP CAES M [[[IVL
PHILIPPO PIO]]
FE]LI AV[GVSTO
PONTIFICI MAX
IMO TRIBV
NICI]AE PO[TES
TATIS] IIII CO[S DES
P P] COH II[II HISP EQ
[[PHILIPP]] DEVOTA
N]VMINI [ET MAIE
STA]TI EORV[M

*[I]mp(eratori) Caes(ari) M(arco) [[[Iul(io) / Philippo pio]] / fe]li(ci) Au[gusto / pontifici max/*5 *imo tribu/trici]ae po[tes/tatis] IIII co(n)[s(uli) des(ignato) / p(atri) p(atriae)] coh(ors) II[II Hisp(anorum) eq(uitata) / [[Philipp(iana)]] devota /*10 *n]umini [et maie/sta]ti eoru[m].*

The reconstruction of the text is plausible, but the 6th row seems not be the perfect solution. The iteration of the *tribunicia potestas* of Philippus Iunior was given as IIII, because

20 The reconstruction of the inscription was made in this case using the photo made by István Vári and graciously sent to me.

also in this case the two years of him being Caesar were given to the time of his rule.[21] In 247 he was *consul I* and *consul designatus*, together with his father.[22]

According this plausible reconstruction the votive texts were written not in the same form with the same abbreviations, see *Felici – Fel(ici); trib(uniciae) pot(estatis) – tribu/nici] ae po[tes/tatis].* It is remarkable that although this adjective was written regularly in full, there are more abbreviated form in the Danube region in Pannonia, Moesia, Dacia and Thracia as *Philip(piana), Phil(ippiana)* and even as *Ph(ilippiana).*[23] Considering these facts, it is then probable that also *Philippiana* was given in these inscriptions differently: *[[Philip(piana)]] – Phil(ippiana)]].*

The statues of these emperors, erected in 247 stood several years long in the auxiliary fort, probably in the *principia*, until they were removed and used as threshold-slabs in the gate of the *porta praetoria*. Considering their poor surface, it happened probably only under Gallienus, and it is quite sure that this operation belonged to the blocking of the fort gates. If it is right, it follows that the blocking of the gates was made not in the forties of the third century[24], but later, at latest in the early sixties under the rule of Valerianus and Gallienus.

Bibliography

CIL XVI. Nesselhauf, H. Corpus inscriptionum Latinarum XVI, Berlin, 1936.

IDR III/4. Russu, I. I. Inscriptiones Daciae Romanae. III/4, Bucureşti, 1988.

Ardevan, R. 2018. Einige Inschriften aus Inlăceni (Dakien), in D. Boteva-Boyanova, P. Delev, J. Tzvetkova (eds.), Jubilaeus VII. Society, Kings, Gods. In Memoriam Professoris Margaritae Tachevae, Sofia, 533–542.

Degrassi, A. 1952. I fasti consolari dell' Impero Romano, Roma.

Gudea, N. 1979. Castrul roman de la Inlăceni (Încercare de monografie). ActaMP 3, 149–273.

Gudea, N. 1997. Der dakische Limes. Materialien zu seiner Geschichte, JRGZM 44. *1–*113.

Kienast, D., Eck, W., Heil, M. 2017. Römische Kaisertabelle. Grunzüge einer römischen Kaiserchronologie. 6. überarbeitete Auflage, Darmstadt.

21 CIL XVI, p. 137.

22 Degrassi 1952, 68. – Philippus Iunior cos I – 247 and *cos designatus*. I follow here the formulating of CIL XVI 152: *consul designatus* only.

23 ED Clauss-Slaby nrs. *Philippian(a)*: EDCS-11000589 in Germania Superior, EDCS-61000016 in Pannonia inferior, EDCS-30100830 in Moesia inferior; *Philippi(ana)*: EDCS-11800294 in Moesia inferior; *Philip(p(iana)*: EDCS-18300348, EDCS-28500209 in Thracia; *Phil(ippiana)* EDCS-74500208; EDCS-74500207; EDCS-74500201; EDCS-75900151; EDCS-75900152; EDCS-75900153 in Hispania citerior (*leg. VII gemina*), EDCS-16600467, EDCS-25500197 in Pannonia superior, EDCS-18300302, EDCS-09900592 in Pannonia inferior; *Ph(ilippiana)*: EDCS-30000416 in Thracia.

24 Gudea 1997, *14.; Visy 2021c, 123.

Komp, R. 2017. Preliminary Field Report on a Geomagnetic Survey of a Roman Auxiliary Camp in the Community of Inlăceni/Énlaka, Romania, 17.10.-20.10.2016, Ephemeris Napocensis 24, 249–258.

Macrea, M. *et al.* 1951. Despre rezultatele cercetărilor întreprinse de șantierul arheologic Sf. Gheorghe – Breţcu, 1950, SCIV 2/1, 285–311.

Székely, Z. 1956. Raport despre cercetările arheologice executate de Muzeul Regional din Sf. Gheorghe între anii 1945–1955, Inlăceni, Almanah (Sepsiszentgyörgy), 31–40.

Visy, Zs. 1977. Intercisa. Dunaújváros in the Roman Period, Budapest.

Visy, Zs. 1988. Kaiserbasen in den Limeskastellen der Provinz Pannonia Inferior. Griechische und römische Statuetten und Großbronzen. Akten des 9. Bronzekolloquiums, Wien, 148–151.

Visy, Zs. 1989. Eine Statuenbasis des Kaisers Volusianus von Lussonium (Paks-Dunakömlőd), Acta Arch.Hung. 41, 385–397.

Visy, Zs. 2003. The ripa Pannonica in Hungary, Budapest.

Visy, Zs. 2017. Inlăceni/Énlaka during the Roman Period, Ephemeris Napocensis 27, 229–248.

Visy, Zs. 2020. Preliminary Report about the Investigation in the Énlaka/Inlăceni castellum in 2019, Angustia 24, 101–117.

Visy Zs. 2021a. Tituli Intercisae reperti. Tituli Aquincenses IV, Budapest.

Visy Zs. 2021b. *Morsa archaeologica et historica I-II. Selected Papers of Zsolt Visy.* Rippl Rónai Múzeum, Kaposvár.

Visy Zs. 2021c. The castellum Énlaka and the eastern limes of Dacia, Angustia 25, 117–140.

Visy Zs. forthcoming. The excavation in the Roman castellum of Énlaka/Inlăceni in 2022–2023, Angustia 27.

Le *centenarium* aux IIIe et IVe siècles : un débat*

Yann Le Bohec

C'est un honneur et un plaisir d'offrir ce modeste hommage à un collègue et ami que j'ai toujours admiré.

La notion de *centenarium* a divisé la critique. Pendant longtemps, elle a été rangée dans le domaine des affaires militaires. Puis des voix se sont élevées en faveur d'une explication civile. Un nouvel examen de la documentation paraît d'autant plus souhaitable que nous avons nous-même évolué vers plus de nuance dans notre propre interprétation. Le travail devrait être facilité (ou compliqué, suivant le point de vue) grâce au petit nombre d'inscriptions utilisables : huit en tout, à notre avis du moins. De plus, le recours au *Thesaurus linguae latinae* rendra service pour sortir de cette ambiguïté[1].

L'auteur de la notice du *Thesaurus*, s'appuyant sur Varron[2], donne une première définition qui pourrait faire consensus (mais une autre hypothèse a été proposée) : *Centenarium, qui centum unitates habet*. Le problème, dans ce cas, est de savoir ce qui doit être compté au nombre de cent. Parmi plusieurs autres, une définition qui intéresse notre propos de très près se trouve également dans cette compilation : *Genus aedificii, fort. castri* [*sic*] *vel burgi* ; elle concerne donc l'architecture militaire, et elle est illustrée par plusieurs inscriptions africaines. En effet, le mot *castra* (toujours pluriel, même pour désigner une seule enceinte) doit être traduit par « camp » et *burgus* par « tour ». Ici, le *Thesaurus* s'appuie sur un article de la Pauly-Wissowa[3].

Pourtant, une voix s'est élevée pour défendre une autre interprétation : le *centenarium* appartiendrait au domaine civil. C'est ainsi qu'A. F. Elmayer a étudié les inscriptions de Tripolitaine qui sont bilingues, qui ont été rédigées en latin et en punique[4] et qui mentionnent des constructions ainsi dénommées, et il en a déduit qu'elles conduisent à une suggestion : il s'agit de demeures civiles ('private dwellings') construites sur des terrains privés. En 1952, au moment de la publication des *Inscriptions of Roman Tripolitania*, il connaissait 35 textes punico-latins[5]. Les documents qu'il a analysés se trouvent tous en

---

* Nous adressons des remerciements à José D'Encarnaçao pour son aide.

1 Hey, *Th.l.l.* III, 1908, col. 812–815

2 Varron, *Ling.*, V, 88.

3 Kubitschek, *R.E.* 3, 1926, col. 1.

4 Levi Della Vida, Amadasi Guzzo 1987.

5 *I.R.T.*, 10–13.

Tripolitaine, dans la partie la plus orientale de l'Afrique, dans une région devenue province entre 294 et 305[6].

A. F. Elmayer a mentionné les trois forteresses les plus connues et les plus septentrionales de cette région, Bu Njem, Gheriat el-Gharbia et Ghadames, qui jouaient un rôle stratégique[7]. Puis il assure que des fermes fortifiées privées, construites par et pour des civils, se trouvaient au sud de ces enceintes, dans le pré-désert, dans une zone étudiée par M. Reddé et située en arrière de cette ligne de fortifications[8], dans les vallées des oueds Soffegin, Zemzem, Ghirza et Merdum ; c'étaient, dit-il, des *centenaria*, constructions à étages datant des IIIe et IVe siècles. Il y voit la présence d'une population de culture néo-punique, parfaitement civile, mais qui a pu jouer un rôle défensif (la relation qu'il établit entre civil et militaire ne nous paraît pas claire). Il en donne des listes impressionnantes, mais les références utilisables, c'est-à-dire confirmées par l'épigraphie, se résument à deux textes, *I. R.T.*, 880, où il n'y a pas d'« indigènes », qui mentionne une construction parfaitement militaire, et *I. R.T.*, 889, texte pour lequel il propose une nouvelle lecture.

1/ *I. R.T.*, 880 = *A.É.* 1950, 128 = 1951, 149 = 1991, 1621 (Saniet Duib) :
Imp(erator) Caes(ar) [M. Iulius Ph]ilippus, invictu[s, Aug(ustus),] | et M. Iul(ius) P[hilippus, Ca]esar n(oster), regionem limi[tis Ten]|theitani partitam et e[ius] viam incursionib(us) barba[ro]|rum, constituto novo centenario [...] | [...]a[...]s prae-[cl]userunt, Cominio Cassiano, leg(ato) Aug(ustorum) | pr(o)pr(aetore), Gallican[o ...,] v(iro) e(gregio), praep(osito) limitis, cura | Numisii Maximi, domo [...]sia, trib(uni).

Dans ce texte, il ne se trouve rien qui fasse référence à la population locale, sauf peut-être le tribun, qui serait alors analogue aux tribuns de Bir ed-Dreder[9] ; mais ces derniers sont bien plus tardifs, car I. R.T., 880 date des années 244–246. Cette inscription a été gravée évidemment à la demande des pouvoirs publics et elle indique clairement qu'un nouveau *centenarium* a été construit pour aider l'armée à arrêter les raids des barbares. Elle désigne un bâtiment construit dans un but purement militaire et plus précisément tactique ; c'est une défense passive. Elle mentionne toute la hiérarchie militaire : du haut vers le bas, les deux empereurs, le légat impérial, le commandant du *limes* (un petit secteur de la frontière militaire) et, tout en bas, un tribun.

2/ *I. R.T.*, 889 = *A.É.* 1951, 10[10], revu par A. F. Elmayer, p. 82 (Gasr ouadi el-Bir, près de Shemech) :
FLABI DASAMA VY BINIM | MACRINE FELV CENTENARI BACARS | SVMAR NAR SABARE S|AVN.

6 Chastagnol 1967.
7 Rebuffat 1985.
8 Reddé 1988.
9 *I. R.T.*, 886.
10 Le Bohec 2006, 103 ; Le Bohec 2022, 66, 175.

A. F. Elmayer traduit: “Flavi(us) Dasama and his son Macrinus, landowners, have made (this) centenarium to guard and protect the whole zone”.

Mais il y a plus compliqué. Et une inscription endommagée, trouvée à Bida, en Maurétanie Césarienne, impose une nouvelle interprétation.

3/ *C.I.L.* VIII, 9010 (Bida)[11] :
M. Au[...] | *mm* [...]*en*, | *ex pr*(*a*)*ef*(*ecto*) *V*, *cen*|*tenarium a fu*|*ndamenta su*|*is sum*(*p*)*tibus fe*|*cit et dedicavit*, (*anno*) *p*(*rovinciae*) *CCLXXXIIII*.
L. 1 : on peut penser à un M(arcus) Au[relius].
L. 5 : *fundamenta* est mis pour *fundamentis*.
L. 6 : L’année de la province 284 correspond à 328 de l’ère chrétienne.

Un nouvel examen de ce texte sème le doute sur la nature militaire du *centenarium* qui y est mentionné. En effet, le personnage dit qu’il était *ex praefecto V*, « ancien préfet, à cinq reprises ». Remarquons d’abord qu’un préfet n’exerçait pas nécessairement un commandement militaire ; il pouvait avoir été préfet de cité, préfet des ouvriers, etc. ; et le chiffre 5 (V), placé après cette charge, fait supposer qu’il l’a exercé à cinq reprises, ce qui irait mieux avec une charge municipale qu’avec un grade dans l’armée. Ensuite, de toute façon il était « ancien », *ex*. De plus, il faut bien voir qu’il n’était pas normal qu’un civil fasse construire un monument pour des militaires.

Évidemment, dans le domaine de la recherche historique, tout est toujours possible. Il semble néanmoins que l’existence de *centenaria* civils est tout-à-fait envisageable.

En revanche, la nature militaire de plusieurs *centenaria* est une certitude.

Dès 1902, et surtout en 1903, P. Gauckler avait rangé ce mot dans le vocabulaire des armées, et il en faisait un masculin ; sur ce dernier point, il s’était trompé, comme la suite des découvertes l’a montré. Il pensait qu’il était un adjectif et qu’il fallait sous-entendre *burgus*, πύργος en grec, soit « tour » en français. Reconnaissons-lui en réalité de nombreux mérites. Il s’appuyait sur trois inscriptions[12] et également sur trois références à des sites appelés *Ad centenarium* qu’il avait prises dans la Table de Peutinger ; ces lieux-dits se trouvaient dans le sud-ouest de l’Afrique-Numidie et les références qui les concernent ont été généralement oubliées[13]. Le premier de ces trois endroits se trouvait entre Lamasba et Zarai[14] ; le second vers Zana[15] ; le troisième entre Vatari et Thigisi, et il correspondait au moderne lieu-dit Fedj Deriasse[16].

Au milieu du XXe siècle, R.G. Goodchild, recourant au matériel trouvé en Tripolitaine, n’avait rien dit d’autre[17] : le *centenarium* était une sorte de tour. Il précisait : ce nom

11 Le Bohec 2022, 39, 193.
12 *C.I.L.* VIII, 8712, 9010, 20215.
13 Miller 1964, col. 889–890 ; *T.Peut.*, II, 2 ; II, 5 ; IV, 1.
14 Miller 1964, col. 919.
15 Miller 1964, col. 924.
16 Miller 1964, col. 940.
17 Goodchild 1949; Goodchild 1976.

venait de *centenarius*, appellation tardive du centurion, forme attestée en Tripolitaine[18]. Plus original sur un point, il ajoutait que la forme *centenare* n'était qu'une déformation de *centenarium*.

Plus récemment, trois collègues italiens, M. Munzi, G. Schirru et I. Tantilo, ont voulu renforcer l'hypothèse militaire, mais en lui donnant une affectation spéciale : le mot *centenarium* serait dérivé de *centenum*, une sorte de céréales, assez rarement mentionnée et consommée par les militaires à les en croire[19] ; du point de vue de la philologie, leur démonstration est tout-à-fait impeccable. Il aurait désigné un grenier fortifié de formes et de dimensions variées, un type de constructions entreprises à partir du IIIe siècle, en Afrique (quelques rares *centenaria* ont été mentionnés hors d'Afrique, mais ils sont tous très tardifs) : « Concerning the etymology, in our opinion, the word *centenarium* comes from *centenum*, which means a kind of a cereal; thus, centenarium indicates a 'fortified grain-house' ». Ils pensaient, par ailleurs, qu'il était possible que d'autres *centenaria* aient été installés dans d'autres régions de l'empire, en particulier dans la péninsule Ibérique ; ils recommandaient la patience dans l'attente de la découverte de nouvelles inscriptions. Ils plaçaient donc ces bâtiments dans le domaine de la logistique ; mais cette branche de l'art militaire ne peut pas cantonner ses activités au seul « blé » ; il faudrait lui ajouter le sel, l'eau, les matériaux comme le bois, le fer, etc.

D'ailleurs, pourquoi limiter la consommation au seul *centenum* ? Nous verrons plus loin que l'hypothèse agricole est à nuancer, à beaucoup nuancer. En effet, les céréales consommées en Afrique étaient le froment (pour les riches, donc en petites quantités), l'orge (pour les pauvres et les animaux), également le millet et le sorgho.

Pour être complet sur ce sujet bien mal connu, ajoutons que la plupart des *centenaria* connus sont situés en Afrique, datent des IIIe-IVe siècles, et que l'hypothèse la plus fréquemment retenue relie ce nom à celui du *centenarius*, forme tardive du nom désignant le centurion[20].

Deux *centenaria* incontestablement militaires ont été repérés et examinés, mais malheureusement peu et mal fouillés. Il s'agit des postes d'*Aqua Viva* en Numidie[21] et de *Tibubuci* dans la Tripolitaine occidentale (sud de la Tunisie actuelle). Le premier nommé est également connu par une inscription célèbre[22].

> 4/ *A.É.* 1942–1943, 81 = 1946, 226 = 1949, 257 (*Aqua Viva*, M'Doukal) :
> *Impp(eratoribus) dd(ominis) nn(ostris duobus) Diocletiano et Maximiano, aeternis Augg(ustis), et | Constantio et Maximiano, fortissimis Caesaribus, principib(us) | iuventutis, centenarium quod Aqua Viva appellatur, ex praecepto | Val(erii) Alexandri, v(iri) p(erfectissimi), agen(tis) vic(es) praeff(ectorum) praet(orio), et Val(erii) Flori, v(iri) p(erfectissimi), p(raesidis) p(rovinciae) N(umidiae), a solo | fabricatum, cu-*

18 *I.R.T.*, 875.
19 Isid., *Orig.*, VII, 3, 12.
20 Le Bohec 2022, 198, 235.
21 Leschi 1941 ; Leschi 1943.
22 Le Bohec 2022, 38, 186.

rante Val(erio) Ingenuo, praep(osito) limit(is). Dedicatum | dd(ominis) nn(ostris duobus) Diocletiano VIII et Maximiano VII Augg(ustis), conss(ulibus).

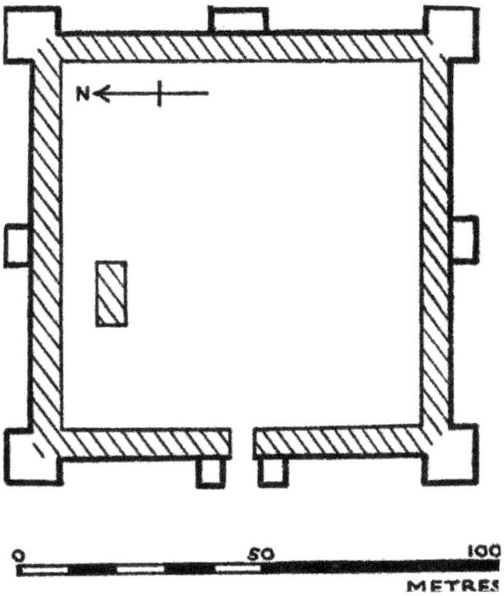

Fig. 1: Le *centenarium* d'Aqua Viva (L. Leschi)

Ce texte est daté de 303, et il mentionne la chaîne de commandement depuis le commandant de secteur (Valerius Ingenuus, *praepositus limitis*) jusqu'aux empereurs en passant par le gouverneur de province (Valerius Florus) et le représentant des préfets du prétoire (Valerius Alexander). Il indique qu'un *centenarium* a été construit depuis le niveau du sol, donc entièrement ; il prouve aussi que le nom est un neutre.

Le *centenarium* d'*Aqua Viva* se trouve près de la source appelée Aïn Naïmia, non loin de M'Doukal, sur le territoire de ce qui fut la commune mixte de Barika[23]. Il n'est connu que par une description rapide de L. Leschi et par un plan médiocre.

Le rempart mesurait 86,80 m. sur 85,90, « à l'intérieur », choix de données peu fréquent, ce qui fait environ 7500 m². À chacun des quatre angles, avait été placée une tour en saillie, comme il était fréquent sous le Bas-Empire, de 3,80 m. à 4,40 (sans plus de précision). Au milieu des murs, on observe d'autres bastions, en saillie, eux aussi, mais de 3,75 à 4 m. Les bastions nord et sud mesurent environ (!) 6,50 m. de largeur, contre 8,50 pour le bastion est, manifestement le plus important à cet égard. La porte est en réalité un couloir de 1,30 m. de large (sans doute 2 m. au moment de la construction) et 3,70 de long ; elle était encadrée par deux tours carrées, elles aussi en saillie, de 4 m. sur 4.

Un élément très important, et qui n'a pas été reporté sur le plan, tient à la présence de casernements périphériques (appuyés sur le mur d'enceinte), qui ont une profondeur de 3,10 à 3,30 m. Le *praetorium*, résidence du commandant du poste, a été identifié au nord, mais il n'en subsiste pas grand' chose. Une grande cour carrée semble avoir occupé le centre de ce camp.

Le *centenarium Tibubuci* est encore plus mal connu, du point de vue archéologique, que celui qui a été vu à *Aqua Viva*. P. Trousset en a donné la dernière description, en suivant fidèlement la notice de P. Gauckler. Il s'agit d'un fortin qui a été érigé en plusieurs phases (sans précisions). Il a la forme d'un heptagone aux angles arrondis, avec un « réduit » en son centre. Les deux archéologues disent qu'il mesurait 110 mètres de longueur, mais ils ne donnent aucune autre indication, ce qui empêche d'en connaître la superficie.

23 *A.A.A.* 37, n° 37.

Le schéma proposé par M. Munzi, G. Schirru et I. Tantilo, d'après P. Gauckler, ne correspond pas à ce chiffre. La partie centrale fait environ 225 m² (15 m. × 15), et il semble qu'un escalier ait mené à un étage ; le rempart extérieur délimite une surface d'environ 900 m². La question est de savoir si le mot *centenarium* désigne le « réduit » central ou l'espace couvert par l'enceinte extérieure. Pour la plupart des commentateurs, la première hypothèse serait la bonne.

Comme il s'y trouve 22 auges, les archéologues en ont déduit que le poste abritait des cavaliers, au nombre de 25 à 30, ce qui correspond à une turme du Haut-Empire, unité commandée par un décurion et pas par un centurion. Une grande citerne avait été aménagée à l'extérieur. Les monnaies trouvées sur le site datent toutes du IVe siècle ; elles vont du règne de Constantin à Eugène.

Un texte complète cette description.

> 5/ *C.I.L.* VIII, 22763 = *I.L.Tun.*, 5 = *I.L.S.*, 9352 = *A.É.* 1902, 47 = 1903, 94 (Ksar Tarcine, *Tibubuci*) :
> *Centernarium Tibubuci, | quod Valerius Vibianus, | v(ir) p(erfectissimus), initiari, | Aurelius Quintianus, v(ir) p(erfectissimus), | praeses provinciae Tri|politanae, perfeci curavit.*

L'enceinte, commencée par un gouverneur a été terminée par un autre ; Aurelius Quintianus est attesté envers 303[24]. Remarquons que, dans cette inscription, seuls les gouverneurs sont mentionnés, sans l'intervention, apparemment, de gradés ; le texte de l'*Aqua Viva* a montré que ces fonctionnaires civils pouvaient intervenir dans le domaine militaire, au moins pour les constructions de fortins, de même que les préfets du prétoire. Il ne faut pas limiter absolument aux activités civiles les compétences de ces personnages.

Plusieurs autres inscriptions mentionnent des *centenaria* dont la nature est plus incertaine.

Faut-il faire confiance à un développement du *C.I.L.*, quand il voit un *centenarium* à Mechta Gara, en Maurétanie Césarienne ? La restitution nous paraît très hypothétique, ne reposant que sur deux lettres bien éloignées l'une de l'autre, un t et un m : [*cen*]-*t*|[*enariu*]*m*[25].

Une inscription de Tripolitaine est plus intrigante : le mot y figure en premier ; hélas, la suite du texte, après un nom d'homme également lisible (sans doute le commanditaire), est incompréhensible[26].

> 6/ *I.R.T.*, 877 = *A.É.* 1950, 209 = 1951, 75 (El-Khadra, Tripolitaine) :
> *Centenarium Marcius Caecilius* | BYMU | 5PAL FESEM A | PERO Y NBAN | EM BUCU BUO | MS AYO NEMA.

24 Chastagnol 1967 ; Lepelley 1981, 343.
25 *C.I.L.* VIII, 8780 = 18016.
26 Le Bohec 2006, 103 ; Le Bohec 2022, 173.

Deux autres inscriptions provenant de sites fort célèbres, ne permettent pas de trancher si le *centenarium* est civil ou militaire ; elles font connaître le *centenarium Solis*[27] et celui qui a été construit près de l'*Aqua Frigida*[28].

> 7/ *C.I.L.* VIII, 8713 et p. 1934 (Bir Haddada, Maurétanie Sitifienne) : [*Impp*(*eratoribus*) *Caess*(*aribus duobus*) *Fl*]*avio Val*(*erio*) *Constantino* | [[*et Va*]*l*(*erio*) *Liciniano Licinio*]], *invictis*, | *semper Aug*[[*ustis*]], *centenarium* | *Solis a solo construxit et dedicavit* | *Septimius Flavianus*, *v*(*ir*) *p*(*erfectissimus*) *p*(*raeses*) *p*(*rovinciae*) *Maur*(*etaniae*) *Sitif*(*ensis*), | *numini maiestatiq*(*ue*) *eorum semper dicatissimus*.

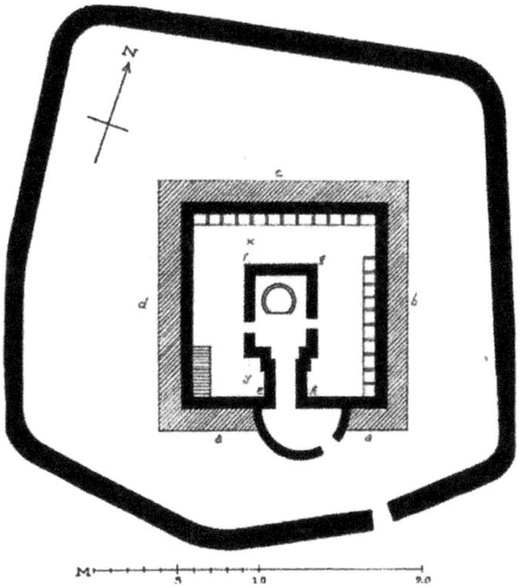

Fig. 2: Le *centenarium* Tibubuci (M. Munzi, G. Schirru et I. Tantilo, d'après P. Gauckler)

Dans ce cas, seule l'intervention du gouverneur, qui a été en poste en 315, est rapportée, sans mention d'aucun autre officier[29]. Toutefois, nous avons vu plus haut que le *praeses* pouvait intervenir pour une construction militaire.

> 8/ *C.I.L.* VIII, 20215 = *I.L.S.*, 6886 (Tala K'frida, Maurétanie Césarienne) : *Impp*(*eratoribus*) *Caess*(*aribus duobus*) *C. Aurel*(*io*) *Val*(*erio*) *Diocletiano* | *et M. Aurel*(*io*) *Val*(*erio*) *Maximiano*, *in*|*victis*, *piis*, *ff*(*elicissimis*), *Augg*(*ustis*), *et Constan*[*tio*] | *et Maximiano*, *nobilissi*|*mis Caesaribus*, *T. Aurel*(*ius*) *Litua*, | *v*(*ir*) *p*(*erfectissimus*), *p*(*raeses*) *p*(*rovinciae*) *M*(*auretaniae*) *Caes*(*ariensis*), *centenarium* | *Aqua Frigida restituit a*[*t*]|[*qu*]*e ad meliorem faciem reforma*|[*vit. Salvis dominis nostris* ! *Multis an*]*nis* ! *Feliciter* !

Les titulatures impériales se placent entre 293 et 305 ; Litua est attesté dès 290[30]. Mais le monument n'a été que restauré ; il est donc bien antérieur. Ici également, le gouverneur est seul mentionné : pas d'officier, pas d'unité.

Le dossier des monuments ayant été présenté, il est possible de revenir sur le sens du mot *centenarium*, problématique qui a été abordée plus haut, à plusieurs reprises.

---

27 Le Bohec 2022, 40, 188–189, 213.

28 Le Bohec 2022, 40, 196–197, 214.

29 Chastagnol 1967 ; Lepelley 1981, 501.

30 Chastagnol 1967 ; Lepelley 1981, 506, 514, 535.

L'explication qui met en rapport *centenarium* avec *centenum*, une céréale, est philologiquement impeccable et intellectuellement séduisante. Nous y ferons toutefois des objections. Pourquoi construire de nombreux bâtiments pour ce seul produit ? Pourquoi privilégier le *centenum*, peu connu, alors que les textes et l'iconographie nous font connaître le froment (*triticum*, *far* ou *siligo*), l'orge (*hordeum*), le millet (*milium*, et pas *centenum* !) et le sorgho (*sorghum*) ? De plus, si le *centenarium* avait été conçu pour la logistique, bien d'autres produits y auraient été entreposés : divers aliments et boissons, surtout de l'eau, du bois, du fer, etc. Enfin, comme on l'a vu plus haut, une de ces enceintes avait un but purement tactique, sans autre fonction.

Il faut alors en revenir à une autre explication, elle aussi philologique, celle qui a été avancée par le *Thesaurus*, qui met le *centenarium* en rapport avec le chiffre cent, *centum*[31]. Donc « cent ». Mais qu'est-ce qui était en cent exemplaires ?[32].

Prenons le cas du *centenarium* d'*Aqua Viva*. Ce qui pouvait y être cent fois, ce n'était pas la longueur du mur : les 85 m. font 250 pieds romains. Ce n'était pas la superficie : les 7500 m.^{2} font 65 000 pieds carrés. Ce n'étaient pas non plus les effectifs : environ 200 fantassins (200 parce que, d'après nos calculs, il fallait 15 000 m.^{2} pour 400 hommes)[33]. Et 25 à 30 cavaliers servaient l'empire à *Tibubuci*.

Le plus simple est de mettre le *centenarium* en relation avec le centurion, devenu *centenarius* au Bas-Empire. Et que le *centenarius* soit apparu peu après ou peu avant le *centenarium* n'est pas une objection : l'épigraphie du milieu du IIIe siècle n'est pas assez riche pour que l'on soit sûr de l'antériorité de l'un ou l'autre de ces deux termes.

Pour le reste, rappelons trois règles souvent oubliées.

D'abord, les Romains n'avaient pas la même conception que les modernes des chiffres, qu'ils arrondissaient volontiers. Un centenaire n'avait pas forcément cent ans : il était « très âgé », et un centurion ou *centenarius*, officier subalterne, commandait normalement moins de cent soldats, plutôt entre 60 et 80. Mais, en cas de besoin, et s'il était reconnu comme très compétent, il pouvait avoir davantage d'hommes sous ses ordres.

Ensuite, il faut se garder de se fier aux « positions stratégiques » pour baptiser *centenarium* une enceinte quelconque. Toutes les agglomérations se trouvent à des positions forcément stratégiques, à un croisement de routes, entre plusieurs autres villes, près d'un défilé, ou d'une autre forme de relief.

Enfin, il vaut mieux éviter de baptiser « *centenarium* » une enceinte en l'absence d'inscription donnant ce nom. Ainsi, on en aurait trouvé en Rétie[34] et J. Baradez avait noté que le fort qu'il avait vu près du lieu-dit *Ad Aquas Herculis* ressemblait à l'*Aqua Viva* ; mais il n'est pas sûr que cette similitude suffise pour en faire un *centenarium*[35].

31 Oxé 1940.

32 Le Bohec 2018, 117.

33 Le Bohec 2018, 115.

34 Schleiermacher 1962.

35 Baradez 1949, 222.

Conclusion

S'il est séduisant d'établir un lien philologique avec la céréale appelée *centenum*, ce rapport semble peu probable pour des raisons de logistique : on ne voit pas pourquoi des bâtiments auraient été élevés et réservés à cette céréale absente des textes concernant l'Afrique. Sans doute, faut-il admettre que ce type de fort tirait son nom de l'officier qui le commandait, un *centenarius*, un centurion.

L'existence de *centenaria* civils aux IIIe et IVe siècles est très possible, mais il n'est pas assuré que toutes les petites constructions de cette époque, notamment les fameux gsurs, soient entrées dans cette catégorie. En revanche des bâtiments à fonction militaire ont bien existé, et au moins l'un d'entre eux avait une fonction tactique : barrer le passage aux raids des barbares.

Bibliographie

Baradez, J. 1949. Fossatum Africae, Paris.

Chastagnol, A. 1967. Les gouverneurs de Byzacène et de Tripolitaine, Ant.Afr. 1, 119–134.

Elmayer, A. F. 1985. The centenaria of Roman Tripolitania, Lib.Stud. 16, 77–84.

Gauckler, P. 1902. Le centenarius de Tibubuci (Ksar Tarcine, Sud tunisien), C.R.A.I., 321–340.

Gauckler, P. 1903. Centenarius [sic], terme d'art militaire, dans Mélanges Perrot. Recueil de mémoires concernant l'archéologie classique, 125–131.

Goodchild, R.G. 1949. The centenaria of the Tripolitanian limes, Dpt. of Antiquities, British Military Administration, Tripolitania, 2, 32–35.

Goodchild, R. G. 1976. Libyan Studies, Londres.

Gsell, St. 1911. Atlas archéologique de l'Algérie, Alger, non paginé ; réimpr. 1997, Alger.

Inscriptions of Roman Tripolitania 1952, Rome.

Le Bohec, Y. 2006. L'armée romaine sous le Bas-Empire, Paris.

Le Bohec, Y. 2018. L'armée romaine sous le Haut-Empire, 4e édit., Paris.

Le Bohec, Y. 2022. L'armée romaine d'Afrique sous le Bas-Empire, Paris.

Lepelley, C. 1979 & 1981. Les cités de l'Afrique romaine au Bas-Empire, Paris, 2 vol.

Leschi, L. 1941. Centenarium quod Aqua viva appellatur, C.R.A.I., 163–176.

Leschi, L. 1943. Le centenarium d'Aqua Viva près de M'doukal, Rev.Afr., 5–22 = *Études d'épigraphie, d'archéologie et d'histoire africaine*, Paris, 1957, 47–57.

Levi Della Vida, G., Amadasi Guzzo, M.G. 1987, Iscrizioni puniche della Tripolitania (Monografie di archeologia libica 22), Rome.

Miller, K. 1964 (réimpr.). Itineraria romana. Römische Reisenwege an der Hand der Tabula Peutingeriana, Rome.

Munzi, M., Schirru, G., Tantillo, I. 2014. Centenarium, Lib.Stud. 45, 49–64.

Oxé, A. 1940. Das Centenarium und seine metrologische Umwelt, Rh.M. 89/2, 127–155.

Picard, G.-Ch. 1956. Néron et le blé d'Afrique, C. T. 4, 163–173.

Rebuffat, R. 1985. Le 'limes' de Tripolitaine, dans D.J. Buck, D.J. Mattingly (édit.), Town and Country in Roman Tripolitania, Papers in honour of Olwen Hackett, B.A.R. Int. Ser. 274, Oxford, 127–141.

Reddé, M. 1988. Prospection des vallées du nord de la Libye (1979–1980). La région de Syrte à l'époque romaine (Armée romaine et provinces 4), Paris.

Schleiermacher, W. 1962. Centenaria am rätischen limes, dans J. Werner (édit.), Aus Bayern Frühzeit. Friedrich Wagner zum 75. Geburtstag (Schriftenreihe zur bayerischen Landesgeschichte 62), Munich, 195–204.

Smith, D.J. 1968. The centenaria of Tripolitania and their antecedents, dans Libya in History, Benghazi, 299–318.

Trousset, P. 1974. Recherches sur le Limes Tripolitanus du Chott el-Djerdid à la frontière tuniso-libyenne, Paris.

Archaeologica

Doctrina armorum: Sulle spade di legno di militari e gladiatori

Giulia Baratta*

Quando si pensa ad armi che rientrano nella categoria delle spade e dei pugnali per consuetudine si è portati a immaginare manufatti di offesa e difesa realizzati in metallo. Così sono, effettivamente, la stragrande maggioranza degli esemplari ad oggi noti rivenuti in tutte le parti dell'impero di Roma, testimoni della presenza di impianti militari o della cruda realtà di una battaglia.

Dagli scavi archeologici, però, seppure in maniera decisamente più sporadica, sono venute alla luce anche spade per così dire "alternative". Si tratta di oggetti realizzati in legno, dunque facilmente deperibili, e per questo motivo scarsamente attestati.

L'immagine che si ha del mondo antico non risponde del tutto al vero perché per alcuni aspetti è ancora legata ad una visione storico artistica dall'impronta neoclassica ma soprattutto lo è per la natura dei rinvenimenti archeologici ove logicamente prevalgono i materiali durevoli, come la ceramica, i metalli e il vetro, a discapito di quelli organici facilmente degradabili e, una volta recuperati, di difficile conservazione. La presenza delle armi di legno, però, non deve affatto stupire. Nell'antichità, infatti, per la sua relativa economicità, per la facile reperibilità e la versatilità nella lavorazione l'uso di questa materia era del tutto corrente[1] per la fabbricazione di un'ampia gamma di manufatti.

Vegezio, tra lo scorcio del IV secolo d. C. e l'inizio di quello successivo, alla fine della parabola del dominio di Roma sui territori conquistati nei secoli precedenti, nella sua *Epitoma rei militaris*, descrive in maniera incisiva l'allenamento dei soldati e dei gladiatori, la cui formazione era improntata a quella dei militari, proprio con l'ausilio di armi di legno (I, XI)[2]:

---

* Università di Macerata, Dipartimento di Studi Umanistici. Questo lavoro si inserisce nell'ambito del progetto del Grup consolidat LITTERA 2021SGR00074 dell'Universitat de Barcelona.

1 Per una panoramica sulle scoperte di oggetti in legno compresi tra la tarda repubblica e l'età imperiale, indicativi dei tanti ambiti di uso di questo materiale si vedano senza alcuna pretesa di completezza Deyts 1983; AA.VV. 1985; De Carolis 1998; Pugsley 2003; Jauch, V., Zollinger, B. 2010; AA.VV. 2012; Hedinger, Leuzinger 2003; Ulrich 2007; Diosono 2008; Fellmann 2009; Cullin-Mingaud 2010; Tegtmeier 2016; Baratta 2022; Sirano, Siano 2022.

2 Testo tratto dall'edizione Vegezio 2003, pp. 88–90.

> 1. *Antiqui, sicut inuenitur in libris, hoc genere exercuere tirones. Scuta de uimine in modum cratium conrotundata texebant, ita ut duplum pondus cratis haberet, quam scutum publicum habere consueuit.* 2. *Idemque clauas ligneas dupli aeque ponderis pro gladiis tironibus dabant.* 3. *Eoque modo non tantum mane sed etiam post meridiem exercebantur ad palos. Palorum enim usus non solum militibus sed etiam gladiatoribus plurimum prodest.* 4. *Nec umquam aut harena aut campus inuictum armis uirum probauit, nisi qui diligenter exercitatus docebatur ad palum.* 5. *A singulis autem tironibus singuli pali defigebantur in terram, ita ut nutare non possent et sex pedibus eminerent.* 6. *Contra illum palum tamquam contra aduersarium tiro cum crate illa et claua uelut cum gladio se exercebat et scuto,* 7. *ut nunc quasi caput aut faciem peteret, nunc a lateribus minaretur, interdum contenderet poplites et crura succidere, recederet adsultaret insiliret, quasi praesentem aduersarium, sic palum omni impetu, omni bellandi arte temptaret.* 8. *In qua meditatione seruabatur illa cautela, ut ita tiro ad inferendum uulnus insurgeret, ne qua parte ipse pateret ad plagam.*

Come per tutte le attività anche per quella militare e gladiatoria esercitazioni ed allenamenti sono fondamentali. Per questi si usavano sagome, i *pali*, come controfigure dei nemici, e pesanti scudi di vimini, gli *scuta de vimine*, e *clavae* in sostituzione delle armi regolamentari per evitare pericolose quanto inutili ferite prima ancora dei combattimenti veri e propri. Vegezio dice esplicitamente che la *clava* sostituisce il gladio, la corta spada con la lama dritta utilizzata dai militari e dai gladiatori[3] che proprio da quest'arma desumono il loro nome. Per *clava*, dunque, non si deve solo intendere un bastone che può ingrandirsi verso una delle sue estremità, come lo è quello brandito da Ercole, la clava per eccellenza, o una mazza con una grossa testa provvista di sporgenze e rinforzi per essere più dannosa, ma anche l'imitazione in legno di una spada usata come arma per esercitazioni. I soldati e i gladiatori non si allenavano dunque con dei semplici bastoni in sostituzione dell'arma da taglio d'ordinanza, l'*arma pugnatoria*[4], ma per acquisire la giusta dimestichezza con delle riproduzioni fedeli di queste realizzate in legno[5] e molto più pesanti degli originali al fine di muscolare il braccio.

Più di quattro secoli prima del tardo testimonio di Vegezio, Tito Livio nel XXVI libro *Ab Urbe condita* descrive gli esercizi dei militari in occasione dell'assedio di *Carthago Nova*:

> *Scipio retentum secum Laelium, dum captiuos obsidesque et praedam ex consilio eius disponeret, satis omnibus rebus compositis, data quinquereme <et> captiuis + cum Magone et quindecim fere senatoribus qui simul cum eo capti erant in naues sex impositis nuntium uictoriae Romam mittit. Ipse paucos dies quibus morari Carthagine statuerat, exercendis naualibus pedestribusque copiis absumpsit. Primo die legiones in armis quattuor milium spatio decurrerunt; secundo die arma curare et tergere ante tentoria*

3 M. Formisano sottolinea come tutti i commenti all'Epitoma mettano in evidenza come gli eserciti descritti siano tratti dal mondo dei gladiatori; cfr. Vegezio 2003, 90, nota 43.

4 Suet. Cal. 54...*battuebat pugnatoriis armis*.

5 E. Saglio nel lemma *clava* scrive che la clava lignea "servant à des soldats romains, n'est autre chose qu'un bâton emplyé pour des exercises d'escrime", cfr. Saglio 1877.

iussi; tertio die rudibus inter se in modum iustae pugnae concurrerunt praepilatisque missilibus iaculati sunt; quarto die quies data; quinto iterum in armis decursum est.

Secondo la narrazione liviana il terzo giorno i militari si sarebbero allenati simulando una battaglia con dei *rudes*. Come in buona parte del XXVI libro, ed in particolare per quel che concerne le vicende dell'assedio di *Carthago Nova*, Livio riprende Polibio[6] che narra lo stesso avvenimento precisando alcune caratteristiche delle armi usate per gli allenamenti. Il passaggio dello storico greco (10, 20, 3), di non immediata comprensione, ha dato luogo a diverse interpretazioni e ad un'ampia discussione[7] in particolare per quel che riguarda le caratteristiche tecniche dell'arma definita da Livio semplicemente come *rudis*. Polibio la descrive nei suoi caratteri essenziali ...ξυλίναις ἐσκυτωμέναις μετ' ἐπισφαιρῶν μαχαίραις.... da cui si deduce che si tratta di una spada di legno con un rivestimento in pelle, evidentemente allo scopo di evitare ferite durante gli allenamenti. Da chiarire rimane la locuzione μετ' ἐπισφαιρῶν secondo molti indicativa della presenza di una rotondità, una vera a propria sfera, verosimilmente in pelle, in corrispondenza della punta della spada che aveva lo scopo di smussarne gli effetti e renderla di fatto inoffensiva[8]. L'ipotesi di un rivestimento totale in pelle comprensivo di una calotta sulla punta della spada risulta abbastanza suggestiva perché con l'arma di allenamento si devono simulare movimenti e tattiche di un combattimento reale ma senza provocare ferite. Rimane però da chiarire perché il sostantivo usato, ἐπισφαιρῶν, è al plurale. Se si trattasse solo dell'imbottitura arrotondata della punta un singolare sarebbe più che sufficiente. Pertanto, sulla scorta di J. A. de Foucault[9], si potrebbe intendere "una spada di legno rivestita in pelle con dei bottoni". La guaina della spada sarebbe dunque corredata da bottoni evidentemente allo scopo di poterla mettere e togliere e più ancora di assicurarne la presa sul corpo dell'arma in modo da non scivolare via durante gli allenamenti. Rimane però anche aperta un'altra possibilità. Le ἐπίσφαιρα potrebbero essere delle semplici sfere di materiale pesante inserite nel rivestimento in pelle della spada, che si dovrebbe immaginare imbottito, allo scopo di appesantire l'arma di allenamento, in maniera maggiore o minore a seconda delle necessità. Sappiamo infatti da Vegezio che queste erano di norma più pesanti delle armi regolamentari.

Sia che i *rudes* e probabilmente anche le *clavae* avessero dunque un fodero in pelle più o meno imbottito con una rotondità sulla punta o che il rivestimento fosse appesantito da sferette di altro materiale, il testimone letterario di una guaina sull'arma in legno sembra confortato dai rinvenimenti archeologici. Infatti gli esemplari di spade in legno riferibili al tipo del *gladius* rinvenute a Vindolanda[10] (fig. 1), Carlisle[11] (fig. 2 a–b) e alla

6 Sulla dipendenza liviana dallo storico greco si veda più di recente Beltramini 2017, in particolare 39.

7 Sull'interpretazione del passaggio di Polibio e di quello di Livio si veda Carter 2006.

8 Cfr. Polybios Geschichte 1961, 710 (trad. H. Drexler); Carter 2006, in particolare 154.

9 Foucault 1972, 119–120.

10 https://www.roma-victrix.com/summa-divisio/armamentarium/pugiones-gladii-et-spathae/rudes.html

11 Caruana 1991, 11–14; McCarthy 2002, 73, fig. 33. L'esemplare intagliato in legno di quercia risale ad epoca flavia (83–84 d. C.) e misura 57,1 cm di lunghezza (14,7 cm corrispondono all'impugnatura), 5 cm di larghezza massima e 1,2 cm di spessore.

Fig. 1: Spada, *rudis*, da Vindolanda: 1 https://www.roma-victrix.com/summa-divisio/armamentarium/pugiones-gladii-et-spathae/rudes.html

Saalburg[12] (fig. 3 a–b) sembrano poco adatti ad essere usati nello stato in cui appaiono ora come armi d'allenamento, sia per lo scarso spessore che per la conformazione poco anatomica dell'impugnatura. Piuttosto, se si vuole scartare l'ipotesi di armi giocattolo[13] o di modelli per la realizzazione di spade in ferro, insegne o elementi decorativi, questi oggetti potrebbero essere l'anima interna di una *rudis* o di una *clava* ormai privi del loro rivestimento esterno che a rigore di logica doveva ricoprire l'arma nella sua interezza, elsa inclusa.

Rispetto ai succitati *gladii* risulta decisamente più realistica una *sica* lignea (fig. 4 a–b) risalente all'ultimo decennio del I secolo a. C. rinvenuta in un pozzo ad Oberaden e riferibile, secondo S. von Schnurbein, a un soldato proveniente dall'area traco-illirica e meno probabilmente ad un gladiatore della categoria dei *Thraces*[14]. L'arma, intagliata in un unico pezzo di legno, presenta un'impugnatura anatomica e potrebbe essere stata usata anche senza un'imbottitura in pelle o con una fodera di sicurezza apposta solo sulla parte della lama.

Se, dunque, allo stato attuale i rinvenimenti di armi lignee sembrano confermare almeno in parte i dati delle fonti scritte, si devono attendere nuove scoperte che in futuro potranno, si spera, chiarire dettagli che oggi sono ancora avvolti nell'alone delle ipotesi ed aiutare a definire più concretamente la destinazione d'uso di questi strumenti e dei loro complementi come lo sono i *pali*[15] (fig. 5) e, soprattutto, contribuire a distinguere tra utensili di allenamento militare e gladiatorio ed oggetti destinati al gioco dei bambini.

12 Jacobi 1934, 21 e tav. III, 1. Il pezzo rinvenuto nel pozzo 51 è realizzato in legno di quercia e misura 42 cm di lunghezza, 3 cm di larghezza e 0,5 cm di spessore.

13 Così N. Albrecht riprende l'ipotesi già avanzata da H. Jacobi sull'esemplare della Saalburg, cfr. Albrecht 2015, 81–82.

14 Schnurbein 1979. La *sica* misura 46,5 cm di lunghezza, di cui 16 cm sono riferibili all'impugnatura e 30,5 cm alla lama.

15 Un probabile esemplare di *palum* è stato rinvenuto a Carlisle nel sito dell'antica *Luguvalium*, McCarthy 2002, 70.

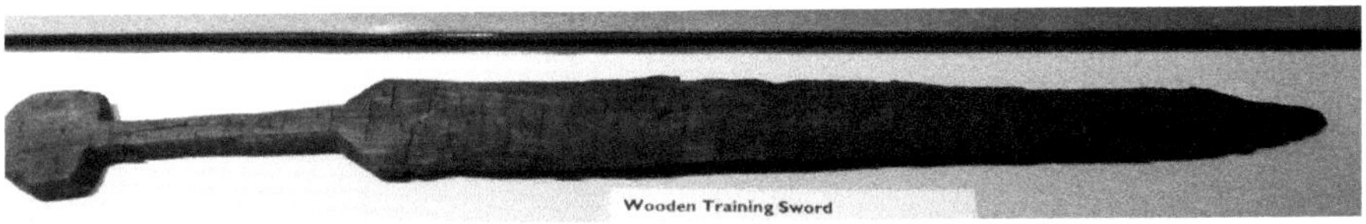

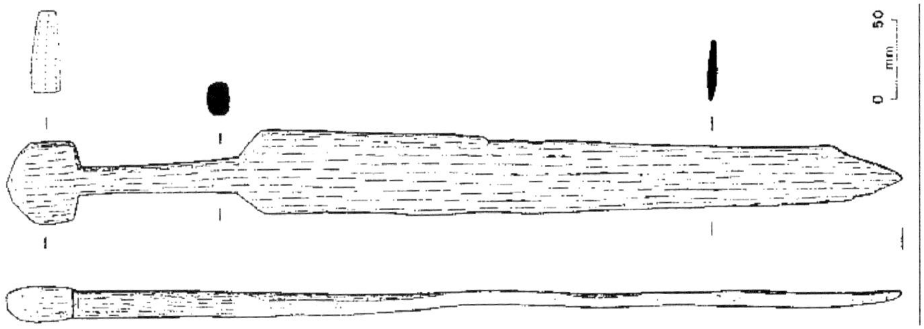

Fig. 2a: Spada, *rudis*, da Carlisle, https://twitter.com/alexrowsontv/status/614486117669322752
Fig. 2b: Spada, *rudis*, da Carlisle, Caruana 1991, 11

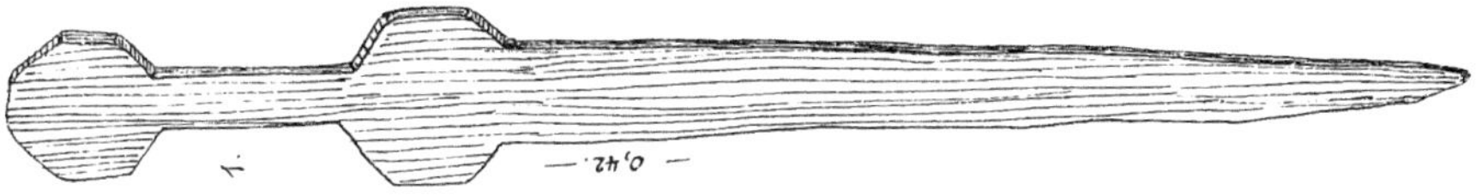

Fig. 3a: Spada, *rudis*, dalla Saalburg, da Bishop 2019, 133
Fig. 3b: Spada, *rudis*, dalla Saalburg, da Jacobi 1934, tav. III, 1

Allo stato attuale, infatti, questo è uno degli elementi di maggiore incertezza. Solo una disamina esaustiva del materiale sino ad ora a disposizione e un approfondito accertamento delle caratteristiche formali dei singoli pezzi potrà contribuire a meglio distinguere tra armi vere e proprie ed oggetti pertinenti alla sfera del gioco[16].

16 È questo il caso, oltre all'esemplare della Saalburg, anche di una serie di armi lignee, tra cui dei *pugi*, ritrovate a Vindolanda e variamente interpretate. A tale proposito si veda http://benedante.blogspot.com/2017/09/wooden-toys-from-vindolanda.html e https://www.bbc.com/news/uk-england-tyne-41225702.

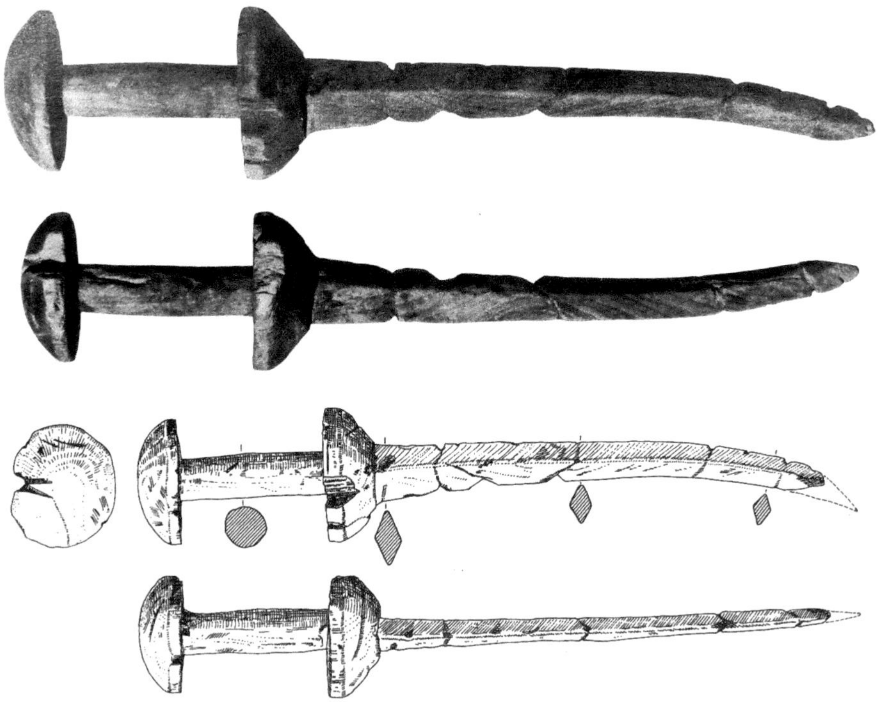

Fig. 4a: *Sica* da Oberaden, Schnurbein 1979, fig. 1
Fig. 4b: *Sica* da Oberaden, Schnurbein 1979, fig. 2

Fig. 5: Probabile *palum*, McCarthy 2002, fig. 30

Bibliografia

AA.VV., 1985, Le bois dans la Gaule romaine et les provinces voisines. Actes du Colloque 1985 (Caesarodunum XXI), Tours.

AA.VV., 2012, Tasgetium II. Die römischen Holzfunde (Archäologie im Thurgau 18), Thurgau.

Albrecht, N. 2015, Römerzeitliche Brunnen und Brunnenfunde im rechtsreihnischen Obergermanien und in Rätien (Studia archaeologica Palatina 1), Mainz.

Baratta, G. 2022, La suppellettile lignea nelle Bucoliche di Virgilio. Aspetti di cultura materiale, Latomus 81, 4, 2022, 729–746.

Beltramini, L. 2017, Commento al libro 26 di Livio, Tesi di dottorato, Corso di dottorato in scienze linguistiche, filologiche e letterarie ciclo XXIX, Università di Padova.

Bishop, M. C. 2019, Warfare through the ages gladiators, New York.

Carter, M. J. 2006, Buttons and Wooden Swords: Polybius 10.20.3, Livy 26.51, and the Rudis, Classical Philology, 101, 2, 153–160.

Caruana, I. 1991, A wooden trainig sword and the so called practice post from Carlisle, Arma 3, 1, 11–14.

Cullin-Mingaud, M. 2010, La vannerie dans l'antiquité romaine. Les ateliers de vanneries et les vanneries de Pompei, Herculanum et Oplontis (Collection du Centre Jean Berard 35), Naples.

De Carolis, E. 1998, I legni carbonizzati di Ercolano: storia delle scoperte e problematiche conservative, Archeologia e territorio 17, 43–57.

Deyts, S. 1983, Les bois sculptés des Sources de la Seine (Gallia suppl. 42), Paris.

Diosono, F. 2008, Il legno. Produzione e commercio, Roma (Arti e mestieri nel mondo romano antico 2).

Fellmann, R. 2009, Römische Kleinfunde aus Holz aus dem Legionslager Vindonissa (Veröffentlichungen der Gesellschaft pro Vindonissa 20), Aagrhau.

Foucault, J.-A. 1972, Recherches sur la langue et le style de Polybe, Paris.

Hedinger, B., Leuzinger, U. 2003, Tabula rasa. Les Helvétes et l'artisanat du bois. Les découvertes de Vitudurum et Tasgetium, Avenches.

Jacobi, H. 1934, Holzfunde, Saalburg Jahrbuch 8, 21–25.

Jauch, V., Zollinger, B. 2010, Holz aus Vitudurum – Neue Entdeckungen in Oberwinterthur, in Archäologie Schweiz 33, 3, 2010, 2–13.

McCarthy, M. 2002, Roman Carlisle & the Lands of the Solway, Charleston.

Polybios Geschichte 1961, Gesamtausgabe in zwei Bänden. Eingeleitet und übertragen von Hans Dexler, Zürich, Stuttgart.

Pugsley, P. 2003, Roman Domestic Wood. Analysis of the morphology, manufacture and use of selected categories of domestic wooden artefacts with particular reference to the material from Roman Britain (BAR int. series 1118), Oxford.

Saglio, E. 1877, s. v. clava, in Dictionnaire des antiquités grecques et romaines, I, 2, Paris, 1237–1238.

Schnurbein, S. von 1979, Eine hölzerne Sica aus dem Römerlager Oberaden, Germania 57, 117–134.

Sirano, F., Siano, S. (eds.) 2022, Materia. Il legno che non bruciò ad Ercolano, Napoli.
Tegtmeier, U. 2016, Holzobjekte und Holzhandwerk im römischen Köln, Köln.
Ulrich, R. B. 2007, Roman Woodworking, New Haven, London.
Vegezio 2003, L'arte della guerra romana, a cura di Marco Formisano, saggio introduttivo di Corrado Petrocelli, Milano.

The Ossuary of "Shelamzion [daughter] of Gozalas of the Village of Ephraia"

Boaz Zissu

An ossuary, supposedly found near Jerusalem, was seized by inspectors from the Israel Antiquities Authority (IAA) and is currently in the IAA's collections. The exact provenance of the ossuary is unknown, but due to its significant inscription, it seems appropriate to present it.[1]

The chalk ossuary (façade rim length 59 cm; façade base length 53.2 cm; narrow side rim length 31 cm; narrow side base length 28 cm; height 29 cm; thickness of walls 2 cm) has four feet and is covered by a vaulted lid (see below). The façade (fig. 1) is adorned with two incised six-petaled rosettes within double circles. In each case, the inner circle has a crude × motif, while the outer one is decorated with a petal motif, executed with a compass. The two rosettes are enclosed by a double rectangular frame filled with a zigzag pattern. A Greek inscription is incised on the center of the otherwise-plain back (see below (fig. 2). A single rosette is incised on each of the narrow faces of the ossuary (fig. 3, 4). The ossuary is intact and in a good state of preservation. Parts of the façade are covered by a fine, uneven, greyish calcitic crust.

The vaulted lid is slightly larger than the box and features two carved depressions that function as handles. It is unadorned except for a small circle incised on the upper part, near one of the corners (fig. 1d). This circle might signify a letter (e.g., a Greek *omicron* or a paleo-Hebrew *'ain*) or might serve as a direction marker. Typically, such markers appear in pairs, one on the lid and another on the narrow side of the box. They were used to ensure correct placement of the lid. In this case, since there is no corresponding mark on the box and the lid is slightly bigger, the lid may have wound up on an ossuary it wasn't designed for. Similar cases are noted by Rahmani (1994, 19–20.).

1 I would like to thank Prof. Leah Di Segni for her useful comments and advice. Special thanks are due to Eli Eskozido, Director General of the Israel Antiquities Authority (IAA) and Yehoshua (Shuka) Dorfman ז"ל former Director General of the IAA, and to Dr. Eitan Klein, Amir Ganor, and Shai Bar-Tura of the IAA's Antiquities Theft Prevention Unit for their assistance. Needless to say, the author bears sole responsibility for this article. Financial support was received from the Krauthammer Fund at the Martin (Szusz) Department of Land of Israel Studies and Archaeology at Bar-Ilan University. The author thanks Debby Stern for her skillful editing of this paper.

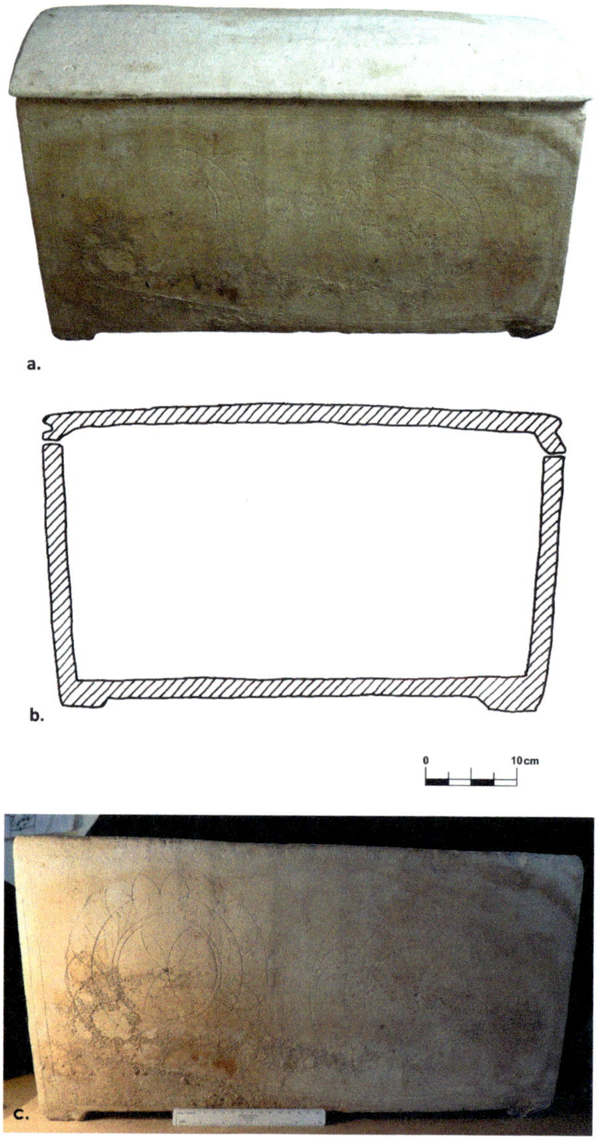

Fig. 1: The ornamented façade of the ossuary
(a. photo; b. section drawing; c. photo of the facade; d., e, f. the lid) (IAA and B. Zissu)

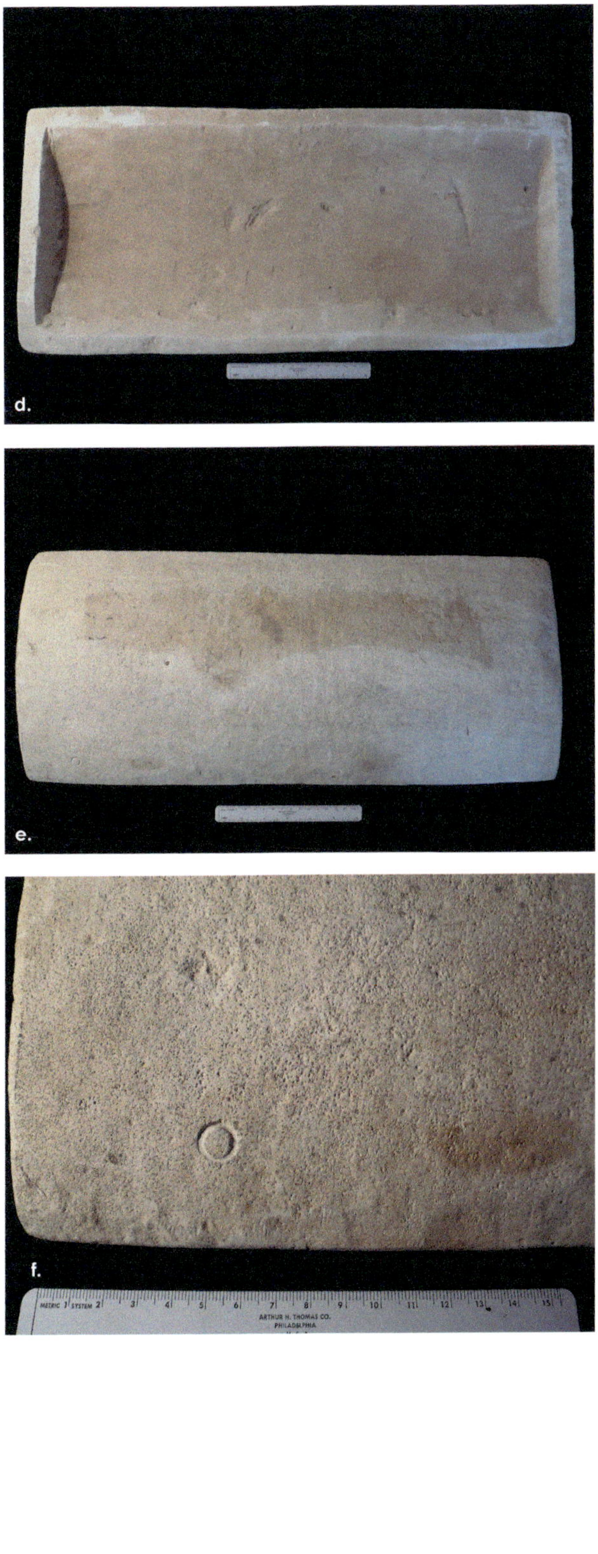
d.
e.
f.

The ossuary is classified within Rahmani's Group B2.[2] Ossuaries of this type, assumed to have been crafted in Judean workshops during the first century CE and until 136 CE (Eshel, Zissu 2020, 34–35), are adorned with finely incised decorations executed with a certain casualness, coupled with compass-aided designs.

The inscription

The inscription (average letter height 20 mm; total length of inscription 43 cm), incised meticulously on the back of the ossuary (fig. 2 and details), reads as follows:

ΣΕΛΑΜΣΙΟΥΣ ΓΩΖΑΛΑ ΚΩΜΗΣ ΕΦΡΕΩΝ

[Bones/ossuary] of Selamsiô [daughter] of Gozalas of the village of Ephraia

The letters are well executed by a skilled hand. A discernible hesitation is apparent in the incision of the first letters. Once the scribe gained confidence, his hand maintained a steady course. This may stem from the scribe's unfamiliarity with the medium or from his position in relation to the surface. The script is formal, in a style common in ossuary inscriptions in Jerusalem and Jericho of the late Second Temple period. On paleographic grounds, the inscription should be dated to the first century CE.[3]

Discussion

(A) The Inscription

Shelamzion

The name of the woman buried in the ossuary was Shelamzion, but it appears here in the genitive as Selamsious, i.e., "of Selamsiô" (a Hellenized feminine form of Shelamzion). Interestingly, the same form appears twice on ossuary no. XX from Tomb H in Jericho.[4]

Shelamzion (meaning "the peace of Zion" or "the wholeness of Zion") was one of the most popular female names among Jews in the Late Hellenistic and Early Roman periods. Tal Ilan has documented 25 epigraphical instances in various forms, including some Aramaic/Hebrew and Greek variants in ossuary inscriptions from Jerusalem and Judea.[5]

Ilan delves into the factors contributing to the name's popularity and raises the question of whether the name was widespread due to its Hasmonean associations, or if it was

2 Rahmani 1994, 21–24.
3 Hachlili 1999, 3a, 10, 11a.
4 Hachlili 1999, fig. IV.12.
5 Ilan 2002, 9, 57, 426–429.

favored within the Hasmonean family because it was already popular. Establishing definitive certainty regarding this matter remains elusive.[6]

Gozalas

The next name, Gozala, is also in the genitive and is apparently not a nickname. We assume it is her father's name. We suggest that this name originates in a nickname, meaning "the fledgling," i.e., "the little/young one."

A *gozal* (גוזל) is one of the birds that Abraham sacrificed in the Covenant of the Parts (Genesis 15:9). In Deuteronomy 32:11, the word denotes a young bird that has not yet grown feathers, and young birds in general.[7] In rabbinical Hebrew, it is used to describe young humans.[8]

Gozal rarely appears as a name. The Hellenized form, Gozalas, appears in an epitaph from Kafr Nasaj in Syria.[9] Sidonius Apollinaris[10] mentions a certain Gozolas of the "natione Judaeus".[11] Leah Di Segni (pers. comm.) highlighted another intriguing case: In a lead weight casting mold discovered in Jaffa, there are three depressions – small, medium, and large – each designated for weights of distinct masses. The same inscription is incised at the bottom of each depression. Y. Kaplan, who published the mold, believed that the name of the *agoranomos* inscribed on the mold was "Youdas Gozomou," a name unrecorded elsewhere, and that each inscription bore a separate date.[12] Di Segni examined the drawings, particularly the third one, which is the best preserved, and proposed that the name could be corrected to read "Gozalou".[13]

Komes Ephreon

The village name is Hellenized and appears here as Ἐφρέων (gen. plural; the epsilon is the phonetic rendering of the diphthong αι.) This village is identified with Ephraia = Aphareama (modern-day et-Taybeh).[14]

It is presumed that in instances where individuals from outside a city or settlement were interred in a local tomb, their original place of residence was often documented. The mention of Shelamzion's place of origin, "the village of Ephraia," is the first known

6 Ilan 2002, 426–429.

7 Through a comparison with תורים (young doves) and בני יונה (young pigeons), a common formulation in the Biblical and rabbinical laws of sacrifices, it is clear that a *gozal* is a young pigeon. This term is also used in a similar sense in Syriac and Arabic (Bilik 1978, 450). In the Hebrew Bible, the words *gozal* (גוזל) and *ephroah* (אפרוח) were used interchangeably to mean "fledgling, chick" (Deuteronomy 22:6–7; Job 39:27). In the Biblical context, the (modern) distinction between *gozal* (גוזל; a young nidicolous bird) and *ephroah* (אפרוח; a young nidifugous bird) did not exist.

8 JT Bava Metzia, chapter 1, halacha 8; BT Pesachim 49a.

9 Bashan; SEG XXVIII, 1349.

10 Book 3, Ep. 4, pl. 58, col. 499.

11 Ilan 2008, 696. The exchange of A/O is common in this region under the influence of Arabic (Di Segni 2006, 589, n. 26; Sartre 1982, 36–37; Di Segni 1998, 438, 451, 452, 454, nos. 34, 35, 58, 60, 62).

12 Kaplan 1981, 412–416.

13 Di Segni 1997, 464–466, and lit. cit. there.

14 Tsafrir, Di Segni, Green 1994, 64; Di Segni, Tsafrir 2015, 393–399.

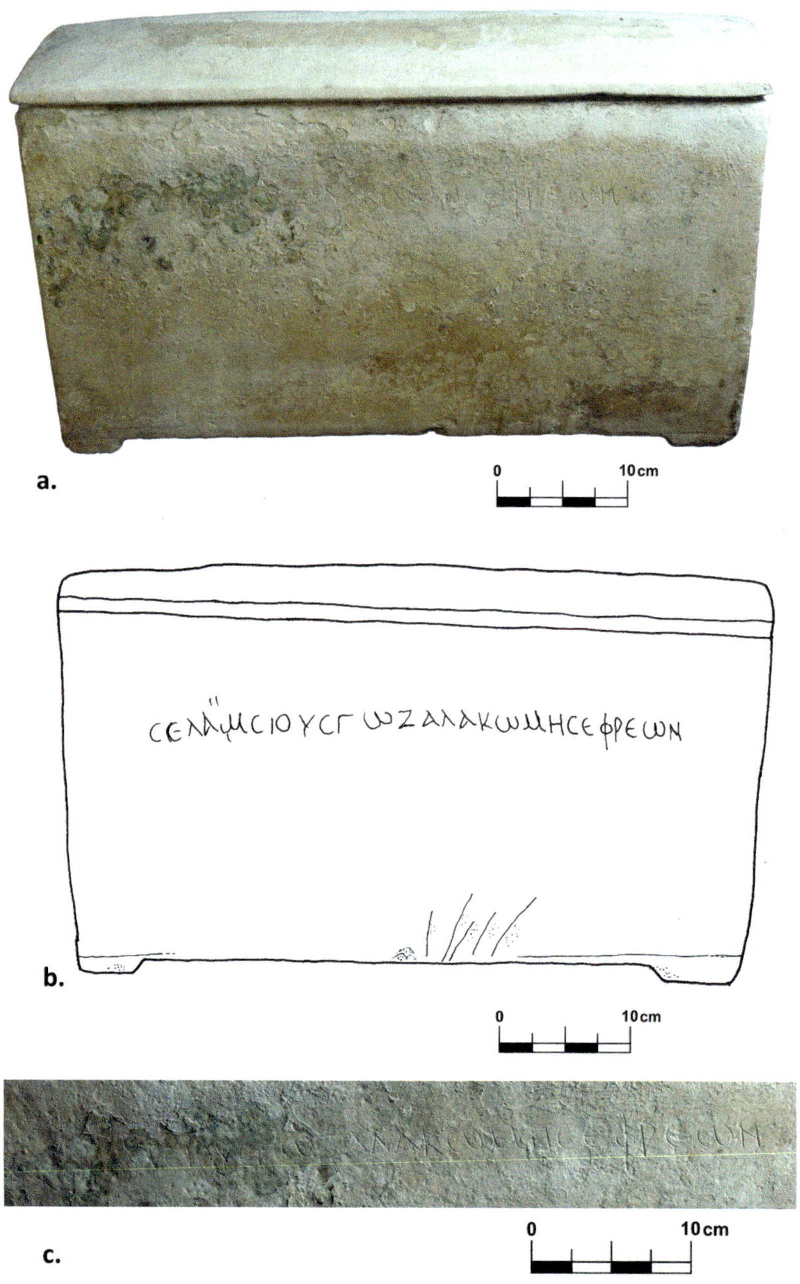

Fig. 2: The back of the ossuary and the inscription (a. photo, b. drawing, c. detail; d,e,f, enlarged photographs) (IAA and B. Zissu)

d.

e.

f.

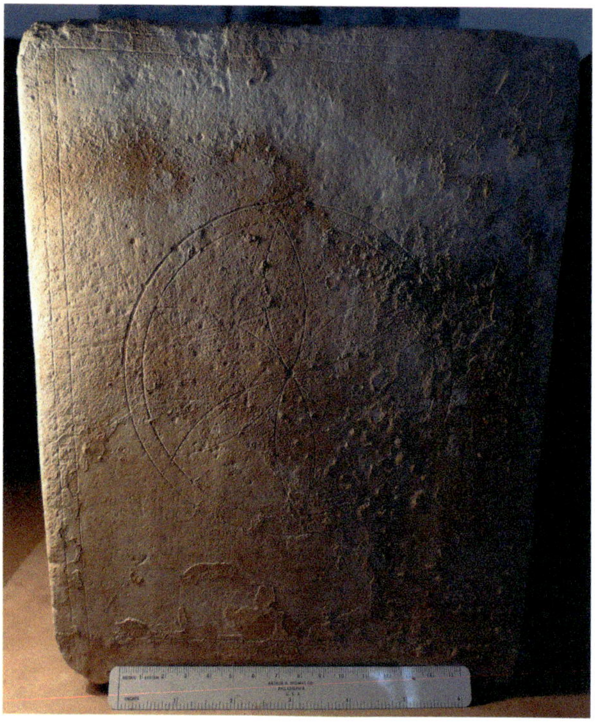

Fig. 3: An ornamented short wall of the ossuary (A) (B. Zissu)

epigraphic reference to this toponym. It also serves as distinct confirmation of its contemporaneous classification as a "village" in the 1st or 2nd century CE. These findings have interesting geographical and historical implications that warrant further discussion.

(B) The Context

(B.1) Ephraia/Apharaema: Historical-Geographical Identification and Archaeological Research

In various periods and places in the Land of Israel, there were settlements whose names were composed of the root עפר.

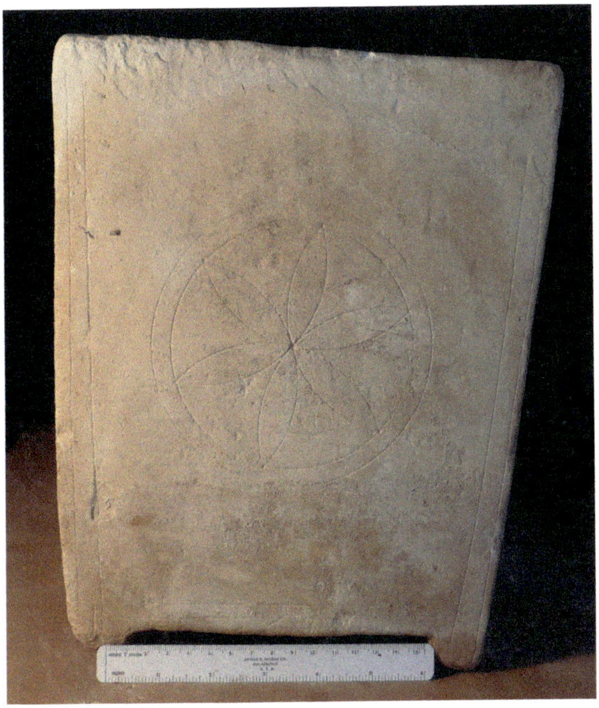

Fig. 4: An ornamented short wall of the ossuary (B) (B. Zissu)

Three forms of this place name appear in the Bible: Ophrah[15], Ephrain[16], and Ephron (Joshua 15:9).[17] In the first two cases, the reference is to the Biblical city of עָפְרָה (Ophrah), situated in the territory of the tribe of Benjamin (the "Land of Benjamin") and identified

15 Joshua 18:23; 1 Samuel 13:17.

16 2 Chronicles 13:19.

17 Joshua 15:9; Biblical Ophrah is where the Philistines camped during their first battle against Saul (1 Samuel 13:17). This is the "Ephrain" mentioned in the story of the war of Abijah son of Rehoboam against Jeroboam son of Nebat (2 Chronicles 13:19). For a discussion of the Biblical toponyms Ophrah, Ephron, and Ephrain/m and various geographical identifications, see Schunk 1961; Heller 1962; Noth 1966, 264–270.

with the village and ancient site of et-Taybeh (fig. 5),[18] approximately 20 kilometers northeast of Jerusalem and 4 kilometers east of the modern settlement of Ophrah.[19]

Apharaema (also known as Aphairema; both Hellenized forms of the Biblical name Ophrah) was a significant village/town during the Hellenistic and Roman periods. Notably, it served as the headquarters of the toparchy (*nomos*) of Ephraim. This was one of the three Samarian toparchies (Ephraim, Ramathaim, and Lod) that were integrated into Judea under an agreement forged in 145 BCE between Jonathan and Demetrius II.[20]

Josephus mentions Ephraim and Bethela when discussing Vespasian's capture of the "Hill Country" in 69 CE. After placing garrisons there, Vespasian led his cavalry to the gates of Jerusalem.[21]

As stated in the New Testament,[22] Jesus, upon realizing that the chief priests and Pharisees intended to apprehend him, relocated with his disciples to Ephraim. He remained there until just before Passover, when he journeyed back to Jerusalem to partake in the festivities: "So from that day on they plotted to take his life. Therefore, Jesus no longer moved about publicly among the people of Judea. Instead, he withdrew to a region near the wilderness, to Ephraim called a city, where he stayed with his disciples."

The place remained significant during the Byzantine period, and the Christian tradition associated with it was not forgotten. At least one church was built, dedicated to Saint George, and in time it was incorporated into a Crusader church.[23] Ophrah is mentioned by Eusebius and Jerome[24] and appears on the Madaba Map as "Ephron also Ephraia, where went the Lord".[25]

During the Middle Ages it was still known as Effrem or Effra; under the Crusaders its official name was changed to Castrum Sancti Helie, but the original name persisted in memory.[26]

***

18 Taybeh (الطيّبة) is a common toponym in this region (Vilnay 1977, 2625–2628). It is an abbreviation of the name et-Tayyibat al-Ism (الطيّبة الاسم) – "The Good Name" or "She with a Good Name." This name was given by the Arabs to several settlements that before the Arab conquest had been called "Ophrat" or "Ophrah." Since the meaning of this word in Arabic (عفرت) is "demon" (or "evil spirit," "bad omen," etc.), the local inhabitants replaced it with a name with a positive connotation (Elitzur 2004, 268–290; 2009, 323).

19 Albright 1923; 1924; Kallai 1971; Elitzur 2004, 268–280.

20 1 Maccabees 11:34; Josephus, Antiquities 13.127; A fresh perspective on the archaeological evidence is offered by Dvir Raviv. His re-examination underscores the idea that prior to the Hasmonean Revolt, the three toparchies were already inhabited by a Jewish population (Raviv 2019).

21 War 4.551.

22 John 11:54.

23 Schneider 1931; Ovadiah 1970, 66–67.

24 Onomasticon 28.4, 86.1; Freeman-Grenville, Chapman, Taylor 2003, 53, 111.

25 Alliata 1999, 63, 67.

26 Ellenblum 1998, 120–126.

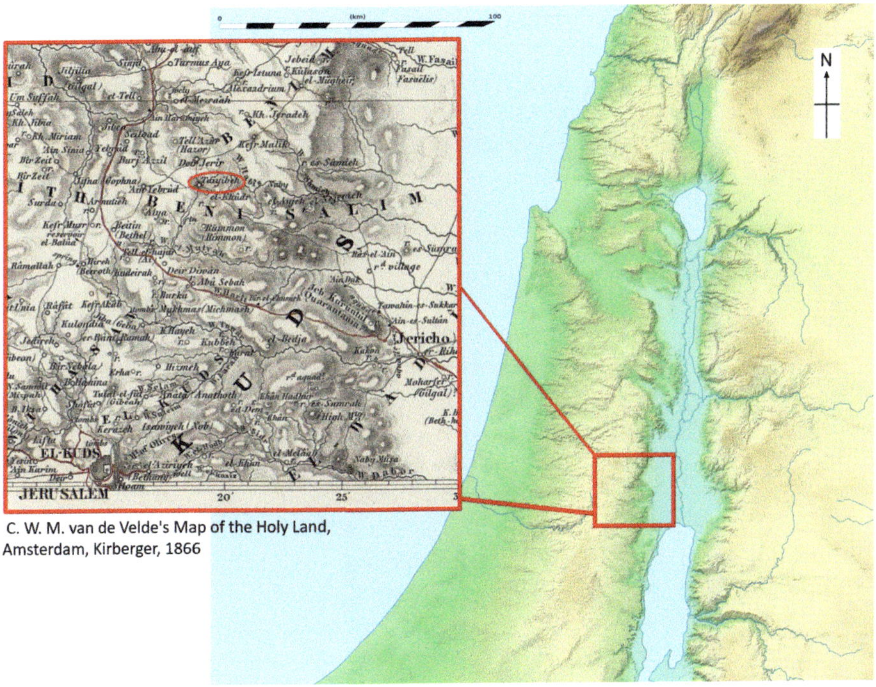

Fig. 5: Location map (B. Zissu)

Already in 1841, Edward Robinson identified Ophrah of Benjamin.[27] Relying on the aforementioned identification with the village of et-Taybeh, Robinson referred to the distance given by Eusebius: "Five miles from Bet-El, to the east".[28] Victor Guérin visited the site, agreed with Robinson's identification, and described various remains, including the Frankish fort.[29] In 1881, the Survey of Western Palestine team found "a large Christian village in a conspicuous position, with well-built stone houses." They provided additional details on the Frankish tower and castle, the ruined church of St. George and various rock-cut cisterns, *kokhim* and arcosolia tombs, and agricultural installations. They also agreed with Robinson's identification.[30]

On July 23, 1934, Salim A. S. Husseini examined a rock-cut burial system found during development works in the village. The system comprised three chambers with *kokhim*,

27 Robinson 1841, 447.
28 Onomasticon 28.4, 86.1, Freeman-Grenville, Chapman, Taylor 2003, 53, 111.
29 Guérin 1869, 45.
30 Conder, Kitchener 1882, 293, 370–371.

accessed through a rectangular shaft. One of the chambers contained five ossuaries, three of them decorated with rosettes.[31]

The site of et-Taybeh was explored in 1982 by Israel Finkelstein, Zvi Lederman, and Shlomo Bunimovitz, who described it briefly as follows: "A large (modern, Arab) village on a commanding hill. The old core of the village is on the summit. A broad view in all directions. The expansion of the (modern) village over the slopes makes pottery collection difficult".[32] They estimated the size of the site at 36 dunams (3.6 ha) and collected pottery from the Iron Age and the Persian, Hellenistic, Roman, Byzantine, Crusader, Ayyubid, and Ottoman periods.

(B.2) Ephraia/Apharaema: The Settlement and Its Status in the Early Roman Period

The inscription on the ossuary explicitly identifies Ephraia as a village (*kome*).[33] In other words, the residents of the area in the 1st–early 2nd centuries CE plainly classified this settlement as a village. This notation holds significance, especially since it is succinctly conveyed through a short funerary inscription, a context in which there was unlikely to be a motive for exaggerating or misrepresenting the settlement's status.[34]

In this context, it is intriguing to examine how contemporary sources define Ephraia and understand the significance of the terminologies employed by these sources.

During the mid-2nd century BCE, Apharaema (Aphairema) served as the capital of a district (toparchy?) designated as a *nomos*.[35] Over time, its status clearly changed, as Apharaema does not appear in Josephus's inventory of Judean toparchies reflecting the situation in pre-70 CE Judea, nor is it referenced in the toparchies' list of Pliny, reflecting the post-70 CE situation.[36]

When describing the story of Vespasian's capture of the "Hill Country" in 69 CE, Josephus defines Ephraim and nearby Bethela as "small towns" (*polichnia*).[37] In the New Testament[38], Ephraim is called a city (*legomenen polin*).

These descriptions are quite intriguing. In the second century BCE, Apharaema (Aphairema) functioned as the capital of a toparchy. However, in our inscription (1st century CE or early 2nd century up to the Bar Kokhba Revolt), it is referred to as a village. In 69 CE, Josephus identified it as a *polis* (city), while the New Testament presents some ambiguity in classifying its status, saying that it was "called a city," potentially suggesting that it had not fully developed into one. What insights can we glean from these varying

31 DoA Mandatorial Archive, et-Tayyibe, file no. 50; Zissu 2001, 30.
32 Finkelstein, Lederman, Bunimovitz 1997, 587–590, site 17–15/81/01.
33 For a discussion of the physical attributes, layout, and characteristics of a village in Judea during the first century CE, see Eshel, Zissu 2020, 21–24; Safrai 1994, 64–77.
34 The inscription was incised in a hidden location and, like other ossuary inscriptions, was not meant for public display.
35 1 Maccabees 11:34; Josephus, Antiquities 13.127.
36 Eshel, Zissu 2020, 18–21.
37 War 4, 551.
38 John 11:54.

designations regarding the status of Apharaema? Can we draw any conclusions about changes in its status over time? This topic warrants further examination.

Various types of settlements existed in Judea during the Early Roman period. Several settlement types are mentioned in contemporary sources, but the use of terminology is somewhat ambiguous.[39] Despite extensive research on rural settlements, there is still no scholarly consensus regarding the terms used in the early sources and their correspondence to the archaeological data.[40]

I will briefly analyze how our primary sources, Josephus and the New Testament, address this matter. It seems that they both distinguish between a city (πόλις) and a village (κώμη) but exhibit inconsistencies in their descriptions.[41] For example, when Josephus refers to Gabara in the Lower Galilee, he alternates between labeling it a city and a village within the same context.[42] Evidently, Josephus tends to elevate the status of certain villages to that of cities when detailing military or civilian activities. This is apparent in cases like Chabulon[43] and Garis[44], to mention just two. It is plausible that Josephus employs the term "city" to amplify the triumph of the besieging (Roman) army in such scenarios. Even Arbela, a village fortified by Josephus,[45] takes on the designation of a city in another context.[46]

Given the inconsistency in Josephus's terminology, it becomes imperative to utilize references wherein he contrasts differing tiers of settlements. Notably, he describes the Lower Galilee as an area encompassing 204 cities and villages,[47] with cities referred to as *poleis* and villages as *komai*. Likewise, Josephus delineates the fortifications he built in prominent cities such as Magdala, Tiberias, and Sepphoris, alongside an array of villages across the Galilee and the Golan.[48] In this context, the designation "city" indicates a central settlement, while references to "villages" pertain to smaller townships.

In contrast, Josephus's depiction of Judea mentions only "cities," prominently Jerusalem but also other ones serving as capitals of toparchies.[49] Consequently, it seems plausi-

---

39 Sartre 2005, 151–239.
40 Safrai 1994, 61–71; Zissu 2001.
41 Safrai 1994, 61–71.
42 Antiquities 3.132; Life 44, 123, 229.
43 Antiquities 2.504.
44 Antiquities 3.129, 5.474.
45 War 1.305; Life 188.
46 Antiquities 12.421.
47 Life 235, 237.
48 Life 188.
49 War 3.54–56, 1.222; Antiquities 14.275; Pliny (Naturalis Historia 5.66–73) also lists a series of Judean settlements, all of them regional administrative capitals. A mere city is called an *oppidum;* only Jerusalem receives the title of a central city, *urbs*. Pliny designates cities like Ascalon and Jaffa as *oppidum*, but villages like 'En Gedi and Gamla also receive this title. The distinction between the levels of settlements is not clear-cut: Pliny distinguishes between two levels of cities based on their size, but his distinction is not uniform and does not conform to precise administrative differentiations. Claudius Ptolemaeus, writing in the 2nd century, employs two terms – "cities" and "villages." In his description of Roman Judaea-Palaestina (Geography 5.15), he does not usually use any terms, except for a series of settlements in the Galilee, which are labelled "cities." As for rabbinic references

ble to infer that the Galilean "cities" served as administrative capitals, whereas the "villages" scattered across the Galilee and other regions were smaller settlements.

Significantly, Josephus's writings lack any systematic terminology for defining lower-level settlements. Consequently, relying solely on Josephus's nomenclature proves unreliable, necessitating a contextual examination of each case. Josephus's *polichnion* (πολίχνιον) is a settlement that, based on its size, importance, and institutions, is somewhere between a village and a city. For example, Josephus refers to 'En Gedi once as a πολίχνιον and once as a πόλις.

A similar situation occurs in the New Testament. The terms employed are "city," "village," and "field building" (*kome, polis, agros*); however, the same settlement is sometimes referred to as a "village" and at other times as a "city." For example, Nazareth, Capernaum, Gergesa, Chorazin, Bethlehem, and Nain are all called "cities," even though they were undoubtedly no more than small towns.[50] But as the authors come to describe the hierarchy of settlements, they use more precise terminology, such as "cities and villages",[51] "field buildings and villages",[52] "cities, villages, and field buildings".[53] In Mark, another term is used – κωμοπόλεις – apparently to denote cities with the legal status of villages.[54]

In conclusion, Josephus and the authors of the New Testament do not use precise terminology. Thus, we can only determine that the writers of that period did not consider precise terminology to be essential, even though they were apparently aware of it.

(B.3) The Archaeological and Cultural Context: Burial Customs in Jerusalem and Judea during the Early Roman Period

The ossuary belongs to the Judean style of the 1st and early 2nd centuries CE and, although its exact origin is uncertain, it was discovered near Jerusalem. Unfortunately, the archaeological context of the ossuary is missing. We will never know at which site it was found, within which burial cave, and what assemblage of finds accompanied it. Therefore, it seems essential to present here briefly the context of Jewish burial customs in Jerusalem and Judea during the late Second Temple period, in order to understand the missing archaeological context.

Archaeological excavations and surveys conducted near Jerusalem have unveiled a remarkable assemblage of about 900 rock-cut tombs within the expansive necropolis en-

---

to this matter, at the top of the settlement hierarchy were big cities, corresponding to the non-Jewish πόλεις. These cities are referred to in the Talmudic sources as *kerakhim* (sing. *kerakh*). They controlled a number of large localities, known in the rabbinic sources as *ayarot* (sing. *ir*). Judean *ayarot* had organized community services, as discussed in a baraitha in tractate Sanhedrin (Sanhedrin 17b). The Mishnah draws a distinction between a city (*kerakh*), a town (*ir*), and a village (*kefar*) (Megillah 1:1, 2:3; Ketuboth 13:10; Kiddushin 2:3; Bava Metzia 4:6, 8:6; Arakhin 6:5, 9:3; Kelim 1:7).

50 Matthew 2:23, 8:28, 8:33–34, 9:1, 11:20; Luke 1:26, 2:39, 4:29, 4:31, 8:10, 8:23, 8:27; Mark 1:33, 2:1, 5:1, 5:14, 5:17.

51 Matthew 9:35, 10:14; Mark 6:11; Luke 8:1, 9:6, 10:10.

52 Luke 9:12; Mark 6:36.

53 Mark 6:56, 5:14; Luke 8:34.

54 Mark 1:38.

circling the ancient city. These tombs have been dated by archaeological methods to the final 150 years preceding the destruction of the city at the hands of the Romans in 70 CE. The diverse array of archaeological discoveries furnishes a robust dataset and facilitates comparison with written sources.[55]

The necropolis, covering a perimeter approximately 3–5 kilometers wide around the city walls, demarcated a spatial boundary between the urban area and surrounding settlements. The tombs, organized in clusters, were carved into the slopes and cliff walls of the valleys.[56]

Each tomb served an extended family and included underground chambers and architectural features. The rock-cut tomb, or burial complex, has two main components: external and internal elements. The external elements include a courtyard, vestibule, tomb markers, and sometimes ritual baths. The courtyard and vestibule were used by pallbearers and mourners. The internal elements were where the bodies were interred. This section includes a burial chamber (or chambers) with benches around a standing pit, burial niches (*kokhim*), arcosolia, and additional burial features. The tomb entrance, usually a small square opening sealed with a fitting stone, marks the border between external and internal elements. In the Early Roman period, Jews practiced "double burial": First, the corpse was placed supine in the burial chamber. After decay, the bones were transferred to a niche or ossuary for secondary burial within the same chamber or complex.[57]

Names in Hebrew, Aramaic, or Greek, many of them distinctly Jewish, were sometimes written in ink or incised on the ossuary. Names may have been engraved onto ossuaries not only to elevate the prestige of the descendants, but also to aid subsequent burial groups in finding a suitable final resting place for relatives of the individual already interred within a specific container.[58]

The distribution of ossuaries is limited to Jerusalem, Judea, and the Jordan Valley. To date, more than two thousand ossuaries have been discovered in various types of tombs, both of the wealthy and the poor, in and around Jerusalem.[59] In other regions, such as Galilee, this practice is less common.[60] Bone collection in ossuaries started in the late 1st century BCE; it persisted in Jerusalem until the destruction of the city in 70 CE, and in the rural areas of Judea until the end of Jewish settlement following the Bar Kokhba Revolt (132–136 CE).[61] Some continuity of (typologically different) ossuaries spanning around two centuries has been noted in southern Judea, but a detailed discussion lies beyond the scope of this study.

55 Hachlili 2005; Kloner, Zissu 2007; Regev 2004.
56 Kloner, Zissu 2007; Shtober-Zisu, Zissu 2018.
57 Rahmani 1994; Hachlili 2005; Kloner, Zissu 2007.
58 Rahmani 1994, 3–59; cf. Semahot 13:8.
59 Rahmani 1994; Kloner, Zissu 2003, 52.
60 Aviam, Sion 2002.
61 Rahmani 1994b; Zissu 2001; Eshel, Zissu 2020.

Given the widespread practice of secondary burial, questions regarding the origin and significance of ossuaries have emerged. Scholars have various perspectives on the purpose behind the introduction of ossuaries in Jewish burial customs.

The "traditional" viewpoint suggests that the appearance of ossuaries was an internal development closely tied to the belief in the resurrection of the dead in their physical bodies. According to this perspective, it was believed that a person's fate in the afterlife was determined twelve months after death, when the flesh had decomposed, and the bones were prepared for their final burial.[62]

An alternative explanation posits that the use of ossuaries represents a hybrid manifestation resulting from the interplay between Jewish burial traditions and Roman culture. This notion arises due to certain similarities in size, shape, and decorations to Roman cinerary urns used for storing cremated remains. From this viewpoint, the introduction of ossuaries is seen less as a testament to Jewish religious faith than as a new social trend influenced by Roman customs.[63] However, it is worth noting that this alternative viewpoint presents some challenges, as according to the established Jewish burial practice the deceased's bones were not subjected to cremation but were instead collected into ossuaries approximately a year after death, following the natural decomposition of flesh at the initial burial site.

Conclusion

Although the ossuary in question was not unearthed through a controlled excavation, its inscription is significant and warrants the attention of scholars.

The first part of the well-executed inscription, which includes the names of the deceased and her father, "Shelamzion [daughter] of Gozalas," aligns with inscriptions typically found on ossuaries from the Early Roman period. However, the reference to the deceased's place of origin, specifically "the village of Ephraia," presents interesting questions.

When individuals from outside a city or settlement were interred in a local tomb, their original place of residence was often documented. The mention of Shelamzion's place of origin, "the village of Ephraia," is the first epigraphic reference to this toponym. It also serves as distinct confirmation of the status of the place as a "village" in the 1st or early 2nd century CE.

These findings have interesting geographical and historical implications concerning Ephraia, also known as Ophrah or Apharaema (Aphairema), a significant location in the Benjamin region. This site is known from the Old and New Testaments, Josephus, and Eusebius and is shown on the Madaba Map. The paper explores the history of the site, its archaeological significance, and its changing status over time.

62 Rahmani 1994; Regev 2004; 2006 and lit. cit. there.

63 Foerster 2005; Levine 2012, 58–62.

Bibliography

Albright, W.F. 1923. The Ephraim of the Old and New Testaments, JPOS 3, 36–40.

Albright, W.F. 1924. Excavations and Results at Tell el-Ful (Gibeah of Saul), Appendix III: Ophrah and Ephraim, AASOR 4, 124–133.

Alliata, E. 1999. The Legends of the Madaba Map, in M. Piccirillo, E. Alliata (eds.), The Madaba Map Centenary, 1897–1997: Travelling through the Byzantine Umayyad Period, Jerusalem, 47–101.

Arakhin: The Mishnah, in. H. Danby (ed.) Translated from the Hebrew with Introduction and Brief Explanatory Notes, Oxford, Oxford University Press.

Aviam, M., Syon, D. 2002. Jewish Ossilegium in the Galilee, in L.V. Rutgers (ed.), What Athens Has to Do with Jerusalem: Essays on Classical, Jewish and Early Christian Art and Archaeology in Honor of Gideon Foerster, Leuven, 151–187.

Bauckham, R. 2018. Magdala as We Now Know It: An Overview, in R. Bauckham (ed.), Magdala of Galilee: A Jewish City in the Hellenistic and Roman Period, Waco, TX, 1–67.

Bilik, A. 1978. Gozal, in Encyclopaedia Biblica, vol. 2, (Hebrew), 450.

BT Pesachim: The Babylonian Talmud, ed. I. Epstein, Mo'ed, vol. IV, Pesachim, London, Soncino Press, 1936.

The Bible. Deuteronomy, Job, Mark, Joshua, Samuel, Chronicles, Maccabees, John, Matthew, Luke,

Conder, C.R., Kitchener, H.H. 1882. The Survey of Western Palestine: Memoirs, vol. 2: Samaria, London.

Di Segni, L. 1997. Dated Greek Inscriptions from Palestine from the Roman and Byzantine Periods, Ph.D. dissertation, Hebrew University of Jerusalem.

Di Segni, L. 1998. The Greek Inscriptions, in M. Piccirillo, E. Alliata (eds.), Mount Nebo: New Archaeological Excavations, 1967–1997, SBF, Collectio Maior 27, Jerusalem, 425–467.

Di Segni, L. 2006. Varia Arabica: Greek Inscriptions from Jordan, Liber Annuus 56, 578–592.

Di Segni, L., Tsafrir, Y. 2015. The Onomasticon of Iudaea: Palaestina and Arabia in the Greek and Latin Sources, vol. 2, part 1, Jerusalem.

Elitzur, Y. 2004. Ancient Place Names in the Holy Land: Preservation and History, Jerusalem and Winona Lake.

Elitzur, Y. 2009. Ancient Toponyms in the Land of Israel, Jerusalem (Hebrew).

Ellenblum, R. 1998. Frankish Rural Settlement in the Latin Kingdom of Jerusalem, Cambridge.

Eshel, H., Zissu, B. 2020. The Bar Kokhba Revolt: The Archaeological Evidence, Jerusalem.

Eusebius of Caesarea, Onomasticon.

Finkelstein, I., Lederman, Z., Bunimovitz, S. 1997. Highlands of Many Cultures: The Southern Samaria Survey [Monograph Series of the Institute of Archaeology 14], Tel Aviv.

Foerster, G. 2005. On the Sources and Meaning of the Custom of Bone Collection (Ossilegium) and Their Burial in Small Stone Chests (Ossuaries) among the Jews in the Land of Israel at the End of the First Century BCE and the First Century CE, in M. Mor et al. (eds.), Le-Uriel: Studies in the History of Israel in Antiquity, Presented to Uriel Rappaport, Jerusalem, (Hebrew), 539–545.

Freeman-Grenville, G. S. P., Chapman, L. P. III, Taylor, J. E. 2003. Palestine in the Fourth Century A. D.: The Onomasticon by Eusebius of Caesarea, Jerusalem.

Guérin, V. 1869. Description de la Palestine: Judeé, Paris.

Hachlili, R. 1999. The Inscriptions, in R. Hachlili, A. Killebrew, Jericho: The Jewish Cemetery of the Second Temple Period, IAA Reports 7, Jerusalem, 142–158.

Hachlili, R. 2005. Jewish Funerary Customs, Practices and Rites in the Second Temple Period, Leiden.

Hachlili, R., Killebrew, A. E. 1999. Jericho: The Jewish Cemetery of the Second Temple Period, IAA Reports 7, Jerusalem.

Heller, J. 1962. Noch zu Ophra, Ephron und Ephraim, Vetus Testamentum 12, 339–341.

Ilan, T. 2002. Lexicon of Jewish Names in Late Antiquity, part 1: Palestine 330 BCE–200 CE, Tübingen.

Ilan, T. 2008. Lexicon of Jewish Names in Late Antiquity, part 3: The Western Diaspora 330 BCE–650 CE, Tübingen.

JT Pesachim: The Jerusalem Talmud, ed. I. Schottenstein, Talmud Yerushalmi, Tractate Nezikin, vol. V, Bava Metzia, London, Soncino Press, 1938.

Josephus, Antiquitates Iudaicae, eds. (H. St. J. Thackeray, R. Marcus, L. H. Feldman, London: Loeb, 1965

Josephus, Vita, ed. H. St. J. Thackeray, London: Loeb, 1926.

Josephus, War: Bellum Iudaicum, ed. H. St. J. Thackeray. London: Loeb. 1928

And move it up, after two other works by Josephus.

Kallai, Z. 1971. Ophrah, Ephron, in Encyclopaedia Biblica, vol. 6, (Hebrew), 322–324.

Kaplan, Y. 1981. Evidence of the Trajanic Period at Jaffa, Eretz-Israel 15 (Aharoni Volume), 412–416.

Kelim: The Mishnah, in H. Danby (ed.) Translated from the Hebrew with Introduction and Brief Explanatory Notes, Oxford, Oxford University Press.

Ketubot: The Mishnah, in. H. Danby (ed.) Translated from the Hebrew with Introduction and Brief Explanatory Notes, Oxford, Oxford University Press.

Kiddushin: The Mishnah, in. H. Danby (ed.) Translated from the Hebrew with Introduction and Brief Explanatory Notes, Oxford, Oxford University Press.

Kloner, A., Zissu, B. 2007. The Necropolis of Jerusalem in the Second Temple Period, Leuven.

Levine, L. I. 2012. Judaism and Hellenism in Antiquity: Conflict or Confluence? Seattle.

Megillah: The Mishnah, in. H. Danby (ed.) Translated from the Hebrew with Introduction and Brief Explanatory Notes, Oxford, Oxford University Press.

Noth, M. 1966. Das Deutsche Evangelische Institut fuer Altertumwissenschaft des Heiligen Landes im Jahre 1965, ZDPV 82, 255–273.

Ovadiah, A. 1970. Corpus of the Byzantine Churches in the Holy Land, Bonn.

Pliny the Elder, Naturalis Historia. Ed. H. Rackham. London: Loeb, 1963.
Raviv, D. 2019. Granting of the Toparchies of Ephraim, Ramathaim and Lod to Hasmonean Judea, Tel Aviv 46(2), 267–285.
Rahmani, L.Y. 1994. A Catalogue of Jewish Ossuaries in the Collections of the State of Israel, Jerusalem.
Regev, E. 2001. The Individualistic Meaning of Jewish Ossuaries: A Socio-Anthropological Perspective on Burial Practice, PEQ 133, 39–49.
Regev, E. 2004. Family Burial, Family Structure, and the Urbanization of Herodian Jerusalem, PEQ 136(2), 109–131.
Regev, E. 2006. Ancient Jewish Style: Why Were Ossuaries and Southern Oil Lamps Decorated? Levant 38(1), 171–186.
Robinson, E. 1841. Biblical Researches in Palestine, vol. 3, Boston.
Safrai, Z. 1994. The Economy of Roman Palestine, London.
Sartre, M. 1982. Inscriptions Grecques et Latines de la Syrie, vol. 13, 1, Paris.
Sartre, M. 2005. The Middle East under Rome, London.
Schneider, A.M. 1931. Die Kirche von et-Taijibe, Oriens Christianum 6, 15–22.
SEG XXVIII. Pleket, H.W., Stroumsa, Guy, G. 1978. Supplementum Epigraphicum Graecum XXVIII, Amsterdam.
Shtober-Zisu, N., Zissu, B. 2018. Lithology and the Distribution of Early Roman-Era Tombs in Jerusalem's Necropolis, Progress in Physical Geography: Earth and Environment 42(5), 628–649.
Sidonius Apollinaris, Epistulae.
Tsafrir, Y., Di Segni, L., Green, Y. 1994. Tabula Imperii Romani: Iudaea Palaestina: Maps and Gazetteer, Jerusalem.
Zissu, B. 2001. Rural Settlement in the Judaean Hills and Foothills from the Late Second Temple Period to the Bar Kokhba Revolt, Ph.D. dissertation, Hebrew University of Jerusalem (Hebrew).

Signacula from Sutor (*Optatiana*)

Sorin Cociş, Vlad-Andrei Lăzărescu*

During the last 30 years, epigraphers have given more attention to the inscribed *instrumenta* category of small finds, as part of the *instrumenta inscripta Latina* class of Roman artefacts encompassing various graphical texts such as words, letters, names, production marks/stamps (*officina*), medical prescriptions, military units' names, graffiti etc. These small finds can provide new insights relating to local military history, economy or daily craftsmanship activities during the Roman time. Recent studies presented at different conferences have led to the publication of collective series dealing with such inscribed artefacts,[1] Roman Dacia making no exception from this new trend, several contributions related to the category of *instrumentum domesticum* being published as well.[2]

Among the *instrumentum domesticum*, *signacula* are probably the best represented group of artefacts. Judging from the perspective of the production material we can account for a great variability, such items being made of iron, bronze, lead, stone, clay or even wood. Out of all these variants, *signacula ferrea* started to be more thoroughly studied after the middle of the 20th century,[3] G. Baratta's seminal paper being among the first attempt at integrating and harmonizing all previously published data concerning such finds.[4] Regarding their function, G. Baratta pleads for their use in marking different types of merchandize or cattle, while not excluding their use in human branding as well.[5] The compiled corpus of finds includes over 50 items discovered all-across the Roman Empire, but unfortunately Dacia was underrepresented (mentioning only one item),

---

* Institute of Archaeology and History of Art Cluj-Napoca, Romanian Academy Cluj Branch, M. Kogălniceanu 12–14, 400084, Cluj-Napoca, Romania, email: scocis@yahoo.com.
Institute of Archaeology and History of Art Cluj-Napoca, Romanian Academy Cluj Branch, M. Kogălniceanu 12–14, 400084, Cluj-Napoca, Romania, email: lazarescu_vlad@yahoo.com.

1 IIL I; IIL II; IIL III; IIL V; IIL VI; IIL VIII.

2 Isac 1991, 57–64; IDR III/6; IDR App. I; IDR App. II; IDR App. III.

3 Klumbach 1952, 1–12; Gherasimov 1959, 339–342; Spitzelberger 1968, 110; Garbsch 1970, 110–112; Gaitzsch 1980, 270; Burger 1987, 116, fig. 102; Visy 1977, 9; Isac 1991, 57–64; Desbat 1991, 323–325; Pietsch 2000, 297–301; Baratta 2004, 189–190; Baratta 2007, 99–108; Krier 2007, 18–22; Mezquíriz Irujo 2007–2008, 212, nr. 26; Pfahl 2012, 200, pl. 80; Cvijetić 2015, 821–825; Ronke 2015, 371–387; Teichner, Dürr 2021, 887, cat. nr. 8–11.

4 Baratta 2007, 99–108.

5 Baratta 2007, 100–103.

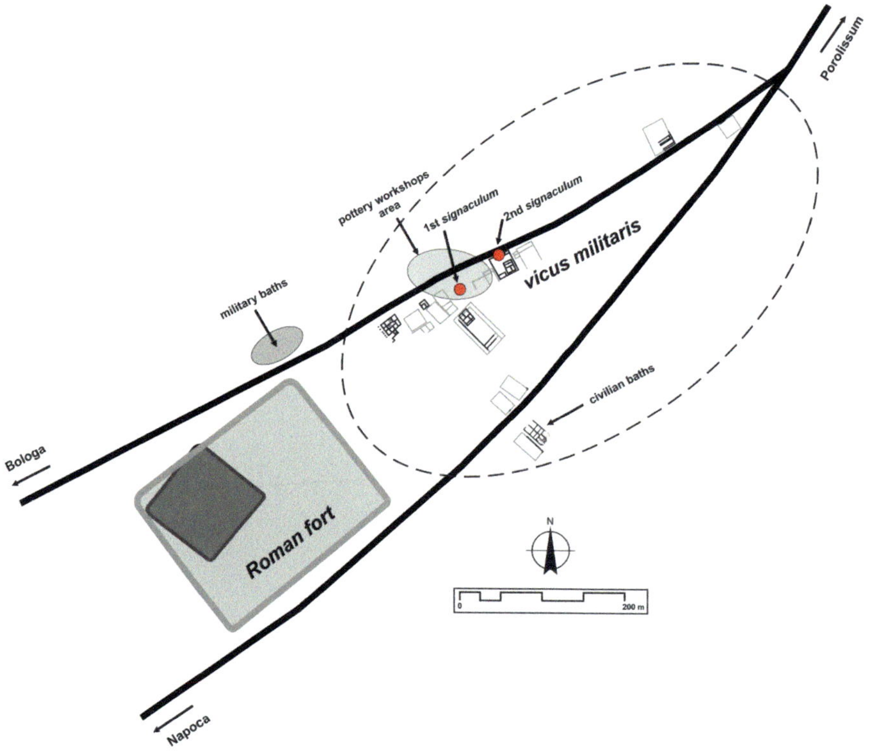

Pl. I: Findspots of the two *signacula* as part of the *vicus militaris* at Sutor (*Optatiana*)

despite the fact that D. Isac's paper on the topic was especially easy to come by,[6] while the Pannonian discoveries are missing.[7] Regarding the province of Dacia, it is highly probable that the bronze *signaculum* coming from *colonia Ulpia Traiana Sarmizegetusa* mentioned by the Italian scholar in her Appendix as bearing the inscriprion "BBB" was erroneously read, a more accurate interpretation of the letters being advanced by D. Isac as "TIB C G/Q".[8] As opposed to the previous class of artefacts, *signacula ex aere* started to be more intensely studied during the last decades,[9] especially for the western Roman provinces.[10]

During the rescue excavations performed between 2021–2022 in the military *vicus* developed in the vicinity of the auxiliary fort at Sutor (*Optatiana*) with the occasion of the

6 Isac 1991.
7 Burger 1987, 16, fig. 102; Visy 1977, 23, fig. 16.
8 Isac 1991, 64, cat. no. 9, "TIB C G".
9 Petcu, Petcu-Levei 2021, 335–348.
10 Feugère, Mauné 2005; Baratta 2014; IIL V (with the literature, see pages 519–579); Braito 2018; Feugère 2020.

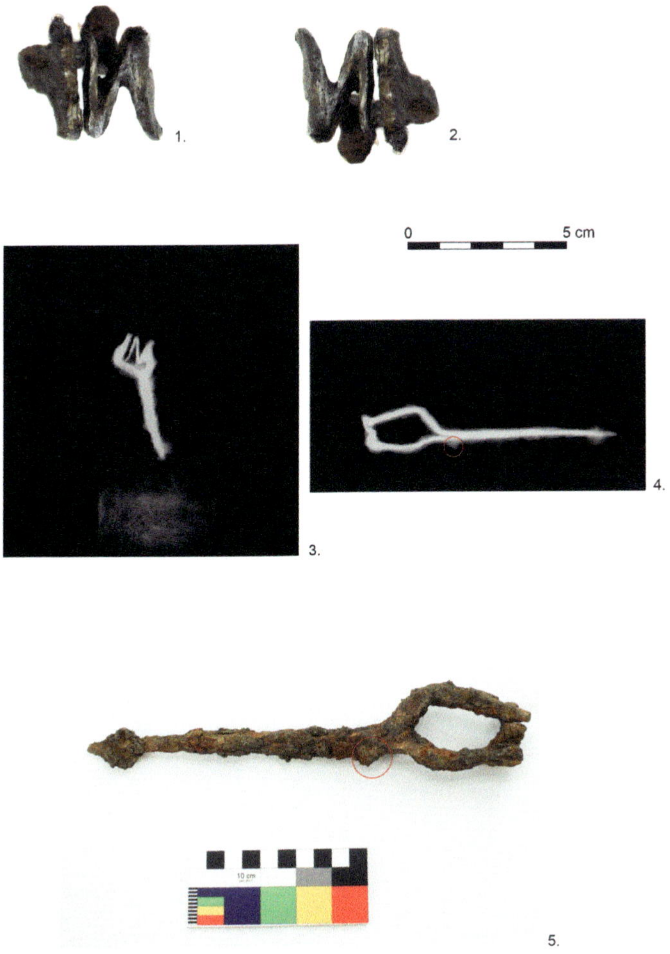

Pl. II: The first discovered *signaculum* found at Sutor (*Optatiana*): 1–2. Photos of the inscription; 3–4. X-rays of the artefact; 5. Photo prior to the restoration process

massive construction works connected with the Motorway A3, a workshops area was documented and fully investigated.[11] From this area, among other small finds that fit within the *instrumentum domesticum* category, two *signacula ferrea* were discovered (Pl. I). The first item was unfortunately only fragmentarily preserved, being forged from a single metal bar.[12] Its preserved dimensions are as follows: height = 24.3 cm; width = 3.9 cm; length of arms = 6.5 cm; rod thickness = 1.6 cm; thickness of the letters = 0.78 cm; height

11 Cociş, Lăzărescu, Socaciu 2021; Cociş, Lăzărescu, Socaciu 2021a; Socaciu, Lăzărescu, Cociş 2023.

12 The artefact was found in S2/2021, small find no. 162, context 1046.

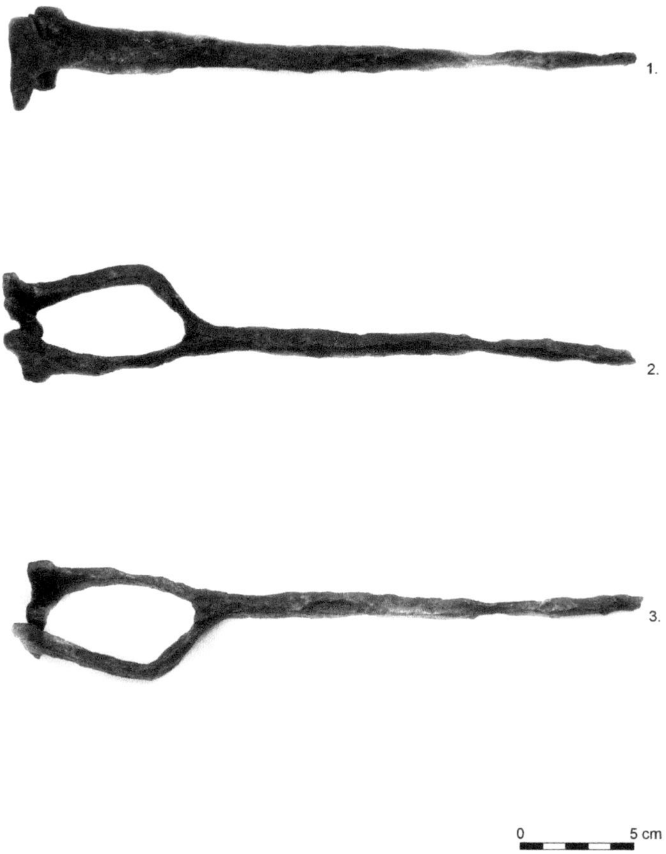

Pl. III: Photos after the restoration process of the first *signaculum* found at Sutor (*Optatiana*)

of the letters = 3.1–3.4 cm. Three “arms” stretch out from the main rod of the artefact. Despite the fact that only two “arms” were preserved after restoration, we can account for an initial “three arms” morphology based primarily upon the X-ray images taken prior to the restoration process (Pl. II/4–5). Each of the three “arms” ended with a corresponding letter as follows: the first letter, partially preserved, corresponds to the letter “N” as the preserved upper arch of the letter suggests (Pls. II/1–2; IV/3–4); the second letter, also only partially preserved, refers to the letter “M” as the upper right part of preserved part indicates (Pls. II/1–2; IV/3–4); concerning the potential third letter, despite the fact that it was missing, we can presume, with good reasons, that we are dealing with the letter “O”. If this hypothesis is correct, we would be dealing with a *signaculum* bearing the name of

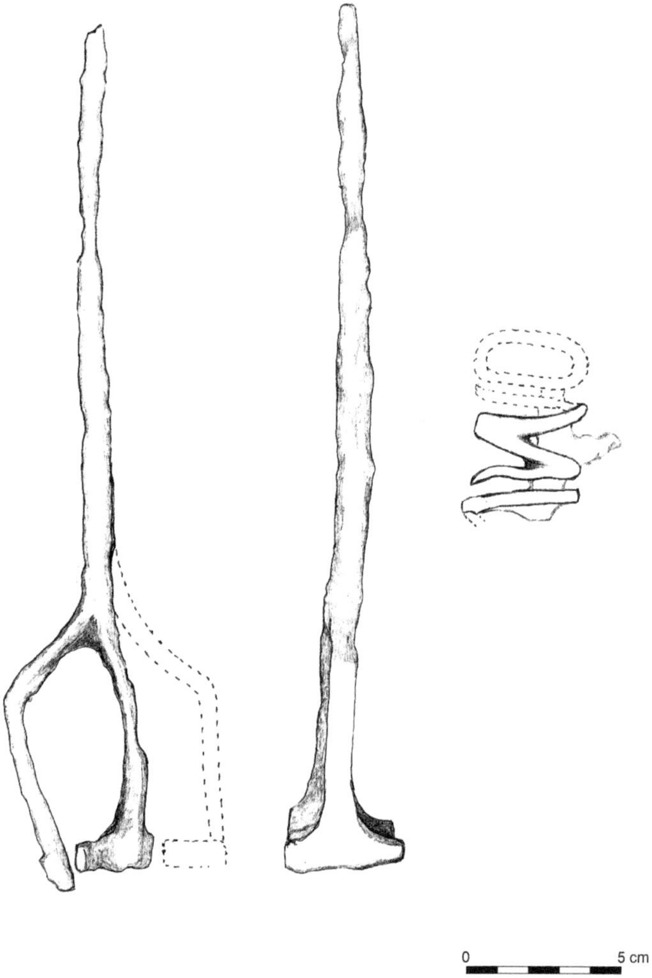

Pl. IV: Drawings of the first *signaculum* found at Sutor (*Optatiana*)

a military unit as other analogies in this respect are well-known,[13] such a reality enabling us to advance the following reading of the text: N(umeri) M(Maurorum) O(ptatianensium),[14] this military unit being attested at Sutor through more than 50 tile stamps recovered during the archaeological excavations or field-walks.[15]

13 Isac 1991, 60–61= Isac 2001, 78–79; Baratta 2007, 106.

14 Cociş 2021, 440.

15 Cociş, Onofrei 2019, 87. The tilestamps at Sutor will be published in a future paper that is currently in preparation.

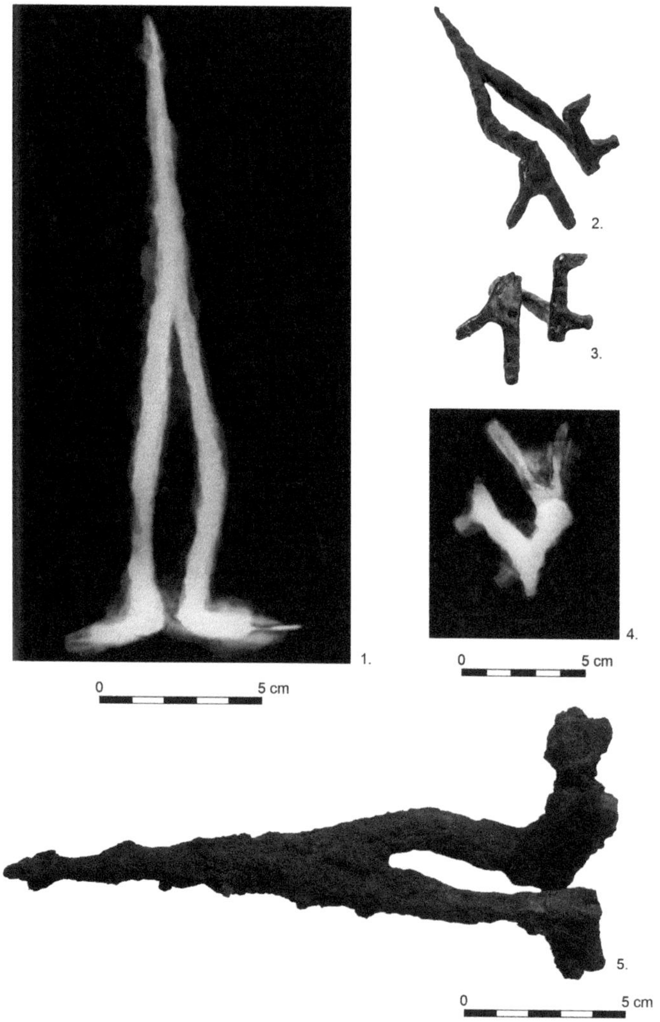

Pl. V: The second discovered *signaculum* found at Sutor (*Optatiana*): 1. X-ray of the artefact; 2–4. Phots and X-ray of the inscription; 5. Photo prior to the restoration process (pictures 2–3 made by S. Odenie, MNIT).

The second *signaculum* is also forged from a single iron bar,[16] its dimensions being: height = 16.7 cm; width = 5.8 cm; length of arms = 9.5 cm; rod thickness = 1.1 cm; thickness of the letters = 0.51 cm; height of the letters = 3.4–4 cm. Although not as certain as in the

16 The artefact was found in S2B-B4/2022, small find no. 362, context 1188.

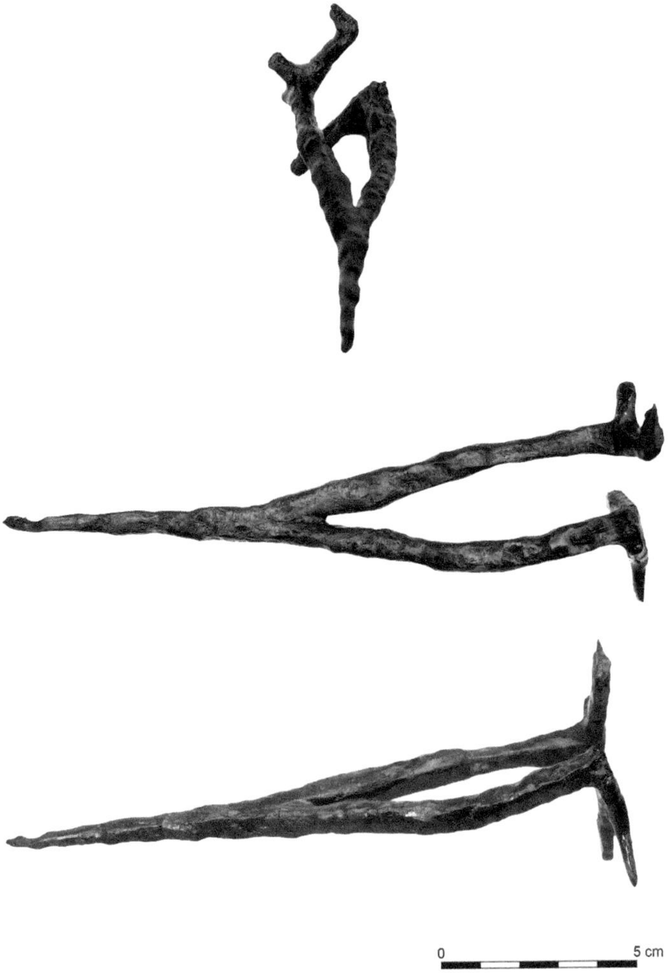

Pl. VI: Photos after the restoration process of the second *signaculum* found at Sutor (*Optatiana*) (pictures made by S. Odenie, MNIT)

first case, we cannot rule out the possibility that, as in the previous case, the *signaculum* would have initially had three "arms", one of these arms being broken since Antiquity (Pl. V/1, 5). Both preserved "arms" ended with corresponding letters, the outer "arm" had what seems to be the letter "V", while the central "arm" was ending probably with the

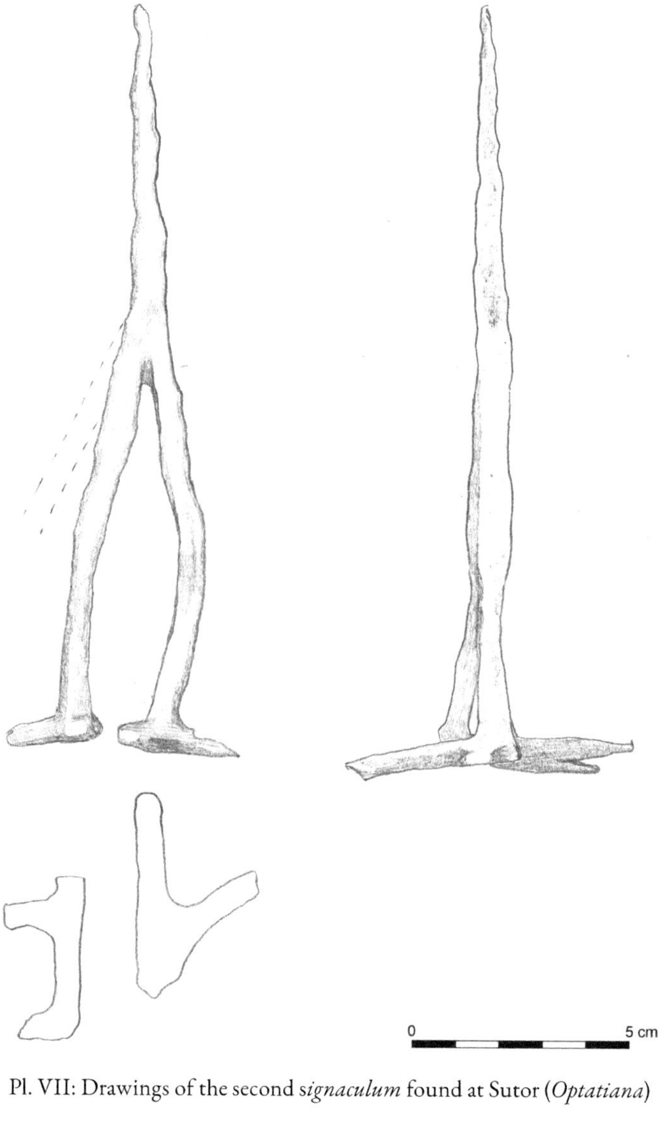

Pl. VII: Drawings of the second *signaculum* found at Sutor (*Optatiana*)

letter "F" or possibly "E" (Pls. V/2–4), a similar combination of letters ("V" + "E") being also known from a *signaculum* discovered at Caşeiu.[17]

17 Isac 1991, 59 = Isac 2001, 77; Abb. 3/1.

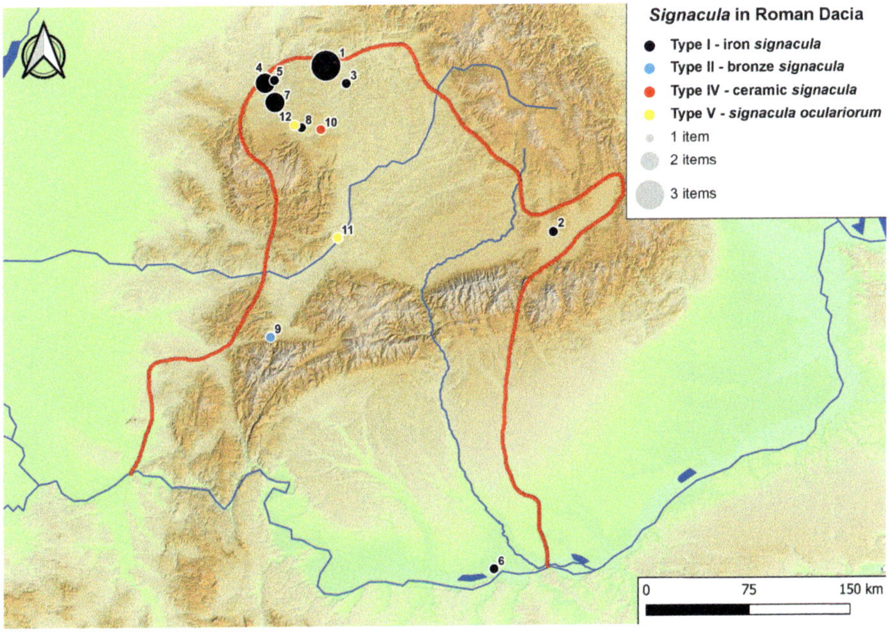

Pl. VIII: Map of the *signacula* found in Roman Dacia

Both *signacula* discovered at Sutor were found in archaeological features that can be dated during the first half of the 3rd century AD.[18] From a typological perspective, both items belong to D Isac's Ist type, being probably used for cattle branding without excluding, based on the archaeological literature, their use in branding also softer materials made of leather, wood or tiles/bricks for example.[19] Following D. Isac's attempt at establishing a unitary typology for the *signacula* in Dacia, we can add new discoveries to his typology and thus create also new types such as: type III including *signacula* made of lead,[20] type IV encompassing ceramic *signacula*, such an artefact being known from Dacia at *Napoca*,[21] or type V including the category of *signacula oculariorum* made usually of stone and having a parallelepipedal shape being inscribed on all faces, two such artefacts being known from Dacia, at Apulum and Gârbou (Sălaj County).[22]

Coming back to the topic of *signacula ferrea* in Roman Dacia, we must emphasize the high number of such artefacts, compared to other neighboring provinces. A number of

18 Sutor 2021, vicus, S2, Small finds nr. 162, context 1046.; Sutor 2022, vicus S2, B4, Small finds nr. 362, context 1188.

19 Isac 1991, 59–60 = Isac 2001, 73–74.

20 So far, no such artefact is known in Dacia.

21 Rusu Bolindeţ 2007, 43, pl. XIII/5.

22 Bologa 1933–1935, 219–222.

14 items are known coming especially from military centers, but also from civilian settlements (Pl. VIII). Compared with the total number of similar items known from the Roman Empire (65 ex.), Dacia is quite well represented, a reality highlighting the fact that the province was fully integrated into the Roman culture and civilization.

Catalogue of *signacula ferrea* in Roman Dacia:

Căşeiu (*Samum*); No. of items: 3 ex.; Complex type: Roman fort; Text: "... EV", "ALN" and "SED"; Chronology: first half of the 3rd century AD; References: Isac 1991, 64, cat nos. 1–3, fig, 5/1–3.

Feldioara; No. of items: 1 ex.; Complex type: Roman fort; Text: "... CN"; Chronology: unknown; References: Isac 1991, 64, cat no. 5, fig, 4/5.

Gherla; No. of items: 1 ex.; Complex type: Roman fort; Text: "... AM"; Chronology: unknown; References: Isac 1991, 64 , cat no. 4, fig, 5/4.

Porolissum; No. of items: 2 ex.; Complex type: unknown; Text: "D ..." and "P ..."; Chronology: unknown; References: Isac 1991, 64, cat. no. 6; Gudea 1996, 244, p. LXII/5.

Romita; No. of items: 1 ex.; Complex type: Roman fort; Text: "XP ..."; Chronology: unknown; References: Matei, Bajusz 1997, 126, pl. LXXV/1.

Sucidava; No. of items: 1 ex.; Complex type: unknown; Text: "AEM"; Chronology: unknown; References: Isac 1991, 64, cat no. 8, fig. 4/8.

Sutor (*Optatiana*); No. of items: 2 ex.; Complex type: *vicus militaris*; Text: "NM ..." and "VE ..."; Chronology: first half of the 3rd century AD; References: Cociş 2021, 440, pl. II–IV.

Viştea; No. of items: 1 ex.; Complex type: Roman villa; Text: "NP ..."; Chronology: unknown; References: Isac 1991, 64, cat no. 7, fig. 4/7.

Bibliography

Baratta, G. 2004. Nota su un ferro per marcare (signaculum) del Museo Archeologico di Spalato, in C. Ciongradi, R. Ardevan, C. Roman, C. Găzdac (eds), Orbis Antiquus. Studia in Honorem Ioannis Pisonis, Cluj-Napoca, 189–190.

Baratta, G. 2007. Una particolare categoria di signacula: Marchi per legno, pellame ed animali, in Acta XII Congressus Internationalis Epigraphiae Graecae et Latinae Barcelona 2002, MonogrSecció Hist.-Arqueológica 10, Barcelona, 99–108.

Baratta, S. 2014. Tre signacula bronzei dalle Isole Baleari (Menorca e Mallorca), Sylloge Epigraphica Barcinonensis XII, 181–192.

Bologa, V. L. 1933–1935. Interpretarea medicală a celor două ştampile de oculişti din Dacia Superioară, Anuarul Institutului de Studii Clasice 2, 219–222.

Braito, S. 2018. Nuovi signacula ex aere dal mercato antiquario online (parte 3), Sylloge Epigraphica Barcinonensis XVI, 265–279.

Burger, A. Sz. 1987. The Roman Villa and Mausoleum at Kővágószőlős, near Pécs (Sopianae), Excavations 1977–1982, Janus Pannonius Múzeum Évkönyve 30–31, 65–229.
Cvijetić, J. Lj. 2015. Roman Hoard of Iron Objects – Notae from the Upper Moesian Limes Roman Hoard of Iron Objects, in L. F. Vagalinski, N. Sharankov (eds.), LIMES XXII Proceedings of the 22nd International Congress of Roman Frontier Studies Ruse, Bulgaria, September 2012, Sofia, 812–824.
Cociş, S. 2021. Un nou signaculum din Dacia romană, Cercetări Arheologice 28, 2, 439–446.
Cociş, S., Lăzărescu, V. A., Socaciu, S. T. 2021. Cercetările arheologice din castrul și vicusul de la Sutor (2001–2021), Cercetări Arheologice 28, 2, 83–130.
Cociş, S., Lăzărescu, V. A., Socaciu, S, T. 2021a. An Overview of the Archaeological Research in the Roman Fort and Vicus at Sutor (Sălaj County), Ehemeris Napocensis XXXI, 223–258.
Cociş, S., Onofrei, C. 2019. Cohors I Brittonum on a tile stamp found at Sutoru, in I. G. Farkas, R. Neményi, M. Szabó (eds.), Artificem commendat opus. Studia in honorem Zsolt Visy, Pécs, 87–93.
Desbat, A. 1991. Un buchón de bois du 1er s. aprés J.-C. recueilli dans la Saóne á Lyon et la question du tonneau á l'époque romaine, Gallia 48, 319–333.
Feugère, M., Mauné, S. 2005. Les signacula de bronze en Gaule Narbonnaise, Revue archéologique de Narbonnaise 38–39, 437–455.
Feugère, M. 2020. Signacula ex aere: épigraphie et matérialité, Le Fil d'ArAr 19/08/2020, https://lefildarar.hypotheses.org/3811.
Gaitzsch, W. 1980. Eiserne Romische Werkzeuge: Studien zur roemischen Werkzeugkunde in Italien und den noerdlichen Provinzen des Imperium Romanum, British Archaeological Reports International Series 78, Oxford.
Garbsch, J. 1970. Eisenfunde aus Eining, Bayerische Vorgeschiteblatter 35, 105–112.
Gherasimov, T. 1959. Anciens outils de fer á marquer, Bulletin de L'Institut Archéologique Bulgare XXII, 339–342.
Gudea, N. 1996. Porolissum. Vama romană, monografie arheologică, Cluj-Napoca.
IDR III/6 1999. Inscripţiile Daciei romane (Inscripţiile antice din Dacia şi Scythia Minor, eria primă), Vol. III: Dacia Superior 6. Apulum – Instrumentum Domesticum, (adunate, însoţite de comentarii şi indice, traduse de C. L. Băluţă), Bucureşti.
IDR App. I 2016. Piso, I., Deac, D. 2016. Inscriptiones Daciae Romanae. Appendix I – Inscriptiones laterum Musei Zilahensis, Cluj-Napoca.
IDR App. II 2016. Piso, I., Marcu, F. 2016. Inscriptiones Daciae Romanae. Appendix II Inscriptiones laterum Musei Napocensis, Cluj-Napoca.
IDR App. III 2016. Piso, I., Ardeţ, A., Timoc, C. 2019. Inscriptiones Daciae Romanae Appendix III Inscriptiones laterum museorum Banatus Temesiensis, Cluj-Napoca.
IIL I. Instrumenta inscripta Latina-Gesellschaftliche und wirtschaftliche Probleme des Romischen Reiches im Spiegel der Gelegenheits und reproduzierte Inschriften, Specimina Nova VII, 1, 1991 (1992).
IIL II. Instrumenta inscripta latina II. M. Hainzmann, R. Wedenig (eds.) 2008. Akten des 2. internationalen Kolloquiums, Klagenfurt, 5.-8. Mai 2005, Vol. 2, Klagenfurt.

IIL III. Instrumenta inscripta III. G. Baratta, S. M. Marengo (eds.) 2012. Manufatti iscritti e vita dei santuari in età romana, Macerata.
IIL V. Instrumenta Inscripta V. A. Buonopane, S. Braito (eds.) 2014. Signacula ex aere: aspetti epigrafici, archeologici, giuridici, prosopografici, collezionistici, Atti del convegno internazionale (Verona, 20–21 settembre 2012), Roma.
IIL VI. Instrumenta inscripta VI. M. Buora, S. Magnani (eds.) 2016. Le iscrizioni con funzione didascalicoesplicativa, Atti del VI Incontro Instrumenta Inscripta (Aquileia, 26–28 marzo 2015), Antichità Altoadriatiche 83.
IIL VIII. Instrumenta inscripta VIII Plumbum litteratum. G. Baratta (ed.) 2021. Studia epigrafica Giovanni Mennella oblate, Scienze e lettere, Roma.
Isac, D. 1991. Signacula aus Dakien, Saalburg-Jahrbuch 46, 57–64.
Isac, D. 2001. Signacula aus Dakien, in D. Isac, Viaţă cotidiană în castrele Daciei Porolissensis, Cluj-Napoca, 70–78.
Klumbach, H. 1953. Pferde mit Brandmarken, Festschrift des Römisch-Germanischen Zentralmuseums in Mainz zur Feier seines hundertjährigen Bestehens 1952, Band 3, 1–12.
Krier, J. 2007. Ein Eisenhortfund der frühen Kaiserzeit aus Goeblingen-‚Miecher', Den Ausgriewer – D'Zeitung vun D'Georges Kayser Altertumsfuerscher 17, 18–22.
Matei, A., Bajusz, I. 1997. Castrul roman de la Romita-Certiae – Das Römergrenzkastell von Romita, Zalău.
Mezquíriz Irujo, M. A. 2007–2008. Instrumentos de hierro para la explotación agropecuaria en época romana, Trabajos de arqueología Navarra 20, 197–208.
Petcu, R., Petcu Levei I. 2021. A Roman bronzes stamp (signaculum ex aere) from Dumbrăveni (Romania) – Moesia Inferior, in S. C. Ailincăi, G. Nuțu, C. Micu, M. Mocanu, A. D. Stănică (eds.), Studii de arheologie și istorie antică în onoarea lui Victor Henrich Baumann cu ocazia celei de a 80-a aniversări, Cluj-Napoca, 335–348.
Pfahl, St. F. 2012. Instrumenta latinae et graecae inscriptae des Limesgebietes von 200 v. Chr. bis 600 n. Chr., Weinstadt.
Pietsch, M. 2000. Ein römischer Viehbrennstempel aus Straubing, Jahresbericht des Historischen Vereins für Straubing und Umgebung, 297–301.
Ronke, J. 2015. Frühes 'Branding the cattle' – Brandmarken für Pferde, Fundberichte aus Baden-Württemberg 35, 371–387.
Rusu-Bolindeț, V. 2007. Ceramica romană de la Napoca. Contribuții la studiul ceramicii din Dacia romană, Cluj-Napoca.
Socaciu, S. T., Lăzărescu, V. A., Cociș, S. 2023. Cercetări arheologice din vicus-ul de la Sutor. Campania 2022, Cercetări Arheologice 30, 1, 85–108.
Spitzelberger, G. 1968. Die rómischen Zielegstempel im nordlichen Teil der Provinz Raetien, Saalburg Jahrbuch 25, 65–184.
Teichner, F., Dürr, R. 2021. Eine römische Eisenwarenhandlung in der dardanischen Bergbaustadt Ulpiana (Moesia Superior), in E. C. Leger, S. Raux (eds.), Des objets et des hommes. Etudes offertes à Michel Feugère, Paris.
Visy, Z. 1977. Intercisa. A római kori Dunaújváros, Budapest.

The worlds of the Living and the Dead – same offerings. An upsidedown perspective from Colonia Dacica Sarmizegetusa

Ovidiu Țentea, Cristian Găzdac, Vitalie Bârcă

The discovery of an offering in Sarmizegetusa's Eastern necropolis from 2018 has given us the chance to revisit the conversation about the importance of placing oblations at Sarmizegetusa. Surprisingly, the offering that has been found nearby a funerary enclosure is almost identical to one discovered in 1932 in a completely different context, close to Trajan's Forum. Our presentation will focus on a comparative analysis of these two findings. Additionally, we will explore two other similar discoveries from Sarmizegetusa to provide contextual analysis.

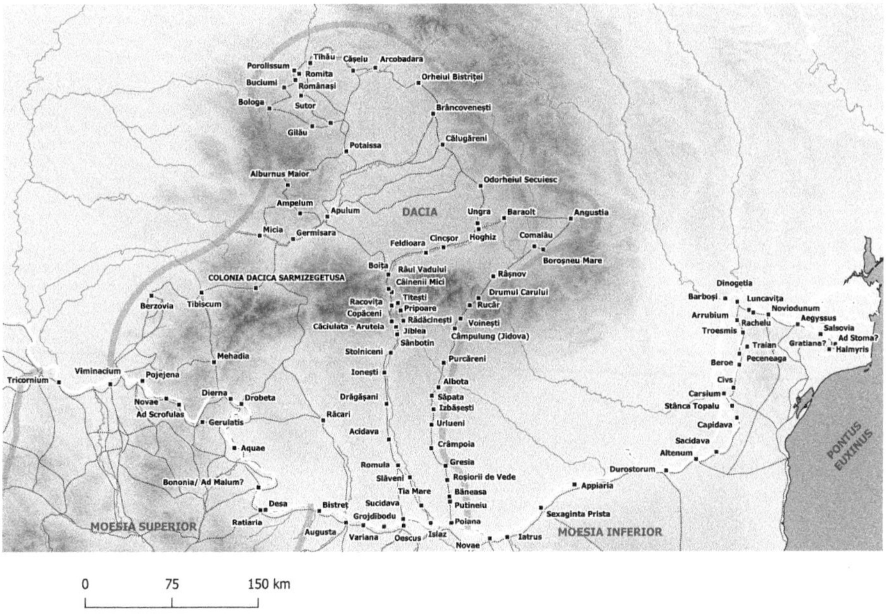

Fig. 1: Map of Roman Dacia

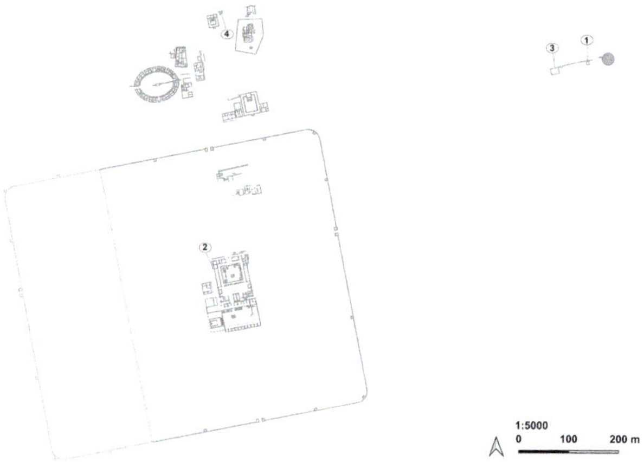

Fig. 2: Colonia Dacica Sarmizegetusa, pointing out the location of the four offerings

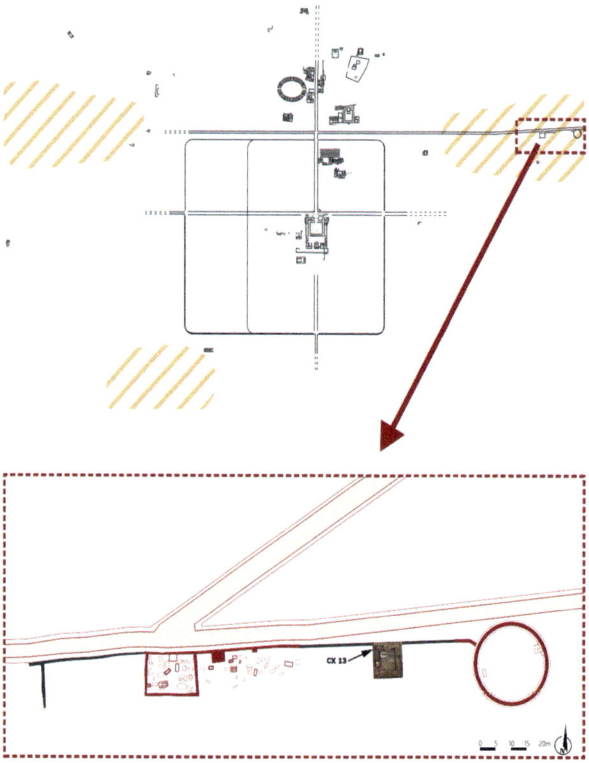

Fig. 3: Colonia Dacica Sarmizegetusa, The plan of the investigations in the eastern necropolis and their location

Fig. 4a: The funerary precinct 2, view from north, on the imperial road
Fig. 4b: Detail on the offering found near precinct 2 in 2018

Fig. 4c: The layout of tiles and gutter tiles in which the offerings was placed

Archaeological research within the Eastern necropolis of the *colonia* have been conducted during various periods: 1934[1], 1982–1984[2], 2001–2008[3] and continuously from 2017 until the present day. In 1934, Constantin Daicoviciu and Octavian Floca discovered the structure known as the *Mausoleum of the Aurelii*. Archaeological digs carried out between 1982 and 1984 explored a burial area situated 80 meters South of the imperial road, facing enclosing structure A. The excavations in the Eastern necropolis undertaken from 2001 to 2008 in the immediate vicinity of the Sarmizegetusa-Ostrov communal

1 Daicoviciu, Floca 1937, 1–27.

2 Allen 1993, 397–400.

3 Egri 2004; Țentea, Egri 2018, 44–47.

road, which largely overlaps with the imperial road, took place at the point called *La Cireş*. Since 2017, ongoing research have occurred in the space located between funerary enclosure A and the so-called *Mausoleum of the Aurelii*.

Archaeological excavations carried out in 2018 resulted in the discovery and examination of a rectangular funerary enclosure (6.25 m × 3.90/4 m), located South of the imperial road. Specifically, within the limits of this enclosure, two cremation graves were ascertaining – one contained a numismatic artifact, specifically a coin identified as an *as*, minted during the reign of Trajan. Both graves were looted in Antiquity[4].

The offering examined in this study (CX 13) was deposited in a ceramic vessel with a lid, over which a small structure made of bricks and tiles was constructed. The arrangement had a rectangular shape (0.7 × 0.40 m) and was situated on the outside, along the Western wall of the enclosure, in close proximity to the imperial road. Three sides of the structure were constructed using bricks arranged in a corner pattern, while the roof was composed of tiles and clay shingles.

Inside the urn (3), six intact bronze coins and one fragmented coin (1) were discovered, along with seven lamps (2), three small fragments of human bones, and two fragmented bones from a small animal.

Subsequently, we will undertake a precise analysis of these discoveries.

1 The Coins

Group of six coins stuck together found beside seven clay lamps. All placed in a ceramic vessel. It must be mentioned here that at the time of discovery a seventh coin was already in a total state of damage – a thick layer of green oxide – therefore, it could not be catalogued or illustrated.

1. Trajan

Nominal: as
Axis: 6; D: 26.6 × 24.7 mm; G: 9.87 gr.

4 Bârcă, Ţentea 2019, 177–181.

Mint: Rome
Dating: 108–110
Obverse: [IMP CAES NERVAE TRAI]ANO A[VG GER DAC P M TR P COS V P P]
Bust of Trajan, laureate, draped on left shoulder, right.
Reverse: [s p q r optimo princi]PI; [S] – C
Abundantia, draped, standing left, holding two corn-ears in right hand over *modius* with corn-ears left, and *cornucopia* in left hand; to right, prow of ship.
Reference: RIC II, 492; MIR 14, 325b.

2. Hadrian

Nominal: as
Axis: 6; D: 25.9 mm; G: 8.99 gr.
Mint: Rome
Dating: 126–127
Obverse: [hadria]NVS [augustus p p]
Head of Hadrian, laureate, right.
Reverse: legend illegible; S – C
Salus standing right, rarely leaning on column, holding a snake and feeding it from a *patera*.
Reference: RIC II.3, 881.

3. Antoninus Pius

Nominal: as
Axis: 12; D: 25.5 mm; G: 10.08 gr.
Mint: Rome
Dating: 140–144
Obverse: [antoninus aug pi]VS P P TR P [cos iii]
Head of Antoninus Pius, laureate, right.
Reverse: [annona au]G; S – C
Annona, draped, standing right, holding two corn-ears in the right hand over *modius* and corn-ears and cornucopia in left; at feet right, prow right.
Reference: RIC III, 675.

4. Antoninus Pius

Nominal: as
Axis: 12; D: 25,5 mm; G: 10,08 gr.
Mint: Rome
Dating: 148–149
Obverse: ANTONINVS AVG – PIVS P P TR P XII
Head of Antoninus Pius, laureate, right.
Reverse: FELICITAS AVG; S – C; COS IIII (exergue)
Felicitas, draped, standing front, head right, holding a long *caduceus*, vertical, in right hand and corn-ears in fold of robe in left.
Reference: RIC III, 860A.

5. Antoninus Pius: Marcus Aurelius (Caesar)

Nominal: as
Axis: 10; D: 26.3 × 24.2 mm; G: 10.79 gr.
Mint: Rome
Dating: 155–156
Obverse: AVRELIVS CAES – [anton] AVG [pii f]
Head of Marcus Aurelius, right.
Reverse: TR POT X – [cos ii]; S – C
Pietas standing, left with right hand dropping incense on a *candelabrum* and holding a box in left hand.
Reference: RIC III, 1333.

6. Antoninus Pius: Faustina II (Augusta)

Nominal: as/dupondius
Axis: 7; D: 26 mm; G: 12.57 gr.
Mint: Rome
Dating: 145–161
Obverse: FAVSTINA – A[ugusta]
Bust of Faustina the Younger, draped, left, hair is elaborately dressed in horizontal lines with ringlets down front: it is coiled in a chignon on back of the head.
Reverse: AVGVSTI – P-II FIL; S C (exergue)

Salus seated left, feeding out of *patera* in right hand snake coiled round altar and holding sceptre in left.
Reference: RIC III, 1391.

2 Lamps

All the lamps are small, with a single burner (*monolychnis*), made of yellowish-brick-coloured paste. Without exception, they display signs of burning on the interior and around the burner area, indicating prior use before being placed in the lidded vessel. Among them, six specimens are miniature medallion lamps of Loeschcke type VIII, and one is a *firmalampen* Loeschke X.

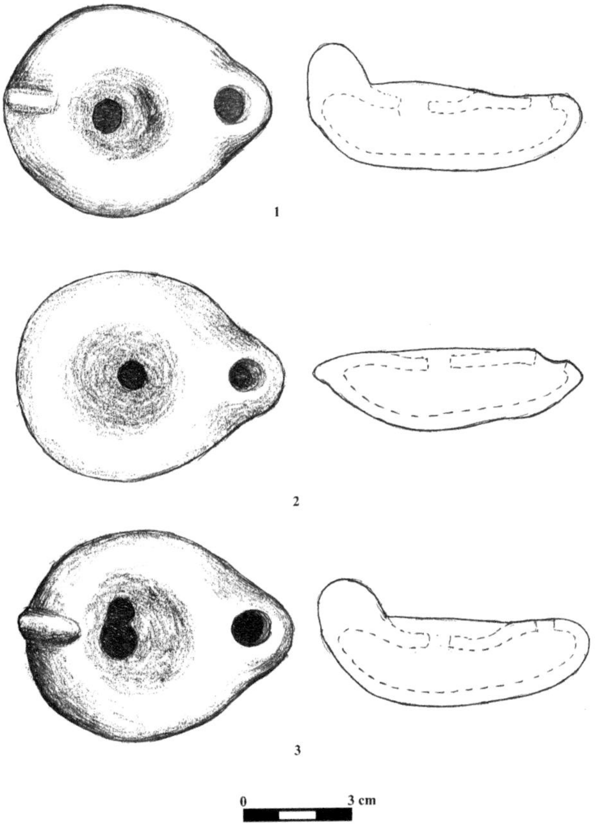

Fig. 5a: Lamps of the offering, drawing 1–3

As suggested by the discs sections, these were likely initially adorned with certain figures or decorations that resulted from wear and repeated duplication over time. There are few examples of type VIII lamps without decoration. The most significant analogies come from the deposition in front of the cult building of the deities *Domnus* and *Domna* at Sarmizegetusa. This deposition comprises nine sets, each featuring a small lamp and a small drinking vessel, placed at the entrance of the temple. The fired clay lamps are medallion lamps, classified as Loeschcke type VIII, and are predominantly well-preserved.[5]

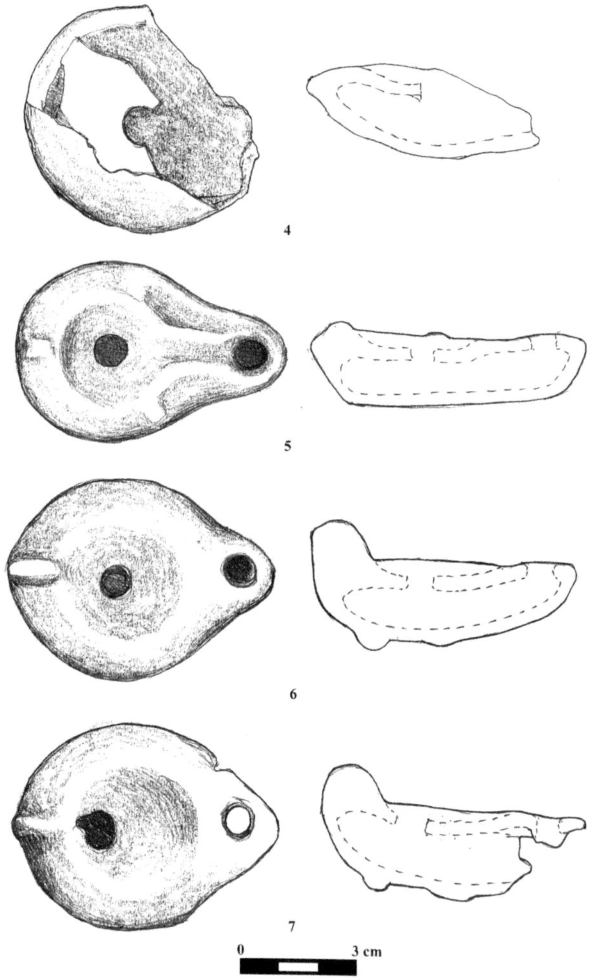

Fig. 5b: Lamps of the offering, drawing 4–7

5 Fiedler, Höpken 2005, 317–320; Fiedler, Höpken 2008, 199- 214, Abb. 9, 12 a, b; Isac, Roman 2006, 54, nr. 82; Roman 2017, 47–54.

3 The vessel

The vessel in which the deposition occurred was crafted on a wheel using a semi-fine greyish paste. It takes the form of a pot with a short, flared rim, a prominently rounded upper body, well-defined shoulders, and a flat bottom. It has a height of approximately 25.7 cm, with a mouth diameter of 23.7 cm and a bottom diameter of 14 cm (fig. 8). The pot closely resembles certain examples associated with Popilian types 2 and 3, representing a prevalent form during the 2nd–3rd centuries AD.[6]

The primary focus of the analysis revolves around the symbolism and message depicted on the reverse side of the seven coins, considering the context of their discovery inside a funerary environment. Furthermore, the examination aims to discern the significance of these symbols and messages to the individual who intentionally placed the coins alongside the lamps in the pot. The temporal span of the issuers, namely Trajan to Antoninus Pius, might be considered as a secondary factor indicating a tentative timeframe for the discovery, which would be during or after the most recent coin issuing date (AD 155–156) (coin no. 5.).

During the Roman imperial era, the coins were produced under the authority of the imperial house and certain local governing bodies. These local authorities were granted permission by the emperor to issue provincial coins. The primary purpose of these coins was to convey a message that aligned with the official image that the governing authority sought to promote among the citizens.

It has been demonstrated that the imperial imagery penetrated into private contexts through coins.[7] If the issuer, as the governing authority, was intentionally conveying a carefully crafted message to the receptor, who is the user of the coin, it is inherent in human nature that the latter may interpret this message and the picture based on their own perspectives regarding many areas of personal life. The issue of personal perspective surrounding the distribution of coins featuring symbols of imperial power during times of crisis has already been pointed out.[8] Similarly, it appears that the coin offerings within the sanctuaries have seen an intentional selection of reverse types to some degree.[9]

In relation to the analysis of coin symbolism within an eschatological framework and beyond, Cl. Perassi has proposed that certain types of coins found in funerary contexts may carry a message associated with various aspects of the funerary ritual. Perassi suggests that individuals may have perceived the imagery on these coins as symbolic representations of their desires for the afterlife.[10] The scholar's approach to the currency user's level of alphabetization offers a noteworthy component of special interest. By integrating both literary and epigraphic sources, Cl. Perassi presents evidence to support the argument

6 Popilian 1976.
7 Howgego 1995, 74.
8 Manders 2007, 281–284.
9 Kaczynski, Nüsse 2009, 93–107.
10 Perassi 1999, 57–68.

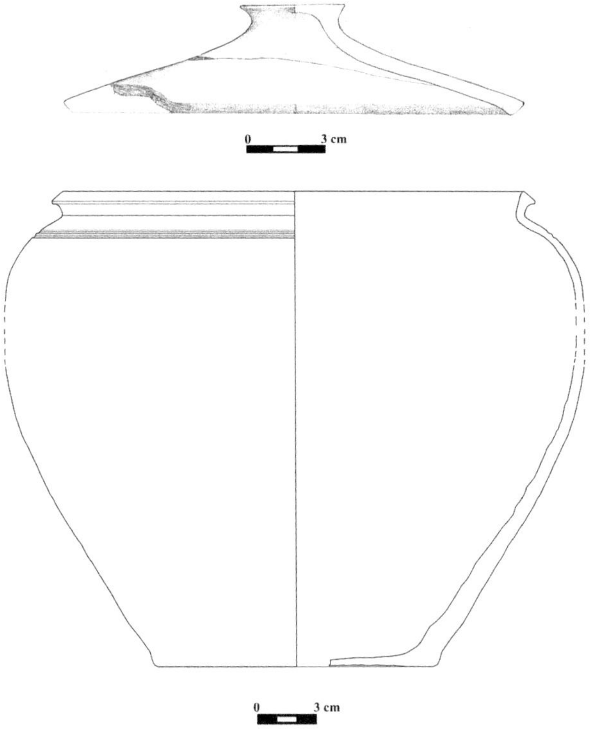

Fig. 6: The offering's vessel

that throughout Roman times, possessing a rudimentary degree of literacy may have been advantageous, but not necessarily obligatory, for individuals intending to utilize coins as offerings.[11]

In certain instances of coin offerings, it becomes evident that the individual responsible for placing the coin within a grave has merged the textual inscription found on the coin with the visual representation portrayed on its reverse side. Conversely, the coins were exclusively chosen based on their depictions that were deemed symbolic of specific ideals and features pertaining to the afterlife.[12]

By employing the approach developed by Cl. Perassi, which involves integrating numismatic elements like design, symbols, and legends with literary and epigraphic sources, it is possible to gain a deeper understanding of the eschatological beliefs held by individuals inside Roman society. This can be achieved by examining the discovery of coins within burial sites.

11 Perassi 1999, 48–52.
12 Perassi 1999, 57–68.

The imagery of the coins under study are referring directly to the moment of passing into the afterlife.

Two of the coins display the iconography of Salus in different positions on the reverse side (coin catalogue nos. 2. 6). The inclusion of Salus on coins within a funerary context should be seen not as a representation of bodily well-being but as a symbol of a benevolent aspiration for salvation.[13] The occurrence of Salus numismatic reverse types in burial sites is a commonly observed phenomenon resulting from the intersection of extensive coin minting practices and the prevailing concern for spiritual salvation.[14]

One coin depicts on revers *Pietas* standing, left with right hand dropping incense on candelabrum and holding box in left hand (catalogue no. 5). This reverse type is included in the category of personifications of benevolent wishes/attitudes in the afterlife.[15] The same eschatological symbolism can be attributed to *Felicitas* (cat. no. 4) considered to be one of the most predominant personifications amongst the benevolent wishes.[16]

The reverse side of the two remaining coins features the personifications of Abundantia (catalogue no. 1) and Annona (catalogue no. 3). H. Nibley posits that these coins may have originated from private *sparsiones*, which involve the act of throwing items as a form of donation.[17] These *sparsiones* took place at ceremonial events that commemorate significant life transitions within a family,[18] including the event of death.[19] However, if we look at the entire assembly of the six coins and the reverse imagery one can easily note that we have a set of benevolent wishes for the dead in the afterlife: *Salus* (well-being), *Pietas* (piety/devotion), *Felicitas* (luck/happiness), *Abundantia* (prosperity), *Annona* (means of subsistence).

The regular placement of lamps in burial sites served to provide *lux perpetua*, or the essential illumination for an underworld journey.[20]

One potential reason in support of this claim is the observation that the seven lamps, which are situated beside the coins in the depicted image, appear to be unused (Fig. 7). The absence of residue near the nozzles is commonly seen as evidence that certain lamps discovered in burial sites were never ignited. Consequently, this observation supports the hypothesis that these lamps were bestowed upon the deceased as symbolic farewell offerings, intended to provide light for their journey to the realm of the underworld.[21] Moreover, the concern for the welfare of the deceased in the afterlife places significant emphasis on the essentiality of light. The lamps would illuminate the darkness of death, the *lux perpetua* of paradise.[22]

---

13 Perassi 1999, 66.
14 Găzdac 2014, 99.
15 Perassi 1999, 58–59, 64.
16 Perassi 1999, 59.
17 Nibley 1945, 516.
18 Nibley 1945, 516.
19 Găzdac 2014, 101.
20 Alföldy-Găzdac 2018, 57.
21 Şöföroğlu, Summerer 2016, 264,
22 Toynbee 1971, 279; Philpott 1991, 192.

The coins serve as a manifestation of the altruistic desires directed towards deceased individuals. The archaeological evidence suggests a recurring correlation between lamps and coins in graves, often with the coin positioned on the lamp's disk.[23] However, the coexistence of seven lamps and seven coins within a single vessel, albeit one coin being totally destroyed by the time of its discovery, raises the possibility of a certain religious or ritualistic significance, as indicated by the presence of human and animal bones.

The most suitable comparison, and the sole one presently known to us, for this discovery originates from a location approximately 600 meters southwest. In the year 1932, a cooking pot with a lid, exhibiting a blackish-grey colour, was unearthed at the Western periphery of the Roman Forum (*Aedes Augustalium*, as it was referred to at that time). The pot was found at a depth of 0.80m. The vessel contained a total of seven clay lamps and an equivalent number of bronze coins, specifically *asses*.[24] (Fig. 7).

Similar to the previously mentioned coins, these seven pieces consist of asses and also ranging from Trajan to Antoninus Pius.[25] At the same time, the coins' reverse visual representation bears striking resemblance to the aforementioned beneficent aspirations for the deceased in the afterlife namely *Abundantia* (3), *Salus*, and *Spes* (Hope). One coin depicts on reverse Iuppiter, seated left, holding Victory.[26] The inclusion of Iuppiter on the coin imagery within funerary context has been seen as a symbol of protection.[27] Regrettably, the presence or absence of additional materials or remains within this vessel has not been specified.

At the first sight, one could seek for a connection between this votive offering and the grandiose Roman architectural complex next to it. Recent academic inquiries have provided insight on the discovery that the area in the Forum (south-eastern corner of the *forum*) near which the vessel storing a set of seven lamps and seven coins was found was associated with the *Aedes Fortunae*.[28]

One potential reason for the correlation between the seven lamps and seven coins could be rooted in the belief that the deceased soul continues to exist in an eternal celestial realm, symbolized by the seven known planets or stars – during the Principate, a planetary association was assigned to each day of the seven-day week.[29] As F. Cumont stated, the great Whole, inhabited by the society of the living and the countless souls of past generations, is conceived as a closed vessel, the outer wall of which is the sphere of fixed stars, where those of the seven planets fit together, and, lower, under the zones of air and vapours in perpetual movement, the immobile terrestrial globe is the stable point

23 Alföldy-Găzdac 2018, 310, 342.

24 Floca 1935, 17–22; Daicoviciu 1938, 407, Fig. 52; 413; Daicoviciu, Daicoviciu 1966, 93, no. 69; Winkler 1975, 120, no. 20; Găzdac, Cociş 2004, 16, 42; https://chre.ashmus.ox.ac.uk/hoard/2593 (accessed on october 18, 2023).

25 https://chre.ashmus.ox.ac.uk/hoard/2593 (accessed on October 18, 2023).

26 https://chre.ashmus.ox.ac.uk/hoard/2593 (accessed on October 18, 2023).

27 Perassi 1999, 54.

28 IDR III/2, 210. Piso, Țentea forthcoming.

29 Bultrighini 2021, 217–240.

around which the entire celestial machine revolves.[30] On this line, a sensitive example is mentioned by the same scholar, a Roman bas-relief from the Copenhagen Museum shows us the sideways busts of a brother and a sister, and the effigy of the little girl is placed on a large crescent and surrounded by seven stars, images of the planets. This motif obviously alludes to the belief that the moon is the abode of innocent souls, like that of this unknown child.[31]

Fig. 7: The ceramic vessel containing seven lamps and seven coins found in 1932 westward of the forum of Ulpia Traiana Sarmizegetusa (after Floca 1935, 18, fig. 1)

Interestingly, within the vessel originating from the eastern necropolis of Ulpia Traiana Sarmizegetusa, a fortuitous discovery was made. It was observed that among the human skeletal remains, there were fragments attributed to individuals of varying age groups, specifically a newborn, a young adult, and an adult.

The epigraphic evidence suggests that *malum astrum* (evil star)[32] may be the cause of premature death.[33] Within the funerary context, Antolini has postulated that celestial terms through "their broad connotation unites in a choral lament not only parents and children, but also and above all, the deceased and the living, those who are gone and those who remain for a short while".[34] The belief in somehow immortality was that the seven planets symbolized the lunar cycle, an astral image of rebirth, because every month it disappears, to then reappear again and grow in splendour.[35]

One of Ausonius' epitaphs just does not let us forget that: "*...perpetuum mihi ver agit inlacrimabilis urna/et commutavi saecula, non obii*" [Tearless my urn enjoys unending spring. I have not died, but changed my state].[36]

Conversely, the placement of the vessel containing seven lamps and seven coins in the *Aedes Fortunae* might carry symbolic significance, particularly for the living. Essentially, it could be interpreted as an *ex-voto* offering. Discovered in a non-funerary context, the

30 Cumont 1949, 6.
31 Cumont 1949, 178, 323.
32 Petronius, 134, 8.
33 Antolini 2009, 861–863.
34 Antolini 2009, 869.
35 Perassi 1999, 58.
36 Epitaphia xxxi – in tumulo hominis felicis, translation Toynbee 1971, 63.

Fig. 8: The gilded silver statuette of Fortuna-Tutela from the hoard of Macon. British Museum: https://www.britishmuseum.org/collection/object/G_1824-0424-1, accessed on November 25, 2023

seven coins, along with the imagery on their reverse sides, implies an expression of benevolence towards the worshiper or an associated individual. Moreover, the inclusion of a coin showcasing Iuppiter suggests a desire for the protection of the supreme god. Within this framework, the seven lamps represent a symbolic manifestation of celestial light, as previously noted.

The occurrence of this *ex-voto* entailing two sets of seven artifacts in an edifice of goddess Fortuna may not be an uncommon phenomenon. An illustrative example is a gilded silver statuette of Fortuna-Tutela found in 1764 in the hoard from Mâcon, France. This statuette potentially mirrors the astrological week. The *poliade* Fortune-Tutela, characterized by two expansive wings, upholds the busts of the seven planets/days and, below them, those of the Dioscuri; these representations essentially depict the movements of the planets and the days of the week, symbolizing the celestial forces that influence a person's destiny, either favourably or unfavourably.[37]

In reflection, the discoveries in Sarmizegetusa's Eastern necropolis reflect a profound continuity between the aspirations of the living and the beliefs surrounding the departed. The intentional selection of benevolent symbols on the coins, echoing desires for prosperity, health, and happiness, underscores an enduring desire for continuity between life and the afterlife. These offerings, encapsulated within a funerary context, transcend mortal boundaries, reflecting a belief that the desires and wishes cherished in life persist into the realm beyond, suggesting an unbroken continuum of hopes and aspirations.

Moreover, the deliberate choice of celestial imagery and the ritualistic placement of lamps and coins within the *Aedes Fortu nae* emphasize an intricate cosmic connection

37 Cumont 1949, 72.

between ancient communities and the metaphysical realm. The unifying concept that benevolent wishes transcend the boundaries of mortality, resonating equally in both worlds of the living and the dead, offers a profound insight into the cultural continuity of desires and beliefs, bridging the gap between human aspirations and the mysteries of the afterlife in ancient Sarmizegetusa.

Bibiography

Alföldy-Găzdac, A. 2018. Charon's Obol. Between Religious Fervour and Daily Life Pragmatism, Cluj-Napoca.

Allen, T. 1993. Interim report on two seasons of excavations of a burial enclosure in the east cemetery of Ulpia Traiana Sarmizegetusa, 1982–1984, Acta Musei Napocensis 26–30, 1/2 (1989–1993), 397–400.

Antolini, S. 2009. Astrosus, astro natus: riflessi epigrafici del tema dell'inesorabilità del giorno fatale, in C. Braidotti, E. Dettori, E. Lanzillotta (eds), OΥ ΠΑΝ ΕΦΗΜΕΡΟΝ. Scritti in memoria di Roberto Pretagostini. Roma, 861–870.

Bârcă, V., Ţentea, O. 2019. Sarmizegetusa, jud. Hunedoara. Ulpia Traiana Sarmizegetusa, Punct: La Cireş – Necropola Estică, Cronica Cercetărilor Arheologice din România, Campania 2018, Bucureşti, 177–181.

Bultrighini, I. 2021. Theōn Hemerai: Astrology, the Planetary Week, and the Cult of the Seven Planets in the Graeco-Roman World, in I. Salvo, T. S. Scheer (eds.) Religion and Education in the Ancient Greek World, Tübingen, 217–240.

Cumont, F. 1949. Lux Perpetua, Paris.

Daicoviciu, C. 1938. Sarmizegetusa (Ulpia Traiana) în lumina săpăturilor, Anuarul Comisiunii Monumentelor istorice. Secţia pentru Transilvania 4, 353–413.

Daicoviciu, C., Floca, O. 1937. Mausoleul Aureliilor de la Sarmizegetusa. Raport preliminar / Das Mausoleum der Aurelier von Sarmizegetusa. Kurze Beschreibung, Sargetia 1, 1–23.

Daicoviciu, C., Daicoviciu, H. 1966. Ulpia Traiana, Bucureşti.

Egri, M. 2004. "Convivio celebrantur amici" : notes on some ceramic assemblages with a funerary character, in: L. Ruscu, C. Ciongradi, R. Ardevan, C. Roman, C. Găzdac (eds.). Orbis antiquus: studia in honorem Ioannis Pisonis, Cluj-Napoca, 502–509.

Fiedler, M., Höpken, C. 2005. Becher und Lampe: weiheigaben von einem Romischen Opfernplatz in Sarmizegetusa, Rei Cretariae Romanae Fautores Acta 39, 317–320

Fiedler, M., Höpken, C. 2008. Rituelle deponierungen im Domnus und Domna-Heiligtum von Sarmizegetusa (Dakien), Mainzer archaologische Schriften Band 10, Mainz, 199- 214.

Floca, O. 1935. Consideraţiuni asupra unor monete barbare-dace. O mică descoperire arheologică la Sarmizegetusa, Deva.

Găzdac, C. 2014. Did Charon read his obol? The message of coin offering in Roman graves from Pannonia, Dacia 58, 95–140.

Găzdac, C., Cociş, S. 2004. Ulpia Traiana Sarmizegetusa. Coins from Roman Sites and Collections of Roman Coins from Romania 1, Cluj-Napoca.

Howgego, Ch. 1995. Ancient history from coins, New York.

Isac, D., Roman, C.A. 2006. Lucernele din castrul de Gilău, in C. Cosma, D. Tamba. A. Rustoiu (eds.), Studia Archaeologica et Historica Nicolao Gudea dicata. Omagiu profesorului Nicolae Gudea la 60 de ani 2001, p. 367–395.

Kaczynski, B., Nüsse, M. 2009. Reverse type selection in sanctuaries? A study of antoniniani found in various contexts, in M. von Kaenel, F. Kemmers (eds.). Coins in context I. New perspectives for the interpretation of coin finds. Studien zu Fundmünzen der Antike 23, Mainz, 93–107.

Loeschcke, S. 1919. Lampen aus Vindonissa. Ein Beitrag zur Geschichte von Vindonissa und des antiken Beleucthungswesens,Zürich.

Manders, E. 2007. Mapping the representation of Roman imperial power in the times of crises, in H. Hekster, G. de Kleijn, D. Slootjes (ed.) Crises in the Roman Empire. Proceedings of the Seventh Workshop of the International Network Impact of Empire (Nijmegen, June 20–24, 2006) Impact of Empire 7, Leiden-Boston, 275–290.

Nibley, H.W. 1945. Sparsiones, Classical Journal 40/9, 515–543.

Perassi, C. 1999. Monete nelle tombe di età romana imperial: casi di scelta intenzionale sulla base dei soggetti e delle scritte?, in O. Dubuis, S. Frey-Kupper, G. Perret (eds.), Trouvailles monétaires des tombes. Actes du deuxième colloque international du Groupe Suisse pour l'étude des trouvailles monétaires (Neuchâtel, 3–4 mars 1995), Lausanne, 43–69.

Philpott, R. 1991. Burial Practices in Roman Britain. A survey of grave treatment and furnishing A.D. 43–410, BAR British Series 219, Oxford.

Piso, Țentea forthcoming. Architecture, religion and ideology in Colonia Dacica Sarmizegetusa (I), in Edited by Szabó, C., Gugl, C. (eds), Sanctuaries in the Danubian Provinces Interdisciplinary Studies in the Archaeology of Religion, Leiden.

Popilian, Gh. 1976. Ceramica romană din Oltenia, Craiova.

Roman, C.A. 2017. Luminatul / The Lighting, in O. Țentea, Al. Ratiu (eds.), Sarmizegetusa. Începuturile Daciei romane / The beginning of Roman Dacia, București, 47–54.

Şöföroğlu, M., Summerer L. 2016. Light for the Dead. Some thoughts on Funerary Lamps in Light of the Hellenistic/Roman Tomb in Kormakiti/Koruçam, in L. Summerer, H. Kaba. (eds.) The Northern Face of Cyprus New Studies in Cypriot Archaeology and Art History, Istanbul, 259–275.

Toynbee, J.M.C. 1971. Death and Burial in the Roman World, London.

Țentea, O., Egri, M. 2017. Necropolele – lumea morților /The necropoles – world of the dead, Sarmizegetusa, in O. Țentea, Al. Ratiu (eds.), Sarmizegetusa. Începuturile Daciei romane / The beginning of Roman Dacia, București, 44–46.

Winkler, J. 1975. Descoperiri monetare în Ulpia Traiana Sarmizegetusa, Sargetia 11–12, 117–134.

Historiographica

Scarlat Lambrino, un Roumain en Lusitanie

José d'Encarnação

On ne saura pas, peut-être, que la Roumanie a été le premier pays à reconnaître la légitimité de la Révolution portugaise du 25 Avril 1974. C'est pour cela que, dans ce cadre, les deux pays ont célébré tout de suite des accords culturels.

Dans la circonstance, est célébré, à Constanza, au mois de Septembre de 1977, le VII Congrès International d'Épigraphie Grecque et Latine, auquel j'ai pu participer, grâce à une bourse de la Fundação Calouste Gulbenkian. Sous invitation, d'autre part, de l'Université de Bucarest, j'ai pu visiter, après, des sites archéologiques et des musées roumains.

Nicolae Gostar (qui nous laisserait, hélas ! l'année suivante, 1978, à l'âge de 56 ans) m'a invité à faire une conférence à son université d'Iaşi ; avec Hadrian Daicoviciu († 1984) j'ai vu la collection épigraphique du musée de Cluj-Napoca et j'ai monté avec lui, à pied, jusqu'à une des forteresses daces, qu'il avait fouillé. Soit au Congrès soit après, à l'Académie Roumaine, j'ai pris contact avec Dionisei M. Pippidi († 1993), Emilian Popescu († 2020), Constantin C. Petolescu, Radu Ardevan (un jeune à ce temps-là), et, naturellement, avec Ioan Piso, du même âge que moi.

Dans le cadre du Congrès, m'a beaucoup surpris, par exemple, le monument refait, sous les ordres du président Nicolae Ceausescu, du *Trophaeum Traiani,* à Adamclisi, et j'ai bien compris pourquoi on voulait célébrer, de nouveau, la défaite de son peuple vis-à-vis l'Occident romain. D'autre part, la visite à *Histria,* cité que, de 1928 à 1942, Scarlat Lambrino avait fouillé[1], m'a beaucoup fasciné.

Lambrino, professeur et épigraphiste

Obligé pour des raisons politiques à abandonner son pays, T. Scarlat Lambrino a été reçu au Portugal, comme l'avait été le roi de Roumanie, Charles II, exilé à l'Estoril, depuis Septembre 1940.

Lambrino a été professeur à la Faculté des Lettres de l'Université de Lisbonne, mais je n'ai pas eu le privilège de l'avoir comme maître d'Épigraphie, puisqu'il est décédé en Aout

1 Le Museu Nacional de Arqueologia, de Lisbonne, en étroite collaboration avec l'Institut Culturel Roumain, de Lisbonne, a présenté, du 30 Octobre au 30 Décembre de 2015, au Grand Salon du musée – justement en hommage à l'excellent travail que Scarlat Lambrino y a aussi développé – une exposition évocatrice de ces fouilles d'*Histria.* Fig. 1. Voir aussi Avram 2004, 705–709.

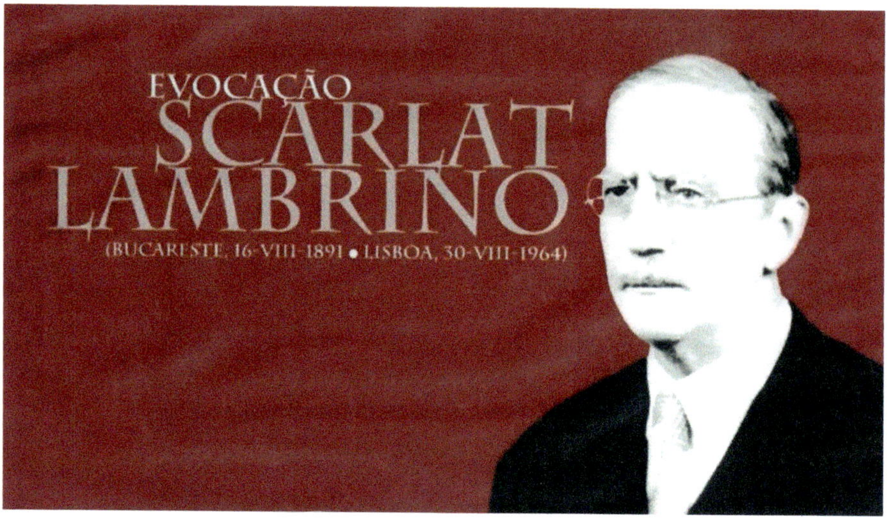

Fig. 1: Affiche de l'hommage pour S. Lambrino à Lisbonne (© J. d'Encarnação)

1964 et, à l'année scolaire de 1965–1966, le responsable de cette chaire était D. Fernando de Almeida, à ce temps directeur aussi du Museu Etnológico Dr. Leite de Vasconcelos (actuel Musée National d'Archéologie), auquel Scarlat Lambrino a donné très précieuse collaboration.

En effet, une des premières activités de Lambrino a été, par suggestion et sous demande d'Almeida, celle de préparer le catalogue épigraphique de ce musée et aussi celui du Musée d'Odrinhas duquel Almeida était simultanément le directeur. Mais, d'autre part, le renommé chercheur roumain a réussi à jeter de nouveaux regards sur d'importantes questions de l'épigraphie lusitanienne et de l'Épigraphie en général.

Je pense pour cela que, dans le cadre de l'hommage à un épigraphiste roumain, peut bien venir à propos mettre en évidence ce que Scarlat Lambrino a fait dans le cadre des études épigraphiques de la Lusitanie.

Les catalogues

D'abord, celui de São Miguel d'Odrinhas.

Lambrino l'a publié au *Bulletin des Études Portugaises et de l'Institut Français au Portugal*[2]. On ne doit pas oublier qu'à ce temps-là le français était, par excellence, la langue véhiculaire des Sciences Humaines et Sociales ! De ce texte a été fait le tiré-à-part avec le

2 Lambrino 1952, 134–176.

18. — Tombe en pierre calcaire, de forme demi-cylindrique: longueur $1^{m}25$, largeur $0^{m}62$, hauteur $0^{m}42$. Elle se trouve sous la galerie qui longe le mur Sud de l'église; creusée et retournée, elle sert de cuve baptismale. Sur un des côtés étroits se trouve l'inscription.

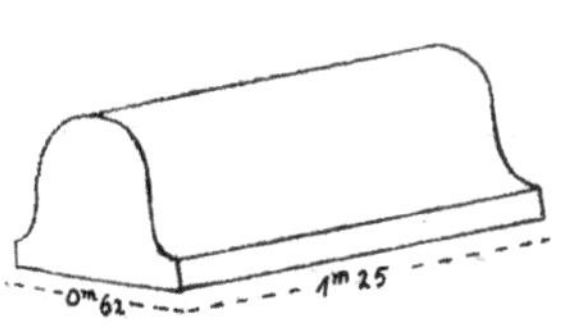

F. Alves Pereira, p. 343, pl. v, fig. 34.

M · VALERIO /////
GAL REBVRRI //////
VALERIA CIVLAN
H S E

Lecture de Pereira: ***M. Valerio,*** **[*M. f(ilio)*], | *Gal(erta tribu) Reburri[no]*, | *Valeria, civ(is) Lan(ciensis).* | *H(ic) s(itus) e(st).* L'endroit où est fixée la pierre ne permet pas le contrôle de la lecture. L. 3, il faudrait peut-être lire: *Valeria, C. [f(ilia)]...***

Fig. 2: Exemple de fiche du catalogue du Musée d'Odrinhas, préparée par Lambrino (© J. d'Encarnação)

même titre, *Les Inscriptions de São Miguel d'Odrinhas,* Coimbra Editora, Limitada, 1953, 48 pages numérotées exprès.

Le recours à la photo n'était pas encore un auxiliaire fréquent et, pour cela, seulement de 5 des 24 monuments y étudiés sont présentés clichés photographiques hors texte, en papier couché.

Un des monuments y présent en photo c'est justement celui du procurateur *C. Iulius Celsus* (nº 24), un monument presque inédit à ce moment, puisque «l'état de délabrement de la face écrite ne lui a pas permis cependant d'en donner une lecture qui ait sens». C'est la référence à F. Alves Pereira, qui a été le premier à se rendre compte, en 1907, de l'existence du monument.

Passé à *L'Année Epigraphique* 1954 253, c'est, en effet, un document auquel on doit faire une spéciale référence dans le cadre de cet hommage, étant donné que, selon l'interprétation de Lambrino, ce chevalier romain, inscrit dans la tribu *Quirina, adlectus in amplissimum ordinem,* a été, très probablement, *missus in Daciam Superiorem,* ce que nous permet de faire une liaison entre les deux territoires romains. En plus, *Celsus* a été *procurator a libellis et a censibus, procurator Lusitaniae, procurator Neapoleos et Mausolei Alexandriae, procurator XX [vigesimae] hereditatium per provincias Narbonensem et Aquitanicam, curator viarum Aemiliae et Triumphalis...*

Avant de déployer – en l'expliquant – le *cursus honorum* de *Celsus,* Lambrino s'interroge sur la raison d'être là cette pierre, avec très vraisemblablement la dédicace à une divinité, puisque, à la fin, on doit interpréter *d(ono) d(edit)* ; et conclut, sans hésitation :

« Elle venait d'ailleurs, du sanctuaire où l'on adorait *Sol* et *Luna* réunis » (p. 18).

On connait très bien, aujourd'hui, le contexte archéologique de ce monument, étant donné que les fouilles y menées par l'équipe du Museu Arqueológico de São Miguel de Odrinhas, sous la direction de José Cardim Ribeiro, ont permis de trouver d'autres autels dédiés à ces deux divinités, ce que nous oblige à croire qu'au temps des Romains cet endroit de *finis terrae* était bien un lieu de pélerinage (disons) pour les magistrats venus de bien loin[3].

Mais il fait aussi ajouter qu'Ioan Piso n'a pas réussi à résister à la magie de ce texte et il est venu exprès l'étudier[4].

Aujourd'hui, avec tant de recours qu'on a heureusement, si d'ordre digital que d'ordre de *corpora* facilement accessibles *on line,* ne sera-t-il pas hors de propos regarder, à titre d'exemple, la fiche nº 18 du catalogue de Lambrino (Fig. 2):

Description courte, dimensions, emplacement, bibliographie, dessin avec les dimensions signalées, lecture, interprétation du premier éditeur ; remarque sur l'interprétation de la 3ème ligne.

Ricardo Campos a, lui aussi, étudié ce monument[5] et nous a permis d'en présenter la photo publiée à la page 223 de son livre. (Fig. 3).

On peut maintenant ajouter que, s'agissant de l'épitaphe d'un citoyen romain d'*Olisipo, Marcus Valerius Reburrus,* puisqu'il a été inscrit à la tribu *Galeria,* l'initiative a été prise par une femme vraisemblablement de la même famille – *Valeria* – dont les liens de parenté avec le défunt ne sont pas indiqués, circonstance qui n'est pas rare à l'*ager Olisiponensis.* D'autre part, son *cognomen* – *Ulan(a)* – seulement se retrouve dans une autre épitaphe d'Odrinhas : celle d'un autre citoyen d'*Olisipo, Quintus Terentius Tanginus,* de l'initiative de son fils (vraisemblablement) *G. Terentius Celer,* et de la mère *Deccia Ulana.* Un *cognomen* dont les 'racines' étymologiques indo-européennes María Lourdes Albertos a bien voulu signaler[6].

C'est, du reste, celui-là un bon témoin pour la réflexion que Lambrino a faite, le premier, à propos des 'racines' de la population de l'*ager Olisiponensis,* à partir de l'examen de son onomastique. En effet, on voit ici la jonction parfaite (on dirait) de l'onomastique latine de bonne source avec l'onomastique de la population indigène. Du nom *Ulana,* par exemple, sont d'ici – jusqu'à présent – les deux seules fois où il est documenté ; *Tanginus* et *Reburrus* sont, depuis beaucoup de temps, considérés typiques de l'onomastique lusitanienne.

Alors, si le catalogue mené à bout par Lambrino est bien innovateur et important, on doit dire que les réflexions faites à ce propos ne le seront moins. Ainsi, après avoir dédié quelques pages à l'interprétation de l'édifice circulaire présent à côté du musée et fait des remarques à propos de la collection épigraphique, il souligne : «Toujours des noms cel-

3 Ribeiro 2019. L'inscription y est étudiée aux pages 17–20, avec photos de détail. Voir aussi, pour l'ensemble de la signification sociopolitique du lieu, Encarnação 2015, 315–328 [accessible à http://hdl.handle.net/10316/32802].

4 Piso 2008, 155–168. Pour d'autres références à ce texte, voir, par exemple, EDCS-51400901.

5 Campos 2023, 222, inscription 2/057.

6 Albertos Firmat 1972, 318.

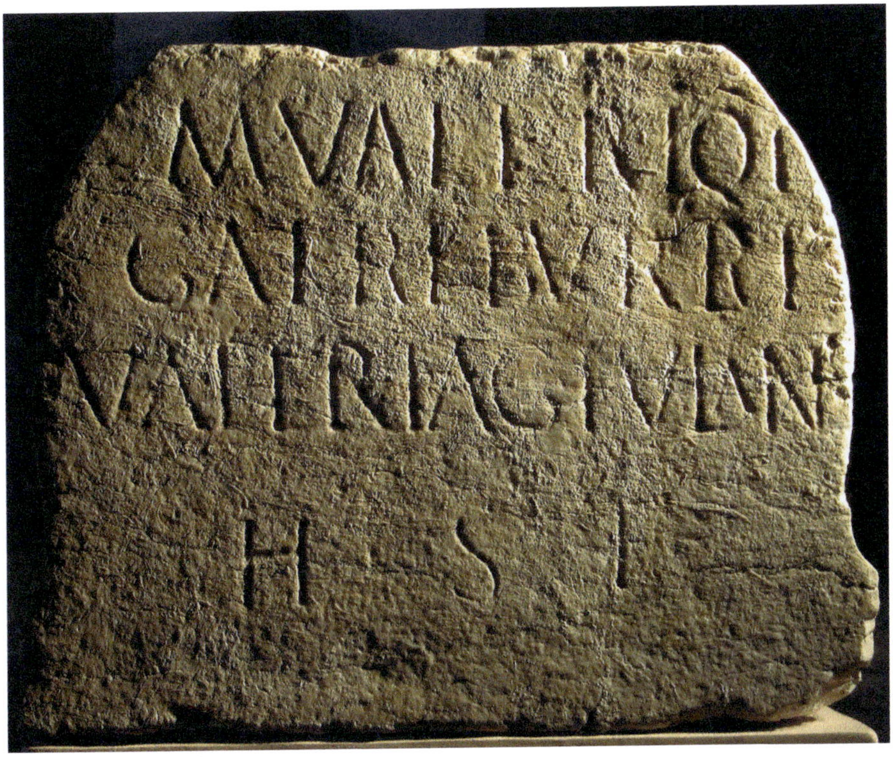

Fig. 3: L'épitaphe de M. Valerius Reburrus (© R. Campos)

tiques apparaissent à côté de beaux noms romains » (p. 36–37) ; la population « s'est bien romanisée depuis que Cesar a créé le municipe *Felicitas Iulia Olisipo.* Mais elle garde très vives encore ses vieilles traditions celtiques », pour conclure :

« Cette population est un témoin, en pleine époque romaine, de la pénétration celtique le long de la vallée du Tage, que nous connaissons par les champs d'urnes qui s'échelonnent depuis Chaminé, près d'Elvas, en passant par Alpiarça, dans le Ribatejo, jusqu'à Alcácer do Sal, au sud de l'embouchure du Tage. Arrivée dans ces parages à la fin du Hallstatt, c'est-à-dire au Ve siècle, elle n'a pas disparu, comme on pourrait le croire. Au contraire, elle s'est maintenue suffisamment compacte et vivace, comme nous le prouvent les monuments examinés d'Odrinhas et d'*Olisipo* » (p. 44).

On pouvait ajouter qu'à Cascais on a trouvé un autel dédié à la divinité *Triborunnis*[7], nom qui doit s'approcher de *Trebaruna,* théonyme dont on a plusieurs témoins à l'actuelle

7 Encarnação 1985, nº 59.

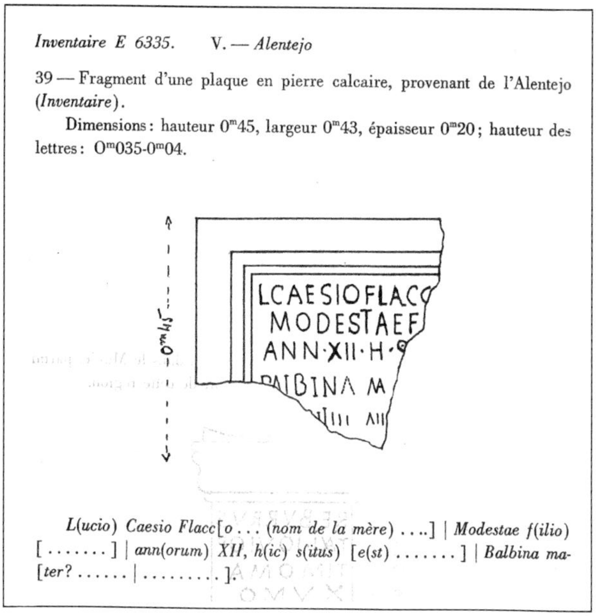
Inventaire E 6335. V. — *Alentejo*

39 — Fragment d'une plaque en pierre calcaire, provenant de l'Alentejo (*Inventaire*).

Dimensions: hauteur $0^{m}45$, largeur $0^{m}43$, épaisseur $0^{m}20$; hauteur des lettres: $0^{m}035$-$0^{m}04$.

L(ucio) Caesio Flacc[o . . . (nom de la mère) . . ..] | *Modestae f(ilio)* [. . . . . . .] | *ann(orum) XII, h(ic) s(itus) [e(st) . . . .]* | *Balbina ma-[ter? . . . . . .* | *. . . . .]*.

Fig. 4: Exemple de fiche du catalogue du Musée de Lisbonne (© J. d'Encarnação)

Beira Baixa, c'est-à-dire, à la partie supérieure de ce couloir auquel Scarlat Lambrino fait mention.

Le catalogue du Musée National d'Archéologie

Celui-là Scarlat Lambrino n'a pas eu, malheureusement, la possibilité de le voir publié, puisqu'il l'a été tout simplement paru aux éditions de 1951, 1956, 1962 et 1967 de l'*O Arqueólogo Português,* la revue du musée[8]. Ce qui donne, tout de suite, une idée de l'énorme travail que l'épigraphiste a fait.

Le schéma utilisé à été le même, comme on peut voir dans la reproduction ci-jointe d'une des fiches, choisie de forme aléatoire:

Ce texte a été repris en IRCP 649,[9] étant donné comme trouvé dans la région nord-est de l'Alentejo, puisqu'on n'a pas eu, pour le moment, d'autre renseignement sur ce monument ; mais la comparaison entre le dessin (Fig. 4) et la photo (Fig. 5) démontre la fiabilité du travail de Lambrino.

8 Lambrino 1951, 37–61; 1956, 5–73; 1962, 279–302; 1967, 123–217.

9 Encarnação 1984 [Le numéro indique le numéro de l'inscription au catalogue].

Fig. 5: Encarnação 1984, nº 649 (© J. d'Encarnação)

Divinités indigènes

Bien certainement l'épigraphiste est resté ébloui par la quantité de monuments dédiés à la divinité indigène *Endovellicus,* tant épigraphiques que sculpturaux, présents au Musée de Lisbonne. L'exhaustif article qu'il lui a dédié, toujours au *Bulletin des Etudes Françaises*[10] en fait la preuve. La vision la plus complète publiée jusqu'à ce moment-là, à propos de cette divinité.

D'abord, Scarlat Lambrino a mis l'accent sur le fait que la divinité soit souvent identifiée comme *deus.* Selon son opinion, ça voulait dire qu'on aurait à voir à une divinité provinciale, puisque ce mot exprimait, en effet, la qualité divine, notamment dans le cas des

10 Lambrino 1951, 93–146.

divinités indigènes, dont cette caractéristique pouvait être mal connue. Plus tard, Lambrino nuancera un peu cette opinion, étant donné que l'adjonction de *deus* se vérifie aussi ailleurs, et non exclusivement dans le cas des divinités provinciales.

En réfléchissant sur les variantes du nom – *Endovellicus, Endovelicus, Indovelicus, Enovolicus, Enobolicus*... – souligne qu'on ne doit pas penser, pour les expliquer, à la négligence ou inhabilité du lapicide. Aujourd'hui, on est bien d'accord : ces variantes reflètent la transmission du nom à travers l'oralité ; étant celui-là un nom méconnu, on l'écrit selon le son perceptible, fait bien compréhensible surtout si on pense que le dieu a été vénéré pas des gens venues de plusieurs parties de la Péninsule, avec langages divers.

En tout cas, pour Lambrino, le nom a bien une origine celtique, opinion qui va dans le sens de l'avis général des chercheurs à cette époque-là, où le 'celtisme' était à l'ordre du jour.

À propos des caractéristiques de la divinité, c'est-à-dire, des 'problèmes' qu'elle – étant invoquée – pouvait résoudre, Lambrino rejette l'avis de Leite de Vasconcelos, qui l'a considéré un dieu médecin :

a. On connaissait bien le dieu Esculape, à cette région de la Lusitanie : il serait, pour cela, difficile d'y ajouter un autre dieu de la Médicine ;
b. C'est vrai que les inscriptions nous apprennent qu'il y avait place pour des oracles ; mais rien ne nous le dit qu'ils soient de nature médicale ;
c. C'est vrai aussi qu'il y a de bas-relief avec la représentation d'une figure masculine où une des jambes donne l'impression de n'être pas très bien, la représentation d'un hémiplégique, on dirait ; alors, le dieu en pourrait l'être le guérisseur. Lambrino, par contre, préfère qu'on voit là la représentation de la divinité elle-même, en train de cheminer et c'est pour cela, explique-t-il, que la jambe est plus courte, elle est représentée en mouvement.
d. Normalement, une divinité médicale vient associée à la présence d'une source d'eaux bienfaisantes ; or, à l'Alandroal pas de source n'a été trouvée.
e. *Endovellicus* devait bien être, de préférence, la divinité des enfers. En effet, sur le côté des dédicaces, on voit le relief d'un sanglier, qui représente la végétation, les animaux ; aussi la palme et la couronne de laurier ; un génie ailé avec des torches... Du reste, c'est bien comme divinité infernale que la divinité donne les oracles, puisque inclusive sur un des textes le dédicant proclame qu'il fait l'ex-voto *ex imperato Averno.*

En mettant l'accent sur la présence de représentations de sanglier surtout au Nord du Portugal datées de la Préhistoire et sur l'existence de monuments funéraires en forme de tonneau (les *cupae),* Lambrino propose une relation étroite le dieu gaulois *Sucellus,* une identification inclusive, idée que, plus tard, a considéré peu acceptable.

Trebaruna a été l'autre divinité qu'a beaucoup attiré l'attention de Scarlat Lambrino[11]. Bien sûrement, parce qu'elle était la 'bien aimée' dc D. Fernando de Almeida, qui lui a dédié un poème ![12]

11 Lambrino 1957, 87–109. Livraria Bertrand a publié en livre, dans la même année, le tiré-à-part de cet article.
12 Almeida 1962, 67–74.

Les idées plus remarquables exprimées dans ce texte monographique ont été reprises à la communication que l'épigraphiste a présenté aux actes du Colloque International sur les Empereurs Romains d'Espagne[13] :

«*Trebaruna* ou *Trebaron(n)a,* qui s'est fait connaître par deux autels d'Idanha-a-Velha et de Lardosa, en Lusitanie centrale, et un de Coria, en Lusitanie espagnole, a son nom formé des racines *treb-* et *runa-*, que déjà d'Arbois de Jubainville avait traduit par « le secret de la maison », considérant ainsi à la déesse une qualité domestique. Mais puisque *treb-* entre dans la formation de noms de peuples, *Atrebates, Arrotrebae,* et de villes, *Contrebia,* et puisque *treb-* signifie «ville» en vieux gallois et en vieux breton, je crois que la déesse est protectrice d'une grande communauté humaine, ville, tribu. Elle est, comme *Tutela Bolgensis,* une divinité nationale » (1957, p. 230).

Étant donné que presque dans le même endroit l'*Igaeditanus miles Tongius* a fait ériger un autel à *Trebaruna* et un autre à *Victoria,* on a pensé à l'hypothèse que *Trebaruna* puisse être une divinité guerrière. Scarlat Lambrino a rejeté l'idée. Pour lui ce n'est pas obligatoire ; par contre, les deux autels montrent un procès de 'romanisation' : *Tongius,* le jeune soldat à peine arrivé à l'armée, ayant encore bien fraîches ses traditions locales, a dédié un autel à la déesse de sa tribu ; après 25 ans de service militaire, une vie dans sa cohorte, il s'est imprégné de la civilisation romaine et, pour cela, retourné, il prie *Victoria*[14].

Conclusion

En total, nous avons plus de deux dizaines de titres dus à l'activité énorme menée par T. Scarlat Lambrino, notamment sur la religion et les peuples anciens.

Au-delà des articles qu'il a écrit, T. Scarlat Lambrino a été invité à faire des conférences, c'est-à-dire, il ne s'est pas limité à être professeur et épigraphiste.

Il a présenté, du moins, trois communications à l'Académie des Sciences de Lisbonne, dont on n'a que les résumés[15] , étant sûr qu'il a été présent à plusieurs séances aux années 60 .

D'autre part, sous invitation de Joel Serrão, éditeur du *Dicionário da História de Portugal*[16], Lambrino a rédigé les entrées «Ebora», «Endovélico». «Epigrafia», «Felicitas Iulia Olisipo».

Dans le *Mensário das Casas do Povo* [Lisbonne] 13 [145], 1958, p. 12, on lit son éloge de la personnalité scientifique de Leite de Vasconcelos, en tant qu'épigraphiste, ce qui nous donne une idée de l'écho du statut intellectuel de Lambrino même au sein des classes ouvrières. C'est, sans doute, un texte intégré à l'occasion des commémorations du centenaire de la naissance de Leite de Vasconcelos.

13 Lambrino 1965, 223–242.
14 Lambrino 1957, 109.
15 Lambrino 1963a, 148–150; 1963b, 245–248; 1964, 121–122.
16 Lisboa, Iniciativas Editoriais, II, 1965.

Aux pages 192 et 193 du nº 79, de l'année 1961, du *Boletim da Sociedade de Geografia,* a été consigné le rapport de la séance mensuel de la Sociedade, le 13 Avril 1961, qui nous est particulièrement séduisant, parce que le président, Dr. Medeiros-Gouvêa, a fait l'éloge de l'orateur dans ces termes :

« Professeur Cathédratique d'Épigraphie et de Civilisation Grecque à la Faculté des Lettres de Lisbonne, où il est en train de développer une activité didactique notable. Enraciné au Portugal, l'illustre professeur a publié ici de très importantes études sur l'origine et l'histoire des Lusitaniens, sur des inscriptions latines et encore à propos d'autres antiquités et religions de la Lusitanie. Il a aussi publié le premier volume d'une « Bibliographie de l'Antiquité Classique ».

Le sujet choisi a été « Ostie, port de Rome Ancienne», dont le président présente, au rapport, une synthèse. On lit, au final :

«La conférence – illustrée avec projection de photographies des trouvailles archéologiques d'Ostie : temples du *Forum,* le théâtre et les termes de la cité, la célèbre Place des Corporations avec ses soixante-dix bureaux des corporations d'armateurs d'Afrique, de la Sardaigne et de la Gaule, quelques édifices chrétiens, parmi lesquels une basilique et un oratoire – a été, à la fin, élogieusement commentée par le président», qui a ajouté: «Cet important travail sera publié dans un des prochains numéros de ce «Bulletin». Hélas ! On n'a pu eu cette chance.

Enfin, pouvons-nous ajouter : il a été un grand Maître, dont on très vivement regrette le peu de temps qu'il a passé parmi nous.

Bibliographie

Albertos Firmat, M. L. 1972. Nuevos antropónimos hispánicos, Emerita 40/2, 287–318.

Almeida, D. F. de, Trebaruna, deusa lusitana, Estudos de Castelo Branco 6, 67–74.

Avram, Al. 2004. Scarlat et Marcelle Lambrino : notes inédites sur les fouilles d'Istros (1928–1940) récemment retrouvées, Comptes rendus des séances de l'Académie des Inscriptions et Belles-Lettres 148–2, 705–709.

Campos, R. 2023. Um Tipo de Monumento Funerário Romano: As *Cupae* Líticas do *Municipium Olisiponense*, Huelva.

Encarnação, J. d' 1984. Inscrições Romanas do Conventus Pacensis. — Subsídios para o Estudo da Romanização, Coimbra.

Encarnação, J. d' 1985. Ara votiva a Triborunnis, Ficheiro Epigráfico 14, nº 59.

Encarnação, J. d' 2015. Era aqui que Febo adormecia (This was the place where Phoebus fell asleep), Estudos Arqueológicos de Oeiras 22, 315–328 [accessible à http://hdl.handle.net/10316/32802].

Lambrino, S. 1951. Inscriptions latines du Musée Dr. Leite de Vasconcelos, O Arqueólogo Português nova serie 1. 1951 37–61.

Lambrino, S. 1951. Le dieu lusitanien Endovellicus, Bulletin des Études Portugaises et de l'Institut Français au Portugal, nova série 10, 93–146.

Lambrino, S. 1952. Les inscriptions de S. Miguel d'Odrinhas, Bulletin des Études Portugaises et de l'Institut Français au Portugal, nouvelle série 16, 134–176.
Lambrino, S. 1956. Les inscriptions latines inédites du Musée Leite de Vasconcelos, O Arqueólogo Português nova serie 3, 5–73;
Lambrino, S. 1957. La déesse celtique Trebaruna, Bulletin des Études Portugaises et de l'Institut Français au Portugal 20, 87–109.
Lambrino, S. 1962. Catalogue des inscriptions latines du Musée Leite de Vasconcelos, O Arqueólogo Português nova série 4, 279–302;
Lambrino, S. 1963a. Os guerreiros lusitanos, Boletim da Academia das Ciências de Lisboa, nova série 25, 148–150.
Lambrino, S. 1963b. Os mosaicos de Torres Novas, Boletim da Academia das Ciências de Lisboa, nova série 25, 245–248.
Lambrino, S. 1964b. Algumas aplicações do Direito Romano na Lusitânia, Boletim da Academia das Ciências de Lisboa, nova série 26, 121–122.
Lambrino, S. 1965. Les cultes indigènes en Espagne sous Trajan et Hadrien, dans Les Empereurs Romains d'Espagne (Actes du Colloque International sur les Empereurs Romains d'Espagne – Madrid, 1964), Paris, 223–242.
Lambrino, S. 1967. Catalogue des inscriptions latines du Musée Leite de Vasconcelos, O Arqueólogo Português 3ª série 1, 123–217.
Piso, I. 2008. Le *cursus honorum* de São Miguel d'Odrinhas, Sylloge Inscriptionum Barcinonensium 6, 155–168.
Ribeiro, J. C. 2019. Escrever sobre a margem do Oceanus: epigrafia e religio no Santuário do Sol Poente (Provincia Lusitania), Barcelona.

Zu den Zeichnungen von Aegidius Tschudi, Politiker und Historiker des 16. Jahrhunderts*

Regula Frei-Stolba

Die Mitarbeit an der Edition der Steininschriften von Vindonissa[1] sowie die fast gleichzeitig laufenden Vorbereitungen zur Publikation des sog. Wettinger-Silberschatzes (Martin-Kilcher S. et al. in Vorbereitung) veranlassten mich, die Manuskripte des in der Alten Eidgenossenschaft prominenten Politikers und Historikers Aegidius (Gilg) Tschudi (1505–1572) nochmals zu untersuchen. Da unser Jubilar Ioan Piso enge Verbindungen zur Gesellschaft Pro Vindonissa und zu Brugg/Windisch pflegte[2], seien ihm die folgenden Zeilen zur Erinnerung an seinen Brugger Besuch gewidmet.

Moderne Editionen antiker Inschriften, so auch jene umfassende der Tituli Helvetici (Kolb 2022), illustrieren jede Inschrift. Falls die Steine verschollen und deshalb keine Fotos möglich sind, werden auch Zeichnungen und Skizzen der ersten Entdecker herangezogen, soweit diese in Manuskripten vorhanden sind.

---

* Danken möchte ich in erster Linie dem Team der Kantonsarchäologie Aargau, dessen Leiter Thomas Doppler, dann Regine Fellmann Brogli, Jürgen Trumm und Ulrich Stockinger; im weiteren der Arbeitsgruppe der Neuedition des Wettinger-Silberschatzes, Heidi Amrein, Christian Weiss und Mylène Ruoss, Landesmuseum Zürich, Stefanie Martin-Kilcher und André Holenstein, Universität Bern; Andrea Schaer, Archäologin, Archaeokontor GmbH Bern; den Bibliothekarinnen und Bibliothekaren aller Spezialbibliotheken, in denen ich Manuskripte konsultierte; schliesslich Benjamin Hartmann für die Durchsicht des Manuskripts und die Hilfe bei der Bildbearbeitung. Ich habe die Anmerkungen bewusst fast nur auf die Zitierung der Manuskripte sowie der wichtigsten Untersuchungen beschränkt. Es ist ein Kapitel aus der Lokalgeschichte, für die es viel Spezialliteratur gibt. Deshalb möchte ich für alle hier zitierten Personen aus dem 16. Jh. auf das Historische Lexikon der Schweiz in der Online-Ausgabe hinweisen (https://hls-dhs-dss.ch), in welchem alle Biographien mit weiterführender Literatur zu finden sind. Die Inschriften werden nur nach ICH, CIL XIII und TitHelv zitiert. Es war verständlicherweise nicht möglich, alle bildlichen Darstellungen auch zu illustrieren. Für die gedruckten Alten Werke verweise ich auf die Digitalisate.

1 Fellmann Brogli et al. 2024.

2 Frei-Stolba 2011. Ioan Piso hielt 2010 an der 114. Jahresversammlung der Gesellschaft Pro Vindonissa einen viel beachteten Vortrag über „Das Heiligtum des Jupiter Optimus Maximus auf dem Pfaffenberg/Carnuntum in Österreich“. Seine Interpretation des Begriffes intra leugam ist massgebend für die örtliche Festlegung des (immer noch nicht gefundenen) vicus von Vindonissa.

Für die Inschriften des schweizerischen Mittellandes bis zum Bodensee sind die ersten[3] Entdecker Aegidius (Gilg) Tschudi (1505–1572), der Autodidakt, Politiker und Historiker, sowie sein Freund und Kollege, der aus dem badischen Bruchsal stammende und in Zürich lehrende Theologe und Chronist Johannes Stumpf (1500–1577/78), schliesslich für die letzten Lebensjahre Tschudis zudem der Theologe, Historiker und Gelehrte Josias Simler (1530–1576), ebenfalls in Zürich[4]. Von der Diskussion zwischen Theodor Mommsen und Salomon Voegelin über die Urheberschaft der ersten Inschriftenkopien sei nur das Resultat genannt: Voegelin konnte zeigen, dass Tschudi als erster römische Inschriften der Schweiz entdeckte und sie Stumpf für dessen gedrucktes Werk zur Verfügung stellte[5]. Die Urheberschaft Tschudis wurde von Mommsen im CIL XIII.2 (fertiggestellt 1888, erschienen 1905) anerkannt und ist seither nicht mehr angefochten worden.

Aus den zahlreichen möglichen Fragestellungen zu den ersten Entdeckern römischer Inschriften im Raume der Nordschweiz soll nun jene nach den Zeichnungen Tschudis herausgegriffen und in den Mittelpunkt der Untersuchung gestellt werden.

Handschriftliche Zeichnungen; Kopisten; Zeichnungen in gedruckten Werken

Das 16. Jh. war eine Zeit des Umbruchs, verschiedene Möglichkeiten der Vervielfältigung und Verbreitung von Information wurden gleichzeitig verwendet. Da war einerseits der immer wichtiger werdende Buchdruck, anderseits gab es noch lange die Zeit der handschriftlichen Reinschriften und der Vervielfältigungen durch Kopisten und Mitarbeiter. Als Zeichnungen Tschudis sollen nur jene Zeichnungen gelten, die er eigenhändig, möglichst nach Autopsie, anfertigte. Sie sind zu trennen von weiteren zeitgenössischen Inschriftenabbildungen, seien sie durch Kopisten handschriftlich erstellt und in Manuskripten tradiert oder in Büchern gedruckt worden. Die handschriftlichen Skizzen Tschudis sind deshalb mit jenen übrigen zeitgenössischen Abbildungen und Drucken von Inschriften zu vergleichen, um sie angemessen würdigen zu können. Es ist dabei notwendig, selbst bis auf die Originale Tschudis zurückzugehen, denn nur die genaue Betrachtung der Skizzen und Notizen Tschudis erlauben auch begründete Aussagen[6].

---

3 Glarean, „der Glarner“ (Henricus Loriti, 1488–1563, geb. in Mollis, Kt. Glarus), der berühmte Gelehrte und Professor, poeta laureatus und Freund von Erasmus von Rotterdam, kopierte neun Inschriften aus Avenches (Frei-Stolba 1992 und 2013). Er wird hier bewusst ausgeklammert.

4 Das frühe 16.Jh. war nicht nur die Zeit der ersten Humanisten, sondern auch die Zeit der Reformation; Huldrych Zwingli, der erste Zürcher Reformator, starb 1531 im Zweiten Kappelerkrieg. Aegidius Tschudi war katholisch, Stumpf und Simler reformiert. Interessanterweise spielte die Konfession für die beiden Historiker der ersten Generation, die beide Schweizer Geschichte schrieben, keine Rolle; in der Politik vertrat Tschudi hingegen eine Politik der katholischen Interessen.

5 Voegelin 1886. Zu Einzelheiten s. unten Anm. 8.

6 Ich danke Philipp Lenz, Stiftsbibliothek St. Gallen für die Auskünfte betreffend die Gestaltung des Codex und besonders für die Diskussionen über die Zeichnungen Tschudis (Besuch vom 20. Aug. 2023).

Eigenhändige Zeichnungen Tschudis finden sich in erster Linie im undatierten Codex SG 1083, den Abt Beda Angehrn (1725–1796), ab 1767 Fürstabt von Sankt Gallen, aus dem Nachlass von Tschudi zusammenstellen und paginieren liess[7]. Nach den Forschungen von Salomon Voegelin[8] (1886), der die darin bewahrten Inschriften als die erste Inschriftensammlung Tschudis identifizierte, begann der Autor die Einträge wohl 1534, als er in seiner ersten Zeit als Landammann von Baden (1533–1535) den in diesem Jahr entdeckten Meilenstein von Wylen (Unterwil, Gemeinde Turgi, Kt. Aargau) beim niederen Schloss in Baden, seinem Amtssitz, aufstellen liess[9]. Voegelin konnte die einzelnen Stufen der Zusammenarbeit zwischen Tschudi und Stumpf zur Edition der Schweizer Chronik 1548 aufschlüsseln und die späteren Zusätze von Tschudi bis vor 1564 ermitteln[10]. Nach diesem Jahr zeichnete Tschudi nach unseren Erkenntnissen nur noch einmal eine Inschrift kurz vor seinem Tod (1572). Es ist nicht einfach, sich im Codex SG 1083 zurecht zu finden, da die Eintragung der Inschriften nicht chronologisch, sondern geographisch von West nach Ost erfolgte, mit leeren Blättern dazwischen[11].

Dann sind im 20. Jh. zwei weitere Bücher mit Zeichnungen und Einträgen aus dem Privatbesitz von Gilg Tschudi aufgetaucht, (1) die in Basel bei Johann Froben 1519 gedruckte Tacitus-Ausgabe und (2) die prächtige Inschriftensammlung, die Peter Apianus (Peter Bienewitz, 1495–1552) mit Bartholomaeus Amantius 1534 in Ingoldstadt drucken liess. In beiden Büchern findet man handschriftliche Einträge Tschudis zu römischen Inschriften aus der Schweiz. Offenbar hatte er die Angewohnheit, einzelne Inschriften auf Innenseiten und Randseiten von Büchern zu schreiben und allenfalls den Stein zu zeichnen.

Die Zeichnung der Isis-Tempelinschrift

Der Eintrag zur Isis-Tempelinschrift aus Wettingen auf der Einbandinnenseite der Tacitus-Ausgabe von 1519 aus dem Besitz Tschudis, die heute in der Kantonsbibliothek

7 Fürstabt Beda von Sankt Gallen konnte 1768 den Nachlass und die Bibliothek Tschudis für die Stiftsbibliothek Sankt Gallen erwerben. Zum Manuskript Voegelin 1886, 56–59; 60- 63. Die Churer Inschriften (TitHelv 721–723) wurden im Codex SG 609 (dort p. 77–83) zusammengebunden. Tschudi hat die Inschriften 1536 gesehen und Beatus Rhenanus zusammen mit dem Manuskript des Buches über Rätien („Die uralt warhafftig Alpisch Rhetia sampt dem Tract der andern Alpgebirgen") zugeschickt. Das Buch über Rätien veröffentlichte er dann nach einigen Schwierigkeiten deutsch und lateinisch 1538.

8 Voegelin 1886, 36–39, 56–65, 133–162.

9 Frei-Stolba 2007, 10. ICH 330; CIL XIII 9075; CIL XVII.2, 595. Der Stein wurde 1712 nach Zürich verschleppt; er befindet sich heute im Schweizerischen Nationalmuseum, Landesmuseum Zürich.

10 Voegelin 1868, 62–63 (erste Sammlung), 63 (nachträgliche Zusätze); Gemäss Frei-Stolba 2000, 145: 1533–1542 sammelte Tschudi Inschriften, schickte das Manuskript 1542 an Stumpf, 1544 sandte Stumpf mit eigenen Inschriftenkopien den Text an Tschudi zurück, 1547 korrigierte Tschudi nochmals alles vor dem Druck.

11 Man vergleiche die Nennung der Inschriften mit den Nummern der paginae des Codex nach Voegelin 1886, 133–162; zudem ist zu beachten, dass p. 69–72 von Stumpf geschrieben wurden.

Aargau aufbewahrt wird[12], besteht aus einem längeren Text zum Fund sowie der Zeichnung mit dem Text der Inschrift. Der bei Froben(ius) in Basel 1519 gedruckte Band war die massgebende Tacitus-Ausgabe jener Zeit; etwa auch Ulrich Zwingli, der Zürcher Reformator, besass sie[13] (Leu 2000, 235 A.10). Die Tacitus-Ausgabe Tschudis ist mit der Schrift von Beatus Rhenanus von 1531 zusammengebunden, was darauf hinweist, dass Tschudi den Eintrag nicht 1519, sondern wohl kurz nach 1531 vornahm[14]. Die erste Publikation des Eintrages erfolgte 1978[15]. Heute verfügt man über eine verbesserte Lesung von Text und Zeichnung der in Wettingen gefundenen Tempelbauinschrift für Isis von Stefanie Martin-Kilcher[16]. Vom etwas langatmigen Text ist hier nur der Anfang von Belang, in welchem Tschudi die Fundumstände beschrieb (Stichworte in modernem Deutsch: „am Glockenturm von Wettingen, ein grosser viereckiger Stein")[17], bevor er auf die mündliche Überlieferung einging. Die Zeichnung entspricht jedoch nicht der Beschreibung, da sich der Zeichner offenbar in freier Eingebung einen Tempel mit Dach vorstellte (Abb. 1). Die späteren Zeichnungen derselben Inschrift in der Apian-Ausgabe wie dann auch im Codex SG 1083 unterscheiden sich von dieser Darstellung, da sie nun einen eingerahmten rechteckigen Block zeigen[18].

Die Einträge in den Inscriptiones sacrosanctae vetustatis

Die Zeichnungen im persönlichen Exemplar Tschudis der damals sehr berühmten, reich ausgestatteten Inschriftensammlung, die Peter Apianus und Bartholomaeus Amantius in Ingolstadt 1534 herausgaben, sind variantenreicher. Apian kannte nur fünf Inschriften aus der Schweiz, die er mit einem prächtigen Rahmen umgab[19]. Obwohl er fehlerhafte Texte publizierte, ist es als Fortschritt zu werten, dass er die Texte der Inschriften als eigenständige Elemente behandelte. Anders ging noch Beatus Rhenanus vor, der kenntnisreich und sorgfältig viele wörtliche Zitate antiker Autoren anführte, aber Inschriftentexte nicht (oder nur ganz selten) als solche kennzeichnete, sondern in seinen Fliesstext

12 Tschudi besass die Ausgabe mit dem Haupttitel: P. Cornelii Taciti Eq.Ro. Historia Augusta actionum diurnalium: additis quinque libris novis inventis ..... Apud inclytam Basileam: ex officina Io. Frobenii [anno 1519]. Signatur: KBA RarF41a. Ich danke Sandra Berger, Leiterin Sammlung und Ringier Bildarchiv, Kantonsbibliothek Aargau, für ihre Hilfe.

13 Leu 2000, 235A.10.

14 Mein Dank geht an Felix Müller, Kantonsbibliothek Aargau, der diese Datierung erkannte.

15 Brüschweiler et al. 1978, 43–44. Abschrift und Fotographie der Notiz Tschudis. Isis-Tempelbauinschrift: ICH 241; CIL XIII 5233; TitHelv 370.

16 Mit Unterstützung von André Holenstein, Universität Bern.

17 „Im dorf Wettingen, nach bim closter des namens und by der statt Baden im Årgow gelegen an dem gloggenthurn/ ist eine alte geschrifft in eim gross vierecketen Stein/...

18 Abb. 2 und Abb. 5 (rechts unten).

19 Petrus Apianus (et Bartholomaeus Amantius), Inscriptiones sacrosanctae vetustatis non illae quidem Romanae sed totius fere orbis summo studio ac maximis impensis Terra Marique conquisitae feliciter incipiunt ... Ingoldstadt 1534, p. 454 u. p. 455.

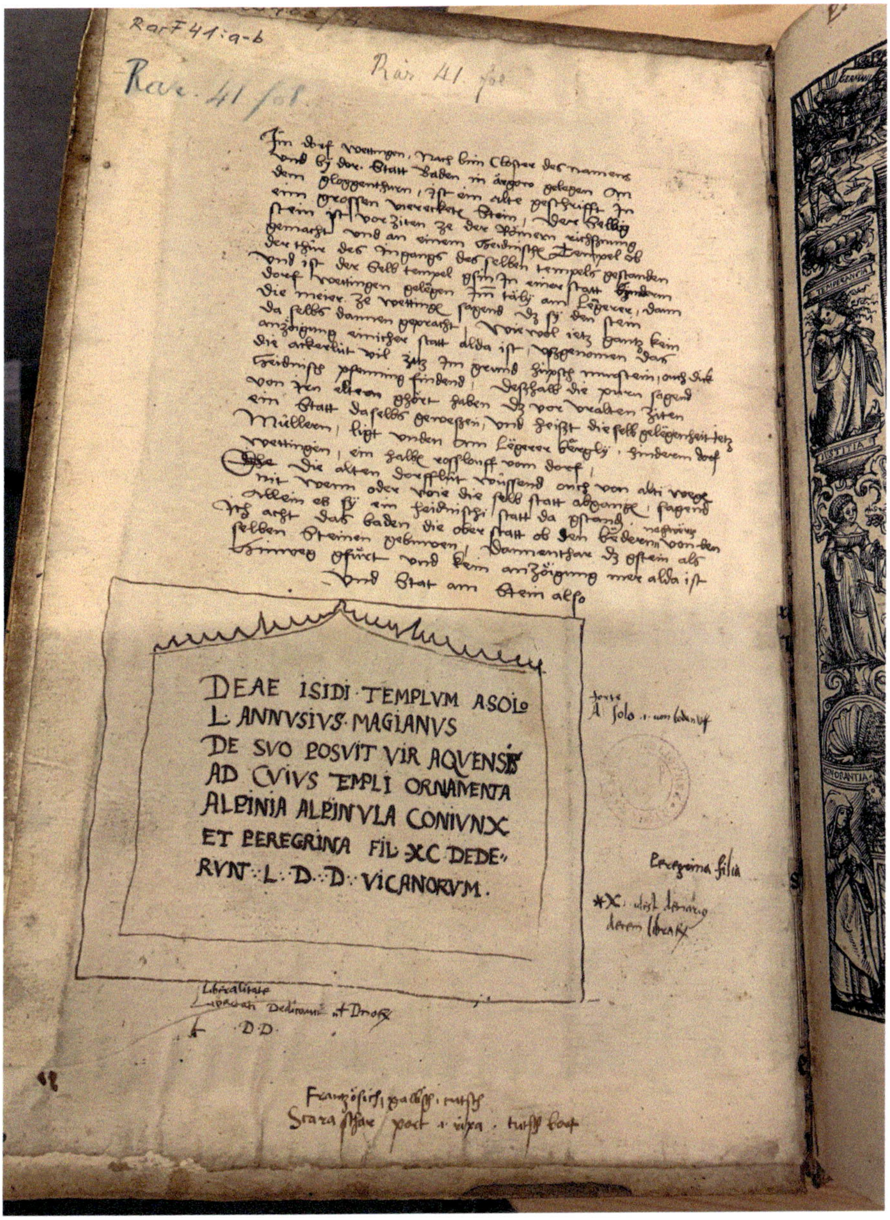

Abb. 1: Skizze zum Fund der Isis-Tempelinschrift aus Wettingen; Einbandinnenseite des persönlichen Exemplars Tschudis von P. Cornelii Taciti Eq.Ro. Historia Augusta … (1519), Kantonsbibliothek Aarau (Kt. Aargau)

einfügte[20]. Tschudi korrigierte die fehlerhaften Inschriften durch einen verbesserten Text; dabei aktualisierte er offenbar bis 1558 die Apian-Ausgabe[21]. Wichtig ist die Feststellung[22], dass Tschudi den Wortlaut der Inschriften verbesserte, auch Angaben zum Fundort festhielt, Zeichnungen – oder besser – Ansätze zu Zeichnungen, aber nur in bestimmten Situationen hinzufügte. So scheint sich die Regel, vollständige Steinplatten mit einer Umrahmung zu kennzeichnen, verfestigt zu haben. Falls ein Stein gebrochen und fragmentarisch war, wurde dies konsequent mit einer Zickzacklinie angegeben. Als Beispiele seien die beiden von Tschudi nachträglich, aber noch vor 1544 gesehenen Fragmente CLAVDI sowie CAL / / O · I genannt[23], ebenfalls die rechts gebrochene Grabinschrift des L. Vecna[tius L.f.] Maximus[24]. (Abb. 2) Anders ging er noch mit dem Grabmonument für Donatus Salvianus, den kaiserlichen Sklaven[25], um: Er verbesserte den Text mit der Bekräftigung „ad formam propriam“[26], fügte aber keine Skizze hinzu, sondern beschrieb den Stein nur als „lapis fere rotundus“. Eine sorgfältige handschriftliche Zeichnung stand dann dafür im Codex SG 1083 (Abb. 3)[27].

Die Zeichnung Tschudis und die Umsetzungen in den Werken anderer Autoren

Das eben erwähnte halbrunde Fragment aus dem Grabmonument des kaiserlichen Sklaven Donatus Salvianus zeigt beispielhaft, dass Tschudi in seinem Bemühen, die ungewöhnliche Form einer Steininschrift zeichnerisch zu erfassen, noch weitgehend allein dastand. Während die Rundung des Steines in der „Schweizer Chronik“ von Stumpf (1548) schon aus drucktechnischen Gründen schematisch und dadurch zu regelmässig abgebildet wurde[28], folgt die Zeichnung im Werk des Janus Gruterus (1603) einer ganz

20 „Vuile/rii in Heluetiis extat inscriptio, qua Auenticenses incolae T. Tertio Seuero ob eius erga se merita donum se posuisse testantur. Ibidem Donatus exactor tributorum in Heluetiis elogium habet. Inscriptiones, quae inter ruinas Auentici reperiuntur, non uisum est apponere.“, „Im schweizerischen Weiler gibt es eine Inschrift, in der die Einwohner von Aventicum bezeugen, sie hätten sie dem Titus Tertius Severus gesetzt wegen seiner um sie erworbenen Verdienste. Ebendort hat auch der Steuereintreiber Donatus ein Elogium bei den Helvetiern erhalten. Die Inschriften, die unter den Ruinen von Aventicum zu finden sind, wollte ich hier nicht zitieren“, so Mundt 2008, 314 und 315.

21 Trümpy 1956, 506; Winteler 1963; Leu 2002, 235–237.

22 Zum Folgenden vgl. die Apian-Ausgabe p. 455; alle genannten Inschriften finden sich auf dieser Seite.

23 ICH 262; CIL XIII 5228; TitHelv 477.

24 ICH 263; CIL XIII 5229; TitHelv 490.

25 ICH 178; CIL XIII 5092; TitHelv 194; vgl. dazu Lieb, Bridel 2009; Eck 2022, 178.

26 Voegelin 1886, 501 A. 14: eine stehende Redewendung.

27 Codex SG 1083, p. 80. Tschudi gab sich offenbar Mühe, die Rundung nachzuzeichnen. Philipp Lenz, Stiftsbibliothekar der Stiftsbibliothek St. Gallen, war der Ansicht, dass er dies ohne Hilfsmittel erreichte; ich übernehme gerne diese Interpretation.

28 J. Stumpf, Gemeiner loblicher Eydgnoschafft Stetten, Landen und Völckeren Chronick wirdiger thaaten beschreybung, Zürich 1548, Bd. 2, Buch VIII, cap.18, fol. 264v. Es musste eine Form im Holzstock geschnitzt werden. Voegelin 1886, 71.

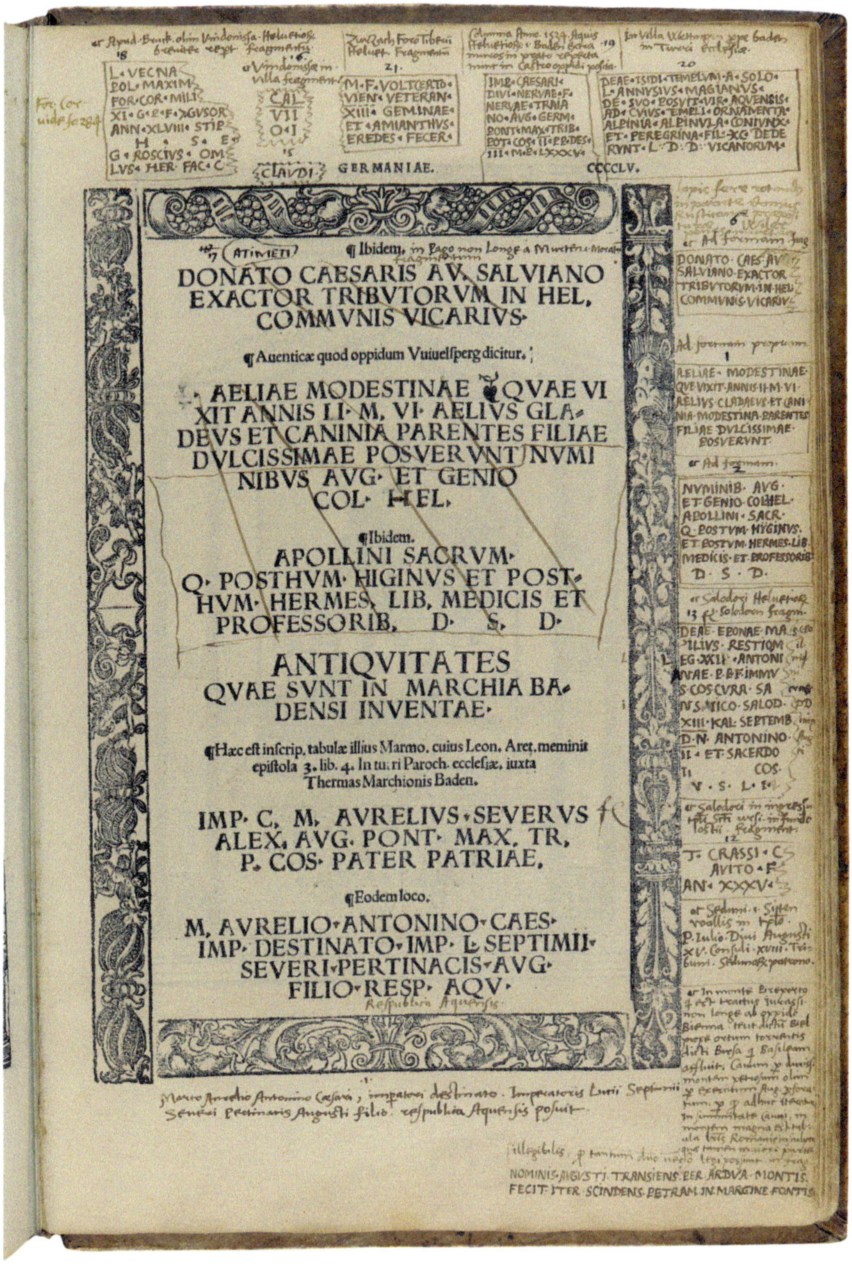

Abb. 2: P. Apianus, Inscriptiones sanctae vetustatis ... (1534), p. 455. Innerhalb des Rahmens: Apians fünf fehlerhafte Inschriften; am Rand im persönlichen Exemplar Tschudis: Korrekturen und Ergänzungen der Sammlung Apians mit Neufunden. Landesbibliothek Glarus (Kt. Glarus)

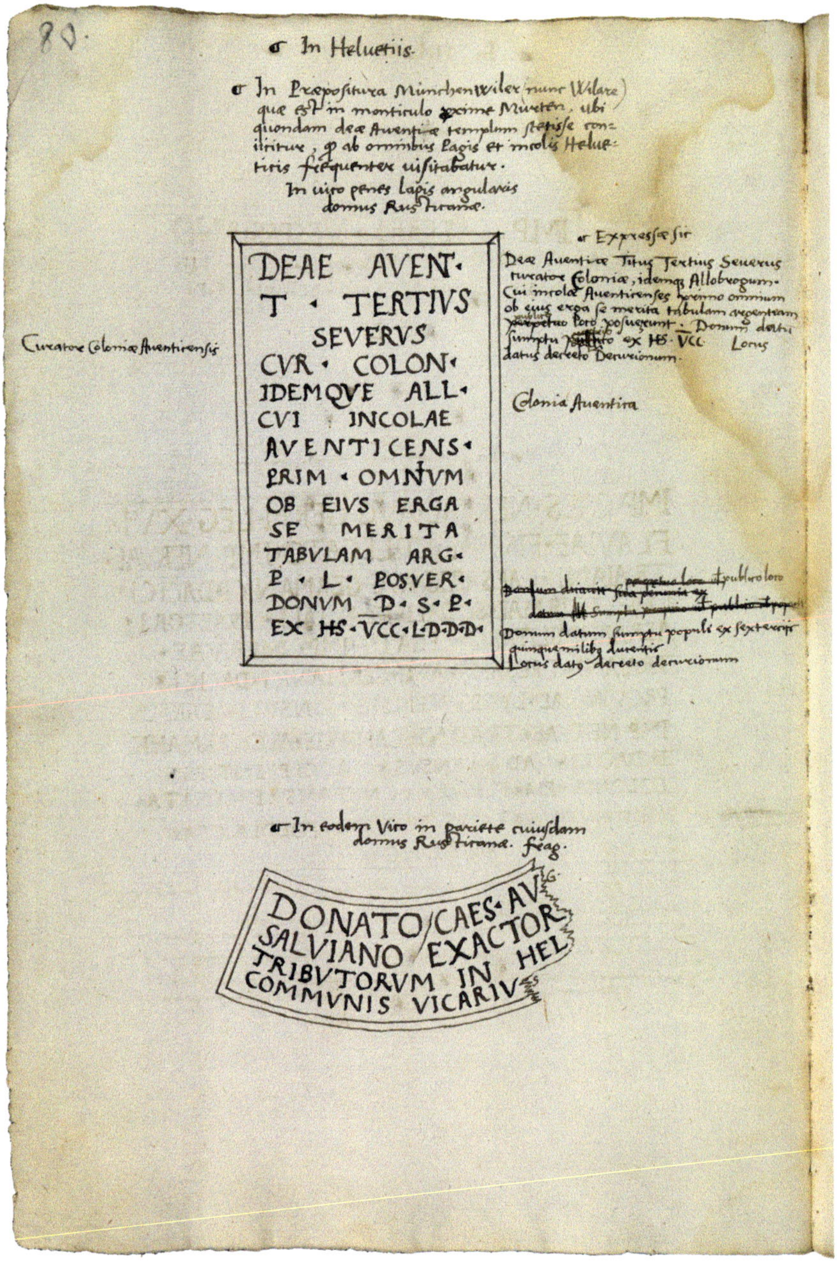

Abb. 3: Handschriftliche Inschriftensammlung. Codex SG 1083, p. 80. Stiftsbibliothek St. Gallen.
Korrekte Zeichnung des heute noch erhaltenen Steinblocks, Avenches.
Grabmal des kaiserlichen Sklaven Donatus Salvianus

anderen Tradition; denn dieser Autor übernahm den unkorrigierten Text von Apian (vgl. oben Abb. 2), und präsentierte ohne Verweis jene phantasievolle Zeichnung, die er in den Inscriptiones antiquae (Leyden 1588) gefunden hatte[29].

Wann zeichnete Tschudi eine vollständige Steininschrift?

Das Beispiel des Grabmonumentes für Donatus Salvianus gibt einen Hinweis auf die Motive Tschudis, einen Stein zu zeichnen: Sobald der beschriebene Stein eine ungewöhnliche Form aufwies, mit anderen Worten nicht eine Steinplatte war, dann versuchte er, diese Besonderheit festzuhalten. Der heute noch erhaltene Teil des Grabmonumentes, der halbrunde Kalksteinblock, wurde gezeichnet eben wegen seiner leichten Wölbung. Ein weiteres Beispiel ist der Sarkophag aus Kalkstein aus Solothurn, den Tschudi zeichnete. Das Steingrab war ursprünglich für eine Flavia Severina hergestellt worden[30], wurde dann aber als Grab des Hl. Ursus gebraucht. Die Steinkiste entdeckte man 1519 beim Abbruch des alten Hochaltars; sie ist heute nach verschiedenen Wiederverwendungen mit wenig beschädigter Inschrift im Steinmuseum von Solothurn ausgestellt[31]. Auch den bereits genannten Meilenstein von Wylen (Unterwil, Gemeinde Turgi), den Tschudi ebenfalls skizzierte, könnte man dazu zählen. Die Zeichnungen dieser Objekte können am Original nachgeprüft werden, da sie heute noch erhalten sind. Sie zeigen, dass Tschudi bemüht war, so realistisch wie möglich zu zeichnen.

Nun gibt es aber Zeichnungen Tschudis von Steininschriften, die heute verloren sind; neben kleineren Fragmenten ohne Aussagekraft sind es drei ganz verschiedene Einträge, die ganz unterschiedlich zu behandeln sind.

Die Grabinschrift für Severia Martiola aus Avenches

Die Grabinschrift für Severia Martiola, gestiftet von ihrem Bruder Severius Marcianus, gehört von Inhalt und Formulierung her zu den gängigen Grabinschriften der römischen Kaiserzeit[32]. Sie taucht noch nicht in den Skizzen der Apian-Ausgabe auf; doch im Codex SG 1083 schrieb Tschudi zur Form: „In eodem oppidulo statua integra in plateis iacens", was dann Stumpf in der gedruckten „Schweizer Chronik" auf Deutsch übersetzte: „in dem selbigen staetli Wifelspurg ligt ein gantze Saul uff der gassen also". Der Begriff statua sowie die deutsche Umsetzung „Saul" bereitete im ersten Interpretationsversuch

29 J. Gruter(us), Inscriptiones antiquae totius orbis romani, in corpus absolutissimum redactae (Heidelberg 1603); Smetii Inscriptionum antiquarum quae passim per Europam liber. Accessit Auctarium a Iusto Lipsio ...Lugduni Batavorum 1588, fol. 168, Nr. 18, Zitat entnommen aus ICH 178.

30 ICH 226; CIL XIII 5181; TitHelv 354.

31 Spycher 1999; ebenfalls TitHelv 354.

32 ICH 202 = CIL XIII 5112 = TitHelv 241: D(is) M(anibus) / Severiae / Martiol(a)e / Sever(ius) Mar/cianus / frater / f(aciendum) c(uravit).

Schwierigkeiten. Was wollte Tschudi sagen? Meinte er eine Säule? Immerhin wurde eine Grabsäule aus Kalkstein, in deren Mitte eine gerahmte Steintafel mit dem Text der Grabinschrift angebracht ist, in Avenches 1886 in der West-Nekropole gefunden[33]. Doch die sorgfältig ausgeführte Zeichnung, die Tschudi zum Text hinzufügte (Abb. 4), löste das Problem: Es handelte sich um eine landläufige Grabstele auf einer Basis, ohne Bekrönung. Offenbar waren die Begriffe wie statua bzw. „Säule" in der Anfangszeit der Epigraphik zeitweise noch etwas unscharf[34].

Die heute verschollene Weihesäule deo invicto

Die zweite Zeichnung Tschudis einer unterdessen verlorenen Weihinschrift betrifft die „Weihesäule" (oder „Weihealtar") aus Baden (Kt. Aargau), die Tschudi sah, zeichnete und beschrieb (Abb. 5), und von der er etwas später erfuhr, dass Ulrich IX. von Montfort sie 1564 mit Erlaubnis der Eidgenossen in seine Antiquitätensammlung nach Tettnang überführte. Da Ulrich von Montfort 1574 starb, mit ihm sein Familienzweig erlosch und der Besitz zudem verschuldet war, kam die Antiquitätensammlung zum Teil in andere Hände, und die Spuren der Inschrift verloren sich. Für die zu Beginn erwähnte Edition des Wettinger Silberschatzes habe ich die Geschichte der Manuskripttradition in allen Einzelheiten aufgearbeitet[35], so dass hier lediglich jene Ergebnisse herausgegriffen werden sollen, die für die vorliegende Fragestellung wesentlich sind.

Während der Fund seit der Ausgabe von Mommsen in ICH 240 und CIL XIII 5236 (cf. pars 4 p. 68) als Votivgabe für Mithras nicht weiter diskutiert wurde, hat TitHelv 371 auf die Zeichnung Tschudis in Codex SG 1083 (p. 67) zurückgegriffen und diese mit der Objektbeschreibung des Autors verbunden. Damit konnten neue Perspektiven eröffnet werden. Die Untersuchung aller mit Tschudi, Stumpf und Simler verbundener Manuskripte zeigt nämlich, dass nur der Eintrag in den Codex SG 1083 die eigenhändige Zeichnung nach Autopsie darstellt, während die zwei Einträge (Fundbeschreibungen, Text der Inschrift und Zeichnungen) im Manuskript Ms. A 105 inhaltlich zwar Tschudis Interpretation wiedergeben, aber von Kopisten geschrieben und gezeichnet wurden[36]. Die Zeichnungen, von denen die erste (Ms. A 105, fol 5r) noch besser dem Vorbild entspricht als die zweite (Ms. A 105, fol 87v), werden deshalb hier nicht weiter diskutiert.

An diesem Punkt ist nochmals auf den Codex SG 1083 und die Forschungen von Voegelin einzugehen. Voegelin konnte zeigen, dass die im Codex SG 1083 aufgeführten Inschriften jene Inschriftensammlung der römischen Inschriften darstellt, die Johannes Stumpf mit Tschudi diskutierte, verbesserte, in seine „Schweizer Chronik" aufnahm und 1548 veröffentlichte. Davon gibt es aber zwei Ausnahmen, zwei Inschriften, die nachher

33 Grabstele von Avenches: CIL XIII 5135; TitHelv 238; vgl. dagegen Codex SG 1083, p. 66.

34 Dies die Schlussfolgerungen aus der Diskussion mit Philipp Lenz.

35 Arbeitstitel: Die verschollene Weihesäule für deo invicto ICH 240; CIL XIII 5236; TitHelv 371.

36 Ms. A 105, Josias Simler, Kollektaneen. „Von Helvetischen Rhaetischen, Wallisischen und diss- auch jenseits der Gebirgen angrenzender Lannde alter Sachen das VIte Buch". Zentralbibliothek Zürich.

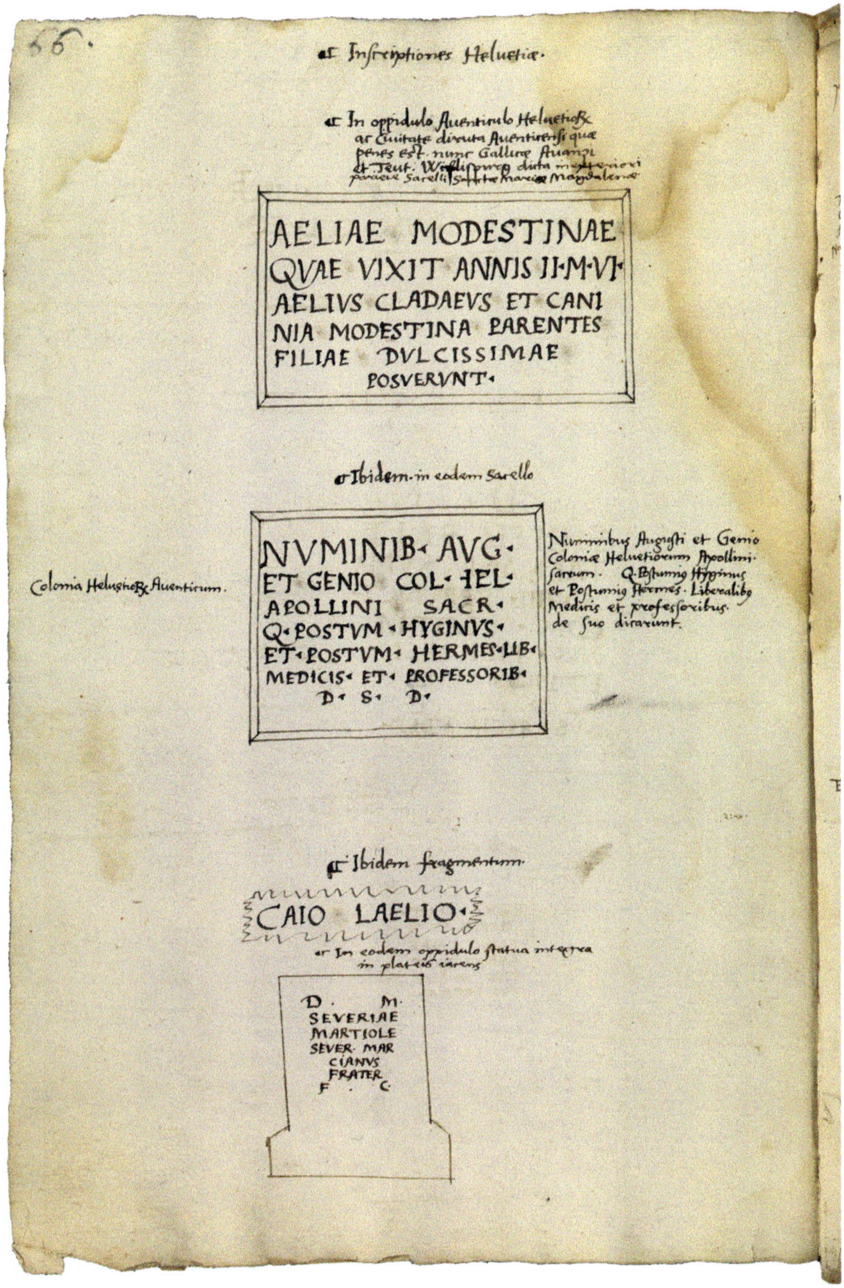

Abb. 4: Handschriftliche Inschriftensammlung. Codex SG 1083, p. 66. Stiftsbibliothek St. Gallen. Zeichnung Tschudis der nicht mehr erhaltenen Grabstele für Severia Martiola

bekannt geworden sind und die Tschudi nach 1548 (und vor 1564) im Codex SG 1083 notierte. Die "Weihesäule" gehört dazu, da sie nicht in die 1548 gedruckte „Schweizer Chronik" von Johannes Stumpf aufgenommen worden ist. Dies lässt sich nur so erklären, dass Tschudi die Inschrift erst nach dem Erscheinen dieses Werkes kennen lernte. Die Datierung des Fundes hängt mit der Anwesenheit von Ulrich IX. von Montfort an den jährlichen eidgenössischen Tagsatzungen in Baden zusammen und kann deshalb festgelegt werden, wie weiter unten gezeigt werden wird.

Hinsichtlich der Inschriftensammlung im Codex SG 1083 handelt es sich also um einen Nachtrag. Tschudi hat neben kurzen Bemerkungen und Umformulierungen nur noch eine weitere Inschrift, die nicht in der Stumpfschen „Schweizer Chronik" veröffentlicht worden ist, als Zusatz im Codex SG 1083 angefügt. Es ist eine heute noch existierende Grabinschrift aus Jona (Rapperswil, Kt. St. Gallen), die er ebenfalls zeichnete[37]. Beide Nachträge sind an ihrer Position auf der betreffenden Seite leicht erkennbar: Die „Weihesäule" ist oben links auf pag. 67 angebracht; man kann sich unschwer das Blatt ohne diese Ergänzung vorstellen. Die Inschrift von Jona ist auf p. 68 unten links an den Rand „geklebt" worden, was bereits Mommsen in CIL XIII 5247 auffiel.

Da die „Schweizer Chronik" von Johannes Stumpf die „Weihesäule" noch nicht enthalten konnte, bildet erst die gedruckte Fassung in der „Gallia Comata" von 1758 den Schluss der Testimonien Tschudis; denn der Plan von Gilg Tschudi und Josias Simler, zusammen eine Publikation unter Einschluss der römischen Inschriften (die nachmalige „Gallia Comata") zu verwirklichen, misslang, da nach dem Tod Tschudis 1572 seine Erben Simler ablehnten. Die Texte gingen unveröffentlicht an die Erben über, unter denen erst Johann Jacob Gallati 1758 das Werk in Konstanz herausgab. Die Erläuterung der Objektgeschichte (erste Hälfte) wie auch die Inschrift blieben dieselben, aber die Zeichnung ist gegenüber dem Original bereits durch die Bedingungen des Drucks verändert worden. Die Objektgeschichte erhielt zudem noch die Information zur Überführung des Steins 1564 durch Ulrich IX. von Montfort nach Tettnang.

Tschudi schrieb im Codex SG 1083, p. 67 (Abb. 5):

> *Aquis Helveticiis in Thermis maioribus in curia posteriori. Lapis forma Baptisterii fere. his annis (durchgestrichen) nup(er) ibidem repert(us).*

In der „Gallia Comata" heisst es dann, p. 144:

> *„Diese Saul, oder Ara, Altar-Stock zu denen Heidnischen Zeiten zu denen Brand-Opffern gebraucht, wurde bey denen Bäderen im hinderen Hof aus der Erden gegraben, die hat der Wohlgeborne Graf Ulrich von Montfort anno Dom. 1564 mit Vergünstigung der Eydgenossen über den Bodensee hinaus in sein Stadt Tettnang geführet."*

37 ICH 237; CIL XIII 5247; TitHelv 402. Die Datierung auf 1531 von TitHelv 402 muss ein Irrtum bzw. ein Druckfehler sein.

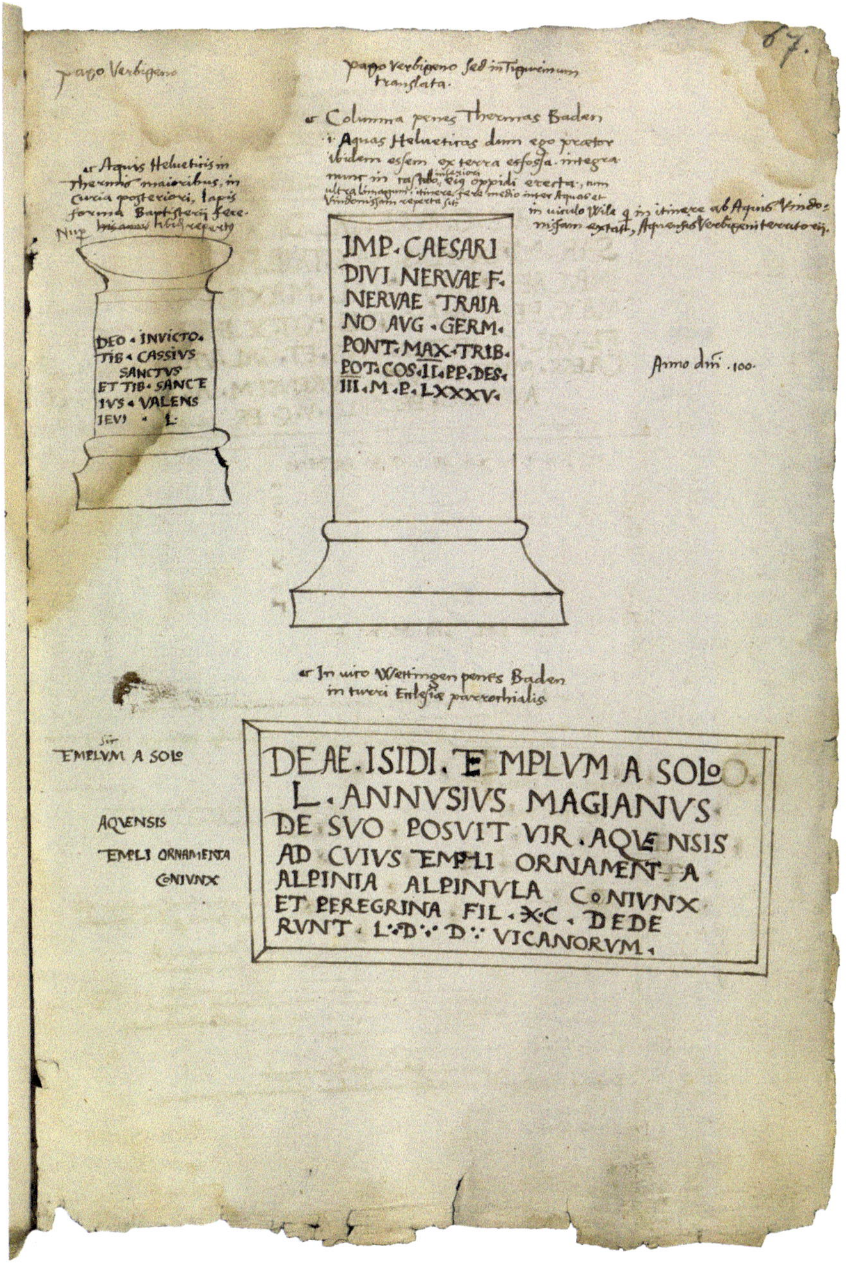

Abb. 5: Handschriftliche Inschriftensammlung. Codex SG 1083, p. 67. Stiftsbibliothek St. Gallen. Oben links als Nachtrag: Zeichnung Tschudis der merkwürdigen „Weihesäule“ deo invicto, die oben einem Taufbecken ähnlich war. Von Ulrich IX. von Montfort 1564 nach Tettnang gebracht

Der bisher kaum beachtete Eintrag von Josias Simler (ohne Zeichnung) sei hier herangezogen, da er wichtige Einzelheiten zur Fundgeschichte enthält[38]. Mommsen zitierte ihn ausschnittsweise in ICH 240 und CIL XIII 5236[39], konnte ihn aber mangels weiterer aufgearbeiteter Quellen nicht auswerten. Dies ist erst im Zusammenhang mit den archäologischen Untersuchungen in Baden erfolgt. Die Informationen Simlers erlauben es, den Hinteren Hof in Baden zu identifizieren, die näheren Umstände des Fundes kennen zu lernen[40], sowie die Rolle von Ulrich IX. von Montfort an den jährlichen eidgenössischen Tagsatzungen von Baden zu würdigen, der seit 1563 dort teilnahm[41]; der reichsunmittelbare Adlige (Geburtsjahr unbekannt, gest. 1575), Landvogt, tätig im Umkreis der Herzöge von Bayern und im Dienst der Kaiser aus Habsburgischem Haus, war zweifellos der ranghöchste Besucher von Baden, sodass die Grosszügigkeit der Eidgenossen, ihm Antiquitäten zu überlassen, verständlich wird.

Tschudi bemühte sich im Codex SG 1083, den Fund zu beschreiben und nach der Beschreibung genau zu zeichnen[42]: Offenbar handelte es sich um eine Säule, die den Text auf ihrem Schaft aufnehmen konnte; ihre Masse sind unbekannt[43]. Der Oberteil der Säule war nicht von einem Kapitell bekrönt, sondern im Gegenteil ausgehöhlt wie ein Taufbecken. Darauf legte Tschudi Wert, er versuchte, etwas Vergleichbares zu finden und betonte diese Sonderform. In der letzten (gedruckten) Fassung schwächte der Autor die Aussa-

38 Simler, Ms. A 102, fol.25r: „anno dom(ini) (vac.) prope vicum calidarum aquarum aliam columnam fere potius aram invenit Theodovirus a Monte hospes tum aulae ut vocant posterioris ad aquas, q(uam) postea ~~ab ips(o)~~ donavit Montfortio [darüber geschrieben, durchgestrichen: ~~huic principi~~] comiti antiquitatum Romanaru(m) studiosissimo, qui illam permissu Helvetiorum Tetnangum avexit. illius unleserlich talis fuit inscriptio. „Im Jahr des Herrn ... beim Dorf der heissen Quellen fand Theodovirus vom Berg, damals Gastwirt des, wie sie sagen, hinteren Hofes bei den Thermen eine andere Säule oder eher einen Altar, den er später dem Grafen Montfort schenkte, einem grossen Liebhaber der römischen Altertümer, der jenen (Altar) mit Erlaubnis der Helvetier nach Tettnang wegführte. Dessen ... Inschrift war die folgende" (Übersetzung R. Frei-Stolba).

39 Man sieht sogleich, dass Mommsen den Text etwas abkürzte, in CIL XIII 5236 aber noch mehr Einzelheiten zu Ulrich von Montfort hinzufügte.

40 Der Hintere Hof oder Hinterhof und der Stad(t)hof in Bäderquartier sind die zwei Gasthöfe, die zinspflichtig waren und ein Traktandum der jährlichen eidgenössischen Tagsatzung bildeten, vgl. Die eidgenössischen Abschiede 1861, Bd. IV, Abt.2, 1091. Theodovicus ist verschrieben (Hör- oder Schreibfehler von Simler) für Theodoricus, latein. für Dietrich. Dietrich II Amberg ist als Gastwirt nachgewiesen. Ich danke Andrea Schaer, Bern, für die Informationen; wir haben gemeinsam diese Texte entschlüsseln können. Für alle Einzelheiten vgl. meinen in Anm. 35 zitierten Beitrag.

41 Nachgewiesen ist seine Teilnahme am 23. Juni 1566 als Gesandter des Kaisers und Landvogt der vorderösterreichischen Lande, der offiziell die Eidgenossen um Hilfe gegen die Türken bat. Die eidgenössischen Abschiede 1861, Bd. IV, Abt.2, Nr. 268, 343 aa.

42 TitHelv 371 geht im Unterschied zu allen anderen Editoren diese Beschreibung ernst. Der Wortlaut der Weihung deo invicto, unter der immer nur Mithras verstanden wurde, steht dieser neuen Interpretation nicht entgegen.

43 Die Angaben des Zürcher Arztes und Naturforschers J.J. Scheuchzer in seiner Schrift über die Bäder von Baden 1732 enthalten Fehler, aber auch den aus einer Tschudi-Tradition stammende Begriff „Altar-Stock". Ich halte trotzdem seine Massangaben eher für errechnet, denn in der Gallia Comata 1758 werden keine Masse genannt, was wohl bedeutet, dass sie auch nicht in der Vorlage von 1571 genannt worden sind.

ge dann zu „Altar-Stock oder *ara*“ ab, die Säule wurde zu einem Altarstein verbreitet, nur der Oberteil, das rätselhafte Becken, ist geblieben.

Bis jetzt ist die von Tschudi beschriebene Form singulär geblieben. TitHelv 371 zieht als mögliche Vergleichsform die Fassung eines Globus, mit anderen Worten eine Statuenbasis in Erwägung, die dann die Büste des Serapis getragen hätte[44]. Das ist bestechend; man wird auf einen vergleichbaren Fund warten müssen. Tschudi beschrieb offenbar sehr ernsthaft einen ihm unbekannten Gegenstand, und es besteht kein Grund, daran zu zweifeln. Oben ist gezeigt worden, dass der Begriff „Saul“ offenbar weiter gefasst wurde und mehrere Formen aufrechter Steinformen umfassen konnte. Sicher ist jedenfalls, dass die Zeichnung Tschudis im Codex SG 1083 die Grundlage für weitere Überlegungen bilden muss.

Die letzte Zeichnung Tschudis

Dank den Forschungen von Hans Lieb (1930–2014) kennt man auch die letzte Zeichnung Tschudis[45] (Abb. 6): Sie betrifft wiederum eine heute verschollene Grabinschrift, die ebenfalls in den Besitz von Ulrich IX. von Montfort gelangte. Die Grabinschrift des Tetto, Sohn des Omullus, wurde 1565 von Bernhard Brand, dem Basler Gesandten, auf der Heimreise von der Tagsatzung in Augst (Kt. Baselland) kopiert und dem Basler Gelehrten Basilius Amerbach mitgeteilt[46]. Er muss auch Pierre Pithou von Text und Ort, aber ohne Zeichnung, informiert haben, der im Sommer 1570 Josias Simler davon berichtete[47]. Simler nahm die Inschrift in seine Unterlagen auf[48] und benachrichtigte Aegidius Tschudi, der am 23. Okt. 1571 Simler für „Inscriptiones so ir mir gelichen“ dankte[49]. Tschudi notierte die Inschrift auf ein Loseblatt, das er als Beleg in sein laufend ergänztes Manuskript Ms. A 105 nach p. 108 einfügte, in welchem dann p. 108 und p. 109 die Ergänzungen zu Augusta Raurica aufgeführt waren.

Tschudi fertigte diese Zeichnung also kurz vor seinem Tode an, freilich nicht mehr nach Autopsie, sondern lediglich nach einem unvollständig übermittelten Text.

44 Mit Hinweis auf Eck 2016.

45 Frei-Stolba 2000, 139. Sehr gerne publiziere ich hier noch einmal die Überlegungen von Hans Lieb, denn ihm verdanke ich die Einführung in die Manuskripttraditionen und in die Handschriftenkunde, die er mir seit 1990 vermittelte.

46 Frei-Stolba 2000, 139–141. Die Abschrift Brands mit Zeichnung und Datum von 10. März 1565 findet sich als Loseblatt p. 24 in den Amerbachschen Scheden, dort wurde sie von Hans Lieb gefunden. Mommsen erwähnte das Loseblatt nicht (Frei-Stolba 2000, 139 Anm. 672).

47 Brief von 1570 (a.d. XIIII Kal. Sept., d. h. vom 19. Aug.) an J. Simler, Zentralbibliothek Zürich, Thesaurus Hottingerianus (Ms. F 36–87), darin Ms. F 60, Brief 572. Vgl. den Inhalt des Briefes in ICH 181, Kommentar.

48 Simler, Ms. A 102, (Titel: Antiquitatum Helveticarum libri III), fol. 41v und fol. 42r.

49 Brief Nr. 54, bei Vogel 1856, 273.

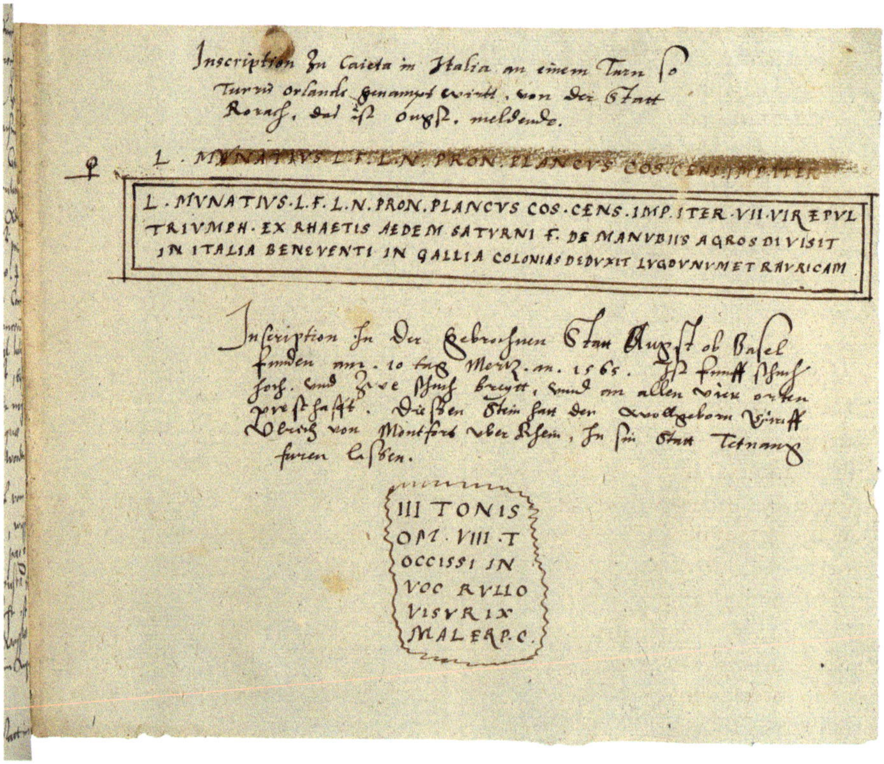

Abb. 6: In J. Simler, Kollektaneen (Von Helvetischen, Rhaetischen...Lannde alter Sachen das VIte Buch), Ms. A 105, Loseblatt nach p. 108, Zentralbibliothek Zürich. Letzte Zeichnung Tschudis. Grabstein für Tetto, Sohn des Omullus. Im Besitz von Ulrich IX. von Montfort

Bibliographie

Brüschweiler R.W. et al. 1978. Geschichte der Gemeinde Wettingen, Baden.

Die eidgenössischen Abschiede 1861. Amtliche Sammlung der älteren eidgenössischen Abschiede, hg. auf Anordnung der Bundesbehörden (EA), Zeitraum 1245–1798, von Segesser Ph. A. et al., Bern. Bd. IV, Abt. 2: Die eidgenössischen Abschiede aus dem Zeitraum von 1556 bis 1586.

Eck W. 2022. Gesellschaft und Administration im Römischen Reich, in A. Kolb (Hrsg.), Aktualisierte Schriften Auswahl, Berlin.

Eck W. 2016. Sarapis und die Legio IV Ferrata. Die Weihung einer Sarapisbüste für das Wohl des Kaisers, ZPE 198, 2016, 211–217.

Fellmann Brogli R. et al. (voraussichtlich 2024). Die Inschriften von Vindonissa. Veröffentlichungen der Gesellschaft Pro Vindonissa [Bandzahl noch offen], Brugg.

Frei-Stolba R. 2013. Die Inschrift über dem Hofportal des Schlosses von Avenches – Zur Rezeption der römischen Antike in der Schweiz im 16. und 18. Jahrhundert, in S. Frey (Hrsg.), La numismatique pour passion. Études d'histoire monétaire offertes à Suzanne Frey-Kupper par quelques-uns de ses amis à l'occasion de son anniversaire 2013, Lausanne, 49–73.

Frei-Stolba R. 2011. Gastvortrag von Prof. Dr. Ioan Piso, Jber. GPV 2011, 107.

Frei-Stolba R. 2007. Der Besuch Trajans in Vindonissa im Jahr 98 n. Chr. Mit einem Beitrag von Jürgen Trumm, Jber. GPV 2007, 3–16.

Frei-Stolba R. 2000. Die Überlieferungsgeschichte der Inschrift ICH 298 = CIL XIII 5295. Der Grabstein des Tetto, in P.-A. Schwarz, L. Berger (Hrsg.), Tituli Rauracenses 1. Testimonien und Aufsätze. Zu den Namen und ausgewählten Inschriften von Augst und Kaiseraugst, Augst. 133–145.

Frei-Stolba R. 1992. Früheste epigraphische Forschungen in Avenches. Zu den Abschriften des 16. Jh., Schweiz. Zeitschr. für Geschichte 42, 227–246

Kolb A. 2022. Tituli Helvetici. Die römischen Inschriften der West- und Ostschweiz. In Zusammenarbeit mit Jens Bartels, Nikolas Hächler, Benjamin Hartmann, Anna Willi, Yannick Baldasarre und mit Beiträgen von Michael Alexander Speidel, Regula Ackermann, Sebastian Geisseler, Bonn.

Leu U. B. 2002. Nicht Tigurum, sondern Turicum. Johann Caspar Hagenbuch (1700–1763) und die Anfänge der römischen Altertumskunde in der Schweiz, Zürcher Taschenbuch, 233–311.

Lieb H., Bridel, Ph. 2009. CIL XIII 5092 – unique vestige d'un monument funéraire?, Bull. Ass. Pro Aventico 51, 59–70.

Martin-Kilcher S. et al. (in Vorbereitung). Der 1633 entdeckte Sakralhort des 3. Jahrhunderts mit Silbergefässen und ein Münzdepot aus Wettingen bei Baden (Aquae Helveticae), Zeitschrift für Archäologie und Kunstgeschichte 81, 2024, Bände 1 und 2.

Mundt F. 2008. Beatus Rhenanus: Rerum Germanicarum libri tres (1531). Ausgabe, Übersetzung, Studien, Tübingen.

Spycher H. 1999. Geschichte der Archäologie im Kanton Solothurn, as. Archäologie der Schweiz 22, 59–66.

Trümpy H. 1956. Zu Gilg Tschudis epigraphischen Forschungen, Schweiz. Zeitschr. für Geschichte 6, 498–510.

Voegelin S. 1886. Wer hat zuerst die Römischen Inschriften in der Schweiz gesammelt und erklärt? Jb. Schweizer. Gesch. 11, 27–164.

Vogel J. 1856. Egidius Tchudi als Staatsmann und Geschichtsschreiber, Zürich.

Winteler J. 1963. Glaronensia. Aus der Geschichte einer Bibliothek, Librarium 6, 27–31.

Explicatio thesauri recens apud Transylvanos reperti – eine Abhandlung des Wolfgang Lazius zum siebenbürgischen Schatzfund von 1543

Fritz Mitthof*

1 Einleitung

Der vorliegende Beitrag bietet die erste vollständige Publikation einer Abhandlung des Wolfgang Lazius (1514–1565), die in der Münchener Sammelhandschrift Clm 9216 enthalten ist.[1] Lazius widmet sich in dieser *Explicatio* der Interpretation eines spektakulären Schatzfundes, der nach seinen Worten kurz zuvor (*recens*) von Fischern im Bett des Strei-Flusses im südwestlichen Siebenbürgen entdeckt worden war. Da der Wiener Gelehrte niemals selbst in Siebenbürgen gewesen ist, dürfte er von diesem Ereignis über Gewährsleute erfahren haben.[2] Die besondere Bedeutung des Textes liegt in vier Aspekten begründet: Erstens handelt es sich um eine der wenigen zeitgenössischen Quellen zu diesem bedeutsamen Fundereignis, das aus der Sicht der modernen Forschung als frühester dokumentierter Fall einer bis heute andauernden langen Reihe vergleichbarer Funde antiker Gold- und Silbermünzen (sowie goldener Armreifen[3]) in der Zone der Orăștie-Berge gelten darf;[4] zweitens hat sich die historische Deutung des Schatzes durch Lazius, der ihn

* Diese Studie ist ein Resultat des vom Verfasser geleiteten FWF-Projekts „Von der Schatzsuche zur Archäologie" (Grant-DOI 10.55776/P23975). – Bei Verweisen auf den nachstehenden Kommentar zur Explicatio (s. unten Abschnitt 7) sind die betreffenden Ziffern mit einem Asterisk markiert (s. unten Anm. 21).

1 Kurze Ausschnitte des Textes wurden bereits von Makkay 1994, 206 und 1995, 342 Anm. 10 sowie von Deppert-Lippitz 2010, 13 mitgeteilt, freilich teilweise fehlerhaft und ohne Übersetzung und Kommentar.

2 Zur Frage, wie Lazius zu Informationen über siebenbürgische Antikenfunde gelangte, s. unten Komm. *23.

3 Hierzu s. unten Anm. 55.

4 Mit dem Ausdruck Orăștie-Berge ist das zu den Südkarpaten gehörige Bergland südlich der Stadt Orăștie gemeint, das aus der Mureș-Ebene nach Süden hin allmählich ansteigt und schließlich vom Mittel- ins Hochgebirge übergeht. Das Gebiet wird durch das schmale Tal eines Flüsschens, genannt Râul Orăștie (im Unterlauf auch Apa Orașului und im Oberlauf Apa Grădiștei), mit einer Gesamtlänge von ca. 50 km erschlossen. In dieses Gewässer münden aus den Seitentälern von Osten und Westen mehrere kleinere Zuflüsse ein. Über die gesamte Zone sind in Streulage die imposanten Reste von Burgen, Siedlungen, Heiligtümern, Wehranlagen und Wachtürmen aus der Blütezeit der

mit König Decebal und dessen Kriegen gegen Trajan in Verbindung brachte, als wirkmächtiges Narrativ erwiesen, das bis heute weitgehend unhinterfragt fortlebt; drittens liefert die *Explicatio* ein Zeugnis für Lazius' Wissensstand zur Geschichte des antiken Dakien, dem in seinem Geschichtsbild eine besondere Rolle zukam; viertens illustriert die Abhandlung die Stärken und Schwächen der Arbeitsweise des Historikers und Altertumskundlers Lazius, die im Vergleich mit anderen Gelehrten des Zeitalters sein besonderes Profil ausmachen, und zwar vor allem im Hinblick auf seinen Umgang mit literarischen und epigraphischen Quellen, aber auch bezüglich seiner historiographischen Akzentsetzungen.

2 Der Inhalt der *Explicatio*

Die Abhandlung gliedert sich thematisch in sieben Abschnitte. Lazius beginnt mit einer knappen Beschreibung zweier Goldmünzen, nämlich einer Münze des Lysimachos (gemeint ist ein postumer Stater des Lysimachos-Typs) sowie einer Münze mit der angeblichen Legende ΣΩΖΟΝ (in Wirklichkeit ΚΟΣΩΝ), die beide mit dem Strei-Schatz zu verbinden seien.[5] Hierauf befasst sich Lazius mit König Lysimachos, den er chronologisch verortet, und mit der von diesem gegründeten Stadt Lysimacheia. Sodann zitiert er den Bericht des Cassius Dio über den Schatz des Königs Decebal, den dieser einst im Fluss Sargetia verstecken ließ und der von Kaiser Trajan nach seinem Sieg über die Daker geborgen wurde. Im vierten Abschnitt begründet Lazius seine Annahme, dass der Strei-Fund als ein Teil von Decebals Schatz zu identifizieren sei. Im Anschluss gibt er mehrere lateinische Inschriften aus der von Trajan gegründeten *Colonia Sarmizegetusa* wieder, die er, was die Örtlichkeit betrifft, mit dem einstigen Königssitz Decebals *Sarmizegetusa Regia* gleichsetzt. Hieran schließen sich Ausführungen zu den drei römischen Teilprovinzen Dakiens an, zu ihrer geographischen Lage und zu Aspekten ihrer späteren Geschichte, sowie zu den Feldzügen der Römer in der Region in vortrajanischer Zeit, von Augustus bis Domitian. Lazius zitiert in diesem Zusammenhang einige Verse aus der Dichtung des Zeitalters: Juvenal, Martial, Statius und Silius Italicus. Den Abschluß der *Explicatio* bilden zwei weitere römische Inschriften, die eine wiederum aus Siebenbürgen, die andere aus Gumpendorf bei Wien.

späteisenzeitlichen dakischen Kultur verteilt (1. Jh. v.–1. Jh. n. Chr.). Im Zentrum befindet sich die Anlage von Grădiștea de Munte bzw. Grădiștea Munțelului, die gemeinhin mit dem in den literarischen Quellen erwähnten Königssitz Sarmizegetusa Regia gleichgesetzt wird; hierzu s. unten Komm. *21–22. Die Orăștie-Berge werden im Westen durch das Strei-Tal und im Osten durch das Cugir- und das Sebeș-Tal begrenzt. – Für einen Überblick zur Geschichte der antiken Schatzfunde in dieser Region s. zuletzt Mitthof 2017; Petac 2018; Mitthof 2022 (mit weiterer Literatur).

5 Zur Identifizierung der beiden Münztypen s. unten Komm. *1–2.

3 Die Sammelhandschrift Clm 9216

Die Sammelhandschrift Clm 9216 (Mon. Jes. 16) 94 fol., die sich aus einer Reihe von originalen Schriftstücken des 16. Jh. zusammensetzt, befindet sich heute in der Bayerischen Staatsbibliothek.[6] Laut Katalog gehört sie zu jener Gruppe von Handschriften, die im Zuge der Auflösung des Jesuitenordens im ausgehenden 18. bzw. der Säkularisierung der bayerischen Klöster zu Beginn des 19. Jh. vom Münchener Jesuitenkolleg an die Hof- bzw. Staatsbibliothek übergeben wurden (daher die ältere Bezeichnung Mon. Jes. 16).[7] Sie trägt den Titel „*Liber antiquitatum*" und enthält neben der *Explicatio* des Lazius eine Reihe weiterer Abhandlungen, Briefe und ähnlicher Texte verschiedener Verfasser und Provenienz zu antiken Inschriften, Münzen und Gemmen sowie zur Altertumskunde.[8] Da die Abhandlung des Lazius und auch andere in Clm 9216 enthaltene Texte mit Sicherheit einige Jahrzehnte vor der Gründung des Münchener Jesuitenkollegs abgefasst worden sind (Lazius verstarb 1565, das Kolleg entstand aber erst im ausgehenden 16. Jh.), muss die Sammelhandschrift zuvor an einem anderen Ort zusammengestellt und verwahrt worden sein.

In Ermangelung einer entsprechenden Dokumentation können über die Ursprungsgeschichte der Sammelhandschrift nur Vermutungen angestellt werden. Mit Blick auf unsere *Explicatio* scheinen sich drei mögliche Szenarien anzubieten. Eine erste Annahme wäre, dass die Abhandlung ursprünglich aus der Bibliothek der „Hohen Schule" zu Ingolstadt stammt, wo Lazius einst studiert hatte und promoviert worden war. Die Hohe Schule wurde 1571 mit dem Ingolstädter Jesuitenkolleg vereint, und von hier aus könnte das Manuskript an das Münchener Jesuitenkolleg weitergegeben worden sein.[9] Ebenso wäre aber auch denkbar, dass Lazius die *Explicatio* auf seinen ausgedehnten Forschungsreisen durch Süddeutschland einer anderen Institution oder Person in diesem Raum überlassen hat, von wo sie ins Münchener Jesuitenkolleg gelangt sein könnte. Als dritte – und vielleicht plausibelste – Variante wäre ein Zusammenhang mit der Augsburger Kaufmannsfamilie der Fugger zu erwägen, da in der Handschrift direkt vor unserer *Explicatio* ein Brief aus

---

6 Deppert-Lippitz 2010, 13 Anm. 11 geht davon aus, dass es sich bei dem vorliegenden Schriftstück nicht um das Original, sondern um eine „professionelle Abschrift" handelt, die Lazius seiner *alma mater* (also der Hohen Schule zu Ingolstadt, s. das Folgende) überlassen habe. In der Tat ist anzunehmen, dass Lazius diesen Text vervielfältigen ließ und an verschiedene Personen oder Institutionen, mit denen er in Kontakt stand, versandt hat; dies entsprach der allgemeinen Praxis des Zeitalters. Man beachte als Parallele besonders den im Folgenden behandelten Briefwechsel des Lazius mit Beatus Rhenanus, in welchem Lazius die Übersendung einer *Explicatio* explizit erwähnt; auch dieser Text handelte, wie es scheint, vom Strei-Fund, ist aber inhaltlich nicht mit der vorliegenden Version des Berichts gleichzusetzen (s. unten Abschnitt 4). Zur Frage nach der Identifizierung des Destinatars unserer *Explicatio* s. das Folgende. In jedem Fall unterscheidet sich ihr sorgfältiges Schriftbild deutlich von dem der in der Österreichischen Nationalbibliothek aufbewahrten autographen *Codices Laziani*, die in einer wesentlich schwerer lesbaren Kursive verfasst sind (so z. B. Cod. 8664, auf den wir im Folgenden mehrfach verweisen werden). Es handelt sich also bei unserer *Explicatio* um eine Reinschrift, die vermutlich von einem Schreiber im Auftrag des Lazius angefertigt wurde.

7 Halm, Laubmann, Meyer 1874, 84–85 Nr. 668.

8 Für eine genaue Inhaltsangabe siehe wiederum Halm, Laubmann, Meyer (wie oben Anm. 7).

9 Siehe wiederum Deppert-Lippitz (wie oben Anm. 6).

Konstantinopel an einen Wiener Agenten der Fugger aus dem Jahr 1555 (fol. 7) und unmittelbar nach dieser (fol. 15) ein Brief aus Bologna an Johann Jakob Fugger (1516–1575) vom Jahr 1536 zu finden sind. Zur Untermauerung dieses Ansatzes ließe sich bemerken, dass Lazius in engem Kontakt mit Vertretern des süddeutschen Handelshauses in verschiedenen Regionen Mittel- und Osteuropas stand, denen er, wie wir gleich sehen werden, unter anderem auch seine Informationen zu Altertümern aus Siebenbürgen verdankte. Hinzu kommt, dass Lazius eines seiner Hauptwerke, die Geschichte der Völkerwanderungen,[10] dem soeben erwähnten J.J. Fugger gewidmet hat. Schließlich ist in diesem Zusammenhang zu beachten, dass die Sammelhandschrift Clm 9216 von Theodor Mommsen (1817–1903) in der Einleitung zu seiner Ausgabe der von Lazius erwähnten Inschrift aus Gumpendorf im *Corpus Inscriptionum Latinarum* (CIL III 4566) explizit als *Codex Fuggerianus* bezeichnet wird, und dass der deutsche Gelehrte überdies davon ausging, dass Lazius unsere *Explicatio* dem J.J. Fugger übersandte, da das folgende Schriftstück in der Handschrift (fol.15), wie bereits erwähnt, diesen explizit als Adressaten nennt.[11]

Ein solches Szenario scheint zwar auf den ersten Blick sehr überzeugend; allerdings bliebe in diesem Fall unklar, wann und auf welchem Weg die Sammelhandschrift Clm 9216 in das Münchener Jesuitenkolleg gelangt sein sollte, in dessen Besitz sie sich ja laut dem Katalog der Bayerischen Staatsblibliothek seit etwa 1800 befand. J.J. Fugger verkaufte nämlich seine Bibliothek im Jahr 1571 an Herzog Albrecht V. von Bayern, der sie in die bereits 1558 begündete Hofbibliothek aufnahm, aus welcher später die Bayerische Staatsbibliothek hervorgegangen ist. Bezüglich der Frage nach dem Entstehungskontext unserer *Explicatio* bzw. nach ihrer Überlieferungsgeschichte ist also unter kodikologischer Perspektive keine sichere Antwort möglich.

4 Datierung

Ein weitgehend gesicherter *terminus post quem* für die Datierung unserer *Explicatio* ist 1543, das mutmaßliche Jahr des Schatzfundes im Strei-Fluss.[12] Weitere Hinweise zu ihrer Abfassungszeit liefern die erhaltenen Teile der Korrespondenz des Beatus Rhenanus (1485–1547) mit Lazius.[13] In einem dieser Briefe vom 30. Juli 1545 dankt Beatus dem Lazius

10 Lazius 1557.

11 Siehe unten Komm. *73.

12 Siehe unten Abschnitt 8.

13 Zwei Briefe zwischen Lazius und Beatus sind im Wortlaut vollständig erhalten; s. Horawitz, Hartfelder 1886, 540–544 Nr. 401: Lazius an Beatus (aus: Cod. 8457, fol. 27a–43b) und 564–568 Nr. 423: Beatus an Lazius (aus: Lazius 1551, lib. I, p. 20–23). Aus diesen ist zu ersehen, dass Beatus mindestens zweimal von Schlettstadt aus an Lazius geschrieben hat, nämlich am 2. Juli und am 30. Juli 1545 (s. Nr. 401, Z. 1–3). Lazius antwortete hierauf aus Wien im weiteren Verlauf des Jahres 1545 (Nr. 401; kein Tagesdatum; Mayr 1894, S. 74 datiert diesen Brief auf den 30. Sept. 1545). Der Brief Nr. 423 des Beatus aus Schlettstadt (ohne Datum) ist vermutlich mit dem vom 30. Juli 1545 gleichzusetzen; in diesem erwähnt Beatus ein früheres Schreiben des Lazius, das dieser offenbar am 24. Mai aus Wien abgesandt hatte und das am 14. Juli bei Beatus in Schlettstadt eingegangen war.

für die Zusendung einer *explicatio thesauri Dacici*, also einer Abhandlung, die dem Titel nach zu urteilen ebenfalls vom Strei-Fund handelte. Dieser Sendung war, so Beatus, auch die Beschreibung einiger neu gefundener römischer Altertümer aus Wien und Umgebung beigefügt, an deren Entdeckung Lazius teilweise selbst mitgewirkt hatte.[14] Lazius hatte dieses Konvolut dem Beatus als Anhang zu seinem Brief vom 24. Mai 1545 von Wien nach Schlettstadt übersandt.

Es stellt sich die Frage, ob der Lazius-Text, der Beatus vorlag, mit unserer *Explicatio* identisch war. Mehrere Indizien sprechen gegen diese Annahme. Zunächst fällt auf, dass Beatus in seiner Inhaltsangabe zu Lazius' Text nur römische Monumente aus Wien und Umgebung nennt, nicht aber solche aus Siebenbürgen; hingegen wird in unserer *Explicatio* ausgiebig über siebenbürgische Inschriftenfunde berichtet, während Wien einzig durch die Inschrift aus Gumpendorf vertreten ist. Zudem besteht das Problem, dass Lazius in unserem Text den *Liber praefecturarum (Romanarum)* verwendet, womit er offenkundig die *Notitia dignitatum* meint,[15] die Beatus zwar bereits zwei Jahrzehnte zuvor in Speyer wiederentdeckt hatte und damals zur Edition vorbereitete, die aber erst einige Jahre nach seinem Ableben, nämlich 1552, im Druck erschienen ist.[16] Lazius kannte von diesem Werk vor seinem Erscheinen nur eine Kurzfassung (*epitome*), die Beatus ihm just am 30. Juli 1545 in Antwort auf sein Schreiben vom 24. Mai desselben Jahres zugesandt hatte;[17] hierbei dürfte es sich um die Indizes gehandelt haben, die in der Handschrift den zwei Teilen des Werkes, nämlich den Listen einerseits für den Osten und andererseits für den Westen des Römischen Reiches, vorangestellt sind und die einen Überblick über alle in dem Werk erfassten Ämter und Provinzen geben.[18] Damit scheint festzustehen, dass unsere *Explicatio* eine überarbeitete Fassung jenes Textes darstellt, den Lazius am 24. Mai 1545 an Beatus übersandt hatte, und dass sie somit von Lazius erst nach dem Eingang des Antwortschreibens des Beatus vom 30. Juli 1545 abgefasst worden sein kann, also nicht vor August oder September 1545.

Einen zweiten Anhaltspunkt und *terminus ante quem* für die Abfassungszeit unserer *Explicatio* liefern Lazius' *Commentarii Reipublicae Romanae* (im Folgenden: *Comm. R. R.*) aus dem Jahr 1551, in denen er einen wesentlich ausführlicheren Bericht über den Strei-Fund bietet.[19] Dort nennt er viele Details zu den Fundumständen, zum Verbleib der Fundobjekte und zum politischen Nachspiel des Fundes, die im vorliegenden Text fehlen. Dies ist ein klares Indiz, dass unsere *Explicatio* vor den *Comm. R. R.* verfasst worden sein dürfte, und zwar vermutlich in einer Zeit, als Lazius mit der Arbeit an diesem Buch,

---

14 Nr. 423 (Horawitz, Hartfelder 1886, 564, Z. 3–5): ... *una cum explicatione thesauri Dacici et monumentis Romanae vetustatis, ad Vindobonnam et locis vicinis partim tua cura, partim forte fortuna repertis.*

15 Siehe unten Komm. *34.

16 Das Werk wurde herausgegeben von Sigismund Gelenius (1497–1554); s. Gelenius 1552.

17 Brief Nr. 423 (Horawitz, Hartfelder 1886, 568, Z. 1–4): ... *quam antiquum illud volumen, quod Noticias cum Orientis tum Occidentis continet ... cuius tibi epitomen hic mittimus* (zur Datierung des Briefs s. oben Anm. 13).

18 Not. dign. Or. 1 und Oc. 1 (ed. Seeck 1876, 1–5 und 103–107).

19 Lazius 1551, Lib. XII, cap. VI (zum Wortlaut der Stelle s. unten Anm. 38).

seinem zweiten Hauptwerk, noch nicht begonnen hatte. Da sein erstes Hauptwerk, die Stadtgeschichte Wiens (*Vienna Austriae*), im Jahr 1546 erschien,[20] können wir mutmaßen, dass er etwa ab diesem Zeitpunkt mit der Abfassung der *Comm. R. R.* begann. Es spricht folglich vieles dafür, die Entstehung unserer *Explicatio* ins Spätjahr 1545 zu setzen; alternativ käme eventuell auch noch das Frühjahr 1546 in Frage.

5 Transkription[21]

[11r] Explicatio thesauri recens apud Transylvanos reperti et per piscatorem quendam in vado fluvii cuiusdam detecti autore Vuolfgango Lazio Viennensi medico.

Numi aurei ex thesauro recens apud Transylvanos opera piscatoris cuiusda[m] detecto, quorum mihi copia fieri potuit, duas Graecas habuere inscriptiones, quarum altera literis his ΒΑΣΙΛΕΩΣ ΛΥΣΙΜΑΧΟΥ[*1], hoc est regis Lysimachi, altera vero ΣΩΖΟΝ[*2], salvatorem vel liberatorem. Quos ego numos a Lysimacho Thratiae & Macedoniae rege signatos annis abhinc 1820[*3] rep[er]io. Vixisse enim Lysimachum, quo tempore inter Romanos ac Pyrrhum Epirotarum regem bellum flagrabat[*4], statim vel non multo post Alexandri Magni aetate[m][*5], anno a condita urbe 468[*6], mundi vero exordio 368[ ][*7] temporum rationem ordinemq[ue] subducenti apparet, ea ferme tempestate, qua Eleazar Iudęorum pontifex Ptolomaeo Aegypti regi septuaginta Bibli[ae] intepretes transmiserat[*8]. Quod Polybij secundu[m] librum legenti manifestum evadit, qui Lysimachum hunc Thraciae regem 124 Olympiade[*9] una cum Seleuco & Ptolomaeo Lago regibus rebus humanis exemptum tradit[*10]. Ab hoc conditam Lysimachiam Thraciae oppidum in confinibus Macedoniae existimo, cuius Antonini Itinerarium[*11], Ptolo[maeus] lib[er] 3 cap[ut] 10 & tab[ula] 9[*12] inter Thraciae oppida meminit, elevationem huic poli constituens 41 grad[us] ½, quod declarat 15 miliariorum Germanicorum[*13] spacio in meridiem ab Adrianopoli[*14] magis declivem Lysimachiam fuisse. Meminit huius & Stephanus Byzantius, De Urbibus, in haec verba[*15]: *Λυσιμαχία πόλις τῆς Θρᾴκης χεῤῥόνησος ἡ πρότερον Κάρδια, ὁ πολίτης Λυσιμάχευς*, id est: *Lysimachia oppidum Thraciae Cherrhonesi, quod prius regio fuerat*[*16], *oppidanus Lysimacheus*. & tantum de numismate isto.

Ad thesaurum revertor, cuius videtur Dion Cassius Nicaeus in Traiano meminisse in haec verba, ut sequit[ur][*17]: *Traianus vero ponte Istrum transgressus bellum magis pro fiducia virium, quam pro studio aut industria gerens, illic com[m]oratus, Dacos tandem subegit,*

20 Lazius 1546.

21 Ergänzte Buchstaben bzw. editorische Angaben (Abkürzungen, Lücken in der Handschrift, Folio-Nummern) erscheinen in eckigen Klammern. Runde Klammern und das &-Zeichen folgen der Handschrift. Zeittypische Abweichungen von der kanonischen Orthographie sind nicht hervorgehoben oder korrigiert. Diakritische Zeichen der Handschrift (Akzente, Punkte, Beistriche etc.) werden nicht wiedergegeben. Großschreibung und Satzzeichen orientieren sich an der modernen Konvention. Zitate, die Lazius aus anderen Werken übernommen hat, sind kursiv gedruckt. Inschriften erscheinen in Majuskeln. Die hochgestellten Ziffern mit Asterisken (*1, *2 etc.) beziehen sich auf die entsprechenden Einträge im folgenden Kommentarteil. Griechische Akzente folgen der Handschrift; für die korrigierte Version s. unten Übersetzung und Komm.

atq[ue] in debellando hoste multa egregij ducis & fortis viri opera aedidit. Complures militum pericula intrepidi adiere, pugnando alij multa fortiter feceru[n]t. Forte eques accepto vulnere de pugna eductus, ut scilicet adhibitis remedijs sanari possit, desperata salute protinus de tabernaculo exivit, nondu[m] enim vis mali vitalia occupaverat, in acieq[ue] constitutus, magna tum iactando, tum etiam faciendo animam efflavit[*18]. *At Decebalus cum* [IIV] *capta regia vicina omnis regio in potestatem po[puli] Ro[mani] venisset, usq[ue] ad captivitatem periclitatus mortem sibi conscivit. Cuius caput deinde Romam delatum fuit. Ita Dacia iuris & ditionis Romanae facta est. Quam mox Traianus in provinciam redegit, urbes condidit, colonos deduxit. Regios vero thesauros, quos Decebalus subter vada Sargetiae amnis haud procul a regia occultaverat, invenit. Fluvium forte rex, captivorum duntaxat manib[us] & opera, averterat de proprio cursu, atq[ue] effosis subinde vadis, in specu magnam vim auri & argenti occuluit, preciosissima quaeq[ue] & eos liquores, qui recondi & observari*[*19] *poterant, eodem congerens. Quibus confectis, ne q[ui]spiam quae gessisset proloqui posset, omnes qui facti conscij erant occidi iussit. At Biculis captivus, cui res cognita erat, abditos thesauros indicavit.* Haec ex Dione.

Ac quanq[uam] reperisse hunc thesaurum Caesarem Traianu[m] devicto Decebalo is tradat, apparet tamen, cum quia in vadis effosis hunc Decebalus occultaverat, ut verisimile, diversis in locis, tum quia Biculi loca non omnia perspecta fuerant, simul quia aquae fluxum vehementiorem, qui fluminib[us] Dacijs per scopulos decurrentibus adhuc visitur, thesaurum distraxisse diversa in loca ac vada rationi consonum est. Atq[ue] propterea non integrum thesaurum, quantum Decebalus occuluerat, Caesarem Traianum reperisse.

Huic accedit, quod is ipse thesaurus recens repertus anno post occultationem 1400[*20] per piscatorem detectus fuerit, & quantum audio parum infra Albam Iuliam, quam Transylvanj appellant. Ubi in loco dicto Varhel vel Gradisca[*21] Sarmizgetusae[*22] regiae quondam Decebali (quam in Ulpiam suam Traianam Caesar Traianus Nerva, nomine mutato, converterat) rudera extant. Quantum ex inscriptionib[us] apparet, ibi & Sargetiae amnis & thesauri reperti in monumentis mentio fit. Quorum mihi quorundam per D[ominum] Stephanum Scher, senatorem Vienn[ensem], & D[ominum] Ioannem Verber Budensem sacerdotem[*23] copia facta est. Quorum quasdam subiungam fidei ergo rapsodias:

DEO HERCVLI
PRO SALVTE IMP.
DIVI TRAIANI
AVGVSTI ET
MARTIANAE
SORORIS AVG.
COLONIA DAC.
SARMIZ.[*24]

SARIS DIVI NERVI
TRAIANI AVGVSTI
CONDITA COLONIA
DACICA
PER
V. M. SCAVRIANV[*25]

FAVSTINAE
AVG
DIVI PII
COL. SARMIZ.[*26]

[12r]

Aliud:
FAVSTINAE
AVG
MAR. AVRELI
ANTONINI
FILIAE
COL. SARMIZ.[*27]

Aliud in quo Sarmiz[getusa] Ulpia Traiana:
M. VLP.
RESTVTO
IIVIR. COL. SARM.
VLPIAE
MARCELLINA
ET RESTVTA FIL.
AE ET HEREDES
T. P. C.[*28]

Aliud in quo Sargetiae mentio:
DEAE ISIDI
PRISCIANVS AVG
COL. SARMIZ METROL.
ET AVRELIA FORTVNA
LIBERTA EIVS AD
SARGE.[*29]

Aliud eiusdem sensus:
DIVO SEVERO PIO
COLONI
VLPIA TRA
IANA SARMIZ.[*30]

De thesauro a Traiano reperto istud ibidem monumentum extat:[*31]
IOVI INVENTORI DITI PATRI
TERRAE MATRI
DETECTIS DACIAE THESAVRIS
CAESAR NERVA TRAIANVS
AVG.
SAC. P.

Porro extat adhuc flumen, quod rudera ista p[rae]terlabitur ac in Marusium paulo infra Albam Iuliam confluit[*32], alveo perbrevi, ubi thesauru[m] (ut inq[ui]t Dion[*33], haud procul a regia & arce) occultaverat Decebalus Daciae rex. Erat vero, si credimus Libro praefecturarum[*34] & Ptolo[maeo][*35] ac Amiano[*36] & Vopisco[*37], triplex Dacia[*38], Ripensis, quam nunc Ulteriorem Hungariam dicimus, Tibisco flumine irriguam, Mediterranea, quam hodie Transylvaniam, seu Germanice Subenburgu[m] appellamus, non (ut falso Annales dicunt[*39]) a septem colliculis sive montibus, sed a ruderibus Zeugniae veteris, cuius Ptolo[maeus], Tacit[us] & Anto[ninus] meminere[*40], quae Seven[*41] postea ab Hunnis barbare nuncupata fuere. Ubi Athilam non semel comitia suae gentis celebrasse, Annales testantur[*42]. Hoc oppidum quod tum metropolis Daciae Mediterraneae fuerat, Germani Saxones, quos eo Carolus Magnus transtulit[*43], suo more Sevenburgum dixere, ceu Hungari suo idiomate hodie Sevesiear[*44] eodem sensu pronunciant, quae vox postea regioni universae accessit. Quod similiter plerisq[ue] in locis accidisse videmus, Mediolano, Ferraria, Mantua, Virtenbergia, Clivio, Iuliaco, Geldria, Mysnia, Brunsvigioq[ue][*45]. Tertiam invenio a Vopisco[*46] distinctam Daciam, quam is novam & Aureliam Daciam vocat, quippe [12v] qui tradit Aurelianum Caesarem, cum desperaret Daciam Mediterraneam tueri, abduxisse inde praesidium & in Mysia collocasse, atq[ue] hanc deinceps novam & suam appellasse Daciam, quam hodie Serviam & Rasciam vocamus, inter Hungariam & Romaniam.[*47] Daciam itaq[ue] Mediterraneam, qua[m] Transylvania[m] hodie & Subenburgum dicimus, primus Octavius Caesar[48] bello adortus est, duobus (si Straboni credimus[*49]) in huius diutini belli usum praecipuis ac maximis Pannoniae urbibus Sirmio[*50] ac Segesta[*51] horreis constitutis, quorum hodie rudera in Petri Varadino & Segednitio[*52] videmus. Sed cum re infecta reducere copias Romani cogerentur, multis postea annis non modo non bello Dacos lacescere[*53] ausi sunt, sed suos insuper limites p[rae]sidio imposito ac limitaneis legionibus XIIII Germanica, Prima Adiutrice Traiana & Septima Galbinia, nec non VI[*54] pro ripa Danubij compositis, male sibi a Dacis deinceps usq[ue] timuere, donec perruptis limitibus primus Decebalus rex Dacorum populabundus Ro[manas] proximas est ausus ingredi provincias, Moesiam inquam & Pannoniam, Dorpaneo Gothorum rege in laboris participatum adsumpto, contra quos Domitianus copias eduxit, sed inauspicato.[*55] Nam & Pompeium Sabinum qui Moesiae post Agrippam praefuerat,[*56] & paulo post Cornel[ium] Fuscum, illum toties ac tantis laudibus a Tacito accumulatum,[*57] cum omni exercitu tum Daci deleverant, ut ex isto Iuvenalis versu apparet:[*58]

et qui vulturibus servavit viscera Dacis
Fuscus marmorea meditatus praelia villa

Meminit & huius rei in epithaphio[*59] Cornelij Fusci Martialis:[*60]

ille sacri lateris custos Martisq[ue] togati,
credita cui summi castra fuere ducis,
hic situs est Fuscus, licet hoc Fortuna fateri:
non timet hostiles iam lapis ista minas.
grande iugum domita Dacus cervice recepit
et famulum victrix possidet umbra nemus.

Huius cladis a Dacis acceptae sub Domitiano ex Taciti autoritate meminit Orosius lib[er] 7 cap[ut] 6,[*61] post quae tempora omnibus contractis auxilijs semel cohercendos Dacorum spiritus Romani existimaverunt. Traianus itaq[ue] Caesar, ad quem imperij tum sunt post Domitianu[m] & Cocceium[*62] fasces delati, eductis quam valdissimis copiis, legiones limitaneas, quae pro ripa Danubij in Pannonijs ac Moesijs compositae fuerant, adiunxit, & recta in Decebalum [13r] movit,[*63] quem, ceu de ipso Dion scriptum reliquit, haud multo negotio demu[m] debellavit, universa Daciae provincia subiugata. Id quod Statius & Silius poetae[*64] & haec quae passim apud Transylvanos, Romae[*65] & in pariete templi in Gumpndorf ad alteru[m] lapidem a Vienna cernuntur inscriptiones contestant[ur]:

Statius lib[er] I Thebaid[is]:[*66]

bisq[ue] iugo Rhenu[m], bis adactum legib[us] Istru[m]
et coniurato deiectos vertice Dacos

Idem lib[er] II Sylvaru[m]:

*Rhenus & attoniti vidit domus ardua Daci**67
*Gallicus es coelo, dis es Germanice condi**68
*non vacat arctoas acies Rhenumq[ue] rebellem**69

Silius lib[er] 2:

*hic & ab arctoo currus aget axe per urbem**70
*Sarmaticis victor compescet sedibus Istrum**71

Inscriptio quae apud Transylvanos:*72
IOVI STATORI
HERCVLI VICTORIAM
M. VLP. NERVA TRAIAN
CAESAR
VICTO DECEBALO
DOMITA DACIA
VOTVM SOLVIT
ASPICE ROMVLE
GAUDETE QVIRITES
VESTRA ISTA GLORIA

Inscriptio quae prope Viennam in pariete templi pagi Gumpndorf:*73
SARI DIV
NERV /
TRA
GER.
MAN. DACI.
ONTIF. MAX.
POT. IIII COS. V

Finis.

6 Übersetzung

[11r] Erläuterung eines Schatzes, der unlängst in Transsilvanien gefunden und von einem Fischer in einem Flussbett entdeckt worden ist, verfasst von Wolfgang Lazius, Arzt aus Wien.

Die Goldmünzen aus dem Schatz, der unlängst in Transsilvanien von einem Fischer gefunden worden ist, trugen, soweit sie zu meiner Kenntnis gelangten, zwei griechische Legenden, die eine lautete ΒΑΣΙΛΕΩΣ ΛΥΣΙΜΑΧΟΥ, das heißt „des Königs Lysimachus", die andere dagegen ΣΩΖΟΝ, „Heiland" oder „Befreier". Diese Münzen wurden meinen Recherchen zufolge von Lysimachus, dem König Thrakiens und Makedoniens, vor 1820 Jahren geprägt. Dass Lysimachus nämlich zu der Zeit gelebt hat, als zwischen den Römern und Pyrrhus, dem König der Epiroten, ein Krieg tobte, kurz oder zumindest nicht lange nach der Zeit Alexanders des Großen, im Jahr 468 nach der Stadtgründung (Roms) bzw. im Jahr 368[ ] seit dem Weltanfang, wird demjenigen deutlich werden, der die Dauer und Abfolge der Zeiten berechnet. Es geschah dies etwa zur selben Zeit, als Eleazar, der Hohepriester der Juden, die siebzig Übersetzer der Bibel zu Ptolemaeus, dem König Ägyptens, schickte. Wer das zweite Buch des Polybius liest, dem wird dies offensichtlich werden. Dieser überliefert nämlich, dass besagter König Thrakiens Lysimachus in der 124. Olympiade zusammen mit den Königen Seleucus und Ptolemaeus Lagus aus dem Leben geschieden ist. Ich nehme an, dass von diesem (sc. Lysimachus) die Stadt Lysimacheia in Thrakien nahe der Grenze zu Makedonien gegründet wurde, die im Itinerarium Antonini sowie bei (Claudius) Ptolemaeus, Buch 3, Kap. 10 und Taf. 9 unter den Städten Thrakiens aufgeführt wird, wobei letzterer Lysimacheia auf 41° 30′ nördlicher Breite legt, was bedeutet, dass die Stadt 15 deutsche Meilen südlich von Hadrianopolis lag. Sie wird auch von Stephanus Byzantius in seinem Werk über die Städte erwähnt, und zwar mit folgenden Worten: „Λυσιμάχεια πόλις τῆς Θρᾴκης χερρονήσου ἡ πρότερον Καρδία, ὁ πολίτης Λυσιμαχεύς“, das heißt: „Lysimachia, eine Stadt auf der thrakischen Chersones, die vorher eine Region gewesen war. Der Bürger der Stadt wird Lysimacheus genannt.“ Soweit also zu dieser Münze.

Ich komme auf den Schatz zurück. Auf diesen bezieht sich, wie es scheint, der folgende Bericht des Cassius Dio aus Nicäa in seinem Buch über Trajan: „Nachdem Trajan die Donau auf einer Brücke überschritten hatte, um Krieg zu führen, mehr aus Vertrauen auf seine Stärke als aus Begierde oder Eifer, setzte er sich dort fest und unterwarf schließlich die Daker. Im Kampf gegen den Feind erwies er sich in zahlreichen Taten als herausragender Truppenführer und tapferer Mann. Die meisten seiner Soldaten zeigten sich in Gefahren unerschrocken, viele zeichneten sich im Kampf durch Tapferkeit aus. So war ein Reiter, der aufgrund einer Verwundung vom Schlachtfeld geführt worden war, damit er durch medizinische Versorgung wiederhergestellt werden könne, als keine Hoffnung auf Rettung mehr bestand, sofort aus dem Zelt gestürzt – das Übel hatte nämlich noch nicht die lebenswichtigen Partien seines Körpers erfasst – und in die Schlachtformation zurückgekehrt, wo er mit großen Worten und Taten seine Seele aushauchte. Decebal aber beging Selbstmord, [11v] nachdem seine Königsburg eingenommen und die gesamte Gegend unter die Herrschaft des römischen Volkes gelangt war und er selbst Gefahr lief, in Gefangenschaft zu geraten. Sein Haupt wurde hierauf nach Rom gebracht. Auf diese Weise geriet Dakien unter römische Rechts- und Herrschaftsgewalt. Trajan richtete das Land unverzüglich als Provinz ein, gründete Städte und siedelte römische Bürger in Kolonien an. Er fand auch die königlichen Schätze, die Decebal im Bett des Flusses Sargetia nicht weit von seiner Burg hatte verstecken lassen. Der König hatte hierzu den Fluss von Kriegsgefangenen durch mühevolle Arbeit umleiten lassen und ließ darauf das Flussbett ausschachten und in dem Hohlraum eine riesige Menge an Gold und Silber verbergen. Alles, was sonst noch von großem Wert war, und auch solche kostbaren Flüssigkeiten, die sich verbergen und verwahren ließen, schaffte er dort hin. Nachdem dies erledigt war, ließ Decebal alle Mitwisser töten, damit niemand über das, was er vollbracht hatte, berichten konnte. Jedoch verriet ein Gefangener namens Biculis, der Kenntnis von der Sache hatte, die Lage der verborgenen Schätze.“ Soweit Dio.

Obschon nun Dio berichtet, dass Kaiser Trajan den Schatz nach dem Sieg über Decebal entdeckt habe, scheint dennoch klar und verständlich, dass dieser auf mehrere Plätze verteilt gewesen sein muss, zum einen weil Decebal, wie es wahrscheinlich ist, den Schatz an verschiedenen Stellen des ausgeschachteten Flussbettes versteckt haben dürfte, zum anderen weil Biculus nicht alle Verstecke bekannt gewesen sein dürften, schließlich auch, weil die starke Strömung des Wassers, die bei den Flüssen Dakiens, die über steile Felsen ins Tal stürzen, bis heute zu beobachten ist, den Schatz weit verstreut haben dürfte. Dies bedeutet, dass Kaiser Trajan nicht den gesamten Schatz, den Decebal versteckt hatte, geborgen hat.

Hinzu kommt, dass der unlängst von einem Fischer zutage geförderte Schatz 1400 Jahre nach seiner Verbergung gefunden worden ist, und dies, soweit ich höre, nur wenig flussabwärts von Alba Julia – so nennen die Bewohner Transsilvaniens die Stadt. Dort, an dem Ort, der Varhel oder Gradisca genannt wird, befinden sich die Ruinen von Sarmizegetusa, dem einstigen Königssitz Decebals (welchen Kaiser Traianus Nerva nach seinem eigenen Namen zu Ulpia Traiana umbenannt hat). Soweit aus den Inschriften ersichtlich, wird an diesem Ort in Steinmonumenten sowohl der Fluss Sargetia als auch der aufgefundene Schatz erwähnt. Hiervon haben mir Herr Stefan Scher, Wiener Ratsbürger, und Herr Johann Verber, Pastor aus Buda, manche zur Kenntnis gebracht. Eine Auswahl der von ihnen mitgeteilten Texte schließe ich zum Beweis an:

Dem Gott Hercules,
für das Heil des Imperators,
des göttlichen Trajan
Augustus, und
der Martiana,
der Schwester des Augustus,
(hat dies geweiht)
die dakische Kolonie
Sarmizegetusa.

... Caesars, des göttlichen Nerva
Trajan Augustus
gegründete dakische
Kolonie
durch
V.M. Scaurianus.

Der Faustina
Augusta,
(Tochter des)
göttlichen Pius
(hat dies errichtet)
die dakische Kolonie
Sarmizegetusa.

[12r]

Ein anderes Monument:

Der Faustina
Augusta,
Tochter des
Marcus Aurelius
Antoninus,
(hat dies errichtet)
die Kolonie
Sarmizegetusa.

Ein weiteres Monument, in welchem Sarmizegetusa Ulpia Traiana (erwähnt wird):

Dem Marcus Ulpius
Restutus,
Duumvir der Kolonie Sarmizegetusa,
(haben dies errichtet)
Ulpia Marcellina
und Ulpia Restuta,
seine Töchter und
Erbinnen
T. P. C.

Ein weiteres Monument, in welchem vom Sargetia die Rede ist:

Der Göttin Isis
(haben des geweiht)
Priscianus, Augustalis
der Kolonie und Metropole
Sarmizegetusa, und seine
Freigelassene
Aurelia Fortuna,
am Ufer der Sargetia.

Ein weiteres Monument im selben Sinn:

Dem göttlichen Severus Pius
(haben dies errichtet)
die Einwohner der Kolonie
Ulpia Traiana Sarmizegetusa.

Von dem Schatz, der von Trajan gefunden wurde, kündet am selben Ort das folgende Monument:

Juppiter, dem Entdecker, sowie Dis Pater
und der Mutter Erde,
nach Entdeckung der Schätze Dakiens,
hat Caesar Nerva Traianus
dies geweiht.

Ferner existiert bis heute der Fluss, der an dieser Ruinenstätte vorbeifließt und nach sehr kurzem Lauf wenig unterhalb von Alba Iulia in den Mureş mündet. In diesem hatte der König Dakiens Decebal seinen Schatz verborgen, unweit der königlichen Burg, wie Dio berichtet.

Dakien aber war dreigeteilt, wenn wir dem Präfekturen-Buch (sc. der *Notitia dignitatum*), (Claudius) Ptolemaeus, Ammianus (Marcellinus) und (Flavius) Vopiscus Glauben schenken, nämlich (erstens) Ufer-Dakien, das wir heute als „Jenseitiges Ungarn“ bezeichnen und das vom Fluss Timiş bewässert wird, und (zweitens) Binnen-Dakien, das wir heute Transsilvanien oder auf Deutsch Subenburgum nennen, und zwar nicht, wie die Annalen fälschlich berichten, aufgrund von sieben Hügeln oder Bergen, sondern nach den Ruinen des alten Zeugnia, das bei Claudius Ptolemaeus, Tacitus und Antoninus (d. h. im *Itinerarium Antonini*) Erwähnung findet und das später von den Hunnen in ihrer barbarischen Sprache als Seven bezeichnet wurde. Dass Attila dort mehrfach Versammlungen seines Volkes abgehalten hat, bezeugen die Annalen. Diese Stadt, die zuvor der Hauptort von Binnen-Dakien gewesen war, nannten die germanischen Sachsen, die Karl der Große dorthin umsiedeln ließ, in ihrer Mundart Sevenburgum, ebenso wie die Ungarn in ihrem Idiom im selben Sinn heute Sevesiear sagen, und dieser Name ging später auf die gesamte Region über. Was auch an vielen anderen Orten geschehen ist, wie wir sehen, so in Mailand, Ferrara, Mantua, Württemberg, Kleve, Jülich, Geldern, Meißen und Braunschweig.

Den dritten Teil Dakiens finde ich bei (Flavius) Vopiscus von den anderen beiden unterschieden. Er bezeichnet diesen als „Neues und Aurelisches Dakien“, aus dem Grund, weil, wie [12v] er überliefert, Kaiser Aurelian, nachdem er die Verteidigung von Binnen-Dakien aufgegeben hatte, die militärische Besatzung von dort abzog und in Moesien stationierte und die Gegend fortan als „sein neues Dakien“ benannte. Heute kennen wir dieses Gebiet, das zwischen der *Hungaria* und der *Romania* liegt, unter der Bezeichnung Serbien und Raszien.

Gegen Binnen-Dakien, das heute Transsilvanien und Subenburgum heißt, hat erstmals Octavius Caesar Krieg geführt. In diesem langwierigen Feldzug hat er sich, wenn wir Strabo Glauben schenken, zweier herausragender Städte Pannoniens, nämlich Sirmium und Segesta, als Stützpunkte bedient und in diesen auch Getreidespeicher errichten lassen. Ihre Ruinen sind heute in Peterwardein und Szegedin zu besichtigen. Damals waren die Römer allerdings gezwungen, den Feldzug ohne Erfolg abzubrechen und die Truppen zurückzuführen. Hiernach wagten sie es für viele Jahre nicht, die Daker herauszufordern, und mehr noch: Da sie seitdem Schlimmes von den Dakern befürchteten, befestigten sie die Grenze und stationierten Grenzlegionen am Donauufer: die XIV. Germanica, die I. Adiutrix Traiana, die VII. Galbinia und auch die VI. Legion. Dieser Zustand hielt an, bis Decebal, der König der Daker, als erster die Grenzlinien durchbrach und in der Absicht zu plündern in die nächstgelegenen römischen Provinzen Mösien und Pannonien einfiel. Er hatte sich für den Kriegszug mit Dorpaneus, dem König der Gothen, verbündet. Gegen diese beiden führte Domitian seine Truppen ins Feld, allerdings ohne Glück. Denn die Daker vernichteten sowohl den Pompeius Sabinus, der nach Agrippa Statthalter in Mösien war, als auch kurze Zeit später den Cornelius Fuscus, den Tacitus so oft und so sehr mit Lob überschüttet, zusammen mit seiner gesamten Armee, wie aus diesem Vers des Juvenal ersichtlich ist:

Und, der seine Eingeweide für die dakischen Geier bewahrte,
Fuscus, in seiner Marmorvilla hat er Schlachten geplant.[22]

Derselben Sache gedenkt auch Martial im Epitaph des Cornelius Fuscus:

Der Leibwächter des erhabenen Kaisers, des Mars in Toga,
dem die Garnison des höchsten Fürsten anvertraut war,
Fuscus, liegt hier. Das darf man, Fortuna, bekennen:
Nicht mehr braucht dieser Stein die Drohungen des Feindes zu fürchten.
Der Daker hat seinen Nacken gebeugt und sich unter unser machtvolles Joch gefügt,
und der Schatten des siegreichen Helden besitzt den ihm dienenden Hain.[23]

Über diese bittere Niederlage, welche die Römer unter Domitian einstecken mussten, berichtet Orosius, 7. Buch, Kap. 6 unter Berufung auf Tacitus. In der Folgezeit gelangten die Römer zu der Überzeugung, dass sie den Kampfesmut der Daker unter Aufbietung aller Mittel ein für alle Mal bändigen müssten. So führte denn Kaiser Trajan, dem die Herrschaftszeichen nach Domitian und Cocceius übertragen wurden, seine stärksten Truppen ins Feld und vereinte diese mit den Grenzlegionen, die in den pannonischen und mösischen Provinzen am Donauufer lagen. Mit diesem Heer ging er geradewegs gegen Decebal vor, besiegte ihn, wie Cassius Dio berichtet, ohne viel Mühe und machte ganz Dakien zu einer unterworfenen Provinz.

Dies bezeugen die Dichter Statius und Silius sowie einige Inschriften, die weit zerstreut in Transsilvanien, in der Stadt Rom sowie in Gumpendorf, von Wien aus am zweiten Meilenstein gelegen, in einer Wand der Kirche zu besichtigen sind:

Statius im 1. Buch der Thebais:
[...] | *vom Rhein, der sich zweimal unserem Joch, und vom Ister, der sich zweimal unserem Gesetz beugen mußte,* | *von Dacern, die man von mitverschworenen Bergen vertrieb.*[24]

Derselbe im 2. Buch der Silvae:
[...] | *wie der Rhein dich eben noch sah und wie das hoch gelegene Haus des erschreckten Dakers?*
[...] | *Gallicus. Du bist im Himmel beliebt, Germanicus* | [...]
Die Zeit fehlt mir, auch noch die Schlachten im Norden zu beschreiben und die Aufstände am Rhein | [...][25]

---

22 Übersetzung: Adamietz 1993, 71.
23 Übersetzung: Barié, Schindler 2013, 437.
24 Übersetzung: Schönberger 1998, 22.
25 Übersetzung: Wißmüller 1990, 9 (vom Verfasser geringfügig geändert). 28. 31.

Silius im 2. Buch:
Er wird durch Rom den Siegeswagen fahren vom Nordpol, | [...] | *(Er auch wird) siegreich die Donaubewohner* [...] *bezähmen in ihrem sarmatischen Wohnsitz.*[26]

Die Inschrift aus Transsilvanien:
Dem Juppiter Stator und dem Hercules (wurde geweiht) diese Victoria. Marcus Ulpius Nerva Traianus Caesar hat nach dem Sieg über Decebal, nach der Zähmung Dakiens sein Gelübde eingelöst. Schau her, Romulus, freut euch, Quiriten, dies ist euer Ruhm.

Die Inschrift, die sich nahe Wien in einer Wand der Kirche des Dorfes Gumpendorf befindet:
... Caesar, Sohn des göttlichen ... Nerva Tra[ianus] Germanicus Dacicus, pontifex maximus, tribunizische Gewalt zum vierten Mal, Konsul zum fünften Mal.

Ende.

7 Kommentar

*1. ΒΑΣΙΛΕΩΣ ΛΥΣΙΜΑΧΟΥ: Gemeint ist ein Goldstater des Lysimachos mit einem durchschnittlichen Gewicht von ca. 8,3–8,5 g. Die Münze zeigt auf der Vorderseite den Kopf Alexanders des Großen nach rechts mit Diadem und Widder- bzw. Ammonshorn und auf der Rückseite die sitzende Pallas Athena mit Schild und Speer, in der ausgestreckten Rechten Nike auf dem Globus haltend, links und rechts flankiert von der Legende ΒΑΣΙΛΕΩΣ ΛΥΣΙΜΑΧΟΥ. Eine genauere Beschreibung als an der vorliegenden Stelle gibt Lazius in Cod. 7688, fol. 189f. (s. unten Anm. 55). Allerdings ist zu beachten, dass es sich, wie wir heute wissen, bei den von Lazius erwähnten Münzen nicht um Originalstücke aus der Zeit des Lysimachos handelt, wovon der Wiener Gelehrte selbstverständlich ausgehen musste, sondern um postume Imitationen, die in späthellenistischer Zeit, insbesondere während der größten Machtentfaltung des Königs von Pontos Mithradates VI. Eupator (regn. 120–63 v. Chr.) im gesamten Schwarzmeerraum und dabei besonders auch in den westpontischen Städten geprägt wurden. Außerdem ist zu berücksichtigen, dass die Statere des Lysimachos-Typs, die in den Orăștie-Bergen seit Jahrhunderten in größeren Mengen gefunden werden, zumindest teilweise eine wesentlich schlechtere Stempelqualität und einen höheren Silbergehalt als ihre Vergleichsmünzen aus den westpontischen Städten aufweisen, was vermuten lässt, dass die dakischen Herrscher im Bereich des politischen Zentrums von Sarmizegetusa Regia Münzen dieses Typs auch selbst produziert haben; zur Thematik s. Poenaru Bordea 1979; Munteanu 2005; Mitthof 2017, 114 Anm. 21 und 144–145; Petac 2018; Strobel 2019a, 195–202; Mitthof 2022, bes. 221–222 mit Anm. 35–36. Wie Petac 2018 und Mitthof 2022 zeigen, sind diese Horte von postumen

26 Übersetzung: Rupprecht 1991.

Lysimachos-Stateren in den Orăștie-Bergen (oder zumindest einige von ihnen) aufgrund ihrer Vergesellschaftung mit Goldstateren der bosporanischen Herrscher Pharnakes II. und Asandros (allerdings nur in extrem niedriger Stückzahl) hinsichtlich des Zeitpunkts ihrer Deponierung ins Jahr 45/44 v. Chr. oder etwas später zu datieren (so der aktuelle Kenntnisstand, basierend auf einer Schlussmünze aus dem 4. Jahr des Asandros als König). Die Horte stammen also aus der Endphase der Herrschaft des Byrebistas (Burebista), der laut antiker historiographischer Überlieferung in etwa zeitgleich mit Caesar, also um 44 v. Chr., gestürzt worden sein soll. Von solchen bosporanischen Münzen, die auch dem Strei-Fund von 1543 beigemengt gewesen sein könnten, wissen weder Lazius noch die anderen zeitgenössischen Autoren zu berichten.

*2. ΣΩΖΟΝ: Bei dieser Münze handelt es sich, wie wir heute wissen, um einen Goldstater mit einem durchschnittlichen Gewicht von ebenfalls ca. 8,3–8,5 g, der auf der einen Seite einen Adler nach links mit erhobenen Flügeln im Perlkreis zeigt, auf einem Szepter stehend und im erhobenen, rechten Fang einen Kranz haltend, sowie auf der anderen Seite, ebenfalls im Perlkreis, einen Konsul, der geleitet von zwei Liktoren mit Rutenbündeln nach links schreitet. Auf dieser Seite erscheint im Abschnitt unterhalb der dargestellten Personengruppe die griechische Legende ΚΟΣΩΝ, nach welcher dieser Münztyp in der modernen Forschung bezeichnet wird, sowie im linken Feld (allerdings nicht bei allen Münzen) ein Monogramm (zwei Monogrammtypen lassen sich unterscheiden). Beide Bildmotive sind von den Rückseiten spätrepublikanischer Münzen inspiriert, nämlich der Adler von einem Denar des Pomponius Rufus (71 v. Chr.) und die Szene mit dem Konsul von einem solchen des M. Iunius Brutus (54 v. Chr.). Dieser Münztyp, dessen Deutung in der neuzeitlich-modernen Literatur seit mehr als fünfhundert Jahren erörtert wird, wirft noch immer viele ungelöste Fragen auf. Fest steht, dass solche Koson-Statere ausschließlich in den Orăștie-Bergen gefunden werden, und zwar ebenso wie die bereits erwähnten Lysimachos-Statere (s. oben Komm. *1) in enormen Quantitäten, und dass daher anzunehmen ist, dass es sich um eine Lokalprägung der dort residierenden dakischen Herrscher handelt, allerdings aus späterer Zeit als die Lysimachos-Statere; s. ausführlich Mitthof 2017 mit der älteren Literatur unter Würdigung aller Erwähnungen des Münztyps in den Werken frühneuzeitlicher Gelehrter, darunter Erasmus von Rotterdam (1520) und Johann Mathesius (1562).[27] Zur Zeit des Lazius war der Münztyp zwar noch recht neu und sein Hintergrund unbekannt; zugleich begannen die Koson-Statere damals aber bereits in der Gelehrtenwelt Mittel- und Westeuropas zu zirkulieren.

Anders als in unserer *Explicatio* wird die griechische Legende ΚΟΣΩΝ bei Erasmus und Mathesius korrekt wiedergegeben. Zugleich bestand für die beiden Gelehrten und ihre Zeitgenossen ebenso wie für alle späteren Bearbeiter des Münztyps das Problem, dass das Wort ΚΟΣΩΝ im Altgriechischen keinen Sinn ergibt und auch kein passender Stadt-, Volks- oder Herrschername sicher überliefert ist. Zwar überwiegt seit dem späten 19. Jh. in der Forschung die Auffassung, dass es sich um einen dakischen König des Namens gr.

27 Es geht um einen Brief des Erasmus von Rotterdam von 1520 an den Fürstbischof von Breslau Johann Thurzo (1466–1520) (s. Mitthof 2017, 117–119) sowie um eine Stelle im Sarepta des Johann Mathesius von 1562 (s. unten Anm. 49).

Κοσων / lat. *Coso* handele, doch ist auch diese Deutung nicht über alle Zweifel erhaben; s. hierzu wiederum Mitthof 2017, 141–143.

Vor dem Hintergrund dieser Aporie war Lazius offenbar bemüht, der rätselhaften Legende durch eine freiere Interpretation dessen, was er vor sich sah (denn er betont ja eingangs, dass er die Münze mit eigenen Augen gesehen hat), einen Sinn zu geben. In seiner Version der Legende ΣΩΖΟΝ ist der Anfangsbuchstabe K zu Σ und der dritte Buchstabe Σ zu Z umgedeutet; ferner ist die Reihenfolge der Vokale Ω und O vertauscht. Lazius scheint also an das Partizip Präsens Nominativ σῷζον zum Verb σῴζω im Sinne von „derjenige, der rettet" (sc. der „Heiland") gedacht zu haben, wie überdies seine lateinische Wiedergabe der Legende mit *salvator vel liberator* bestätigt. Aber auch diese eigenwillige Herleitung ist sprachlich nicht ganz richtig, da der Maskulin des Partizips eigentlich σῴζων lauten müsste; σῷζον wäre die Neutrum-Form.

In seinem Parallelbericht über den Strei-Fund von 1543 in den *Comm. R. R.* von 1551 berichtet Lazius nur noch vom Lysimachos-Stater und nicht mehr vom Koson-Stater (s. unten Anm. 38); es steht also zu vermuten, dass er den letztgenannten Münztyp zwar im Moment der Abfassung unserer *Explicatio* mit dem Fund verband, diese Ansicht später aber stillschweigend geändert hat.

*3. *annis abhinc 1820*: Die Angabe ist ungenau. Wenn wir entweder das mutmaßliche Fundjahr 1543 (s. unten Abschnitt 8) oder das oben in Abschnitt 4 genannte mutmaßliche Abfassungsdatum unseres Textes 1545 ansetzen, würden wir in die Jahre 276 bzw. 274 v. Chr. gelangen. Tatsächlich war Lysimachos aber seit 305/4 König von Thrakien und seit 285/4 König von Makedonien, und er verstarb bereits 281 v. Chr. In Lazius' Rechnung fehlen also mindestens 5 Jahre. Auch die folgenden Angaben des Wiener Gelehrten zur Datierung des Lysimachos sind unpräzise (s. unten Komm. *4–*7). Wie wir gleich sehen werden (s. unten Komm. *7), hat sich Lazius in Fragen der Zeitrechnung der Chronologie des Beda Venerabilis (672/3–735) bedient, doch wird Lysimachos in diesem Werk nicht erwähnt; Beda war ihm daher in dieser Frage allenfalls indirekt eine Hilfe. Hinzu kommt, dass die Herrscher der Diadochenzeit bei Beda, ausgehend vom angenommenen Schöpfungsjahr 3952 v. Chr. (s. wiederum unten Komm. *7), gegenüber ihrer tatsächlichen Zeitstellung etwa 40 Jahre zu spät angesetzt werden.

*4. *inter Romanos ac Pyrrhum Epirotarum regem bellum flagrabat*: Roms Pyrrhoskrieg datiert in die Jahre 280–275 v. Chr.

*5. *post Alexandri Magni aetate(m)*: Verstorben im Jahr 323 v. Chr.

*6. *anno a condita urbe 468*: Nach varronischer Zählung (Beginn der Stadtgründungsära Roms im Jahr 753 v. Chr.) wäre dies das Jahr 286 v. Chr.

*7. *mundi vero exordio 368[ ]*: Die letzte Ziffer am rechten Rand des Blattes ist verloren. Möglich ist die Ergänzung einer Zahl von 3680 bis 3689. Gemeint ist offenkundig die Weltära nach den Berechnungen des Beda Venerabilis, auf dessen in Mittelalter und Neuzeit einflussreiches Werk mit dem Titel *De temporum ratione* Lazius an der vorliegenden Stelle mit seiner Formulierung *temporum rationem ... subducenti* anspielen dürfte. Für diese Annahme spricht auch die unmittelbar folgende Eleazar-Episode (s. unten Komm. *8). Zur Zeit des Lazius existieren zwei Ausgaben des Werkes (Beda 1529 und 1537). Vom Jahr 3952 v. Chr. ausgehend, das bei Beda als Schöpfungsjahr angesetzt wird, würden wir mit dem

Zeitfenster *anno mundi (a. m.)* 3680–3689 in die Jahre 272–263 v. Chr. gelangen. Wenn wir aber als alternativen Orientierungspunkt die von Beda explizit verzeichneten Herrschaftsantritte der beiden ersten Ptolemäer heranziehen, so werden diese von ihm wie folgt datiert (Beda 1529, fol. 54 bzw. 1537, 79): *a. m. 3669* für Ptolemaios, Sohn des Lagos (= 323 v. Chr.), und *a. m. 3707* für Ptolemaios Philadelphos (= 283 v. Chr.). Auf dieser Grundlage würde der Zeitraum *a. m. 3680–3689* den Jahren 312–303 bzw. 310–301 v. Chr. entsprechen.

*8. *Eleazar etc.*: Der Legende nach geschah dies unter Ptolemaios Philadelphos (regn. 285/283–246 v. Chr.). Lazius übernahm diese Episode offenkundig aus Beda (s. oben Komm. *7), wo es zu Philadelphos wie folgt heißt: *Eleazaro pontifici multa Hierosolymae & in templi donaria vasa transmittens, LXX interpretes petit, qui scripturam sanctam in Graecum verterent.* – *Iudęorum*: Unser Schreiber verwendet einzig an dieser Stelle *ę* (= *e caudata*) für *ae*.

*9. *124 Olympiade*: 284/283–281/280 v. Chr. Diese Information übernahm Lazius aus Polybios; s. den folgenden Komm. *10.

*10. *Quod Polybii secundum librum legenti*: Die Stelle findet sich in Polyb. 2, 41, 1–2; dort wird neben den drei von Lazius genannten Herrschern Lysimachos, Seleukos und Ptolemaios, dem Sohn des Lagos, auch Ptolemaios Keraunos erwähnt: Ὀλυμπιὰς μὲν ἦν εἰκοστὴ καὶ τετάρτη πρὸς ταῖς ἑκατόν ... καιροὶ δὲ καθ' οὓς Πτολεμαῖος ὁ Λάγου καὶ Λυσίμαχος, ἔτι δὲ Σέλευκος καὶ Πτολεμαῖος ὁ Κεραυνὸς μετήλλαξαν τόν βίον. – *Ptolomaeo Lago*: Richtig wäre der Genitiv *Lagi*.

*11. *Antonini Itinerarium*: Diese Angabe des Lazius ist nicht richtig: Lysimacheia kommt in diesem antiken Straßenverzeichnis, das in seiner frühesten Fassung auf die severische Zeit zurückgeht, nicht vor.

*12. *Ptolo. lib. 3 cap. 10 & tab. 9*: In der Kapitelzahl irrt Lazius; richtig wäre *cap. 11*. Die kompletten geographischen Koordinaten von Lysimacheia lauten bei Ptol. 3, 11, 13: 54° 10′ 41° 30′ (ed. Stückelberger, Graßhoff ^{2}2017, 332–333).

*13. *15 miliariorum Germanicorum spacio*: Lazius meint hier entweder die deutsche Landmeile (ca. 7530 m) oder aber die geographische Meile (ca. 7420 m). Beide waren in seiner Zeit gebräuchlich. 15 Meilen entsprachen demnach ca. 113 oder 111 km. Dies kommt der tatsächlichen Entfernung von Hadrianopolis (Edirne) nach Lysimacheia (Bolayır) recht nahe; s. auch den folgenden Komm. *14.

*14. *ab Adrianopoli*: Der Grund, warum Lazius Hadrianoplis (Edirne) als Referenzort nennt, ist möglicherweise darin zu suchen, dass diese Stadt an der wichtigen Diagonal- oder Militärstrasse lag, die den mittleren Donauraum und Balkan mit Istanbul verband und daher Kaufleuten und Reisenden (darunter auch Gelehrten) aus dem Habsburgerreich oder Süddeutschland bekannt gewesen sein dürfte. Hiervon zeugt beispielsweise das nur wenige Jahre nach der Abfassung unserer *Explicatio*, nämlich 1553, erschienene Itinerar des Antonius Verantius (Antun Vrančić, 1504–1573), in welchem dieser den Weg von Buda nach Hadrianopel beschrieb (*Iter Buda Hadrianopolim*; s. Mommsen, CIL III, p. 4; Sorić, Jurić 2021). Das Manuskript des Verantius war Lazius möglicherweise schon vor der Drucklegung bekannt (s. unten Komm. *23 zu Verantius als einem möglichen Informanten des Lazius über Altertümer).

Ptolemaeus nennt für Hadrianopolis die geographischen Koordinaten 52° 30′ 42° 45′ und für Lysimacheia 54° 10′ 41° 30′ (Ptol. 3, 11, 12 und 3, 11, 13; ed. Stückelberger, Graßhoff [2]2017, 330–333). Lazius hat offenbar bei seiner Berechnung der Distanz zwischen den beiden Städten den Ost-West-Abstand von 1° 40′ vernachlässigt und sich darauf beschränkt, die Nord-Süd-Distanz von 1° 15′ in Meilen umzurechnen. Dabei scheint er die Rechnung sogar noch weiter vereinfacht zu haben, indem er die in seiner Zeit übliche Gleichung 1° = 15 (geographische) Meilen anwendete; s. den vorangehenden Komm. *13.

*15. *Meminit huius & Stephanus Byzantius de urbibus*: In korrekter Form lautet das Zitat wie folgt: Λυσιμάχεια· πόλις τῆς Θρᾴκης χερρονήσου, ἡ πρότερον Καρδία. ὁ πολίτης Λυσιμαχεύς (Steph. Byz., Ethnica Λ 114; ed. Billerbeck 2014, 238).

*16. *quod prius regio fuerat*: In den Ausgaben des Stephanus Byzantius, auf die Lazius in seiner Zeit zurückgreifen konnte, war keine lateinische Übersetzung enthalten. Diese dürfte also von Lazius selbst stammen. Wie Lazius dabei zur Wiedergabe des Namens der Stadt Kardia mit dem Wort *regio* gelangte, bleibt unklar. Vielleicht bezog sich seine Deutung auf den Umstand, dass die Einwohner von Kardia (Bakla-Burun) im Jahr 309/8 v. Chr. von Lysimachos umgesiedelt wurden, um seine Neugründung Lysimacheia (Bolayır), die als künftige Reichshauptstadt konzipiert war, zu bevölkern (zur Gründungsgeschichte und Lage von Lysimacheia s. Lichtenberger, Nieswandt, Salzmann 2015).

*17. *Dion Cassius Nicaeus in Traiano meminisse in haec verba, ut sequit(ur)*: Das folgende längere, weitestgehend wortgetreue Zitat stammt aus einem von Erasmus von Rotterdam herausgegebenen Werk, in welchem dieser verschiedene lateinische Quellen zur Kaisergeschichte zusammengestellt hat, und zwar Sueton, die Historia Augusta, Aurelius Victor, Eutropius und andere spätantike Autoren, daneben aber auch den griechischen Autor Cassius Dio, und zwar unter Rückgriff auf die lateinische Übersetzung von Giorgio Merula (1430–1494). Allerdings bot Merula nicht nur eine Übersetzung der indirekt überlieferten Fragmente des Dio (Xiphilinos) zu Trajan, sondern eine abgerundete Erzählung in biographischer Form, die das Originalwerk gar nicht besaß. Dies hatte zur Folge, dass Lazius und seine Zeitgenossen sich auf ein „Buch" des Dio über Trajan bezogen, das so in der antiken Überlieferung niemals existiert hat (bekanntlich besteht zwischen der Serie der Kaiserviten des Sueton, die mit Domitian endet, und derjenigen der Historia Augusta, die mit Hadrian beginnt, eine Lücke; zu Trajan existiert keine ausführliche antike Biographie).

Die vorliegende Stelle findet sich in Erasmus (Merula) 1518, 174–175. Vorlage der Stelle ist Cass. Dio 68, 14 (= Xiph. 232, 28–234, 16). Neben marginalen Abweichungen bietet der Passus drei sprachliche Varianten zur dionischen Version: 1. Trajan führt laut Dio den Krieg δι' ἀσφαλείας μᾶλλον ἢ διὰ σπουδῆς; Merula macht hieraus: *magis pro fidutia virium, quam pro studio aut industria*; 2. Der schwerverletzte und todgeweihte Reiter zeichnet sich bei Dio durch große Waffentaten aus: μεγάλα ἐπιδειξάμενος; bei Merula heisst es hingegen: *magna tum iactando, tum etiam faciendo*; 3. Biculis heißt bei Dio Βίκιλις und wird nicht als Gefangener, sondern als Gefährte (ἑταῖρος) des Königs bezeichnet. Lazius gibt denselben Passus übrigens auch in seinen *Comm. R. R.* wieder (Lazius 1551, p. 1093). Zur sprachlichen Einordnung des mutmaßlich dakischen Namens Βίκιλις, der ansonsten unbezeugt ist, s. Dana 2014, 35: „probablement corrompu".

*18. Erasmus (Merula) 1518 (s. oben Komm. *17) hat *afflavit.*

*19. Erasmus (Merula) 1518 (s. oben Komm. *17) hat *reservari.*

*20. *recens repertus anno post occultationem 1400*: Da Trajan die beiden Kriege gegen Decebal in den Jahren 101–106 n. Chr. führte, würde Lazius die Entdeckung des Strei-Schatzes mit dieser Bemerkung in die Jahre 1501–1506 setzen und damit um etwa vierzig Jahre nach hinten verlegen, was unmöglich ist. Das tatsächliche Fundjahr 1543 ist anderweitig gesichert (s. unten Abschnitt 8), und überdies will Lazius uns mit seinem Traktat einen rezenten Fund bekannt machen. Zugleich ist nicht anzunehmen, dass Lazius der Annahme war, der Dakerkrieg sei in die 40er Jahre des 2. Jh. n. Chr. zu datieren. In der Chronik des Beda, die Lazius für die Chronologie der Diadochenzeit verwendet (s. oben Komm. *7), wird zwar der Dakerkrieg Trajans nicht explizit erwähnt, aber immerhin die Regierungszeit des Kaisers korrekt mit *a. m.* 4049–4068 (= 98–117 n. Chr.) angesetzt. Es handelt sich an der vorliegenden Stelle also um eine Ungenauigkeit oder Unachtsamkeit entweder des Lazius oder aber des Urhebers der vorliegenden Reinschrift.

*21. *in loco dicto Varhel vel Gradisca*: Lazius meint die beiden unter der lokalen Bevölkerung Siebenbürgens seit alters für den Platz gebräuchlichen Toponyme Várhely (ungarisch) bzw. Grădişte (rumänisch). Die Identifikation mit der trajanischen *Colonia Sarmizegetusa* stand zur Zeit des Lazius aufgrund der von dort stammenden epigraphischen Monumente, in welchen der Name der Stadt oftmals erscheint, außer Zweifel. Was Lazius und seinen Zeitgenossen allerdings noch unbekannt war und sich erst durch die moderne Forschung herausgestellt hat, ist die Tatsache, dass der Königssitz sich an einem anderen Ort befand, der ca. 30 km weiter östlich in den Orăştie-Bergen lag. Hingegen wurden im Bereich der trajanischen Kolonie im Hatzeger Land keine Spuren einer vorrömischen Siedlung festgestellt. Es existierten in der Antike also zwei Plätze mit dem Namen Sarmizegetusa, das königliche (*Sarmizegetusa Regia*) und die Kolonie (*Colonia Ulpia Traiana Augusta Dacica Sarmizegetusa*). Zur Verwirrung um die beiden Sarmizegetusae, die bis in neueste Publikationen anhält, hat nicht unerheblich beigetragen, dass beide Plätze seit Jahrhunderten die beiden auch von Lazius erwähnten Bezeichnungen Várhely und Grădişte tragen, zwei Toponyme, die beide unspezifisch für „Burgort“ (= im Sinne einer alten Ruinenstätte) stehen und im südosteuropäischen Raum auch anderswo anzutreffen sind. Daher ist zur Vermeidung von Verwechslungen ein klärender Zusatz erforderlich, so im vorliegenden Fall „Grădişte am Berg bzw. am Muntsel“ (Grădiştea de Munte / Grădiştea Muncelului) für den dakischen Königssitz und „Grădişte im Hatzeger Land“ (Grădiştea Haţegului) für die römische Kolonie.

*22. *Sarmizgetusae*: Dies ist die einzige Stelle in unserer *Explicatio*, an welcher das dakische Toponym von Lazius ausgeschrieben wird. Ansonsten belässt er es bei der Abkürzung SARMIZ. (besonders in der Transkription der von ihm weiter unten mitgeteilten Inschriften). In der heutigen Forschung wird als Standardschreibung die Form *Sarmizegetusa* verwendet (vor allem auf Grund von Inschriften aus der trajanischen *Colonia Sarmizegetusa*, in denen der Name ausgeschrieben ist, die Lazius aber noch nicht bekannt waren). Hingegen verzichtet Lazius auf das E zwischen Z und G; so auch in *Comm. R. R.*, p. 1094. In Lazius' Ungarn-Karte (s. unten Komm. *32) wird der Name überdies mit Z im Anlaut geschrieben: *Zarmizgetusa*. Für beide Schreibweisen gibt es antike Vorbilder, die

Lazius allerdings ebenfalls noch unbekannt waren; zu den antiken Namensvarianten und ihrer Bewertung s. Mitthof 2014.

*23. *per D(ominum) Stephanum Scher, senatorem Viennensem, & D(ominum) Ioannem Verber Budensem sacerdotem*: Diese beiden Informanten über Inschriften Siebenbürgens erwähnt Lazius auch an anderer Stelle in seinen Manuskripten, so in Cod. 8664, fol. 77 und in Cod. 7967, fol. 60 (s. Mayr 1894, 25).[28] Stephan Scher (auch in der Form Scherr) ist für 1530/1 als Leiter der Filiale der Fugger in Siebenbürgen und für 1540–1547 als Wiener Ratsbürger bezeugt.[29] Johannes Verber aus Buda / Ofen (in Cod. 8664 immer in der Form Ferber) wird von Lazius als eifriger Sammler transsilvanischer Altertümer gewürdigt. In Cod. 7967 erweckt Lazius sogar den Eindruck, dass er die Kenntnis der dakischen Inschriften ausschließlich diesem verdankte.[30] An anderer Stelle hingegen nennt Lazius unter seinen Quellen eine Sammlung siebenbürgischer Monumente von Verber und Vrantius (*monumenta Transylvaniae a Verber et Vrantio collecta*). Gemeint ist mit Letzterem der kroatische Adlige, Bischof, Diplomat und Gelehrte Antonius Verantius (Antun Vrančić; zu diesem s. oben Komm. *14). Ein solches Werk lässt sich allerdings nicht anderweitig nachweisen.

Hingegen ist es überaus erstaunlich, dass Lazius weder an dieser Stelle noch sonst irgendwo in seinen Schriften jene früheste und bedeutsamste frühneuzeitliche Sammlung von Inschriften Dakiens erwähnt, die zu seinen Lebzeiten unter Gelehrten bereits allgemein kursierte, nämlich die Sylloge des Johannes Mezerzius (Megyericsei János, 1470–1516). Dieses Werk erfasste das gesamte damals bekannte Material und enthielt etwa 120 Titel, darunter auch jene aus Sarmizegetusa. Es ist zwar nicht im Original erhalten, kann aber aus verschiedenen Schriften, die nach 1516 entstanden sind, vollständig rekonstruiert werden.[31] Eine besondere Rolle spielt dabei die in einer Handschrift der Bibliotheca Ambrosiana überlieferte Sammlung des Mariangelus Accursius (Mariangelo Accursio, 1489–1546), die ihrem Titel zufolge die Abschrift einer Sammlung darstellt, die Accursius aus Siebenbürgen und Ungarn (vielleicht auf seiner Reise in diese Länder 1522) erhalten und dann während eines Aufenthaltes in Deutschland an Anton Fugger (1493–1560) übersandt hatte.[32] Mommsen vermutet, dass Lazius eben diesen verlorenen Codex des

28 Das genaue Zitat in Cod. 8664, fol. 77 lautet wie folgt: ... *mihi sunt sincere communicata partim per D. Stephanum Scherr senatorem Vienn., qui quondam in Transilvania dominorum Fuggerorum institorem egerat, partim per dominum Iohann. Verber Buden. sacerdotio et annis rerumque experientia praeclarum* (zitiert nach Mommsen, CIL III, p. 154–155).

29 Zur Person Reinhard *et al.* 1996, 142: „TO29: Scher, Stephan TO291: Faktor/Siebenbürgen TO292: 1530/1531"; s. auch Deppert-Lippitz 2010, 13.

30 Cod. 7967, fol. 67: *Romanas inscriptiones in sarcophagis ac saxis admiranda diligentia a Joanne Verber Budensi passim animadversas* (Zitat nach Mayr 1894, 26 Anm. 1); zur Rolle Verbers s. auch Mayr 1894, 73.

31 Mommsen behandelt alle handschriftlich oder im Druck erhaltenen Sammlungen, die für Dakien aus Mezerzius schöpften, sehr ausführlich in CIL III, p. 153–156.

32 *Exemplar vetustarum inscriptionum et scholiorum ex archetypo libello olim ad me ex Dacia et Hungaria misso, quem de Germania misi ad D(ominum) Ant(onium) Fugger(um) MDXXXVIII* (zitiert nach: Mommsen, CIL III, p. 154).

Anton Fugger auf Vermittlung von Scher zur Einsicht erhielt und in Wirklichkeit hieraus seine Kenntnis der dakischen Inschriften schöpfte, da die Versionen des Lazius mit denen des Accursius weitestgehend übereinstimmen (CIL III, p. 154–155). Von diesem mutmaßlich aus Mezerzius übernommenen Material gibt Lazius aber in unserer *Explicatio* nur eine kleine Auswahl wieder, während er in Cod. 8664 mehr Inschriften aufgenommen hat (daneben existiert auch noch Cod. 7967, der laut Mommsen aber nur Kopien der Inschriften aus Cod. 8664 bietet). Außerdem veröffentlichte Lazius einige dieser Inschriften auch im Druck in seinen *Comm. R. R.* von 1551.

24. DEO HERCVLI | PRO SALVTE IMP. | DIVI TRAIANI | AVGVSTI ET | MARTIANAE | SORORIS AVG. | COLONIA DAC. | SARMIZ.: Bei der Wiedergabe dieser Inschrift in Cod. 8664, fol. 77 hat Lazius die korrekte Schreibung MARCIANAE statt MARTIANAE. Mommsen reiht die Inschrift, dem Urteil des Mezerzius folgend, unter die Falsae ein (CIL III 67). In der Tat ist das Formular aus mehreren Gründen zweifelhaft oder schlicht unmöglich. So wäre eine Weihung *pro salute etc.* für einen verstorbenen Herrscher (*divus Traianus*) undenkbar. Diese Stelle ließe sich allerdings mit einem kleinen Eingriff emendieren, indem DIVI durch NERVAE ersetzt wird. Gleichzeitig ist allerdings zu bemerken, dass wir ansonsten keine Monumente für *Marciana soror Augusti* aus der Zeit vor ihrem Tod und ihrer Divinisierung im Jahr 112 besitzen. Da Marciana überdies irgendwann nach 105 zur Augusta erhoben wurde, wäre das mögliche Zeitfenster für die Abfassung einer solchen Inschrift, wie sie von Lazius hier wiedergegeben wird, auf die Gründungsphase der Kolonie beschränkt. Bekannt sind hingegen aus anderen Teilen des Römischen Reiches Monumente für die divinisierte Schwester Trajans vom Typ *Divae Marcianae Augustae sorori Imp. Caes. Traiani etc.* oder ähnlich. Vielleicht gab es auch in der Colonia Sarmizegetusa ein solches Monument, das dann zwischen 112 (Tod der Marciana) und 117 (Tod Trajans) errichtet worden sein müsste, jedoch in der Überlieferung seit Mezerzius irrtümlich mit einer Weihung für Hercules verbunden wurde.

*25. SARIS DIVI NERVI | TRAIANI AVGVSTI | CONDITA COLONIA | DACICA | PER | V. M. SCAVRIANV: Diese Gründungsinschrift der Colonia Sarmizegetusa ist in jedem Fall authentisch. Sie wird auch in den Wiener Handschriften des Lazius erwähnt, besonders in Cod. 8664, fol. 76–77, wo sie sogar in verschiedenen Fassungen erscheint. Seit Mommsen ist sie in den maßgeblichen epigraphischen Corpora erfasst: CIL III 1443 = IDR III/2, 1. Im Jahr 1990 wurden bei Grabungen zwei zuvor unbekannte Fragmente gefunden, alle anderen Teile sind nur handschriftlich überliefert. Zum aktuellen Kenntnisstand s. Piso 2006, 214–217 Nr. 2 (= FVSarmiz 2). Hiernach sieht die Rekonstruktion des Monuments wie folgt aus: *Auspiciis / [Imp(eratoris)] Caes(aris) divi Nervae f[il(ii)] / [Nervae] Traiani Augusti / [Germ(anici) Dac(ici)] condita colonia / [Ulpia Traiana Augusta] Dacica / [Sarmizegetusa] per / [D(ecimum) Terenti]um Scaurianum / [legatum eius pro pr(aetore)].*

*26. FAVSTINAE | AVG | DIVI PII | COL. SARMIZ.: Diese und die folgende Inschrift sind offenbar zwei Versionen einer Ehreninschrift für Faustina Minor (130–176 n. Chr.), Tochter des Antoninus Pius (der zum Zeitpunkt der Errichtung des Monuments bereits verstorben war) und Ehefrau des Marc Aurel. Das Original ist verschollen. Lazius erwähnt beide Versionen auch im Cod. 8664 fol. 76–77. Mommsen nahm die vorliegende

Fassung, ergänzt um das Wort *filiae* aus dem zweiten Text, als die authentische Version (*exemplum sincerum*) ins CIL auf, und von hier gelangte sie auch in die IDR: *Faustinae | Aug(ustae) divi Pii | filiae | col(onia) Sarmiz(egetusa)* (CIL III 1449 = IDR III/2, 75). Allerdings ist einschränkend zu bemerken, dass bislang keine weiteren Parallelen für ein Ehrenmonument der jüngeren Faustina, das nur den Vater und nicht zugleich auch den Ehemann nennt, bekannt geworden sind. Von daher bleiben Zweifel bestehen, ob die Inschrift in dieser Form vollständig überliefert ist; s. den folgenden Komm. *27.

*27. FAVSTINAE | AVG | MAR. AVRELI | ANTONINI | FILIAE | COL. SARMIZ.: In dieser zweiten von Lazius mitgeteilten Version der Inschrift der Faustina Minor wir die Geehrte fälschlich als Tochter (und nicht als Ehefrau) des Marc Aurel bezeichnet. Mommsen betrachtete sie als interpolierte Fassung (*exemplum interpolatum*) und erwähnt sie daher im CIL nur im Kommentar.[33] Sie fehlt folglich auch in den IDR. Hingegen sind beide Inschriften in EDCS aufgenommen worden, als CIL III 1449a (EDCS-26600886) und 1449b (EDCS-79500129). Tatsächlich dürfte es sich aber gar nicht um zwei verschiedene Monumente handeln, sondern um Teile ein und desselben Monuments. Das Versehen von Lazius' Gewährsleuten ließe sich leicht damit erklären, dass im Original sowohl der Vater der Faustina als auch ihr Ehemann genannt waren. Für diese Textversion gibt es viele Beispiele aus anderen Teilen der Römischen Welt.

*28. M. VLP. | RESTVTO etc.: Auch diese Grabinschrift der Ulpia Marcellina und Ulpia Restuta für ihren Vater M. Ulpius Restutus ist verloren. Lazius erwähnt sie ebenfalls im Cod. 8664, fol. 77. Der Text scheint authentisch überliefert zu sein. Nach heutiger Rekonstruktion lautet er wie folgt (mit geringfügig von Lazius abweichender Zeilentrennung): *M(arco) Ulpio / Restuto / IIvir(o) col(oniae) Sarm(izegetusae) / Ulpiae / Marcellina / et Restuta fi/liae et heredes / t(estamento?) p(onendum) c(uraverunt)* (CIL III 1520 = IDR III/2, 448).

*29. DEAE ISIDI etc.: Eine weitere authentische Inschrift, die heute nicht mehr existiert. Bei Lazius erscheint sie wiederum auch im Cod. 8664, fol. 77. Der Lesetext der Weihung lautet: *Deae Isidi / Priscianus Aug(ustalis) / col(oniae) Sarmiz(egetusae) metrop(oleos) et / Aurelia Fortunata / liberta eius* (CIL III 1428 = IDR III/2, 228). Zu beachten ist aber, dass die Schlusszeile AD SARGE., die sich wohl auf den Fluss Sargetia beziehen soll (*ad Sargetiam*), bei allen anderen Autoren, die die Inschrift überliefern, nicht enthalten ist und selbst bei Lazius im Cod. 8664, fol. 77 fehlt. Zudem ist der Name des Flusses in keiner antiken Inschrift nachzuweisen, sondern nur literarisch überliefert. Es handelt sich somit offenkundig um einen erfundenen Zusatz des Lazius.

*30. DIVO SEVERO PIO etc.: Der Text ist authentisch und dürfte korrekt überliefert sein; Lazius erwähnt das Monument ebenfalls im Cod. 8664, fol. 77. Das Original ist verschollen. Der Lesetext lautet wie folgt: *Divo / Severo Pio / colonia / Ulpia Tra/iana Aug(usta) / Dacic(a) Sar/miz(egetusa)* (CIL III 1452 = IDR III/2, 78).

---

33 Theoretisch könnte es sich zwar auch um die gleichnamige Tochter des Marc Aurel handeln (Annia Aurelia Galeria Faustina, 150/1–vor 180), doch ist diese Annahme unwahrscheinlich, da diese Faustina keine besondere politisch-dynastische Bedeutung besaß und daher die Existenz eines solchen Ehrenmonuments in der Peripherie des Reiches ungewöhnlich wäre.

*31. IOVI INVENTORI etc.: Es handelt sich um eine berühmte, bei vielen Autoren der frühen Neuzeit erwähnte Fälschung. Sie erscheint bereits bei Mezerzius. Der Text ist gänzlich frei erfunden und entspricht in keinem Teil antikem Formular. Lazius zitiert ihn an zwei weiteren Stellen, nämlich im Cod. 8664, fol. 76 sowie in den *Comm. R. R.* (Lazius 1551, p. 1094). Mommsen führt die Inschrift unter den Falsae (CIL III 69*), allerdings in zwei Fassungen, die von der des Lazius leicht abweichen.

*32. *flumen, quod rudera ista p[rae]terlabitur, ac in Marusium paulo infra Albam Iuliam confluit*: Der Strei-Fluss mündet ca. 70 km flussabwärts von Alba Iulia bei Simeria in den Mureș. Er fließt aber keineswegs an Sarmizegetusa vorbei, weder an der Königsburg (s. oben Anm. 4) noch an der trajanischen Kolonie, sondern erreicht, von Petroșani her aus südöstlicher Richtung kommend, zunächst das Hatzeger Land, wo er sich nach Norden wendet. Die Distanz vom Ufer des Strei bei Hatzeg bis zur Kolonie Sarmizegetusa beträgt knapp 20 km in südwestlicher Richtung. Lazius' Worte zeigen, das er mit der Geographie der Zone nicht sonderlich gut vertraut war. Dieser Verdacht bestätigt sich bei einem Blick auf die Karte der Länder der ungarischen Krone (*Regni Hungariae descriptio vera)*, die unter der Anleitung von Lazius erstellt und im Jahr 1556 in Wien herausgegeben wurde:[34] Zwar lässt sich der Lauf des Strei-Flusses (*Istrygy fl[uvius] olim Sargetia*) gut nachzuvollziehen, doch wird das Hatzeger Land (*Haczag/Haczak Vallis*) mit der Kolonie Sarmizegetusa (*Varhel Ulpia Traiana Zarmizgetusa*) links seines Oberlaufes viel zu weit im Osten verortet, und die Städte Hunyad und Deva erscheinen sogar in völlig Verkennung ihrer wahren Lage nicht westlich, sondern östlich seines Mittel- bzw. Unterlaufes.

*33. *Dion*: s. den von Lazius weiter oben zitierten Passus aus Cassius Dio (Xiphilinos).

*34. *Libro praefecturarum*: Gemeint ist die *Notitia dignitatum* (so der Titel des Werks laut Handschrift). Dieses Verzeichnis aller Zivil- und Miltärbehörden des spätrömischen Reiches wurde um 1525 von Beatus Rhenanus in einer Handschrift des Speyerer Domstifts neuerlich entdeckt, nachdem italienische Humanisten bereits einhundert Jahre zuvor darauf aufmerksam geworden waren. Beatus ließ Lazius eine Kurzfassung (*epitome*) zukommen, auf die dieser sich gestützt haben dürfte, als er unsere *Explicatio* verfasste; vermutlich handelte es sich dabei um die beiden Indexkapitel Not. dign. Or. 1 und Occ. 1 (s. oben Anm. 17). Die *Notitia* enthält Einträge zu allen Provinzen des Reiches, so auch zur *Dacia Ripensis* und *Mediterranea* (Or. 1, 55 und Or. 42: *dux Daciae ripensis*; Or. 1, 77: *consularis Daciae mediterraneae*; Or. I 121: *praeses Daciae ripensis*; ed. Seeck 1876, 3–5 und 95).

*35. *Ptolo[maeo]*: Die Informationen bei Ptolemaeus zu Dakien beziehen sich auf die früheste Phase der Provinzgeschichte; er erwähnt daher auch nur eine Provinz Δακία und noch keine Unterteilungen derselben (Ptol. 3, 8; ed. Stückelberger, Graßhoff ²2017, 312–313), s. unten Komm. *38.

*36. *Amiano*: Ammianus Marcellinus bietet in seinem Geschichtswerk *Res gestae* sporadisch Informationen zu den geographischen und militärisch-administrativen Verhältnissen des Donau- und Balkanraumes im dritten Viertel des 4. Jh n. Chr. und darunter

34 Die Karte wurde in den folgenden Jahrzehnten in den von Abraham Ortelius herausgegebenen Atlanten unter dem Titel *Hungariae descriptio Wolfgango Lazio auct(ore)* mehrfach koloriert nachgedruckt.

auch zu den beiden rechtsdanubischen Provinzen *Dacia Ripensis* und *Dacia Mediterranea*; s. unten Komm. *38.

*37. *Vopisco*: Gemeint ist Flavius Vopiscus Syracusius, einer der angeblich sechs Verfasser, denen die in der *Historia Augusta* enthaltenen Kaiserviten laut überliefertem Text zugewiesen werden. Wie wir heute wissen, sind diese Personen und auch die Vorstellung eines Autorenkollektivs fiktiv; der tatsächliche Verfasser der *Historia Augusta*, der im ausgehenden 4. Jh. wirkte, bleibt unbekannt. Den Text kannte Lazius vermutlich aus der oben erwähnten Sammlung von Kaiserviten des Erasmus von Rotterdam von 1518; s. oben Komm. *17. Im besonderen bezieht sich Lazius im Folgenden auf die *Vita Aureliani*. Vopiscus nennt in dieser Biographie an einer Stelle zwei dakische Provinzen, die alte *Dacia Transdanuvina*, d. h. die am linken Ufer der Donau gelegene trajanische Provinz, und das neue, von Aurelian geschaffene Dakien am rechten Ufer des Flusses (HA Aur. 39, 7; zum Wortlaut der Textstelle s. unten Komm. *46); an anderer Stelle erwähnt er auch die *Dacia Ripensis* (HA Aur. 3, 1).

*38. *triplex Dacia*: Die von Trajan geschaffene Provinz Dakien wurde im Laufe des 2. Jh. in drei Teilprovinzen untergliedert: im Zentrum *Dacia Apulensis* (Hauptstadt Apulum), im Norden *Dacia Porolissensis* (Hauptstadt Porolissum) und im Südosten *Dacia Malvensis* (Hauptstadt Romula-Malva). Zusammengefasst wurden sie als die *tres Daciae* bezeichnet (s. Piso 1993 und 2013). Nach Räumung dieser Gebiete durch die Römer unter Aurelian wurde auf dem rechten Donauufer auf dem Boden der Provinzen Ober- und Untermösien eine neue dakische Provinz eingerichtet. Dieses rechtsdanubische Dakien wurde unter den Nachfolgern Aurelians in zwei Provinzen unterteilt: *Dacia Ripensis* / Ufer-Dakien (Hauptstadt Ratiaria) und *Dacia Mediterranea* / Binnen-Dakien (Hauptstadt Serdica); zu dieser Thematik s. zuletzt Mitthof, Matei Popescu 2023.

Die soeben erwähnte ältere, kaiserzeitliche Gliederung der dakischen Provinzen bleibt bei Lazius unerwähnt; die betreffenden Details waren ihm wohl noch unbekannt. Auffällig ist hingegen, dass der Wiener Gelehrte bei der Verortung der spätantiken dakischen Provinzen, die er aus den ihm vorliegenden Quellen kannte, ein schwerwiegender Fehler unterläuft. Er lokalisiert diese Provinzen nämlich fälschlich links der Donau: Die *Dacia Ripensis* identifiziert er als die Region östlich des *Tibiscus*, während er die *Dacia Mediterranea* mit Transsilvanien gleichsetzt. Dabei stiftet er noch zusätzliche Verwirrung, indem er den antiken Namen *Tibiscus* nicht auf den Fluss Timiş bezieht, wie es eigentlich richtig wäre, sondern auf die Theiß (deren antiker Name aber *Pathissus* lautete), was es ihm im Übrigen erlaubte, für dieses Gebiet die zeitgenössische Bezeichnung *Hungaria Ulterior* zu verwenden. Dasselbe irrige Konzept ist auch in seiner bereits oben Komm. *32 erwähnten Karte anzutreffen (*Regni Hungariae descriptio vera*; Lazius 1556): Der Schriftzug *Dacia Ripensis* findet sich in dieser östlich des Mittellaufes des *Tibiscus*, unterhalb der Einmündung des Someş, während die Legende zu Transsilvanien vollständig wie folgt lautet: *Transylvania Herdel olim Dacia mediterranea*. Dass andere Gelehrte seiner Zeit die Dinge bereits richtiger sahen, zeigt ein Eintrag in den *Annales ducum Boiariae* des Johannes Aventinus / Johann Turmair (1477–1534); s. unten Komm. *39. Dort wird die Situation korrekt umschrieben (Aventinus 1554, Lib. II, cap. 4, p. 143): *inter has (sc. Moesiae* *superior und inferior) fuit Dacia ripensis, octava provincia, quam Romani cis Danubium amissa Dacia transdanubiana fecerunt.*

*39. *ut falso Annales dicunt*: Auf welches Werk sich Lazius hier und weiter unten bezieht, bleibt unklar. In den *Annales ducum Boiariae* (s. oben Komm. *38), die von ihrem Autor Aventinus 1521 abgeschlossen wurden, ist keine entsprechende Stelle zu finden; zudem erschien dieses Werk erst postum im Jahr 1554 im Druck.

*40. *a ruderibus Zeugniae veteris, cuius Ptol[omaeus], Tacit[us] & Anto[ninus] meminere*: Es ist unklar, worauf Lazius sich hier bezieht. Ein antikes Toponym *Zeugnia (vetus)* existiert nicht, weder in Dakien noch anderswo in der antiken Welt, und es erscheint daher auch nicht bei den drei von Lazius genannten Autoren. Der einzige ähnliche lautende Ortsname, der in der antiken Überlieferung bezeugt ist, wäre Zeugma am Euphrat; immerhin schiene ein Schreib- oder Kopierfehler von *Zeugma* zu *Zeugnia* durchaus denkbar. Dieses Zeugma wird auch von Ptolemaeus, Tacitus und dem Itinerarium Antonini erwähnt, war also Lazius vermutlich bekannt, kann aber wegen seiner entfernten Lage am Ostrand des Römischen Reiches an der vorliegenden Stelle keinesfalls gemeint sein.

*41. *Seven*: Lazius bezieht sich hier allem Anschein nach auf den ungarischen Namen von Sibiu (lateinisch: Cibin(i)um; deutsch: Hermannstadt), der Nagyszeben (Groß-Szeben) lautet, nach dem namengebenden Fluss Szeben / Zibin / Cibin. Seine Überlegungen sind jedoch unhaltbar. Die tatsächliche Herkunft des Namens Siebenbürgen ist zwar nach wie vor ungeklärt. Zu vermuten ist aber am ehesten ein Zusammenhang mit der mittelalterlichen lateinischen Bezeichnung *Septem Castra*; weniger überzeugend scheint dagegen eine Herleitung über „Sieben Sachsenstädte" (*Septem Urbes*) oder „Sieben Stühle" (*Septem Sedes*); zur Problematik s. Hochstrasser 1998; Schuller 1999.

*42. *Annales testantur*: S. oben Komm. *39.

*43. *Germani Saxones, quos eo Carolus Magnus transtulit*: Die Ansicht, dass die Siebenbürger Sachsen Nachfahren des germanischen Volkes der Sachsen seien, die Karl d. Gr. nach Siebenbürgen habe umsiedeln lassen, wurde von Antonius Bonfinius / Antonio Bonfini (1427–1502) in seinem Werk *Historia Pannonica sive Hungaricarum rerum Decades* von 1543 vertreten (s. Armbruster 1978, 25), von wo sie Lazius übernommen haben dürfte. Tatsächlich erfolgte ihre Ansiedlung aber, wie wir heute wissen, erst im hohen Mittelalter, und die Bezeichnung „Sachsen" ist nicht in ethnischem Sinne zu verstehen, sondern als sekundäres Exonym. Der Dialekt der Siebenbürger Sachsen, die sich aus Gruppen von Einwanderern aus verschiedenen Teilen Deutschlands zusammensetzten, ist überwiegend vom Moselfränkischen geprägt.

*44. *Sevesiear*: Die Lesung scheint sicher, aber die Deutung unklar. Es existiert kein solches Toponym, weder auf Ungarisch noch auf Rumänisch. Möglicherweise bezieht sich Lazius auf Segesvár, also den ungarischen Name der Stadt Sighişoara (deutsch: Schäßburg). Das Zustandekommen der verderbten Namensform ließe sich dann eventuell wie folgt erklären: Zunächst könnte Lazius den tatsächlichen Namen Segesvár zu **Sevesvar* umgedeutet haben, um seine These vom ursprünglichen Landesnamen **Sevenburgum* zu stützen (der ungarische Namensbestandteil -vár steht bekanntlich für -burg). In einem zweiten Schritt könnte der Kopist, der die Reinschrift unserer *Explicatio* anfertigte, die

Form seiner Vorlage **Sevesvar* irrtümlich mit *Sevesiear* wiedergegeben, also *ie* statt *u* geschrieben haben.

*45. *Mediolano, Ferraria, Mantua, Virtenbergia, Clivio, Iuliaco, Geldria, Mysnia, Brunsvigioq[ue]*: Für Lazius sind dies Beispiele, dass ein Ort oder Herrschaftssitz einer ganzen Region oder Landschaft seinen Namen verleihen kann.

*46. *invenio a Vopisco*: Zum Autor s. oben Komm. *37. Lazius bezieht sich hier auf HA Aur. 39, 7: *cum vastatum Illyricum ac Moesiam deperditam videret (sc.* Aurelian*), provinciam Transdanuvinam Daciam a Traiano constitutam sublato exercitu et provincialibus reliquit, desperans eam posse retineri, abductosque ex ea populos in Moesia conlocavit appellavitque suam Daciam, quae nunc duas Moesias dividit* (ed. Hohl 1965, 178–179).

*47. *Serviam & Rasciam ... inter Hungariam & Romaniam*: Während Lazius die beiden zuvor behandelten dakischen Provinzen irrtümlich links der Donau vermutet, sucht er das dritte (Aurelianische) Dakien rechts der Donau, auf der gegenüberliegenden Flusseite von *Hungaria* und *Romania*, was grundsätzlich richtig wäre. Allerdings ist die geographischen Lage, die er diesem Gebiet zuweist, nach Westen verschoben und zudem in südlicher Richtung zu weit gefasst. Serbien erstreckte sich längs der Donau bis in die Region wenig unterhalb des Eisernen Tores, und Raszien (Raška), als politisches Gebilde oder historische Landschaft betrachtet, lag weitab von der Donau, südöstlich von Serbien, an der Grenze zum heutigen Montenegro und Bosnien-Herzegowina. Allerdings scheint möglich, dass Lazius hier gar keine solche konkrete Differenzierung im Sinn hatte, sondern die Verbindung *Servia & Rascia* als vagen Sammelbegriff für alle serbischen Gebiete gebrauchte, vor dem Hintergrund der synonymen Verwendung der ethnischen Bezeichnungen Serben und Raizen. Mit *Romania* schließlich meint Lazius offenkundig Oltenien und die Walachei, also die Gebiete östlich von Transsilvanien und links der Donau. In Wirklichkeit befand sich das rechtsdanubische Dakien jedoch deutlich unterhalb des Eisernen Tores, hauptsächlich auf dem Gebiet des heutigen nördlichen Bulgarien. Dies ist eine Region, die offenkundig bereits außerhalb des geographischen Gesichtsfeldes des Lazius lag.

*48. *Octavius Caesar*: Gemeint ist Kaiser Augustus, geboren als C. Octavius, dann durch Caesars testamentarische Adoption den Namen C. Iulius Caesar führend, schließlich seit 27 v. Chr. Imperator Caesar Augustus. Die Namenskombination Octavius Caesar hat er zu keinem Zeitpunkt getragen.

*49. *si Straboni credimus*: Meines Wissens gibt es keine Strabo-Stelle, welche die folgenden Aussagen des Lazius belegen würden. Ausführlicher äußerst sich der Geograph nur zu Segestike (= Segestica), und er betont dabei den Wert des Platzes als Operationsbasis für einen Krieg gegen die Daker: ἡ δὲ Σεγεστικὴ πόλις ἐστὶ Παννονίων ἐν συμβολῇ ποταμῶν πλειόνων, ἁπάντων πλωτῶν, εὐφυὲς ὁρμητήριον τῷ πρὸς Δακοὺς πολέμῳ (Strab. 7, 5, 2 [313, 30–32 C.]; ed. Radt 2003, 296). Hingegen nennt Strabo Sirmium nur einmal kursorisch, und zwar Seite an Seite mit Siscia, das er nahe bei Segestike verortet:[35] ἐγγὺς

35 Siscia war jener Teil von Segestica, in welchem das römische Militärlager entstand; später wurde der Name für die aus diesem Lager hervorgegangene römische Zivilstadt verwendet, während das Toponym Segestica außer Gebrauch geriet.

δὲ τῆς Σεγεστικῆς ἐστι καὶ ἡ Σισκία φρούριον καὶ Σίρμιον, ἐν ὁδῷ κειμέναι τῇ εἰς Ἰταλίαν (Strab. 7, 5, 2 [314, 15–16 C.]; ed. Radt 2003, 298). Zur besonderen Bedeutung dieser Plätze sowie des Flusses Save für die Logistik im Illyrienkrieg Caesars des Sohnes (des späteren Augustus, bei Lazius Octavius Caesar) in den Jahren 35–33 v. Chr. s. Strobel 2019a, 224. Zur Gleichsetzung von Segestica = Siscia = Sisak s. unten Komm. *51.

*50. *Sirmio*: Das heutige Sremska Mitrovica.

*51. *Segesta*: Richtig wäre Segestica (Name der Stadt in vorrömischer Zeit) bzw. Siscia (Name der Stadt in römischer Zeit)[36], das heutige Sisak am Mittellauf der Save. Möglicherweise hat Lazius das Toponym mit dem der Stadt Segesta auf Sizilien verwechselt.

*52. *rudera in Petri Varadino & Segednitio*: Hier irrt Lazius abermals ganz erheblich. Petrovaradin/Peterwardein an der Donau (gegenüber Novi Sad) und Segedinum (Szegedin/Szeged) an der Theiß – dies dürfte mit *Segednitium* gemeint sein – liegen weitab vom Savetal und damit auch von Sirmium und Segestica. Die Form *Segednitium* ist m. W. ansonsten nirgends belegt und vermutlich ein ähnlicher Lapsus des Lazius wie Segesta für Segestica, s. oben Komm. *51.

*53. *lacescere*: l. *lacessere*.

*54. *legionibus XIIII Germanica, Prima Adiutrice Traiana, & Septima Galbinia, nec non VI*: Als Quelle für die Nennung dieser Legionen dürfte Lazius sich vor allem auf Tacitus sowie auf Inschriften aus Wien und Umgebung gestützt haben. Der Beiname *Germanica* wurde von keiner römischen Legion jemals offiziell geführt; er ist nur einmal auf einem Grabstein für die frühkaiserzeitliche *Legio I* bezeugt (CIL XII 2234). Stattdessen meint Lazius an der vorliegenden Stelle zweifellos den gängigen Beinamen römischer Legionen *Gemina*, der ihm aus lokalen Monumenten vertraut gewesen sein dürfte, und zwar in erster Linie für die *XIV Gemina* (Standort unter Trajan vorübergehend in Vindobona, dann dauerhaft in Carnuntum), eventuell aber auch für die *legio XIII Gemina* (Standort in flavischer Zeit vorübergehend in Vindobona, dann in Apulum). Die *legio I Adiutrix*, aufgestellt im Jahr 68 und seit Domitian in Brigetio (Komárom) stationiert, war Lazius vielleicht ebenfalls aus lokalen Inschriften vertraut, doch irrt er sich hinsichtlich des Beinamens *Traiana*, den diese Legion niemals geführt hat. Die *Legio VII*, aufgestellt von Kaiser Galba und seit Vespasian benannt als *VII Gemina*, erscheint unter dem Beinamen *Galbiana* bei Tacitus (Tac., Hist. 2, 86). Schließlich gab es in der Kaiserzeit nur zwei „Sechste", von denen die eine (*VI Ferrata*) in Syrien, die andere (*VI Victrix*) zunächst in Germanien und später in Britannien lag. Allerdings hielt sich die *VI Ferrata* im Jahr 69 vorübergehend auf dem Balkan auf (Tac., Hist. 2, 83; 3, 46); s. Strobel 2019a, 267–268. Da die Legion von Tacitus nur als *Sexta* bezeichnet wird, war Lazius ihr Beiname unbekannt.

*55. *Dorpaneo Gothorum rege in laboris participatum adsumpto, contra quos Domitianus copias eduxit*: Zu den Feldzügen Domitians gegen die Daker s. Strobel 1989 und 2019a, 268–273. Von einem Anführer der Gothen namens Dorpaneus berichtet Jordanes in den *Getica*, und Lazius dürfte die Information aus diesem Werk bezogen haben (s. unten Komm. *56). Die anachronistische ethnische Bezeichnung Gothe steht dabei für Geten =

36 S. die vorangehende Anm. 35.

Daker. Die Form Dorpaneus ist verderbt; gemeint ist Diurpaneus *rex Dacorum*, der 85–86 Krieg gegen Rom führte. Unrichtig ist auch, dass Diurpaneus und Decebal gemeinsam gekämpft haben sollen. In Wirklichkeit betrat Decebal erst nach der Niederlage und dem Tod des Diurpaneus die Bühne; s. Strobel 1989, 39–40 und 62–63 sowie 2019a, 270.

*56. *Nam & Pompeium Sabinum qui Moesiae post Agrippam praefuerat*: Mit *Agrippa* meint Lazius den Statthalter Mösiens während des Vierkaiserjahres C. Fonteius Agrippa (PIR² F 466; Stein 1940, 32–33), den er aus Jordanes kannte, wo der Sachverhalt ähnlich formuliert wird: *cui provinciae tunc post Agrippam Oppius praeerat Sabinus* (Jord., Get. 13, 76: ed. Mommsen 1882, 76). Agrippa wurde im Frühjahr 70 bei einem Angriff der Roxolanen besiegt und getötet; s. Strobel 2019a, 268–269. Hingegen steht *Pompeius Sabinus* für Oppius Sabinus, ebenfalls ein Statthalter Mösiens (PIR² O 122; Stein 1940, 34), der im Sommer 85 die erste der beiden schweren Niederlagen Roms unter Domitian gegen die Daker erlitt, nachdem letztere unter ihrem König Diurpaneus in seine Provinz eingefallen waren. Zu diesen Ereignissen s. Strobel 1989, 42–43 und 2019a, 269. Lazius' Namensversion *Pompeius Sabinus* ist leicht erklärbar; in manchen Jordanes-Handschriften steht tatsächlich an der soeben zitierten Stelle *Po(m)peius* anstelle von *Oppius*.

*57. *Cornel[ium] Fuscum, illum toties ac tantis laudibus a Tacito accumulatum*: Cornelius Fuscus war *praefectus praetorio* unter Domitian in den Jahren 81–86; s. PIR² C 1365; Absil 1997, bes. S. 154–155 Nr. 25. Er wird von Tacitus in den erhaltenen Teilen der Historien mehrfach erwähnt; seinen Aufstieg verdankte er der Tatsache, dass er Vespasian im Bürgerkrieg gegen Vitellius unterstützt hatte. Von Domitian im Sommer 86 als Oberbefehlshaber für eine Strafexpedition gegen die Daker unter Diurpaneus jenseits der Donau ernannt, erlitt er wie schon Oppius Sabinus (s. oben Komm. *56) eine vernichtende Niederlage und blieb auf dem Schlachtfeld; s. Strobel 1989, 53–54 und 2019, 269–270.

*58. *et qui vulturibus servavit etc.*: Iuv., *Sat.* IV 111–112; *servavit*: l. *servabat*; *praelia* : l. *proelia*.

*59. *epithaphio*: l. *epitaphio*.

*60. *ille sacri lateris custos etc.*: Martial., *Epigr.* VI 76; *ista*: l. *iste*.

*61. *Orosius lib[er] 7 cap[ut] 6*: Gemeint ist Orosius VII 10, 3–4: *bellum adversum Germanos et Dacos per legatos gessit (sc.* Domitian*) pari rei publicae pernicie .... nam quanta fuerint Diurpanei Dacorum regis cum Fusco duce proelia quantaeque Romanorum clades, longo textu evolverem, nisi Cornelius Tacitus, qui hanc historiam diligentissime contexuit, de reticendo interfectorum numero et Sallustium Crispum et alios auctores quamplurimos sanxisse et se ipsum idem potissimum elegisse dixisset* (ed. Zangemeister 1866, p. 463–464).

*62. *Cocceium*: Kaiser Nerva, mit bürgerlichem Namen M. Cocceius Nerva.

*63. *Traianus ... recta in Decebalum movit*: Zum Verlauf der beiden Kriege Trajans gegen Decebal in den Jahren 101–102 und 105–106 s. Strobel 1984 sowie Strobel 2019a, 273–283 und 2019b, 268–325.

*64. *id quod Statius & Silius poetae*: Lazius erweckt den Eindruck, dass die folgenden Verse sich auf Trajans Erfolge beziehen; tatsächlich ist aber Domitian gemeint.

*65. *Romae*: Lazius führt im Folgenden keine stadtrömischen Inschriften an. Denkbar wäre, dass er sich hier nicht auf Inschriften, sondern auf die Reliefs der Trajanssäule bezieht, die einen Bildbericht von Trajans Dakerkriegen bieten. Zur Rezeption dieses berühmten Siegesmonuments im 15.–16. Jh. s. Heenes 2017.

*66. *bisq[ue] iugo Rhenu[m] etc.*: Stat., *Theb.* I 19–20. Die fünf Verse aus Statius, die Lazius hier und im folgenden anführt, finden sich genau in dieser Reihenfolge auch in der *Germaniae exegesis* des Franz Friedlieb (1495–1553); s. Friedlieb 1518, Liber V, cap. VIII: *De Domitiano etc.*, fol. 124. Dies ist deshalb bemerkenswert, weil die Verse im Original teilweise unverbunden sind. Es besteht daher der Verdacht, dass Lazius sie in dieser speziellen Kombination aus Friedlieb übernommen hat. Diese Annahme wird weiter untermauert durch den Umstand, dass bei Friedlieb kurz zuvor auch die zwei ebenfalls unverbundenen Verse aus Silius Italicus zu finden sind, die bei Lazius nachfolgen. Was hingegen die beiden vorangehenden Stellen aus Juvenal und Martial betrifft, so werden diese zwar in Friedliebs Werk eine Seite zuvor ebenfalls angeführt, aber nur zum Teil; es fehlt nämlich bei Friedlieb gegenüber Lazius jeweils ein Vers. In diesem Fall muss Lazius also eine andere Vorlage bzw. eine Originalausgabe der Werke benutzt haben. Freilich ist zur Annahme einer Abhängigkeit des Lazius von Friedlieb einschränkend zu bemerken, dass letzterer teilweise Lesarten hat, die von Lazius abweichen: *haec fateri* statt *hoc fateri*, *lapis ille* statt *lapis illa* und *servabat* statt *servavit.*

*67. *Rhenus & attoniti vidit domus ardua Daci etc.*: Stat., *Silv.* 1, 1 (*Ecus maximus Imp. Domitiani*), 7.

*68. *Gallicus es coelo, dis es Germanice condi*: Stat., *Silv.* 1, 4 (*Soteria Rutilii Gallici*), 4; *condi* : l. *cordi*.

*69. *non vacat arctoas acies Rhenumq[ue] rebellem*: Stat., *Silv.* 1, 4 (*Soteria Rutilii Gallici*), 89. Das R in *arctoas* ist über dem C geschrieben.

*70. *hic & ab arctoo currus aget axe per urbem*: Sil., *Pun.* III 614. Das R in *arctoo* ist wiederum über dem C geschrieben.

*71. *Sarmaticis victor compescet sedibus Istrum*: Sil., *Pun.* III 617.

*72. IOVI STATORI etc.: Auch diese Inschrift ist eine bekannte und vielfach zitierte Fälschung, die völlig von der Diktion echter römischer Inschriften abweicht. Sie war offenkundig schon in der Sylloge des Mezerzius enthalten. Lazius erwähnt sie außer hier noch im Cod. 8664, fol. 77 sowie in den *Comm. R.R.*, p. 215 und 1094. Bei Mommsen erscheint sie unter den Falsae (CIL III 70*).

*73. *in pariete templi pagi Gumpndorf*: Es handelt sich um Fragmente einer Bauinschrift Trajans, die in der dem Hl. Ägidius geweihten Pfarrkirche zu Gumpendorf vor den Toren Wiens vermauert waren. Lazius berichtet an verschiedenen Stellen über ihre Existenz (außer hier auch in *Comm R.R.*, p. 216 und 1161 sowie in seiner Wiener Stadtgeschichte: *Rerum Viennensium commentarii*, Basel 1546, p. 37), und er gibt sie dabei in verschiedenen Fassungen wieder. Es ist dies die einzige in unserer *Explicatio* mitgeteilte Inschrift, die Lazius in Autopsie studiert hat (vermutlich war dies auch der Grund, warum er sie überhaupt anführt, denn eine inhaltliche Verbindung zum Thema der *Explicatio* besteht nicht).

Mommsen druckt im CIL die verschiedenen Versionen des Lazius ab (CIL III 4566 + p. 1045), was singulär ist, und er führt dabei zum einzigen Mal in CIL III unter den Werken des Lazius auch unsere *Explicatio* als Autorität an (ansonsten stützt er sich für die von Lazius behandelten Inschriften auf Cod. 8664; s. oben Komm. *23). Im Lemma zur Inschrift CIL III 4566 bezeichnet Mommsen unsere Handschrift als *Cod. Fuggerianus (Monac. Lat. 9226)* (richtig wäre 9216), und in der zugehörigen Einleitung zum Kapitel Pannonia Superior, wo er unter den Schriften des Lazius ebenfalls unsere *Explicatio* erwähnt (was er in der Einleitung zum Kapitel Dakien nicht tut), führt Mommsen noch weiter aus: ... *codex Monacensis Lat. 9226, in quo inter alia missa ad Iac. Fuggerum inest Lazii explicatio thesauri recens apud Transylvanos reperti et in hac titulus unus Vindobonensis* (CIL III, p. 480). Mommsen ging also davon aus, dass Lazius unser Exemplar der *Explicatio* dem J. J. Fugger übersandt hatte (s. oben Abschnitt 2).

Zur Geschichte der vorliegenden Inschrift ist zu bemerken, dass die besagte Ägidiuskirche sowie die Ortschaft Gumpendorf schon während der Ersten Türkenbelagerung Wiens von 1529 (also nur wenige Jahre bevor Lazius auf die Inschrift aufmerksam wurde) erhebliche Zerstörungen erlitten hatte, ebenso wie dann nochmals bei der Zweiten Belagerung von 1683. Im späteren 18. Jh. wurde die Kirche dann an einem benachbarten Platz völlig neu errichtet. Im Mauerwerk dieses Neubaus wurden im Jahr 1962 zwei Fragmente der Inschrift wiederentdeckt und freigelegt. Für Bildmaterial und Literaturhinweise s. den Eintrag in der Lupa, Nr. 4830 (http://lupa.at/4830).

8 Der Schatzfund von 1543: Datierung, Umfang, Fundort und politische Folgen[37]

Die einzige genaue Angabe zum Datum des Schatzfundes, die Lazius in der *Explicatio* macht, nämlich *thesaurus recens repertus anno post occultationem 1400*, ist offenkundig fehlerhaft (s. oben Komm. *20). Ob es sich um einen Lapsus des Wiener Gelehrten oder aber um einen Fehler des Kopisten handelt, der die Reinschrift des Traktats erstellt hat, ist nicht zu entscheiden. An anderer Stelle in seinem Werk gibt Lazius einen weiteren präzisen Hinweis auf das Fundjahr, und zwar in den *Comm. R. R.*, wo er die Umstände des Fundes ausführlich beschreibt.[38] Auch die dortige Angabe *ante annos circiter octo* lässt

37 Zum Folgenden s. Mitthof 2017, bes. 115–120 mit den neuzeitlichen Quellen und der modernen Forschungsliteratur; dort noch nicht erwähnt: Petac 2018, 14–15.

38 Lazius 1551, Lib. XII, cap. VI: *De paganis et villis Romanis, Romanoque in vulgo idiomate*, p. 1094: *Huius thesauri reliquum ante annos circiter octo, in eodem fluvio Sargetia, quem Valachi Istrigij appellant, inventum est hoc eventu: Navigabant ex Marisio per ostium Valachi piscatores in Istrigam, & cum forte ad truncum arboris cimbas admovissent, conspicati sub aqua aliquid quod valde splenderet, cum illud efferre fuissent agressi, magnam vim aureorum extulerunt. Qua re alacriores effecti, fundum diligentius rimati, pervenerunt postremo ad aedificium quoddam parvum sub undis, instar loculi. Cuius fornicem, quia arbor enata, vetustate decidens, ad ruinam tracto aedificio aperuerat, omni diligentia perscrutati, ingentem vim nummorum aureorum (qui magna ex parte Lysimachi Thraciae regis Graecam inscriptionem ostendebant) milia (ut ex fide dignis audivimus) plus quam quadringenta, & massas insuper auri sectiones gravis ponderis. Quibus domum delatis, atque inter se divisis, cum Albam Iuliam ingressi, aurificibus ostendissent nummos, & valorem sciscitarentur, res palam facta, Georgium Monachum, qui tum pupilli regij nomine Transylvaniae praesidebat, excivit, ut rei inquisitionem faceret. Fecit ille quidem, & multa adhuc milia vel inventoribus ademerat, vel de novo in aedificio memo-*

sich allerdings nicht sicher umrechnen, da das Referenzdatum unklar bleibt; am ehesten dürfte es sich um das Jahr 1551 handeln, auf welches das Vorwort des Werkes datiert ist (das Werk selbst ist ohne Datum). Hiervon ausgehend wird der Strei-Fund von der heutigen Forschung allgemein ins Jahr 1543 gesetzt. Diese Annahme wird gestützt durch einen Brief des Kronstädter Reformators Johann Honterus (ca. 1498–1549) an Sebastian Münster (1488–1552), der in den Jahren 1544–1549 abgefaßt wurde und in welchem Honterus den Schatzfund mit knappen Worten vermeldet.[39] Andere Quellen, aus denen sich das Funddatum präzise bestimmen ließe, existieren nicht.

Zum Umfang des Schatzes berichtet Lazius in den *Comm. R. R.*, dass dieser, wie er aus verläßlicher Quelle erfahren habe, aus mehr als 400.000 Goldmünzen[40] und weiteren goldenen Artefakten bestanden habe. Eine solche Menge, die – bei einem durchschnittlichen Gewicht von 8,3 g je Münze – mehr als 3.300 kg Gold entsprochen hätte, ist allerdings wenig glaubhaft.[41] Vermutlich liegt abermals ein Lapsus des Lazius (oder des Buchsetzers) vor, und das Zahlwort *quadringenta* steht eigentlich für *quadraginta*. Jedenfalls reduzieren einige spätere Autoren die Zahl stillschweigend auf 40.000 Münzen,[42] also etwa 330

---

rato invenerat. Caeterum certiores ante facti, qui antesignani huius reperti erant, cum aliquot oneratis plaustris in Moldaviam procul aufugerunt. Et hactenus de inventione Dacici thesauri.

39 Honterus, in: Teutsch 1883: *Ad Sargetiam aurei antiqui plurimi a piscatoribus reperti cum inscriptione ΒΑΣΙΛΕΩΣ ΛΥΣΙΜΑΧΟΥ, ex altera parte ejusdem regis effigie.*

40 S. oben Anm. 38: *milia (ut ex fide dignis audivimus) plus quam quadringenta.*

41 Anders Makkay 1995 (wie oben Anm. 1), der die Zahl 400.000 für glaubwürdig hält.

42 So etwa Tröster 1666, Erstes Buch, cap. XIII, p. 61–62: *Daß aber dieser Schatz / in mehr / als einer Grufft beygelegt sein muß / ist daher zu sehen; denn ohngefährt um das Jahre 1543. Schiffeten etliche Wallachische Fischer / so daselbst bey der vormals so köstlichen Stadt / in einem geringen Dörfflein / von ihnen Gradisca geheissen / wohnen; aus dem Möresch in den Fluß* Sargetia, *den sie* Stryg *heissen / als sie aber die Zille an eines Baumes Stock anhängten / wurden sie gewahr / daß etwas in dem klaren Wasser überaus schön glänzete / und als sie versuchet / zogen sie einem Hauffen Goldmünzen heraus / welches sie denn aufmunterte / etwas genauer da zu suchen / daselbst funden sie ein Gewölb / wie eine Todengrufft gebauet / welches von einem alten niedergefallenen Baum an einem Ort eingeschlagen war / daraus erhuben sie mehr als 40000. Goldmünzen / so des* Lysimachi, *der nach* Alexandri *Tod König in* Thracia *worden / Griechische Uberschrifft hatten / darzu ein grosse Menge von ungeprägten Gold-Blechen. Diese Wallachen nun giengen auf Weissenburg hinein / fragten bey den Goldschmieden / was die Münzen wehrt wären / dadurch wurde der Handel dem Mönch Georgen, so damals in Siebenbürgen* Gubernator *war / verrahten / welcher noch von etlichen der Schatz-Gesellen / und aus dem Strom viel tausend solche Lysimachische Münzen krigett / davon Keyser* Ferdinando *zwey tausend zugesendet / so alle zween Ducaten schwer waren.* – Tröster setzt also den Lysimachos-Stater (ca. 8,3–8,5 g) auf 2 Dukaten = ca. 7 g, was etwas zu gering ist. Etwa zur selben Zeit schätzt ein anderer Autor, nämlich Mathias Miles (1639–1686), den gesamten Fund auf 100.000 antike Goldstücke, mit einem ebenfalls nicht ganz genauen Gewicht von je 3 Dukaten (also etwas mehr als 10 g): *Alß Castaldus seyn Heer nach Hause ließ zu wintern / kam ihm unterwege diese erfrewlige Post zu: Nahe bey Deva, da vormahls Ulpia Trajana gestanden/ an dem Fluß Strigh (genant) haben die Pawren unter einem alten Bawm / welches Wurzeln das Wasser ganz unterwaschen / etwa gleisendes gesehen / wie sie zu Mittag ihr Vieh wollen tränken. Deswegen sich in Fluß begeben / und etwa fleissiger nach gegraben / biß sie einen über alle maß reichen Schatz übebrkommen: Oben war eine güldinne Schlange / gleichsahm wie ein Hütter darauffgesetzt / (welche nach Georgii Todt Ferdinandus überkommen) sonst güldinne Münzen waren unzählig vill / auff einer Seitten hatten sie Lysimachi, auff der anderen Göttin Victoriae Büdnis gepräget / und mach-*

kg Gold, was zwar immer noch sehr viel wäre, aber nicht undenkbar scheint. Allerdings ist zu bedenken, dass alle behördlich dokumentierten Hortfunde solcher Münzen, die in der betreffenden Zone, den Orăștie-Bergen, in den letzten 200 Jahren getätigt wurden, jeweils mehrere hundert bis mehrere tausend, aber nicht mehrere zehntausend Münzen umfassten.[43] Es ist also gut möglich, dass auch die Zahl 40.0000 übertrieben war. Jedoch ist an der Tatsache des Fundes kaum zu zweifeln, da derartige umfangreiche Münzschätze in dieser Gegend bis auf den heutigen Tag immer wieder auftreten.

Skepsis besteht auch hinsichtlich des genauen Fundortes des Schatzes.[44] Zunächst ist die Identifizierung des Flusses Strei (ungarisch: Sztrigy)[45] mit der antiken Sargetia, die schon bei Honterus[46] vorkommt und seitdem von den meisten Gelehrten geteilt wird, eine bloße Vermutung.[47] Sie basiert zunächst auf dem ähnlichen Klang der Namen, ohne dass sich in sprachwissenschaftlicher Hinsicht der jüngere aus dem älteren zwingend herleiten ließe. Zudem eröffnet die Angabe der antiken Quellen, dass die Sargetia an Sarmizegetusa Regia „vorbeifloss", auch andere Optionen einer Identifizierung: Die Königsresidenz liegt nämlich genau betrachtet auf einem Bergrücken zwischen zwei engen Tälern mit kleinen Wasserläufen, die sich an dessen westlichem Fuß zur Apa Grădiștei vereinen, die von hier nordwärts zum Mureș fließt, während der Strei-Fluss zwar parallel hierzu verläuft, aber ca. 15 km westlich, jenseits von Bergketten und Tälern, in einer weiten Ebene (s. oben Anm. 4). Auf welchen der beiden Wasserläufe sich die antiken Autoren beziehen, ist nicht sicher festzustellen. Theoretisch wäre sogar möglich, dass sie in Wirklichkeit einen der weiter östlich gelegenen, von Süden nach Norden verlaufenden Flüsse wie Cugir

ten im Gewicht unser gutten Duckaten 3. Die Pawren hatten schon vill davon vertuscht / biß es richtbahr worden / und waren sehr reich davon worden: Jedoch was noch überblieben / und aus ihren Händen genommen / wurde auff 20000 Duckaten geschätzet / und Ferdinando durch Joh. Baptistam Castaldum überschicket / nebenst zweyen güldinnen Büldnissen Nini und Semiramidis, so nachmahls Carolo V. zu einem Anreiz und Anleitung Ferdinandum auch weitter in Siebenbürgen mit seiner Hilffe zu stärken / wurden verehret. Daß also dieser Vorrath in allem mit dem Theil / so Castaldus für die Kriegs-Knecht behalten / auch die Pawren verschaffet / auff die 300000 Duckaten auffs genawste gerechnet wurde: Diesen Schatz / hatte vormahls der Thracier, und Dacier oder Siebenbürger Könige Decebalus (wovon droben) aus Furcht des Römischen Keysers Trajani, damit er nicht den Römern zu theill wurde / vor seinem Tode in diesen Fluß vergraben (Miles 1670, p. 45).

43 Zu den größten dokumentierten Funden zählt der von Șeșu Căprărețel aus dem Jahr 1998 mit angeblich ca. 3.600 Münzen des Lysimachos-Typs sowie beigemengten nordpontischen Münzen; s. Mitthof 2022, 228–230.

44 Siehe Mitthof 2017, 116–117.

45 Lazius und andere neuzeitliche Autoren verwenden variierende Schreibweisen des Flussnamens: Lazius 1551, 1094: *Istrigij* und *Istriga*; Lazius 1556: *Istrygy*; Tröster 1666, 61: *Stryg*; Miles 1670, 45: *Strigh*.

46 S. oben Anm. 39.

47 Zu den wenigen Ausnahmen zählen etwa Winkler 1972, 188–192; Munteanu 2002, 256–260; Petac 2018, 15, die erwägen, die Sargetia mit dem Orăștie-Fluss zu identifizieren. – Es scheint in diesem Kontext auch bedeutsam, dass Lazius in seiner Karte von 1556 nur den Strei-Fluss darstellt, während die ältere *Tabula Hungariae* von Lazarus Secretarius und Georg Tannstetter aus dem Jahr 1528 sowohl den Strei-Fluss als auch den Orăștie-Fluss zeigt. Lazius war sich dieser möglichen Alternative für eine Identifizierung der Sargetia also nicht bewusst.

oder Sebeş meinten. Hinzu kommt drittens, dass zu den Umständen des Schatzfundes zwei verschiedene Versionen existieren: Der einen zufolge, die wir auch von Lazius kennen, soll der Schatz im Bett des Strei entdeckt worden sein, nach der anderen hingegen in einer alten Burg am Abhang eines Hügels.[48] Viertens ist zu bemerken, dass die beiden eingangs erwähnten Münztypen, die Statere des Koson- und des Lysimachos-Typs, entgegen dem von Lazius in unserer *Explicatio* erzeugten Eindruck, der im Übrigen bis heute in der Forschung allgemein geteilt wird, niemals vermischt gefunden werden. Die einzigen Quellen, die beide Münztypen in einem Atemzug nennen, sind Lazius, allerdings nur in unserem vorliegenden Text, sowie der in Böhmen wirkende Reformator und Lutherschüler Johann Mathesius (1504–1565) in einer Predigt aus dem Jahr 1562.[49] Es handelt sich also um zwei Berichte aus der Ferne. Zudem erwähnt Lazius bei der Schilderung des Strei-Fundes in den *Comm. R. R.* von 1551 die Koson-Statere nicht mehr.[50] Hinzu kommt schließlich fünftens, dass die beiden Stater-Typen des Koson und des Lysimachos in den Orăştie-Bergen schon lange vor dem Strei-Fund und vermutlich sogar zu allen Zeitaltern immer wieder gefunden wurden und daher auch in Siebenbürgen und gelegentlich sogar weit über dieses hinaus zirkulierten. Dies zeigt etwa der oben erwähnte Brief des Erasmus von Rotterdam vom Jahr 1520, in welchem der Koson-Stater erstmals beschrieben wird.[51]

---

48 Zu nennen ist diesbezüglich besonders der Bericht des Centorio degli Hortensii 1566, p. 198–199, der von der Version des Lazius nicht unerheblich abweicht: *Imperoche Deva era una buonissima & abbondante terra, & in sito che participa del piano, e del colle con un Castello assai forte, appresso di cui non molti anni inanzi in un castello overo palazzo antico poco discosto dalla terra tutto disfatto, e rovinato, fu ritrovato un grandissimo thesoro da alcuni villani in questo modo, che essendo molti di piovuto e per la violenza dell' acque che giu da quel poggio venivano precipitosamente correndo, fu discoperto un numero infinito di monete, o vogliamo dire, di medaglie d'oro, nelle quali era da un lato la imagine di Lisimaco, e dall' altro una vittoria di peso di duoi in tre scudi l'una, sovra lequali (cessato il nembo) percotendo il sole, fece da loro venire un splendore maraviglioso, dal quale fermati i detti villani, e correndo colà a vedere ciò che poteva essere, rimasero attoniti per allegrezza nel remirare tanta quantità di medaglie d'oro, & aprossimandosi per pigliarle, vi trovarono un serpente d'oro, ilquale fu poi mandato dal Castaldo a Ferdinando, ch l'hebbe nella morte di Frate Giorgio con una parte di quei Lisimachi, percioche anticamente coloro che sotterravano i suoi thesori, vi ponevano in segno di fida custodia, e somma, vigilantia i serpenti appresso, e dopo che i villani ne hebbero pigliato a piu non posso, se n'hebbe di quelle che avanzarono tanto, che valeva piu di venti mila ducati, perche fu fama per havere in quel luogo habitato il Re Lisimaco, che ve ne fussero piu di cento mila, de' quali Ferdinando n'hebbe, come si disse, mille medaglie, & il Castaldo da trecento in circa, e tra l'altre cose notabili che vi si trovarono, furono due medaglie d'oro, una del Re Nino, e l'altra della Reina Semiramis ch'ambe si mandarono a donare a Carlo Quinto, e per tutta quella provincia non c'è huomo di qualche aspettatione, che non ne habbia quantità, cosi grande fu la somma ritrovata.*

49 Mathesius 1562 (1618), 65–66: *Zu unseren zeiten hat man in Siebenbürgen ein Gewelb gefunden / welches ein kläffteriger Bawm der drauff gewachsen / im umbfallen entblösset hat / das ist steck voller geschlagener Goldgülden gelegen / der ich etliche gesehen / auff einem stehet Greckisch /* Basilij Lysimachon, *auf eim andern stehen drey Bilder / darunter (wie ich lese)* Koson, *auff der andern Seiten ein Phenix in seinem Neste / Es wigt aber einer mehr als zween Ungerische Gülden / diese Gülden hat endlich das Tagwasser auß dem Gewelb in grund gestösset / darvon ein Custer ist reich worden / welche sich endlich Georg Münch hat angemasset.*

50 S. oben Anm. 38.

51 S. oben Komm. *2.

Auch Lazius berichtet kurz nach 1551, als König Ferdinand ihm die Lysimachos-Statere zeigte, die diesem vom Condottiere Castaldo aus Siebenbürgen übersandt worden waren (hierzu s. das Folgende), er habe solche Münzen schon einige Jahre zuvor zu Gesicht bekommen, und zwar bei Kaufleuten, die sie von der walachischen Landbevölkerung Siebenbürgens angekauft hatten.[52] Diese Mitteilung könnte sich auf den Zeitraum ab 1543 beziehen, aber auch auf frühere Jahre und damit auf ältere Funde. Aus all dem folgt, dass Lazius eine sichere Zuordnung solcher Münzen zu einem konkreten siebenbürgischen Hortfund von Wien aus nicht möglich war, und es ist daher sehr gut möglich, dass er in unserer *Explicatio* zwei Münztypen unterschiedlicher Fund-Provenienz, die zwar aus der Zone der Orăştie-Berge, aber nicht unbedingt aus demselben Schatz stammten, miteinander in Verbindung gebracht hat.

Der Strei-Fund hatte, wie bereits angedeutet, politische Folgen.[53] Zu Beginn verkauften die für uns anonymen Finder die Münzen vor Ort oder brachten sie heimlich über die Landesgrenzen in die Moldau. Bald darauf bemächtigte sich Georg Martinuzzi („Mönch Georg"; 1482–1551), Bischof von Großwardein, Vormund des jungen Königs Johann Sigismund Zápolya und Gubernator in Siebenbürgen, der noch greifbaren Teile des Schatzes. Georg wurde im Jahre 1551 auf Veranlassung des Giovanni Castaldo (1493–1563), eines Condottiere Karls V., ermordet, wobei der Schatzfund eine wichtige Rolle gespielt haben dürfte. Allerdings wurden später in seinem Besitz nur 1.000 bzw. 4.000 Lysimachos-Münzen gefunden – möglicherweise auch dies ein Hinweis, dass der Strei-Schatz deutlich kleiner war, als von Lazius und den anderen Zeitgenossen berichtet. Castaldo übersandte 1.000 Lysimachos-Statere nach Wien an König Ferdinand,[54] wo sie von Lazius untersucht wurden.[55]

52 Zum Zitat s. unten Anm. 55.

53 Siehe Mitthof 2017, 115–116.

54 Hierzu existiert ein Brief Castaldos an Ferdinand vom 30. Jan. 1552; s. Bucholtz, 1838, 585–586. – Tröster (s. oben Anm. 42) spricht dagegen von 2.000 Lysimachos-Stateren.

55 Lazius berichtet hierüber in Cod. 7688, fol. 189f. (zitiert nach Mayr 1894, 57 Anm. 2): *Quoniam de thesauro monachi constabat Caesari, mox ab obitu mille Lysimachos ac draconem aureum pondere quingentorum ducatorum Caesari ceu spolium Viennam transmissit, cum meliorem sibi abegisset partem. Porro non illos solum mille aureos conspexi, quorum quilibet trium ducatorum habebat pondus, a Caesare ipso mihi ad interpretandum exhibitos, verum etiam a mercatoribus passim, qui a Walachis in Dacia emerant, pluribus antea annis oblatos conspexeram, quorum erat omnium eadem inscriptio idemque symbolum, videlicet facies iuvenis imberbis, diademate cincti in capite, in quo duo cornua hircina eminebant, et in altera parte icon Palladis sedentis cum inscriptione Graeca: Βασιλεως Λυσιμαχου, id est regis Lysimachi.* – Mit dem *draco* im Gewicht von angeblich 500 Dukaten (= ca. 1,7 kg), von dem Lazius hier spricht und der zusammen mit den Münzen nach Wien übersandt wurde, ist vermutlich ein dakischer Armreif gemeint. Derartige spiralförmige Objekte aus Gold, deren beide Enden den Köpfen und Vorderteilen von Schlangenwesen ähneln und die, soweit heute bekannt, im Durchschnitt ca. 1 kg wiegen, sind bei einigen Münzhortfunden in den Orăştie-Bergen als (apotropäische?) Begleitobjekte entdeckt worden (s. Spânu 2010). – Es sei an dieser Stelle nochmals betont, dass weder hier noch in anderen Quellen zur Martinuzzi-Affäre jemals Koson-Münzen erwähnt werden, was die oben dargelegte Vermutung bestärkt, dass solche im Strei-Fund nicht enthalten waren.

9 Beobachtungen zur Arbeitsweise des Lazius

Unsere Explicatio liefert Einblicke in Lazius' Arbeitsweise und Verlässlichkeit. Eine ganze Reihe von antiken Autoren bzw. Werken werden von ihm explizit als Autoritäten angeführt und dabei auch inhaltlich weitgehend korrekt wiedergegeben:[56] Ammianus (Marcellinus), (Cassius) Dio, Juvenal, Martial, Orosius, Polybius, (Claudius) Ptolemaeus, Stephanus Byzantius (*de urbibus*), Silius (Italicus), Statius (*Thebais* und *Silvae*), Tacitus, Vopiscus (= Historia Augusta, *Vita Aureliani*) sowie ein Auszug, vermutlich die Indizes, aus dem *Liber praefecturarum* (= *Notitia dignitatum*). Nur im Fall von Strabo sowie des *Itinerarium Antonini* entsprechen seine Angaben nicht dem überlieferten Text. Daneben hat Lazius offenkundig auch Beda Venerabilis' Werk über die Zeitrechnung (*De temporum ratione*) und Jordanes' *Getica* benutzt, ohne dies explizit zu vermerken. Einmal ist der Gebrauch von Tacitus eindeutig erkennbar, ohne dass Lazius dies explizit sagen würde. Im Falle von Stephanus gibt er ein wörtliches Zitat auf Griechisch wieder. Diese Angaben sind fast immer nachvollziehbar. In manchen Fällen hat Lazius die von ihm zitierten Autoren nur indirekt verwendet. Den Cassius Dio kennt er aus der Version des Merula, die bei Erasmus abgedruckt ist. Ähnliches gilt vermutlich auch für die Verse des Silius und Statius, die er in dieser Kombination möglicherweise der *Germaniae exegesis* des Franciscus Irenicus / Franz Friedlieb (1495–1553) entnommen hat.

Denselben Eindruck erweckt sein Gebrauch zeitgenössischer gelehrter Literatur. An einer Stelle scheint sich Lazius auf das Werk *Historia Pannonica sive Hungaricarum rerum Decades* des Antonius Bonfinius / Antonio Bonfini (1427–1502) zu stützen. Außerdem gibt es vielleicht Bezüge zu Werken von Johannes Aventinus / Johann Turmair (1477–1534) und Antonius Verantius (Antun Vrančić, 1504–1573), doch ist dies unsicher. Unklar bleibt, welches Werk Lazius mit den *Annales* meint, auf die er sich in Bezug auf die Geschichte Attilas und der Hunnen beruft.

Lazius' chronologische Berechnungen zur Zeitstellung des Lysimachos im zweiten Abschnitt der *Explicatio* sind nicht völlig konsistent. Er nennt hier geringfügig divergierende Daten. Völlig aus dem Rahmen fällt seine Angabe, der Strei-Schatz sei 1400 Jahre nach seiner Verbergung entdeckt worden. Hier liegt offensichtlich eine grobe Ungenauigkeit des Wiener Gelehrten oder ein Versehen des Kopisten vor. Die Berechnung der geographischen Distanz zwischen Lysimacheia und Hadrianopolis anhand der Koordinaten des Claudius Ptolemaeus erweist sich hingegen als vergleichsweise präzise. In krassem Gegensatz hierzu stehen seine fehlerhaften geographischen Angaben zur Lage der spätantiken dakischen Provinzen, zur falschen Identifikation antiker Orte mit modernen Plätzen (Segestica bzw. Sirmium mit Peterwardein und Szeged) und zur unhaltbaren Herleitung des Landschaftsnamens *Subenburgum* (Siebenbürgen) aus einem ungarischem Toponym *Seven / Sevesiear* (= Segesvár?) über die Zwischenstufe *Sevenburgum* unter Gleichsetzung dieses *Seven* mit einem antiken Ort namens *Zeugnia* (= *Zeugma*?), der weder in den von

56 Für die Details s. oben Abschnitt 7.

ihm genannten Quellen noch anderswo belegt ist: Die Ausführungen des Lazius zu diesen Punkten sind allesamt unhaltbar.

Dasselbe Schwanken des Lazius zwischen solider und quellentreuer Forschung, ungewollter Fehldeutung und dem bewussten Erfinden von Fakten ist auch bei seiner Behandlung epigraphischer Zeugnisse festzustellen. Von den zehn Inschriften, die Lazius in unserer *Explicatio* mitteilt, hat er nur eine in Autopsie gesehen; diesen fragmentarischen Text gibt er sehr verläßlich wieder, und er enthält sich auch jeder Spekulation über seine genaue Bedeutung. Die anderen Inschriften sind ihm, wie er sagt, von Informanten aus Siebenbürgen zugetragen worden. Sieben von diesen Inschriften sind echt, zwei hingegen ganz offenkundig Fälschungen, die allerdings schon vor Lazius bekannt waren und deren „Erfindung" daher nicht diesem anzulasten ist. Hingegen ist es sehr auffällig, dass Lazius die wichtigste Autorität seiner Tage für Inschriften aus dem antiken Dakien, nämlich die Sylloge des Mezerzius, weder in unserer *Explicatio* noch in seinen übrigen Schriften jemals erwähnt, obschon ein Vergleich seiner Transkriptionen mit den überlieferten Versionen des Mezerzius vermuten lässt, dass entweder Lazius selbst oder aber seine Gewährsleute ihre Kenntnis dieser Monumente in Wirklichkeit aus Mezerzius schöpften. Möglicherweise wollte Lazius die tatsächliche Herkunft dieser Informationen verbergen. Nur in einem Fall jedoch hat er zu einer authentischen Inschrift, die auch von anderen Autoren überliefert wird, ein Textelement hinzugedichtet, und zwar in der Absicht, die Lage der Colonia Sarmizegetusa am Fluss Sargetia nachweisen zu können, was für die Lokalisierung des Schatzfundes eine wichtige Erkenntnis gewesen wäre. In diesem an sich belanglosen Fall können wir, wie es scheint, Lazius als „Fälscher" entlarven.

10 Lazius und die Legende vom Schatz des Decebal

Lazius ist der früheste für uns fassbare Autor, der einen Zusammenhang zwischen dem spektakulären Goldfund vom Jahr 1543 und der antiken Überlieferung vom (legendären) Schatz des Decebal herstellt. Wir wissen heute, dass diese Deutung schon deshalb falsch ist, weil die damals entdeckten Münzen, nämlich Statere des Lysimachos-Typs, bereits mehr als 150 Jahre vor Decebals Herrschaft, im Zeitalter des Byrebistas (Burebista), geprägt und deponiert wurden. Zugleich ist es aber auch höchst fraglich, ob Lazius der Erste war, der eine solche Verbindung gesehen hat. Im Gegenteil: Wir müssen damit rechnen, dass die Erzählung von Decebals Schatz, die Cassius Dio (vermittelt über Xiphilinos und Merula) der Nachwelt überliefert hat, in den humanistisch gebildeten Kreisen der Gesellschaft Transsilvaniens der frühen Neuzeit[57] und vielleicht sogar unter der einfachen Landbevölkerung damals längst bekannt war und daher der Fund des Jahres 1543, sicherlich nicht der erste seiner Art, sofort in diesem Sinne gedeutet wurde. Wichtigster Beleg für diese Annahme ist die Existenz zweier frei erfundener Inschriften, deren Text damals in Siebenbürgen zirkulierte. Sie waren offenbar bereits in der Sammlung des 1516 verstor-

57 In diesem Sinne auch bereits Winkler 1972, 190; vgl. Petac 2018, 15.

benen Mezerzius enthalten. Ob sie von Mezerzius selbst oder schon zuvor von einer anderen Person erdichtet wurden, ist nicht zu klären. In jedem Fall bezogen sie sich nicht auf den Fund von 1543, sondern auf einen älteren Schatzfund. Diese beiden Inschriften und das mit ihnen verbundene Narrativ wurden aber erst anläßlich des Fundes von 1543 von Lazius und anderen Gelehrten außerhalb Siebenbürgens aufgegriffen und durch ihre Publikationen in anderen Teilen Europas bekannt gemacht.

Zudem ist aus den Akten der habsburgischen Verwaltung Transsilvaniens zu den Schatzfunden von Koson- und Lysimachos-Stateren von 1802–1804 deutlich zu ersehen, dass in der lokalen Bevölkerung der Region allerlei historische Sagen und abergläubische Vorstellungen über die Hintergründe des antiken Goldes verbreitet waren.[58] Wir können daher sogar noch einen Schritt weiter gehen und vermuten, dass das damals in Siebenbürgen allgemein bekannte Narrativ vom sagenhaften Schatz im Bett des Flusses Sargetia von den Findern und anderen Profiteuren des Goldes ganz bewusst aufgegriffen wurde, um ihren Zeitgenossen einen plausiblen Fundort, den Strei-Fluss, zu benennen und zugleich den wahren Fundort zu verschleiern. Der tatsächliche Ort des Schatzfundes von 1543 dürfte nämlich in den Orăştie-Bergen zu suchen sein (wie nicht zuletzt der Bericht des Centorio degli Hortensii vermuten lässt).[59] Von dort stammen alle siebenbürgischen Funde von Stateren sowohl des Lysimachos- als auch des Kosontyps, die in den folgenden Jahrhunderten bis auf den heutigen Tag bekannt geworden sind.

Literaturverzeichnis

Lazius-Handschriften

München, Staatsbibliothek (Reinschrift)
  Clm 9216, fol. 11r-13r
Wien, Österreichische Nationalbibliothek (Autographe)
  Cod. 7688 [Hist. prof. 223 et 224]
  Cod. 7967 [Hist. prof. 156–158]
  Cod. 8457 [Hist. prof. 165]
  Cod. 8664 [Hist. prof. 216]

Gedruckte Werke des Lazius

Lazius, W. 1546. Viennae Austria. Rerum Viennensium commentarii in quatuor libros distincti, Basileae.
Lazius, W. 1551. Commentariorum Reipublicae Romanae illius, in exteris provinciis, bello acquisitis, constitutae, libri duodecim, Basileae s. a. (laut Vorrede 1551).
Lazius, W. 1556. Regni Hungariae descriptio vera, Viennae.

58 Mitthof, Mádly 2015.
59 S. oben Anm. 48.

Digitalisat der Universität Basel: https://www.e-rara.ch/bau_1/doi/10.3931/e-rara-12901
Lazius, W. 1557. De gentium aliquot migrationibus sedibus fixis ..., Basileae.
Lazius, W. 1558 (1605). Historicarum commentationum rerum Graecarum libri duo, Hanoviae (Erstausgabe 1558).
Lazius, W. 1598. Reipublicae Romanae in exteris provinciis bello acquisitis constitutae commentariorum libri duodecim, Francofurti (postume und revidierte Zweitausgabe der *Comm. R. R.* von 1551).

Neuzeitliche Textausgaben und Literatur (16.–17. Jh.)

Aventinus, J. 1554. Annales ducum Boiariae.
Beda 1529. Bedae Presbyteri Anglosaxonis viri eruditissimi De natura rerum et temporum ratione libri duo, ed. Ioannes Sichardus, Basileae.
Beda 1537. Bedae Presbyteri Anglosaxonis ... opuscula complura de temporum ratione diligenter castigata atque illustrata veteribus quibusdam annotationibus ..., authore Iohanne Noviomago, Coloniae.
Centorio degli Hortensii, Ascanio 1566. Commentarii della Guerra di Transilvania, Vinegia.
Erasmus (Merula, G.) 1518. Ex Recognitione Desiderii Erasmi Roterodami: C. Suetonius Tranquillus. Dion Cassius Nicaeus. Aelius Spartianus. Iulius Capitolinus. Aelius Lampridius. Vulcatius Gallicanus v.c. Trebellius Pollio. Flauius Vopiscus Syracusius. Quibus adiuncti sunt Sex. Aurelius Victor. Eutropius. Paulus Diaconus. Ammianus Marcellinus. Pomponius Laetus Romanus. Ioannes Baptista Egnatius Venetus, Basileae, 171–180: Dionis Cassii Nicaei Traianus Nerva Georgio Merula Alexandrino interprete.
Friedlieb, F. I. 1518. Germaniae exegeseos volumina duodecim a Francisco Irenico Ettelingiacensi exarata, Hagenau.
Gelenius, S. 1552. Notitia utraque cum Orientis tum Occidentis ultra Arcadii Honoriique Caesarum tempora, Basileae.
Mathesius, J. 1562 (1618). Sarepta, darin von allerly Bergwerk ..., (Widmung/Vorrede von 1562), Die Ander Predigt, Leipzig.
Miles, M. 1670. Siebenbürgischer Würg-Engel / oder Chronicalischer Angang des 15 Seculi nach Christi Geburth / aller theils in Siebenbürgen / theils in Ungern, und sonst Siebenbürgen angränzenden Ländern / fürgelauffener Geschichten, Hermanstadt.
Tröster, J. 1666. Das Alt- und Neu-Teutsche Dacia. Das ist: Neue Beschreibung des Landes Siebenbürgen ..., Nürnberg.
Zamosius, S. 1593. Analecta lapidum vetustorum et nonnullarum in Dacia antiquitatum, Patavii (neu abgedruckt in: Lazius 1598).

Moderne Ausgaben und Übersetzungen antiker Autoren

Adamietz, J. 1993. Juvenal, Satiren.
Barié, P., Schindler, W. 2013. Martial, Epigramme (Gesamtausgabe), Berlin, 3. Aufl.
Billerbeck, M. 2014. Stephanii Byzantii Ethnica, Volumen III: Kappa–Omikron, Berlin.

Hohl, E. 1965. Scriptores Historiae Augustae, Volumen II, Leipzig 1965.
Mommsen, Th. 1882. Iordanis Romana et Getica. Berlin.
Radt, S. 2003. Strabons Geographika, Band 2. Buch V–VIII: Text und Überlieferung, Göttingen.
Rupprecht, H. 1991. Silius Italicus, Punica. Das Epos vom Zweiten Punischen Krieg, Mitterfels.
Schönberger, O. 1998. P. Papinius Statius, Der Kampf um Theben, Würzburg.
Seeck, O. 1876. Notitia dignitatum, accedunt Notitia Urbis Constantinopolitanae et Laterculi provinciarum, Berlin.
Stückelberger, A., Graßhoff, G. ²2017. Klaudios Ptolemaios, Handbuch der Geographie, 1. Teil: Einleitung und Buch 1–4, 2. Auflage, Basel.
Wißmüller, H. 1990. Statius, Silvae, Neustadt/Aisch.
Zangemeister, C. 1866. Pauli Orosii Historiarum adversum paganos libri VII, Wien.

Moderne Literatur

Absil, M. 1997. Les préfets du prétoire d'Auguste à Commode, Paris.
Armbruster, A. 1978. Die rumänischen Chronisten und die Herkunft der Siebenbürger Sachsen, Zeitschrift für Siebenbürgische Landeskunde 1, 24–30.
Bucholtz, F.B. von 1838. Geschichte der Regierung Ferdinands des Ersten, Band IX: Urkundenband, Wien.
Dana, D. 2014. *Onomasticon Thracicum*. Répertoire des noms indigènes de Thrace, Macédoine orientale, Mésies, Dacie et Bithynie, Athènes.
Deppert-Lippitz, B. 2010. Thesauro monachi – Der grosse dakische Goldfund aus dem Strei (1543), Annales Universitatis Apulensis. Series Historica 14/I, 9–27.
Halm, K., Laubmann, G. von, Meyer, W. 1874: Catalogus codicum latinorum Bibliothecae Regiae Monacensis, Bd.: 4,1, Codices Latinos (Clm) 8101–10930 complectens, München.
Heenes V. 2017. Zu den Kopien der Reliefs der Trajanssäule im 16. Jahrhundert: Zwei neue Zeichnungen eines unbekannten Rotulus, in F. Mitthof, G. Schörner (Hrsg.), Columna Traiani – Trajanssäule. Siegesmonument und Kriegsbericht in Bildern, Wien, 271–278.
Hochstrasser, G. 1998. Siebenbürgen – Siweberjen bedeutet Zibinumschließung – Cibinbërgen, Zeitschrift für siebenbürgische Landeskunde 21, 192–195.
Horawitz, A., Hartfelder, K. 1886. Briefwechsel des Beatus Rhenanus, Leipzig.
Lichtenberger, A, Nieswandt, H.-H., Salzmann, D. 2015. Die hellenistische Residenzstadt Lysimacheia: Feldforschungen in der Zentralsiedlung und der Chora, in A. Matthaei, M. Zimmermann (Hrsg.), Urbane Strukturen und bürgerliche Identität im Hellenismus (Die hellenistische Polis als Lebensform 5), Heidelberg, 163–192.
Makkay, J. 1994, The Treasures of Decebalus, Specimina Nova Universitatis Quinqueecclesiensis 10, 1, 151–215.
Makkay, J. 1995, The Treasures of Decebalus, Oxford Journal of Archaeology 14, 333–343.
Mayr, M. 1894. Wolfgang Lazius als Geschichtsschreiber Österreichs, Innsbruck.

Mitthof, F. 2014. Sarmizegetusa? Zu den Varianten eines dakischen Toponyms in den lateinischen und griechischen Quellen, in: I. Piso, R. Varga, R. (Hrsg.), Trajan und seine Städte. Colloquium Cluj-Napoca, 29. Sept.–2. Okt. 2013, Cluj-Napoca, 233–244.

Mitthof, F. 2017. *Vexatissimi nummi*: 500 Jahre numismatische Forschung zu den Koson-Münzen, Acta Musei Napocensis 54/I, 105–168.

Mitthof, F. 2022. Die Analyse eines siebenbürgischen Schatzfundes durch Abbé Eder im Jahr 1803: Goldstatere der bosporanischen Herrscher Pharnakes II. und Asandros in Vergesellschaftung mit solchen des Lysimachos-Typs, in B. Woytek, D. Williams (Hrsg.), Ars critica numaria. Joseph Eckhel (1737–1798) and the Tranformation of Ancient Numismatics, Wien, 211–244.

Mitthof, F., Mádly, L. 2015. Ein Golddepot aus der Zeit des Horea-Aufstandes? Zur Geschichte eines siebenbürgischen Schatzfundes aus dem Jahre 1796, in I. M. Balog, I. Lumperdean, L. Mádly, D. Ţeicu (Hrsg.), Multikulturalismus, Identität und Diversität. Historische Perspektiven. Festschrift für Professor Rudolf Gräf zum 60. Geburtstag, Cluj-Napoca, 183–194.

Mitthof, F., Matei-Popescu, F. 2023. Gab es im Jahr 283 n. Chr. zwei dakische Provinzen südlich der Donau? Zur Lesung und Deutung der Inschrift *AE 1912, 200 = ILBulg 188*, in L. Mihailescu-Bîrliba, I. Piso (Hrsg.), Roman and Natives in the Danubian provinces (1st–6th c. AD), Wiesbaden, 553–565.

Munteanu L., 2002. Despre descoperirile monetare de tip Kosōn, Arheologia Moldovei 25, 2002, 253–270.

Munteanu, L. 2003. Despre emiterea monedelor de tip Kosōn, Arheologia Moldovei 26, 241–264.

Munteanu, L. 2005. Quelques considérations concernant les découvertes des monnaies d'or de type Lysimaque dans la Dacie intra-carpatique, in V. Cojocaru (Hrsg.), Ethnic Contacts and Cultural Exchanges North and West of the Black Sea from the Greek Colonization to the Ottoman Conquest, Iaşi, 237–254.

Petac, E. 2018. About the Sarmizegetusa Hoard from 1998 and the Possible Chronology of Burebista's Campaign to the Black Sear Border, Notae Numismaticae / Zapiski Numizmatyczne 13, 13–28.

Piso, I. 1993. Fasti provinciae Daciae, I: Die senatorischen Amtsträger, Bonn.

Piso, I. 2006. Le Forum vetus de Sarmizegetusa I (Colonia Dacica Sarmizegetusa I), Bucureşti.

Piso, I. 2013. Fasti provinciae Daciae, II: Die ritterlichen Amtsträger, Bonn.

Poenaru Bordea, Gh. 1979. Les statères ouest-pontiques de type Alexandre le Grand et Lysimaque, Revue Belge de Numismatique 125, 37–51

Reinhard, W. *et al.* 1996. Augsburger Eliten des 16. Jahrhunderts. Prosopographie wirtschaftlicher und politischer Führungsgruppen 1500–1620, hrsg. von W. Reinhard, bearb. von M. Häberlein, U. Klinkert, K. Sieh-Burens und R. Wendt, Berlin.

Schuller, W. 1999. Siebenbürgen – ein Toponym mit rechtshistorischem Hintergrund, Zeitschrift für siebenbürgische Landeskunde 22, 119–122.

Sorić, D., Jurić, T. S. 2021. The Textual Transmission of Iter Buda Hadrianopolim, a Travelogue by Antun Vrančić, Povijesni prilozi 61, 397–427.

Spânu, D. 2010. Zur Analyse der Goldspiralen von Grădiştea de Munte, Rumänien, Das Altertum 55, 271–314.

Stein, A. 1940. Die Legaten von Moesien, Budapest.

Strobel, K. 1984 Untersuchungen zu den Dakerkriegen Trajans, Bonn.

Strobel, K. 1989. Die Donaukriege Domitians, Bonn.

Strobel, K. 2019a. Südosteuropa in der Zeit von Republik und Principat: Vorgeschichte, Etablierung und Konsolidierung römischer Herrschaft, in U. Brunnbauer, K. Clewing, O.J. Schmitt (Hrsg.), Handbuch zur Geschichte Südosteuropas, Band 1: Herrschaft und Politik in Südosteuropa von der römischen Antike bis 1300, 1. Teilband, Berlin / Boston, 131–322.

Strobel, K. 2019b. Kaiser Trajan: Eine Epoche der Weltgeschichte, 2. Auflage, Regensburg.

Teutsch, G.D. 1883. Ein Schreiben des Honterus – angeblich – an Sebastian Münster, Korrespondenzblatt des Vereins für siebenbürgische Landeskunde VI, 6, 61–67.

Winkler I., 1972. Consideraţii despre moneda "Koson", SCIV 23, 173–199.

King Matthias and Peisistratos

György Németh

There are many Hungarian folk tales about the righteous King Matthias Corvinus, and one them is set in Cluj (Kolozsvár),[1] both the birthplace of Matthias and the home of celebrated Ioan Piso.

When King Matthias heard that the wicked judge in Kolozsvár was oppressing the poor, he went to Kolozsvár, dressed as a commoner. He was waiting in front of the judge's house when a servant grabbed him and dragged him in to see the judge. The judge forced the disguised king to carry logs into his yard. Matthias had his name secretly engraved on three logs. In the evening, tired, he stood in front of the judge and asked to be paid for the day's work. The ignorant judge did not pay, but gave Matthias twenty-five lashes. After returning to Buda, the king appeared again in Kolozsvár with a distinguished company. He brought out the three logs bearing his name, confronted the judge with his deeds, and then expelled the evil judge and his servants from the city.[2]

There are three main parts of the story: 1) The king in disguise spies on the evil judge; 2) The judge beats the disguised king, thinking that he is a mere commoner, and 3) Matthias returns with a royal entourage, chases the judge away and saves the poor people from tyranny.

István Székely published his chronicle in 1559, in which he quotes King Matthias's conversation with a poor man, whom he eventually freed from serfdom for his uprightness.[3] Székely does not write that Matthias was in disguise, but had the poor man known he was talking to the king, he would have been less outspoken.

In history, we do not know many kings or princes who went among the common people in disguise to find out how they lived and what their problems were. The most famous ruler about whom such stories were told was caliph Harun al-Rashid.[4] However, he mingled with the common people primarily for amusement, not to punish the unjustly privileged. It also happened that he was beaten like King Matthias, because he was not recognised. It is unlikely, of course, that the caliph would have really behaved in this way,

1 ELTE University, Budapest. ORCID 0000-0001-8708-8102. For the earlier version of the paper in Hungarian, see Németh 2019, 71–80.

2 Magyar Népmesekatalógus (The Types of the Hungarian Folktale): MNK 921 IV*

3 Székely 1559.

4 Suedfeld 2004, 480.

but these legends were so well known that they even made it into the *One Thousand and and One Nights* collection.[5]

We know of few rulers from antiquity who went about in disguise among the people, but those who have survived are said to have dressed up for their own amusement. Cleopatra's husband, Antony, frolicked with his royal wife in the streets of Alexandria, but they had no thought of punishing or rewarding their subjects: "and when by night he would station himself at the doors or windows of the common folk and scoff at those within, she would go with him on his round of mad follies, wearing the garb of a serving maiden. For Antony also would try to array himself like a servant. Therefore he always reaped a harvest of abuse, and often of blows, before coming back home; though most people suspected who he was. However, the Alexandrians took delight in his coarse wit, and joined in his amusements in their graceful and cultivated way; they liked him, and said that he used the tragic mask with the Romans, but the comic mask with them."[6]

Even in disguise, Caligula and Nero could not hide their own depravity, so their adventures were even less like the tales of King Matthias than the escapades of Antony and Cleopatra: "But he could not even then conceal his natural disposition to cruelty and lewdness. He delighted in witnessing the inflictions of punishments, and frequented taverns and bawdy-houses in the night-time, disguised in a periwig – and a long coat."[7]

> "After it was dark, he used to enter the taverns disguised in a cap or a wig, and ramble about the streets in sport, which was not void of mischief. He used to beat those he met coming home from supper; and, if they made any resistance, would wound them, and throw them into the common-sewer. He broke open and robbed shops; establishing an auction at home for selling his booty. In the scuffles which took place on those occasions, he often ran the hazard of losing his eyes, and even his life; being beaten almost to death by a senator, for handling his wife indecently. After this adventure, he never again ventured abroad at that time of night, without some tribunes following him at a little distance."[8]

In the above-mentioned chronicle of István Székely, we can read about King Matthias sneaking into the besieged city of Vienna in disguise, in order to personally gather information about the enemy. The source of this story is an Italian humanist working at King Matthias' court, who tells about Matthias' disguised spy, but Antonio Bonfini also claims that the disguised king went to the Turkish camp, where he spent the whole day selling barley near the Turkish leader's tent.[9] When Matthias returned to his own camp,

5 Clot 1989.

6 Plutarch, *Antonius* 29.1–2.

7 Suetonius, *Caligula* 11.

8 Suetonius, *Nero* 26.

9 Bonfini 4.8.262: *Cum prope Turcos castra metatus esset, sic vires hostium exploravit. Pagano nanque subornatus amictu cum uno tantum comite se cum iumento inter eos, qui commeatus in hostilia castra conferrent, insinuavit; cum eo pervenisset, toto die pro tabernaculo Turci hordeum vendidit; ingruente nocte se incolumem in sua castra recepit. Scripsit ad hostem se pridie eius castra penitus explorasse, ven-*

he even sent a message to the Turkish leader about the food that was brought into his tent all day. The Turkish leader was frightened so much that he withdrew with his army the next day. In reality, of course, the king did not risk his life with such pranks. Bonfini drew the story from Plutarch, who had Sertorius spying in disguise in the Celtic camp: "In the next place, when the same enemies were coming up with many myriads of men and dreadful threats, so that for a Roman even to hold his post at such a time and obey his general was a great matter, while Marius was in command, Sertorius undertook to spy out the enemy. So, putting on a Celtic dress and acquiring the commonest expressions of that language for such conversation as might be necessary, he mingled with the Barbarians; and after seeing or hearing what was of importance, he came back to Marius."[10]

Bonfini not only knew Greek and Latin, reading ancient authors in Italy or in Buda in the famous Bibliotheca Corviniana, but he also knew how ancient classical writers flattered the rulers of their time. Bonfini was also a master of flattery. Based on his ancient sources, he not only embellished the deeds of the living monarch, but also the figure of Louis the Great, the Knight-King of Hungary. According to Bonfini, the king went around among the people in disguise, punishing unjust judges and tax collectors, and inquiring about opinions of the king's actions. He even corrected his own decisions when the people complained about them.[11]

Bonfini attributed the same deeds to King Matthias when he described him as a just ruler. The story of the judge in Cluj can be described using this model. But, as we can see, the stories of ancient rulers in disguise did not fit this model. There is only one ancient story in which the ruler was not recognised by the poor man, and on hearing his honest answers the ruler rewarded him. This was the story of Peisistratos and the peasant ploughing on Hymettus. The scene is recorded in Aristotelian *Constitution of the Athenians* (though the author is certainly not the eminent philosopher):

> "For it was when Peisistratus was making an expedition of this kind that the affair of the man on Hymettus cultivating the farm afterwards called Tax-free Farm is said to have occurred. He saw a man at farm-work, digging mere rocks, and because of his surprise ordered his servant to ask what crop the farm grew; and the man said, 'All the aches and pains that there are, and of these aches and pains Peisistratus has to get the tithe.' The man did not know who it was when he answered, but

didisse rustici sub persona hordeum ad tabernaculum eius et, quo maiorem dictis fidem faceret, ferculorum numerum et epularum cuncta genera retulit. Que cum hostis accepisset, timore perculsus postero die castra solvit veritus Corvinum regem non modo ad vallum sibi occursurum, sed in medio tabernaculo invasurum.

10 Plutarch, *Sertorius* 3.2.

11 Bonfini 2.10.474: *Ne plebs ac rustica multitudo gravioribus, quam par est, tributie et portoriis a questoribus et prefectis oneraretur neve iniquis iudicis gravaretur afficereturve rapinis, dissimulato sepe habitu veluti callidissimus explorator vicos et oppida lustravit perscrutaturus mores publicanorum et prefectorum et eorum iniurias ex plebis querimoniis recogniturus, quod idcirco a clementissimo principe factitatum aiunt, ut non minus optimatum quam plebis curam gerisse videretur. Quin etiam sepissime subornatus de moribus regis percontabatur et e simplicium responsis sese ipse quandoque castigav*it.

Peisistratus was pleased by his free speech and by his industry, and made him free from all taxes."[12]

The only problem is that Bonfini could not have known the *Constitution of the Athenians* yet, because in his time it was still hidden in the sands of Egypt in two papyrus fragments.[13] Fortunately, a codex of the Corviniana preserved a version of the story: "Once when Peisistratus was journeying through the country he saw a man on the slopes of Hymettus working in a field where the soil was exceedingly thin and stony. And wondering at the man's zeal for the work, he sent some of his company to inquire of him what return he got from working ground like that. And when the men had carried out the command, the farmer replied that he got from the field only grievous pains; but he did not care, since he gave the tenth part of them to Peisistratus. And the ruler, on hearing the reply, laughed, and made the field exempt from taxation..."[14]

Bonfini adapted this story to the figure of the just King Matthias, which turned out so popular that centuries later it became part of Hungarian folklore, and most Hungarians, when asked what they know about King Matthias, will immediately reply that Matthias was just.

Bibliography

Bonfini, A. 1936. Rerum Ungaricarum Decades. Leipzig.

Clot, A. 1989. Harun Al-Rashid and the World of a Thousand and One Nights. Saqi Books, London.

Németh, G. 2019. Mátyás király álruhája, in A. Bárány *et al.*, Hunyadi Mátyás és kora, Debrecen, 71–80.

Rhodes, P.J. 1993. A Commentary on the Aristotelian Athenaion Politeia. Oxford.

Suedfeld, P.2004. Harun al-Rashid and the Terrorists: Identity Concealed, Identity Revealed, Political Psychology 25/3, 479–492.

Székely I. 1559. Chronica ez vilagnac yeles dolgairol. Krakkow.

12 *Athenaion Politeia* 16. 6.

13 The two large fragments of the papyrus reached Europe in 1879 and 10 years later (Rhodes 1993, 1–3).

14 Diodorus Siculus 9. 37.

Among wise men the game goes: Deceneus and Alfonso X of Castile

Juan Ramón Carbó García

In 2021, Spain celebrated the eighth centenary of the birth of King Alfonso X of Castile and León (1252–1284). He remains one of the most reliably famous and well-studied monarchs, not just of medieval Iberia, but of the entirety of the European Middle Ages. Whether as "the Learned King", "el Sabio", or "the Wise King", Alfonso's reign and his exceptional literary, scholarly, and juridical work have attracted scholarly attention regularly and reliably for years[1].

Several were the fields of knowledge that attracted the interest of the wise king, and several were the languages in which they were expressed. Both the choice of those fields and those languages did not take place at random but in connection with a broad project of reform of his kingdom. The books acted as true pillars, and not as cultural amusements or marginal additions to the work of government. All these books proclaim the king as their author, hardly mentioning the Christian and Jewish scholars with whom he surrounded himself to write them. The purpose was for Alfonso X to appear as a model of wisdom before his subjects and, with this, to cement a monarchy in whose head were the kings. In his vision, these were vicars of God on earth.

The areas of knowledge addressed by Alfonso X aspired to dominate the three times in which humanity organizes the axis of its life on earth –the present, the past and the future– as well as the time that awaits beyond death: eternal life. In the very broad theme of his literary production, we could contemplate law as the ordering of the present, history as the teaching of the past, science as the knowledge of the future, and finally the cult of the Virgin Mary as the support of divinity, in relation to the Hereafter.

Today, in the Spanish National Library, five original Alfonso's codices (or close to his workshop) are preserved: the "Fuero real" (1255), the "Libro complido de los judizios de las estrellas" (c.1254), the "Libro de las cruzes" (1259), the first part of the "Grande e general estoria" (c. 1270) and the first version of the "Cantigas de Santa María" (c. 1270). In addition, there are also luxurious copies of other works composed by order of the Learned King, such as the astrological treatise on the constellations, called " Libro de las figuras de

1 E.g.: O'Callaghan 1993; O'Callaghan 1998; Doubleday 2015; Kennedy 2019; O'Callaghan 2019.

las estrellas fixas", with Renaissance decoration, or the "Siete Partidas" that belonged to the Catholic Monarchs.

1 Alfonso X and his legal reform

The centrality of legal reform to the reign of Alfonso X, and in particular the significance of the famous "Siete Partidas" law code has been demonstrated since the last thirty years. The project that created the Alfonsine codes was initiated under his father, Fernando III, who ordered his son to complete it. These codes were essentially completed in two stages: the "Espéculo" (which was a law code itself, but probably intended as a guide for judges) and the "Fuero Real", likely promulgated in 1254 and 1256, were followed by the later expansion on his original work, the "Libro de las leyes", better known as the "Siete Partidas", which was completed in 1265. Alfonso and his court made different justifications for this major revision of Castilian legal practice. In this way, the wise king emphasized not only the expediency of a uniform law code for his realm, but the well-ordered society dedicated to the common good, which could be produced by a systematic revision like that[2].

The divine origin of the king's power was emphasized, as was his superiority in all temporal matters. The codes made extensive use of the theory of the two swords, the temporal and the spiritual, which should work jointly. Nevertheless, the king's authority in temporal matters was pre-eminent. The king's duty to his people, especially his duty to promote and enforce justice, and the people's duty to obey the king were paired[3]. Defense of the realm was a rather more straightforward issue, dealt with at some length in the various pieces of the Alfonsine code. Perhaps most striking is the notion, found in the fourth of the "Siete Partidas", that men have a great debt to the land to love it, increase it, and die for it.

The code covers the different forms of ownership of land and other forms of property, as well as the proper conduct of and regulations for commercial enterprises. In addition to covering the landed rights of the monarchy, Church, and nobility, the third Partida describes common property rights, rental property, and even the ownership of wild animals. The Alfonsine code made provisions for contract law, lending, and the payment of debts. The king enacted extensive market regulations, including attempts to set fair prices and wages, and to discourage guilds and private price-fixing. Fairs and foreign trade were encouraged, and the royal duties and taxes set.

A vast array of criminal conduct is described, from fraud to heresy to murder, and beyond. The array of punishments that the law might prescribe included execution (only for serious crimes), exile, imprisonment, mutilation, humiliation, and court-imposed fines. Though the king reserved the right to pardon convicted criminals, the emphasis of the code was on the maintenance of public order, and the exemplary punishment of those who threatened it.

---

2 O'Callaghan 2019, 21.
3 O'Callaghan 2019, 42.

The achievements of Alfonso X in the realm of legal scholarship and reform are especially noted in the long shadow that the "Siete Partidas" would cast down the centuries, both in Spain and in the wider world. The ideals of law, order, and governance are envisioned in the Alfonsine codes, demonstrating the remarkable vision of the king to create a society in which carefully considered laws made justice available to all.

2 The historiographical work of Alfonso X and the transmission of the figure of Deceneus

To the great work of legal reform of the wise king we must add, for our immediate interest in this study, his great historiographical work, the culmination of Castilian production in this area in the thirteenth century. This is the "Estoria de España" –also known as the "Primera Crónica General de España"[4]–, written from 1260 on the initiative of King Alfonso X the Learned.

The monarch actively collaborated in its drafting, and it was the first extensive history of Spain written in the Romance language. It covered chronologically from the biblical and legendary origins of Spain to the immediate history of the kingdom of Castile under Fernando III[5].

This great work of the Alfonsine desk is divided into four parts: the first of them constitutes a history of Rome, since the medieval kings of the European nations considered themselves heirs of the Roman Empire; the second part is dedicated to showing the history of the barbarian kings, the Gothic kings among them, being the direct ancestors in the Peninsula; the third is a history of the Asturian kingdom and, finally, the fourth, a history of the kingdoms of León and Castile. However, as in the chronicles of the time, it goes back to the most remote past found in the Bible, specifically to Moses, to continue with myths and legends mixed with Greek sources and ancient history[6]. Very diverse works were used for its composition, such as the Bible, classical Latin historiography, ecclesiastical legends, medieval chansons de geste in the Romance language, and works made by Arab historians. But among all of them stand out the two great Latin chronicles that constituted the most complete knowledge of the history of Spain in the thirteenth century: the "Chronicon mundi" by Lucas of Tuy and the "Historia de rebus Hispaniae" by Rodrigo Jiménez de Rada; although the work team of Alfonso X also used other medieval Latin chronicles[7].

---

4 Menéndez Pidal 1977.

5 Catalán 1962; Catalán 1992; Crespo 2000.

6 Estévez Sola 2004; De Carlos Villamarín 1993.

7 Dyer 1990; Fernández-Ordóñez 1992, 138–158; Fernández-Ordóñez 1999; Fernández-Ordóñez 2000.

2.1 *Lucas of Tuy*

Lucas of Tuy represents the continuation of the tradition coming from Isidore of Seville. He was born at the end of the twelfth century. He developed his ecclesiastical career as a canon of the collegiate church of San Isidoro de León in the first part of the thirteenth century. During the last ten years of his life until 1249, as bishop of Tuy, he carried out his historical work, in which the "Chronicon mundi" (approximately between 1230 and 1238) stands out[8]. This is but an extension of Isidore's "Chronicon de sex aetatibus". In the first part we will find a complete paragraph about Trajan, even longer than that of Isidore. When, in a second book, he reproduces without modifications the "Historia Gothorum", some elements of the identification between Goths and Getae that Isidore had etymologically developed make a reappearance[9].

We can find examples of Gothicism everywhere in the work of Lucas of Tuy. When he deals with the time after the fall of the Kingdom of Toledo, he will continue to refer to the peninsular Christians as "Goths", both in his interpolations and when the information from any source differs[10]. The touchstone of Hispanic Gothicism will be the conception of organized resistance in the north of the Peninsula against the Arab invaders, in the Pyrenees, the Cantabrian Mountain range and the Galician mountains, a conception that would continue to be transmitted much later. The Christians who resisted Islam in those areas were called Goths by Lucas of Tuy[11].

On the other hand, by highlighting the virtues of the Goths, he departs from the myth of the undefeated Visigothic army, only surpassed in civil strife, following the extensive reference of Isidore in his "Historia Gothorum" on the courage and military capacity of the Goths, identified with the Getae[12]. By considering blood nobility as an indispensable condition to be able to stand out for their courage and mastery of arms, the supreme nobility of the Goths is indirectly proclaimed. This has its most evident testimony in its excellence on the battlefield. And it is very likely that the proclamation of such nobility constituted a veiled expression of Leonese exaltation, given that the kings of León were considered the legitimate heirs of the Visigothic monarchy[13].

2.2 *Rodrigo Jiménez de Rada*

Practically contemporary of the "Chronicon Mundi" of Lucas of Tuy is the "Historia de rebus Hispaniae sive Historia gothica" of the Toledan archbishop Rodrigo Jiménez de Rada (c. 1170–1247), in which the history of the Peninsula until the year 1243 is de-

8 Linehan 1997; Martin 2001; Falque 2003; Fernández Gallardo 2004.

9 Falque 1998.

10 Lucas de Tuy, Chron. mun., IV.3. 21–22; 5. 16; 35. 21–22 y 45; 36. 5; 37. 5 y 67; 40. 3; 45. 5; 57. 25; 70. 50; 77. 55; 83. 42.

11 Lucas de Tuy, Chron. mun., III. 63. 42–46.

12 Isid., Hist. Goth., 66–70; Carbó García 2015, 62–65.

13 Lucas de Tuy, Chron. mun., II, Prologus.

scribed[14]. Jiménez de Rada continued to draw notably inspiration from Isidore of Seville, but he also relied heavily on the "Getica" of Jordanes. From this, as we shall see, he would take complete passages referring to the mythical past of the Goths. In the thirteenth century, the work of Jordanes had a remarkable influence on the Iberian Peninsula, since the kings sought to legitimize themselves through the Visigothic "ancestors" and were going to appropriate the history of the Goths[15]. The Isidorian tradition also remained in this century, which sees the arrival of these new sources from Europe that will feed the chroniclers of this time. Nevertheless, the identification between Getae and Goths and the etymological theory of Isidore had practically lost their value until that moment.

For the elaboration of his work, Jiménez de Rada followed the model of the "Crónica najerense", and the "De rebus Hispaniae" would become one of the main sources for the historical work of Alfonso X the Learned. It would have a very important impact on the conception of peninsular historical writing and, in addition, in the thirteenth century several translations would be made in peninsular vernacular languages. For this reason, it would significantly influence the conception of a dominant unitary history of Spain until the fifteenth century[16].

The nature of the commissioned work is what determines the historical perspective in the writings of Rodrigo. In the case of Lucas of Tuy, if we know that he made his work commissioned by Queen Berenguela, Jiménez de Rada composed his own at the request of King Fernando III. This king, Alfonso's father, must have felt somehow dissatisfied and required a history that covered from the most remote peninsular past to his time. It is also possible that Jiménez de Rada could also be the one who indicated to the monarch the deficiencies of the "Chronicon Mundi" of Lucas of Tuy and the need of a peninsular, Hispanic, complete history. Perhaps he was even looking for the primacy of the city of Toledo over that of León, in which Lucas of Tuy wrote his work[17]. King Fernando III is interested in the peninsular past, the antiquities of Spain, not only in the search for identity and dynastic legitimation, in such a way that the tradition coming from Isidore was insufficient for this task[18].

In his preliminary reflections, the starting point is the need to present the past with an exemplary character, an approach that he takes from the "Etymologiae" of Isidore[19] and he develops later. He takes up the initial idea of transmission of the past as an example but directing his interests towards the communication of science and the mechanical arts. Thus, instead of listing the liberal arts, he mentions the disciplines that supposedly interested him, such as astronomy, geometry, botany, and pharmacology. And once he demonstrates the usefulness and necessity of writing, he points out the exemplary usefulness of

---

14 Fernández Valverde 1987.

15 Svennung 1967, 21–33; Eliade 1985, 80–82; Busuioceanu 1985; Happ 2000, 13–21; Carbó García 2004; Dana 2008, 179–181.

16 Jerez Cabrero 2003; Catalán, Jerez Cabrero 2005.

17 Rodrigo Jiménez de Rada, De reb. Hisp., Praefatio.

18 Fernández Gallardo 2004, 67.

19 Isid., Etym., I, 2–3.

the history of monarchs, for which he highlights four virtues: wisdom, courage, liberality, and justice[20]. In this way, the objects of study in his work are, as he himself affirms, the antiquities of Spain, the peoples who have invaded it, the origin of the Spanish kings and their great deeds[21]. For this, the Gothic origin not only of the reigning dynasty but also of the high Hispanic nobility will be defended by Jiménez de Rada, with an evident legitimizing purpose sought by and for all of them[22]. The Castilian-Leonese high nobility – or the part of that with which the Toledan had a closer contact – showed at this time an interest in the history of the Goths in search of their own legitimacy[23].

The political transformations in the reign of Fernando III, the definitive union of León and Castile and the military advance towards the Muslim south made necessary a reevaluation of historical memory –a fashionable concept in our days–. They needed an ideology that unified the different territories of the Crown and a historian who could give them a common past[24]. In it, the Gothic story plays a main role. Hence the importance of Jordanes' work for Jiménez de Rada, although the Isidorian tradition continued to be "the central axis of the conception of the Hispanic past, endowed with an intense Gothic inspiration"[25].

The new character of the "Historia de rebus Hispaniae" of Jiménez de Rada, which will serve as a source and model for later historians even in the same thirteenth century, is also shown in the action of completing the historical account with chapters destined to clarify the origins. In these, he follows traditions and varied sources that he does not always identify, reaching the legend and myth. Some of these elements were already found in Orosius, in Isidore of Seville or in the closest in time, Lucas of Tuy, but until the appearance of the work of Jiménez de Rada, those legends and myths had not been gathered in a whole nor had they been added to a history of Spain in the form of a chapter on the origins[26]. Despite this, in the historical part itself, Jiménez de Rada manifests a fairly pronounced critical spirit, the result of a concept of culture and moralization about history that is characteristic of the time in which he writes his work. He also resorts to Arab sources to contrast his data, an aspect to highlight since, at that time, aspects such as society or economy were only treated by Arab historiography[27].

20 Rodrigo Jiménez de Rada, De reb. Hisp., Praefatio.

21 Quia igitur placuit vestrae excellentiae Maiestatis, meae requirere ignorantiam parvitatis, ut si quae de antiquitatibus Hispaniae, et de iis etiam quae ab antiquis vel modernis temporibus acciderunt, meae memoriae occurrissent, petitioni vestrae describere laborarem, et ut a quibus gentibus calamitates Hispania sit perpessa, et Hispanorum Regum origo, et eorum magnalia (...) per scripturae meae indaginem ad diligentiae nostrae notitiam pervenirent.

22 Rodríguez 2003; Rodríguez 2004. Igitur quia magnorum petitio me coegit Gothorum originem et acta describere, (...) usque ad mea tempora contexui et descripsi.

23 Wulff 2003, 38–39; Moxo y Ortiz de Villajos 2000, 273–277; Fernández Gallardo 2004, 72.

24 Lomax 1977, 588.

25 Fernández Gallardo 2004, 73.

26 Carbó García 2004, 202.

27 Pick 2004.

Precisely one of the myths that he collects in his chapter on the origins of the Hispanic people is our subject of study on these pages, the myth of the wisdom of the Goths, which gains a moral meaning, as it will appear in later historians and writers and in relation to the exposed virtues of the Castilian-Leonese kings[28].

In his story, Deceneus reappears. Jiménez de Rada will make of him an example of wisdom and good government for the new Hispanic rulers, heirs of the Gothic tradition transmitted by Isidore and reactivated in the thirteenth century. It will also include Zalmoxis and some Dacian traditions, elements all of them taken, now, from Jordanes, who had mixed the history of the Goths with those of the Getae and Dacians in his "Getica"[29]. Through Jordanes and the independent Hispanic tradition represented by Isidore of Seville, Jiménez de Rada introduced the myth and history of the Getae and Dacians -previously appropriated for the Goths- into the history of the Hispanic people[30]. Thus, he affirms that, in the time of Sulla, a certain Dicineus (sic) would have taught the Visigoths all philosophy, physics, theoretical and practical disciplines, logic, the arrangement of the twelve signs, the movement of the planets, the growth and decrease of the moon, the course of the sun, astrology and astronomy, the natural sciences ...[31]:

> "Deinde regnavit in Gothis Borvista, et venit ad eum in Gothiam Dicineus, quo tempore Silla in Romanis habuit principatum. Et Diciney consilio Germanorum terras quas nunc Franci detinent occuparunt, et dedit ei Borvista fere regiam potestatem (...) Gothi autem hoc comodum, hoc salubre, hoc votivum, hoc agendum in agendis et in iudiciis iudicabant, quod Dicineus eorum consiliarius aprobabat. Ipse autem mores eorum barbaricos inmutavit, ipse fere omnen philosophiam, fisicam, theoricam, practicam, logicam, disposiciones XII signorum, planetarum cursus, augmentum lune et decrementum, solis circuitum, astrologiam et astronomian et naturales sciencias Gothos docuit et ex beluina ferocitate homines et philosophos instauravit. Hec et alia Dicineus Gothis pericia sua tradens mirabiliter enitiot apud eos, et non solum mediocribus, immo et regibus imperavit. Elegit preterea nobiliores et prudenciores fecitque sacerdotes, quos ad theologiam instituens vocavit speciali nomine "pilleatos", et quia tyaris capita paliabant arbitror sic vocatos. Decedente vero Dicineo pene pari veneration Eumosicum habuerunt, quia nec impar in solercia habebatur. Etenim rex et pontifex ob sui periciam illis fuit et in summa iustitia populos iudicabat, Et hoc rebus humanis exempt succesit in regno post multa tempora Dorpaneus".

Some of this knowledge that Jiménez de Rada highlights in the Goths we know that Jordanes had taken from the ancient references to Deceneus and the Dacians of the first cen-

28 Carbó García 2004, 203.
29 Carbó García 2015, 23–66.
30 Svennung 1967, 26–30; Busuioceanu 1985, 124–141.
31 Rodrigo Jiménez de Rada, De reb. Hisp., 1. 15.

tury BC and I AD[32]. This agrees with the aforementioned interests of Jiménez de Rada towards the communication of science and mechanical arts and the disciplines that should interest him especially. In fact, chapter XV of his work, "De sapientibus Gothorum et consiliariis eorundem", is nothing but an excursus on Deceneus, whom he includes in a place of honor along with Zeuta and Zalmoxis –whom he calls Zalmoxes– among the "philosophers" of the Goths[33]. Jiménez de Rada had to know the theories at the University of Paris on the translatio studii, which in the case at hand would have been carried out directly thanks to the Visigoths. They would have transferred their philosophical and cosmological knowledge learned in the east when they settled and were identified with Hispania[34]. From the study of the first books of his work we can see to what extent he used Jordanes and Isidore. In them, the Toledan archbishop was guided especially by the "Getica" of Jordanes. Sometimes he literally transcribes it, with unimportant stylistic modifications, and other times he summarizes it. It is in the moments when he decides to expand the text when he transcribes or summarizes parts from the "Etymologies" or the "Historia Gothorum" of Isidore. In rarer cases, even from Orosius. And the verses he quotes from Lucan or Virgil come from references to Jordanes or Isidore. Of course, he does not differentiate between Goths and Getae, and like Isidore, he begins his chapter of the history of the Goths by going back to Magog, son of Japheth. The etymological theory of the identification between Getae and Goths proposed by Isidore will also be collected in its pages, although not without certain modifications resulting from the confrontation with what was exposed by Jordanes[35].

In Jiménez de Rada, the Gothic myth related to the origins of the people who were going to be considered "founder" of Spain will be projected in the history and reality of the Iberian people, containing the identity and the appropriate past of the Getae and Dacians of Antiquity in it. However, these do not constitute by themselves the direct object of appropriation, but indirectly they are appropriated when the true object of that appropriation at that time –the Goths and their history– is taken by Jiménez de Rada on behalf of King Fernando III for the legitimization of the reigning dynasty over León and Castile and legitimization of the high nobility too. They had those same interests in enhancing their origins by appealing to the "glorious past" of unity of the different territories of the Peninsula under the Goths: a people whose remote antiquity –and consequently, the greater prestige and power of legitimation it could confer– would be reinforced by the repetition of passages about the legendary origin of the Goths, as it had been elaborated at the time by Cassiodorus and Jordanes from ancient sources.

32 Iord., Get., XI, 67; 69–73.

33 Rodrigo Jiménez de Rada, De reb. Hisp., 1. 10 y 1. 13.

34 Dana 2008, 179–180; Rucquoi 1998, 739–740.

35 Alarcos 1937.

2.3 *The Decenean model for Alfonso X*

The encyclopedic and exhaustive character of the knowledge of the thirteenth century finds in the historiographical work promoted by Alfonso X its fullness, surpassing in quality the two great chronicles that preceded it and with the difference of the use of Castilian versus Latin[36].

The intense Gothicism present in medieval Hispanic historiography, which was based on the Isidorian tradition and was stimulated from the political ideology of restoration of the Visigothic monarchy was a determining factor in preventing a search for the ancestors of the inhabitants of the Peninsula. The renewal and overcoming promoted by Fernando III with respect to the limited previous dynastic interests allow to investigate the most remote past by raising the question of the origins of the nation and the necessary research for that purpose. In the "Estoria de España", we find the idea –already developed by Jiménez de Rada– of some original peninsular inhabitants and different invasions that successively devastated Spain, as can be seen in the translation of the passage taken from Jiménez de Rada, which lists these calamitous invasions: Hercules, Romans, Vandals, Silings, Alans and Suebi[37]. By contrast, the mention of the "Spanish" people is reiterated without leaving any doubt about the identity of the inhabitants of Spain who suffer these invasions. But when the time comes to deal with the arrival of the Visigoths, a problem arises, because it could not be presented as another invasion, like the previous ones, so that it would be alien to the Spanish identity, to those "espannoles" who inhabited Spain, and the simplest solution is chosen: omit the problem, so that the Goths appear, even without any link, together with the Spanish people. The arrival of the Goths supposes a new dominion, but not one more like the previous ones, but the one that generates the legitimacy on which the dynastic rights of Alfonso X and all the previous and subsequent kings are based. The recourse to Gothicism was inevitable, both from the perspective of the political arguments related to dynastic identity and those that supported the idea of Reconquista. The Hispanic historiographical tradition from Isidore onwards had consolidated an image of the past that at that time could not be renounced. It would have meant calling into question the collective identity that was sought to confer on the Spanish people, as inhabitants of that national entity whose origins were also sought, the medieval Hispanic nation[38].

When reading the history of the Goths in the "Estoria de España", it seems that for Alfonso X, promoter of Spanish culture, reformer of laws and cultivator of all sciences

36 Fernández Gallardo 2004, 79–80.

37 Rodrigo Jiménez de Rada, De reb. Hisp., Praefatio: «(...) ortum eorum qui primo in Hispaniis habitavere, et bella Herculis quae exercuit super eos, et quae Romani mortis iudicia intulere, et quibus Vándalos, Silingos, Alanos, et Suevos exitiis consumpserunt (...) compilavi (...)». Alfonso X el Sabio, Estoria de España, Prólogo: «Et esto fiziemos por que fuesse sabudo el comienço de los espannoles, et de quales yentes fuera España maltrecha; et que sopiessen las batallas que Hercoles de Grecia fizo contra los espannoles, et las mortandades que los romanos fizieron en ellos, et los destruymientos que les fizieron otrossi los vandalos et los silingos et los alanos et los suevos...».

38 Fernández Gallardo 2004, 83–87.

and arts, from music and literature to astronomy and astrology, the figure of Deceneus – called by him Diçeneo or Dicineo – will not only be that of the wise advisor of Burebista – whom he calls Boruista –, but will become a model for the monarch himself. So Alfonso X the Learned lists Deceneo's activities, repeating Jiménez de Rada, who in turn followed Jordanes' account[39]:

> "Empos esto regnò en los godos Boruista, et uino a ell en Goçia uno que llamauan Dicineo. Et fue esto en el tiempo en que Silla era consol en Roma et tenie el principado. E leuantos este rey Boruista por conseio daquel Dicineo, et priso las tierras de los Germanos, las que tienen agora los Francos, et dio Boruista a Dicineo por ello fascas tod el poder del sennorio. E los Godos dalli adelant por que ueyen al so rey et assi mismos muy bien aconseiados daquel Dicineo, lo que el les conseiaua et tenie por bien aquello iudgauan por cosa prouechosa et de salut et de sanctidat en las cosas que ellos auien de fazer. E aquel mudò entrellos las costumbres que auien entonçes non tan buenas; et este Dicineo ensennò a los godos fascas toda la filosophya et la fisica, et la theorica et la practica, et la logica, et los ordenamientos de los doze signos, et los cossos de los planetas, et el cresçer et le descresçer de la luna et el cosso del sol, et la astrologia, et la astronomia, et las sciencias naturales. Et sacolos duna braueza que trayen antes a manera de bestias saluages, et ensennò los a seer mansos et philosophos. Et sobresto escogiò Dicineo de los mas nobles, et mas entendidos, et fizò dellos sacerdotes et obispos, et diò dellos que prendiessen theologia et llamò los pileatos por nombre de pileus que dicen el latin por sombrero de cauallero; et segund departen los sabios esto era por las mitras de que trayen cubiertas las cabeças, cuemo los caualleros las suyas de los sombreros. Et murio este Dicineo, et ouieron en logar del otro que dixieron Eumusico, sabio cuemo ell, et onrraron lo los Godos poco menos que a aquel, ca tanto fue sabidor aqueste que por rey et por obispo le tenien ellos entresi, et uidgaua este en sos pueblos toda iusticia muy complidamientre. Et pues que murio este Eumusico, ouvieron por rey a grand tiempo depues otro quel llamaron Dorpaneo, segund que adelante cuenta la estoria".

And along with Deceneus and Burebista, Zalmoxis also appears in the Alfonsine chronicle, although his figure is eclipsed almost entirely in the Spanish chronicles by that of the intellectual "Goth", Deceneus. In the case of Alfonso X, it is said of Zalmoxis that "cuentam las estorias que fue muy sabio to marauilla enla filosophya"[40].

In the thirteenth century, the Castilian-Leonese chronicles of Lucas of Tuy, Rodrigo Jiménez de Rada and Alfonso X the Learned represent –progressively– the Spanish national exaltation against the northern neighbour. If in France it was sought to reaffirm the Trojan origin of the French people, mixed with the Germanic origins, in León and Castile Tubal, Hercules and especially the Visigoths are chosen as ancient ancestors, in search of affirming a consciousness of their own identity, unity and independence against

39 Alfonso X el Sabio, Estoria de España, cap. 388.

40 Alfonso X el Sabio, Estoria de España, cap. 393.

France and the main European powers, such as the Holy Roman Empire or the Papacy[41]. And with the Goths, the most outstanding characters of the ancient history of the Getae and Dacians, such as the aforementioned Deceneus, Burebista or Zalmoxis, are perfectly integrated into the history of the Spanish people when dealing with the legendary origins of the Visigothic people, always with an exemplary and legitimizing intentionality. In the specific case of Deceneus, we find the clearest model of a reformer and wise man for Alfonso X.

Bibliography

Alarcos, E. 1937. El Toledano, Jordanes y San Isidoro, Boletín de la Biblioteca Menéndez Pelayo 17, 101–129.

Busuioceanu, A. 1985. Zamolxis, sau mitul dacic în istoria şi legendele spaniole, Bucharest.

Carbó García, J. R. 2004. Godos y getas en la historiografía de la Tardoantigüedad y del Medievo: un problema de identidad y de legitimación socio-política, Stvdia Historica: Historia Antigua 22, 179–206.

Carbó García, J. R. 2015. Apropiaciones de la Antigüedad. De getas, godos, Reyes Católicos, yugos y flechas, en Anejos de la Revista de Historiografía 3, Madrid.

Catalán, D. 1962. De Alfonso X al Conde de Barcelos. Cuatro estudios sobre el nacimiento de la historiografía romance en Castilla y Portugal, Madrid.

Catalán, D. 1992. La Estoria de España de Alfonso X: creación y evolución, en Fuentes Cronísticas de la Historia de España, nº 5, Madrid.

Catalán, D., Jerez Cabrero, E. 2005. «Rodericus» romanzado en Aragón, Castilla y Navarra, en Fuentes Cronísticas de la Historia de España 10, Madrid.

Crespo, J. B. 2000. La "Estoria de España" y las crónicas generales, in I. Fernández-Ordóñez (ed.), Alfonso X el Sabio y las crónicas de España, Valladolid, 107–132.

Dana, D. 2008. Zalmoxis de la Herodot la Mircea Eliade. Istorii despre un zeu al pretextului, Iaşi.

De Carlos Villamarín, H. 1993. Las antigüedades de España: fundadores y reyes míticos en la literatura medieval, en Colección Tesis en microficha Univ. Santiago, Santiago de Compostela.

Doubleday, S. 2015. The Wise King: A Christian Prince, Muslim Spain, and the Birth of the Renaissance, New York.

Dyer, N. J. 1990. Alphonsine Historiography: The Literary Narrative, in R. I. Burns (ed.), Emperor of Culture. Alfonso X the Learned of Castile and his Thirteenth-Century Renaissance, Philadelphia, 140–158.

Eliade, M. 1985. De Zalmoxis a Gengis-Khan. Religiones y folklore de la Dacia y de la Europa Oriental, Madrid.

41 Rucquoi 1992, 341–352.

Estévez Sola, J. A. 2004. Los orígenes míticos de Hispania en las Crónicas españolas de la Edad Media, in J. Mª Candau Morón, F. J. González Ponce, G. Cruz Andreotti (eds.), Historia y mito. El pasado legendario como fuente de autoridad. Actas del Simposio Internacional de Sevilla, Valverde del Camino y Huelva, 22–25 de abril de 2003, Málaga, 365–388.
Falque, E. 1998. La Translatio s. Isidori en el Chronicon mundi de Lucas de Tuy, in P. Linehan (ed.), Life, Law and Letters: historical studies in honour of Antonio García y García, Studia Gratiana XXIX, Roma, 213–219.
Falque, E. 2003. Lucas Tudensis, Chronicon Mundi, in Corpus Christianorum, Continuatio Mediaevalis LXXIV, Turnhout.
Fernández Gallardo, L. 2004. De Lucas de Tuy a Alfonso el Sabio: idea de la historia y proyecto historiográfico, Revista de poética medieval 12, 53–119.
Fernández Valverde, J. (ed.) (1987). Roderici Ximenii de Rada, Historia de rebus Hispaniae, in Corpus Christianorum, Continuatio Mediaevalis LXXII, Turnhout.
Fernández-Ordóñez, I. 1992. Las Estorias de Alfonso el Sabio, Madrid.
Fernández-Ordóñez, I. 1999. El taller historiográfico alfonsí. La Estoria de España y la General estoria en el marco de las obras promovidas por Alfonso el Sabio, in J. Montoya y A. Rodríguez (coord.), El Scriptorium alfonsí: de los Libros de Astrología a las "Cantigas de Santa María", Madrid, 105–126.
Fernández-Ordóñez, I. 2000. El taller de las Estorias, in I. Fernández-Ordóñez (ed.), Alfonso X el Sabio y las Crónicas de España, Valladolid, 61–82.
Happ, K. 2000. Der Goticismus in Spanien, in Hauptseminar: Nationale und regionale Identität in Schriften des europäischen Humanismus, Humboldt-Universität zu Berlin, Berlin, 1–35.
Jerez Cabrero, E. 2003. La Historia gothica del Toledano y la historiografía romance, Cahiers de Linguistique et de Civilisation Hispaniques Médiévales 26, 223–239.
Kennedy, K. 2019. Alfonso X of Castile-León: Royal Patronage, Self-Promotion, and Manuscripts in Thirteen-Century Spain, Amsterdam.
Linehan, P. 1997. On Further Thought: Lucas of Tuy, Rodrigo of Toledo and the Alfonsine Histories, Anuario de Estudios Medievales 27, 415–436.
Lomax, D. W. 1977. Rodrigo Jiménez de Rada como historiador, in Actas del Quinto Congreso Internacional de Hispanistas, Burdeos 2–8 de septiembre de 1974, Bordeaux, 587–592.
Martin, G. 2001. Dans l'atelier des faussaires. Luc de Túy, Rodrigue de Tolède, Alphonse X, Sanche IV: trois exemples de manipulations historiques (León-Castille, XIIIe siècle), Cahiers de linguistique et de civilisation hispaniques medievales 24, 279–309.
Menéndez Pidal, R. 1977. Primera Crónica general ó sea Estoria de España que mandó componer Alfonso el Sabio y se continuaba bajo Sancho IV, en 1289, Madrid, 3ª ed. (1ª ed. 1906; 2ª ed. 1955).
Moxo y Ortiz de Villajos, S. 2000. Feudalismo, señorío y nobleza en la Castilla medieval, Madrid.
O'Callaghan, J. 1993. The Learned King: The Reign of Alfonso X of Castile, Philadelphia.

O'Callaghan, J. 1998. Alfonso X, the Cortes, and Government in Medieval Spain, Burlington.
O'Callaghan, J. 2019. Alfonso X, The Justinian of His Age, Ithaca.
Pick, L. 2004. Conflict and Coexistence: Archbishop Rodrigo and the Muslims and Jews of Medieval Spain, Oxford.
Rodríguez, A. 2003. De rebus Hispaniae frente a la Crónica latina de los reyes de Castilla: virtudes regias y reciprocidad política en Castilla y León en la primera mitad del siglo XIII, Cahiers de linguistique hispanique médiévale 26, 133–149.
Rodríguez, A. 2004. Sucesión regia y legitimidad política en Castilla en los siglos XII y XIII. Algunas consideraciones sobre el relato de las crónicas latinas castellanoleonesas, in I. Alfonso, J. Escalona, G. Martin (coord.), Lucha política, condena y legitimación en la España medieval, Annexes des Cahiers de Linguistique et Civilisation Hispanique Médiévale, Lyon, 21–41.
Rucquoi, A. 1992. Les Wisigoths fondement de la "nation Espagne", in J. Fontaine, C. Pellistrandi (eds.), L'Europe héritière de l'Espagne wisigothique, Madrid, 341–352.
Rucquoi, A. 1998. Contributions des *studia generalia* à la pensée hispanique médiévale, in J.M. Soto Rábanos (ed.), Pensamiento medieval hispano. Homenaje a Horacio Santiago-Otero, Madrid, 739–740.
Svennung, J. 1967. Zur Geschichte des Goticismus, Uppsala.
Wulff, F. 2003. Las esencias patrias. Historiografía e Historia Antigua en la construcción de la identidad española (siglos XVI–XX), Barcelona.

INDEX LOCORVM